B

Henry Cowell

Henry Cowell

A Man Made of Music

JOEL SACHS

OXFORD
UNIVERSITY PRESS

OXFORD
UNIVERSITY PRESS

Oxford University Press, Inc., publishes works that further
Oxford University's objective of excellence
in research, scholarship, and education.

Oxford   New York

Auckland   Cape Town   Dar es Salaam   Hong Kong   Karachi
Kuala Lumpur   Madrid   Melbourne   Mexico City   Nairobi
New Delhi   Shanghai   Taipei   Toronto

With offices in

Argentina   Austria   Brazil   Chile   Czech Republic   France   Greece
Guatemala   Hungary   Italy   Japan   Poland   Portugal   Singapore
South Korea   Switzerland   Thailand   Turkey   Ukraine   Vietnam

Published by Oxford University Press, Inc.
198 Madison Avenue, New York, NY 10016

www.oup.com

Oxford is a registered trademark of Oxford University Press

Library of Congress Cataloging-in-Publication Data
Sachs, Joel.
Henry Cowell : a man made of music / Joel Sachs.
p.   cm.
Includes bibliographical references and index.
ISBN 978-0-19-510895-8
1. Cowell, Henry, 1897–1965.
2. Composers—United States—Biography. I. Title.
ML410.C859S23   2012
780.92—dc23
[B] 2011040686

Research for this book was funded in part by a grant from the National Endowment for the
Humanities, a Federal Agency, in Washington, D.C.

1 3 5 7 9 8 6 4 2

Printed in the United States of America
on acid-free paper

To my beloved family
and in memory of Sidney Cowell, who did not live to read it.

CONTENTS

PART SIX   WORLD TRAVELER

ACKNOWLEDGMENTS

Of the countless people who deserve credit for assisting me in preparing this book, none are as important as my family, who put up with it and sustained me from collapsing under its weight; my daughter and son kept me cheerful by treating the book as some kind of endless family joke. For its actual completion, I am indebted to Angelica Kyang, who constantly encouraged me as I faced the difficult process of assimilating the vast amount of material.

I am especially grateful for a grant from the National Endowment for the Humanities that enabled me to conduct research in New York, Boston, Moscow, Washington, several parts of California, and elsewhere. My grant officer, Elizabeth Arndt, and Darcy Hector Soong, who helped write the grant application, were immeasurably supportive. Emily Good, now an executive at BMI, was my invaluable research assistant in the initial stages. Sidney Cowell made the project possible by providing me with complete access to the Cowell papers, annotated copies of her personal correspondence, information about some little-known actors in this drama, and fresh insights (plus occasional confusion) in letters to and conversations with me.

To the staff of the research division of the New York Public Library's Library-Museum of the Performing Arts, no words of thanks are sufficient. I especially cite Jean Bowen (chief of the Music Division at the time this project began), George Boziwick (current chief), Frances Barulich, Charles Eubanks, Tema Hecht, Bob Kosovsky, Richard Jackson, and John Shepherd. Wayne Shirley of the Library of Congress generously gave me a pre-publication copy of his article on the *Hymns and Fuguing Tunes*. He and his colleagues saved me having to travel to Washington by providing answers to many questions. H. Wiley Hitchcock helped unravel some fascinating puzzles about Sidney Cowell.

Other helpful libraries and institutions include the Bartók Archive, Budapest (László Somfai); California State University Library, Long Beach; Carnegie Hall (Kathleen Sabogai, associate archivist); Columbia University (Oral

History Research Office, Sarang Lee, editorial assistant); Composers' Union Library, Moscow; Glinka Library, Moscow; Martha Graham Dance Company (Aaron Sherber, music director); John Simon Guggenheim Foundation (G. T. Tanselle); Harvard Club of New York; Charles Ives Society (James Kendrick, attorney); the Jewish National University and Archive, Jerusalem (Zmira Ruveni); The Johns Hopkins University Medical School Archive; Mills College (Janice Brown, archivist); The Juilliard School (Jane Gottlieb, vice-president for library and information resources; Jeni Dahmus, archivist); the Louisville Orchestra (Robert Birman, chief executive officer); The New School University Library and Archive (Carmen Hendershott and Jill Luedke); Paul Sacher Stiftung, Basel (Felix Meyer, director, and his staff); San Francisco Public Library Historical Photograph Collection; Sherwood Conservatory of Music, Chicago (Allison Scott-Williams, director of programs and admissions; Caroline Girgis, interim director of programs and admissions); Stanford University (Green Library); Temple of the People, Halcyon, California (Eleanor Shumway, guardian-in-chief); Vassar Alumnae Association; Wesleyan University (Olin Library, Valerie Gillespie, assistant university archivist); Yale University (Beinecke Library, Department of Manuscripts and Special Archives, and Irving S. Gilmore Music Library); Universal Edition, Vienna (Eric Marinitsch); and the UCLA Ethnomusicology Archive (Aaron Bittel, archivist).

Individuals who assisted me include Fariba Amini, Charles Amirkhanian, Peter Bartók, Amy Beal, Eugene Becker, Paul Binkley, Peter Binkley, Chester Biscardi, Peter Burkholder, Eugenia Choi, Dierdre Ní Chonghaile, Thomas J. Cottle, Laurel Fay, Michael Frishkopf, Scott Gac, Don Gillespie, Michael Hicks, Pascal Ianco, Kerry King, Stephen Kinzer, Roberto Kolb, David "Uncle Dave" Lewis, Amy Nelson, David Nicholls, Carol Oja, Robert Parker, Louis Pine, Howard Pollack, Adelaide Reyes, Frans van Rossum, Ralph Samuelson, Brian Silver, Kenneth Silverman, Mark Slobin, Judith Anne Still (for providing letters from Henry Cowell to her father William Grant Still), Eleanor Sutter (my hostess in Moscow during a month of research), Richard Teitelbaum, Judith Tick, Jean Seward Uppman, William Weber, Chou Wenchung, Elektra Slonimsky Yourke, and Izaly Zemtsovsky.

The following persons graciously gave their valuable time for interviews: Mildred Baker, Jack Beeson, Henry Brant, John Cage, Sidney Cowell, Lou Harrison, Harold and Barbara Tufty, Jean Seward Uppman, Frank Wigglesworth, and Dr. Joseph Wortis.

I am especially grateful for the pioneering bibliographers of Cowell—William Lichtenwanger (who compiled the indispensable catalog of Cowell's music), Bruce Saylor (author of an annotated listing of 239 books and articles written by Cowell), and Martha Manion (for her truly backbreaking bibliography of 1,359 writings about Cowell going through the early 1980s).

Reviews of Cowell's concerts were graciously translated by Kolbeinn Bjarnasson (Icelandic), Eugene Brogyanyi (Hungarian), Andrew Dobrowolski (Polish), Hiromi Fukuda (Japanese), and Eleanor Sutter (Slovak).

I have saved for the last the most important people who assisted with final form of this book. I am grateful beyond measure to Mary Belanger for her tireless labor in editing the final manuscript with astounding thoroughness. Almost as tireless was George Boziwick, who started to read the book so that he could find a little something to say for the back of the book jacket, and read it with the greatest of care, providing invaluable feedback. Linda Solow Blotner prepared the excellent index. And, finally, it has been a delight to have had the full, warm support and incredible patience of Oxford University Press's superb American office— Suzanne Ryan (editor of books on music), Caelyn Cobb (editorial assistant), Joellyn Ausanka (senior production editor), Patterson Lamb (copy editor), and the wonderful design, production, and promotional staff.

To anyone who has inadvertently been omitted from the lists, I extend my most profound apologies.

INTRODUCTION

Despite this book's subtitle, "A Man Made of Music," the complexity of Henry Cowell's life made it impossible to fit a "life and works" into one volume that the reader could hold without risking carpal tunnel syndrome. Since Oxford University Press made it clear that two volumes were not an option, I could only tell the full, unusual, and long-awaited story of this extraordinary man by greatly restricting my discussion of his music. To do so has been painful, since his wonderful music is badly in need of re-discovery. I therefore hope the reader will always keep in mind that Henry Cowell was primarily a composer and that his music amply rewards efforts to get to know it. A fair amount of it was recorded during his lifetime, and although those LPs are no longer in print, they may be found in many libraries. In recent years, some LPs have been re-released on CD, recording has resumed, and performances are becoming more frequent. Among the larger studies of his music are Steven Johnson's survey "'Worlds of Ideas': The Music of Henry Cowell," in *The Whole World of Music—A Henry Cowell Symposium*; Joscelyn Godwin's *The Music of Henry Cowell*; Peter John Schimpf's *A Transcultural Student, Teacher, and Composer—Henry Cowell and the Music of the World's Peoples*, and Jeremy Brown's articles on his band music.

Although I was a graduate student at Columbia during Henry Cowell's final two years there, I did not meet him because, unknown to most of us, he was already very ill and rarely came to the music department. My interest in him arose through his music, to which I was introduced by Cheryl Seltzer and Peter Perrin, the founders of the new-music ensemble Continuum. His piano, chamber, vocal, and chamber-orchestra compositions gradually became part of my repertory as a pianist and conductor. The coincidence that his mother and my mother share a birthday or the fact that most of the Cowells' later New York apartments were in my own neighborhood may have added subliminally to the urge to investigate him. That process began in 1988.

Now, at the end of the eternity that this book has taken, an apology is overdue to those who waited for it. I deeply regret that his widow Sidney Cowell—whom I liked tremendously—my colleague H. Wiley Hitchcock, and most of the people who kindly allowed me to interview them did not live to read this book. I confess, however, that a knowledgeable person, who shall remain anonymous, suggested only half-facetiously that I write slowly, lest I complete it during Sidney Cowell's lifetime. Otherwise I would be bombarded with corrections, largely of imagined errors. As I got deeper into the materials and saw Sidney's hair-trigger response mechanism in action with other authors, and became aware of the errors, confusion, and contradictions that infected her later writings and some of our conversations, I realized the seriousness of that warning. As it happened, however, deliberate delay was unnecessary. Sidney passed away in 1995, after a long and distinguished life. I still had years of work ahead, and missed her greatly.

The longevity of my labors had two principal causes. One is the richness of my life and activities over these twenty-three years, including the incomparable joy of teaching at The Juilliard School; playing in and conducting the ensemble Continuum and co-directing it with Cheryl Seltzer; creating, directing, and conducting the New Juilliard Ensemble; creating and directing Juilliard's *Focus!* Festival: directing Juilliard's concerts at MoMA's Summergarden festival; and performing and lecturing internationally. All those wonderful experiences deepened my understanding of the world in which Henry Cowell functioned but delayed the birth of this book.

The chief reason for its prolonged gestation, however, is a kind of indigestion that followed reading the massive documentation of his life. The bulk of it resides in the gigantic collection of Henry Cowell's papers at the New York Public Library for the Performing Arts, at Lincoln Center. It contains tens of thousands of letters, press clippings, photographs, and myriad other documents, as well as copies of his music manuscripts. (The original music manuscripts, and Sidney Cowell's papers that are not relevant to her husband's life, went to the Library of Congress.) The Library for the Performing Arts also contains the extant papers of the New Music Society [Cowell's concert, publishing, and recording venture] and of several of Cowell's close associates. If that were not enough, archives in other libraries and secondary sources are endless. To paraphrase an old commercial, "I can't believe I read the whole thing!" and I am sure that there is more material hiding somewhere.

Digging through it, however, was great fun. Whereas many composers have a few adventures and otherwise quiet lives, Henry Cowell's history is a chain of adventures, involving seemingly the entire international music world, right up to the final collapse of his health. Telling the story therefore also required attaining some background in the history of American musical institutions; the commercial and cultural development of modern California; musical life during the

Depression; the new technologies of the 1920s and 1930s; American communism; Soviet cultural policy; California penal law; American propaganda in World War II; the Cold War and Red scare of the 1950s; the CIA's secret sponsorship of experimental culture in the 1950s and 1960s; and many other topics.

It is, of course, neither possible nor desirable to include such a mountain of information in one book. Detailed research into several aspects of his life has already led to fascinating articles, and more will doubtless follow. This book is the first attempt to tell the whole story.

Because money plays a major role for someone as immersed in the business of music as was Henry Cowell, I have included some of that information. Raw numbers are misleading, however. I am grateful to my former doctoral advisee Eugenia Choi, who led me to the Web site Measuring Worth, which facilitates converting old amounts into modern values. Of that site's various mechanisms I opted to use purchasing power, since in the end we are trying to imagine how Henry Cowell lived (www.measuringworth.com/ppowerus).

Finally, a word about how Henry Cowell's name appears. A biography in which Schoenberg is called "Arnold" is unimaginable because he was Viennese, and the Viennese custom of addressing even very close friends as Herr X or Frau Y survived most of the last century. Virtually no one called Schoenberg "Arnold." In the United States, on the other hand, one is immediately on a first name basis with virtually everyone in sight, especially on the West Coast and in the arts. Almost everyone addressed Henry Cowell as Henry. Furthermore, his adventures began almost at birth, a time of life when one could hardly refer to him as "Cowell." Once the usage "Henry" was established in this book, there was no turning back.

Henry Cowell

Prologue

Of the Three Ladies, Henry, and Some Others

All biographies are shaped in some way by their sources, and the biographer needs to consider seriously the way those sources themselves were shaped and the motivations of the shapers. The complexity of Henry's life in particular requires a preliminary visit with the three women who, believing that a biography would have to be written, created the archive of his papers.

The first of them, Henry's mother Clara (or Clarissa) Dixon Cowell, a professional writer, saved her own papers and the scraps of his early life, and wrote an extensive memoir of his first eighteen years. The second collector, Olive Thompson Cowell, was Henry's second stepmother, that is, his father Harry's third wife. An experienced researcher, she knew that any scrap of evidence can be useful. Accordingly, once she began to appreciate his talents, she amassed everything she could and wrote copious notes about their conversations, his lectures, his professional activities, his musings, and her own assessments of him. Although some of her literary legacy seems colored by the expectation that she would live on through her services to Henry, and much of her writing tends toward hagiography of Henry and his father, Olive's papers are indispensable.

The third hoarder was Henry's wife, Sidney Robertson Cowell. A brilliant, determined, reserved yet fiery woman with extraordinary talents as a writer, photographer, folklorist, and musician, Sidney far surpassed Olive as a preserver of paper. The most objective of the three women, she loved Henry yet could be very critical of him. That duality gives special weight to her writing, which steers clear of hagiography, even at its most positive. Unfortunately, the same is not true of what she had to say about Olive and Harry; her pervasively negative feelings complicate any effort to understand them. After Henry's death, even as Sidney tried to put him behind her and get back to her own life, she remained so immersed in his story that she could not stop pondering him in endless statements, taped depositions, and letters that often contradict one another. She must have sat at her typewriter continuously for thirty years. Fortunately, many of her commentaries can be evaluated by comparing them with letters and other documents contemporaneous with the original events.

Her laudable efforts to make a record of her husband's life led to intense controversy, however. At some stage, possibly as early as their marriage in 1941, she decided that the story of his imprisonment on a morals charge should not be told for the first time outside the context of a full biography. Conversations that I have had with many musicians and music lovers strongly support the Cowells' fear that, like the late-Renaissance composer Don Carlo Gesualdo, Henry would be remembered only for his brush with the law. After Henry's death, Sidney feared—probably correctly—that he would be made a martyr for homosexual rights, something he never wished. She was especially bothered because she did not feel he was homosexual and never established whether he was even bisexual, as he thought, or not particularly sexual at all. Accordingly, the Cowell papers were closed for fifty years after his death. Although that restriction is neither uncommon nor uncommonly long, it only increased the tendency toward the "Gesualdo effect," which in turn justified her decision to control the context in which the story would be revealed. Unsurprisingly, although her decision made sense, she was declared obstructive and suspected of cleansing the archive to protect his image. The presence of very negative material in the archive, much of it written by her, led me to conclude quite the opposite—that she never hid the truth or destroyed anything. It was the lack of any context that alarmed her, not the facts, which, on many levels, are tragic. Her anger at researchers who attempted to tell the story seemed further evidence of her will to alter history, but in fact she already had turned over complete use of the documents to Richard Franko Goldman and then to Hugo Weisgall, neither of whom followed through with the book they promised to write. When she then tried to write Henry's biography by herself, her insatiable curiosity twisted her into knots. Later she turned to me and was so disappointed that I could not finish the book quickly that she shortened the period of exclusive access to the documents. I did not attempt to explain that she was partly responsible for the complexity of the task because of her confusing commentaries, or that she had spent some seven years working on the biographical section of the Cowells' book about Ives, whose life was far less eventful than Henry's.

Sidney's compulsion to supply the biographer with every detail of her husband's life, and her wonderful writing style, makes her a compelling but extremely problematic witness. It is almost impossible to determine whether some of her statements represent what Henry told her or are her own opinions, except when she would write, with her characteristic orthography, "I do n't know. I forget." On the whole, I have tried to write this book using her contributions primarily when they originated at or near the time of an event, such as her long letters from California when she was working toward a pardon for Henry. The problems arise with her later statements, some of which contribute unique and valuable material, some of which—especially her dozens of "self-interview" tapes, with their "corrected" transcripts—are so muddled as to be useless. I have tried to be clear about what is reliable and what cannot be verified.

Henry himself also is responsible for the enormity of the archive, although he sometimes added to the stash passively by not troubling to throw anything away, even unused Paris metro tickets from the 1920s. (He treated his compositions completely differently, blithely giving away unique copies of his scores.) His many published interviews are both helpful and confusing because, as Sidney described him, he was extremely truthful but given to embroidery, which is entertaining but unhelpful to the search for accuracy. Especially troublesome is the fascinating, two-day interview by Beate Gordon in 1962 for the Columbia Oral History Project, the only source for some events, such as his tennis games with Schoenberg. Learning the details of his strokes in his last decade prompted me to ask Mrs. Gordon if she remembered his state of mind during the interviews. She answered that he showed no apparent effects of his strokes and was completely communicative. Age itself was not a problem; he was only sixty-five at the time. Sidney, however, said he could get very confused and speak convincingly but inaccurately.

I do not believe that Henry was determined to improve upon the past. He seems instead to have been like so many of us who, in retelling a story, unwittingly decorate it. I believe that he told his story the best way he could, in his famously vivid style, but his memory of events in the distant past probably changed subtly as he retold his autobiography in innumerable lectures and interviews spanning some four decades. It was like a long game of "telephone," but with only one participant. For example, in the Columbia interview he placed his lesson with Rachmaninoff several years too early. There was no reason for him to do that deliberately; the lesson was but one of the many interesting moments in his development. Unfortunately, that error had Rachmaninoff talking to a teenager rather than a composer in his early twenties and casts the story in a very different light. Yet like many events in Henry's life, it was too amusing to omit.

Michael Hicks has raised the question of Henry's dating of his compositions, imputing to him a desire to place his innovations earlier than their true birth dates. This may be so; but Sidney offered an equally convincing explanation—that Henry's book of "compositorial dates" reflected the time when he felt a piece was ready to be shown, which sometimes was long after he first conceived it. The well-known piano piece "The Tides of Manaunaun" is one example. Although it reached its final form in 1917, Sidney thought he probably worked on it for about five years and may even have played it in one or more preliminary forms. That may be why it is dated 1912 in the published score; but that date refers to a performance that he completely mis-recollected! In the end, it does not matter particularly. He indisputably was the first pianist in the twentieth century to use his forearms to play the piano, and to play directly on the piano strings. A few years more or less do not change the picture materially. (The dates of his later pieces seem to be reliable.)

Another intriguing question is how and why some misinformation about Henry kept circulating in the early years. For example, he was erroneously called a pupil of Rachmaninoff and Ornstein in the press several times. Had he exaggerated during an interview or did the press feed on its own initial error? There is no way to know. Sidney believed very strongly that he did not lie, and I tend to lean in favor of her characterizations because I always found her so honest and self-effacing. In that, I was not the only one. She once told me, with a sweetly puzzled expression, that Harmony Ives and Charlotte Ruggles, two "real New England women," considered Sidney, a comparatively brash Californian, one of their type. With respect to integrity, she considered it a high, if misplaced, compliment. She certainly did not want to live on through Henry.

Henry knew fairly early that he should try to assemble both incoming letters and the letters that he wrote, but it was after his death that Sidney realized the urgency of getting copies of his letters from their recipients because important information could be lost if the heirs to Henry's friends sold their documents haphazardly. Ultimately, she succeeded in getting originals or copies of the most important letters. Unfortunately, those written to him in San Quentin Prison were lost. They had to remain there when he was let out on parole; they should have been returned to him when he was pardoned, but it was then wartime and he was both busy and extremely reluctant to get involved with prison authorities, fearing that the yellow press would get wind of it and fan the old embers into a new scandal that could destroy his hard-won reentry into society. By the time Sidney inquired about them, long after his death, they had vanished. The loss of those papers also prevented her from compiling a list of people to whom he wrote from San Quentin. She therefore could contact only the most obvious, closest friends to get copies of his letters. Nevertheless, she obtained copies of so many that the collection of his outgoing correspondence seems deceptively complete. There is no way to know what she missed. And with no possibility of retrieving the letters that he received, the "conversations" will always be unidirectional.

In the 1970s, Sidney also commissioned invaluable interviews with Henry's most important associates, many of whom were already quite old and burdened with flawed memories. Those interviews produced another bumper crop of contradictions. Some recollections can be cross-checked against original documents; in other cases, fanciful reminiscing can be detected. At still other times one can only hope that the witness was reliable. Several of them certainly were not. I decided that by the late 1980s it was pointless to try to re-interview most of them, since their days with Henry were even more distant by then. I opted to seek out those with whom an interview might prove fruitful.

Despite the fact that the Cowell papers must be used very carefully, they contain unparalleled evidence of the international musical world of 1910 to 1965, and the evidence of a life that reads like a novel—full of noble acts, promises kept and promises broken, unprecedented ideas about music, thrills, tragedies, political intrigue, and even sex. In a novel, a character like Henry Cowell would probably seem hopelessly improbable. Indeed, even he had some surprises when he looked at the documents of his amazing history.

PART ONE

CHILD TO MAN

|| 1 ||

Clarissa, Harry, and Their Child

A perfectly ordinary marriage certificate states that Henry Clayton Blackwood Cowell and Clara Davidson were joined in matrimony on February 25, 1893, by a justice of the peace in Oakland (California) Township. When it surfaced years later, Henry Cowell was amazed that his parents ever legalized their union and his birth.[1] His error about his own legitimacy is understandable, given the thicket of stories surrounding his parents' peculiar blend of the conventional and unconventional. Information about his mother was scarce until some fifteen years after her death, when Olive, his father's third wife, questioned Clara's first son, Clarence Davidson, a Des Moines businessman. Clarence generated virtually the only available history of their mother's ancestry and early years. The following chronicle, largely his, was fleshed out by Olive and Sidney, Henry's widow. Its accuracy cannot be verified because Clarence, having no documents, relied upon his memory.

Clara Belnap Dixon—usually called Clarissa—was born on November 30, 1851, at Hennepin, Illinois, a small town on the Illinois River thirty miles north of Peoria, to Samuel Asenath Dixon and Bethshua Nash Dixon.[2] Bethshua's respectable English lineage led back to one Thomas Nash, who settled in Boston in 1638, and later moved to Connecticut, where he attained sufficient status to co-sign the "Fundamental Agreement" regulating civil and religious affairs of the Quinnipiac colony, now called New Haven. His descendants gave Nashville, Tennessee, its name.[3] Concerning Clarissa's paternal lineage, the Dixons, Clarence remembered only their Scotch-Irish origins. Olive, however, excavated a connection with Jeremiah Dixon, the eighteenth-century English astronomer who, with Charles Mason, determined the "Mason-Dixon Line" that later separated slave and free states. Clarissa's immediate forebears, the Illinois Dixons, were mostly farmers; Clarence thought that Clarissa's father was a mechanic and wagonmaker, but he may have been a cabinetmaker.[4] Clarissa was the second of five children. The family moved at some point, for all the children attended free public school and church in Amityville, near Eddyville, Iowa,[5] a typical Midwestern farming community some forty miles southeast of Des Moines. Clarence did not know the Nash's religious convictions, but the fundamentalist Dixons trained their children very strictly, even teaching them a roundabout route to school to keep them from passing the house of a reputed atheist.

Surprisingly, Clarence said nothing of Clarissa's defining moment, which was recorded by Sidney, who must have learned it from Henry, who probably heard it from Clarissa. That is: when Clarissa was seventeen (around 1868), at the moment for "testimony" in the church service, she stood up and announced that, having lost her belief in the tenets of the church, she was renouncing her membership.[6] She sensibly left town. In Kirkville[7] she met and married George Davidson, a farm boy, with whom she settled in Eddyville, six miles west. Their son Clarence was born around 1871.[8] Now about nineteen and determined to improve herself, Clarissa attended a private school at nearby Ottumwa. The costs were a burden; their parents provided very little assistance. Seven or eight years later she studied unspecified subjects at Penn College, Oskaloosa, and took some classes for teachers at Ottumwa. She became one of a half-dozen teachers in Eddyville, working for some eight years largely in Cedar and country schools. Clarence said she also wrote fiction. That was an understatement: she was passionate about writing, and not just fiction.

Clarence's almost breathless description of his father evokes the man's immense energy. Like Clarissa, George Davidson was an achiever. He briefly operated a livery business, went to school with Clarissa, studied law locally, carried mail, and was elected mayor of Eddyville. After moving to Kirkville, he was elected justice of the peace and president of the school board, bought and sold real estate, built cheap housing for coal miners, conducted an undertaking business, operated a mill, owned a large general store, and sold agricultural implements. His strength far from depleted, he studied law at Northwestern University and practiced in Ottumwa. The law soon became secondary as he began accumulating valuable property in several states and became active in third-party politics. Clarence was proud of his father, a leading man in the community, popular, reliable, and intelligent.

Clarence painted a warm and loving domestic scene in which George treated Clarissa with tenderness. A mature couple, they managed their household finances jointly. She was a good mother, housekeeper, cook, and dietician; did not spend much time visiting with friends and neighbors; was an average reader with a small library of books and magazines. Clarence thought Clarissa read some Shakespeare, and "paid some attention to the Bible." She even sent him to Sunday School in a Campbellite church. Another bout of religious doubts turned her to Spiritualism, reflected, perhaps, in her poems about a beautiful sunset or landscape. She sang in "an alto voice of splendid tone but not strong." A brunette who turned gray early, 5'1", slender to average until she reached about fifty, she was "considered handsome" when young, but later did not mind how she dressed as long as she was neat and clean. She was endlessly patient, cheerful, optimistic, idealistic, truthful yet tactful, generous. Although somewhat retiring by nature, she formed many close friendships, "particularly with those of talent beyond the ordinary. . . . She abhorred vulgarity and vulgar persons; used correct language herself, and was anxious that I do likewise." Neither she nor George drank or smoked.

Clarissa seemed to Clarence a typical product of the nineteenth-century Midwest. He was right up to a point. He listed, but did not remark upon, the implications of her social and political interests. Instead of frequenting conventional women's clubs, she attended Central Labor Body, Communist, and Anarchist meetings in Chicago, and other political gatherings. Using a toy typesetting device, she produced a political leaflet, and she functioned as a kind of unremunerated information service about reform and women's suffrage for local newspapers. Clarence considered his mother a clear thinker and talented writer but observed that her devotion to reform led her to write for publications—such as the Chicago *Sentinel, The Spiritual Offering, New Thought, The American Nonconformist,* the *Iowa Farmers' Tribune*—that circulated widely but could not pay writers.

In short, the idyllic rural American scene masked an underlying social conflict. And that was not the only conflict. Clarissa and George soon had "separate quarters," says Clarence. After she began to teach, Clarence lived with his paternal grandparents, where Clarissa would visit him on Saturdays and George on Sundays. This separation, he thought, was temporary, because "a comfortable home was later established." Clarissa, however, told Henry that she and George separated within a year of her marriage because she refused to submit to sexual relations, which she found distasteful. Henry added that Clarissa was the driving force behind George's ambitions but considered his business practices unethical.[9] From Clarence's vantage point, however, the marital problems developed gradually over about fifteen years, when, after "calm discussions," his parents terminated twenty years of marriage.

Above all, Clarissa, an aspiring writer, had to escape the stifling atmosphere of rural Midwestern fundamentalism. In 1890 she took the train alone to San Francisco, a city with more-or-less everything one could want—a lively colony of unconventional writers, the spirit of a big city, a multicultural environment, the pioneering spirit of the West, abundant land nearby, tremendous amounts of money, concentrated in the pockets of the heirs of the great mining and railway magnates, and a superabundance of poverty and crime.[10] Clarissa, it has been suggested, may have been drawn to the "bohemianism" of the literary community, but we do not know precisely which aspects of San Francisco appealed to her.[11] If she was the driving force behind George, she may have been attracted to the potential for literary success in that West Coast center of the arts world. The cheap land also made buying or building a house far more feasible than in New York. At the time, however, Clarence did not know where or why she had gone, and did not see her again for twenty-six years. He neglected to say that when he ran away from home at fourteen, he may have freed Clarissa to seek her own fortune.

The divorce, finalized on March 15, 1892, raised the probability of ostracism in finer San Francisco society in the unlikely event that Clarissa entered it. Fortunately, the calm of their parting encouraged her to expect her share of their assets and some support from George. The collapse of his finances not long afterward probably justified her dim view of his business practices. Still worse, it deprived her of desperately needed security.

Clarissa, however, had some basis for believing she could develop a career. As early as 1883 her essays and stories were attracting fan letters from around the country and she was being solicited by magazines in the nation's largest cities. One editor also sought a romantic relationship with her. From 1889 to 1891 she was assistant editor of an anarchist weekly, *The Beacon*. In San Francisco, she teamed up with a young Irish immigrant to publish a fortnightly anarchist paper, *Enfant Terrible* (1891–92),[12] with which she built a following. One sample of her contributions unmasks the underlying temperament of this ex-housewife who was anything but placid.

> The clergyman has no more right than the clown to marry people. The judge has no more right than the jail-bird to sentence people. The policeman has no more right than the pauper to arrest people. The tax-collector has no more right than any other thief to filch people's property. The legislator has no more right than the lackey to make laws. I have no reverence for God, nor parents, nor sovereigns, nor presidents, nor popes, nor bishops, nor dead bodies, nor ancient institutions; in short, I have no reverence for any person or thing.

In "Relations Between Parents and Children," published in the New York journal *Liberty* (1892), she asserted that a parent cannot be compelled to support a child, though he can be compelled not to "aggress upon it." Parents can prevent acts but cannot compel the performance of an action. Parents defeated their aims by applying them unintelligently—confusing, for example, the responsibility to provide clothing with the urge to create attractiveness. As a teacher she had seen parents brush off an intelligent question, replying, "You will learn when you are older." Often, she observed, such questions concerned the matter of omnipotent government. Worst of all, when a child was about six, or even younger, its parents abdicated their responsibility by entrusting its education to the church and the state, criminal institutions that inculcated a spirit of subordination, teaching children to submit to cruelty. "The State uses money robbed from the parents to perpetuate its powers of robbery by instructing their children in its own interest. The church also, uses its power to perpetuate its power. And to these twin leeches . . . are the tender minds of babies entrusted for education." Society's failings conspired with parental errors, leading children to lie, steal, and act violently. "Reason," she said, would bring people to rebel against inequalities. "Then parent and child shall not be master and slave, a relation distasteful to reasoning people, but they shall be friend and friend."[13]

The Clarissa Dixon of the early 1890s thus was perfectly suited to the individualistic world of San Francisco, as was her co-publisher of *Enfant Terrible*, an Irish immigrant named Henry Cowell, known as Harry. When they met around 1891, she was about forty, he about twenty-six. He too was from a respectable family. The Cowells of Logadowden, County of Dublin—whose arms were registered at Dublin Castle in 1771—produced a host of military men and Protestant clergymen. An ancient clan in the north of Ireland, they descended from an Irish monarch whose grandfather had been baptized by St. Patrick.[14] At some point the Cowells cooperated with, and were favored by, the English invaders.

Harry was born in Carlow, County Clare, Ireland, some twenty miles south of Kildare, on February 6, 1866, the eldest of six children of George Cowell, later the Dean of Kildare Episcopal Cathedral (1890–1913), and Jennie Blackwood Cowell, who died when Harry was a teenager. He attended "public" (that is, private) school and Trinity College, Dublin, but dropped out. It has been suggested that Harry was drawn to a spirit of separatism,[15] but he left Ireland for more mundane reasons. After his father remarried, neither he nor his eldest brother Dick could abide their new stepmother or her son. George Cowell bought into a farm near Vancouver on their behalf, and they left for a new existence.[16] Dick found western Canada congenial, but Harry tired of rural life and moved to the Bay Area sometime in the late 1880s, yearning for a literary community.[17] He soon fell in with the anarchist philosophers, including Clarissa Dixon. The rest of his life in that period is obscure.

Two knowledgeable sources, both claiming the authority of Harry's and Henry's words, painted diametrically opposed portraits of Harry. His garrulous third wife, Olive Thompson, could effuse boundlessly.

[In Canada] Harry loved the wilderness and the Indians in particular. He supported himself with rough work and never wrote home for money. His sensitive nature made it impossible for him to go "native." Drinking, chasing women, and gambling were impossible for him, the while [*sic*] he sat in the corner of a saloon reading his Shakespeare. He was much interested in poetry. After making some money selling books in Vancouver, he managed to get to San Francisco which attracted him for its literary life. Democratic and liberal by nature, he tried lecturing and writing being very much interested in Darwin, Huxley and the like, definitely avaunt-guarde [*sic*]; but it was very difficult . . . Associated with artists and writers, and met Clarissa Dixon in this group. . . . Harry and she, who was much older, lived together, as philosophical anarchists, and shocked all their friends.[18]

Sidney Cowell, Harry's later daughter-in-law, could also hold forth about Harry at length, equally unobjectively, and unrelentingly negatively. She saw him as an aspiring poet who was utterly self-absorbed, a "non-stop talker" who contributed nothing to the history of anarchism and attained upward mobility through serial marriages. When she met Harry's very congenial family in Ireland in the 1950s, she noticed that those who remembered him thought he was not good for much, because, in the words of one relative, "whatever it was, it would have to be something where Harry could count on being admired."[19]

Clarissa's only written comment followed their divorce. By then her initial attraction to Harry had faded. "[Harry] is a writer, a thinker who has chosen to be clever because cleverness is pleasing and thought is not. Perhaps it would be more just to say he was driven to be clever, Need being his driver. He is an essayist, a story-writer and a poet." (Even Sidney grudgingly admitted that some of his poetry was very fine.) Fortunately, Olive's romanticizing and Sidney's demythologizing can be blended with the observations of other dramatis personae into a moderately unimpressive image.

The early days of their relationship may well have been smooth, however. Clarissa and Harry rapidly found their way among the literary set of San Francisco, though it is not certain when they met writers and poets like Ambrose Bierce, George Sterling, and Mary Austin.[20] They wrote articles and poetry, published their anarchist journal, and clearly had much in common when they married in February 1893, a year after her divorce. Their address may already have been the small house that Harry built in the foothills west of Menlo Park, a site eventually denominated 2156 Harkins Avenue, a short street near Avy Street and Alameda de las Pulgas. Even twenty years later a friend was struck by the crudity of the surroundings. The street, still unimproved, became impassable mud when it rained. He remembered walking-boards along the side of the road, so rough was it.[21] They may have been "irresistibly drawn to Menlo Park's blend of Irish and bohemian cultures," as Michael Hicks suggests,[22] but Harry told Sidney a simpler story: they settled in Menlo just in time to become members of the first class at Stanford. Yet while Henry apparently believed the story, the dates seem incorrect,[23] and Sidney dismissed it as another of Harry's tales.[24] They may have intended to study there, but apparently never did.

Menlo Park had many advantages over San Francisco. The pioneering spirit characteristic of late nineteenth-century California made it a natural haven for the penniless. Squatting was a normal method of obtaining property. With Stanford University still under construction—it opened in 1891—discarded building material abounded; Harry used an old redwood for shingles. Olive said that he got lumber in exchange for typesetting at the *Palo Alto Times*. A mild climate, with almost no rain from May to September and only occasional frosts, simplified building a house. Sidney says, "[Their house] was no more than minimal shelter, and at first a roofed pavilion with screens on three sides and old blankets for curtains. This became a sleeping porch as the house acquired one and then two rooms, with small porches back and front."[25] Twenty years later it still did not have running water.[26] The property is easily recognized now by its unusually small lot.

Another surprising discovery: Harry and Clarissa purchased their land on September 6, 1894, for $125 [2010: $3,270],[27] taking a short-term loan.[28] This correct act of buying land, at a time and in a place where poor people were either given land by major landowners or simply appropriated it, puzzled Sidney as much as Harry and Clarissa's wedding. Either they never reconciled their philosophies with their middle-class backgrounds, or Sidney overestimated the totality of their commitment to anarchist principles. The issue is far from trivial, considering how much of Henry's personality has been attributed to his parents' outlook.[29]

On March 6, 1897, Harry submitted the final payment for the land. Five days later, on March 11, their baby emerged as Henry Dixon Cowell—a conventional name for a highly unconventional child.

2

Henry

Unlike some famous childhoods, Henry's is not shrouded in mystery. In 1914, Clarissa felt so driven by fate to document his development that although mortally ill, she began drafting a biographical sketch, amplifying it until her strength gave out.[1] While her almost mystical view of her son can hardly be called objective, her powerful influence on Henry renders her essay indispensable. Not that one has any options; it contains virtually the only information about a childhood that never could be dismissed in a sentence or two.

The adoration that both colors and corrupts her story enters at once. She declared that much about her baby could not be accounted for "on generally-accepted scientific principles. He seems to be part-angel and wise with inexplicable wisdom. He has taken much away from my old cock-suredness about the nature of being. He has also added material to my stock for renewal of speculations."[2] Expecting to mother Henry according to the precepts of her own essays, she was amazed by the changes that he worked upon her. He was "born cold," she says. Since all the manuals on mothering condemned cuddling, she placed him in the middle of a big bed. Still he was cold. Hot irons did no good. Finally, a mother of seven (probably her neighbor, Mrs. Harkins) urged her to take Henry in her arms. Suddenly Clarissa abandoned her battle against this traditional role of women. "Gladly I became an old-fashioned mother as far as cuddling is concerned. From that day forward I warmed my baby in the best of myself, soul and body." Soon he was declared physically perfect by one physician. "He was beautiful beyond the ordinary, with an indescribably spiritual quality of loveliness impossible to convey in words or to be caught in a photograph." The Scotch Club of San Francisco later pronounced him the most beautiful child in the city. "Crowds used to gather about him—on streetcars, railway trains, and in streets. He was happy in it all, but wholly unspoiled." Photographers (among them Arnold Genthe, the celebrated documenter of San Francisco street life), painters, and sculptors would ask her to let Henry pose for them, but apart from a few Genthe photos, she always said "no."[3] She believed

Henry understood that this attention would ultimately stop, but it looks like the roots of Henry-the-performer. Unfortunately, many of her photographs were lost in the fire triggered by the 1906 earthquake.

Unwilling to repeat what she considered her immature mothering of Clarence, Clarissa, with Harry's acquiescence, decided to give Henry the maximum amount of freedom compatible with safety. The social reformer Anna Strunsky Walling, who witnessed that period while a student at Stanford, described Clarissa as permissive "to use an understatement."[4] Nurturing him became a kind of scientific study of free choice. "As soon as he was able to look about with steady eyes," Clarissa continued, "I arranged brightly colored fabrics around him. Invariably his eyes, after some wandering from one color to another, rested on pink. Pink was accordingly made his own—pink dresses, pink hood, pink sacque. Remembering this, I wonder he did not tire of pink. I think I overdid the lavishing of his favorite color upon him."

His instinct for physical beauty had a strange result. When it was time for him to wear trousers, he objected to their ugliness. Clarissa: "He said he wished to be a girl and wear dresses because they were prettier than boys' clothes. Up to the age of about [eight] Henry frequently dressed himself in gay attire, castoff finery of ladies, the most beautifully colored silks and finest fabrics he could command." What may seem like deviant behavior became a spectacular performance as he began calling upon neighbors under the name "Mrs. Jones." His love of pretty things became so well known among their friends that women contributed their old dresses, ribbons, lace, and such "until he had a large trunkful to draw upon for his full-dress parades." Soon the neighbors' children started joining him in the game, which resembled a fancy dress ball. Henry usually wore a large sofa cushion on his head in lieu of a hat; no real hat was enormous enough. Otherwise, says Clarissa, his costumes usually displayed great taste.

Whether or not Henry was exceptionally intelligent—Clarissa heard him speak at least 272 words by the age of two—she treated him that way. After she taught him about "property rights," he began to give his possessions to his friends. (Later in life he would give away casually the only copy of a composition, and, according to Sidney, was not particularly upset when he was robbed.)[5] Allowed the long leash—physical punishment or any other use of force was unthinkable[6]—he would became engrossed in one or another aspect of life and later reject it. An obsession with cleanliness was temporary; a period around the age of six when he could not be trusted to keep a promise gave way to a compulsion to teach people not to be naughty. According to Sidney, as an adult he was compulsive about honorably fulfilling promises.[7]

His alert, inquisitive nature forced his parents to choose between their ingrained resistance to formalizing his education and their responsibility to answer his questions. Clarissa called it "Groping Among Educational Methods— I do the groping. The child leads." Because they would not make him study one

thing when he wanted to learn another, he learned very quickly, devoting his energies at various times to geography, botany, music, or other subjects. Spelling
and arithmetic were barely touched.

When Henry was about three they moved to San Francisco, spending a few
weeks on Bernal Heights while Harry completed a house in the Mission district,
at 2517 ½ Castro Street, at 30th Street,[8] near the end of the Noe Street streetcar,
a "steep spot [in Henry's later recollection] with nothing but wild flowers &
rocks around."[9] Clarissa did not say why they moved; they may have wished to
be closer to their San Francisco literary friends, especially the Strunskys, whose
nieces became Henry's playmates.[10] Financially, the move was ill-advised. Early
in 1901, Harry took a job as a proofreader at the state offices in Sacramento,
earning $33 [2010: $873] a week, boarding in a private home, and saving every
cent to pay for the new house, which they nearly lost. His letters suggest a well-
intentioned dreamer who was deluding himself and everyone around him. He
told Henry of the "literary life" they would enjoy, but reality kept him in Sacramento for the whole session of the state legislature, which ended in mid-March.
Henry came to resent his absences,[11] but Anna Strunsky (Walling), looking back
sixty years to those days, remembered Henry bathed in overwhelming love.[12]

As to that literary life, one of the few details that Henry retained was an
encounter while waiting for a streetcar in Berkeley. A ditch-digger who happened to hear Harry and Clarissa discussing writing proved to be self-educated
but with "astounding ideas and great clarity of speech." The laborer, Jack London, accepted Harry's invitation to see them for the first of many visits when
Henry was about seven.[13] Henry clearly remembered "playing with his children
while the parents talked, and thinking of Jack London as being most kindly
towards children . . . and being well understood by them. . . . I was immediately
drawn and attracted to him." Although Henry thought that Harry was the one
who persuaded London to write about his experiences, Sidney was doubtful—
"just one of Harry's tales about himself."[14] The story seems plausible in part
because of another connection: Anna Strunsky, the Cowells' neighbor, and London were close friends.

Harry's absences and other unspecified problems eventually took their toll.
Clarissa's next actions may have been suggested by her handsome, autographed
set of Laura Smith Wood's "Epigrams of Love, Woman and Marriage," which
urged women to resist subjugation, be independent, live their own lives; be financially independent; and seek men who recognize and support such a status.
When Henry was about six (around 1903), they moved without Harry to a larger
house at 1611 Laguna Street near Post, close to San Francisco's Asian district
and not far from the Strunskys.[15] Clarissa intended to earn their support by
taking in roomers. She does not say whether anything specific precipitated their
separation, but elsewhere we learn that she denied Harry sex because it was no

longer needed for reproduction. She happily terminated such "dirty" contact between man and woman.[16] Or did she reject Harry because he had commenced relations with a French-born singer and distinguished voice teacher, Henrietta (or Henriette) Grothwell, with whom he occupied the Castro Street house after Clarissa left?[17] The time sequence is not known. Harry may have become involved with Henrietta because Clarissa had ended their sex life; he was only in his thirties. His guiltlessness is implied by the fact that the separation did not alienate Anna Strunsky, who remained close to Harry until he died.[18]

According to Henry, when Harry and Henrietta began living together, she did not know he had a wife and child. Upon learning the truth, she went to Clarissa to apologize and they became friends. Henry and Henrietta also bonded. "About this time Henrietta asked me what she might bring me the next time she came. I asked for a kaleidoscope, but this was too modest for Henrietta's ideas & she arrived with an expensive great magic lantern. I cried."[19]

On December 8, 1903, Clarissa divorced Harry "without reproach" so that he and Henrietta could marry. She never expressed her heartbreak in any letter or in her biography of Henry, but wrote a very sad poem about the discovery that her husband no longer loved her. Henry remembered Clarissa saying that she had assumed she would lose Harry because she was so much older, but had not expected it to happen so soon.[20]

In her first divorce, Clarence's age and disappearance rendered the question of custody moot. This time custody of their child was of great concern since Harry could earn a steady income but Clarissa was an impoverished freelance writer. Recognizing the depressing reality, she even considered not fighting to keep Henry. The prospect of having to take responsibility for the boy, however, may be what prompted Harry to put Henry in her hands and agree to provide child support of $10 [2010: $256] per month, which he maintained until Clarissa and Henry left the Bay Area in 1906 and which he continued irregularly afterward.[21]

Meanwhile, Clarissa and Henry lived on Laguna Street until an increase in her earnings from writing encouraged her to abandon the rooming-house enterprise and move back to Menlo Park in mid-1905. Eight-year-old Henry had to say good-bye to his Asian playmates.[22] Laboring indefatigably at her writing, she received acceptances and rejections. Yet even if she had sold everything she wrote, any writer without a great reputation had to produce a torrent of essays, short stories, and poems to survive. These hardships were amplified by a series of tragedies. Late in 1904 Clarissa had lost a beloved aunt;[23] the following summer, a brother who battled alcohol and depression committed suicide. Fortunately, her rapid exit from that Iowa church had not cost her the love and support of her Midwestern family, whose warm, uncomplicated letters cheered her as she struggled to support her son.[24]

Up to this point the only corroborating witnesses to Clarissa's narrative have been Anna Strunsky Walling and Henry, neither of whom had a flawless memory. Long after Henry's death, in investigating the next period, his widow, Sidney Cowell, located another witness, Angela Joulie Kiefer, who confirmed some aspects of the story while adding a little confusion. The contradictions suggest that Mrs. Kiefer, who was in her mid-seventies when she responded to Sidney's 1975 inquiry, may have combined her recollections of 1905 with others from after 1910, when Henry's and Clarissa's situation was quite different. Nevertheless, her picture of their corner of Menlo Park around 1905–10, is invaluable.

The population of the Menlo Park of 1905 was so small that someone building the first house on the block could name the street. (The entire San Francisco Bay area, including the East Bay, had only 543,000 residents in the 1900 census, but was growing rapidly.)[25] The heterogenous community ranged from professors at the expanding university, some from very fine families, to laborers, mostly immigrants, some of them very poor. The Joulies (Mrs. Kiefer's family), for example, lived in a large house near what is now the Alameda de las Pulgas;[26] their neighbors had eleven children, with a Mexican mother and an English father. None of the local children were Henry's age, however; Henry's neighbors, the Harkins (who evidently named the street), had seven, all older than he. Angela Joulie was several years younger. The Harkins's four boys—the only other boys in the neighborhood—would play tricks on him. "Poor Henry didn't know what it was all about. He didn't think it was funny and the boys would sit there and just howl." Mrs. Kiefer could not describe the tricks, for "I never had a boy around me."[27]

She remembered Clarissa as somewhat strict, though not a nag. Henry was always helping her in the garden or with similar little jobs, not out playing. Mrs. Kiefer felt that he was isolated from people and detached, either because he was an only child totally wrapped up in music, or because the population of the area was so sparse that people were forced to live independently of one another, without close neighborhood contacts. Everybody did chores; she milked the cows and brought them in from the pasture. When boys were needed, the Harkins boys would be hired. Henry, however, had nothing more than his music. While Mrs. Kiefer avoided the temptation to call his childhood "misspent," she felt it was not much of a childhood.

She also remembered Henry rarely turning up at Las Lomitas school. In fact, his education was a burning issue for Clarissa, who knew that he needed contact with children his age, and she needed time to write. When the time came for a decision, Clarissa had to choose between not sending him to the local public school or abandoning her doctrine that the public school system was unjustifiable because it homogenized instead of reinforcing natural heterogeneity, and abused democracy in forcing voters to pay school taxes.[28] In the end she convinced herself that he would withstand the schools' "process of reduction to pulp . . . with little or no intellectual or spiritual hurt." Unfortunately, she never considered that he might literally be beaten to a pulp. That was a serious miscalculation. Whereas their cabin in the Santa Clara Valley was two miles from the center of Menlo Park, and almost as far from Stanford, both of them pleasant places, "the [one-room] country schoolhouse, a half-mile away, in our district, was also in the district of a number of very rough children. There were some boys 14 to 17 years old who were worse than rough; they were ruffians, as I afterward learned to my horror." She had not exactly prepared the way properly. Photographs show him looking like "Little Lord Fauntleroy." His appearance, small size, and huge vocabulary, made an attack almost inevitable. He must have told Sidney what happened next. She wrote,

> After school during the first week he was caught by some rough older boys who challenged each other to capture his large head of uncut curly blond hair with their lassos. He was dragged along the ground by a rope that tightened around his neck, and when his head hit a rock the big boys abandoned their rope and ran off. Henry was feverish for several days but as soon as the mark on his neck healed he said he liked the teacher and the other children, and he wanted to go back. This time a larger group of older boys circled him in the yard to take turns bloodying his nose and blackening his eyes; a blow left his jaw with a permanent slight twist. The teacher said frankly she could not control these big fellows and Mrs. Cowell concluded the situation was impossible. . . . She learned later that some hazing of newcomers sometimes took place, but she seems not to have realized what a challenge Henry's appearance presented, in a community where most boys wore overalls with bibs and had their hair trimmed very short at home around an inverted bowl.[29]

Mrs. Kiefer attributed the attacks to Henry's lack of a brother or father to protect him, and to possible racial antagonism among the boys, who were mostly Portuguese or Spanish, some with Mexican and/or Indian blood, and some of them quite big. Clarissa withdrew him from the public school and taught him at home a short time every day for the next eleven months.

His interest in music had already asserted itself. He is said to have sung phrases from folksongs before he could even talk.[30] Henry recalled Clarissa singing the folksongs of the Ozarks, and Harry singing Irish tunes. His first instrument was a mandolin-harp presented by a family friend. "Soon I began to improvise and they thought I had talent. You know what that means. If you have gifts when you're young, parents always imagine that they're for playing on an instrument rather than composing for one." When he was only four-and-a-half, a young musician who lived nearby gave him a quarter-size violin, but even that was too large, and Clarissa bought a smaller one. A year later, he had his first lesson, with Sylvia Holmes, the daughter of Henry Holmes, a Londoner born in 1839 who had enjoyed a successful career as a young man before joining the faculty of the Royal College of Music. In his mid-fifties, Holmes moved to San Francisco, where his best-known pupil was the Canadian-born virtuoso Kathleen Parlow. When a hand injury forced Sylvia Holmes to give up teaching, her father stepped in. On January 15, 1903, seventy-five-year-old Henry Holmes taught five-year-old Henry Cowell for the first time.[31] Holmes accepted Henry on the condition that he alone would determine what music the boy played and, Henry says, "there would be none of this nonsense of modern music, such as Schubert and Schumann. So I was raised on Haydn and Mozart and a little bit of early Beethoven. Late Beethoven he said was what started all this downpour of dissonant music." Within two years he was playing Mozart and Haydn. When Harry and Clarissa asked whether he might try some nineteenth-century music, Holmes reluctantly allowed Cherubini, a safe choice. The old man "really thought that music came to its senses only in the middle and late Eighteenth Century and that there was not much to do about it before or after. Now maybe that's why I broke out and became an enfant terrible, I don't know."[32]

The first obstacle to progress was physical. "Both doctors," Holmes's wife wrote Clarissa, "agree that the warmth and sensitiveness of the spine is a symptom demanding an inquiry. They both also agree that the child should live out of doors, & undertake no kind of study." Furthermore, when Henry's practicing began to fall off, Holmes had to be "gently, tenderly severe" with the boy and declined to see him unless he committed himself seriously.[33] Holmes eventually relented, but not for long. After he pointed out a mistake that Henry could not rectify, he exclaimed, "I don't see why you keep making the same mistake!" Accustomed to dealing with adults as an equal, and clueless about the deference that Holmes expected, Henry retorted that he could not hear Holmes if he spoke while Henry was playing "and you put me out." Lessons ended abruptly and unpleasantly. Having lost his teacher, Henry continued to practice Spohr's *Violin Method* by himself. Meanwhile, Holmes's friends convinced him to take back this very promising pupil. They never understood one another, however. In the late summer of 1905, he had a few sessions with another violinist, Karl Becker, but as symptoms of chorea were increasing, a doctor advised "avoiding the violin and its associations." Clarissa estimated that between 1902 and the fall of 1905, when he was eight and one-half, Henry had had weekly lessons for a total of about eight months. At his most advanced he was playing easy movements from Mozart, Haydn, and Beethoven sonatas.[34] When Henry was eight, Harry began taking him to play the violin around San Francisco, unconcerned about the pressure that was causing him to develop an irritability foreign to his nature, facial tremors, and other symptoms. Hearing Harry talk about auditioning him for vaudeville, Clarissa laid down the law.[35] "At nine I retired. My career as a violinist had finished." His "retirement" would probably have come anyway: Holmes died a few months later. Mrs. Kiefer did not even remember that he had played the violin until her husband reminded her. Strangely, Clarissa mentioned little more about the violin than Henry's ability at age five, less than four months after commencing violin studies, to play simple tunes at sight, rarely playing a wrong note though making rhythmic mistakes.

The search for other early musical influences collides with Henry's conflicting recollections. In 1962 he said that Harry and Clarissa never introduced him to any of their musical friends;[36] but a year later he recounted being taken to dinner in Berkeley at the home of the celebrated accompanist Fred Maurer—who had worked with Nelly Melba and Marcella Sembrich—and accidentally discovering there, among twelve musician-guests, that he had perfect pitch.[37] Other episodes may have been forgotten.

Unlike his violin studies, living on Laguna Street, situated between the Japanese and Chinese districts, had an extremely positive impact on six-year-old Henry's musicality. According to Sidney, his Japanese, Chinese, Tahitian, and Filipino playmates taught him their singing games, and he heard koto music in Japanese homes. Singing the songs of his Asian playmates became so much a matter of course that he came to consider their music his own, a natural complement to his mother's Tennessee songs and his father's Irish tunes. The many distinguished Asian political refugees in San Francisco included Indian musical virtuosi who sometimes let Henry listen from a corner of their room. Henry's solo trips to Chinatown alarmed Clarissa because the neighborhood was riddled with violent criminals, but she was confident that Henry's only goal was to hear music,[38] which he did at a club of elderly Chinese refugee musicians, spectacular performers who played above an old Chinatown restaurant and could be heard from the street, where Henry and other admirers sat on the curb and listened. He also heard Chinese opera before he ever heard a Western opera, because Clarissa knew the importance of opera but could not afford tickets for Western opera. By hearing "a little bit of everything from everywhere," including classical music, he learned to respect the world's many musics. No one, he said, ever told him that Western music was supposed to be superior.

But how could he be a musician without a piano? His answer became his personal credo. It is, however, not clear where or when the events he describes took place; it could have been San Francisco or Menlo Park. His reference to playing with the kids suggests that he was not as isolated as Mrs. Kiefer remembered.

> I said to myself, "A composer uses his mind, he hears sounds in his mind so he doesn't need any other musical instrument except his mind." I

decided to be a composer at this point. All the children I played with
went in from four to five in the afternoon, exactly, to practice the piano,
and of course, everybody was out again at 5:01 to play. I didn't want to
be left out of such activity, so for one hour every day I practiced in my
mind. I sat down at the desk and practiced listening to sounds in my
mind. I did this very methodically, and I think this is a point. It has to do
with education, it has to do with method in composing. Although I
lived among people who were very romantic about composition, I
myself supplied a method, and this method was to cultivate my mind to
hear sounds which became more and more complicated as time went
on. I remember starting to hear, in my mind, the sound of melodies,
first a melody as played on the piano, then on a violin. Then I found out
what the oboe sounded like and added this, then voice, and so on. After
I had done this a while I hit on something which is really one of the
secrets of composers. That is that when you listen to two or more
sounds at the same time, you don't try to listen to two things at once,
you listen to the combined unit that these sounds make and then you
are listening to one thing. In this way I trained myself then to hear harmony as well as melody. And, of course, the rhythm was part of the
composition. By the time I got to the age of about thirteen and finally
earned enough money to buy an old, decrepit piano, I had already gone
through a great deal. . . .[39]

His story is all the more compelling because his parents thoroughly approved
of music and gave him all the encouragement he could have needed, but believed
so strongly in inspiration that formal study of music seemed superfluous if not
deleterious to his growth. Clarissa's Spiritualist background may have led her to
regard inspiration as a mystical and supernatural force, whereas Harry's attitude
seems to stem from a Romantic view of the inspired virtuoso as an admired
public figure. The result was the same, however: an inspired composer did not
need to study, and no amount of study would help an uninspired composer. "It
was only when I was about sixteen that people said to me, 'Well, really, these
compositions of yours are wonderful, but you just *have* to study.'" He could not
really regret his unconventional self-training and background, however: it was
the wellspring of his conviction that one should be free to draw upon all musical
materials, an attitude that he considered typically American.[40]

This stimulating if isolated life suddenly changed at 5:14 A.M. on April 18,
1906. Henry and his mother were staying with friends in a two-story house not
far from Menlo Park. When the earthquake hit, the steps from their upper-story
room crumbled, taking them along; outside, they had to make their way across
the bricks of the collapsed chimney. Fortunately, damage in the immediate area

was comparatively light; their own house survived but was littered with broken plates. Many Stanford buildings had been destroyed, however, and water mains were ruptured. The next day, they were horrified by the glow of San Francisco burning in the north. Clarissa's reference to losing her photographs in the fire suggests that the house in San Francisco was destroyed. Aftershocks, which continued for years, were extremely frightening. When Harry arrived after biking for two days, he, Henry, and Clarissa went to see crevices at the San Andreas fault. The earthquake must have been one reason for Henry's recurring bad dreams; he was still terrified two years later.[41] Some 3,000 buildings were destroyed and 500–600 people died. An enormous exodus began: one railroad reported moving some 216,000 people. Only 175,000 remained after the fire.[42]

Clarissa also must have known that with employment in the city at a halt except for the reconstruction industry, a writer of political essays and fiction had few prospects. With nearly $100 [2010: $2,500] saved from her writing, on May 22, 1906, Clarissa and Henry headed for her relatives in the Midwest[43] on their way to New York.

|| 3 ||

Years of Voyage

The next three-and-one-half years can be pieced together from Clarissa's biography of Henry, letters, and stories that he later told Sidney. His complex relationship with his father may be inferred from an exchange that began with Henry's pithy farewell: "Dear papa we are going to start tomorrow so good-bye. Henry D. Cowell."[1] Realizing that his son might never return, Harry lamented that they could have had another hour down by the creek if he had known they were about to leave. Henry's apology—that they did not know when they would start out—makes sense in the chaos after the earthquake. When weeks passed without a letter from Harry, Henry suffered greatly. In fact, he had written, but the letter only caught up with Henry and Clarissa in Kansas, where they were visiting her sister and brother-in-law Jennie and James Guilbert. The mollified Henry described their situation, enclosing a flower. "thair are seventy pigs on the farm. it is fun to hear them squeal. the school is the nearrest naber . . ."[2] They stayed there, in the endless plains of western Kansas, for three weeks, eighteen miles from Banner at the Guilberts' 480-acre farm, near a bluff with prehistoric fossils that fascinated Henry. Their closest neighbor was a mile and a half away; the post office, seven miles. Aunt Jennie, outraged that nine-year-old Henry lacked religious education, took him to a Sunday "entertainment," at which children recited biblical verses. He was amazed by the atmosphere and the low regard in which music was held. Here was a land where secular music effectively did not exist. Clarissa was so appalled that she wished she had taught Henry arias rather than folk songs.[3]

In mid-July they went to Cashion, Oklahoma, some twenty miles northwest of Oklahoma City, to visit Clarissa's father and her youngest brother. Since everyone belonged to a "Holiness sect," they had to attend church, where the pastor delivered a fiery sermon accusing sinners of bringing San Francisco's fate upon it. Later, Henry realized that two of the sinners were his mother and himself. In moments of meditation, the quiet of the church would be shattered by sudden outbursts of screaming. Henry was again perplexed, having never heard of Holy Rollers.[4]

They finally got to her son Clarence's Des Moines home around August 1, 1906. When Clarissa found a job as editor of the women's page of a farming magazine,[5] she rented a little house at 1428 Walnut. At sixty-six degrees the weather seemed cold to Henry. He spent his time reading *The Faery Queen, Siegfried,* and books by May E. Wilkins, a famous author of stories for young people, and writing his first known composition, a melody composed to his own words about traveling the seas and never returning to San Francisco. One can imagine Harry's and Henrietta's reactions when they received it.[6]

In September, needing time for work, Clarissa compromised her principles and sent Henry to school, the first time in more than a year. Nine-and-one-half years old, he combined great intellectual strengths with such poor penmanship, spelling, and arithmetic skills that the school had no idea where to place him. Assigned to third grade, he attended regularly for about four months until a long period of poor health culminated in an operation to remove his tonsils and adenoids around his tenth birthday, March 11, 1907. Clarissa doubted that it affected his school work, since almost nothing was new to him except drawing. Local educational methods confirmed her negativity about public school. He was prohibited from reading further ahead in the book than the lesson of the day; the art teacher sent him home because he insisted upon using pink and brown together.[7]

Nevertheless, he was promoted and had barely begun the fourth grade when he contracted measles and scarlet fever. A few weeks later he crawled home from school in terror after suffering convulsions, which no one at school noticed. Fortunately, the problem was chorea and not epilepsy. He may have been having small attacks for up to four years.[8] A friend who must have heard the whole story only a few years later added that the children ridiculed him because he sucked his thumb until a late age, distorting his jaw and giving his smile a rather sweet, lopsided effect. Neither the friend nor the children in Des Moines knew that the distortion resulted from the beating he had taken at school in California.[9] Clarissa was advised not to send him back to school. Although it would limit her time for writing, she was delighted to educate her boy by herself. Formal schooling, which, in her opinion, had brought him only physical pain, was over. Henry enjoyed referring to his third-grade certificate of promotion as his highest academic degree until he received an honorary doctorate in 1953.

Clarissa's approach to homeschooling was shaped by her belief that Henry should follow his interests and not be pushed to learn subjects that bored him. She felt justified and delighted when a phrenologist at the fairgrounds proclaimed that Henry entirely lacked the Bump of Deference. Respect yes; but deference, never! (A pity that Henry Holmes died without learning what caused their friction.)[10] Her teaching was also supported, perhaps unknowingly, by the librarian of the local children's library, who permitted Henry to browse through the adult section, assuming he was reading only superficially. Clarissa kept a running list of his readings, but since she did not pinpoint the time when he read each one, we shall put aside the list for the moment.

The infrequency of Harry's letters gnawed at Henry, especially as he longed for news about Henrietta. Struggling to maintain communication, he sent Harry an imaginative little story called "The Inchanted Palace," but his signature "Henry Dixon" had to have hurt. The few letters of the next months mix good cheer with much bad news—from Henry, reports of cold weather, a cousin's death from cancer, and a joke; from Harry, an inquiry about whether Clarissa needed money, and a message from Henrietta that Henry should write her. On March 9, 1907, two days before Henry's tenth birthday, Harry sent Clarissa a bit of money and fifty cents to cheer him after an operation to remove his adenoids. Although Harry was doing some lecturing, he was in difficult straits. To his credit, he does not seem to have evaded child support. He simply had no money. Instead of hostility, Clarissa's acknowledgment of his contribution to the "Henry-get-well fund" expressed distress that her poems were faring reasonably well while her best work was being rejected.

By May 1, Henry had recovered from a bad reaction to the ether anesthetic used in his adenoidectomy. From Harry, the usual story: he had hoped to send money, but had not been paid for a lecture at Berkeley. Still unreconciled to Henry's "retirement" from the violin, he touted Kathleen Parlow's success in St. Petersburg. Subsequent letters are unrevealing. Harry would drop in at once if he had an airship; Harry was sorry about Clarissa's repeated misfortunes; Harry had money for Clarissa but was pickpocketed. In June, sister Jennie's husband died. It was all fairly ordinary family business until September 11, when Harry reported that he had received a composition from Henry. Henry's last known letter from Des Moines is dated September 25, 1907. In his personal style of spelling and grammar he told Harry that he had seen three operas—"'The Wiserd of Os,' 'the Mrs. Wigges of the Cabbage Patch', and 'The Cat and the Fiddle.' But all of them are so changed that I would not know them . . . I have a cold. Mama's hair is coming out. . . . I forgot tell you how glad I was to receive the money, so that I could go to the opera, and I thank you for it very much." He may be referring to his first encounter with Western classical opera, Il Trovatore, which inspired him to write his own opera, using Longfellow's "Golden Legend" as a libretto. The one surviving melody became the second theme of the piano piece "Antinomy."

The summer freshness of their room turned into an oppressive cold. Alarmed that Henry and Clarissa never answered one of his letters—it apparently never arrived—Harry realized that if something happened to her, her relatives might deprive him of his son. He therefore requested legal guardianship. Clarissa's prompt authorization suggests that her trust in Henrietta overcame her reservations about Harry. She may also have been alarmed at her hair loss, since she was only fifty-six.

Henry, however, had two more things to celebrate. The pansies growing in his first garden won him a gold medal and $2 [2010: $47.90] in a children's competition, and Clarence's wife had given him one of her two pianos.[11] According to Clarissa, "It was very old, but well made, and usable through the middle range of the keyboard." The engagement of a piano teacher did not comfort Harry, however, who kept feeding Henry reports about Kathleen Parlow in the royal palaces of Europe.[12] Considering his dismal record with the violin, and Harry's serial failures, it is hard to imagine Henry buying the idea that the violin was the route to glory.

Fortunately, Clarissa knew better than to linger in Des Moines; she really was a city girl. In late winter, after receiving $100 [2010: $2,390] for a children's book that had been accepted by a New York publisher, she prepared to move on. Shortly after Henry's eleventh birthday (March 11, 1908), they went to New York, settling at 222 East 33rd Street.

Her dreams of success in New York were shattered decisively. The extreme financial distress into which they quickly sank may explain why Clarissa's memoir is relatively quiet about the New York years. Her description of the struggle for a livelihood as "increasingly strenuous" was a gigantic understatement; in one year there she earned less than $200 from writing. Literary life was a roller-coaster. First Harper and Brothers rejected her novel *Janet and Her Dear Phebe* because it was neither juvenile nor adult; then Frederick A. Stokes & Co., a noted publisher of fiction, overcame its reservations about the novel's commercial prospects, offered her a $100 advance on royalties payable after the first thousand sales, moved the book immediately into production, and took first options on her next five novels, with increasing royalty rates. She must have been ecstatic until, shortly after the proof stage of *Janet*, Stokes rejected one book and deferred deciding about another, pending sales figures for *Janet*. *Janet and Her Dear Phebe*, which appeared in February 1909, was warmly received by the press, but only 310 copies were sold in four months. In fact, it is a fine book, but truly straddled the borderline between teenage and adult. Politely but decisively, Stokes dropped further options.

The publication of *Janet and Her Dear Phebe* was a fleeting moment of brightness in New York. Characteristically, her biography of Henry says little more than "I worked hard on my poor little short stories that nobody would buy . . . and Henry . . . a splendid comrade . . . was more than ever dependent on the Public Libraries . . . and Life, itself, for an education."[13] Tactfully hiding the seriousness of their situation from Harry, she could not be completely silent. Wouldn't he consider going back to the printing business? "I should be very glad if we could get along without asking your help, but at present everything is so uncertain, I should like to lean a little, if I could find something to lean on." Harry's own problems were multiplying, however. He sold the house on Castro Street because Henrietta could not climb the stairs. Now they were living in a tent on Baker's Beach while he built a new one.[14] He also seemed to have retreated from his old principles. While assenting to her plans for Henry's homeschooling, he urged that Henry "see something of the inside of public schools" if his health improved.[15] In August (1908) he finally sent $10 [2010: $244] in child support.[16] Grateful Clarissa harbored no ill will; she was most concerned that his new house be earthquake-resistant. "Henry cannot get over the earthquake terror. He is afraid you and Henrietta will sometime suffer from one."

Since June 15 they had been caretakers during the renovation of a townhouse at 24 West 12th Street. Clarissa assured Harry that she only had to protect the house, fulfill the insurance requirement that it be occupied, answer the bell, and keep the steps and sidewalk clear. Their above-average pay ($15 a month [2010: $367]) perhaps compensated for the discomfort incumbent upon living in a once-fine house that was being reconstructed, with lime dust everywhere. Henry, who enjoyed climbing the scaffolding for a view, had a peculiar visit to the intersection of art and mammon after the kindly workmen built him a swing. One day, while he was swinging and singing, someone complimented his voice and threw him a quarter. He was mortified at being paid to sing like a beggar.[17]

When the renovations neared an end they had to relocate. The arrangement had been satisfactory enough that Clarissa sought another caretaker's job. She told Harry, "We may get only our rent next time, but that would mean a good deal, here." If she did not find a position, they would look for a cheap place across the river, presumably in Brooklyn. Happily, they never had to cross the waters. In September, when the renovation was complete, they moved to a new home at 525A East 72nd Street, and again at the end of January 1909, to 160 Waverly Place, near Greenwich Village, whose café life was beyond their means.

Despite the hardships, she did not regret coming to New York. Des Moines was too limited, California was endlessly frustrating. New York seemed to have been preordained. She was confident that life held a place for her and she would "be getting fitted into [it]." The city also provided the stimulus that Henry needed. "[He] loves a land of art galleries and libraries, and big grand opera advertisements—even if he can't go in and pay for a seat." Looking back half a century later, he recalled getting his first exposure to symphonic music at a concert with Mahler conducting the New York Symphony, but didn't remember a thing about it.[18] His passion for stamp collecting that taught him geography, history, and politics drove Clarissa to distraction and hinders the establishment of a chronology because he tore the stamps and postmarks from almost every letter of that time. Later, to her relief, he diverted his attention to amassing a complete set of pre-earthquake streetcar transfers.[19] His verbal skills grew rapidly, which is more than can be said of his spelling. He wrote Harry about tall buildings, mosquitoes that "turn boys into hamburger steak," grass and trees visible from their window.

Clarissa was sometimes reproached for bringing up Henry "in ignorance" by keeping him out of school. She admitted that formal schooling might have filled some holes in how she schooled him but largely regretted her inability to give him more time or hire a tutor. Nevertheless, he studied history, especially of ancient cultures; travels in Alaska, Australia, Chile, China, Holland, Iceland, India, Japan, Korea, Labrador, Norway, and Panama; sciences including astronomy, geology, mineralogy, natural history, zoology, physiology; biographies of political figures and musicians (Beethoven, Liszt, and Mendelssohn); great literature (Keats, Lamb, Shakespeare), art, and fiction.

He read Stainer on harmony, Mason on orchestration, and Prout on musical form. These, however, pale in comparison with what he was attempting to accomplish in his mind out of necessity, because he had no other instrument but intensely desired to hear music. On those few occasions when he could attend a concert, he would "rehearse" the pieces he liked so that he could listen to them over and over in his mind, making a special effort to get the right tone color, since color would easily "shade off into something indeterminate." Suddenly, original ideas started popping into his mind, totally beyond his control. He thought these experiences were what his circle called "inspiration." It all happened so quickly that he could not write down the ideas. He determined to "practice" until he could control longer and longer ideas and improve his command of tone color. Gradually he could "turn on a flow of [the ideas] at will," and write them down. Yet they usually proved uninteresting when he played them. He concluded that the composer's mind was far superior to that of any performer, and that only about 10 percent of musical ideas can be realized even at the best performance.[20] The disappointment must have come later, because he had no piano in New York.

New York touched Henry's social consciousness. He noticed the hundreds of thousands of destitute, and that most cultural life was off limits for poor people like him. There were some resources, however. While he and Clarissa only went where admission was free, they had the Metropolitan Museum on certain days, Central Park, Riverside Drive, Morningside Park. When they lived downtown they would go to Cooper Union, the Astor Library, Hearn's department store (which had a fine collection of carved ivory and some good paintings), and Wanamaker's, which had free concerts where Henry could hear an orchestra.[21] If invited to an artist's reception, they accepted. "We used to walk lingeringly past great opera-houses when world-famous singers might be heard within by those who could pay for seats; but Henry never asked me to buy tickets. Young as he was, he understood our necessities."

By October 1908, Henry had read 150 books and his stamp collection—as he told Harry—"is growing so fast that you can see it grow. Indeed, just today I received twenty-eight."[22] Music fared much worse, however. Before they moved to New York, he had had five lessons. During their one year and four months in New York Clarissa remembered Henry touching a piano only once, for a few minutes "when we were visitors where he was left to his own devices in the parlor." At least she, while no richer for it, had become part of the literary world. *Who's Who in America* wanted her biography;[23] her publisher, Stokes, remained in touch; and Romeike's newspaper cutting service (to whom we owe the enormous collection of clippings from the height of Henry's performing career) solicited her business regarding reviews of *Janet*. There was business for Romeike, but not for Clarissa. With sales peaking at 400, neither royalties nor contracts were on the horizon. She never received a penny for *Janet*.

Henry felt confident of what he learned in a city so rich in free resources, but now he wanted to return to California. He was reading a lot but mentioned no friends.[24] He did not tell Harry that he accidentally locked himself in a closet and screamed in terror for three hours. One friend of later years said that the incident explained the panic that she sensed beneath Henry's outer serenity.[25]

Clarissa's memoir of the time in New York is touching and alarming enough without the dramatic climax, about which she is silent. Indeed, there is no written evidence of the disastrous winter of 1908–9. Years later, Henry told Sidney that friends found the two of them in bed starving and freezing, and took them home to their small apartment, where they lived for an unspecified period, dependent upon their hosts, who also were poor. According to Sidney's account, the man sold souvenir postcards and Henry tried to help him with his deliveries but was too weak and ill to do much. Eventually the Society for the Improvement of the Condition of the Poor provided money for food and train fare to their nearest solvent relative, Clarissa's widowed sister Jennie Guilbert in rural Kansas.[26] They left New York in mid-June, 1909. The journey's many delays only magnified Henry's desperate desire to see Harry and Henrietta.[27]

Penniless, they had to stay with Jennie for about a year. Harry's infrequent letters included a poppy and a dollar for Christmas, 1909, which Henry put into his "California fund." They had not celebrated Christmas. He longed to be in San Francisco for the mammoth celebration of the opening of the Panama Canal and impatiently awaited passing through the tail of Halley's Comet. His craving for California, part sadness and part fantasy, was reinforced by the conditions of their lives. Jennie, reasonably affluent after her husband's death, had turned into a penny-pinching, dour matron who made them work extremely hard for their keep. She considered book-learning an indulgence, music perhaps even worse. Schools were only open for the short period between the last harvest and spring plowing. Henry was slightly cheered when Jennie allowed him to plant a flower garden outside the kitchen window to improve the view.[28]

When he wrote Harry from Kansas for the last time in late July (1910), it was 110 degrees in the shade. "The praries are not good company . . ."[29] Finally Clarissa sold a story for enough money to buy train tickets to California. By October they were back in Menlo Park.[30]

4

The Turning Point

They found their home wrecked and looted after standing empty so long. Neighbors housed them as thirteen-year-old Henry restored it; Clarissa was too ill to help.[1] When they finally moved in, he slept on an old door laid across makeshift supports until Harry brought bedsprings and a mattress fashioned from a muslin bag stuffed with wild oats.[2] They were down to their last $100 [2010: $2,370]. With Clarissa's writing producing no income and Harry unable to offer much help, Henry became the sole provider. He worked at the local schoolhouse as assistant janitor, earning $12 per month, although he did not show up there as a pupil, and got $4 a month to clean a neighbor's chicken houses. Venturing into the foothills of the Santa Cruz Mountains, in a region where a mountain lion had recently attacked a man, he collected ferns and flowers to peddle around Menlo Park.[3] His best source was an old well, into which he would descend in the well bucket, whose rope was past its prime.[4] Says Sidney, "Later Henry realized that in his zeal for saving time by offering his plunder for sale to the nearest houses, he must often have sold his customers the produce of their own fields." The steep, downhill return trip could be hazardous because his bicycle had no brakes, so he slowed it with big branches tied to the back.[5] When ferns were so plentiful that he could not sell them, he became an entrepreneur, enlisting Harry to market his pickings in San Francisco.[6] After business collapsed in midsummer (1911) "because most wild things have died down and people won't buy what isn't there! . . ." he made rustic hanging baskets. At some point he began cultivating bulbs.[7]

Henry's musical and social skills were also improving, thanks to the "Toyon Club"—named for a berry native to Menlo Park—of which he was secretary, chairman of the entertainment committee, and an actor in plays. Angela Joulie Kiefer recalled that the club, started by the neighborhood children for weekly get-togethers, met at her large house. Everyone was welcome—that is, anybody from the four or five families in the area, some of which were filled with children. They worked up little plays, and the children would dress Henry to play roles to an audience consisting of little Angela and her sister. She remembered his performances as "from another world"; they made the children howl with laughter. Even his old tormentors, the Harkins boys, could not contain themselves when they heard his improvised atmospheric music on the piano. ". . . There was something there he was trying to bring out. Every once in a while he'd stop and he'd say, 'Oh! Did you hear those bells ringing!' To him, what he did at that particular moment, to him it sounded like bells ringing in the background. . . . 'I'm going to do it again, see if you hear it.' And that's how he got started. From that, that's what he called it, wasn't it, clusters?"[8]

All of this was taking place in the first half of 1912, many months before his earliest known notated tone-cluster piece, "Adventures in Harmony" (1913), which therefore may represent the end, not the beginning, of a period of experimentation. (The famous "Tides of Manaunaun," published with the date 1912, actually comes from 1917, at least in the form in which it is known.)[9]

A tone cluster is a chord in which all intervals are seconds. (Henry eventually called it "secundal harmony.") These chords, which can be found as early as the eighteenth century, were part of the arsenal of the piano virtuoso Leo Ornstein (1893–2002). Henry later found that Vladimir Rebikov (1866–1920) used them in Russia.[10] Henry, however, wished to use them with more than a handful of pitches. Lacking enough fingers, he expanded the resources of pianism by using the flat of the hand, the side of the fist, or the entire arm. This too was not entirely unprecedented. Daniel Steibelt's late eighteenth-century "battle pieces" included passages played with the flat of the hand, and Ives had used a board to produce oversized clusters in the "Concord" Sonata; but Henry would not have known either of them. He might, however, have heard of the ex-slave Blind Tom, a virtuoso pianist who used them in his own Civil War battle pieces.[11] While a conventional musician daring enough to use such chords might balk at the unconventional physical requirements, Henry had no such inhibitions, especially not in the Toyon Club. Mrs. Kiefer may be right that his celebrated pianistic technique was born there, and the hilarity of the Toyon kids began a long tradition of listeners being distracted from the musical end by the physical means. But even the use of hands and arms was the distillation of a larger process. Mrs. Kiefer tells us that "when he decided to play with his feet, well, then the boys just went into ecstasy. We had a chair . . . a desk chair . . . that reclined back. . . . He'd sit back here, and with his feet he'd play, you know, like he would with his hands. With his toes. . . . He manipulated his toes somehow and he'd get up there, and we'd just sit around and I tell you . . ."

Mrs. Kiefer also described the dramatic impulse behind his performances. He would sit and think, and then say "'Well, I guess I'll play this now.' And he'd start out, and he'd tell us what he was singing about." His musical narratives would ramble on as he visualized his stories. Clearly the programmatic associations of Henry's music began very early. If her memory is correct, tone clusters did not simply begin as a translation of the sound of waves breaking on the California coast, as Henry later said.[12]

The Toyon Club was also one of many reasons that Henry was cheerful in the summer of 1912. The physical development resulting from menial labor bolstered the confidence of this teenager once tormented by bullies. He proudly told Harry that he had the grip of a sixteen-year-old (42½ pounds) and a lung capacity equal to seventeen-year-olds. Despite his short legs, Henry came second in a track meet, beating boys of seventeen and eighteen. The blooming of Leopard Lilies suggested a new, lucrative product. And he discovered a hot springs in the hills hidden amid the worst tangle he had ever seen.[13] He resumed using the surname Cowell, saw more of Harry and Henrietta, and had Harry's jokes published in the Toyon Club's newsletter.

Meanwhile, his life had changed suddenly and dramatically. Exactly what brought him together with Stanford Professor Lewis M. Terman in the fall of 1910 has been the subject of several colorful but unverifiable stories. One account, from Sidney and presumably based on statements by Henry, says that he was herding cows for a dairy in the pasture just below the Alameda de las Pulgas, next door to Professor Terman, whose lawn the cows threatened. It is strange that Mrs. Kiefer did not mention this story, since it was her family's cows that he was herding, but she was young at the time. Another version, equally unverifiable, has Henry meeting Terman while selling flowers. A third version, recounted by a Menlo Park contemporary, claims that Terman learned about the young man from Dr. Percy E. Davidson, a Stanford professor experimenting with the use of phonetics in teaching reading.[14] Whatever really happened, Henry impressed someone so strongly that Terman, a thirty-four-year-old professor of educational psychology who is best known as inventor of the Stanford-Binet IQ test and was studying extremely gifted California children, realized he had found his "control," an unschooled boy necessary for his research about whether intelligence tests measured innate gifts or the fruits of education. He offered Henry fifty cents an hour [2010: $12] to spend approximately two hours per evening, thrice weekly, taking intelligence tests. It gave Henry some extra money and he could do it when he was too tired for anything else.

Terman kept copious notes on their encounters and published several detailed reports that refer to Henry, giving us a view of him through the eyes of this trained educator and social scientist. His evaluation, in *The Intelligence of School Children*, was published some seven years later, when Terman had the benefit of some distance from his subjects. His notes on the interviews with Henry add important details. Taken together, Terman's documents are the best account, other than Clarissa's, of Henry as his life in music commenced.

Conspicuously absent from Terman's analysis is any reference to influences other than Clarissa, whom he admired. He seems to have discounted Harry from the outset, and if Henry offered anything to contradict him, Terman ignored it. He called Henry "odd and interesting in the extreme," especially because he spoke or drawled in a quaint, stilted manner that may have resulted from knowing many books and few children. His eyes were devoid of self-consciousness, his clothes were "often ragged and always ill-fitting; his hair hid his ears and straggled down to his shoulders; his face and shoulders twitched occasionally with choreic spasms." (Recurring attacks of chorea had tapered off into a kind of nervous twitching that had almost disappeared by 1911.)[15] "Everybody considered Henry as queer, not to say freakish."

Henry told Terman that he and Clarissa read to each other and had endless discussions about religion, politics, literature, and art. He had read more than 300 books before he was fourteen and, according to Terman, could converse about socialism, atheism, science, and other subjects with "greater breadth of knowledge and much deeper understanding than the average university senior." Yet his spelling was dismal, and he knew only the four fundamental arithmetic operations and simple fractions. His stunning ability to concentrate on music was a liability at work, because "if employed to weed a lawn he was likely to forget what he was doing while trying to compose and whistle a tune. His janitor work was hardly more successful." He read every evening for two or three hours, sometimes even more; in New York he had finished two books a day. Amazed to discover what he had devoured by the age of fifteen, Terman assembled a list of books classified by the age when Henry read them, noting Henry's assessment of them.[16]

Henry marked "excellent" all of the books that he read between the ages of eight and ten, before leaving San Francisco: *Alice in Wonderland, Black Beauty, Wizard of Oz, Queen Zixi of Ix,* fairy tales by Grimm and Hans Christian Andersen, *Gulliver's Travels, Arabian Nights, Robinson Crusoe, Swiss Family Robinson.* Between the ages of ten and twelve his favorites books (marked either superior or excellent) included six novels by Mark Twain, two by Dickens, Hjalmar Hjorth Boyesen's *Queen Titania,* and three collections of his short stories. Among the older literary classics, which he found "superior," were *Orations* of Demosthenes; two volumes each of plays by Aristophanes, Euripides, Sophocles, and Aeschylus; Shakespeare's *Pericles* and "King Henry"; Balzac's *The Hated Son.* He did not particularly like Jules Verne. Nonfiction included two geology and two mineralogy texts; histories of countries from all over the world; a book on stamp collecting and a book on how to recognize minerals at sight (marked "medium"); studies of Zoroastrianism and Islam.

After returning to California—aged thirteen to fifteen—he continued to read fiction, including four Dickens novels, Jack London's *The Call of the Wild,* and

Hawthorne's *Grandfather's Chair*. But nonfiction became his primary interest. He devoured books on Greek art and biographies of major figures in American history, including Booker T. Washington's autobiography, *Up from Slavery*. Clarissa's homeschooling was clearly effective, its lapses notwithstanding.

Terman was extremely impressed that Henry's treks for flowers had led to a mastery of botany that seemed equal to his musical accomplishments. He had read university textbooks in New York's libraries before the age of twelve, developed a remarkable knowledge of California wildflowers, and knew the principles of plant breeding. He even considered making a career in botanical science, but his irregular education had foreclosed the possibility of matriculating at a university.[17] All in all, Terman was amazed.

According to Sidney, Henry also went to Stanford's botany department for advice and information but found the faculty so oriented around nomenclature and lines of descent that he could learn nothing about a plant's environmental needs and its habits of growth. Nevertheless, he learned about plant identification and brought a previously unknown wild orchid to a professor, who said the flower would be named for him, though it never was. Sidney also claimed that Stanford professor and president David Starr Jordan, one of America's most important zoologists, introduced him to Luther Burbank, who taught him how cross-pollination could improve the bulbs he was growing for sale. Henry then developed an improved yellow marigold, which soon could be found all over the Stanford neighborhood. Although her story remains uncorroborated, apparently a newspaper article entitled "Our Boy Burbank" was Henry's first mention in print. Unfortunately, it has resisted discovery. Somebody or something, however, inspired Henry to trade plants for bulbs, which he then planted to produce blossoms for sale and more bulbs.

In February 1912, Terman began assigning Henry timed writing exercises. Brief but pungent, they present a self-portrait of Henry's philosophies and independent personality that is almost unequaled because he almost always guarded his innermost thoughts. That tendency is already visible in Henry's response to Terman's request for an essay about himself. He instead chose as his subject another Henry Cowell, the son of a wealthy Massachusetts family, who went to California in 1849, the Gold Rush year, started a successful hauling business, and eventually quarried lime, bought ships, exported cement, and accumulated huge land holdings. Henry Cowell State Park and Cowell College at the University of California, Santa Cruz, are named for him, not our man. This "other" Henry Cowell had lived in the affluent Atherton district of Menlo Park. Henry, dressed in ragged clothes, once called upon the deceased cement man's elderly daughters in their mansion and received a rude brush-off. Sidney thought that the women were offended at the idea that there might be a family relationship and that they might be considered Irish.[18] This rebuff, and conversations at

home, may explain his namesake's effect upon Henry's normally gentle temperament. Given ten to fifteen minutes to write an essay, five and one-half minutes
sufficed to uncork pure vitriol.

> There once was a man, (now dead) who was named Henry Cowell. I
> have heard more than one man say that he was the meanest man that
> ever lived. He kept a cement work in Santa Cruz hiring labor at a low
> price and saving for himself all the time, always at the expense of others.
> as is natural such a man became very wealthy. instead, however, of
> trying to do any good with his money he devoted it to the undoing of
> others. this horrible monster was murdered, finely [probably means fi-
> nally], but the criminal was never found. I am very glad! this is all I
> know about Henry Cowell.[19]

"Above is a true story," noted Terman. Not quite. Cowell was shot in the
shoulder in a land-boundary dispute and died of his wound after first appearing
to recover. It cannot be proven that he exploited labor, but it would not have
been a novelty then.[20]

Terman must have insisted that Henry write another essay about himself.
Timed at six and one-half minutes, it produced Henry's view of his dual interests
and an eerie prediction of his life span.

> Henry Cowell. born March 11, 1897. Died probably about 1960. it has
> been called upon me at the present age (2108) A.D. to procure data and
> write the biography of this obscure person. how I am expected to do it
> I know not. Henry Cowell was a very ordinary man, who cultivated
> flowers extensively and successfully, and whom [sic] some records say,
> made feeble attempts to compose music, which was rotten, but I, per-
> sonally, do not believe this. the only thing for which he might be at all
> noted, was the producing of a new and slightly better kind of garden
> beet. as this is all I can find about this person I will come to an end.

Other essays display the lack of sentimentality that became Henry's hallmark.
It took him a bit under five minutes to say that he really did not care about Stanford's architecture so long as the buildings served their purpose. In "The Last
Leaf on the Tree," dated February 22, 1912, Henry took about seven minutes to
produce a paragraph that is at once reflective, oddly detached, and entertaining.

> The last leaf on the tree is not the leaf for me. there are other leaves
> much more beautiful and while I am very sorry to see it go, I guess I can
> get along without it, especially as there are other leaves on other trees

this time of year, and in fact in Cal. all year round. if you wish this leaf you can have it. the tree sheds it's leaves in order that it may put forth much finer ones in spring, and then my leaf will be much the finest. just what this tree means by shedding its leave this time of year I do not know. anyway. it is much out of order, on this account, come to think of it, I believe I wish that leaf after all. so good bye.

Finally, in a tiny statement entitled "The Things I have thought most about while at work during the last few days" Henry admitted his lack of focus in the workplace: ". . . anything that I happened to be doing, for the most part. I improvise music, always different, which goes through my head, when my brains are not taxed in any other way, for the most part."

If the essays seem dispassionate, regular conversations with Terman early in 1912 elicited personal musings that rarely escaped his lips later in life. Terman was impressed by the energy he put into hearing good music, even when he could not afford it. Henry admitted that conditions in New York discouraged him. "In NY when I was 11–12 years old, mother ill, owed 20.00 rent & had only 60 cts—did not know whether we could get another cent—made me ill—my twitches came back." But he said he did not spend much time daydreaming about this misfortune; he preferred improvising music in his head. Because he always had something to do, such as a ramble in the woods, he had not felt lonesome since he was small. Now, in 1912, he confined himself to composing music and hybridizing flowers. He thought Clarissa probably initiated his interest in flowers even though she never grew them, but he told Terman that he never had help either with the flowers or in selecting books about them. It is impossible to determine whether the omission of any reference to Burbank was an oversight, a clue that they had not yet met, evidence that they never did meet, or an attempt to avoid sharing credit.

Stubborn independence and rationality permeates all the conversations, such as their discussion of the Bible. He had read it all and especially enjoyed the history of the Jews, which he had found nowhere else. Yet the Bible's many truths declined in his estimation because of absurd meanings that had been attached to them. Asked if he had been taught this attitude, he said that no one had influenced him to disbelieve any of the Bible. "I believe or disbelieve as I like." Clarissa certainly must have sown the seeds of doubt, but Henry either forgot or wanted to seem mature. Asked how he made decisions, Henry explained that he had been taught to reason things out ever since he was small. Most of his ideas originated in himself; he would not adopt any idea without a good reason, for once he had noticed how people oppose ideas, he needed reasons to choose his own. For example, he hoped that in *The Origin of Species* he might find explanations of things he had not learned from studying botany. Nothing in Terman's notes suggests that Henry attributed his attitude to Clarissa's independent spirit, but it was so constant in his life that he may never have imagined an alternative.

One of Henry's most striking conversations with Terman concerned politics (February 22, 1912), two weeks before Henry's fifteenth birthday.[21] He claimed that he had never read about politics but only picked up some things in conversations and formulated a point of view that recognized society's complexity. Whether or not he was entirely forthcoming about his sources—Clarissa and Anna Strunsky's voices sing loudly—his ability to assimilate ideas is impressive. He defined socialism as (in Terman's rapid paraphrase) "a way of ordering things of politics & industry in which prac all indus would be governmental," and anarchy as "no government." In the ideal government, he said, everyone would have the sense to look after himself. But that would not happen for 2,000 years—maybe never. Although socialism might be better than the present state of affairs, Henry would not support it until a real plan was worked out. Behind his arguments is an implicit awareness of the nationwide debate that ended when the Sixteenth Amendment to the Constitution legalized federal income tax, to which Clarissa-the-anarchist was almost certainly hostile despite her passion for social justice. He was wary about the advent of socialism, which could bring people to delegate their charitable instincts to the government and reduce overall support for the arts. Original ideas would disappear because "people would be as alike as sheep," their individuality crushed, and their personal rights limited. People could be ordered isolated from others without the right to get mail, and without recourse to the courts. Religion would have no chance. He also felt tremendous inequity in American laws, and injustice everywhere, such as in the repression of labor unrest. Capital punishment should be abolished: "Govt has no right to commit murder. Hires thousands of murderers all the time, soldiers and sailors."

Their final conversation (February 24) concerned Henry's social instincts. He had had intimate friends all his life—two older girls, boys three years younger. Now he didn't have any time, but he liked to play with younger ones, and they liked him to. He preferred girls because of the bullying behavior of boys. In fact, he used to hate boys and would be happy if there were none; boys ridiculed him and stole what he was carrying home to his mother; fourteen- and fifteen-year-olds would beat him. Groups of boys were troublemakers; athletes were ruffians. Henry did not even like the fairly nice boys in Menlo Park. Terman must have found it all exceptionally interesting since one of Henry's few male friends around this time was his own twelve-year-old, Frederick, a member of The Toyon Club who got to know Henry around the time he and Clarissa returned, played with him occasionally, and shared his interests in wildflowers and botany.[22] Henry said he liked most adults, and had many friends, whom he especially admired for their playing or singing.

Henry's self-image is largely consistent with later observations of his character. For example, he said that anger played a very small role in his nature: bumping his head made him angrier than any person except bullies. He was neither jealous nor covetous. While he used to suffer from bouts of pity, especially in New York, where he saw so much poverty, he admitted that he didn't feel pity when he didn't see the poor, nor did he regard himself as poor. He admitted to some fears. An awful terror of the dark had finally dissipated. Nightmares and little snakes frightened him, but not snakebites; he had even killed six or seven rattlers, but liked lizards. He was not afraid of death and had gotten over his fear of earthquakes, but was afraid of a cyclone he once saw right over his house in Kansas, and was somewhat afraid of lightning, for he once "was shocked." Punishment did not worry him: he was never sent to bed for a punishment, nor deprived of anything. Confirming Clarissa's observation, he admitted to telling lies when he was six or seven, but since he was nine he had been truthful. When he did wrong, he talked to himself.

While Henry talked freely about his inner world, he had very little to say about music. He told Terman that when playing the violin he would get so nervous that in fifteen minutes he could hardly stand still, and suffered cramps, yet he claimed to have enjoyed it anyway. The piano attracted him because its large range helped him compose. Practicing gave him pleasure, but he needed lessons; he had had only four or five. Right now he was practicing on an organ for about half an hour every day. (The organ may have been at a Roman Catholic church in Redwood City whose priest or organist had begun telling him about the history of church music in 1911; his organ teacher was probably Benjamin Blodgett, the Stanford organist. Since Blodgett had studied with Liszt, who studied with Czerny, who studied with Beethoven, Henry later called Beethoven one of his musical ancestors.)[23] He had composed and could write down his music, but he preferred improvising to playing from notes. Apparently his improvising antedated the performances at the Toyon Club; he said that when he was small he enjoyed improvising for crowds of people, which was encouraged.

In *The Intelligence of School Children* (1919), Terman wrote that what impressed him more than Henry's IQ (131) was his intellectual versatility. Terman's tests added to Henry's new sense of self: he had a vocabulary of 15,500 words, 50 percent more than the average for fourteen-year-olds. Henry could hardly wait to get more test results.[24] Elsewhere Terman said he was impressed that Henry's musical talent had "survived all the vicissitudes of poverty and illness," but noted that he had abandoned any ambition to be a great performer because of his nervousness and the ruinous effects of hard labor upon his hands. He now concentrated upon composing and had written out "numberless compositions."[25] About thirty pieces are known, all but two of them for piano.

To return to the piano. According to Clarissa, just around the time that Terman began his interviews, Henry announced that he needed a piano; quite possibly the conversations with Terman bolstered his confidence in becoming a musician. First they bought a worn-out instrument, a relic from a boy's school, for $60 [2010: $1,420]—all their remaining money. Henry paid $20 down and the rest in $5 monthly installments to avoid depleting their reserves.[26] Soon he was practicing so much that he did not even have time to write Harry. By July 1912—when he was marketing the Tiger Lily—he had written five waltzes.[27] It was the tip of the iceberg of little piano pieces.

The piano teacher to whom he referred, Edith Partridge, at eighty-four gave her story to Sidney.[28] She was born in London in 1893, four years before her family moved to Menlo Park, where the Partridges prospered. Partridge Avenue, off Camino Real, probably was named by her family. Later she married one of those annoying Harkins boys.[29] In 1910, when Henry returned to Menlo Park, Edith, now seventeen, had studied piano for six years at a "conservatory" in San Jose run by the Sisters of Notre Dame. It was insufficient to give her real musical sophistication, but perhaps adequate to help him. Edith, however, said that she actually was Henry's third music teacher since he stopped playing the violin. The first, surprisingly, was Clarissa; the second was Edith's future sister-in-law Mrs. Charles Harkins, who gave him a few lessons. (The teacher who was supposedly engaged in Des Moines was never mentioned again.) Soon Henry was working from books assigned to him by Edith, who taught him weekly in exchange for gardening.[30] The experience was the opposite of his agonies at the violin. He was prompt, regular, and practiced hard. She began assigning more pieces from a G. Schirmer collection and standard instruction books. Clarissa recorded that he played Heller's "Tarantelle," Chopin's "Military" Polonaise, and the first movement of the "Moonlight" Sonata. Edith did not refer at all to abnormal pianism. She certainly did not teach it to him, and he probably never played such things for her.

At the end of May, a young Stanford graduate came to the house and gave Henry some instruction. Clarissa says, "We felt sorry they had not met sooner. Yet that one evening worked a revolution in Henry's method of writing down his compositions. He had not known how to do it. It seems incredible that he learned it in one evening, but he asked information on points that had puzzled him. He remembered every answer he received."[31] Since he was already playing published piano pieces, his problem may not have been conventional musical notation but a way to notate the tone clusters that were already part of his programmatic performances. Clarissa added that although Henry generally worked alone, in the next year or so he had two or three composition/harmony lessons from one Arthur Lewis, whom Sidney identified as an oboist in the San Francisco Symphony.[32]

Angela Kiefer remembered how much Henry loved to come to her house, where the doors were always open and the girls loved to see him. She thought that the real reason was her family's piano, a Jacob Zech square grand, the only grand in Menlo Park. She recalled her father attaching a brace to keep the top up so it would not come crashing down on Henry's arm. He may have been in the piano, playing directly on the strings, but he may just have played with alarming vigor. Had the piano not vanished, it might have helped determine whether Henry could have been playing on the strings more than a decade before the premiere of the stringpiano piece "Aeolian Harp." Most of his known stringpiano pieces were written for a Steinway B.[33]

By the autumn he knew he needed a better piano at home. In October, 1912 they bought one for $235 [2010: $5,450],[34] which Henry and Clarissa could not possibly have afforded. That piano, not the Joulies' Zech, brings us to a remarkable group that changed Henry's life and, one can fairly say, the course of American music.

5

The Expanding Circle

Around the time of Terman's interviews, Henry's social circle began to expand with such tremendous consequences that we must pause to become acquainted with the new friends who steered his life out of poverty and isolation. The first concrete sign was the $235 piano, whose "angel" was Ellen Rolfe Veblen, a central figure in Henry's life for nearly two decades. In 1888, Ellen, the twenty-nine-year-old daughter of a wealthy Minnesota family, defied her parents to marry a college friend, the young economist Thorstein Veblen, whose brilliance immediately won him a job at the University of Chicago, which later dismissed him over a flamboyant extra-marital relationship. In 1906, when Stanford University came to Veblen's rescue, Ellen loyally accompanied him to Menlo Park.

The Veblens rented out a room in their cottage to Robert Duffus (1888–1972), an eighteen-year-old Stanford student who became one of America's most distinguished journalists and a good friend of Henry. Duffus affectionately described Ellen as "relying on the inward and unprovable experience," in contrast to her husband, who was "rooted . . . solidly in the provable fact." She was as imaginative and sparkling as he was logic-bound and silent, "in her thinking and feeling . . . as purely feminine as a human being could be." Too whimsical to be called an intellectual, she was (at least to Duffus) in no way Thorstein Veblen's inferior. When Duffus got to know her she was approaching fifty and seemed strangely old. She took "no particular care for personal appearance, unless it was a whimsical delight in suiting her own taste and mood, without regard to prevailing styles. She can never have been beautiful, but she had the charm of quaintness."[1]

After a recurrence of Thorstein Veblen's amorous wanderings, Ellen campaigned successfully for his dismissal from Stanford and divorced him in 1911. Meanwhile, her eccentricities intensified. She believed she was a psychic "and perhaps actually was," says Duffus, "in the sense that she seemed to hear, see and experience things that other persons did not." She seemed at home in northern California, which, "like the weird region around Los Angeles, had its mystics." Unquestionably a dreamer and poet, Ellen was fated to become a friend and confidant of Clarissa and her gifted boy, who returned to Menlo Park just as the Veblen marriage exploded. Ellen, Clarissa (her contemporary), and Henry, a very needy trio, soon found one another in the little community. Judging from the history of Henry's pianos, that would have been early in 1912, about the same time that he met Terman.

Although Duffus got to know Henry extremely well, he mentioned Ellen's relationship with him only in passing. The full story was provided by Evelyn Wells, the adopted daughter of close friends of Ellen Veblen. Like Duffus, Evelyn had the power of observation that later made her a renowned journalist and a colorful witness of the epoch. She told Sidney that late one afternoon "Mrs. Veblen opened her door on the San Francisquito Creek to a tired, smudgled little boy who without a word held out to her a bunch of blossoms." Ellen told Evelyn that she bought them, "'those dreadful wilted weeds. He was like an angel, looking up at me.'" Ellen and Henry immediately began taking walks, "botanizing," gathering mushrooms, getting their stomachs pumped because of mushroom poisoning. During one walk, Ellen suddenly discovered Henry's musicality. As re-told by Evelyn Wells, "He was singing a song without words. 'What is that?' she asked, puzzled. He gave her a fawn's glance. 'Mine.'" A scene from a Grade B movie, with Ellen's personality it rings true. Henry began visiting her, playing her fine piano until she helped him replace his battered upright. Her gift of much of the cost of the piano was certainly the best thing she could have done for him.[2] It was symptomatic of a relationship for which the word "intense" is another monumental understatement. Clarissa said that she immediately loved Ellen[3] and intended to repay the money.[4]

Childless Ellen virtually adopted Henry. In July 1913, when she brought him to see two productions at Carmel, Takeshi Kanno, a Japanese Theosophist poet, happened to hear him playing the piano and asked him to provide music for his new poetic drama, *Creation Dawn*. By assembling parts of previous compositions, Henry completed the score in about a week and returned to Carmel for the premiere in the Forest Theater, where he played the piano hidden from the audience behind a screen of green leaves. This was probably his first true public performance. Clarissa could not contain her joy. "After it was all over the woods rang with Henry's name. 'Henry Cowell! Henry Cowell!' was shouted over and over and over. Henry was surrounded by boys offering candy, and by men and women offering congratulations."[5] He suddenly had a public persona, and not just as a gifted pianist-composer. An observer remarked, "Strange, weird and macabre was this performance of the Japanese poet's drama . . . and over all, the music of a piano played in a manner so new, so ultra modern, that it seemed another instrument."[6]

Clarissa's joy was a happy parenthesis in her difficult life, as chest pains, coughing, and hemorrhaging convinced her that she was suffering from tuberculosis. Concerned that she would not survive another winter in the shack, Ellen invited her (and Henry) to stay at her home in Carmel, which was sunnier and warmer than Menlo Park. They remained until March 1914.[7] Ironically, Ellen's ministrations destroyed Clarissa. Instead of seeing a doctor, she moved her bed out of doors for fresh air and to isolate herself, thereby giving the real culprit, breast cancer, time to take root. Two mastectomies ensued, both unsuccessful.[8]

About the same time Henry met Ellen, or perhaps even a little before, his path crossed that of another local intellectual, John Varian (1863–1931). Varian's name is familiar to lovers of Henry's piano piece "The Tides of Manaunaun," which bears a motto from an Irish myth as retold by him. Indeed, he, not Harry, is the chief source of the Irish component of Henry's early compositions, which are more closely connected with Gaelic mythology than with Irish music. Whereas Harry apparently had hardly a good word to say about the land of his youth,[9] Varian was utterly devoted to it. Understanding Henry therefore requires understanding Varian, and understanding Varian's strengths and eccentricities requires a look at the family's role in Ireland's troubled history.[10]

The name Varian is not Irish but some sort of Roman derivative found throughout Europe. In the seventeenth century, two Varian brothers are believed to have emigrated from France to Ireland, where they became officers in Cromwell's brutal army and were rewarded with estates. When they made the mistake of falling in love with Irish girls, the English retaliated by confiscating their property, driving the boys to switch sides and become the first of three Varian generations of anti-English guerrillas. In 1723, as the English burned the hills of Kerry to destroy the fighters, Isaac Varian, a popular musician and dancing master, and a direct ancestor of John, took refuge in Cork. There the family prospered as brushmakers, spawning musicians, writers, artists, craftsmen, and tradesmen who also were political and social activists, and religious freethinkers. The nineteenth-century Varians were Unitarians, Irish nationalists, and lively members of Dublin's intellectual circle. Like the Irish Cowells, they were people of social standing.

The Varians were also immersed in Theosophy, a spiritual movement rooted in the ancient world and non-Western cultures, which attracted many adherents after the founding of the Theosophical Society in the 1870s. Believing that everything contained in the universe was unified, Theosophists elaborated their ideas through a philosophy combining elements of spiritualism, the occult, the world's religions, and science. It was a natural haven for highly intelligent people, some of whom, like John, sought a community that could be a real home.

John, now married, worked in the family brush business, but did not get along with his brother, who was in charge. Furthermore, the damp climate and the dusty factory aggravated his asthma. A suggestion that the dry air of California would improve his health prompted him to take his wife to America. In 1894 they arrived in New York, visited relatives in Washington, and took the train to San Francisco, where the foggy summer induced one of John's worst asthma attacks ever. Heading north, they met up with their Dublin friend Ernest (Harry) Harrison. Failure followed failure. They eventually returned to Washington, DC, but lacking professional training and crippled by asthma, John barely covered their expenses. In 1898, after their first son, Russell Harrison Varian, was born, they went to Philadelphia, where John had Theosophist friends and Harry Harrison joined them. Harry and John then hitchhiked to Syracuse, New York, to investigate a new Theosophical sect, the Brotherhood of Man. Russell and his mother—pregnant again—followed. Sigurd Fergus Varian was born in Syracuse in 1901. John worked there as a masseur in a Turkish bath until it closed in 1902 and his fortunes plummeted again. Early in 1903, relatives helped them move to Palo Alto, California, where John, the eternal optimist, opened a chiropractic office. Their third son, Eric, was born there the following year.

Around then, the Syracuse Theosophists moved to Halcyon, north of Santa Barbara, California, where they built their "Temple of the People" around an existing sanatorium. An early advertisement[11] for the community describes the Halcyon Sanatorium as a fashionable resort and a refuge for invalids and sufferers from stress and exhaustion. Unstated was the increasingly Theosophist orientation of the settlers, whose tents gradually were replaced by cottages as Halcyon turned into a real community. When I visited it in the 1990s, it retained its peacefulness, its little wooden houses and silent lanes resembling a summer camp at Rest Hour. In those days, however, its residents were despised as crazy radicals.

The Halcyon Theosophists then opened a branch in Palo Alto called "The Temple Square," whose meetings turned the Varian home near the Stanford campus into a magnet for faculty and students, writers, artists, musicians, businessmen, and professionals. The group enjoyed music and conversation embracing politics, social reform, economics, psychology, Irish mythology and British-Irish relations. As they listened to John singing old Irish songs in English and Gaelic, which was banned in Ireland, and telling stories of English brutality and Irish martyrdom, they absorbed his intense nationalism.

Theosophy was thus embedded in southern California, with a strong branch in the south San Francisco Bay area, not far from where Henry lived. Its adherents included wealthy people from the Chicago and New York areas who summered in the West, especially at Carmel, which was being developed as an artists' colony. Through them and the nature of Theosophy itself, anyone involved in the California Theosophical colonies could become part of a transatlantic network of like-minded souls.

The Varians were natural friends for the Cowells, but although the two families knew of one another, they did not cross paths until about 1910 or 1911, when thirteen-year-old Henry happened to meet Russell and Sigurd Varian, boys of about twelve and nine, as they cycled around Menlo Park. Having learned of their father, Henry was delighted to be invited home.[12] John, who had heard that a young composer supported his invalid mother by selling lily bulbs, welcomed him cheerfully. Gawky and freckled Russell came in from the back yard, where he was building an airplane from a cigar box and rubber bands, and proceeded to explain his machine right over the manuscript of a "sonata" for violin and piano that Henry offered to him.[13] Although Russell preferred his airplane to Henry's sonata, it was clear that he, John, and Henry—and later Sigurd Varian and the Harrisons' son George—had a future. A family friend's 1931 account of this event glows extravagantly with John Varian's aura.

> And I doubt not that in that very moment the poet and the composer looked at one another in soul recognition across the ages and the Gods approved. . . . The singer had met his poet and the poet his singer, coming together thus in this quaint way, with its touch of unconscious Irish humor, on a momentous day. A day of portentous and prophetic skies whereunder the rhythmic thunders of creation were to break forth in new-formed music and distinctive song.[14]

While this description, so appropriate to the author's postmortem tribute to John, seems overwrought, Dorothy Varian, Russell's widow, felt it accurately described the enormous and lasting effects of the family's friendship with Henry, and vividly portrayed the atmosphere around this poet-bard, who is associated with many of Henry's best-known compositions. Its author may have been unaware of the equally fruitful relationship between Henry and the Varian boys. Strangely, Clarissa does not mention the family in her "biography" of Henry. Many of his youthful political ideas may have germinated in the Varian house, however.

John, a real character with a bushy beard, bright red nose, and huge blue eyes, was not having an easy time. Patients paid late, and he could not work when his asthma attacked. As a result, they often ran out of food. When the 1914 California legislature mandated licensing of chiropractors and masseurs, John, lacking the medical training required for the exam, lost his clients. He was tempted to homestead in the undeveloped Los Padres mountains, near Carmel, but recognized that the boys' education might suffer from the isolation. When Harry Harrison's wife suggested that the Varians take over her post office and small store in Halcyon, they moved there. John quickly gave Halcyon an Irish flavor.

John was clearly a wonderful person, but it must be added that he was tainted by a streak of prejudice whose sole virtue was its inclusiveness. Like many Irish intellectuals, he was anti-Catholic; he also was at least to some degree anti-Semitic, extremely anti-British, and in the 1920s became anti-French. It speaks of the bitterness of Irish history, but John reportedly kept his prejudices from undermining his essential warmth and gentleness.

He already had resumed writing poetry, much of it lyric reworkings of Irish epics with obscure meanings. Soon he hatched a plan to write operas or musical plays based on Irish legends, which would be given at the Halcyon community's August Conventions, using as performers his many musical friends, especially Henry. The first opera was to be *The Building of Bamba*, based on the Irish myth of the creation, whose subject matter suggested incorporating "the sweet music and magic of the Great Harp of Life, played by Lir, the God of Love, which the legends said could be heard all across Ireland"—that is, a gigantic harp, which John and the boys spent years trying to construct, hamstrung by their lack of money. *The Building of Bamba*, with music by Henry, but without the harp, was not completed until 1917.

Henry, now virtually a member of the Varian family, spent extended periods with them at Halcyon. He often showed up there at around Convention time, which, according to Clarence Weaver, a young friend in the community, was "a gala time of programs and religious meetings and social activities," at which many interesting people turned up. Everyone, Weaver said, was impressed by "a brilliant young man by the name of Henry Cowell. Dr. Dower, the Guardian of the community, said 'Henry is a wonderful boy, if he doesn't burn himself out.'"[15]

John Varian's artistic relationship with Henry permeates his early music, but the precise nature of his effect on Henry's personality is almost indeterminable. While Varian may have partly fulfilled his longing for a real father, Henry also might have preferred someone more practical than Varian or Harry, and definitely did not share their sentimentality. Nevertheless, John was an excellent friend and mentor, whose failures in life did not stem from a want of trying. Halcyon itself assumed great importance in Henry's life for years, offering him science, spirituality, a community of brilliant young people, and Varian's poetry and passion for music. While he does not seem to have bought into its religious aspects, he unquestionably felt the community was his home.

As the relationship between Henry and the Varians flowered, Henry and Veblen's young friend Evelyn Wells were also drawn together; born in 1899, she was two years his junior. Although they saw less of each other after Wells married in 1920 and Henry's travels increased, he visited her whenever he was in San Francisco. She became a syndicated reporter, a feature and editorial writer for Hearst's *San Francisco Call-Bulletin*, a writer of fiction, a poet, a ghostwriter, a speechwriter for political and military figures of World War II, a Hollywood writer, and the recipient of many awards. After decades in California, she separated from her husband and moved to the Hudson River valley, not far from Henry and Sidney. About a year after Henry's death, Sidney began a correspondence with her that lasted until Wells's death in 1984. Skilled at observing people, she gave Sidney an unparalleled description of her relationship with Henry when they were teenagers, filled with memories so powerful that she could barely stand to revive them.

Evelyn's adoptive parents were a Chicago-based minister and his wife with whom the Veblens, for unexplained reasons, were living around 1904.[16] When Veblen was hired by Stanford, they all lived near Menlo Park as "one family." As the Veblens' domestic problems were erupting again, the Wells family moved to San Jose, where "Veblen" went into hiding with them, drawing pesky reporters day and night. The Veblen hiding with Evelyn's family must have been Thorstein, however, not Ellen, who became convinced that they sided with him over the divorce and broke off contact. The split finally healed around the time Ellen and Henry met—approximately 1912—and Ellen soon brought him to meet Evelyn and her family in San Jose. Evelyn, now about twelve, recalled the moment. She instantly resented this boy about whom Ellen so frequently talked, with whom she now had to share her affection. Soon, however, they were the closest of friends. Even a summary of their relationship dispels the myth of a young Henry benefiting only from the affections of much older women. The rascally Evelyn was a good counterweight to Ellen's unbridled adoration and, she thought, helped keep Henry from becoming too full of himself.

Like the Varians, the Wells clan became another family for Henry. He and Reverend Wells "loved each other as only chess players can." Mrs. Wells was always "Mother Wells" to Henry. He would help her, play with the pets, and then go off to the big piano in the living room. Henry had their front room with their instruments all to himself "and we crept in to hear him working on the Tides of Manaunaun. He never seemed to mind." Sometimes she and her brother Wesley would copy Henry's music manuscripts. "Once he said people made money copying music, which amused Wesley and myself because it was work we loved doing and were very proud of the results—neat pages in india ink, and blotless." Their work may explain why some early manuscripts are not in Henry's hand.

They played word games in an invented language, always seeming to know what the other one wanted to say, or spent evenings with Ellen Veblen composing poems jointly; they loved reading poetry together. (Sidney thus was wrong in saying that Henry lacked any interest in poetry, although it could have lessened in later life.) He taught Evelyn to sing, and to sing duets in fifths, always out of tune. "It was perfectly dreadful and we loved it. Everyone hated us when we sang. He also tried to teach me piano but my hands, while no smaller than his, could not stretch. He had me stretching them, in busses, on trains when we made one of our rare expeditions to San Francisco." She spent months at a time in Palo Alto, staying with Ellen near Henry's home, and going to campus concerts where Henry would patiently explain musical instruments and advise her how to listen.

Sometimes they would hike with Ellen Veblen, sometimes with the Wells family, even with Evelyn's vegetarian cat. Evelyn liked to think that Henry's fondness for cats in later life came from his love for her cats and dogs in those years.

Pranks were Henry's specialty. After hiking turned him into an expert mountain climber, he led a terrified Evelyn across a precarious razor-back granite ledge over the water at Carmel, promising to show her a land where no one had ever trod, but when they finally arrived, there was a beach with picnickers. She felt like an idiot. Another joke, probably unintended, arose from Henry's botanical experiments. He planted rows of daffodils in his garden along with rows of garlic, and "the bulbous plants crossed and there were horrible little green budlike daffies that smelled like garlic. This could only have happened to Henry, we said." She thought it related to his later love of food and his excellence as a cook.

A trip to San Francisco required them to save money. Ten cents [2010: $2.25] got them the cheapest seats at the Orpheum Theater, where they could see touring stars such as Nazimova, Pavlova, Ruth St. Denis, and Ted Shawn.[17] At home, Ellen would play classical music so Evelyn and Henry could indulge their dancing habit. "It amused her that we each danced toes up, like Oriental dancers. We had each lived near Chinese and Japanese neighborhoods and had become accustomed to Oriental music." She attributed their dissonant singing to it. "'It takes perfect pitch to sing offkey,' Henry explained (to encourage me in the awful caterwauling)."

Looming over everything, however, was the burden of Clarissa, which Evelyn Wells and Ellen Veblen helped Henry to bear. Evelyn called Clarissa "a gentle, exquisite presence. . . . To her, poetry and music repaid all the injustices in the world, and many had come to her. But she had Henry. No kinder, gentler son ever lived." Evelyn had mixed feelings about Harry, calling him a blowhard, a womanizer (though she never actually saw him in that capacity), and above all, a neglectful father. She admired, however, Harry's generous praise of others, especially Ellen. But Evelyn's antagonism increased when Harry later walked out on Henrietta. Certain that Henry's "fatherlessness" affected him very deeply, she concluded that his patience and his sense of amusement at human foibles saved him.

Evelyn's view of Henry as a teenager is encapsulated in two sentences: "I know he had lived through more than young folk should ever suffer, but outwardly at least it had not changed him. He had a faunlike quality but his capacity for making and holding friends was rare and very human." Above all, she said, he was brave.

"Brave" also characterizes Jaime de Angulo. He was born in Paris in 1887, the scion of an ancient Spanish family, whose stultifying domestic atmosphere drove him to emigrate at eighteen. In the United States he found his true calling as an adventurer. Beginning as a cowboy in Colorado, he then went to San Francisco, then to Guatemala, returning to San Francisco one day before the earthquake. After fighting blazes until the emergency ended, he attended medical school in San Francisco. At twenty-one (1908) he began studying medical research at The Johns Hopkins University, where he met Cary Fink, a student from a wealthy Louisville family, about two years older and, in Jaime's estimation, a "free type," whose notion of life concerned advanced ideas of socialism, freethinking, and feminism. (She later translated the I Ching.) Gui (pronounced "ghee"), Jaime's daughter by his second marriage, said that Cary "brought out the best in him, and they found each other intellectually stimulating for as long as they were in contact, some twenty years."[18]

Jaime got a job at Stanford in 1912. One day, as he walked by the Cowell home, he was intrigued by music emanating from it, which sounded vaguely like Schumann or Schubert. He refused to believe Henry's tale of having composed it himself until he was shown pages in scribbled notation.[19] Duly impressed, Jaime became Henry's friend despite the ten-year difference in age. Something Jaime told Gui years later prompted her to describe Henry as "already quite eccentric."[20] This description cannot be taken at face value, however. While Henry may have been eccentric, he also may have used his love of a good prank to become the resident eccentric to his new friends, whose own singularities may have magnified any latent eccentricity in Henry. Jaime himself gave new meaning to the term "eccentric." In a telephone conversation in 2002, Gui de Angulo echoed a statement by Henry Miller that her father later developed into a kind of madman.[21]

That was in the future, however. Jaime impressed Clarissa as "a man of temperament, insight, mental quickness, searching intellect driven by whirlwinds of glorious excitements over the beautiful in art or nature. . . . He and Henry love each other ardently."[22] Jaime, Cary, and Henry spent time together until the summer of 1914, when Jaime abandoned eight years of medical training to become a cattle rancher, eventually buying land in the wilderness of Big Sur south of Carmel, just below the point where the Sur River meets the coast.[23] Jamie's ranch became Henry's destination on many hiking expeditions. One can imagine the charisma of this adventurer for whom riding forty miles on horseback seems to have been normal.[24] Yet while Jaime can seem like another California delusionary, dreams did not suffice for him. He eventually made himself into one of the pioneers of American anthropology, doing endless field work and translating native American languages.

Soon after meeting Henry, de Angulo took it upon himself to improve his young friend's grasp of science. He told Henry to read a book on chemistry and write a 500-word essay about what he had learned,[25] later repeating the process with other subjects. In the fall of 1913, he enlisted Henry in his neurological study of the apparent disappearance of certain insects from San Francisco; Henry's job was to collect the relevant "bugs." Bug-collecting continued until

December, when the insects reappeared in San Francisco and Jaime asked Henry to observe them to facilitate comparing their habits in San Francisco and Carmel.[26] Jaime reviewed acoustical science to prepare for discussions with Henry, but Henry already knew more about it than he did. In fortifying Henry's well-developed scientific disposition, Jamie must have encouraged him to find logical explanations for his musical innovations. Jaime also shared Henry's interest in music, learning Chinese flute, combing Chinatown for a good instrument, and sending Henry a sketch for a libretto or a program for three pieces about a tropical forest.[27]

Although impressed by Henry's raw ability, Jaime constantly advised him to study and achieve breadth.[28] He also warned Henry, from personal experience, that "all trouble comes from too much opening of the mouth!" Form your opinions, he said, but there is no need to pass them along.[29] Henry, he counseled, would find his own way if he stuck to his beliefs but avoided being stubborn.[30] He cautioned him that Ellen Veblen might be "somewhat insane, but how much I don't know. I think you will have to sweep her judgment aside many times." On the other hand, his wife Cary should be heeded. "Her criticisms are often burning, but they are usually just." Cary de Angulo played a quieter role in Henry's life, giving him good advice and generous financial assistance even after the de Angulo marriage fell apart in 1914 and she moved to upstate New York.

Above all, Jaime encouraged Henry to remain strong and not be bound by the rules. The greatest lesson that Henry learned, however, was to reject the otherworldliness represented by Harry, John Varian, and Jaime himself.

Jaime, John Varian, and Ellen Veblen were colorful, to say the least. Yet none of those adult admirers, other than Terman, helped Henry as concretely as Samuel S. Seward, a Stanford professor of English. Their relationship also can be traced back to events early in 1912, when Henry came to the attention of the San Francisco musical world by playing one of his compositions at the Pacific Musical Society's anniversary celebration at the Palace Hotel, a huge social event attended by more than a thousand members and guests. Henrietta, who was in the receiving line and participated in the informal concert, had brought Henry, but the brochure does not mention him because his performance had not been planned. Sidney only learned about it from a postcard to his mother that subsequently disappeared. For a long time, Henry considered this evening his official debut. Decades later, he concluded that his career should date from the first reviewed concert, in 1914. The 1912 date persists in biographies, however.[31]

After that performance, Terman asked Sam Seward and Jaime de Angulo to formulate a plan of assistance. Seward agreed to help with English, and Jaime with science. The challenge was to find the right composition teacher, because Henry resisted studying anything that was not a response to questions originating in himself. Furthermore, as Sidney said, "What others considered desirable for him might be very different from what Henry felt he needed."[32]

Above all, he needed an income that would free him to complete his education and relieve him of some of the burden of caring for Clarissa. The de Angulos committed themselves to giving him $10 [2010: $232] per month. When they increased it to $20 in June 1914, Clarissa was ecstatic: "O . . . there is goodness in the world . . . loveliness most glorious."[33] She thought that Lewis Terman and his friend Seward were responsible, but the increase came from Cary de Angulo, who had already split up with Jaime.[34] Subsequent donors included Cary de Angulo's college friend Edna Smith, whom Henry met at the ranch, and Seward's friend Judy Dawson (later Mrs. Armitt Brown), who became involved late in 1913 after bringing a pudding to Henry and Clarissa at Christmas, only to discover that they had almost nothing else to eat. All of them remained loyal for years. Judy Brown sent Henry money even during the Depression, and continued to send something to Sidney after Henry's death.[35]

Too practical to leave donations to individual motivation, and lacking personal wealth, Seward had the skills to organize and maintain a formal fund and excellent connections to nourish it. After Seward's untimely death in 1932, Henry told his widow that he had been "responsible for my being educated, and that it is highly probable that without his aid, I would never have been able to have a public career, nor to have developed culturally."[36] Sidney Cowell, who knew the Sewards well when she was young,[37] described him as "endlessly kind and helpful in personal ways as well as with HC's writing of English."[38]

Seward needed all his diplomatic skills to convince Henry that further education was urgent, for he knew that Henry resisted "received wisdom." He wisely avoided broaching the subject of a composition teacher, but it happened that Henry was encountering compositional problems and was open to consulting with someone. Seward also asked if Henry would like to learn to write as well as he talked, to which Henry responded positively, "declaring that he had already thought of some things he wanted to write about, and that he would welcome help."[39] He may be the person who persuaded Harry in the autumn of 1913 to take Henry to instructors of piano and theory around the Bay Area in search of a teacher and evaluations of his prospects.

Seward himself began collecting professional testimonials for a serious fund-raising effort. Terman's formal report about Henry, intended for fund-raising, is of special value because it is more detailed than the description in *The Intelligence of School Children* six years later. After using about every available intelligence test and statistics from several countries, he concluded that Henry's "general mental ability is of a degree so high that it is not met with in more than one case out of five hundred, or possibly not oftener than one case in a thousand." Terman reduced his estimate in 1919, not revealing whether he was taking into account subsequent studies or had inflated it in 1913 to help raise money.[40]

At the beginning of 1914, Seward formally established the fund and began soliciting.[41] In January, his good friends the de Angulos held a social event for some local ladies at their ranch. When Cary got home, Henry was merrily chopping kindling wood. After dinner and some preliminary "fun," he played several piano pieces and what he called his "orchestra piece," to the "astonishment and delight" of the group. Then Seward introduced Henry, who spoke extremely engagingly, leading one woman to propose Walter Damrosch, the conductor of the New York Symphony, as the person to help him. Seward in turn asked her if the Peninsular Musical Association, which sponsored concerts in Palo Alto, could arrange something for him, but the woman didn't think they'd understand.[42]

Seward also arranged for Henry to play for Elizabeth Bates, a young piano teacher, and her wealthy mother. Observing their powerful reaction to his music, he told them that Henry had had no instruction and had heard no classical music at all—a fib that secured their financial support. Half a century later, Elizabeth Bates could still remember Henry "with his big inquiring eyes, rosy cheeks, usually wearing a big sombrero type shade hat," and exuding boundless curiosity and determination. He told her he was training himself to hear many melodies at once, and "had got it up to fourteen." She recalled trembling for her family's Steinway parlor grand as he played his "tone-clusters and other experimental devices," and realizing to her relief that he knew what he was doing. "My piano never suffered from his manipulations." "Other experimental devices" and "manipulations" suggest that he already was playing directly on the strings.[43]

When Elizabeth told her colleagues in the San Francisco Musical Club about Henry, every teacher offered him free lessons. None of them was suitable, but her speech led to Henry's true debut at a Club meeting on March 5, 1914, in the Hotel St. Francis, the event that Henry mistook for the 1912 performance. Billed as "a program of descriptive and orchestral music," the concert opened with a group of his pieces and the Andante from the Sonata Op. 26 (presumably Beethoven's, and more likely Op. 27 No. 1), one of his few public performances of another composer's music. The concert then continued with a recitation of Schilling's "Young Olaf" with piano, and Mozart's Concerto in A Major, probably using other pianists.[44]

Aware of the potential impact of Henry's performance, and leaving nothing to chance, Seward had gotten two of San Francisco's most important critics, Ana Cora Winchell of the *San Francisco Chronicle* and Redfern Mason of the *Examiner*, to attend. Winchell—who started badly by identifying Henry as the son of the cement man—called him utterly original, childlike for his years, but "his ideas outstrip his appearance . . ." As to the music, she remarked that the very title of his opener, "Adventures in Harmony," revealed his greatest strength—his command of color and grandeur. After some semi-comprehensible words of praise, she concluded that Henry's work still showed some immaturity, but "its instinct is big and needs but reasonable discipline . . ." By any standards, it was a rave review, with the headline proclaiming, "Lad Shows Signs of Real Genius."[45]

Mason had more mixed reactions. The music was "lawless, without a trace of counterpoint"; on the other hand, Henry knew how to get his ideas "across the footlights." Convinced that Henry had not the faintest notion of "what is meant by development," he advised packing him off to Germany, "where he would be out of the reach of idolizing women folk who mistake anarchistic rhapsodizing for inspiration."[46] According to Evelyn Wells, Mason's comment about the idolizing women folk infuriated Henry, who assumed he meant Ellen Veblen.[47] He later admitted that Mason was correct, an awakening for which Seward, Terman, and de Angulo could be thanked.

According to a reviewer, the Musical Association performance also led a San Franciscan to contribute enough money to justify planning six months of lessons with a fine teacher.[48] (Henry identified the sponsor as a German baron who wanted to send him for lessons with Richard Strauss.) The plan was temporarily shelved by Clarissa's illness, the absence of teachers during the summer, and a peculiar injury to Henry's leg. An infected, scraped heel caused a muscle spasm that doubled his lower leg back so that he could not straighten it out. When a doctor suggested surgery or even amputation, Henry refused and translated his fury into the piano piece "Anger Dance." Eventually an osteopath cured his problem.[49] Then the outbreak of war made a trip to Europe impossible.[50]

As of October Seward had raised nearly $335 [2010: $7,540] from donors in Palo Alto and San Francisco, of which a little more than half remained. Thanks to Henry's frugality, Seward estimated that he could get through the year.[51] He already had had some piano lessons—apparently gratis—with a professionally trained teacher, Carrie ("Mother") Carrington,[52] an Englishwoman of about fifty from a musical family, who had trained at the Royal Academy of Music and in Germany.[53] He credited her with teaching him the few pieces he ever learned. Sidney said that Mother Carrington also arranged for him to receive $5 [2010: $113] for playing at the Ladies' Music Club of Salinas "in what he remembered as his first performance before an audience of complete strangers." Mother Carrington also obtained proper concert attire for him.[54]

Along with piano lessons, Henry finally got to hear more orchestral music, which was in its infancy in San Francisco. In 1909, when the city had largely recovered from the earthquake, fire, and massive corruption that slowed the reconstruction, local music lovers impressed by performances of Damrosch's New York Symphony Orchestra founded the Musical Association of San Francisco, which created the San Francisco Symphony two years later. In 1913, its conductor, Henry Hadley, who may have heard about Henry from the oboist who gave him a few lessons, invited him to attend rehearsals, which Henry regarded as his first instruction in composing for instruments other than the piano. "So while [Hadley] didn't do anything for me in the way of spoken lessons, it was a great lesson and a great favor to me, and I have always admired him greatly on this account."[55] The connection with Hadley was what permitted Seward to approach him for a letter of recommendation. Henry's remark that he heard his first symphony orchestra when Karl Muck conducted the Boston Symphony at the 1915 Panama-Pacific International Exposition, is therefore mistaken unless he meant that it was the first orchestra he heard in a concert.[56]

Henry's life was accelerating rapidly. He began giving voice lessons and advertising his services as a teacher of voice, piano, and harmony, charging 50 cents per lesson,[57] made an appearance as a singer in a recital by Henrietta's students,[58] and learned the fox-trot.[59] A Stanford student who had met Henry when he sold flowers to her mother wanted to study his heredity.[60] He became friendly with Ansel Adams, later a master photographer who then was a thirteen-year-old avid pianist living next door to Harry and Henrietta.[61] While Clarissa and Ellen returned again and again to the perpetual mess of his clothing, other people were comfortable introducing him to their wealthy friends.

Prospective teachers overwhelmingly admired his talent but seemed too old-fashioned. Finally Harry brought Henry to Charles Seeger, a quirky, brilliant Harvard graduate with broad experience as a teacher, composer, and conductor who was only twenty-six when he was invited to chair the music department at the University of California in Berkeley. He had been there a year when Henry auditioned.[62] Mightily impressed, Seeger accepted him and wrote a recommendation for Seward's use. Although Seeger's statements about that epoch are sometimes marred by errors and his desire to receive due credit for his work,[63] his recollections were validated by Sidney, who heard Henry's side of the story, had known the California circle firsthand, and was capable of disagreeing with anyone, including Henry (posthumously) and Seeger. The following account is based on Seeger's comments, the only source about Henry's education in that period apart from scattered remarks by Henry himself.[64]

Seeger understood that the most unusual aspect of Henry's and Harry's visit was its very occurrence. He saw that Terman's, Seward's, and de Angulo's relentless chipping away at Henry's resistance had made him realize that composers— not just performers—had to study.[65] Seeger was immediately won over by the young man, "to all external appearances a very disheveled farm boy" who played the piano with his elbows and fists. He assured Henry that his music was "right in line with music history," while observing his ignorance of that history. Recognizing the "first brilliant talent of my teaching experience," Seeger agreed to supervise his education without fee.[66] Ultimately he was amazed to see Henry emerge as "the most unregenerately unromantic and anti-sentimental musician of our times . . . and the most self-sure autodidact I ever met." He was wrong about Henry's ignorance of other music, however, though much of it was non-Western. Seeger claimed to have supervised Henry's music studies until 1919, but after 1917 they interacted more as colleagues and friends.

Seeger offered Henry three options: (1) abandon "free" composition and totally devote himself to academic disciplines; (2) continue to compose freely while Seeger acted as a source of technical information and did not actually teach him; or (3) pursue free composition and academic disciplines concurrently. Since he did not want to teach Western traditional music in the usual manner but could not ignore tradition completely, the third path was the only option, and Henry became Seeger's first student of composition. Seeger arranged special status for him at the University of California in Berkeley, then a small school with a tiny music program. In three grueling days each week, he had lessons there with two of Seeger's colleagues, Edward Stricklen (1880–1950), a fine and very conservative teacher of harmony and history,[67] and a Mr. Dowden, who taught sight-reading. For strict sixteenth-century counterpoint he sent Henry to Wallace Sabin (1869–1937), a British-born San Franciscan. Uda Waldrop (1885–1951) gave Henry piano lessons in San Francisco until the logistics of travel became impossible. One afternoon a week, Henry and Seeger explored new music. Henry also took courses in physics and philosophy at Berkeley[68] and weekly English lessons with Seward at Stanford.

Adhering to this program was not easy for Henry, whose responsibilities for Clarissa's care caused him to miss some sessions.[69] He took a 4:45 A.M. train from Menlo Park to San Francisco, caught the ferry to Berkeley, and walked to the music department for an 8:00 A.M. class.[70] He would go to Seeger's studio for the afternoon and often remain for the evening or stay overnight with Seeger and his wife. Seeger played what he could for Henry—his own music, Schoenberg's Opus 11, some Scriabin, some Stravinsky—and urged him to study Debussy, Satie, Ravel, and others. As soon as a new Schoenberg score arrived, he would pass it along. Seeger also claimed to have introduced Henry to other intonation systems and to associated rhythmic concepts. He later said that he never quite decided which of them got more pleasure from those sessions.

Henry was quickly accepted by Seeger's students. The advanced group of three young women and two men—one of whom was Glenn Haydon, Berkeley's first graduate in musicology[71]—loved Henry, who soon began to coach them unofficially. By no later than the third year, he was a teaching assistant, helping Walter Spalding's students with harmony and counterpoint.[72] These fine relationships were marred, however, by Henry's physical state. When the girls finally asked Seeger to persuade Henry to bathe and to get his clothes

cleaned, and Seeger declined because he did not want Henry to feel conde-
scended to, the girls pushed him into the music building's bathroom and made
him wash.

Seeger had no doubts about Henry: "He was my most talented student and
it was a great pleasure to open to his alert and sensitive mind the beauties of
the monuments of musical art, and to discuss with him the potentialities of
the twentieth century—many of which he [later] so notably developed in
himself or aided in others." They talked endlessly about everything; Seeger
called Henry one of the best conversationalists he had ever met; his criticisms
of concerts were far more advanced than any others that he had encountered.
According to Seeger's biographer Ann Pescatello, he tried out his ideas on
Henry, refined them fifteen years later with Ruth Crawford, and turned them
into the book *Tradition and Experiment in (New) Music*.[73] The long gestation
time makes it impossible to know precisely what they discussed, however.
Seeger also expressed his strong opinions as a Marx-loving conscientious ob-
jector who thought the British Empire ought to be abolished. Henry's interest
in socialism and Marx blossomed; the title of his piano piece "Antinomy" (a
pair of opposites) emerged from a discussion they had about Kant, Hegel, and
Plato.

In Seeger's new and "rather tentative" class in dissonant counterpoint, Henry
soon outstripped everyone. There was, however, the problem of Henry's stubbornness, which Seeger considered typical of autodidacts. Seeger never gave
him assignments, which he thought Henry would not have done. Only once did
he make a suggestion, which was to change a note in his first symphony. "I felt
the issue was worth making because the work was almost orthodox and might
give him a chance of performance. But Cowell was adamant. Ten years later,
almost to the day, he volunteered out of a clear sky that I had been right. I remember feeling I must have been wrong."

Henry brought Seeger his most experimental pieces—perhaps the highly dissonant "Dynamic Motion," or his first String Quartet,[74] but refused to show him
folklore-based compositions like "The Tides of Manaunaun."[75] Nevertheless,
two aspects of Henry's music struck Seeger with particular force: he used "commonplace materials in some compositions and new or unusual materials in
others," and he liked extra-musical titles, "the more irrelevant and whimsical the
better." Henry himself later said that his style was based on the title "or vice
versa," and both materials and title "were meant to fit." Seeger, however, thought
the titles were superfluous. To Henry, the most important goal was that chords,
rhythms, and other materials be either more conventional or less, in accordance
with the demands of the subject. This concept remained his credo. In later years,
he frequently said that his search for consistency sometimes led him to use experimental material, and sometimes not, depending on which resources were

appropriate to the idea. He never accepted the notion that a composer should cultivate a single musical style and apply it to all his music.

They both knew he would have to deal with a hostile or apathetic public. Henry was far from naive, Seeger added. "We spent no small amount of time in planning assaults, in the form of concerts, upon New York, Paris, and Berlin, in which elbows, string-plucking, and fantastic titles figured largely."

Perhaps the most interesting question is why Henry, so self-assured, studied with Seeger at all. Sidney said that he was uneasy at being unable to extend his compositions. The music of those years certainly supports the idea that he had the same conceptual problem as many early Romantic composers: by thinking in complete melodies, he foreclosed the possibility of extension through development and could not see how to invent new relationships. Henry's later writings also imply that he craved a historical and scientific justification for his music. He soon realized that he needed to know where such music fit into the flow of history.

Seeger felt his greatest contribution was his acceptance of Henry's ideas when other musicians called him a silly experimenter. He did not think he changed Henry. "My conservative friends have always wondered why I did not teach him to be a respectable musician. My liberal friends have never given me credit for teaching him anything. He himself swiped many of his best (and some of his worst) 'ideas' from me, and occasionally acknowledges it." But perhaps Seeger did not have enough time. His irascibility and opposition to the war led him to take a sabbatical, from which he never returned to Berkeley.[76]

‖ 6 ‖

Beginning Bi-coastal Life

After two fruitless mastectomies, Clarissa shuttled between her bed in the garden and a lounge inside, sank into depression, and died on May 15, 1916. When all the people present at her deathbed turned to look at him, Henry went completely deaf for a few moments. "Then . . . [he told Sidney] I thought, 'I won't hear Mama's voice again.'" Without saying anything he bicycled off to the Wells home in San Jose, arriving there in the evening, followed by Ellen Veblen.[1] (Evelyn Wells offered the somewhat less dramatic story that she and Henry took a streetcar to her place.) Later Veblen moved in with Henry to keep him company until he finished the term at Berkeley.

Clarissa bequeathed to Clarence the manuscript for a novel, some poems, articles, and short stories intended for young people's magazines. None of them had any monetary value. Henry received the remainder of her estate, which was not settled until two decades later, when the house was sold for $350 [2010: $7,170], leaving him $248 after the commission and fees, and ending Clarissa's fight for independence pitiably.[2]

Despite having to tend to her endless needs in those final months, Henry had completed a substantial body of music and may already have begun a theoretical treatise with Seward's aid.[3] When the semester ended, Henry, Ellen, and Evelyn went to Carmel, where he and Evelyn participated in a performance of scenes from *A Midsummer Night's Dream*, in which Henry played Bottom and choreographed the children dancing as fairies. Sidney, who was one of the children in the audience, later recalled "a shaggy-headed figure in a grey sack . . . [who] peered up from behind a wall . . . must have been Henry."[4]

A visit with the Varians[5] helped him escape the sadness of his little house. At Halcyon he had excellent and stimulating friends—the Varian boys, George Harrison, Franklin Wolff, Clarence Weaver, some young women. Despite its reputation, Halcyon was decidedly not a last resting place for social misfits. Russell Varian and George Harrison considered it "an ideal place in which to grow up,"[6] a warm, close-knit community near a fantastic beach and open countryside—a paradise where teenagers could hike, swim, think, dream. People had no money and fewer pretensions. Looking back on those days, Harrison observed that the older generation of idealists had spawned a brilliant and highly motivated second generation determined to break new paths for the common good.[7] Russell grew into a first-class inventor, Sigurd became senior pilot for Pan American's dangerous Mexican and Central American routes. Later the brothers created Varian Associates, one of the world's leading high-technology companies. Eric, the youngest brother, became an important breeder of Arabian horses. George Harrison rose to be chairman of physics at MIT; Clarence Weaver chose a more conventional life as a dentist and teacher; and, of course, there was Henry. The only member of that circle to remain immersed in Halcyon's otherworldliness was Franklin Wolff, a graduate student in mathematics at Stanford in the mid-1910s who later abandoned the profession to seek enlightenment and attracted a following as a mystic-philosopher.[8]

Halcyon thus had everything that interested Henry—science, spiritual life, Varian, and these excellent young friends. Halcyon valued Henry, who brought his own music and other recent compositions, including a two-piano version of *The Rite of Spring*, which he played with Jane Dower, the wife of the Guardian.[9]

In mid-summer (1916), Henry spent a month there, giving a course of eight lectures on music.[10] Then he, Franklin Wolff, and Russell and Sigurd Varian set off on a fifteen-day, 300-mile hike through the spectacular, largely uninhabited mountain country along the coast between Halcyon and Carmel.[11] A grand opportunity for them to exchange ideas, it is preserved in a long letter from Russell that suggests a Henry very different from the little weakling beaten up by bullies. They started somewhere near Halcyon, walked north about twenty-two miles, and spent most of that first night trying to get used to sleeping on the ground. The next day they covered about the same distance; then, after breakfast at Cambria, they hiked along the coastal cliffs toward their next camp, north of San Simeon, the headquarters of William Randolph Hearst's ranch, and "the last town of more than two houses on the trip." A very rough place, its locals could be expected to threaten some very nasty behavior. Fortunately, Russell added, the men just stared at them. After passing San Carpoforo the boys entered the coast trail proper, traveling a thousand feet above the sea, on precipices so steep that the ocean seemed to be below them. The gray water would appear and disappear below as the fog rolled up the mountain. They camped near a "talkative mountain stream. Everyone felt made over as soon as we came to the mountains." On the fourth day, after seeing in the fog a double circular rainbow, with another large, faint rainbow of the ordinary variety above it, they passed through an area with not a single occupied house, arriving at a campsite in a narrow canyon a quarter of a mile deep, a gorgeous virgin forest. A falling stone started them thinking about mountain lions, tested their will to sleep, and spooked their mule, which once had been attacked by a mountain lion. The remaining days included many storms, two of them violent, and the discovery of two large enamel bathtubs in the middle of nowhere.

After reaching the de Angulos' ranch in Big Sur, they returned to Halcyon, where Henry remained until it was time to go to Menlo Park for an October vocal recital with two new songs. In the end he canceled it, however, because he needed to pack. Seward had understood that, in losing his invalided mother, Henry had gained his freedom. It was time for him to reshape his life in New York. Ellen Veblen told Evelyn Wells, "I pity him so in the loneliness that is coming . . . Who knows whether he will come back again? People don't generally *leave* New York." She longed to fulfill Henry's wish that she accompany him.[12]

After a pleasant sojourn with Clarence in Des Moines, Henry eliminated a sight-seeing stop in Washington and settled in at 30 Bank Street, in the West Village. A week later he moved to 151 West 15th Street, which he hoped would be his permanent address. Rather than feeling lonely, he soon had many connections who opened up an urbane new world, thanks to acquaintances from Carmel, a watering place for many wealthy Easterners.[13] A friend of Seward brought him into contact with people who applied the radical political ideas that he had absorbed in California. Henry told Ellen, "You wouldn't think of any of his friends as being radical, would you? And yet this one walked from her home on 123rd St. down town every day of the street car strike, after the company was running 'scab' cars, just through principle. And a very interesting talker about labor trouble she is, although she teaches English at Columbia." Another person had nearly been killed while participating in the violent 1915 Standard Oil strike at Bayonne, New Jersey.[14]

Other contacts came through Cary de Angulo's college friend Edna Smith, with whom Henry dined a few days later; Seward enlisted Cary and Edna to visit potential donors in the New York area.[15] Henry's nervousness about poverty in New York suddenly erupted, however, when a communications problem prevented his withdrawing money wired by Seward.

He immediately started to take advantage of New York's cultural life, attending music and dance performances. Sophistication is evident in his comparison of Maud Allen with Pavlova.[16] Later he saw Diaghilev's Ballet Russe twice, with Nijinski as the lead, in *Til Eulenspiegel*, *Afternoon of a Faun*, and *Petroushka*, his favorite. "There Nijinski died in a wonderful way, quivering for so long." Hearing the New York Symphony play Strauss and Wagner convinced him of Strauss's inferiority.

With some trepidation Henry told Ellen that he had joined the Temple of the People.[17] He assured her that he had become a Theosophist only out of curiosity. "I never could join anything where you had to believe something. But [the Temple] present[s] instructions to you, to take as you will and these are so logical, so scientific, and so nearly in accordance with my own experiences, that I felt like persuing [*sic*] them farther."[18] Ellen appears not to have responded. One can imagine her fretting that Henry would settle into the comfortable community and lose his motivation, or that the Temple's teachings would pollute his originality. Above all, childless Ellen may have been jealous of the community and the Varians in particular. Her worries about Henry being lonely in New York probably reveal more about her than him. Even she later turned to Theosophy and became a member of Halcyon.

In fact, Theosophy had a lot to offer Henry. Its teachings centered upon a set of basic tenets, most of which were compatible with his individualism—to formulate spiritual truths without formulating a creed; to set forth a philosophy of life harmonious with divine law; to study the sciences and their "fundamental facts and laws"; to promote the study and practice of the arts and their benefits for human welfare; "to extend belief and knowledge from the known to the unknown, from the physical to the super-physical; and ultimately to reach an understanding of the spiritual teachings which have been given to mankind from time to time"; and to promote knowledge "of a true social science based on immutable law, showing the relationship between all people, between each person and God, and between humanity and nature."[19] The Temple emphasized the individual, and the need for individuals to work together voluntarily for the common good. Not much "belief" was involved, and hardly any aspect of the basic principles contradicted Henry's mode of living.

Above all, music was considered the foundation of true education, a manifestation of the Sixth Sense—the "Sense of Understanding"—"because it is common to all people and is understood by all without definite training, independent of nationality, environment or any other exterior requirement." Its cultivation, and its promotion among the masses, was therefore a priority for humanity.[20] Unfortunately, Theosophical ideas tended to mutate into semi-comprehensible invocations of cosmic forces, which might not have deterred Henry, but repelled Robert Duffus—Ellen's lodger—who called the movement "fantasy, wishful thinking and logic mixed in about equal parts."[21]

Although Henry's guiding principles clearly had some roots in Halcyon, even Sidney did not know the depth of his commitment. In 1974 she located Clarence Weaver in the hope that he could enlighten her. Weaver himself had undergone the entire educational process of the Temple, drawing away only when university education offered an alternative view of life. He remembered Henry attending meetings and having a reverential attitude and a loving relationship with everyone there. He could not imagine him being untouched by the experience.[22] Alas, he did not actually *know* Henry's feelings. He was right about one matter, however: Halcyon could only sustain someone with a monastic personality. Just as it did not sustain Clarence Weaver, it ultimately lost its grip on Henry and his friends.

For the moment, the omnipresent spirit of John Varian and his family sustained Henry's involvement. Despite Varian's impracticality, he had recruited another sponsor, his friend Elizabeth (Mrs. F. H.) Moss.[23] Varian also had musical projects for Henry, which are preserved in Henry's expanding portfolio of piano music relating to Irish myths.[24]

Halcyon and other California connections opened many doors into New York society. Dr. Frederick Bartlett, a noted pediatrician about twenty years Henry's senior,[25] had taught at Stanford University for two years at the turn of the century and seems to have known Ellen Veblen; his wife, once a singer, knew Ysaÿe and Busoni. Mrs. Bartlett introduced him to many musical friends, including the manager of Steinway Pianos, who showered him with free concert tickets and made him an "elite depositor" at an "elite bank," whose president placed Henry on his "Opera list," which meant Henry would occasionally be given tickets.

His excitement is palpable as he recounts being taken to dinner atop a thirty-story building by a friend of Seward who was "not bothered by heights." He expected to meet Leo Ornstein, the famous young radical modernist pianist-composer, at a dinner party, and was about to see Cary de Angulo.[26] Another rich, cordial, female helper with good connections brought Henry to the Boston Symphony and a concert by Percy Grainger, and introduced him to four noted teachers, namely, the virtuoso pianist Sigismund Stojowski,[27] Frank Damrosch (the director of the Institute of Musical Art, forerunner of The Juilliard School), Rubin Goldmark (remembered as the teacher of Aaron Copland and George Gershwin), and Arthur Battelle Whiting.[28] Through Whiting Henry met Charles T. Griffes, and the two played their music for one another. Meanwhile, Seeger sent calling cards of other potentially useful contacts, whom Henry quickly pursued. The list of interesting experiences seems endless. He heard "the charming old Paderewski" play and sat next to him at another concert. He had every reason to enjoy New York and took full advantage of it. What he would not have heard is modernist music, which effectively did not exist in the New York of the 1910s. If he noticed the flourishing world of innovative visual arts, he did not mention it.

New York's promise increased Henry's desire to share it with Ellen Veblen. His new apartment, with two grand French windows, was comfortable and large enough for "an enchanting Knabe grand of moderate size [that he had rented]. You can imagine how much fun I am having with it. It fills about half the room." Ellen too would be comfortable there, he kept insisting. Were they lovers, or was Ellen a substitute mother? The question is moot; her crushing financial burdens made a visit unlikely.[29]

Eventually, letters to Ellen Veblen began to refer to loneliness and friendlessness. Henry was only nineteen years old and had recently lost his mother; his father's few letters contain little more than philosophizing. His California friendships retained their strength, however. It is impossible to know whether the loss

of his California life wore upon him as much as Ellen thought.[30] She told Evelyn
Wells that Henry was discouraged,

> not at all well, and finds no one who knows as much about music as
> Mr. Seeger. [Seeger was expected in New York but had not yet ar-
> rived.][31] Says the NY ideals are very low, and evidently he hates it all.
> <u>Just you wait</u>, and see what turns up. If he comes back and wants to go
> to Berkeley, maybe we'll move up, and get a flat, and he will give you
> lessons and you will pose for the Univ. Art classes, and I'll try to cook,
> and everything will go swimmingly.[32]

Nothing seems farther from Henry's experiences so far. His discouragement
seems to be her wishful thinking.

His California life flourished in letters. Among his young correspondents
were the Liberty sisters, the very musical daughters of a Theosophist family,
with whom Henry had a long, close relationship. Bright, witty, and charming
Agnes breathes affection in a neat handwriting that makes her seem conventional in comparison with her older sister Lola, who expresses herself more
formally but in a bold, eccentric, hand, in exclamations like, "I was rejoiced
[sic] to hear of your efforts in behalf of the attainment of the technique of
bodily care and fitness. . . . By the way, we are charmed with the map of your
heart and grateful for any location!"[33] Henry had given one of them voice
lessons and discussed his ideas with them around the dining table, though
their contributions, colored by Theosophical mysticism, were not the stuff
of theory textbooks.[34] Lola was remarkably perceptive about Henry's development. "You are so far keeping pure and directing an inflow of cosmic consciousness. Had your present evolution been reversed, you might have
become as a polished mirror, reflecting all about you because you could do
nothing else, which is so frequently the case with indefatigable book
readers."

Such letters would have convinced Ellen that Henry was being sucked into
the Theosophist maze. Either he was open to Lola's spiritual bombardment, or
he enjoyed her way of expressing it. Once again, Henry leaves us guessing. A
certain frivolity is suggested by his response to Ellen's question about the fourth
dimension: "If you will write to Franklin Wolff at Halcyon, he will send you
things about the 4th, 5th, 6th, and 7th dimensions! All very amusing. I haven't
been able to follow them, because I don't know enough of the three . . . I must
practice now . . ."[35]

By mid-November 1916, Seward had produced enough money for him to
stay in New York through the spring. He had heard the Kneisel Quartet, whom
he contemptuously described as "nice," coincidentally the same term used by

Ives, whom Henry only met a decade later. He was about to go to the Metropolitan Opera for the first time, to see *Tristan und Isolde*, already had tickets for *Der Rosenkavalier*, and would attend *Parsifal* at Thanksgiving—all free, thanks to the bank president. After seeing *Tristan* he wrote, "I never enjoyed music as I did last night at 'Tristan', for while in a concert they mix bad and good, this is great from start to finish."[36]

Although Henry was getting an unparalleled education in some respects, other aspects of it began to erode his good mood. A friend's introduction to Frank Damrosch may have facilitated his late registration at the Institute of Musical Art, which Damrosch had founded and still directed. At first Henry cheerfully wrote Harry of the warm welcome accorded him. He expected to study orchestration with Damrosch, piano with Arthur Newstead—a celebrated British virtuoso who had recently joined the faculty—and counterpoint with Percy Goetschius. That does not seem to be what happened. In late November, practicing and counterpoint exercises left little time for anything exciting. Even worse, the general standard of instruction disappointed him. On November 22 he wrote Ellen, "The people there are all cads, but they seem to know what I want to. I don't know how long I can stay there, though, under their severe personal treatment. I am to meet Percy Grainger and Leo Ornstein. Maybe I shall study with one of them."[37] His time at the Institute ended abruptly. Disgusted with the quality of instruction, Henry handed in a Bach chorale harmonization as if it were his own, received it back filled with corrections, and complained to Damrosch, adding that the historical lectures of Waldo Pratt were filled with inaccuracies and that the counterpoint classes of Percy Goetschius abounded with unwarranted freedoms. He had opened his mouth exactly as de Angulo had warned him not to. Damrosch responded by kicking him out of the school without refunding his tuition money for the rest of the year, which had been paid in advance. Henry withdrew on January 15, 1917.[38] Damrosch had simply lived up to his reputation as authoritarian and paternalistic. He gave the students no choice about courses, enforced strict codes of behavior and dress—the latter was certainly not Henry's cup of tea—and even exerted strong influence on students' reading and other spare-time activities. Many of them got fed up but could not change the school. The only remedy was to leave.[39]

Henry, however, muddied the waters with two versions of their confrontation. He told Terman that he went to Damrosch, who listened until he foresaw the trend of Henry's speech, then broke in and told him (as Terman transcribed the narrative) "that since he is so unappreciative of what they have tried to do for him he may no longer consider himself one of their pupils—in a word, that they want nothing more to do with him!" Terman does not mention the trick with the chorale, but his notes contain a coda that Henry omitted in his later version. When Seeger told Damrosch that Henry was the Institute's most promising pupil, Damrosch enthusiastically gave Henry a letter of recommendation to an unnamed musician.[40]

Other evidence, however, implies a much less amicable parting. In 1921, when Henry's career as a pianist was growing, his manager produced a circular stating that "Mr. Cowell has studied principally in New York, where he entered the Institute of Applied Art [sic] and later coached with Leo Ornstein." The statement is accurate, but the absence of the exit conditions triggered Damrosch's temper when he saw a copy.

> Your record shows that you attended the Institute of Musical Art about seven weeks during which period you had seven lessons on the piano, six in Theory and were absent from eleven lessons in Ear-training. Your theory teachers expressed no opinion concerning your work during the few weeks you attended. Your piano teacher's opinion on your work was entirely unfavorable and under these circumstances, I consider it an unwarranted impertinence for you to claim you have been a student at this Institute.

He strongly "suggested" that in the future Henry omit references to the Institute of Musical Art.[41]

While some members of the Seward circle were alarmed by the rupture of his relationship with Damrosch, the twenty-nine year-old writer Maxwell Anderson—who probably met Henry while studying at Stanford—wrote, "It is with pleasure that I note your ejection from the Damn-rosch institution. Are you too wild and woolly for them? And is the Ornery Ornstein the only alternative? It seems to me that there should be a purgatory between heaven and hell."[42]

Henry's revulsion at the limits of traditional education, at least as practiced at Damrosch's Institute, may have had a reasonable basis. His self-education, leavened with the sessions with Seeger, may have put him far ahead of the Institute's teachers. He also may have been driven by his mother's hostility to institutional education, or may simply have been ornery. Whatever the reason, in this phase of intellectual ferment, when he sought a theoretical basis for his music and an appropriate place in the musical world, the staid Institute was definitely wrong for him.

At Christmastime (1916), Seeger, having resigned from Berkeley, arrived in New York. He and Henry roamed the city, walking back and forth on the Brooklyn Bridge repeatedly, discussing ideas for music and for Henry's career. The conversation continued when Henry visited Seeger and his "elegant New England family" at Patterson, New York.[43] Agnes Liberty was with him in spirit, sweetly writing about practicing her singing in major sevenths and fourths in order to learn pieces that Henry had given her—songs by Schoenberg and, of all people, Strauss. Her irresistible pen picture of herself and Henry giving a recital shows her singing Schoenberg and trembling as Henry plays the piano—but the picture lacks her face and his hands.[44]

With the Institute of Musical Art behind him, Henry hoped to study with either Leo Ornstein or Percy Grainger, both of whom he anticipated meeting early in 1917.[45] Although Ornstein was Henry's rival as an ultramodernist pianist, Henry exuded admiration of him, considering Ornstein's technique superior to Paderewski's.[46]

While no meeting with Grainger is known, getting to Ornstein was something of a saga. Henry told Terman that the music critic of the *New York American* urged Ornstein to see him, but Ornstein claimed to be too busy to waste time on just another young composer. When the critic, who had "made" Ornstein, accused him of being less modern than Henry, Ornstein agreed to a two-minute meeting when Henry could give him a couple of compositions. Ornstein then invited Henry to come that evening to his room, hidden among labyrinthine passages behind a hardware store on 42nd Street. After cordially explaining that he had interrupted his busy schedule to practice Henry's music for two hours, Ornstein told him it was "crude, but . . . the material was there." (Not that his views were tempered by age: Ornstein was only twenty-five, five years older than Henry.) Henry was "working in the dark, he needed only to find himself." Ornstein declared Mischa Levitzky, another young virtuoso gaining national acclaim, "far less promising" and threw Levitzky's music in the wastebasket. They arranged for Henry to study with Ornstein when he spent two months in California and then "to betake himself to a quiet place for study and composition."[47] Henry was not pumping himself up for Terman's benefit; Ornstein verified this account in a February letter of "opinion and advice."[48] They finally got together late in 1917[49] when Ornstein played in San Jose,[50] but there is no evidence that Henry ever studied with him, nor was he correct in saying that Ornstein imitated clusters after hearing Henry play in 1915, which was much earlier than their first encounter.[51]

Henry returned to Menlo Park in early February 1917. With his friends at hand, letter-writing declined, the picture of his life becomes vague, and we become dependent upon Sidney's commentaries, which say that he quickly called upon Cary de Angulo, accompanied by Ellen Veblen. Cary supposedly claimed that this was the first time she heard him perform, which is not true, since she had attended both the performance of *Creation Dawn* and the fund-raising dinner in January 1914. It might have been her first exposure to Henry's techniques, however, because she disapproved thoroughly. When Henry responded that it shouldn't make any difference *how* he produced his music so long as he produced

it, Cary had to agree with him. He could not ignore, however, this trusted supporter's vision of dangers in how his music "looked" to the listener, though he
did not act on it until much later.[52] Sidney could have heard about the incident
from Henry, but the source was probably Cary, for someone told Sidney that
Henry showed unconcealed curiosity about Cary's houseguest Edna Smith,
whom he had already met at least once. About her, more in due course.

That was also the time when Henry met Sidney Hawkins (decades later, Sidney Cowell), a thirteen-year-old freshman at fashionable Castilleja High School
for Girls.[53] The intermediary was Henry's patron Elizabeth Bates, the supervisor
of Sidney's daily piano practice. Bates told Sidney that if she played for a famous
musician who had just returned from New York, "something might come of it."
Sidney found out only later what Elizabeth had in mind—namely, that Sidney
would ask her wealthy parents to help him. The odds were fair; her mother already
had given two young painters money to study in Paris, had heard Henry play, and
was intrigued by reports of his talent. "She might perfectly well have sent him for
two or three years to New York (Europe being impossible in 1917 because of the
war) if anyone had just asked her." Henry never brought up the subject, and that
was that. Elizabeth Bates, of course, was ultimately correct in thinking something
would come of it, but she had in mind the wrong "something."[54]

On March 1, 1917, ten days before Henry's twentieth birthday, the Termans
had him over to dinner, the occasion when he told them about meeting Ornstein. Terman seized the opportunity to assess the effect of living in New York
upon his mentee.[55] His notes on the conversation show the difficulty that he
soon faced when writing about Henry for *The Intelligence of School Children*. He
had to remember Henry as he was in 1914, not by what he had become through
their close relationship.

His description of Henry in 1917 is unique in its detail. Upon arriving home,
Terman found Henry helping Mrs. Terman in the kitchen. Henry seemed
unchanged except more mature, a little less freakish in his looks and manners . . .
"Our boy must be fulfilling his promise. The busiest of musicians would not be
willing to give so much time to him did they not feel him to be a kindred soul."[56]

In response to questions about his mental processes, Henry reported the end
of "disagreeable" dreams that had bothered him in earlier years. Now he dreamed
only in music, frequently the most beautiful music he ever heard. It could not be
described except that it was loud and compelling, its tones purer than real tones,
and not resembling any instrument. He remembered the music upon waking,
but it disappointed him when he wrote it down. Such dreams did not come more
often when he was composing than at other times. They might last all night, and
sometimes, if he awoke, they would resume after he fell asleep again. Once, when
he could not fall asleep, he read an article on Ornstein with some excerpts from
Ornstein's compositions that kept him awake thinking of Ornstein's genius. To

Terman's surprise, Henry said that he sometimes dreamed music when he was not asleep. It would break in upon him at almost any time, so vividly that he was surprised that other people could not hear it. It was distinguished from real music by being louder and "more heavenly in quality. . . ." Sometimes its force nearly swept him off his feet. Yet when he wrote down the sounds, they too were disappointing.

He said he did not await inspiration; he could work at any time. Composing was a process of working out in detail a theme "that has already presented itself to me in a flash. This flash comes as a musical scheme, rather fully organized. It is instantaneous, so that after seconds it seems a memory. When it comes I have it. There is no trouble remembering it, even for months. But as soon as I have written it down I forget it." These flashes were fully-organized schemes of a composition, not melodies, not "intellectualistic" but emotional, although they could have intellectual elements. "It comes as an outburst—a volcanic outflow. I do not create it. It comes. But it must be given material form, and I may work long hours to get the scheme down in a form which adequately represents it."

Terman noted in conclusion that Henry told his story "in language almost literary. No college professor of English could have improved upon it. And it was so natural. His conversation breathes intelligence. I had the feeling that no unschooled boy who was not a genius of the first order could speak thus."[57]

Other than that visit with the Termans, the remainder of 1917 offers almost no news, since almost no letters survive. On March 6 and 29, Henry and a soprano gave recitals in Palo Alto and San Francisco. The most noteworthy relic of their collaboration is a review in the *Palo Alto Times* stating that "Les Ornskein" had undertaken the "direction of Henry's further studies"—which was only true if Henry followed his advice—and that Henry proposed "a forward reach of the piano into the realm of Cubism. Liszt was wont to use the tips of his fingers and of his nose. Cowell is not thus anatomically limited." The *Examiner* review said that Henry was believed to be at the "Damrosch Musical Institute." Fortunately, Damrosch was unlikely to see it.[58]

Considering all the playing Henry had been doing, it is disheartening that he was almost never paid. Without the Seward fund, he would have been in deep trouble. Fortunately, he had time to compose and expand his theoretical ideas. His major project, music for Varian's *The Building of Bamba*, grew into some form of musical pageant that was premiered in August by Temple members at the Temple of the People and repeated in Carmel and Palo Alto. Sidney recalled that while it may have expressed the ideals of the Theosophist community, it distressed friends who were hoping for something really grand. They apparently had good reason to be disturbed. She heard it in Palo Alto "without being able to make head or tail of it, the performance was so painfully bad."[59] Its only surviving movement, the prelude, is "The Tides of Manaunaun," whose sweeping melody, sonorous tonal harmonization, and tone-cluster coloring have made it one of Henry's best-known pieces.[60] While "The Tides of Manaunaun" may have originated up to five years before, Henry himself associated it with *The Building of Bamba*, and apparently did not consider its precursors definitive.

Henry's ability to interact with the spiritual concepts of the Temple of the People can be seen in the aftermath of some classes he gave there in August. His explanation of "dissonance" led to a larger communal discussion of dissonance, consonance, harmony, and life that climaxed with an article in *The Temple Artisan* by the Guardian-in-Chief, an excellent specimen of how a straightforward discussion of compositional tools could be transformed into an exposition of cosmic forces.[61] Henry's ongoing presence at Halcyon is no surprise, but it is unexpected to find, in the same issue of *The Temple Artisan*, a poem by Harry about the Temple's handsome sanctuary. Harry's connection with Halcyon is otherwise unknown.

All in all, it was a productive summer. Although the young Henry is remembered as a composer for piano, his music for *Bamba* is only a fraction of his many songs and choral pieces from those years. He attributed his interest in the voice to a few singing lessons with Henrietta, whose students he also occasionally accompanied at lessons. He quickly found, however, that poetry helped him find a sense of form in his music.[62] He also completed several *Ings* (intricate etude-like pieces for piano), and the "Quartet Romantic," for two flutes, violin, and viola, to which we shall return in the next chapter.

In the fall of 1917 Henry's Halcyon friend Clarence Weaver arrived at Stanford and stayed briefly at Henry's house. Weaver recalled that the area was still so crude that one could hardly imagine it. "I would say he just lived on Mud Street." Harkins Avenue was still virtually impassable in the rainy season. They cooked together, made music, and enjoyed the area. Henry composed continuously. They would have jam sessions—Weaver on violin, which he didn't play well but loved. He remembered Henry's great rapport with nature and the impression that he practically had enough knowledge to qualify him for an advanced degree. "Henry told me that one evening when he was walking through this area and the scenery was very beautiful and an inspiring sunset came out over the ocean, he was just enthralled by the flooding into his mind of the beautiful composition known as *Exultation*. He just heard the whole thing. So he didn't have to compose it. All he had to do was just write it down." Weaver remembered him as a lovely young man.[63]

Henry ended up remaining in California for the rest of 1917. With the United States now fighting in Europe, all young men had an uncertain future. A friend in New York wondered if his absence meant he had been drafted. "I think your stature would not mitigate [sic] against you since they lowered the height requirements. Personally, I don't think you are strong enough for the army, but then I suppose they know best. . . ."[64]

7

Genesis of a Theoretical System

In contrast to Terman, who was studying Henry's intelligence and, one might say, persona, Seward simply had to improve Henry's spelling, grammar, and writing style. Unlike Seeger, he did not encounter the autodidact's resistance because Henry knew his limitations. Assignments to write about music, rather than conventional subjects like his summer holidays, were the perfect stimulus. Henry's initial achievements survive in a notebook with five essays on musical topics datable to 1915 or 1916, some of them corrected by Seward: "Modern Music," "Schoenberg," "Concord and Discord," "Which Poems to Set to Music" (an examination of the properties of poetry), and "Conducting" (the baton as an instrument). These essays are especially interesting views of Henry's development because he was not trying to prove anything about his intellect; he was just trying to improve his writing. Already, however, he was preoccupied with making modernism understood for what it is, rather than for what it is not, and for finding modernism's roots in tradition.

His ideas probably stemmed from discussions with Seeger, which usually ended in the complete intermingling of their individual thoughts. While Seeger did not mention the particulars of their discussions, they can be deduced from the syllabus of his Introduction to Musicology. Translating the term "musicology" as "the science of music," Seeger surveyed the development of scientific, critical, and artistic approaches to music; the "general sciences" of music—rhythm and harmony—using mathematics, physics, physiology, psychology, and so on; the merging of science with art; the logic of methodical thought as viewed by the artist; and artistic logic itself. More clues reside in Henry's jumbled notations on the syllabus, which refer to the relationship between what he called "the consonance in dissonance" and the overtone series, and his idea of "consonant rhythm." He imagined dissonant harmony balanced by consonant (i.e., clearly synchronized) rhythm, and vice versa. It is impossible to know whether these notes refer to his own thoughts or something Seeger said, however.

Seeger was not his only companion in discussions, and the essays for Seward hardly touch upon Henry's bubbling cauldron of ideas. Theories of music and sound surely were in the air during the 300-mile, late-summer hike with Russell and Sigurd Varian and Franklin Wolff in 1916. Since music was central to Halcyon life, the convergence of science and music in these young people was almost inevitable. While the nature of Franklin Wolff's and George Harrison's interest in music is not known, and Sigurd Varian was only fifteen, Russell Varian is inextricably linked with Henry's development.[1] His genius was surprising for someone who had been left back in grade school four times because he could not master reading, spelling, and arithmetic. (His widow thought that in the mid-twentieth century he would have been diagnosed as dyslexic and treated accordingly.) Tall, ungainly, nearsighted, with buck teeth, up to four years older than his schoolmates, he was taunted as dumb and "touched in the head." He was saved from illiteracy by Stanford professor Dr. Percy E. Davidson, the pioneer in teaching reading through phonetics who also may be the person who "discovered" Henry.[2] Like Henry, Russell was an outsider to conventional education. At the time of the great hike, he was already demonstrating his scientific brilliance.

The relationship between their thinking might only be speculative if Russell had not contracted chicken pox shortly after Henry left for New York in the fall of 1916. Lying in bed, he passed the days studying light, heat, acoustics, and electricity. He had lost interest in his father's dream of a gigantic harp once he learned of the audion bulb, a triode vacuum tube invented by Lee de Forest in 1906 that played a central role in telephone systems and radio.[3] Its possible consequences were the subject of an intriguing correspondence between Russell and Henry that apparently expanded upon their conversations during the hike. Russell envisioned the audion bulb being used to produce just intonation and quarter tones, and developed an elaborate plan for a keyboard controller "as flexible as the piano," although it might require several players. After further thought, he refined his keyboard into a pressure-sensitive device. In a cryptic reference to an earlier conversation, he also suggested a kind of voice synthesis. The audion bulb, Russell realized, could transmit music thousands of miles by radio, and probably make it receivable for 600 to 800 miles with an ordinary $25–$30 wireless set.[4]

Henry responded with his own ideas of rhythm, pitch, and notation.[5] At the Institute of Musical Art rhythm was "a really neglected subject," he said. Since the rhythmic complexity of counterpoint developed early—Seeger's course studied fourteenth-century polyphony—he reasoned that rhythm grew from a more primeval thought process than melody or harmony, that "people grew intelligent about it first." He already had deduced that rhythmic relationships could be conceptualized in the same terms as pitches.

Anyway, counterpoint is practically built on rythms working against each other, almost entirely, however in consonant ratios, that is, either 2, or 3, or 4 notes against one, which, in tonal ratios, would be the same as the octave, the fifth, and the octave above again, the very simplest consonances, the same which charichterized [*sic*] the tonal style of those times also. When people discovered Harmony of tone, they used unison rythms also, and that is what still clings.

Ragtime's syncopations had prompted Henry and Russell to think that rhythm could also be considered consonant or dissonant. Henry wrote Russell that ragtime's syncopations manifested "an embryonic tendency toward dissonant rhythm, of a more complicated ratio" using lines moving at two "*rates* of speed at once . . . so that in steady rhythm the ratios would still come out, in other words you use steady rythms in counterpoint to each other, and the rag uses unsteady rythms in harmony!" He knew of no one "doing new things with counterpoint." Anticipating the ideas of Conlon Nancarrow by more than three decades, he continued, "Another interesting counterpoint with rhythm, would be to have one steady movement getting steadily faster, against another getting steadily slower . . . Another idea is different rythmic figures in counterpoint as regards rate of speed. A lot of new kinds of notes will have to be invented to write this down, as it is impossible, with our limited present supply." His enthusiasm was uncontainable, especially as the academicism in New York was really getting under his skin: "Everyone here composes along old lines, or merely stupid new ones, using discords without reason. You have heard and are hearing more of the best present day music in Halcyon than is produced in all this big city." He closed, "Send along some more schemes!"

Russell responded with an article about de Forest[6] explaining the audion bulb's applicability to broadcasting. A hint of post-1945 sine-wave generators and synthesizers was already in the air: de Forest had an audion that could produce sustained pitches in a broad range of tone colors. People were already foreseeing an electronic improvement over the organ. Russell imagined a multimedia application coordinating pitch ratios, rhythmic ratios, and "light ratios," which seems to have meant ratios of the frequencies of different colors. He already imagined an electro-mechanical machine to produce those rhythms. Although it would not be able to produce pitches, he believed it could become a real instrument cheaply. They never found out because they never had the money to build their inventions.[7]

It is a pity that Henry's correspondence with Russell temporarily ended at this point, because their ideas, some of the freshest of that entire epoch, were at the core of Henry's evolving theories as he moved from speculation to reason. His next direction can be seen in a collection of undatable leaves probably written around 1916 and recopied later. One sheet proposes classifications for extraordinary harmonic relationships. Fused chords with names like "polychord" are treated as if they are single bodies capable of functioning contrapuntally against similar bodies, producing "counterpolychords." His chart of relationships stretches to extremely complex structures, running from counterpoint of different chords (counterchord) to counterpoint of contrachordal sections as units (megacounterchords). Other notes evoke Theosophical thoughts while emphasizing reasoned composing.

> A certain expression of my music is that of interpreting as best I may the universal sounds going on always. The music will then neither have definite beginning or end, being a slice of something going on forever. It must sound like a mixture of all things, and no one should sound above the others, unless some one thing, such as human sympathy or passion, could sing out, with accompaniment of natural sound. Each moving part must be very logical in itself, and in its relationship, else it will all be a mere jumble, and not expressive of the form and relationship of things. . . . Let my music attempt to express this great cosmical fact, the unity of all things, though seemingly removed, into one great tone.

The quest for unity of materials stretched to a "counterpoint of dynamics," which in turn could bring about "dynamic positive pitch"—that is, the ability to remember absolute dynamic levels. One paragraph concerns a "melody by omission," that is, a melody whose shape emerges from lacunae in the texture, somewhat like the imaginary melody in Schumann's "Humoreske." Such a melody could be played in counterpoint to a real melody.[8]

In a short time Henry had taken giant steps beyond his essays for Seward, although his ideas were still a jumble. Seeger, who was convinced that Henry was not interested in other ideas, greatly underestimated his curiosity. Asked years later about possible influences on Henry, he dismissed Helmholtz, a copy of which was on his desk, because Henry could not read German. But Henry had sources beyond Seeger. He had already impressed de Angulo with his knowledge of acoustics. His treatment of string vibrations and the overtone series could have developed further in discussions with Russell Varian about John Varian's plan for the gigantic harp. He could have read A. J. Ellis's translation of Helmholtz, *On the Sensations of Tone* (1875). Speculation is probably unnecessary, however. On his loose sheets of ideas, Henry mentioned Sedley Taylor's 1873 *Sound and Music*, subtitled "a non-mathematical treatise on the physical constitution of musical sounds and harmony, including the chief acoustical discoveries of Professor Helmholtz." An exceptionally thorough explanation of acoustics for the layman, it is almost certainly the source of Henry's extensive knowledge of the subject, which had taken Jaime de Angulo completely by surprise. In addition to basic acoustics, Taylor discussed experiments with multiple tuning forks to measure interference, which Henry and Russell attempted to replicate until they found that German-made tuning forks could not be imported because of the war.[9] Taylor talked about the acoustical foundations of intervals and chords, physical explanations of consonance and dissonance, the physics of the voice, combination tones, and even an experiment using sirens as tone generators to measure acoustical phenomena that Henry said he once undertook with a Stanford graduate student.[10]

Sidney also underestimated Henry; she thought that he "would have dismissed any music theorist completely as having nothing to contribute to what he had on his mind." It is strange that she did not know about the conversations with Russell and Sigurd, and that both she and Seeger failed to notice the depth of Henry's studies and thinking. In short, the view of Henry as an autodidact uninterested in the ideas of others is far too limited and may speak to Seeger's own insecurities and Sidney's misunderstandings.

Whatever their source, Henry was soon working out his ideas as a full-sized treatise, published more than a decade later as *New Musical Resources*. We shall give him time to finish it before examining it. In the meantime, never intending his ideas to be confined to a theoretical system, he began applying them in two compositions that explored his theory of coordinated pitch, rhythmic, and metric relationships. The underlying idea was that the mathematical ratios represented in sound by vibration ratios—for example, the fifth is 3:2—can be represented simultaneously by the same ratios of rhythms, erecting a sturdy framework for a composition. The idea of coordinated pitch and rhythmic relationships resurfaced in the extended serialism of the 1950s, though in a different form and not in formulations by Henry.

His first compositional application of the idea is the phenomenally complex *Quartet Romantic* for two flutes, violin and viola (1915–17). The second piece, *Quartet Euphometric* ("Euphonious Meter")—begun in 1916 and completed in 1919, is still difficult, but less experimental in tone and much shorter. In addition to its remarkable rhythmic-metric coordination, the *Quartet Euphometric* is permeated with "dissonant counterpoint," an emancipation of the dissonance that seems even more extreme than Schoenberg's and was central to Seeger's nascent compositional method.[11] Henry had first tried writing dissonant counterpoint in January, 1916, in a little canon called "Dissonant Counterpoint," an experiment for himself and Evelyn Wells "who," Sidney says, "was always willing to try anything."[12] In April, he expanded the idea into the *Quartett Pedantic*. Yet, as Henry pointed out in his 1964 introduction to the printed score of *Quartet Euphometric*, his melodies are much more conjunct than in the European style of the time, and the texture is far more polyphonic than harmonic. His goal was a systematically conceived, expressive piece in which he never repeated himself literally. Although the early tone-cluster pieces are considered quintessential Cowell, *Quartet Euphometric* is a more stunning conceptual achievement, and shows tremendous growth beyond the more complex but perhaps less spontaneous *Quartet Romantic*.

Henry, however, realized that complex rhythmic counterpoint was a thing of the future. After witnessing the difficulty his friends had in executing such rhythms, "he concluded that a mechanical means would be needed before composers could hear them and players could play them."[13] With regard to the *Quartet Romantic*, he was absolutely right: it waited sixty-one years until it could be played, and even then it required a click-track.

8

Henry Goes to War

When the United States entered the Great War on March 20, 1917, British-Irish relations were so abysmal that the Americans were asked not to draft Irishmen for fear they would be sympathetic to the Germans. As the grandson of an Irishman, Henry took an option to be considered legally Irish and exempted from the draft.[1] Unfortunately, a new agreement early in 1918 would have compelled him to fight in the Irish army.[2] Recognizing that his days as a civilian were numbered, he enlisted rather than risk the consequences of compulsory service.[3] A few weeks before his twenty-first birthday, he volunteered at Oakland for the medical corps "for the duration of the war," giving his occupation as "student." The enlistment papers contain the earliest description of him: blue eyes, brown hair, ruddy complexion, five feet two and three-quarters inches tall. His vocation was given as "musician"; he had no ratings for marksmanship, gunnery, horsemanship, battles, engagements, skirmishes, or expeditions.[4] Henry, all in all, was no soldier.

Evelyn Wells was devastated by the possibility of Henry going to battle. At the very least, his hands could be damaged or destroyed. Somehow this eighteen-year-old, who had just been hired by the *San Francisco Call-Bulletin*, persuaded her editor to place an article about him on the front page. Although Henry was impressed, her victory had no effect. One day in March (1918) she accompanied him to his San Francisco departure point. He wore "a baggy uniform & puttees he could not wrap properly so they kept flapping loose all over Market Street. We laughed & laughed as he knelt, wrapped, tucked in, & I tried to help. Then he boarded a streetcar & left & all at once I realized he was going to war & might not be seen again. And I stood on the pavement before the emporium & bawled like a baby."[5]

After ten days at Angel Island in San Francisco Bay he went east by train via New Orleans, an odd route that gave him an unforgettable view of a southern spring filled with blooming trees and shrubs he had never seen.[6] Following a brief visit with his friend Dr. Fred Bartlett in New York, he arrived at Camp Crane, Pennsylvania, the training ground for military ambulance crews, assigned to Evacuation Ambulance No. 8.[7] (He did not know how to drive.)[8] Henry was in the same camp as Seward,[9] who had enlisted eight months earlier in the Stanford Division of the USA Ambulance Service.[10] But if they planned it that way so they could work on Henry's treatise, it was to no avail. Just about when Henry arrived, Lieutenant Seward was sent to France, attached to the French infantry as Commandant of the USA Ambulance Service, for which he was later named Chevalier of the Legion of Honor and awarded La Croix de Guerre.

Camp Crane had been crafted from an agricultural fairground right in the middle of Allentown, Pennsylvania. The grandstand was headquarters, the cattle sheds and poultry buildings were the sleeping quarters, and the mess hall was installed in underground rooms. The historian of the unit wrote, "Some men complained of feeling like animals in a zoo, but others recorded fond memories of a 'beautiful town,' where they met girlfriends, and friendly families who cooked and threw parties for ambulance corps members." The population of the camp was an odd mixture of men with higher education and medical training, and others who thought that ambulances were better than trenches. Photographs show them in standard wool uniforms, with medical belts holding bandages, tourniquets, gas masks, scalpels, clamps, needles, thread, and other instruments. Ford cars were used as ambulances because they were easily dismantled and reassembled. Twenty thousand men passed through the camp in the two years after America's entry into the war.[11]

Henry's first assignment was the kitchen, where he cooked for 800, suffering through an exhausting twelve-hour shift but earning $8 [2010: $116] monthly in extra pay and every second day off. (He and a certain Abrams got the jobs because their names came first on the list.) He tried to fry eggs by dropping them into deep hot fat without removing their shells, but they exploded.[12] Just eating could be risky. One day the baked beans were revolting; a soldier/cook had washed his clothes in the pot and forgot to take them out. The pork and beans had been piled right on top.[13] Michael Hicks's inference that this job was extremely demeaning for Henry, "who had never fit in with the well-bred college crowd,"[14] is unlikely to be correct. Many of his closest friends came from the college crowd, including Edna Smith, Cary and Jaime de Angulo, Seward, Seeger, Terman, Fred Bartlett, and Edna's friends in New York. Henry never refers to such a problem.

The regular days off were extremely useful because Camp Crane was within easy reach of New York. Henry developed warm relationships with Ornstein and a new friend, the composer Carl Ruggles, whom he apparently met through Dr. Bartlett.[15] The days off also gave him time to finish his Symphony.[16] He wanted to set some poems by Harry and the "International Hymn," but creative work at the camp became impossible. When the men received typhoid and typhus immunizations on April 2, they naturally—and incorrectly—assumed that they were about to be sent to the front.[17] By June, Henry was back in music, having obtained the commandant's authorization to form a band by interviewing all the men who came through the camp.[18] He conducted it until the arrival of an experienced bandmaster, Theodore Otto, at which point Henry became assistant conductor, librarian, dormitory officer, arranger, copyist, and a kind of apprentice flutist, with the rank of corporal.[19] He rehearsed the band, selected the music, and became skilled at forecasting which popular tunes would be the rage, so that their band could be the first to play the hits. Henry was happy to let Maestro Otto do the conducting, feeling talentless and burdened by an uncertain beat, an amusing liability considering his espousal of complex rhythms.[20] Otto fondly remembered their "walks and talks."[21]

The situation was, however, odd to say the least. Although nominally an ambulance unit, eighty-one musicians were detailed as a band, using their own instruments until October 1918, when the camp commander purchased new ones from the entertainment fund.[22] It may or may not have been a good band, but it toured the area and developed a certain renown. One local newspaper probably exaggerated in saying that it comprised the leading musicians of the country, some of whom had played with the best American symphony orchestras, but there may have been some top people in it.[23] It may be the same group as the well-known Allentown Marine band.

Terrified that war eventually would engulf Henry, Ellen Veblen hatched a brilliant scheme to get him discharged: he and Evelyn should marry. Evelyn was amused but embarrassed, as was Henry, then home on leave. She could not forget their conversation. "'I understand,' he said, in that oblique humorous approach that was funnier than anything he could put into words, 'that Ellen R [Veblen] has done me the honor of offering you my hand.' We both went into hysterical laughter over this. Nothing of that nature [was] between us, we were pals and quarreled often, at least I did, he was beyond argument, and treated any of my tantrums with a loftiness that made me more furious than ever, invariably."[24]

The whole experience in Camp Crane seems to have been reasonably tolerable. Henry's privileged position gave him little taste of ordinary military life, but Olive Cowell (Henry's later second stepmother) said that he had "very little social life outside, although one woman invited him to her beautiful home. Army life was boring and the time was sterile as to ideas and compositions."[25] Doubtless Henry told her so, but he later grasped the value of his new experience with band instruments.

In the fall of 1918, when word came that they would soon be transferred to an Italian contingent and sent abroad, band rehearsals gave way to gas mask drills.[26] Then the fighting suddenly ended. Not Henry's war, however. At the end of 1918, still stuck at Camp Crane, he fell victim to a flu epidemic that was laying the camp low and then to chicken pox. From his sickbed on New Year's Day he answered a recent letter from Russell Varian. "My head, having been filled full of much rubish [*sic*], has been constantly vomiting, and is now ready to hold ideas once again. I am beginning, through the inspired medium of having chicken pox, and being in bed, to seriously consider the mechanistic development of musical technology and other charming points . . . I have been longing for a little reciprocating of ideas, and your letter fell like a delicious hot tamale on a goulash-oppressed tongue. I would much relish another."[27]

Later in January the band members should have been discharged, but the company commander, stuck with the new instruments for which money was owed, persuaded the commander of Fort Ontario, on Lake Ontario, north of Oswego, to acquire his own band by assuming the debt on the instruments. The entire Camp Crane band was then transferred north and illegally kept past its term of service.[28] With mounting frustration Henry asked Harry to write to the commanding officer of Camp Ontario requesting a discharge "on the grounds of my being an unusual musician, deserving to return to studies. The more stress that can be laid on my talent, the better, and the sooner it is sent the better."[29] He urged Ellen Veblen to appeal to the general in command of the Eastern Division, who had the authority to discharge him.[30] His friends did what they could, but he still was in the army. At least life was comfortable in this camp, which was right on the lake, and "pleasanter than flat Pennsylvania."[31] He used the time to write a trio for violin, cello, and piano. "It is sheer rot," he said.[32]

In February 1919, Seeger complained to the secretary of war that the commanding officer of Camp Crane had not even answered his inquiries about Corporal Cowell. With some license he said that the amount in the fund to support Henry's education was the equivalent of one of the better class of scholarships in American universities "and would allow him to continue his study in New York with Mr. Ruggles and myself (we give him our instruction etc., gratis) for an indefinite time to come. I am about to have published Twelve Piano Pieces of his and with a little time spent in revision his two String Quartets and a Symphony will be ready for performance." Seeger suggested that Corporal Cowell was more valuable for the country as a composer than as a soldier, now that the crisis had passed.[33] Nothing is known of the publication plan, which may have been a sham. Meanwhile, the commanding officer of Fort Ontario wrote Ellen that it was difficult to discharge members of the medical corps, like Corporal Cowell, because of the need to handle the thousands of wounded soldiers daily returning from overseas. (Apparently they needed a band for that.) Ellen commented to Henry that she hoped things were not as bad as they would seem from the commander's reply. Henry said nothing about the wounded in his letters.[34]

The matter plodded on. While Henry was neither tending to wounded soldiers nor nursing his band skills, he took a long furlough to visit New York. After his medical ambulance service terminated in February, he was assigned to General Headquarters. Then the end was finally in sight because Seeger actually had persuaded the secretary of the army to intervene. On April 3, Henry was on leave in Menlo Park;[35] on May 6 he was finally discharged at Fort Ontario, by direct order of the secretary of war.[36] He was entitled to wear two silver service chevrons, and received travel pay at reduced railroad rates to Oakland, California. Henry celebrated at the Grand Canyon in mid-May and arrived in San Francisco a free man. Seward also had to wait until April to be discharged. As he was not a band musician, however, he would not have been sent to Camp Ontario. The reunion with Henry had to wait until they both were in California.

Strangely, Ellen Veblen did not learn of his discharge until a month later. Either Henry decided to put some distance between them or she had gone off on one of her wanderings. John Varian remarked sometime in these years that "she is a big soul with queer Karma on."[37]

‖ 9 ‖

Marketing Henry

Henry now resumed composing with real vigor, completing just in June a four-movement Piano Sonata, an a cappella setting of Psalm 121, and songs to texts by Harry, John Varian, and Robert Burns. In July and August, he wrote short pieces for cello solo and for piano, a sonata movement, a song to words by Keats, and finally finished the *Quartet Euphometric*. Seward threw himself so completely into working with Henry on his theoretical treatise that his fiancée joked about feeling threatened by it. She had to put up with it for eleven more years.[1]

As he pondered how to earn a living, a career as an unorthodox composer-performer seemed plausible, given his music's perverse appeal to the press. Not that he had much choice: a third-grade diploma did not open doors to jobs, and he did not play traditional repertory. He had to sell himself as an unconventional American, to a public committed to the European masters. That process produced some of the more amusing episodes in music history, but Henry had to live it, as he learned from a critic's response to his first postwar performance, in June 1919. Henry had told the audience that "Amiable Conversation" was based upon the tones of Chinese speech and could be imagined as a chat in a Chinese laundry between two Cantonese, one with a high-pitched voice, the other with a low voice.[2] The *Call's* reinterpretation:[3] "In the 'Amiable Conversation' Cowell appears to have had in mind a futuristic musical cocktail. Beginning on a basis of Chinese melody he works up a dash of Celtic harmony, mixes it with a 'shake well before using' variety of Yiddish intensity and tops it off with a sprig of Oriental politeness." "Dynamic Motion" evoked a Futurist manifesto: "'Dynamic Motion' is a musical impression of the New York subway. The clamor in the subterranean darkness, the wireless-like crossing of many minds huddled together, and rushing along insanely under the earth, a touch of horror and jagged suspense, and then the far light in the tunnel and the dizzying jerk at the end. The subject of 'Dynamic Motion' spreads like a disease through the music...." Henry, we are told, is a figure to reckon with: Ornstein is said to be playing several of his works, and (Walter) Damrosch will produce one of Henry's symphonies in New York. Wishful thinking with long shelf-life, it suggests that the anonymous writer was fed information by Henry, Harry, or Seward. He or she is unlikely to have been an "enemy," however. The most logical candidates are *Call* writers Evelyn Wells and Robert Duffus, both of whom understood how the symbiotic relationship between Henry's music and the press's appetite for sensationalism increased the value of marginally outrageous reviews to Henry's career.

Henry's shaky memory of dates colors his story of a lesson with Rachmaninoff around this time. When he talked about it in 1962, he erroneously placed their encounter in approximately 1914 or 1915, when Rachmaninoff could not come to the United States because of the war. Furthermore, the piece he showed him was not composed until 1917. In fact, the Rachmaninoffs stayed in Menlo Park in the summer of 1919, and their daughter took a class at Stanford with Samuel Seward, who arranged for Henry to show the master his music. The two therefore met when Henry was twenty-two, not a precocious eighteen-year-old.

> ... And so I went to his home and, being inexperienced, took with me several hundred compositions, and was of course asked to select one. I selected a small piece, a two page work for piano ["Fleeting"], and Rachmaninoff kindly took this piece and examined it through an eyeglass for just two hours without saying anything whatsoever. Then he got out a small red pencil, and he put a tiny red circle around 41 notes in these two pages, and he handed it to me with a smile and with great courtesy, and said, 'There are 41 wrong notes in your composition.'
>
> So then I said, 'What makes you think they are wrong?' and he said, 'They are not within the rules of harmony.' 'But,' I said, 'do you really think that people now, in composing, should follow the rules of harmony?' He said, 'Oh, yes. These are divine rules, the rules of harmony.' Then he was very kindly and said, 'I too, when I was a boy, sometimes wrote wrong notes.'

Henry wrote that the session was unrewarding and Rachmaninoff was uninterested in the piece. Nevertheless, they parted cordially. Although Rachmaninoff led a very isolated life, they met socially at Stanford once or twice, and later in New York, Chicago, and elsewhere. "He always remembered me. . . . He always singled me out for a warm conversation, because I had been the first musician that he met after he came to this country."[4]

Although the story shows signs of embroidery, Rachmaninoff's reaction must not be dismissed as hopelessly conservative. Showing him "Fleeting" rather than a cluster piece probably was a mistake. While Rachmaninoff would have thought using arms and elbows was absurd, "Fleeting" could have been even more puzzling. The general context is conventional—a melody-and-accompaniment piece in ABA form, played with ten fingers—but freely dissonant counterpoint is set against a tonal accompaniment, making most notes seem wrong. It would be interesting to see precisely which ones Rachmaninoff singled out, but Sidney filed the score "in some special place" and never could find it.[5]

After a summer devoted almost exclusively to composing, Henry headed east in October, taking the train that passes through the spectacular Royal Gorge, near Pike's Peak, Colorado. There, at an altitude of more than 10,000 feet, he suffered a nosebleed and what he called a "bad heart," which could have been an early warning of the cardiac problems that plagued his later years.[6] In Chicago he visited some of Ellen Veblen's old friends, almost certainly including Georgia Kober, a Chicago pianist sympathetic to modernism, whom he may have met at Carmel, where she often visited her sister. Kober became one of Henry's most devoted supporters and friends.

In New York, Elizabeth Moss, a sponsor and friend, had found him a pleasant front room on the first floor of 440 West 34th Street, for $8 [2010: $101] a week. When an irate neighbor complained about his practicing he found better lodgings at 411 W. 45th Street[7] and began searching out every opportunity to play. He quickly got his fill of the publishing world. The Teller company offered to publish "Dynamic Motion," its four "Encores," and some songs—if he would pay $260 [2010: $3,280] to underwrite the costs.[8] Schirmer rejected his music; Carl Fischer offered to accept it if he would pay about $250 in printing costs and assume responsibility for advertising. That deal seemed so promising that Henry enlisted Harry to place the scores at San Francisco's largest music store and sell them to "not too close" friends.[9] Fischer's offer withered, however. Meanwhile, he was wasting his time negotiating with an unreliable publisher for a book of Clarissa's poetry that Ellen desperately wanted to underwrite.[10] October thus ended with a bumper crop of frustration, and Henry snapped up Seeger's offer of a springtime ride to California, relishing the prospect of teaching in the music department Seeger (fruitlessly) hoped to start at Stanford.[11] Then he received an offer from the New York branch of Breitkopf and Härtel,[12] whose stature, European connections, and commitment to advertise him internationally as the year's "specialty" were powerful attractions. In return, Henry had to guarantee the sale of at least 200 copies in the first year and play the pieces in important concerts in America's large eastern cities. Breitkopf would advertise the performances but Henry had to rent the venues, unless he got a famous artist to play his pieces, in which case Breitkopf would waive guarantee.[13]

Breitkopf's proposal and Henry's blossoming friendships improved his mood. Dr. Bartlett enrolled him as a guest member of the Harvard Club, "which is so swell that I am completely staggered whenever I enter it."[14] Ruggles agreed to advise Henry about his "symphony,"[15] read it with his orchestra at the Rand School, and perform it if it were not too difficult. His request that Henry orchestrate a piano piece and perform it with the orchestra may account for the new version of "What's This?"[16] Seeger had no particular plans to suggest, other than getting "a little notoriety in New York."[17] Nothing could have been easier, as can be seen in some late autumn concerts sponsored by the New York *Globe*, where Henry now had two friends, Maxwell Anderson and Robert Duffus. A preliminary announcement for a late November concert for the Stowaways, a club of typographers and designers from the major New York newspapers and magazines, shows where he was heading. He was labeled "a revolutionist in music. We call him a Cubist because we can find no other word to describe him. Leo Ornstein . . . says of him, 'He is too strong for me,' or words to that effect. . . . He will be at the luncheon next Saturday (November 22nd). Come and look him over!"[18]

He immediately performed in two more *Globe* events at the auditorium of Wanamaker's department store on Broadway at 8th Street, where a conservative concert series featured artists such as mezzo-soprano Ernestine Schumann-Heink. At the first one, on November 29, he played some thirty of his pieces, and Charles Isaacson, the *Globe's* music editor, spoke about "Modernistic Music and Henry Cowell." The *Globe* (the sponsor) waxed appropriately enthusiastic in words probably written by one of Henry's friends: "A great composer is Henry Dixon Cowell, a discovery of the first rank. His recital developed into an ovation . . ." His second *Globe* performance, two weeks later, was part of Isaacson's lecture on "Beethoven and the People," a topic of uncertain relevance to Henry.[19]

It is almost impossible to assess his state of mind in these crucial years, because he rarely revealed it, and hardly anyone else bears witness to his development in that busy winter of 1919–20. If he was shaken by news that Sigurd Varian had contracted tuberculosis, his surviving letters do not mention it.[20] An amusing parody of Harry's poetry that he concocted for Ellen Veblen shows that he still had a sense of humor.

Although Breitkopf's insistence that he find performers for his music must have seemed impossible to fulfill, California connections linked him to Grainger, Ornstein, and now the current rage, Mischa Levitzki, the twenty-one-year-old Russian emigré whose music Ornstein had literally trashed. As a result, by early January Henry was again excited. He found a new advocate in Ethel Leginska, a twenty-four-year old pianist who only five years later became the first woman to conduct a major American orchestra. Leginska, he told Ellen, had switched her allegiances, pronouncing "Antinomy" "better than anything [Ornstein] ever wrote," proposed introducing him to Ernest Bloch, and asked him to "criticize her things for her." He was sure she would play some of his music.[21] Moreover, Breitkopf encouraged him to write two short orchestral pieces, claiming that they could get performances by the New York Philharmonic, the Philadelphia Orchestra, and the Detroit and San Francisco symphonies. They also promised to work for performances of his music by the stars of the day—Grainger, Leginska, Ornstein, Rudolf Ganz, Ossip Gabrilowitsch, Josef Hofmann, Levitski,

Heifetz and Max Rosen—but only Grainger is known to have played it, and not until decades later. The head of Breitkopf's American branch guaranteed to pay *all* publishing and nearly all advertising expenses, if Henry paid advance royalties and a small portion of advertising. Those "royalties" actually were honoraria to entice the performers to play the music, and could total some $3,000 [2010: $32,600]. Seeing no alternative to making the investment,[22] Henry asked Ellen to have Seward broach the subject to Edna Smith, Cary de Angulo's wealthy college friend; he said he could not propose it himself.[23] Thanks to Seward, Edna's sponsorship made Henry the first American avant-gardist published by a major European company.

Henry's exit from the Institute of Musical Art has been called the end of his formal musical training. In fact, he enrolled in the Institute of Applied Music in New York[24] to study fugue with R. Huntington Woodman, an organist and former pupil of César Franck who was only two years older than Henry.[25] It is even possible that this school, and not the Institute of Musical Art, is the establishment referred to in the brochure that infuriated Frank Damrosch. Henry said he learned from Woodman counterpoint that Franck had highly organized but never written down, and therefore considered Franck part of his family tree.[26] A double fugue for Woodman consumed his life. "An awful job," he told Ellen, "but I have the solace that my fugue teacher says I have mastered the subject."[27] Woodman even gave him a letter certifying his "all-around musical ability in the line of composition, with counterpoint and fugal styles in particular," authorizing him to refer to this in any brochures, and adding, "I have found your work very interesting intelligent and in many ways original."[28] Henry now had the license for fugue-writing that Satie joked about. He also seems to have hoped for another session with Rachmaninoff. Seeger's description of him as an unteachable autodidact no longer was applicable.[29]

Irritations and disappointments persisted. All in all, Henry radiated the vague discomfort that arises from seeing how good plans sometimes do not produce solid results. Clarence, distressed by Henry's frustration, urged him to give up music and become his business partner in Des Moines.[30] A warm letter from Russell Varian describing a trip to Yosemite may be what prompted Henry to tell Harry that he was coming back to California if nothing happened in New York.[31] Then almost on cue, something happened. On May 2, after a brief service at the Church of St. Mark's in-the-Bouwerie, on East 10th Street, Henry, introduced by Robert Duffus, spoke informally about "Musical Imagination To-day and Tomorrow," playing some illustrations.[32] Reverend William Guthrie, mightily impressed, offered to arrange performances at the MacDowell Club and the National Arts Club, and, most important of all, proposed that Henry move to a little room in the chapel rent-free in exchange for talks and performances at the church.[33]

Now certain that he would return to New York in the autumn, Henry left for California, entrusting Clarissa's poetry to Maxwell Anderson, whose warm farewell note is his last known letter to Henry. Henry's presence in Menlo Park for the spring of 1920 drew Ellen back from Halcyon, suspending their letters just as Henry must have had a lot to say about his sputtering career.[34] News is therefore almost nonexistent. His uncertainties may explain why he wrote almost no music, however. An August engagement at Santa Barbara in an unappetizing concert entitled "A Night in Spain"—a mishmash of salon songs, an aria from *Tosca*, and dance, punctuated by Henry's music[35]—implies that he either was desperate for work or owed someone a favor. The fall of 1920 found Henry extremely busy, making his debut as a journalist by reviewing a recital for the *Palo Alto Times*,[36] drafting an elementary piano method for the children of Halcyon,[37] and working on two pieces for Georgia Kober, "Prelude Diplomatique" and "Fabric." In "Fabric" he used specially shaped noteheads to represent unconventional subdivisions of the whole note, such as fifth-notes, seventh-notes, and ninth-notes. As Breitkopf's publication of his piano pieces neared the proof stage, Henry became uncomfortable about the agreement. Sidney thought that he was offended by the idea of a subsidized publication, but since he had initiated the appeal to Edna Smith, it is more likely that he worried about the requirement to secure performances by major artists.[38] Amid all those projects, he found time for hiking, prompting Russell Varian to remark, "I am afraid Henry is the only person around here who still has a desire to walk. The people of the future won't have any legs. Everyone wants to ride every where they go."[39]

Henry now had to prepare a full concert for November 6 in Palo Alto's Community House, whose directors envisioned it as a tribute to the publication of his music and a benefit for the piano fund, hopefully not because they feared having to pay for repairs after Henry was finished with it.[40] Among the collaborating artists was May Mukle, a world-famous English cellist—the "woman Casals," as Russell Varian put it, remarking that her participation was a real triumph for Henry.[41] An undated review in the Cowell papers, apparently referring to this event, says there was an overflow crowd.[42] No doubt; publicity had been going on for five months during which reality was swamped by compound errors and exaggerations. For example, of the four musicians named by the *San Francisco Chronicle* as Henry's New York teachers—Ornstein, Rachmaninoff, Leginska, and Woodman—only Woodman fits the description. The statement that Ornstein was playing his music and Henry was "rapidly winning recognition from other artists" also must be understood loosely.[43] As such stories were recycled, however, they gradually turned into truth. At least the concert showed a sign of tangible progress: he played some of his "elbow music" without being met by laughter.[44] Breitkopf was excited by a report that Mukle planned to play Henry's Sonata on her own programs, another evidence-free assertion.[45]

The four reviewers finally treated Henry as a mature musician. Redfern Mason, in the *Examiner*,[46] acknowledged that his education was paying off, though he was concerned about the brevity of the compositions, as if Henry were "incapable of sustained concentration of thought." Like Mason, Ray Brown, in the *Chronicle*,[47] did not consider the possibility that the classical forms had outlived their usefulness. On the other hand, Edith Daley, in the *San Jose Evening News*,[48] had no such reservations. Under the headline "Palo Alto Musical Genius Plays at Community House," she rhapsodized about the second movement of the Cello Sonata: "One sits in silence giving the use of one's very soul to the man's hands touching the responding keys and the woman-hands magically drawing a vibrant bow across the emotions. . . . 'The Tides of Manaunaun' . . . touches depths of forgotten things and sweeps one on great waves of feeling—straight up to nearness with the Infinite. Henry Cowell is worth while. He has conquered his own soul, caught it and held it to pour it out in tonal beauty that makes life sweeter for all of us."

Evelyn Wells provided the antidote in the *San Francisco Call and Post*.

> Those who have heard Cowell appreciate the wide range covered by his playing. So wide is this range, indeed, that many who had heard the music of the young Californian before wisely chose their seats in the rear of the hall, in order to get as far out of range as possible. Cowell's compositions are like the better order of paintings, one must stand far back, at respectful distances, before order results from chaos, and the colorful motes of sound resolve into one theme. . . .
>
> Cowell closed the program with a selection called "Antinomy." Hitherto the program had been almost undemonstrative. But Cowell cast all musical ethics to the winds, and played with an abandon and interpretive ability that caused many to watch the piano nervously, for "Antinomy," if played correctly, is harder on a piano than several spring movings.
>
> Cowell was merciless, and in splendid physical condition, apparently, for the ordeal. In fact, one pained musical critic remarked that this was no place for him; the sporting editor should have been sent instead.
>
> To be fully appreciated, Cowell should be heard and not seen. Apparently the composer himself realized this, for in response to the encore he rendered the delightful little "Dance of the Brownies," a product of his earlier youth. This faylike touch toned down the after effects of "Antinomy," and restored to the audience the mood brought by the more comprehensible and beautiful compositions of the evening.[49]

She may or may not have been avenging herself for Henry's pranks and obstinacy, but Ruggles rejoiced that her assault had done him a big favor.[50] Her perceptive remark about being heard and not seen underlined Henry's fundamental dilemma: the visual spectacle drew publicity but undermined some very appealing music. A sixteen-column-inch feature in the *Globe and Advertiser* on October 31 made that California concert big news even in New York. Reminding the reader that modernists like Stravinsky, Ornstein, and Scriabin gradually won public acceptance, the writer named Henry the "coming musician of America"—modernistic but classical. "I predict for Cowell a most brilliant career. He is a modest, quaint character. You only need to see him to know that he is genuine, different, musical, and poetical."

Now either life turned tranquil or the lack of correspondence creates a pleasant illusion. Around the turn of 1921, he wrote a few piano and vocal pieces, worked on an article he was writing with Duffus,[51] and gave two concerts. In February, after visiting the De Angulos in Carmel,[52] he spent a few weeks finishing some piano pieces, songs, a short violin and piano piece, and a movement for string quartet. Having completed his treatise but lacking a publisher, he wrote up the first statement of his theoretical ideas as "Harmonic Development in Music," a three-part series in the *Freeman*, a New York arts journal.[53] Presumably the ideas were Henry's and Duffus, his co-author, smoothed the prose for their target, the intelligent listener and thinker, rather than the convinced modernist.

In Part I, on progress in the arts, Henry staked out a position completely at odds with the criticism of his music as destructively modernist. Instead of aligning himself with radical revolutionaries who wanted the new to destroy the old, he distinguished between radical progress and anarchy, and emphasized study of the classics. Like Schoenberg, Henry argued that a successful modern composition must begin with a well-conceived structure, which was to say that the concept of beauty as "pleasing" had to be replaced by the ancient definition of beauty as perfection, a perfection resting on the physical reality of the overtone series. Like Schoenberg, he saw the history of harmonic development as a series of steps toward more remote regions of the overtone series. Unlike Schoenberg, however, he did not consider the major and minor seconds the next logical destination, because they do not exist in the overtone series. While he was far from alone in noticing the discrepancy, he seems to be the first to observe that small intervals from the overtone series are freely employed in some non-Western cultures, and to call for careful study of other cultures by Western musicians. He predicted that microtones would be used when the limits of our intonation system were reached, if one developed a "keener perception of the overtones." (Henry and Duffus could not have known about microtonal experiments by Ives or Haydn Wilson, an obscure nineteenth-century Englishman, but they might have read Busoni's proposal for a sixth-tone scale.) Henry's approach to microtones is also distinctive, however, because he linked them to non-Western music. Small intervals, used commonly in Arab music, might first be perceived only as passing tones, but eventually would generate their own harmonies. The limit of usable overtones, he wrote, "is fixed only by the delicacy of our hearing and the flexibility of our tastes." He concluded that the time for microtones was still remote because components of music other than harmony still needed exploration. One of those components was time. Henry proposed that rhythm, meter, and tempo were all capable of variations "beyond the accepted practice."

In contrast, Henry's other two proposed paths of development—tone clusters and polyharmony—seem comparatively ordinary because they draw upon the familiar tones of the chromatic scale. They were, however, even more unusual than microtonality, because they undermined the primacy of the single pitch as a musical unit. This is obvious in the case of tone clusters, but polychords, defined as the "simultaneous employment of different chords instead of single tones as harmonic units," also led away from the dominance of the single tone. Henry's clusters already suggest that nearly any sound—even pure noise—could be legitimate material for music. While that notion has become almost mainstream thanks to Henry's later students Lou Harrison and John Cage, in 1921 it must have seemed completely bizarre to anyone other than Edgard Varèse.

"Harmonic Development in Music" opened fascinating prospects for a new view of modernity. Music, Henry and Duffus concluded, still had "its undiscovered continents. As an art and as a science the work of exploration has just begun; and this, for a jaded world, is perhaps a sufficient moral." Irrespective of whether all of its ideas are original, and which man was responsible for its final formulation, these articles coherently presented ideas that could both explain the present and herald future sound-worlds. Less analytic than prescriptive, they opened new paths rather than dwelling upon the old. Yet although the essays are intriguing, they may not have circulated beyond the journal's immediate readership. The Cowell papers contain only the lukewarm reaction of the *San Francisco Chronicle*'s Ray Brown.[54] Wider dissemination remained a challenge.

In March 1921, just about the time when "Harmonic Development in Music" appeared, a rumor spread that Henry suffered a hemorrhage and might have contracted tuberculosis.[55] He was fine, but discouraged, sick of running around trying to peddle his music[56] and playing at trivial concerts. He found respite in a few quiet weeks at Halcyon,[57] where he gave piano lessons using his elementary piano instruction method, raising the community's hopes for a well-organized music program respecting the highest traditions and correlating "the fundamentals of the science and art of music with the fundamentals of occult philosophy and the Wisdom Religion."[58] Then he spent a week at Carmel and hiked for a hundred miles at Yosemite, finally arriving at Menlo Park in late September, ready for a "long deferred" dinner with Harry.[59] All his efforts had generated very little income,[60] leaving him dependent upon his sponsors. As of October 31, Seward had disbursed $500 [2010: $6,500] of the donations, leaving a balance of $106. Henry took his situation very seriously, submitting detailed itemizations of his expenses, and, at Seward's urging, strengthened his bonds with his biggest donors, Edna Smith and the Browns,[61] whose generosity is nothing short of amazing. Armitt Brown secured the publication agreement with Breitkopf with a guarantee of $1,000 [2010: $12,200].[62]

In the fall Henry moved into his tiny room at St. Mark's in-the-Bouwerie, lecturing and performing in exchange. The slightly outrageous Reverend Guthrie encouraged him to play cluster pieces "largely to shock the church-goers."[63] His ecumenical institution was a perfect setting for Henry's unusual talks, which highlighted music from outside the Western concert tradition. On November 20, after the service, he played "a few lively descriptive compositions influenced by Oriental music" and assisted with the communal singing. Two weeks later the topic was "Peasant Folk Songs Sung for the First Time in America: . . . Folk Music Harmonized and New Music Composed by Henry Cowell." In retrospect, these were only mild hints of what was to come.

Even if such minor tasks provided free rent, they dispersed his energy, so that the only compositions he completed in the latter part of 1921 were very small occasional pieces, including a canonic Christmas greeting for Dane Rudhyar (a friend from Halcyon), a waltz for another friend, and a song for Harry. A few other pieces possibly stemming from this time include a little nonet for Ruggles's birthday (which was the same day as Henry's) and some incomplete vocal and instrumental music. He warded off homesickness by corresponding with Halcyon friends and some poor and barely literate children at Menlo Park. In early December 1921, he returned to California. During a short stay at Halcyon, he heard about "interesting experiments of an electronic nature . . . relative to the influence of tone on disease,"[64] which he reported in *The Temple Artisan*. His enthusiasm for the idea that a sustained tone or a sustained fifth interact with the bloodstream to aid diagnoses of diseases, or the idea that tuberculosis responds to E flat and B flat, syphilis to E and B, and strep to C and G, seems over the top, but twenty-first-century research continues to probe the use of sound in certain therapies.

Shortly after the New Year, Ignaz Paderewski came to nearby Santa Barbara in his private railcar. Having given his personal assistant a three-day holiday, he hired Henry, who had met Paderewski's niece. His principal job was to prevent anyone from disturbing the Paderewskis' relaxation.

I knew at this time that Paderewski's regular fee was $5000 [2010: $65,000] and so when somebody knocked on the train door, and I went out to open it, there was Mr. Cornelius Bliss, a man whose standing hardly needs to be questioned. [Bliss was a rich merchant and former secretary of the interior.] He said that he wanted very much to invite Mr. Paderewski to play at his regular fee for a few invited guests. So I thought that perhaps

I really should let Paderewski know this. I knew he was pipe-free [*sic*] and I thought maybe he would like to pick up $5000. Paderewski was annoyed, for the one and only time. He said, "I thought I asked you not to bother me about anything like this." So then I knew better, after this time, and I had to tell Mr. Bliss that this couldn't be arranged . . . [Paderewski] was a kindly man, and a man who always acted as through he were talking to a prince. It was nothing except high society for him, no matter if you were not. Even though his secretary was not, he still talked as though I were. He gave me rather small amounts of things to do. I copied a few notes for him. He liked to play for me and see if I could find any flaw in the playing, as a composer. He was disappointed because I couldn't. If I had found one, I would have been more valuable to him.[65]

Little else is known of Henry's movements in the first months of 1922, but the time was not without its notable moments. At a concert in the Palo Alto Women's Club on his twenty-fifth birthday, he tried to compensate for the brevity of the thirteen pieces by grouping them into roughly-fashioned categories, essentially cycles of character pieces of which one, *Three Irish Myths* (later called *Three Irish Legends*), became a staple of his tours. The concert's big novelty was "Sword of Oblivion," which is played directly upon the piano strings. Although Henry said "Aeolian Harp" was the first "stringpiano" piece, he dated it 1923, and as of 1922 it had not shown up on programs. Whichever had precedence, he certainly was reformulating the limits of the piano.

On March 31 he was back in New York, appearing as a guest in Ruggles's lecture on modern music at the Whitney Studio Club.[66] Louise Vermont, writing in the *Greenwich Villager*, contributed her bit to Henry's press kit while probably enhancing attendance at a forthcoming program when she was to sing Henry's song "April."[67]

Then [Ruggles] introduced an American composer, who, according to Mr. Ruggles, "had something original to say with guts in it," Mr. Henry Cowell. Cowell said it with a wallop. One piano sounded like six of them. People stood up and watched this little fellow while the rolling sound wrapped them round and overwhelmed them with its dynamic force. For a closing number Cowell played one of his amazing compositions which he calls Dynamic Motion. At the finish of it three women lay in a dead faint in the aisle and no less then ten men had refreshed themselves from the left hip.[68]

Three weeks later, a letter of condolence from Seward hints that the sudden death of Edna Smith cost Henry far more than a benefactor.[69] Up to now the only signs of her in the Cowell documents are their meeting at the de Angulos' ranch at least six years earlier, her contribution to the fund for Henry's welfare, their dinner in New York in 1916, and her subsidy of the publication of his piano pieces. If they corresponded, the letters have perished. A note from John Varian saying "Why not bring her along & let us see what she is like?" could refer to Edna, but its date is unknown.[70] Chats years later with Judith Dawson Brown and Samuel Seward's widow Amy, however, plus some evidence from the 1930s, showed Sidney that their relationship was not simply funder-grantee. Apparently referring to approximately 1920, she wrote,

> Once back in California, he took a fresh look at an exquisite girl named Edna Smith whom he had met through the de Angulos before he left for the Army. Judith Dawson Brown, at whose dinner table in Palo Alto the two renewed acquaintance, was still amused, when she told me about it 45 years later, at the rapidity with which they lost all sense of other people and fell blindingly in love from one minute to the next. "They seemed to feel that they shared some weighty secret" Judy told me affectionately. . . . Mrs. Seward mentioned to me how alike the two were in their look of youthful eagerness and in their physical frailty, and she too spoke of their sharing "some wordless joy." Both friends had been struck by a sense the two seemed to have of a deep and private bond for which there were no words, unlike the many couples whose engagement gives them a sense of happy discovery and open triumph that they want to share. Edna and Henry achieved what he called "an understanding" and were presently talking of a future engagement, the next step toward their marriage.[71]

Sidney believed that Edna was a Philadelphian two or three years Henry's senior, who had received a large inheritance when orphaned at eighteen. Actually, she was about twelve years older than he,[72] one of three daughters of a prosperous Aurora, Illinois, industrial family. The girls were wealthy in their own right and, according to the *New York Times*, the wealthiest women in Aurora. Initially educated by private tutors and in an elite school in New Jersey, at Vassar Edna got to know Cary Fink, later Cary de Angulo, who was a year ahead. Brimming with curiosity, she took classes in English, French, German, Latin, mathematics, chemistry, history, Bible, economics, philosophy, biology, physiology, and art, and received the bachelor of arts degree in 1907. Her whereabouts in the subsequent seven years included Ann Arbor, Michigan, and California. Like her two sisters, Edna used her money for social causes, establishing a home for dependent children in Aurora around 1914, a school in New York for the education of poor children, and eventually a similar school in Carmel. She also underwrote Jaime

de Angulo's studies of Indian languages.[73] Henry could not have seen her during
military service, because she and her sister Genevieve went abroad in the YMCA
canteen service.[74] In 1920 she began a Ph.D. program in botany at Columbia
University.[75]

In the middle of the spring term of 1922, she and one of her sisters decided to
spend Easter vacation at a resort hotel in New Jersey. On April 15, they picked
violets along the railway about 150 feet from an unprotected crossing, chatted
with some local people, got in the car and headed across the tracks. A locomotive hit the car on the driver's side, threw it seventy-five feet, and tossed their
bodies twice that distance. Edna, who appears to have been trying to escape, was
badly mangled. Because it was the third fatal rail crossing accident in eleven days,
it became front-page news.[76] Otherwise Edna would remain almost unknown.

Sidney's mistake about Edna's age is not trivial. As his father had done, Henry
was to marry a woman many years his senior. Like Harry and Clarissa, their mutual attraction seemed grounded in their intellectual interests. She was musical,
intelligent, wealthy, generous, and apparently beautiful—in short, very eligible.
He, by all accounts, was kind, funny, and obviously very gifted. Both were passionate about botany. They might have made a fine couple, even though their
backgrounds and education were so different. "Henry was grieved to the heart
and resentful at a cruelty of fate that was far from what he had been brought up
to expect of life," said Sidney. Years later he told her in a rare moment of revelation that Edna's death was "the only pain that could compare with his mother's
loss six years before." Even after so long, "it was still hard for him to speak of that
memory of lost perfection."[77]

That sad story would rest, were it not for Sidney's talent for making the simple
complex by producing contrary versions of a story, or adding contradictory evidence as she sought completeness. She says that Henry told her that their relationship had a sweet innocence: he was allowed to kiss her on the day she said
she would marry him, but then had to wait until they married.[78] Yet elsewhere
she says Henry never really acknowledged that they were engaged, only that they
had "an understanding." When she questioned him on this, "Henry was a bit
offended and would not return to the subject. He did once say to me that they
would have married sometime, but that the discovery that she was wealthy and
had contributed to the fund for his education had 'put him off,' for a while, as he
expressed it. (He was amused to discover that my family was, or rather had been,
wealthy . . . because he had made the same mistake with Edna.)"

Apparently Amy Seward gave Sidney the idea that Edna's wealth was an issue,
that both Sewards knew Henry would never accept being financially dependent
upon his wife, and that he fretted about how to support her. Says Sidney, "He and
Edna seemed to be living in a happy dream with nothing resembling reality to
shadow it."[79] Her comments about the publication subsidy probably originated

with Henry, but lack of corroboration confuses what seems like a clean narrative. Sidney states that Edna and Sam Seward conspired to have Edna underwrite the publication of fifteen pieces, and that when Henry discovered their ruse, he was "deeply shaken and offended," having thought his music had been accepted only on its merit.[80] Actually, we know that Henry asked Seward to solicit her sponsorship. Sidney also claimed to have learned from Seward himself that Henry tried to stop the publication. If Edna and Seward had cooked up the idea even before Henry thought of enlisting her, however, presumably Breitkopf would not have told Henry to find a sponsor.

Sidney also thought that Henry's dismay and indignation sent Edna sadly off to South America with a famous naturalist, but Henry suggested that Edna sponsor the publication after she had already departed for Brazil. According to Sidney, by the time she returned from Brazil, Seward "seems to have persuaded Henry to be a little less stiff-necked" and they reconciled. There is no trace of such tension in Henry's letter to Ellen asking her to contact Edna—only a need to rush to get the agreement with Breitkopf sealed. To add to the confusion, Sidney surmised that since Henry was accustomed to friends helping him, his feelings for her must have caused his embarrassment. She was wrong, however; Henry apparently never told Sidney that her sponsorship was his idea, which he may have forgotten or suppressed. Amy Seward's and Judy Brown's descriptions seem to eliminate the possibility that Henry was exploiting Edna. Nevertheless, Henry's feelings about her remain a mystery.

Sidney believed, however, that the whole business had a lasting effect on American music. Because Henry felt guilty that Edna's money had given him an advantage over other composers, he wanted to give his colleagues something in return. She attributed his attitude to the "philosophical anarchist principle of mutual aid and non-competition that he took seriously as long as he lived," and decided that it explained at least in part his "untiring helpfulness toward other composers."[81] Her view is logical but cannot be corroborated.

Seward's concerns after Edna's death, however, transcended Henry's personal feelings. If her estate did not pick up the obligation to pay Breitkopf and Härtel, the publication would be jeopardized.[82] Unfortunately, the trail goes cold here. In 1962, Anna Strunsky Walling, who seemed to know many details, wrote that Henry used a settlement from Edna's estate to pay for his debut tour, but no documentation could be found, nor did Henry refer to it. Anything he wrote Seward about it disappeared when Seward discarded his correspondence.[83]

In any event, Henry had no time to brood; a string of performances on both coasts awaited him. These concerts offer an opportunity to assess his image, now that he was no longer a prodigy, a matter that extends beyond the immediate issue of his biography. Reviews, irrespective of whether they mirror the reactions of audiences, can attract or repel new listeners. The sheer quantity of reviews of

Henry's concerts therefore had to affect readers' general perceptions of new music.

Only a few days after Edna's death, he played again at St. Mark's. Considering its location on the edge of the Lower East Side, the presence of any "significant" person was unusual. This concert, however, put Henry by chance into contact with one of the most important people in his developing circle. A woman whom Henry had met with his mother "while we were all running from a cow in an open field in Oakland when I was six or seven"[84] brought Blanche Walton, an accomplished pianist in an era when well-bred women did not pursue public careers. By the time Henry met her, she was one of the leading patrons of new music in New York. Walton immediately became Henry's close friend and supporter.

It is perhaps a measure of Henry's growing renown that Louis Bromfield of *Musical America* and Pitts Sanborn of the *Globe* covered the concert, making it a kind of New York pre-debut despite the church's apparent insignificance. (Henry's official New York debut took place two years later.) They even said all the right things.[85] Shortly thereafter he played at Wanamaker's in an afternoon event sponsored by the *Evening Mail*. A kind of variety show, it included the New York Ladies Quartet, other musicians, and a talk entitled "Music and Statesmanship" by Fiorello La Guardia, the president of the New York City Board of Aldermen, a candidate for the House of Representatives, and, much later, the popular mayor of New York, who would have drawn a crowd.[86]

At the end of June Henry stopped in Denver to play a public concert at the home of a rancher and stockbroker. The *Denver Express* sounded an old refrain about exaggeration, eccentricity, and further study, dismissing Henry's technique as "the sort of thing affected by Leo Ornstein before he discovered that Americans had outlived the necessity for an appeal a la P. T. Barnum."[87] Luckily, in those days of multiple local newspapers, even a small city could generate a torrent of contradictory punditry. The *Rocky Mountain News*[88] printed an especially powerful endorsement of his music.

In reporting that Henry was leaving for New York, the *Denver Post* had him pointed in the wrong direction. Back in the East, however, a performance of his music at a house concert in Greenwich, Connecticut, was a double novelty: his music was invading the preserve of the exclusive, and Henry himself was not playing.[89] The event included a talk on Henry and modernity, and a performance of "The Tides of Manaunaun" by Margaret Nikoloric, who had met Henry at a cocktail party and became extremely important to him. A fund-raiser attended by all the fashionable of Greenwich, this seemingly obscure concert was reported in both a local newspaper and the *New York Times*, igniting a little controversy reaching to the City. The Greenwich critic called his piece "without question the most important work of recent years," the most important step forward since Debussy's *Pelléas et Mélisande*.[90] Although the *New York Times'* anonymous writer[91] wrote less portentously, he provoked an outraged reader to ask, in terms exquisitely 1920s, why such ugly and meaningless noises deluded the fashionable into believing this was the music of the future. "Parlor and boudoir Bolsheviki have for some time been imbibing political and economic theories equally extravagant and ridiculous, while propagandists who have been bamboozling them have held 'the tongue of contempt in the cheek of scorn.'" Although he too sounds a little ridiculous, he was a product of the anti-communist hysteria that only three years earlier had led to the destruction, by hundreds of soldiers and sailors, of a socialist newspaper's offices and a raid of the Rand School, where Ruggles had his orchestra.[92]

That a private performance could trigger such outrage is impressive enough. That news of his minor concert would appear in the *San Francisco Call*[93] suggests the hand of Evelyn Wells and may explain why Henry, the modernist composer, was treated as a hometown hero upon arrival. The *Palo Alto Times* described him as "exultant over new triumphs in musical circles of New York."[94] Of course, the immediate goal was to publicize Henry's next concert, which it reviewed on July 28 under a headline proclaiming his "Genius for Daring Originality."[95] The first Californian to take the East by storm, Henry was becoming a symbol of Bay Area culture and musical modernism even as (or perhaps, because) his music triggered anti-modernist rants elsewhere.

He stayed in California for four months in mid-1922, performing and hiking, but composing very little. On the way from Santa Barbara to San Francisco, he and the Los Angeles pianist Richard Buhlig spent a night at Halcyon, where both of them played.[96] An unidentified friend heard Henry say, "It's a funny thing about composers: if they write just like everybody else people are bored; and if they don't, nobody will listen!"[97]

The press, meanwhile, had discovered that Henry's music sold papers. A new publicity barrage touted an October concert at the Palace of Fine Arts that was promoted as Henry's San Francisco debut. Now, however, most comments were extremely positive. When the concert was postponed until November, Henry profited from a second round of publicity. So much talk about new "classical" music makes one wonder if the motivation was admiration of Henry, California chauvinism, or simple journalistic self-interest. By any measure, he was a good act and the rescheduled concert was a landmark in the growth of music in San Francisco, the grand opening of an elaborately renovated, 500-seat hall left over from the 1915 Panama Pacific International Exposition.[98] This appearance was by no means Henry's first in San Francisco, but probably his first major public performance. Since the concert celebrated the centenary of César Franck, it is not obvious how Henry fit in, nor is it obvious that Henry's participation had any bearing on the huge attendance of the press, which, eight years after his San Francisco debut, still had diametrically opposite views of him. A review in Chicago's nationally circulated *Musical Leader* shows that at least this critic listened to the music and to Henry's talk. Under an unpromising headline—"San Francisco Ensemble Presents Ultra-Modern Music. Local Composer Resorts to Weird Measures"—the writer praised the music and its scientific basis in overtones. Henry's good suggestion that the audience listen with its eyes closed was useless. "The effect was so startling, every eye 'peeked' with excusable curiosity to find out how this musical pioneer worked out his problem. He certainly has the courage of his convictions, and sails on the uncharted seas of the musical world."[99]

So far, so good. In November he opened a tour in the Los Angeles region, which still was a new market for him.[100] A joint concert at the Pasadena YWCA with Arthur Farwell[101] was a warm-up for Henry's performance at Hollywood High School on November 21, billed as Los Angeles' only opportunity to hear "a creative genius."[102] "Eclectic" hardly does justice to the affair, a benefit for the Community Chorus, including "two charming local dancers" from the Ballet Russe.[103] This must be the event to which Henry referred in a letter to Harry: "I played a concert for 16,000 people at Hollywood last night—unfortunately, they don't pay!" Surely he meant 1,600, unless the concert was out of doors, but in any event, according to one newspaper, it was the largest concert of the season.[104] Henry told *Holly Leaves* that he wanted a piano upon which he could get an "octave" (an octave cluster) by striking a single key so that he could realize the cluster polyphonies about which he theorized.

Henry's dramatic style of performing helped ensure that the critics heard what he intended. With the spread of his music to other performers, however, he had to worry about the survival of his "children" at their hands. Indeed, a performance by another pianist triggered Henry's first written expressions of concern about the problem. The occasion was Margaret Nikoloric's November 15 performance of "The Tides of Manuanaun" at the Town Hall, then one of New York's leading recital venues. The *New York Tribune* critic snidely wrote, "As for . . . the effect of laying the forearm on the keys for a thunderous roll . . . it may or may not be magnificent, but it is certainly not music." Then someone—probably Ruggles—told Henry that she played well but too slowly at the climax, and that the critic was second tier. As a consolation, he added that "Tides" was the only work encored.[105]

Henry returned to San Francisco for another recital on December 13. Although his "first San Francisco appearance" had already taken place twice, a brochure fudged the issue by correctly calling this concert his first *solo* recital in San Francisco.[106] Pre-concert puffs[107] warned that this would be Henry's last recital there before he sailed to Europe on January 11. In one version his publishers were sending him abroad; in another, a wealthy San Francisco patron was sponsoring the trip.[108] The pre-concert publicity included an exceptionally interesting article, a front-page interview by Evelyn Wells in the *San Francisco Call*,[109] nearly two full columns, with a large photograph, declaring "Composer Would Write Jazz. Classical Composer Envies Berlin. Respect Syncopation, Plea." This statement, Henry's first about jazz, shows his naïveté about it. He regretted his failure to write jazz and envied Irving Berlin; he saw a kinship between jazz and Chinese music in that both are principally instrumental; jazz was an improvement upon "soulless" ragtime and the stagnant sentimental song; jazz was "the first distinctive music America had to offer the world." Unfortunately, he wrested the origin of jazz away from black America.

> Nearly everyone will assure you wisely that it comes from the South, from negro syncopation. But after a glance into the negro melodies it seems to me jazz sprang direct from the heart of America, from the people themselves, from everywhere. Just as folk songs come from the people, Irving Berlin, not an ordinary musician in the common sense, but master of his jazz art, accepts melodies from everywhere—from the people.

Henry's talk of the vitality and Americanness of popular art is surprising because his own music was so utterly divorced from it. The spirit of jazz, most loosely defined, is manifested only in *Six Casual Developments* for clarinet and piano (1933). This interview, however, was far from Henry's last word on the subject.

His programming increasingly shows his desire to make his music more accessible. For the December 13 concert he grouped his music into units entitled "Earlier Style," "Later Style," "Little Pieces," and "Irish Legends," and provided program notes that inexplicably omit the much-regurgitated story of "Amiable Conversation." No matter. The headline writer returned with "Ugliness in Composer's Music Matter of Deliberate Choice, Writes Critic After Concert," not bothering to mention Redfearn Mason's generally positive attitude. "People may not like this music, but they cannot be indifferent to it, for the aesthetic urge is powerful, and, in spite of occasional dissonances of lacerating brutality, the sense of wonder and beauty which they diffuse remains in my mind. . . . Watch Cowell. He will do something distinguished yet, and the people who are sending him on a tour of Europe are benevolently wise."[110]

Mason (in the *Chronicle*) also had advice for Henry about the music world's growing preoccupation with Americanism. "Music must speak the lingo of good Americans or it will forever be a pallid imitation of the work of foreigners." Rather than write scores reflecting his Irish culture, why should Henry not "tell the story of those Irish pioneers and cattle rustlers who led audacious lives in Arizona and New Mexico? If he is a wise lad—and he undoubtedly has a touch of genius—he will steep himself in Bechdolt's stories [of the settling of the West] and give us something really American."[111]

As 1922 came to an end, Henry should have felt generally encouraged by his status and prospects for a successful trip to Europe. His name had been made a symbol—for better or worse—of fresh, young American music, thereby legitimizing his methods of playing. While nay-sayers abounded, in the West he was a cultural hero. Nationally, some journalists called him America's first true musical genius. He had a publisher, and other artists were beginning to play his music. His personal qualities projected powerfully in his commentaries; he spoke well with interviewers. In Des Moines, even the mere possibility that he would stop off to see Clarence on his way east was considered newsworthy.[112] None of this negated the truth that sustaining himself as a concert pianist would be a phenomenal battle. For almost any musician, the number of concerts required to generate a good living precludes serious composing. Halcyon's Guardian, Dr. Dower, had every reason to worry that Henry would burn himself out.

Henry's first foreign tour has been described as a "bold, typically bohemian adventure"[113] in which Henry would teach Europe his tricks. While a trace of this attitude may have conditioned his decision to go, Henry was doing no more than virtually every aspiring performer did and still does—attempting to build the reputation in Europe that would bring fee-paying work worldwide. Letters of recommendation to potentially useful strangers in London, to Fritz Kreisler, Schoenberg, and Busoni, were what a career-minded composer-performer needed in order to reap the maximum benefit from a tour.[114]

The letters to Schoenberg and Busoni must have come from Richard Buhlig (1880–1952), a Chicago-born pianist who had studied with Theodore Leschetitzky and was one of Busoni's favorite pupils. According to Sidney, Buhlig had been on the verge of a great career when he became terrified of solo performing and turned to teaching. He had been attempting to give Henry a systematic pianistic technique and believed so strongly in the importance of Henry's performing in Europe (again, according to Sidney) that he raised money for it among his friends.[115] Henry had just missed Buhlig at the Institute of Musical Art, where he taught from 1918 to 1920. Although John Cage later claimed that Buhlig did not take Henry seriously, Buhlig suggested that Henry delay his departure until April, when he would make one of his periodic trips to Berlin and could introduce him to the musical world. (According to the brochure that infuriated Frank Damrosch, Henry was to have left for Europe the previous October.) Thus, after arriving in Menlo Park, and obtaining his first passport, Henry suddenly changed his plans and returned to Los Angeles, almost certainly to play for Buhlig.[116] To assure an up-to-date program for Europe, he also needed to focus upon composing. The current project, "The Vision of Oma," looked as if it would be considerably longer than the earlier three Irish pieces that he played as a suite. A big concept, it has fifteen tempo changes in twelve pages of manuscript. He thought it also would be suitable for singing and could be used in a theatrical piece planned by Varian.

On his twenty-sixth birthday, March 11, 1923, "Exaltation" was performed in Pasadena by the English pianist Winifred Hooke, an accomplished violinist who became a pianist and studied with Buhlig in Berlin. An exponent of modernism and a rare teacher who encouraged her pupils to play new music, she introduced many new works to Los Angeles, including Franck's *Symphonic Variations*, Debussy's and Ornstein's cello sonatas, and Scriabin's *Poeme d'extase*, and became one of Henry's most important West Coast allies. That event was unusual because Henry talked about his ideas but another pianist performed his music.[117]

Henry returned to northern California for April concerts at Berkeley and Mills College, where he gave the first known performance of the polyrhythmic "Fabric."[118] Almost no personal news comes down to us from this period; his correspondence with Ellen Veblen again trickled to a halt. Meanwhile, Mme. Nikoloric's concert in Philadelphia showed how a single new piece on a traditional program could attract attention. Eighty-five percent of the review concerned "The Tides of Manaunaun," which brought virtually the entire audience to its feet. "So enthusiastic and insistent was the applause that, for an encore, she rendered the latter half of the number again."[119] To be sure, "The Tides" combines accessibility with novelty in a way that continues to surprise and dazzle audiences nearly a century later.

On the eve of their departure for Europe, Henry's first recording became available as a roll playable on electric or mechanical pianos. His suggestion that Varian get the roll for the Halcyon pottery collection[120] is a wry reflection on his enduring struggle. He would need a huge infusion of fortitude as he set off to bring American modernism to Europe.

PART TWO

INTERNATIONAL ULTRAMODERNIST VIRTUOSO

10

The Trio

In the winter of 1922–23, Olive Thompson, a thirty-five-year-old professor of international relations at San Francisco State College, went to her favorite French restaurant, where she happened to sit at the same table as Harry Cowell. Being a generation younger, she did not pay much attention to him until he began to talk about his son Henry. Noticing that Harry too was "of good stock," her imagination was piqued. He, meanwhile, was falling in love with her. They were an unlikely combination. Harry, with no formal education after his teen years, had gifts for poetry, sports, and gab. Olive, on the other hand, had excellent credentials. Born in 1887 near New Haven, Connecticut, to what she called "old New England stock,"[1] she went to New York with her mother after her parents' marriage disintegrated, and eventually had to fend for herself. A Pulitzer scholarship put her through Barnard College, which awarded her the B.A. in 1910. After teaching in a girls' school, she studied in Europe until the outbreak of war forced her to return. When Harry met her she had just received the M.A. degree from Berkeley and served for three years on the faculty of San Francisco State College (now San Francisco State University), where she eventually founded the Department of International Relations.

Harry soon discovered that Olive surpassed even Clarissa in the oddity of her relationships with men. She never saw her father after her parents split up and claimed she did not miss him. Educated in and employed by single-sex institutions through her early career, she had had little contact with men her age. Although she lived alone and, in her words, craved love, her preconceptions of the ideal husband had led her to reject all suitors. She had given up the thought of children, partly, she said, after seeing the suffering in the trenches in Europe. A noble sentiment, indeed, but her colorful writing style makes one wonder if she actually saw the trenches or imagined them. It is not an idle question, since her volubility on the subject of Henry and Harry makes her a crucial witness.

One Sunday afternoon, after Olive and Harry attended a concert, she asked him home to dinner. Her romantic account implies that they ended up in bed, and that he thoroughly enjoyed the experience. Olive explained that she had "freed [herself] sexually" (as opposed to Clarissa, who had freed herself from sex). They became lovers at once, "two very liberated human beings." Because (she wrote) such encounters were not unusual for her, she was surprised to discover that she found herself in love and, consequently, in a very awkward situation. If their affair became public knowledge, she would lose her job, and they could not marry because Harry was still married to Henrietta. The enforced secrecy and separation explains why Henry wrote to Harry and Olive individually for a few years.

Olive's first encounter with Henry impressed her indelibly. "Such a striking out-of-this-world expression, revealing his uniqueness, his exceptional creativity. Yet a gentle, kind face, though such individuality." Olive, Harry, and Henry soon became a threesome. Henry would come to San Francisco weekly to have dinner and talk about music; on camping expeditions, they caught up on his news.[2] Olive relentlessly struggled to bring Harry and Henry closer, succeeding partly because her boundless affection for Harry made him so likable. The tone of her letters sometimes suggests, however, very strong feelings for Henry. She was only ten years older, closer in age than Edna Smith had been. If she secretly longed for him, however, she never let it surface. Convinced of his genius, she dedicated her formidable energies to his success. Without her, Henry's phenomenal accomplishments over the next thirteen years would not have been possible.

The Henry of her first acquaintance was a peculiar mixture of innocence and professionalism. While strongly focused on his career, he was also reasonably adept at balancing the pressures of New York with his desire for the peace of rural California. Neither his brilliant gifts nor his mushrooming exposure in the press seemed to have gone to his head. In part urbane and cultured, a superb conversationalist accustomed to mixing with the wealthy, he was still notoriously careless about his appearance. While generous sponsorship provided for his modest needs, he perceived that his unconventional education undermined prospects for security.

Biographer Michael Hicks has made the case that he was a "bohemian."[3] His parents in some senses met a standard definition of "bohemian," that is, living an unconventional lifestyle within a kind of colony, in their case the Bay Area writers. They also had a strong vein of middle-class values, however, and their anarchist outlook argued for taking extreme responsibility for one's actions. Clarissa's entire life was guided by a powerful sense of political ideals and feminist convictions. She stuck doggedly to her unsuccessful fight to provide for herself as a writer at a time when women had few decent options other than marriage. Harry was closer to a bohemian, but his negligence and unreliability repelled Henry. Some of Henry's larger circle also were poor role models. Ellen Veblen, a real bohemian, was deeply troubled. Although Jaime de Angulo contributed enormously to Henry's growth and confidence as a person and as a scientific thinker, he was also an impossible man.

John Varian could be considered a middling model. Eccentric and poetic, visionary yet earthy, he also was a practical man attempting but failing to be a normal, wage-earning citizen. He and his wife became Henry's surrogate parents and reinforced Henry's own desire to give his best to the world. Thanks to them, Halcyon was almost as much Henry's home as it was for the children who grew up there.[4]

Seeger, Seward, and Terman were true guardian angels who taught Henry to pursue his goals rationally and with extreme self-discipline. His contemporaries understood how to prepare the way for productive lives. Russell Varian, Sigurd Varian, and George Harrison grew into important scientists; Robert Duffus and Evelyn Wells became prominent journalists; Edna Smith combined intelligence, motivation, and generosity. To all of them was now added Olive, the consummate achiever.

With the influences weighted heavily on the side of practicality-as-a-servant-of-vision, Henry had come to understand the practical foundation needed for success. While recognizing that American music lovers generally were ignorant of modernist aesthetics and ideas, he also knew that they could be open-minded, since most of them were not obsessed with the European musical tradition. Friends like the Varians, Lewis Terman, Sam Seward, Fred Bartlett, Jaime de Angulo, and Armitt Brown—as well as Harry—proved that the American male's disdain for the arts was not universal and the admiration of artistic innovation was possible. He therefore had some reasons to feel that he could win converts to his spectacular and unconventional music. Although frustration was almost certain, Henry, like Schoenberg, was sustained by the faith that his music was historically inevitable, and that his ideas could open new worlds for composers. If building this career meant getting attention, his music was his perfect tool.

11

Conquering Europe, First Attempt (1923)

The European debut tour was a huge gamble. Henry, a pianist-composer from a country with no record of compositional excellence, the first American modernist to perform in Europe since Leo Ornstein nearly a decade earlier, would face journalists who were unprepared for his music and extremely cynical. He was also stepping into a maelstrom in which classical music was a cult, virulent nationalism and racism were politicizing anti-modernism, and, in reaction to the horrendous reality of the past war, even the old modernists—composers and visual artists—sought stability in neoclassicism. The conventional European audience, armored against novelty, would proclaim him guilty until proven innocent. He would also have to win over the European modernists, newly conservative or not, who were likely to reject his unconventional emphasis on sound as opposed to individual pitch. The extreme Dadaists, on the other hand, might think his music too mild. Everyone could dismiss his unorthodox performance techniques as a typically American sales swindle.

In May 1923 he saw what he faced. After Frederick Bristol, an American pianist, gave the first European performance of the guileless "Tides of Manaunaun," a London reviewer loaded his imagination and fired. ". . . As to forearm music, the public will now know what to expect, since forewarned is forearmed. . . . This is something quite new in piano technique, and represents another triumph for the land of sewing machines and typewriters. But it is a dangerous precedent, as the next step, obviously, is a part of the player's nose."[1] Henry, however, knew how to profit from the sarcasm. The article got to Los Angeles critic Bruno David Ussher, who gave him good publicity by protesting its anti-Americanism.[2] At the same time, Ussher, who understood the indisputable provocativeness of Henry's music, cautioned that the piano might not be the best place to apply his theories of sound. In other words, the visual impact of his performance methods could be a liability. He also implied that Henry's allusions to Irish culture might provoke English hostility.[3]

Meanwhile, Henry, Richard Buhlig—who knew Berlin well—and the young pianist Wesley Kuhnle gathered in New York in preparation for their voyage.[4] Kuhnle, a nephew of the critic Henry Krehbiel, had studied in Los Angeles with Buhlig and planned to continue lessons with him abroad.[5] Henry considered him mildly talented but stunted artistically by illness.[6] Fortunately, Kuhnle was a complainer who vented his frustrations in long letters home that supply most of the information about their journey—such as Buhlig's initial advice to get both German and Austrian visas because the increasing power of the communists might block them from entering Germany.[7]

The tour was going to be costly and had to have backing, though the source is not clear. If, as has been believed, Edna Smith left Henry money for this purpose, the paperwork is gone. Olive claimed to have paid, but Henry said the first trip was financed by Sam Seward, which is to say, the educational fund.[8] Sidney thought Buhlig's friends Aline Barnsdall, an oil heiress, feminist, anarchist, drama producer, and backer of Frank Lloyd Wright, and Mrs. Harry Chandler, the wife of the publisher of the Los Angeles *Times*, also helped.[9]

At the end of May they sailed on the crowded S.S. Bremen, tossing and rolling in very high seas. After recovering from extreme seasickness they spent evenings at cards since, according to Kuhnle, the music on the ship was "pretty bad," and attempts to play the ship's excellent Ibach grand were thwarted by the turbulence. One night they both played in an entertainment in the large dining room, a benefit for the suffering people of the Ruhr. Other performers included an impressive young violinist named Leo Linder, the ship's orchestra, and assorted acts such as Sammy, Sambo, and Mammy in "Eine Unterhaltung in Alabama" (A Chat in Alabama). Henry accompanied a few salon songs. In such a context, "The Tides of Manaunaun" surely did not go unnoticed.[10]

When they docked in Bremen after twelve days,[11] Henry immediately was overcome by its old-world quaintness. Kuhnle, Buhlig, Henry, and an unnamed fourth person (almost certainly Linder) treated themselves to a meal at the Rathskeller, whose magnificence surpassed anything Henry had never seen. Nor had he seen the benefits of hyperinflation for the holder of hard currency. Enormous portions of soup, fish, meat, fowl, dessert, and a rare wine cost 80,000 marks—ninety cents [2010: $11.50].[12] Seventy-five cents got them from Bremen to Berlin, where Buhlig—apparently on Busoni's recommendation—took them to Pension Bruhn, 65 Nürnbergerstrasse, near the Zoo railway station and Kurfürstendamm. The manager of the highly music-friendly establishment, Elsa Schmolke, would never have foreseen that she would join this drama as her pension became Henry's European base.

In the first few days they spent less than twenty dollars for several meals, about a dozen taxis, hotel, railway, and tips.[13] With the mark at 94,000 to the dollar, Henry's large room cost eighteen cents a day, including breakfast and

lunch; renting a grand piano cost seventy-eight cents a month; the best seats at
the opera, thirty cents; an ordinary taxi ride, sixteen cents; a meal in the best restaurant, twenty-one cents, a new suit, seventeen cents, and so forth. On a dollar a
day—he told Harry—one could live like a prince. "It is, however an impossible
situation, and I am not going to be the kind of foreigner who takes advantage to
purchase luxury at the expense of the poor here. It is dreadful to get used to
making change." But 94,000 was a mere way station. Soon the dollar yielded
280,000 marks; three days later, 740,000. Cultural immersion in one of the
world's liveliest cities was utterly painless to the pocketbook. Henry heard magnificent performances of Handel's *Julius Caesar* and Wagner's *Flying Dutchman*.
Even the summer season was "unbelievably brilliant," he wrote while planning a
trip to the Leipzig Bach festival. He thought life could hardly be cheaper, but it
soon became virtually free with hard currency.[14]

Buhlig promptly brought him (without Kuhnle) to dinner with his old friend
Artur Schnabel,[15] a forty-one-year-old celebrity pianist and quirky composer.
Henry's playing turned him into a Cowell fan, although he heeded his manager's
warning never to play modern music in public. He and his son Karl Ulrich
learned a few of Henry's pieces, and Schnabel offered to try to get Henry a Berlin
concert sponsored by either the Composers' Society or the Melos Society, a performance of his orchestral music, and an engagement at World Music Days, the
festival started by Busoni's new International Society for Contemporary Music.
Schnabel then invited distinguished musicians to a gathering at which he and his
son played Henry's pieces; arranged for Henry to visit the grandchildren of Felix
Mendelssohn (who still lived in the composer's house); and introduced him to
Hermann Scherchen, the conductor and founder of the Melos Society, an
important force in the new-music world.[16]

Kuhnle and Henry developed a pleasantly symbiotic relationship. Henry
learned the geography of Berlin and, as Kuhnle said, did "the steering" when
they went out; Kuhnle knew German, which was incomprehensible to Henry.
They briefly considered sharing the costs of joint concerts in two cities selected
from Cologne, Copenhagen, Prague, Stuttgart, and Zürich.[17] On June 22 they
went to Leipzig, where Henry must have discussed arrangements for an autumn
concert. In the violent political climate they needed a police permit to return to
Berlin.[18]

Henry now engaged Wolff & Sachs, Berlin's largest concert management, to
produce concerts in Berlin and Vienna, and other German performances if the
budget permitted. Concerts were scheduled for Munich, Leipzig, Berlin, and
Hamburg (later canceled); additional recitals looked probable for Vienna and
Paris; a London date had yet to be set. Soaring inflation so reduced the dollar
cost for self-sponsored recitals in Germany that Prague or Copenhagen seemed
potentially feasible within the budget. Henry, however, sensed the shadows:

"One feels ... that any sort of sudden change, either financially or otherwise, is possible of happening."[19]

Even the normally dull summer months were charged with activity. After a brief holiday in the Alps, Henry completed a piano piece tentatively entitled "Mastadon," which Buhlig urged him to play in Berlin. The Melos Society auditioned him on Schnabel's recommendation. Planning continued. Although Henry could not afford seventy-one dollars [2010: $958] to pay for a concert in Budapest, he knew that he needed press notices from outside Germany. Meanwhile, he learned that in the United States, Ampico (the player-piano manufacturer) and Knabe might reach some kind of "financially advantageous arrangement" with him.[20]

Most of the summer was spent in Berlin, where Henry and Kuhnle played at a house party at the end of July.[21] Visits by Buhlig's wife and the English-born California pianist Winifred Hooke relieved Henry's homesickness but not his craving for letters from Harry. No other travel is alluded to in letters or his passport. (The Alpine holiday may have been in Bavaria, since the passport contains no stamps for Switzerland.)[22] A looming general strike suggested the merits of decamping for London, but trains had become so unreliable that they considered flying.[23] It would have been Henry's first trip by airplane, but in the end, he and Buhlig opted for quiet, inexpensive Vienna.[24] Kuhnle, fed up, went to London alone and then to New York, leaving no one to record the finer details of the tour.[25]

From Vienna, Henry went briefly to Paris to see his sponsors Judy and Armitt Brown,[26] confer about the concert planned for the Salle Erard, and visit with his first stepmother, Henrietta. Getting her agreement to divorce Harry so that he could marry Olive was easy because she never intended to go back to him, having unilaterally sold their house without splitting the proceeds. Harry soon had his freedom and Henry enjoyed two weeks with Henrietta as guide and interpreter. They maintained an intermittent but loving relationship for the remainder of her life.

In early September, after seeing Versailles, he returned to Vienna[27] to prepare for his European debut in Munich's Hercules-Saal on October 11. His program, well-balanced between conventional and extraordinary performing techniques, included *Sechs 'Ends'* (Six Ings), *Three Irish Legends*, *Four Encores to Dynamic Motion*, and assorted other pieces. With the German mark still plummeting, the concert cost virtually nothing. The response of the audience of about 150 is unknown, while the unpleasant reaction of the newspapers is all too obvious. One critic suggested that cabarets engage Henry.[28] The Munich *Post*, noting that Henry was Anglo-Saxon (and thus perhaps detestedly British but at least not Jewish), observed that, unlike Schoenberg, "Cowell's extremity is in his method of performance ... A witty friend remarked 'If he sat down on the keys one could talk of expressionistic "Afterkunst" [backside art].'"[29]

That article appeared on October 15, the day of Henry's performance at the Feurich-Saal in Leipzig, a concert that gave him priceless material for forty years of autobiographical lectures. The excitement of the evening was described by the *Volkszeitung*.

> Henry Cowell composes music of traffic and industry bustle, of noise in shops, factories and of the street. In order to exhaust it thoroughly, he needed here and there the forearm and elbow; a wonder that he did not use the tip of his nose also, and the opposite parts of the body. The artistic mission of this apparently Anglo-Saxon youth was greeted either with amazement, laughter, or rage, according to the state of mind of the hearers who had to bear these unchained piano acrobatics patiently. Several of the "Irish Legends" alone pricked one's ears, since here, in spite of everything, something of a mystical-mythical tune manifests itself, but otherwise . . .[30]

The *Leipziger Neuste Nachrichten* wished that the program had included German commentary to clarify whether the unrestrainable laughter of the young women resulted from the success or failure of the pianist. The *Abendpost* felt that ultimately the event was taken with good humor, despite the brawling.[31] Brawling? Henry's first account of it appeared three months later in the New York *Evening Mail*, headlined "Strong-Arm Pianist."

> The most exciting concert I ever gave was in Leipsic. When I played the final piece ["Antinomy"] (the loudest I have, and many say the loudest piano piece in the world) the audience was yelling and stamping and clapping and hissing until I could hardly hear myself. They stood up during most of the performance and got as near to me and the piano as they could. It did not bother or embarrass me exactly, but of course it rather keyed me up. Some of those who disapproved my methods were so excited that they almost threatened me with physical violence. Those who liked the music restrained them.[32]

Such events lend themselves so well to elaboration that this description, and the one Henry served up many years later, may need to be taken with a lot of salt. He recalled, "Well, there were a few very enthusiastic people, but there were more than a few who were not enthusiastic at all. . . ."

> The hall [in Leipzig] was comfortably filled. I didn't know anything about Europe at all, and I thought, well, they have plenty of people who play conservative music, they'd be more interested if I play something

less conservative. So I started in [*sic*] one of my less conservative pieces, and a gentleman jumped up from one of the front rows and shook his fist at me and he said, "Halten Sie uns fuer Idioten in Deutschland?" "Do you take us for idiots in Germany?" Then someone in the back said, "Who are you to speak for Germany. You're not very important yourself."

Upon which, this loosened the tongues of the auditors, who then began discussing the nature of the music. The music got louder and louder, so that the people, in order to be heard over it, had to talk louder and louder. Finally a bunch of young fellows in the back said, "You are just doing this to irritate us, and you are doing it to insult the names of Bach and Mendelssohn who lived here, and we give you one minute to get started out." So then another group said, "No, even if he does play like this, we'll show him that we're gentlemen. Let him play!" After one minute, the first group started up onto the stage, and the second group jumped onto the stage, and the two groups had an awful fight on the stage. Police were called. The police came onto the stage and arrested 20 young fellows, the audience being in an absolute state of hysteria— and I was still playing![33]

Henry was taken completely by surprise, but the argument was less about his music than about Leipzigers' code of behavior. In the end, he was almost forgotten since the music could hardly be heard in the uproar, but, as he told Sidney, the sensation of leaving the stage at intermission with his knees shaking was "interesting." The only threat to him personally was a promise that he would be helped on his way if he did not leave by himself. While he never again encountered a near riot like this one, he had learned the lesson that German audiences felt obligated to stay for the entire event and register their disapproval by whistling on their big housekeys.[34] He got off comparatively well. Joseph Szigeti encountered violence and stinkbombs in the 1920s.

By the time the Leipzig reviews appeared, Henry had already returned to Vienna for his debut on October 31, at the Neuer Saal der Burg, which drew about 350.[35] This event was comparatively peaceful. One man kept yelling "Schluss, Schluss" (Stop, stop!), refusing to desist even when the audience shushed him. Julius Korngold, the leading critic,[36] damned his music as the "Gipfel atonales Denken," the "peak of atonal thought." Henry used the line in his next circular.[37] Later he heard that Korngold's son Erich had had to sit through his music played by Schnabel.[38] Once again, the nasty bits found their way to an unidentified American newspaper, whose declared agenda this time was not to support Henry but to counterbalance some recent positive reviews of him.[39] The route through which news circulated now revealed itself: Henry had made Harry into an effective press agent.

Vienna's standards shone brightly in the *Allgemeine Zeitung*'s description of Henry as a "highly peculiar fellow who takes himself seriously, but . . . goes to the piano and music with an American ease, as if it was a matter of boring through a tunnel, or otherwise to hew through a technical knot, and that for us in this country, does not do at all."[40] The *Wiener Morgenzeitung*'s Erwin Felber praised "an honest but confused talent that is temporarily expending itself in futuristic sound-experiments."[41] Paul Stefan, a supporter of new music, found the concert interesting only from a sensational viewpoint. Yet to be fair, Henry's lack of extended compositions might have bothered even a committed pro-modernist.

In Vienna he stayed with the poets Louis and Jean Starr Untermeyer, where he met the tenor Roland Hayes, initiating a long, close collegial relationship.[42] The few scraps about his adventures include a ticket to the ballet, a copy of Kurt Schwitters's Dada journal *Merz*, and a libretto for Schoenberg's *Gurrelieder*, which was performed the day after his concert. He met Alban Berg, who asked for permission to use tone clusters. "Berg was such a wonderful, hearty person, appreciating a joke, and always full of laughter. It's hard to think of him as being the composer of such gruesome tales as 'Wozzeck' and 'Lulu.' But he got all of this gruesomeness out of his spirit, probably, by writing the music. So he is the nearest to a Rotary Club member type of anybody I met in Europe at all, hearty and hale, slaps you on the back, laughing at jokes, his own and other people's, and so on."[43]

All the while, Paris papers heralded his forthcoming concert in paid announcements disguised as news items emphasizing moderated modernism—that is, Henry's music expresses his personal vision without any larger agenda. One "article" shrewdly admitted that many critics do not appreciate his work, presumably to pique the interest of Parisians addicted to sensationalism.[44] Henry was surprised to find that his manager announced him as Henri Cowell, hoping to spare him the fate of an unknown foreign pianist with a small publicity budget.[45]

The Paris debut took place on November 17, 1923, at the Salle Erard. Attendance is unknown; the press responded more-or-less as usual. The Paris *New York Herald* heard "little melody and little harmony, even discordant" but granted that the audience liked and encored "Antinomy."[46] *Comoedia*'s Paul Le Flem was so positive that Henry commented, "None of my Paris criticisms after the concert were paid for in any way."[47] (The problem of bribery in Paris persisted for many decades.) *Paris Soir*'s Louis Vuillemin was stupefied that a piano could be so solid. Again Henry, obviously amused, wrote, "Not paid for." Raymond Petit, in *Revue Musicale*, conceded that Henry's harmonies were "not without producing a certain effect," but warned that Henry's search for a language was preventing him from finding something more real and musical.[48] To be sure, the combination of tonal melodies with clusters can strike some people as artificial.

Despite the predominant cynicism, Henry considered the concert a great success, without hissing or other demonstrations. "Tides," "Antinomy," and the superb new "Piece for Piano with Strings" were encored, and the prestigious art exposition Salon d'Automne invited him to repeat his program on December 16 with Yvonne Daunt, the British principal soloist of the opera ballet, dancing to some of his music. Henry extracted passages from *Le Soir* and *Le Figaro* that had "a very nice tone," and wrote a feature about the tour for the San Francisco *Call,* for nationwide circulation.[49]

Before the second Paris concert he rushed back to Berlin to play under the sponsorship of the Melos Society, which had been won over by Schnabel's support and Henry's audition. This time four of the six reviews were to some degree positive. The *Vossiche Zeitung,*[50] while acknowledging the public's interest in the music, wished that such unusual means had produced a more unusual music, a comment applicable to some early pieces but not to the new "Piece for Piano with Strings," a powerful work on a grand scale that uses an astute mixture of his techniques and lacks any pictorial content. *Berliner B-Z am Mittag's* Adolf Weissmann also was not convinced by the music, but liked Henry's adventurous attitude to sound. Calling the resultant "noise" a kind of American Futurism, he pronounced Henry "an interesting American type, a conclusive force for a nation. . . . As a musical sportsman, he arouses the fantasy of the observer no less than that of the listener, and opens up a view into an intermediate realm (*Zwischenreich*) of art. I would not want to have missed it."[51] Oscar Bie, the Berlin correspondent for the *Basel National Zeitung,* called him a representative of those who have found a counterbalance to the consonance and harmonic *Baulichkeit* (structuring) of the old school. Henry underlined the sentence "Er spielt fabelhaft gut" (he plays fantastically well). Bie had his reservations nevertheless. "Sometimes there flashes a wave of feeling and lyricism, but the whole is subdued to the cold law of that *Struktivität* (structuralism) which is the skeleton of modern art."[52] To the anonymous critic of the *Berliner Tageblatt,* however, the most striking feature "was that an organization of [Melos's] artistic quality . . . could invite professionals to witness such nonsense."[53] The scorecard pleased Henry, who concluded that reactions were better in Berlin than in Leipzig because Berliners were better versed in new music.[54]

When Henry left Germany on November 26, the unexpected was happening: the mark had passed four trillion to the dollar, and Adolf Hitler had attempted a coup in Munich. Henry went to see his grandfather in Dublin, which had its own problems. Although advised not to play there because of residual instability from the armed revolt against the British two years earlier, he asked a Theosophist friend of Varian to help organize something, but a performance was impossible.[55] Not that a little family holiday was such a bad thing, and Harry wanted news of his father, whom he had not seen for some forty years. Grandfather George was happy that Henry was "simple and unaffected," without a swelled head.[56] Henry, however, found himself in an awkward position. Because his only contact with the

Episcopal Church was the eccentric St. Marks-in-the-Bouwerie, he was embarrassed when his distinguished clergyman-grandfather asked him to describe the
difference in worship between St. Marks and St. Patrick's, Dublin, where Henry
had to sit in the bishop's pew as a model for the congregation to follow.[57]

Henry then visited an uncle in Birmingham[58] en route to his December 10
concert at Aeolian Hall in London, which unfortunately competed with Bartók's
performance with the well-known violinist Adila Fachiri, Joseph Joachim's
grandniece.[59] Tension surrounding the impending general election also threatened to affect attendance.[60] Henry played his usual program, with the addition of
"Piece for Piano with Strings," which Le Courier Musical had recently asked to
publish, making it his first piece to be printed outside the United States.[61] Again,
there is no record of the size of the audience, a significant segment of which was
reporters.[62] Notices, mostly recirculated through the wire services, appeared in
thirteen papers on the day after the concert alone, and that was just the beginning. The following day brought reviews in ten more papers in Aberdeen, Bath,
London, and Paris. Over the next month at least twenty-eight articles followed,
ranging from uncomplimentary to abusive. By now, if Henry was not a household name, it was not the fault of the newspapers. Some highlights:

> Daily Mail (London)—"Newest Piano-Playing. The Elbow Touch,"
> with comments about the ceiling collapsing, etc.
> Daily Express (London)—Headline: "Elbow Pianist. A Wonderful
> Test for the Instrument." A compliment for the Broadwood piano "that
> it stood this high-spirited American handling so well."
> Daily News (London)—Headline: "Piano Played with Elbow. Fin-
> gers too Limited for Mr. Cowell. Result Like a Nursery in Rebellion."
> Evening News (London). "Talk about a kitten on the keys! You might
> think a full-grown hippopotamus was step-dancing there. But we are
> afraid Mr. Cowell does not go far enough. He is hampered by his early
> Academic training. What the public wants is a man who dives off the
> deep end of the piano and crashes full length upon the keys. That will
> be really great. And if the result is fatal either to the performer or those
> who come to listen so much the better."
> Liverpool Echo—Headline: "Strong Arm Pianist," over a short item
> apparently taken from London's Daily Mail: "One of Mr. Cowell's works
> was entitled 'What's This?' What, indeed? The answer would be too
> colloquial for print."

In London Henry stayed in the enormous house of soprano Lady Dorothy
Mayer and her husband Robert Mayer, founder of a renowned series of children's
concerts. One morning around seven o'clock he went downstairs to practice,

unaware that there was another guest, who was awakened and descended in his bathrobe, mystified by the sounds. It was Bartók. As they chatted, Henry expressed his disappointment in the results of his concert in Paris, where "you can't just go in and expect anybody of real importance to be there. Nobody at my concert amounted to anything." Bartók told Henry to go right back to Paris, and he would arrange a concert that everyone would attend. He was as good as his word.[63]

Sometime after they parted company, Bartók requested Henry's permission to use tone clusters. Henry replied that he would be most happy. Unfortunately, Sidney could not locate Bartók's letter when she started organizing Henry's papers in the 1940s, and thought it might have been stolen. Regarding the story's authenticity, she wrote that as Henry was "fanatically honest about such things and given to understatement where his connection with other famous people was concerned," she believed his account.[64] While the surviving Bartók papers contain nothing to or from Henry,[65] Bartók's works of the next few years include many cluster-like chords.

Another London adventure could have been done without. While traveling around the city, Henry lost a package of scores. Says Sidney,

> He was of course distraught, but was directed to New Scotland Yard where the lost scores arrived almost as soon as he did. It seems unbelievable (but not if like me you were married to Henry Cowell for 25 years!) that later on the same day he forgot the same lot of scores again in a taxicab. When he turned up at New Scotland Yard for the second time, a kindly detective located his scores for him and sent him home in a police car. This nearly precipitated a crisis in Lady Mayer's domestic arrangements, for she had a new butler who protested he was not accustomed to a household where official police cars delivered guests, and for a few days she was afraid she would lose him.[66]

With his London recital behind him, Henry returned to Paris.[67] An excellent connection, "the Steins" (Gertrude Stein and Alice B. Toklas) had instigated the concert in the Grand Palais for the Salon d'Automne, arranged for Henry to make piano rolls for Pleyel, gave him a valuable early fifteenth-century music manuscript, and got Matisse to write a letter of introduction to Stravinsky, who happened to be away. At some point, perhaps on this trip, Henry began running into Stravinsky at parties. He said he once counted twenty-seven encounters with Stravinsky—only at social events—but never felt he got to know him, in part because Stravinsky lived behind what Henry called a wall of "Parisian politeness."[68] No matter that we do not know how Henry met the Steins; considering the effort that he put into meeting people, nothing should be a surprise.

A singer introduced him to Henri Prunières at *La Revue Musicale*, who invited Henry to his home to discuss modern music and wrote about him in the Paris papers.[69] Bartók assembled a group including Ravel, Falla, Honegger, Milhaud, Prunières, Roussel, Stravinsky, "all the people that really counted for anything in the way of creative music in Paris. They came, because Bartók invited them and said, 'This is going to be good.'" (Henry's reference to Stravinsky suggests a slip of the memory, since he was not in Paris then.)[70]

There is no record of that concert, which Sidney thought was a private event sponsored by a socially prominent patroness, and similar to one in London.[71] Other private events also are shrouded in their very privacy. An article in the *Herald* leaves a trace of one such evening, however—Henry's mid-December visit to the studio of the painter Lester Rosenfield for an evening of literature and dance, amid a distinguished crowd from the entire spectrum of the arts, including Jean Cocteau. The centerpiece was Miss Constant Lounsbery's reading of her *Poèmes Vecus* (in French and English), which must have interested Henry because they were based upon the principle that any thought may be expressed by a rhythm,

> the combination of words giving certain sound vibrations which produce rhythms suitable to the feeling of the poetry itself. . . . The poems were embodied in dance form, while two voices, that of a man and of a woman, recited the stanzas on a given note and in the tempo required by the meaning and the natural flow of the words. The stage, softly lighted, was arranged in Oriental fashion, with a curious Indian curtain at the back, and Oriental rugs and cushions on the floor, on which were seated the two "Voices" . . . both dressed in gorgeous Oriental costumes. The drummer . . . [a woman] costumed like an Arab boy, squatted on the other side of the floor and beat rhythmic accompaniments, intoned on stage. The dancer . . . professionally known as Nadja appeared before the curtain as the "Body," expressing in rhythmic movement what sound and musical rhythm simultaneously conveyed. . . . Miss Constant Lounsbery herself joined the "Voices" for certain of the poems, and was a striking figure in a rich Indian robe and turban.[72]

On Sunday afternoon, December 16, Henry played for the joint performance with Yvonne Daunt, who danced to "Exultation," "Second Episode," "Voice of Lir," and "Advertisement." The one surviving review, in the *Herald*, contains a rare serious observation that Henry used his arms to produce orchestral effects.[73] While the French press declined to attend,[74] his day *en français* was approaching. Beginning on January 23, 1924, notices of his London concert, largely copies of one another, appeared throughout France, and even in Casablanca, French Morocco.

Through their mutual mimicry a little originality shines, such as "never thought anyone could go farther than Satie. . . ."[75] An Orléans newspaper, combining reports of acoustical experiments in Moscow with a remark in *Pravda* that the promotion of such music helps push the world toward socialism, concluded that Henry was a Soviet agent.[76]

Before leaving for New York, Henry made piano rolls for Pleyel's "La Pleyela," a novel variant of the pianola. He may have been right about "Antinomy" being the loudest piece ever written: the technicians thought it might require too much wind pressure to be practical. Proofs needed reading for "Piece for Piano with Strings," scheduled for publication by *Le Courier Musical* in January. He finally left for Cherbourg on December 29. Despite rough seas and daily gales, he did not get sick, enjoyed the weather, and docked in New York on January 10, 1924.[77]

While Henry did not enjoy the abuse heaped upon him, the only trace of a reaction is his muted and businesslike assessment for Harry.

> I have ordered both a French and an English Press-Clipping bureau to send clippings to you, so you will undoubtedly have seen the tremendous, though unpleasant publicity I have had in England. It will be noticed, however, that the best papers (Times and Observer) gave quite good notices. It is not only very hard to get a good word from either of these papers, but also very hard to get a notice at all, as they seldom review unknown artists. Altogether I have gained tremendously from the European trip, and feel I would have a good welcome if I go back.[78]

Henry could hardly have complained about the quantity of press coverage. The sarcasm and insults may or may not reflect the audiences' reactions, however; the press, especially in Europe, reveled in mudslinging. Ten days on shipboard sufficed for him to find good material among the morass of insults— excellent, brief quotations suitable for publicity. When told of his clever feat, Sidney first indignantly insisted that he was too honest to falsify reviews, but was mollified by assurances that he did not invent phrases. He simply trimmed judiciously.[79] His correspondence increasingly shows his sharp commercial instincts. Knowing that he could become a *succès de scandal*, he had Harry circulate anything that was usable.

All in all, the tour was a good investment. Invitations to be an American correspondent for *La Gazette Musicale* and a Lyons newspaper were the first of many that would be extended over the years.[80] Henry had matured through his travels, functioned without knowing the languages, overseen complex international organizational problems, and learned the arts of concert production and publicizing. An invaluable foundation for any career, for Henry they became essential.

The best lesson concerned his perspective on the musical world. Years later he concluded that he had been better received in the United States, where his compositions were "recognized as sounding like music, and people had this more or less direct response, whereas in Europe it broke all the traditions, and they were more worried about tradition-breaking than they were about how it sounded, at first."[81] Nevertheless, while everything suggested that his future lay in his own country, he was not about to surrender. He knew that Europe could no longer ignore American modernism.

Attacking the American Market

The tour concluded on February 4, 1924, with Henry's official New York debut, produced by Judy Brown's friend Arthur Judson, one of America's most powerful managers.[1] Persuaded that his music would attract crowds, Henry rented Carnegie Hall's main auditorium, seating more than 2,800 and costing between $700 and $900 [2010: $8,930–$11,500], plus stage labor and box office charges.[2] Most of his program comprised very recent pieces, which he again grouped as if each section were a multimovement composition.

Judson, capitalizing on Henry's growing notoriety, circulated advertisements trumpeting "'Tone Clusters' *What are they?* They are the latest musical device of an ultra-modern composer. They are played with the forearm./ *Who devised them?* HENRY COWELL /and he will demonstrate them at his recital at Carnegie Hall. . . ."[3] The strategy drew leading movie companies to film Henry for the still-silent newsreels that were shown in movie theaters nationwide.[4] Here was a rarity: a pianist who could make an impression without sound. Newspapers proved helpful with apparently unpaid publicity quoting the best of the European reviews. Breitkopf circularized the concert although Henry's contract did not obligate them to do so. As to the yield, the *New York Telegram and Evening Mail* reported numerous empty seats, while the *Herald* referred to "a large audience, of which a noticeable portion appeared to be easily fed up." A tenth of Carnegie Hall's 2,800 seats would have been a big crowd for a modernist, but Carnegie Hall lacks attendance records that could resolve the conflicting descriptions.

The sheer quantity of reviews evokes the heyday of print media. The first morning yielded eight, with a score of three for, five against—not magnificent, but better than in Europe. The worst articles belong in a comedic anthology; the best showed Henry gaining prominent champions. Pitts Sanborn (*Telegram and Evening Mail*) declared that the musical community unquestionably showed interest in Henry, while those who expected a circus were disappointed. Since the music was full of color, melody, and evocativeness, he could not see why one should *not* strike the strings, or why Henry should not use limbs when ten fingers did not suffice. The *New York Herald's* W. E. J. Henderson found "extraordinary and genuinely musical effects . . . So, after all, the advocates of the new methods win, for probably only Mr. Cowell can weave these singular, sonorous effects."

A week later, the *New York Telegraph* printed Ben Deacon's priceless "Kid Knabe Takes Heavy Punishment, But Is on His Feet at End of Bout." Henry, he wrote, would have been better with a good sledgehammer; the concert would have been a good assignment for the sporting editor, and on and on. The damage done, Deacon admitted that Henry was serious and he (Deacon) was not. He knew nothing about music, but liked it visually and enjoyed some of it musically.

New York newspapers were but the beginning. The Cowell archive contains reviews from twenty-four cities in sixteen states, spread nationally, and there may have been many others. Prose about heavyweight pianos, knuckles, and so forth made Henry a media star. One engaging headline, from Bridgeport, Connecticut, read: "California Boy Assaults Piano for Art's Sake . . . A Neo-Leo Ornstein. Pianist Produces Bowling Alley Music but Critics Remain Bored."

From *Musical America*, "Plaint of a Pedal-Point":

> I want to be a cluster
> And with the clusters stand,
> Just like the other modern tones
> Played without use of hand!
> When youthful virtuosi
> Start banging keys with fist
> I sigh to think I'm orthodox.
> Oh my, what thrills I've missed!

Henry now played at a tea given by the Pictorial Photographers of America[5] to promote the February 17 Town Hall concert, a "Second Recital by Henry Cowell" offering "More 'Tone Clusters.'" Since two closely spaced concerts seems risky, the turnout at Carnegie Hall was either quite good or it was too late to cancel the contract with The Town Hall. This time, publicity sensationalizing Henry's music was balanced with quotations emphasizing his seriousness of purpose. While no program survives, reviews indicate that he played essentially the same program as at Carnegie, with the addition of three other pieces including the very grand "Vision of Oma," probably in its first performance.[6] Attendance is described as light, though it is anybody's guess what "light" means for a new-music program in a theater seating more than a thousand.

Another rush of articles about the Carnegie concert appeared on the same day as the Town Hall recital. Then the deluge resumed nationally. *Musical Courier* (Chicago) returned to the sports image: "There are to be musical contests at the Paris Olympiad next summer. Should not America send as its representative

Henry Cowell, whose fist and elbow work have won him such fame? If expounders of the piano, why not pounders, too?"[7] The *New York Herald*, however, reminded its readers that although Henry's devices "do not promise much, other things that seemed to mean little have become part of the stock in trade of music."[8]

Henry correctly inferred that the American press was beginning to accord him an open-minded hearing while the Europeans resisted novelty, especially if it were American. On both continents, however, a recital by Henry remained a license for writing rubbish. After publishing yet another athletics parody, the *Montreal Star* recognized the paradox that the "entire musical profession is puzzling over the unprecedented conduct of Cowell, the most puzzling phase of his work being the excellent quality of his music."[9] A *Brooklyn Standard Union* interviewer, visiting Henry's West 8th Street apartment, loved hearing him play in private, without "critics willing to devastate a reputation for the sake of a witticism."[10]

Nevertheless, converting notoriety into a *succès de scandale* takes time, during which Henry needed to eat. Occasional sneers that his "tricks" were enriching him could not have been further from the truth. Decent fees for performances were rare; composing and writing brought in only a bit of extra money. Although he lived most of the year rent-free—but without running water—in Menlo, or at Blanche Walton's homes in New York and Bronxville, his life would have been untenable without help from his sponsors. Something had to change before his marginal existence devoured his inner strength. A more lucrative performing career required shifting listeners' attention to his music and away from the fireworks. While sarcastic reviewers did not necessarily reflect the reaction of the audience, the average newspaper reader knew only what was printed.

To obtain the trust of booking managers, Henry had to change the terms of the discussion. Self-sponsored recitals and flamboyant reviews were not the answer, nor was a manager like Arthur Judson, for whom Henry's account was small potatoes and who never got him a single engagement. Louise Vermont, the singer with whom he had performed in 1922, suggested he talk with her husband, William Gassner,[11] proprietor of the Concert Guild, a small agency. She correctly felt he might take a personal interest in such an unusual act. In April 1924, Gassner signed a one-year agreement as Henry's American and Canadian manager. Henry had to provide $175 [2010: $2,230] for a postal campaign and retained the power to block unauthorized expenditures. A 25 percent commission on all engagements closed by Gassner gave him an incentive to obtain good fees. Henry, however, had to pursue new contacts as vigorously as ever. Although Gassner was not entirely effective, he was a good man who understood that lecture-recitals could be sold more readily than pure concerts. Ultimately, through Gassner's and Henry's own promotion efforts, Henry gave some forty to sixty concerts a years in the 1920s. [12] They kept renewing the contract for most of the next twenty years.

After the Town Hall recital, Henry went on the road, opening at the end of February in Chicago. The general tone of the Chicago critics shows either that his ideas were no longer outrageous, or that those critics were serious. For once, they concurred that the large audience received him enthusiastically. While the expenses exceeded the receipts, there were important long-term gains, thanks to Henry's friends in Chicago's lively musical world. Pianist Georgia Kober, president of the Sherwood School,[13] was very fond of Henry as a man and a composer. Through either Kober or Arthur Judson, he met Djane Lavoie-Herz, the wife of Judson's Chicago representative, Siegfried Lavoie-Herz, and a friend of Henry's friend Dane Rudhyar.[14] A prominent piano teacher, salon hostess, and Theosophist, Lavoie-Herz had gifted young piano students including Gitta Gradova and Ruth Crawford, who quickly became Henry's friends. The Herzes also introduced him to wealthy, music-loving members of Chicago's Jewish community, and to seventeen-year-old Alfred Frankenstein, who later became his powerful supporter as music critic of the *San Francisco Chronicle*.[15]

On the way to California, Henry probably stopped as usual to see his halfbrother Clarence and Clarissa's Iowa family. We hear of him next on April 14, when he played for the American College Salon in Oakland. This concert seems to be the first occasion when he offered a formal pre-concert lecture, which he called "Musical Resources of Modern Composition."[16] A week later, in publicizing Henry's coming concert for the Western Arts Association, the *San Francisco Call* printed a warm interview portraying him as a traditionalist who does not assert a kinship with "such extremists as Ornstein and Schoenberg and Bartók and Percy Grainger." That seems like nonsense, but it is also true that Henry's pervasively melodic aesthetic gave many of his supposedly radical piano pieces a strongly conservative flavor that critics rarely noticed.[17]

After two more Bay Area concerts, he commenced a series of lectures at the San Francisco Conservatory. Like Harry, he found public speaking easy; unlike Harry, he saw its professional potential. Olive, convinced that his life would demand good documentation, now set up an archive into which went everything from scraps of paper to important documents and countless letters including many from friends in Menlo Park who were not professionally "useful"—even the first letters from Elsa Schmolke, his Berlin landlady, who addressed him intimately as "Lieber, kleiner Henry . . ." (Dear little Henry) while employing the formal third-person case. Olive also tried to help Henry behind his back, such as confiding with Gassner that audiences were disturbed by his inability to look neat.[18]

His personal appearance implies either a small ego or a lack of professionalism. Whichever was true, he also had no money—not even enough to visit Halcyon. He finally got there for the Theosophists' Convention in early August 1924.[19] That is the last news of his whereabouts until November, when, after concerts in San Luis Obispo and Santa Fe, he returned to New York to play and lecture. Performances of his piano music on both coasts and in Caracas, by Edwin Hughes, Winifred Hooke, and Frederick Bristol, provided seasonal cheer.

On the last Sunday of 1924, although he was no longer using his free room at St. Mark's in-the-Bouwerie, Henry repaid the congregation's generosity with a day-long event whose long-term consequences even he could not have antici- pated. This "Symposium on Exotic Music" opened with a talk "on the peculiar- ities of Oriental Music, illustrated by Instrumentalists" who played music of Japan, India, and China that must have been unfamiliar to almost everyone.[20] Asked whether this concert might have been the first public presentation of extra-European music in the United States, ethnomusicologist Dr. Adelaide Reyes responded that it almost certainly was, at least for a white audience. Anti- immigrant and especially anti-Chinese sentiments were so powerful that the only other possible venues would have been in Chinatown or in freak shows at the P. T. Barnum circus. The 1882 Exclusion Act, which kept Chinese out of the United States, was not repealed until 1943.[21]

Considering Henry's busy concert career, it is not surprising that half of the thirty compositions known to originate in 1924 are for piano. He also completed fifteen other pieces, some of them for Leo Linder, the violinist he had met en route to Berlin. *Ensemble*, for string quintet and thunder-sticks, is his first ex- tended chamber work. Among the songs is the lovely "Where She Lies," a me- morial to Edna Smith with poetry of Edna St. Vincent Millay, which Eva Gauthier premiered at The Town Hall in 1927. Henry's progress in controlling longer forms can be heard in the "Piece for Piano with Strings" and the ensemble compositions. An orchestral piece, *Some More Music* (a sequel to the 1922 *Some Music*), may also have been written in 1924.

In early 1925, Henry's frenetic schedule included, in rapid succession, a con- cert sponsored by the New York City Board of Education, an interview with a Rome paper, a private performance for a wealthy crowd including the patroness Elizabeth Sprague Coolidge, and a concert in the Manhattan Opera House. He completed another piece for violin and piano for Leo Linder and wrote an article for *Musical America*. Celebrities abounded: as Edwin Hughes's guest at the New York Musicians' Club, he met Furtwängler, Kneisel, Rubin Goldmark, and his old nemesis Frank Damrosch. His career seemed to be accelerating, but Mrs. Varian gave him a new suit because his only one had worn out and he had no money for another.[22]

Henry now commenced his long, stormy collaboration with Edgard Varèse, to whom (Olive says) he was introduced by Ruggles.[23] Varèse's International Com- posers' Guild (ICG) by now had completed three seasons of concerts of the new- est music. While Henry may have been honored to be put on its International Advisory Board, Varèse ruled it with an iron fist. Henry almost immediately endangered their relationship by expressing reservations about Varèse's new en-semble piece *Hyperprism*.[24] Nevertheless, on February 8 the International Com-posers' Guild became the first New York organization to perform Henry's music. Varèse chose *Ensemble*, probably counting on its thunder-sticks and Henry's name to generate publicity. He bet well. Just as Henry's pianistic techniques were looking like old news, the thunder-sticks landed him another newsreel and a bi-coastal radio broadcast. Well publicized and widely reviewed, the concert gave Henry's unorthodox reputation a new impetus.[25]

The thunder-sticks, perforated boards on ropes twirled above the head, opened another door out of the Western musical mainstream, as Henry explained in a program note. "The thunder-stick is an ancient American Indian instrument, used by the Aztecs and many tribes of the Southwest in initiation ceremonies. It is with them a sacred thing, to be used only by a priest, and at night, so that the cause of the sound may not be known to the listener. It produces a soft whirring, not unlike that of the wings of a quail in flight, which is employed in *Ensemble* to form a sus-taining background for the other instruments in two of the movements."

The thunder-sticks provoked strong reactions, though not the ones that Henry wanted. One of them broke loose from its handle, flew right past the con-ductor and nearly hit one of the music critics, prompting *New Yorker* magazine to suggest selling accident insurance with concert tickets.[26] Some reviewers dis-missed the sticks as a novelty; others reacted as if a major crime had been perpe-trated. Not a single writer noticed that *Ensemble* may have been the first Western composition to incorporate a non-Western instrument as a soloist, nor did any-one mention Henry's idea that the piece could be played on any combination of instruments with the correct range and balanced tone colors. In 1963 he finally eliminated the thunder-sticks, not because of their tendency to distract the listener—which he recognized—but because they could not achieve the canonic crescendo-diminuendo that he wanted. By then they had become an attraction, however. Although Sidney kept trying to get the thunder-sticks out of the piece after Henry's death, she rarely succeeded.[27]

The Guild concert ended another winter in New York. On his way west in early March, 1925, Henry played in Chicago amid a "veritable whirl of meeting folks of importance." After his renewed encounter with Ruth Crawford, he started her career by including her in his lectures about modern composers.[28]

Henry's long absence rescued him from entanglement in a New York scene bubbling with antagonisms. After the previous ICG concert, Ruggles fumed that Varèse's newest piece was an improvement "in as much as that it held together better. But when he tried to write a melodic phrase it was the rott'nist thing you ever heard. Charlie [Seeger] is right when he says: 'Varese should stick to his per-cussion. For when he tries to write music it is the vilest stuff in the whole world.' ... I felt like a king when I went home from that concert. You know what I mean."[29]

Henry knew why Ruggles felt like a king, but also knew that Ruggles could undermine his relationship with Varèse, whose support he could not afford to lose, since the ICG dangled the hope of a cost-free New York appearance. Sensing that Varèse might back out of his commitment to program Henry's first string quartet, *Quartett Pedantic*, he began planning a concert at Aeolian Hall, toward which Blanche Walton contributed $500 [2010: $6,220]. After pondering the joint orchestral program that he and Ruggles had discussed, he concluded that it was too expensive and began planning a chamber program for February 2, 1926, including the Quartet.[30] That meant that the ICG performance six days later was no longer a premiere. Varèse must have been furious.

By this point, Henry was one of the most discussed composers since the premiere of the *Rite of Spring*. He had a committed manager and some exceptionally fine performers playing or singing his music. Opportunities as a writer were increasing; his lectures were widely praised. Yet Henry kept his thoughts about it to himself. Any blossoming egotism must have been arrested by the press's insults. One sign of modesty is his continuing interaction with the poor neighborhood children of Menlo Park, and his monthly checks to his old teacher, Mother Carrington. Halcyon was still in the picture, though increasingly marginally.[31] Indirect evidence shows that Henry was in touch with other old friends, but, apart from John Varian, only Terman shows up in the letters, usually in the context of an annual follow-up to his study of the gifted. Henry's most personal revelations can be gleaned from letters to Olive and Harry. Although in his late twenties, he still expressed being "overcome" when they approved his program notes, and asked their advice about problems with his hair and scalp. In addition to small gifts of money, Olive gave him $450 [2010: $5,600] toward the cost of another European trip, which she co-sponsored with his long-time patron, Judy Brown.[32] By now it is clear that Olive was a woman of means.

Considering his fragile financial position, the idea of starting a major new project that was unlikely to produce income seems completely counterintuitive. The first hint of something keeping him unusually busy in California is found in a letter from Varèse of June 7, 1925, which refers to Henry's intent to program *Octandre* on a California concert that could not have been a typical Cowell recital. Indeed, in August he announced the debut of "The New Music Society of California," which would present works already premiered by the International Composers' Guild. For the inaugural concert, in Los Angeles, Adolph Tandler's Little Symphony would play music by Ruggles, Varèse, Arthur Bliss, Stravinsky, and Dane Rudhyar.

The Society had germinated the previous winter, when Varèse suggested that Henry organize and direct a San Francisco branch of the International Composers' Guild. In exchange for the affiliation—more-or-less a franchise—Henry obligated himself to arrange at least one concert per season with a chamber orchestra, and observe the ICG's policy of presenting only premieres.[33] Varèse must have hoped that a western branch would renew the ICG's prestige, which sank in 1923 after his unflinching enforcement of his premieres policy drove Claire Reis and other important board members to secede from the ICG and form the rival League of Composers.[34] From Henry's perspective, the link would be an important resource for music in California.[35] He, however, may already have contemplated starting a new organization based on the League of Composers, E. Robert Schmitz's Pro Musica, or Berlin's Melos Society, which Rita Mead, the chronicler of the New Music Society, thought was the real model, not knowing that Varèse had initiated the plan. To avoid the factionalism plaguing most new music activities, Henry looked for compositions of the highest quality regardless of personal style. His nonpartisanship was quickly recognized and widely admired, the more so because he continually sought his colleagues' advice.

While aware that the New Music Society would not solve his financial problems, Henry also knew the value of a power base. Although he does not say why he started it in Los Angeles rather than San Francisco, he may have been impressed by the rapid expansion of its musical life. The Los Angeles Philharmonic Society, founded in 1878, began giving orchestral concerts ten years later; the Los Angeles Symphony was started in 1898; a Women's Orchestra of Los Angeles played from 1893 to 1913; chamber music concerts began in 1904. When Adolph Tandler, a Viennese conductor, took over the Symphony in 1913, he embraced American music and music by women. The modern Los Angeles Philharmonic (the orchestra, as opposed to the society) was founded in 1919 and supported for fifteen years by a single philanthropist. Hollywood Bowl concerts began in 1922 under Alfred Hertz. Then Los Angeles began growing exponentially as unimaginable wealth was drawn to the barren hills by oil and unlimited sun for filming. Although Henry had seemingly limitless social contacts in the San Francisco area, Buhlig may have persuaded him that the resources of money and performers were stronger in the south. Rudhyar, however, perceived a real risk because the profoundly conservative musical community still considered Debussy radically modern.[36]

Henry left almost no evidence of how he planned his society and its marketing strategies. Although he listed himself as "Organizer," he was its mastermind and source of energy. At some point he enlisted pianist Winifred Hooke as treasurer and subscription manager. A "Resident Cooperating Committee" consisting of Arthur Bliss, Henry Eichheim, and Dane Rudhyar, and a Non-Resident Advisory Board comprising Eugene Goossens, Carl Ruggles, Carlos Salzedo, and Edgard Varèse, probably were no more than window dressing. Ten musicians, spouses, or leading patrons were acknowledged as "guarantors." In addition to programming, hiring, and publicizing, Henry had to assemble a board and find financial support. His first thoughts were Mrs. Walton and the Browns, but they were not going to suffice.[37] According to Olive, Buhlig had the map to the potential goldmine that was Los Angeles.[38] The principal sponsor was Buhlig's wealthy friend Aline Barns-dall.[39] Anna de Mille (the sister-in-law of movie magnate Cecil B. de Mille and mother of choreographer Agnes de Mille) sent $25 [2010: $311] for a box at the first concert, admitting that it was odd for her to be a patron of music that she hated.[40] When Wesley Kuhnle expressed curiosity about Henry's financial stake, he pointedly replied, "I never heard of any Society which pays anything to any composer and I certainly do not derive any benefits from it. The only money I ever made on my compositions is $4.50 [2010: $56] royalties on "The Tides." Here's to the heart-ache, As ever yours, Henry-in-a-hurry."[41]

The first concert took place on October 22, 1925, in the ballroom of the Bilt-more Hotel; admission was $1.65 [2010: $20.50].[42] While the publicity flier proclaimed the new society "an affiliate of the International Composers' Guild," the credit was accidentally left off the concert program. Knowing Varèse's vola-tility, Henry asked Harry and Olive to keep the flier as evidence of the credit for the connection.[43] Rather than dwell on the relationship between the New Music Society and the ICG, however, Henry told the audience that the New Music Society aimed "to present musical works embodying the most progressive ten-dencies of this age, and disseminate the new musical ideas," comparing the era with the fourteenth century, when avant-gardists were "anathemized by the all-powerful Pope in terms strikingly similar to those used by the academic critics of our present day." Like the Church that attacked unconventional com-posers, the "Big Orchestras and the Big Publishers refuse them the means of livelihood as well as of expression."

That first program, slightly different from the one originally announced, was filled with significant advanced composers—Milhaud, Ruggles, Varèse, Orn-stein, Schoenberg, and Rudhyar. Conspicuous in its absence was Henry's own music. For an orchestra, he secured the cooperation of Adolph Tandler's Little Symphony. Henry Eichheim and Tandler shared the conducting; Arthur Bliss, who was listed on the promotional flier, had already moved back to England.[44]

Press coverage included an attractive advance piece in the *Los Angeles Times* a week before the concert.[45] The most comprehensive and comprehending review was written by Bruno David Ussher for *Saturday Night*, the details of which are less important than his general interest in and sympathy for the event, and his unfortunate dislike of Varèse's *Octandre*. Most important, the article could tempt a music lover to attend a future concert. An *Examiner* interviewer said nothing about the concert because she became distracted by Henry's idea for a new piano with four extra keys in the treble and bass and an octave pedal (to play clusters). "'The new pedal will solve many of my problems,' said Mr. Cowell. 'I have had to use the forearm for many effects because of the piano [*sic*] limita-tions. It is the same when I am writing for the instrument. I hear an idiom which must be brought to the world through a piano as yet unborn.'"[46]

A week after the concert, Henry left for New York, stopping in Salt Lake City,[47] playing in Salinas, Kansas,[48] and in Chicago and its suburb Winnetka, where he was accorded celebrity treatment. Among the "four wealthy Jews" who presented him was the mother of the famous murderer Richard Loeb. ("She is a delightful woman, and I think very courageous to appear socially.")[49] While in Chicago he got promises of performances by pianist Gitta Gradova and basso Alexander Kipnis (who does not seem to have honored his word).[50]

In Winnetka he performed with a folk singer named Clara Bloomfield, whose original name was Klara Lilien, a "titled Polish lady" with excellent connections in Warsaw. Conquered by Henry's unaffected charm, she offered to arrange concerts for him there and in Krakow—for which he would be paid a small fee[51] — and gave him introductions to the director of the Warsaw artists' club "Polonia," an American singer living in Paris who knew "everybody that counts" in Warsaw, and a Warsaw critic. If they took an interest in him, he could count on a large and appreciative audience and the attendance of other critics. In Lwów (now Lviv, Ukraine), her family would take care of him.[52] She also had a friend with "no end of friends and connections in Vienna," and a cousin in The Hague. With a date in Vienna already set, a second European tour now looked promising. (Henry reciprocated with contacts for performances in French Canada.)[53]

He continued to Montreal, where he was again treated like a celebrity, thanks to his growing personal network. Mary Lloyd, a friend of Cary de Angulo and wife of the chairman of McGill's Botany Department,[54] made the Montreal visit a whirlwind of receptions, performances, and interviews. His concert, co-sponsored by the Faculty of Music and the Departments of Physics and Psychology, became the first of many engagements sponsored by psychology departments over the next decade. Henry called it "unusually successful," with an overflowing hall and many people standing.[55] At one event, he met the botanist Vladimir Ulehla, the head of the science department at Masaryk University in Brno, who promised him concerts in Prague, Brno, Pilsen, and Mährisch-Ostrau. At a grand tea in his honor, the Czech consul-general promised to help Ulehla arrange the Prague concert.

On Saturday morning Henry attended synagogue with a prominent local violinist and teacher named Brant, probably his first experience with Jewish worship. For the Brants' twelve-year-old son Henry it was a turning point. After reviewing the boy's music, Henry urged his father to bring him to New York to study, which he did four years later, changing Henry Brant's whole life.[56] After the service Henry (Cowell) visited the head of a girl's school before an evening reception at the Lloyds' brought the trip to an exhausted end. The press gave him a warm sendoff.[57]

The trip to Chicago and Montreal was exceptionally profitable because, for once, promises were fulfilled. Uhlela became an ardent ally; Gitta Gradova performed Henry's music at Aeolian Hall in New York alongside compositions by Rudhyar,

Scriabin, and Ruth Crawford—reportedly the first public performance of her music. The *Musical Courier* reveled in the progress that modernists from the American West had made in a just few years: "From the virgin West stretching from Chicago to the Coast perhaps a new spirit is revealing itself. And we must free ourselves from centuries-old prejudices in order to listen to those songs of the new generation."[58]

Henry must have been in a fine mood in December 1925,when he arrived at Blanche Walton's home in Bronxville, to be greeted by another new suit from Mrs. Varian and a blizzard of business. Parts had to be copied for approaching orchestral performances in Los Angeles and New York; "Aeolian Harp" and "The Harp of Life"—a new piece similar to "The Tides of Manaunaun"—were going to be published by Breitkopf.[59]

His positive experiences in the Chicago area may have catalyzed his vision of using joint ventures to broaden the scope of the New Music Society. The first project was to be a recital by Gradova in San Francisco in early March 1926, with her manager providing one third of the costs. Weighing the drawing power of such a well-known pianist against the lack of money for advertising, however, Henry knew that contributors would be needed. Although he wanted to reward Gradova for performing his music and writing about him in *Musical America*, he eventually decided that the project was not feasible.[60] Nevertheless, he could see how the New Music Society would enhance his prospects for effective professional relationships, that is, deal-making.

Now that Olive had immersed herself in his entire existence,[61] Henry's letters to her become something of a journal of his life. He reported more engagements in America, requests for articles, concerts in Europe, and a projected trip to Havana with Leo Linder, all expenses paid. There were impending or promised performances of his music by tenor Roland Hayes and pianists Edwin Hughes, Margaret Nikoloric, and Calmon Lubovitzki; Hughes constantly had to repeat "The Harp of Life" at concerts in Ohio. Breitkopf accepted the *Suite for Violin and Piano*, with Blanche Walton paying a third of the costs, a huge improvement over the earlier full subsidies. Carlos Salzedo invited him to be a member of the "endorsement committee" of his National Association of Harpists. Above all, Walton had decided to back singlehandedly the $1,200 [2010: $14,800] cost of a New York recital, and divide the box office between Henry and Linder. Olive's help would not be needed beyond $100 she had already sent.[62]

Gassner now renewed his commitment to manage Henry with a three-year exclusive contract updated with agreements about receipts from radio and mechanical reproduction. All appearances west of a line drawn north and south passing through Denver were to be under the direction of the "Western Management of Henry Cowell," namely, Olive,[63] saving Henry from having to pay Gassner a fee for engagements that he could not possibly have arranged and keeping Henry in control of work in California.

If Henry was convinced that the West was more open to his ideas than the East, he was rudely awakened when Tandler's Little Symphony gave the Los Angeles premiere of parts of *A Composition* for ensemble, with Winifred Hooke as soloist on stringpiano. The hall was full, but the critics were unanimously unconvinced. Even his old supporter Bruno David Ussher felt that Henry had entered a musical cul-de-sac. "Mr. Cowell is too sane, not to realize that he has made a plaything out of an instrument."[64]

Whatever the value of *A Composition*, Ussher was right. To grow as a composer, Henry had to shed his reputation as an ultramodernist pianist. He therefore proposed that his next New York appearance, February 2, 1926, at Aeolian Hall, be the joint orchestral concert that he and Ruggles had often discussed. It was too expensive, however; Mrs. Walton's gift would only be a step toward the total costs, some four to six times as much.[65] Retaining the general concept, he reduced the concert to a chamber music program billed as Leo Linder's New York debut, with world premieres of *A Composition* for stringpiano with ensemble (of which only parts had been played) and *Chapter in Seven Paragraphs* for string quartet; the New York premiere of the *Suite for Violin and Piano*, and five piano pieces. He engaged top-quality performers, principals or members of the New York Philharmonic and internationally known solo and chamber players. A sympathetic pre-concert feature in *Musical America*[66] quoted Henry's much recycled remark that he had tried to catalog the sounds he had created on the piano but gave up at 165. Gassner earned no points for the article, however; it was the work of Henry's California friend Ray Brown.[67] Henry promoted his concert at a meeting of the Bohemians (New York Musicians' Club) and benefited from Roland Hayes's performance of "The Fairy Fountain" at Carnegie Hall.

In comparison with the uniform snickers at Henry's 1923 concerts, the reviews represented a large range of opinion. Hostility and sarcasm abated, as did nationwide circulation of sensationalized articles. Several writers, who may have derived their comments from an article by Pierre Key, said that they didn't like the music but were startled to meet people who did. Henry's experiments impressed some; others wrote that the experiments obstruct his talent. Some lukewarm reactions may have resulted from overblown expectations of a spectacle, however. Descriptions of the audience at the Aeolian Hall concert also diverge. Some writers emphasized a warm reception, others cited laughter and rushing for the exits. There is not even a consensus about the size of the crowd. Henry's report to Harry was, however, unequivocal. He called the concert a grand success, with a cordial audience of 1,200—an odd estimate since the hall is described as seating 1,100. In this case, some evaluation is possible. The financial returns imply an audience with 500 to 900 paid admissions. Presumably free tickets were also distributed. "I played numerous encores, and took five bows after the orchestra number. 'The Banshee' had to be repeated." There was much less amusement in the audience than in the past, and the critics seemed much more serious. Linder, however, who had been a success elsewhere, was "a rank failure" in New York.[68]

Henry's letters manifest remarkable resilience and an ability to find the positive amid the discouraging. Indeed, his stamina in the face of vicious negativity is impressive, especially because an element of the press sometimes seemed determined to discredit him.[69] The concert was a milestone in other senses. It was Henry's final major New York recital and the end of the road for Aeolian Hall, which closed shortly thereafter. The space became a dime store.[70]

After the concert he reported more good news. A promotional recital at Knabe Hall drew representatives of Knabe's Ampico player-piano division and "buyers" for music clubs and universities in Iowa, Michigan, Missouri, and New York. Gassner claimed to have persuaded Knabe to give Henry a salaried tour next season. Curwen was about to issue the song "Manaunaun's Birthing"; Breitkopf had published the *Suite for Violin and Piano* and accepted "The Harp of Life," but had postponed publishing "Aeolian Harp" until they could determine the likely future of the stringpiano. It sat on Breitkopf's shelf until Quincke published it in Los Angeles in 1930 and is now one of Henry's most popular piano pieces.[71]

That report to Olive and Harry was written from shipboard as Henry and Linder sailed to Europe.

Europe Again (1926)

Henry used the transatlantic sail to write two articles and contemplate a peaceful life in California.[1] When they arrived at Schmolke's pension in late February, conditions in Berlin had changed enormously. With the German economy stabilized by the renegotiation of war reparations, prices were about the same as in America.[2] What Henry did not report was much more consequential—an unstable government, a near-civil war between left and right, bookstores selling Hitler's newly published *Mein Kampf*. In Italy, a socialist delegate to parliament had been murdered by the fascists; Poland teetered on the edge of dictatorship. Henry, nevertheless, hoped that this tour would be calmer and more productive than the first one.[3] He immediately dove into endless organizational problems, studied a bit of Polish, met many Berlin musicians at a party hosted by Buhlig, and enjoyed a cordial visit with Schnabel, who invited him to dinner with Schoenberg after his Warsaw concerts. All the while Henry had to keep tabs on business back home.[4]

His career seemed to be advancing. More and more pianists were programming his music; a dancer was to choreograph a piece; the Quintet with thundersticks had been promised a spot in the November Gruppe's next season, in exchange for Henry producing something by its director, Max Butting, in California. To Henry's amazement, a German children's book contained a story about his playing.[5]

For the Berlin concert, Henry again diversified his program by featuring Linder in three pieces. Assuming there would be advantages in giving the critics advance exposure to his music, he played privately for Rudolf Kastner and Adolf Weissmann. It paid off with a reasonably sympathetic notice from Kastner acknowledging the audience's warmth,[6] and a short, pleasant note by Weissmann in *B.Z. am Mittag* (March 30). Otherwise, most critics remained suspicious, hostile, or frivolous. The quantity of reviews—twelve—compensated for their mixed quality, however. *Tageblatt*'s "K.W." compared his music to watery MacDowell and alluded to an unwanted humorous effect of the programmatic content. Two reviews, one by Stuckenschmidt, were reprinted in Paris and Prague.

Henry and Linder played on March 29 at the Polish Artists Club in Warsaw. Despite their reservations about the quality of Henry's compositions, the press's warm reception of his color palette and his methods of playing portended an open-minded attitude in Eastern Europe and revived the question of how much the usual sarcastic reviews mirrored the audience's response. *Express Czerwony* (Red Express), said that while the critics, with their professional, noble bearing "had uncertain facial expressions—smile to be pleasant or mad?—Music lovers right from the start applauded with bravos . . . moved by the originality of invention and the undeniable value of the interpretation."[7] Henry later told the *Los Angeles Times* that he had to stop his performance to convince the audience that he actually was playing a normal piano. Otherwise he had nothing to say about Poland,[8] or about Linder, whose name is conspicuously absent from the reviews.

On the other hand, he left plentiful documentation of their stay in Czechoslovakia. Although Stuckenschmidt had written only lukewarmly about him in Prague's *Auftakt* (Upbeat), Henry found allies among the ethnic Czechs, especially scientists. Vladimir Ulehla, the Brno botany professor at Masaryk University, whom he had met in Montreal,[9] arranged a lecture-recital at the Association of Moravian Composers and a concert sponsored by the Moravian Urania, a "people's" cultural and educational association, where Henry prefaced his performance with an introduction about his background, the American rural and urban landscape, and the rational foundation of his work.[10] In Prague, František Pospíšil, director of the Moravian Museum, arranged a lecture-recital at the Conservatory and a concert under the auspices of Prague's Society for Modern Music.[11] Henry especially enjoyed a tour of Alois Hába's Department of Quarter-Tone Music at the Conservatory. A vocal ensemble using extended techniques must have been the inspiration for Henry's astonishing score *Atlantis*, for orchestra and three howling singers.

Before the Brno concert, conservative music lovers kept asking Ulehla if Henry's music was "serious enough."[12] Nevertheless the hall was full, with Janáček, the association's president, in attendance and "most enthusiastic."[13] A reviewer, the contemporary-music pianist and writer Dr. Ludvík Kundera, expressed reservations about the compositions but was persuaded that Henry was not a charlatan.[14] The Prague recital—preceded by a lecture by Henry on overtones—was also packed, with twenty-five people standing. "There was an amazing pitch of enthusiasm demonstrated by the audience," he wrote his parents, "who applauded and called for me to play many encores. Nearly all the most famous composers of this country were present, and many critics." Hába stated publicly "that my music was not only new, but also well written, and showed fine invention." Janáček, he added, made a similar statement.[15]

A trip with Ulehla and Pospíšil was the highlight of his stay in Czechoslovakia, and in many respects a turning point in his life. A two-hour train ride from

Brno, a ride on a local railway, and a drive across roads designed for oxcarts, brought them to the foothills of the Carpathian Mountains, where Henry admired brightly colored houses, costumes, and local paintings that showed "much greater artistic grasp than the works of many who live in Greenwich Village attics, and make high pretensions." He was the first American to visit Velka, a village where the peasants wore traditional costumes "of colors so gay as to beggar description." Although they often resented outsiders, they knew and loved Pospíšil, accepted his friends, and invited them to folk dancing in the town hall, with "an orchestra of old men who happened to play [a kind of bagpipe], together with trumpet and clarinet, and who knew the traditional music of the district. This tradition, perhaps centuries old, includes many effects we have considered to be of recent invention in 'modern' music, many things not to be found in any known music new or old, and above all, a method of procedure of its own." Henry "committed the extravagance" of spending $2.00 [2010: $24.63] for two small pieces of embroidery, one of them two centuries old.

He also realized that because travel and communication between villages was very problematic, every village had its own culture, "and probably one could find a new basic music every few miles, each quite different from the other in conception. Fascinating possibility! Be that as it may, I heard only the music of one such district, and it seemed to me important enough to form the basis of a new art music, a new conception of what may induce musical pleasure." Not a single urban Czech musician that Henry met had any conception of the distinctiveness of rural music, however, or any interest in going to hear it. Well-educated Moravian composers adapted folk music by squeezing it into a Germanic theoretical framework, leaving it devitalized and with "very little resemblance to the fresh music of the mountains. Yet those who write in this fashion are fervently convinced that they are writing Czechish music, and the rest of the world knows Czechish music only through their works."[16]

With activities in Czechoslovakia complete, he and Linder went to Vienna for a concert in the small auditorium of the Musikverein on April 21, attended by several hundred. Of the two extant reviews, the one in the *Wiener Morgenzeitung* perceptively emphasized the new world of overtones in Henry's music and urged the readers to keep an eye on him.[17] The other critic consigned Henry to the variety hall.[18] A visit with Alban Berg is the only other thing Henry mentioned about their stay. They then made the short trip to Bratislava for concerts on April 22 and 23, before audiences of several hundred. One reviewer referred to booing, several to laughter; some of them insisted that Henry's techniques were not new, others thought they were really novel; some called the music uninteresting, others, fascinating. Another writer doubtless spoke for many countrymen in warning against letting European art "be replaced by the art of America, Africa, Asia, the art of the Zulukafiors, etc." It seems that most of the audience enjoyed the concert while some musicians disliked it intensely.[19] Like Henry, one critic recognized that an audience could not be blamed for reacting against music about which it had received no guidance.

They must have left for Poland before receiving a depressing letter from Bartók describing a very bad season in Budapest and advising him not to lose money playing in an empty hall for hostile critics.[20] A concert in Budapest had already been arranged for April 28 in the great hall of the municipal auditorium, however. (Henry probably paid all the expenses since no sponsoring body was credited.) Linder, growing tired of playing Henry's music and unhappy about being ignored by reviewers, opened with some short eighteenth-century pieces. Unfortunately, Bartók's instincts were correct, at least about the press's hostility and mirth. The metaphor of boxing and the "Euro-American art market's" obsession with novelty sold well. Henry was not even credited with inventiveness, and Linder came off badly in two of the three reviews.[21] The audience may have felt otherwise, however, because Henry later said that he found an astounding interest in new music in Hungary, Czechoslovakia, and Poland.[22]

Henry may have recalled telling Olive and Harry before leaving for Europe that Linder felt calm,[23] a comment with alarming implications that "calm" was not Linder's normal state. Indeed, Linder refused to play at the next concert, in Venice,[24] forcing Henry to insert more solos and costing him the variety that he had wanted. Fortunately, the critic of *Gazetto di Venezia* got past the acrobatics to find the music so noteworthy, curious, and suggestive that "the audience was taken by it and compensated the artist with effusive applause."[25] Other papers took the same line although they felt that too many pieces were similar.[26] The critic of *l'Italia* earned a place in Sidney's later compilation of "Especially Horrendous Early Reviews": "The music of Cowell is the ultimate modern degeneration of the *basso continuo*. The audience seemed to enjoy having its hair stand on end, for it applauded long and warmly." Despite the humor, the passage gave a positive impression of the audience's response, which, according to Henry, started cold and "[grew] into warm applause at the end." An expected anti-demonstration did not materialize.[27]

In Paris he was greeted by a letter from Linder declining to play if he had to play the thunder-stick piece again.[28] He had disappeared to the companionship of an American woman who surprised Henry with a check for $30, which he returned to avoid being indebted to her,[29] although he could have applied it to the $50 [2010: $616] price of new fliers and the nuisance of revising all the remaining concerts. He wrote John Varian that although the tour had been "surprisingly successful, with large and enthusiastic houses and better press notices," he was sick of the whole business. "I suppose I should be full of news, but I am not—I do nothing except give concerts, and the much business connected with them—enveigling people into going—I do not think I shall try playing in Europe again, but hope to visit the Orient in two years." Varian's warm reply cheered him,[30] as did a letter from Schmolke, who complained that Henry had no time for her.[31] A very upsetting letter from Ellen Veblen, however, was her last extant communication. Extremely ill, she was turning into a kind of hermit.[32]

Linder's cancellation wrecked Henry's plan to present Paris premieres at his concert in the Salle Pleyel on May 21 and forced him to concoct a completely new program to avoid repeating his 1923 performance. The reviews say nothing of Henry's impact. (Linder was still listed on the program, which must already have been printed.) An undocumented private performance of "The Banshee" gave Paul Henry Lang a story that he loved to tell his students decades later, when he and Henry were colleagues at Columbia.[33] In 1926, Lang was studying musicology at the Sorbonne and probably met Henry through Henri Prunières, whom Lang was assisting. When Henry requested Lang's help at a private concert, Lang replied that his only instrument was bassoon, but Henry said not to worry, just wear a black tie and appear at a certain house. At the performance, Lang said, "I held the pedal and Henry climbed into the piano!"

Very little else is known about his time in Paris. Two new-music societies proposed to arrange something for him, but he never again performed there. Gian Francesco Malipiero gave him a letter of introduction to Stravinsky, but there is no evidence that they met this time,[34] which was too bad in view of Henry's growing contempt for his latest music.[35] A visit with Henrietta can be presumed.

Henry now went to Dublin to see Harry's father. In Galway and Kildare he was surprised to hear Gaelic spoken openly; it was Year Four of the Irish Free State and the language was now legal. Such moments helped him to forge a connection with his paternal culture as it existed then, not just as he knew it through Varian's retelling of the myths. In Birmingham he visited his Uncle Huntley, who took him to Shakespeare's home in Stratford, Kenilworth Castle, and Tintern Abbey.[36] From there he went to London for a Wigmore Hall recital on June 16 without Linder. Fortunately, Paul Bechert's report about the Vienna concert, which had just appeared in *Musical Times*, was extremely positive.[37]

The press coverage of the London concert, however, was distinguished almost entirely by its quantity. Eight articles appeared immediately after the concert, most of them in tabloids that behaved in character. The *Daily News* got his name wrong; The *Star*'s review was headlined "Piano Punching"; the *Daily Telegraph* was all sarcasm. Only the *Daily Mail* acknowledged that "The Banshee" "struck the audience's fancy and we encored it" but could not resist saying that "the housemaid at home, when she dusts the piano, often gives us an unconscious imitation of Mr. Cowell's art."[38] The *Evening Standard*'s view might be regarded as complimentary. "He has a mighty left, and his ring-craft is much to be admired. Executants in this effete land who wish to get talked about should plan to have themselves given a few lessons by this pianist from 'the wide, open spaces where men are men.'" The *Westminster Gazette* lamented that Henry overlooked the possibility of using the nose, knees, and feet, wondering if the "much fun and roars of laughter" was attributable to the music or his commentaries. *Eve* offered its best pun: Cowell made "a decided hit." Although the *Sunday Express* compared him with the great clown Grock, it at least admitted that Vienna had listened to him seriously. (Presumably the writer had seen Bechert's review.) "Mr. Cowell played several of his own compositions consecutively. He might try playing them all at once by lying down on the keyboard."

In this obnoxious atmosphere, two of nearly two dozen other reviews deserve mention for their rare rationality. The *Musical Herald*:

> One's only difficulty is to try to form any opinion on a new medium on the limited experience of one concert. This much can be said. One listened with an extraordinary exhilaration—an exhilaration which persists in one's recollection. There were strong demands for repetition in several cases, but it was only in "The Banshee," the most extreme of his pieces, that Mr. Cowell yielded to them. In "The Harp of Life" an extraordinarily massive climax was worked up by the use of double arpeggios played by both forearms, clustering round fortissimo chords. We understand that in the States, Mr. Cowell has many determined followers. When more of them have played his music here, it will be easier to forecast its future.[39]

The Sackbut's editor Ursula Greville came down on Henry's side with a nononsense attack on incompetent journalists. Critics are necessary, she wrote, because of their clear vision and honest desire to serve the art, "yet, when a definitely new problem is presented to our critics, they do not even attempt to function, as at Henry Cowell's recent concert, whereof the various notices appearing the next day were mostly filled with any sort of cheap witticism and contained none of the considered judgment on a novelty that the critics were invited (and presumably paid) to write."[40] (Disclosure: she was married to Kenneth Curwen, one of Henry's publishers.)

Making It in America, Scene 2

Back in the United States, Henry had good news in the form of a concert that for once paid a decent fee. Unfortunately, there was also bad news: Copland had publicly called him "essentially an inventor, not a composer," though allowing at least that "his most interesting experiments have been those utilizing the strings of the piano. The *Banshee*, when performed in a small room, is musical noise of a most fascinating kind. Perhaps if Cowell develops along these lines he may even make a distinctive path for himself as composer."[1] Henry attributed the slap to Copland's desire to be the sole leader of American music. One must grant, however, that if all that Copland knew was pieces like "The Tides of Manaunaun" or "The Banshee," in which arrestingly fresh techniques are combined with extremely simple melodies, his attitude is understandable. "Piece for Piano with Strings," conventionally played pieces like "Dynamic Motion" or the extraordinary rhythm studies for chamber ensemble, might have struck him differently. The damage was done, however. Copland's disparaging assessment was certainly a major cause of the competitiveness with him that marred Henry's next decade.

After a few weeks with Blanche Walton in Bronxville,[2] Henry drove to California, stopping as usual to see Clarence in Des Moines. The known events of the summer of 1926 lay at the extremes: Harry's third and lasting marriage, to Olive, and the death of Ellen Veblen at sixty-seven. She had settled at Halcyon almost penniless, and when the Halcyoners realized she was dying, they simply delivered her to Evelyn Wells's parents, who could do nothing more than ask Stanford to take charge of arrangements. Adding to the indignities, an obituary dwelt on Thorstein Veblen rather than Ellen, though it honored her patronage of Henry.[3] She had bequeathed the Halcyon house to him, another one in Carmel to Evelyn Wells, and a brooch and her remaining cash to Evelyn's mother. Since all houses in Halcyon were owned in common, however, Henry received next to nothing. Evelyn did no better. The Carmel house probably was valuable, but the papers of ownership were incomplete.[4]

Sidney's later attempt to make sense of the relationship between Henry and Ellen foundered on the absence of tangible information. Three of her poems are so passionate that, as Evelyn wrote Henry and Sidney in 1962, they were "the sort of thing one would be reluctant to expose to those who do not know the almost terrible innocence and purity of her love. Her poetry is her emotional history and it breaks the heart."[5] Sidney inferred that they drifted apart because Henry became nervous about her desire to join him in New York and rejected her proposal too bluntly. If so, he probably was even more uncomfortable for having originally encouraged her. It seems more likely that her instability was the villain.

Evelyn Wells felt that without Ellen, "Henry Cowell would have been but he would have been longer finding the way and her adoration of him helped at a time when there was no one to help him, when his mother was dying, and there was no hope in his life." Attributing her own success as a writer to Ellen's inspiration, Evelyn added, "Henry and I were well aware of what she meant for us. She was our spiritual guardian, and her intelligence, her love of the outdoors, of games and play, above all music and poetry and art, were poured over us."[6] Her demise, along with Clarissa's death, Jaime de Angulo's increasing eccentricity, and rapid development of the virgin West Coast, was another sign that Henry's California paradise was becoming a fading dream.

Henry's relationship with his father was still vexing. Sometime around 1926 Olive took notes on Henry's comments about Harry.

> Perfectly inscrutable—never can tell how he is going to act. "I don't know him at all." Temperament of an artist—He feels that he has been a failure, and that I carry on. [illegible] over everything—always—a mask of which he is unconscious. Will never go out of his way for anyone. Likes only those people who are really interesting and have brains. Age is telling on him. Tries to avoid reverting to childhood. Notions he has are preconceived—sometimes of his former self. Thinks he is a wit and wants to live up to his former self. Never had a paternal feeling toward me, although acted the part to perfection but unconscious of what he was doing. His early environment still has hold of him hence his efforts to rebel. Has always been interested in music, and became interested in me when I began to show achievement in music.

Here too, the truth is elusive. Olive's love for Harry blinded her to his weaknesses; Harry may still have been acting out the role of the good father; Henry may have been unready to acknowledge any of Harry's genuine love, which Olive saw embodied in the picture of Henry that Harry kept on his washstand—"the favorite son."[7] One thing is certain, however—Henry was very happy to give him jobs that would help advance his own work, and Harry was equally happy to help. The case can even be made that Henry was exploiting him.

Henry's only major concert for the rest of 1926, at San Francisco's Fairmont Hotel on October 31, garnered mountains of publicity but few important engagements. He later remembered traveling widely without experiencing protests or disturbances, but only playing at private or semi-private events that Gassner mustered through Henry's friends.[8] The public seemed difficult to arouse because radio and recordings catered to popular taste and concert programs rarely ventured beyond the customary. Thanks to the lull, however, Henry had time to compose and run the New Music Society.

One private event, at which, surprisingly, Linder played, was a prelude to the New Music Society's November 20 concert at the Los Angeles Biltmore Hotel. By now, the organization had expanded: Winifred Hooke was treasurer; the conductor Tandler replaced Arthur Bliss on the Resident Cooperating Committee. The Non-Resident Advisory Board comprised Bliss, Alfredo Casella, Ruth Crawford, Alois Hába, Malipiero, and five Hungarians—Bartók, Pál Kadosa, Kodály, István Szelényi, and Imre Weisshaus. The concert embraced the stylistic diversity that was rapidly earning Henry friends—quartets by Milhaud, Casella, and himself, Schoenberg's Op. 23 piano pieces and Rudhyar's *Moments* for piano; and the string version of Ruggles's *Lilacs* and *Angels*, which was encored. Henry concluded the concert playing his brand-new "Sleep Music of the Dagna" for piano strings, "The Trumpet of Angus Og" (a diatonic tone-cluster piece), and "The Snows of Fuji-Yama," a pentatonic tone-cluster piece. Reduced circulation of the reviews through the wire services implies that Henry's notoriety was wearing off. The *New York Times* claimed that the New Music Society was organizing annual exchanges of music with many groups in Europe,[9] but the moment was not quite ripe for such grand plans to yield concrete results .

To settle accounts with the New Music Society's sponsor, Aline Barnsdall, Henry had to miss Thanksgiving with Harry and Olive.[10] This may have been the occasion when Barnsdall pulled out, causing Henry to move the concerts to San Francisco. From then until the end of the year, his only public performances were lecture-recitals. In San Jose he spoke while dressed in an "heirloom of a [Czechoslovak] peasant family bestowed upon him in recognition of his work in gathering and preserving the folk songs of that nation." (That was unquestionably an exaggeration.)[11]

After "Harmonic Development in Music," Henry published no articles for four years. When he resumed writing in 1925, clarity, directness, and informality—combined with an authority denied to most journalists—brought him a continuous series of commissions from magazines and newspapers. Unique professional experiences added spice to his appeal for rational thinking and good collegial manners. His search for a scientific basis for modernism was much deeper than public relations, however; it was the natural union of his twin talents.

His articles of ca. 1925–27 summarize his thinking as his career was gaining momentum.[12] Foremost in his mind was the damage to modernism wrought by composers who turned "modern" just to seem new. Since music lovers eager to evaluate new compositions received no guidance from the feeble press, they excoriated all modernist ideas, unaware of the difference between fine music and incompetent imitations. The larger reputation of American music was also damaged when compositions with very little merit were performed with real enthusiasm, creating the impression that this was the best that the country had to offer. The obsession with defining an "American sound" was also destructive because it sidelined excellent composers, such as Ruggles, whose music did not meet the criteria. Henry frequently assailed the influential Parisian-Stravinskian neoclassicism as pure note-spinning. For a truly new experience he recommended Varèse, who had virtually eliminated harmony and most melody.

Yet if it seems that Henry's overall aim was to promote modernism, he also defended composers of quality who were conventional harmonically but explored innovations in melody and rhythm. He himself was already moving in a new direction as he followed his instinct to avoid slavish adherence to any single style. His new *Suite for Violin and Piano* (1925), for example, combined neo-baroque gestures with tone clusters.

The culminating article of the mid-1920s, "The Process of Musical Creation," was suggested by Sam Seward, completed in June 1925, and published in *The American Journal of Psychology*,[13] signed "Henry Cowell, Stanford University." Intended for psychologists, "The Process of Musical Creation" formalizes the 1917 discussion with Terman (surveyed in Chapter 6), where Henry described how he learned to hear music in his mind, rejected inspiration, and sought to control sound. The entirely internal process of working in pure sound—learning to hear in multiple layers, gradually becoming able to write down one part while not forgetting the rest, and dealing with the disappointment that the "external" version was so weak in comparison with the internal—had convinced him that a performance cannot realize more than about 10 percent of the composer's vision, that nothing was as "rich and beautiful" as that internal image. However, he also learned to write at any time, "controlling a flow of musical sounds at will" and shutting off the flow when he did not have time to work. By the time of this article, experience had taught him that after the long, internal process of finding the finest form for his ideas, he could barely change a note in the written-out form of a composition. (It became his life-long practice simply to move on to another piece if he felt serious flaws in one that was newly completed.) He also was unable to discover "the exact relationship . . . if there be one, between my musical creations and the experiences which have preceded it, either immediately or remotely."

He could only say that his musical ideas "seem to be an exact mirror of my emotions of the moment, or of moments which I recall through memory."

Henry's remarks were especially timely because one of the fruits of this very productive period is the celebrated stringpiano piece "The Banshee," a kind of etude based on the sonic properties of piano strings when rubbed, stroked, and strummed in different ways. It is a perfect example of his stylistic dualism: the stunning effects are embedded in a simple, conservative structure. "The Banshee" is inextricably associated with its title, which tells of the Irish household ghost that wails as it ascends to Earth to fetch the spirit of the departed. Seeing how titles can distract the listener from perceiving the composition itself, he considered removing them from concert programs. In 1929 he told Nicholas Slonimsky, the versatile Russian émigré pianist, conductor, and composer whom he had met early in 1928:

> The interest in the Banshee, for example, is not that it suggests a Banshee, but in the remarkable number of subtle qualities of tone, and the way in which they are built into musical form. The name of the Banshee was added after the piece was written, to give the musical idea to people who do not have good enough ears to take interest in the music itself, without some exterior prop, such as a literary suggestion. The fact that the title proves to be a good one, insofar as it has a strong suggestion of reality in the music, does not remove the purely musical values from the music, nor should the title cause the music to be discredited as such . . . [14]

This issue of the illusory relationship between a composition and its title became one of Henry's major concerns and may explain why more and more of his music bears generic titles like Suite or Composition. Moreover, those pieces demonstrate that his description of his lack of a compositional "manner" was not just rationalization. His ability to write in dramatically opposed styles, which Seeger noticed a decade before, has remained one of the most intriguing and perplexing aspects of his music. Like his writing, his music stems from his search for novel solutions for individual problems.

"The Process of Musical Creation" also is a sign of Henry's growing relationship with the world of academic psychology. On December 9, 1926, he spoke at Stanford's psychology department, where Paul Farnsworth (1899–1978), then in his second year on the faculty, was conducting research into the psychology of music.[15] Since Terman was unable to attend he solicited two reports on Henry's visit that are excellent portraits of him at nearly thirty. Dorothea Jensen, Terman's assistant, said "I had somehow expected him to be somewhat taller than he is—he is perhaps 5 ft. 3 in. tall, and probably weighs about 130 pounds— Dr. [Walter] Miles says he impresses him as being more slight than when he has seen him previously. . . . Although Henry is rather neat and fairly well dressed, he is not what one would call scrupulously neat in dress and personal appearance. Although poverty does not now press him so closely as it used to, I gather that he is not becoming wealthy by any means."

Some twenty to thirty people heard Henry's talk, "The Psychology of Music as it Relates to Composers," which focused on current research rather than Henry's personal development. According to Jensen, his material and his excellent English made a strong impression. He dwelt on experiments, using some 200 University of California students, on perception of consonance and dissonance, which showed that some of them found combinations universally accepted as consonances to be dissonant; and some combinations called discords were found consonant. (A report by Farnsworth said that Henry was involved in the experiment, but not when or how.) He criticized textbooks for not taking into account changes in harmony, citing as evidence some chords that in popular music remain unresolved and proposing that jazz therefore could be a better guide to what people currently thought was permissible. Testing interested Henry greatly; but he felt that the widely praised Seashore tests of musicality did not reveal true talent. He ended by playing some of his pieces and discussing the acoustics behind them.

In touring the psychology laboratory with Henry, Jensen saw that he understood the mathematics and physics of Farnsworth's experimental equipment. She concluded that he was "much more of the scientist than I had ever thought one with such marked musical ability could be," and recommended that Stanford furnish Henry facilities to work out his ideas experimentally.[16]

Paul Farnsworth, who was very well informed about the newest ideas, had his own quarter-tone organ, and knew Henry already, thought Henry understood sound as well as any acoustician and knew the possibilities of the piano better than any piano builder. His combination of artistry and scientific ability was extremely striking; his ideas, while not the product of controlled laboratory conditions, were novel and led to important results. He was impressed by the serenity with which Henry received the caustic opposition to his work. "He probably rationalizes this by the knowledge that all musical radicals have been laughed at and maligned at first. . . . Cowell's early tics seem to have practically disappeared. His general health seems good . . . His buoyancy is most apparent and his laugh pleasant. . . . Henry Cowell combines a most pleasing personality with extraordinary musical talents. Altho a radical he appears to be close enough to tradition to be accepted. He is still able, however, to disturb the musical conservatives not a little."[17]

After the New Year the general mode of Henry's life continued. Concerning his performances from early 1927 until his departure for his third European tour two years later we need only observe that he covered a lot of the United States, encountering so many irritations and empty promises that he would gladly have given up the whole enterprise and stayed in California if he had not needed the income. At the same time, his frequent concerts reduced the shock of his methods and led to better press even in small towns where he had never previously played. Reviewers describe large, responsive audiences, musicians snapping up copies of his music, and so on.

While he would have preferred that his music speak for itself, his unpretentious lecturing and writing did wonders for his public image. "Buyers" who engaged artists for concerts, however, remained unpersuaded. After Henry performed for the Associated Managers in September 1928, the frustrated Gassner warned him that he needed financial backing to mount a major campaign. Even so, Henry would still have to exploit his personal contacts.[18] According to Sidney, the endless aggravation made Henry a very nervous performer.[19]

The next best thing to major sponsorship was to have his own power base. His integrity kept the New Music Society from becoming a vehicle for his sole benefit, but he was not above making reciprocal arrangements, as he sought opportunities for all composers. When he saw that unconventional American scores could not be found in Europe,[20] he realized that the problem of giving new music maximum exposure was even greater than he had imagined. Interested performers could not get scores because commercial publishers avoided unusual music. Without performances, new languages would never be absorbed. Henry concluded that composers urgently needed to get their music into print if their audience was to be greater than those few who attended rare concerts.

Sensible people without a reliable income would be cautious about launching a second project that promised to drain personal resources. Fortunately, Henry, undeterred by realism or common sense, decided to create a quarterly magazine of new scores. Before he could begin, however, one problem needed attention— the matter of whether Charles Seeger had once had the same idea. Around 1915 Schirmer had invited Seeger to edit a new journal called *Musical Quarterly*. When Seeger, uninterested in talking *about* music, demurred, Oscar Sonneck was appointed. Although *MQ*'s format was unrelated to Henry's vision, he did not want Seeger to feel he had stolen an old idea. Seeger responded that he could not have cared less. His increasingly leftward orientation had led him to dismiss concert music as the music of the elite. He also doubted that he would have thought about a score-publishing project in 1915, when there was essentially no American avant-garde to publish.[21]

Shortly after arriving in Menlo Park at the end of April 1927, Harry, Olive, and Henry went to the ocean near Cazadero, where they camped in a canyon by moonlight. "So exquisite I could hardly sleep," wrote Olive. "We talked a lot on this trip about the possibility of his publishing some music and hit upon the title

New Music as the most satisfactory. Harry and I gave him the first hundred dollars to start New Music; a few others also contributed."[22] The quarterly journal, containing only scores and no prose at all, would be unparalleled anywhere in the world.[23] In retrospect, Seeger felt that the timing was right. *New Music* began to appear just as American music was making a transition from elitist to a broad middle-class pursuit.[24]

Henry immediately solicited Blanche Walton's support, emphasizing that his magazine would have more permanent value than a concert.[25] Without even waiting for her response he started gathering scores. Ruggles agreed to let Henry publish "Lilacs," from *Men and Mountains*, and found backing to print the other movements as well,[26] ensuring that *Men and Mountains* would be the distinguished debut volume of *New Music Quarterly*. Blanche Walton's $100 [2010: $1,230][27] guaranteed the magazine's first issue. Henry planned to cover costs through subscriptions, of which, as of early July 1927, he already had thirty-six before even beginning to solicit.[28] Subscriptions, in fact, were crucial: a single mailing had devoured the contributions. He began by approaching his Halcyon friends and ultimately signed some 8,000 letters of solicitation, adding personal notes on many of them.[29] Meanwhile, he broadened the New Music Society's advisory board with Alban Berg, and persuaded Leopold Stokowski to lend his name as an Honorary Member. The second volume was assigned to Rudhyar's *Paeans*; Ornstein offered material for the third issue,[30] to which Henry added music by Imre Weisshaus. The first year was rounded off with Carlos Chávez's *Sonatina*. In committing the fifth volume to Ruth Crawford, *New Music* became her only publisher.

It was soon obvious that even the subscriptions would not cover the bills and *New Music Quarterly* needed a sponsor. This time, a fortuitous dinner engagement came to the rescue. One evening the previous winter, pianist Margaret Nikoloric—who had recently recorded "Tides" for player-piano—and her husband Arthur, a Serbian-born lawyer,[31] had dined with the wealthy insurance executive Charles Ives and his wife. Mrs. Nikoloric, who knew Ruggles through Henry, had never heard of Ives.[32] Upon learning that he composed, she realized the importance of introducing Henry to him. Although Henry knew of Ives, Seeger and Ruggles had convinced him that he was a phony whose music was not worth a look. As a result, he never saw any until 1927, a year after Ives stopped composing.[33] Henry never said who or what changed his opinion.[34]

In his first letter to Ives, July 27, 1927, Henry requested his music, solicited a subscription, and offered him honorary membership on the advisory board of the New Music Society.[35] Ives accepted, apparently thinking that Henry had in mind a circulating library.[36] Henry then extended his hope for a meeting—which Ives's poor health and Henry's absence in California had so far prevented—offered additional copies of *New Music Quarterly*, and repeated his desire to receive Ives's compositions.[37] This simple exchange forged a relationship that ensured the long-term life of *New Music Quarterly*, the rapid growth of American composition, and the first broad circulation of Ives's music. It also was an early instance of the problem that historians have faced since the late 1920s, because their letters imply conversations by telephone, which was newly available to private subscribers. Fortunately, they wrote often enough to permit tracking their friendship's progress.

From the beginning, Henry understood the need for diplomacy.

> When I first met him, he was still in his office. He had a couch in his office, and received me lying down. If we began to talk about anything really interesting in music, he would turn red and have a little heart attack. And . . . you had to avoid certain subjects entirely. I found out, he didn't like Haydn, as I found that you mustn't mention Haydn at all. He didn't like [Walter] Damrosch, so you mustn't mention Damrosch. I finally found out about Damrosch, because as a young man Ives had taken Damrosch a Scherzo. This Scherzo was in three-four and two-four simultaneously, and so then Damrosch took this and said, "Well, young man, make up your mind."
>
> Ives was so angered by this, to think that Damrosch wouldn't consider the matter of playing both two and three together at the same time, that he'd always had this awful peeve about Damrosch. He lived right across the street from the Mannes School, and he would sometimes shake his fist at it, because of the fact that [Mannes had] married into the Damrosch family.[38]

Ives promised to contribute $50 [2010: $628] per month. Moreover, "when he found out that *New Music* . . . was a nonprofit undertaking, whose slogan was: 'If it will sell, we won't accept it,' he allowed me to publish his works." Nevertheless, Henry assumed ultimate financial responsibility, which obligated him to cover annual deficits of up to $100.[39] At the same time, Henry was a godsend to Ives. After almost everyone had rejected his music out of hand, he finally had an advocate.

As Henry realized that he could not handle the swelling workload while touring, he enlisted the free labor of Blanche Walton, Olive, and Harry. The only employee was a boy hired in the summer to distribute circulars, which Walton spread around New York;[40] Harry supervised the card file of subscriptions; Olive, who had commenced an extended leave of absence from her college to study and travel, took over management of the New Music Society's concerts, kept the books, lent her address as the office, and slogged away at mailings, correspondence, banking, circularization, paying bills, printing, and endless other tasks. By the time she and Harry left in December 1928 for an eighteen-month trip around the world, she desperately needed a break.[41] Friends like Djane Herz, Ruth Crawford, John J. Becker, and Dane Rudhyar eagerly helped because *New Music Quarterly* was conceived as a cooperative in which the composers would share any profits.[42] (Ives flatly refused to accept any money.) Becker, who had responded to a circular, became one of Henry's closest friends and associates, working strenuously to find support for him in the Midwest. The group kept expanding, as more and more composers and friends of new music recognized the value of the journal.

By mid-September 1927, the publication had 225 subscribers. Henry was so resourceful in developing mailing lists that Rudhyar foresaw a New Music Publishing Company for books about music. "Think of it! We might become millionaires, publishing ultra-modern music! Would it not be sufficient to die from laughter?" Before long, Henry and his friends had corralled some 700 subscribers, about half of whom canceled when they discovered what kind of music was being published.[43]

Gradually an eclectic philosophy emerged. Instead of restricting *New Music Quarterly* to modernists, Henry published any music of quality that was "so new in character as to be difficult to place with the general run of publishers."[44] His friends did not always agree with his choices, however. Selecting Rudhyar's *Paeans* taught him how little support Rudhyar enjoyed in *New Music's* circle. When Blanche Walton worried that Rudhyar's music would compromise the journal's standards, Henry responded that *Paeans* were the best thing he had other than Ruggles's piece, and Ruggles, who had recommended Rudhyar,[45] set a very high standard. Furthermore, because *New Music* was a California publication, he wanted to have something by a resident Californian, of whom Rudhyar was the best.[46] Unfortunately, Walton's opinion was shared by reviewers, who overwhelmingly rejected the issue,[47] causing an alarmed Olive to suggest that Henry approach his board for recommendations about new works. Always ahead of her time, she suggested he find a female composer from Mexico.[48]

Henry's labors as a publisher explain why he composed only one song and one, or possibly two, piano pieces, in all of 1927. His swollen correspondence is packed with searches for music, obtaining manuscripts, dealing with printers, mailing and shipping problems, reading proofs, on and on. Bruised feelings had to be salved. In order to bolster the confidence of composers, he took out copyrights in their names, permitting them to withdraw a composition any time a commercial publisher wanted it. According to Virgil Thomson, as of the twentieth anniversary (1947), only one piece had been withdrawn.[49]

Gradually *New Music's* inclusiveness dissolved collegial doubts. Seeger, however, found it all too *recherché* and intellectual to be useful for society. After a brief look at each issue, he gave it away. Ruggles and Rudhyar seemed amateurish to him; Ruth Crawford's music seemed undisciplined. Later he acknowledged that the experimentation produced more and more musical journeys, and that *New Music* is a record of it.[50] What he could not foresee was the place eventually earned by the best of those composers. In *New Music Quarterly*, a panorama of those years, the most conspicuous missing name was Henry's own. Although an adept promoter, in the context of *New Music* he considered self-promotion improper.[51] The illuminating details of the New Music Society and its publications can be found in Rita Mead's *Henry Cowell's New Music, 1925–1936.*

Despite Henry's reservations about the effectiveness of concerts for circulating music, he continued to present New Music Society concerts, but moved them to the Bay Area for 1927–28. A year's membership, for $5 [2010: $62], included reserved seats at the concerts and a subscription to *New Music Quarterly*. The first concert in the San Francisco area, on October 25, 1927, which also was Henry's conducting debut, included Schoenberg's Wind Quintet, Ruggles's "Angels" and "Lilacs," and Varèse's *Octandre*. The second concert, in Palo Alto on November 30, was a recital of new Hungarian piano music by Imre Weisshaus; the third, on January 18, 1928, presented pianist Winifred Hooke in music by Ravel, Debussy, Berners, Bloch, Cowell, Kodály, and Bartók. For the fall of 1928 there were programs by pianists Arthur Hardcastle and Richard Buhlig, and violinist Dorothy Minty, who played an Ives Sonata. Contradictory reviews make an objective assessment of the concerts impossible. The programs are impressively broad, but the performances are said to have been below standard because financial limitations forced Henry to rely upon his friends. Alfred Frankenstein, who vividly recalled the concerts' deficiencies, felt Henry was more concerned to get the music performed than to ensure that it was performed well.[52]

Despite Henry's cultivation of good collegial relations, when he, Olive, and Harry resumed their travels, the concerts were suspended until the fall of 1929. The details of these concerts and the reactions to them are also found in Rita Mead's history of *New Music*.

It is easy to see that the New Music Society's concerts and periodical could have consumed all of Henry's time. Thanks to his skill at enlisting the help of family and friends, however, he could fill his life with additional projects. The next one involved Varèse, fresh from losing the battle of the New York new-music groups. After swearing that he would never again start an organization, he astonished his wife by unveiling the Pan American Association of Composers (PAAC), a composers' group conceived to serve all the Americas. While Louise Varèse assumed that it was her husband's idea, Carlos Salzedo, Henry, and Carlos Chávez all said that Chávez broached it to Henry during a cross-country drive. Convinced of its potential, they took it to Varèse, who brought in Salzedo a few weeks later.[53]

In his study of the PAAC, Deane L. Root suggested that the motivation stemmed from Latin American nationalism.[54] That may have been true for

Chávez, but Varèse saw it as a tool to battle European neoclassicism, which he called academicism, "an evil thing, for it stifles spontaneous expression. . . . It is not that I believe music should be limited to a passport but rather that today very little music is alive in Europe."[55] His agenda may not have been strictly stylistic, however. The original membership suggests that Varèse also was at war with those who had seceded from the International Composers' Guild (ICG), many of them Jews including Aaron Copland, Claire Reis, and Lazare Saminsky. A pernicious undercurrent of racism also stained some other PAAC members, making anti-Semitism one of the few things about which Ruggles and Varèse agreed.

Whoever generated the idea, it was natural to include Henry. As a member of the Advisory Committee of the International Composers' Guild and the founder of its California filial, he seemed to be a Varèse loyalist. Furthermore, he had a valuable constituency of his own (which Virgil Thomson incorrectly remembered as all-WASP). Whether or not Henry shared Varèse's resentment of the League of Composers and Copland, he was attracted to Chávez's vision of inter-American musical exchange.

An early circular announced that membership in the PAAC would be restricted to citizens of the Americas, but the initial group of sixteen had only three Latin Americans—Chávez and Revueltas from Mexico, and the Uruguayan Eduardo Fabini. The Americans and Canadians were Henry, Ruth Crawford, Howard Hanson, Roy Harris, Charles Ives, Colin McPhee, Dane Rudhyar, Carl Ruggles, William Grant Still, Adolph Weiss, and Emerson Whithorne. Salzedo and Varèse were French-born. Its executive board consisted of Varèse, president, and four vice-presidents—Whithorne, Ruggles, Chávez, and Henry.[56] The society promised to sponsor "the production of its members' works throughout the Americas, in order to promote the music of all the Americas and stimulate composers to make still greater effort toward creating a distinctive music of the Western Hemisphere." Surprisingly, considering Varèse's involvement, its program policy repudiated the ICG's by emphasizing repeated performances, though presumably in different cities. Henry told his parents that the C. C. Birchard company was going to publish a PAAC magazine in English and Spanish, that the PAAC planned branches in Mexico and South America, that government support would be sought, and that it eventually would give orchestral concerts of its members' music in New York.[57]

Other frenzied activity ensued just as Henry was bringing *New Music Quarterly* to life. In late February 1928, he informed Ives that the PAAC wanted to include "Emerson" in a concert series in New York in April, suggesting Buhlig as the pianist.[58] Meanwhile, Chávez was planning the PAAC's first concert in Mexico City, with Henry's *Sinfonietta*, Varèse's *Intégrales*, and music by Revueltas, Rudhyar, and Whithorne,[59] as well as arranging for the Havana Symphony to play PAAC works.[60] Flutist-conductor Georges Barrère agreed to include a PAAC composer's work in all ten of his ensemble's 1928–29 Carnegie Hall concerts and many others on tour. When Ives offered moral support, Henry suggested he donate money instead, "since as you know, it is always very hard for a bunch of composers ever to find money to carry out the sort of plans I have just disclosed."[61] Ives responded with regular backing to both *New Music* and the PAAC.[62]

In mid-September Varèse proposed that Henry and Whithorne take charge when he moved back to Paris.[63] Actually, Henry already was running it. Since no PAAC-sponsored concerts could be organized in 1928, he earmarked Ives's initial contribution of $125 [2010: $1,590] for a catalog of members' works that would be used to solicit performances.[64] Then everything ground to a halt. At the end of November 1928, Henry wrote Ives that Chávez had lost interest, Varèse was away, the catalog had gone nowhere because the composers did not submit their works-lists, and an incomplete catalog seemed useless. Some composers were blocking any action out of reciprocal jealousies. Henry concluded that the New Music Society needed Ives's $125 more than the PAAC.[65] Ives told him to do whatever seemed best.[66]

All this explains why Louise Varèse remembered so little of the PAAC—only that when her husband was in Paris, Henry was the active member.[67] Actually, without Henry's persistence, the organization would have died quickly. A simple debut concert was finally organized for March 1929, at Birchard Hall, with music of Chávez, Villa-Lobos, Paniagua, and the Cubans Caturla and Roldán. Then Henry left for Europe and the PAAC again went into hibernation.

The combination of *New Music Quarterly* and the PAAC tightened Henry's relationship with Ives. Until late 1928 much of their correspondence concerned the overwhelming problems of engraving the second movement of Ives's fourth Symphony when the engraver could not make head or tail of the manuscript. (Henry offered to copy the first page himself as a model.) Ives insisted on paying the entire cost of the fourth Symphony issue, which was expensive to produce and ship. Other business besides the periodical and the PAAC included the larger matter of Ives's music, which might have languished without Henry's relentless hunt for performers willing to tackle works like "Emerson" or even parts of it. He programmed Ives's first Violin Sonata on a New Music Society concert in San Francisco on November 27, 1928, and planned to include something in a projected concert of American music by the Berlin chapter of the International Society for Contemporary Music (ISCM) the following fall.[68] His articles on American composers consistently placed Ives at the top. Henry bent his usual rule against prose in *New Music Quarterly* by printing Ives's impressive "Conductor's Note" to the fourth Symphony.

Soon they developed a social relationship. Henry visited Ives in New York and at West Redding, Connecticut; Ives invited Henry to hear Ravel perform, attended a Humphrey-Weidman dance concert when Doris Humphrey danced to "The Banshee" with Henry playing, and invited Henry to stay in his New York apartment until he found his own place. Although for a long time the two addressed each other as "Mr. Ives" and "Mr. Cowell," their affectionate letters imply that Ives came to regard Henry as a son. Henry, of course, might be suspected of using Ives for his money, were there not overwhelming evidence of his determination to bring Ives's music to the world.

It is amazing that Henry had any time to compose. Yet from the beginning of 1928 until his next trip to Europe fifteen months later he completed nine piano pieces, including three extremely beautiful "Irish" pieces ("The Fairy Bells," "The Leprechaun," and "the Fairy Answer"), "Euphoria" (or Euphonia; his handwriting is ambiguous), and a set of children's pieces. Three orchestral compositions of this time—the tone-cluster Piano Concerto, the *Irish Suite* for piano and small orchestra, and the *Sinfonietta*—retain a small place in the repertory. He also worked on a choral piece for John J. Becker as well as two songs.

As if all this were not enough for one man, lecturing was increasingly occupying his time. While his correspondence contains many details of the negotiations, the lectures usually survive only as titles because he spoke off-the-cuff. Thanks to a newspaper report, a brochure, and Olive's handwritten notes, the talks that he gave in the Bay Area in the fall of 1926 show how one lecture gave lay listeners a good overview of modernist trends and their place in history.

He began by surveying composers who broke the rules of their time, and how their work was received, beginning with the ancient Greeks. Then he showed how the use of new intervals culminated in Bach's establishing a harmonic logic that reigned through Wagner's day. Although that harmonic language became accepted as a set of inviolable rules, Henry believed that "rules" are merely traditions formulated as guides for students.

As a prelude to discussing modernism, he cited Strauss's introduction of "strange" intervals that were (according to Olive's notes) "unacoustical"—that is, out of the main line of musical development and removed from the physical laws of the overtone system. Turning to modernism, he explored discord and concord as concepts stemming from psychological reactions, using excerpts from Wagner, Debussy, Schoenberg, Stravinsky, and Hába, the Czech microtonalist, as illustrations, and explained modernism's roots in the overtone series. "Smoothness of harmony" was determined by the presence or absence of acoustical beating. His brief history of new harmonies used examples from Rudhyar's chords built on the perfect fifth, Schoenberg's augmented fourths, his own tone clusters, and Milhaud's polytonality. He credited Ruggles with the greatest development of dissonant counterpoint since Bach.[69]

He far preferred Schoenberg to Stravinsky, praising in particular Schoenberg's ability to avoid repeating himself. He then briefly surveyed trends represented by Goossens, Honegger, Malipiero, Bartók, Ornstein, Ruth Crawford, Varèse, and others, not restricting his list to composers who appealed to him.

His favorite Americans were Ornstein, Rudhyar, Ruggles, Varèse, and, surprisingly, Copland. (He had not yet encountered Ives.) He mentioned the quarter-tone piano, Busoni's third-steps, sliding tones, and clusters as well as new rhythms, and he envisioned a new instrument that could produce smaller intervals. His real break with tradition, however, was once again his belief that the route to innovation lay beyond the Western "civilized" world, in extra-European music. "When a composer arrives who adds this to the new material in harmony and melody, whose control of the wider field is masterly enough to handle it and whose inspiration demands it, we shall at last have a figure in the musical world as great if not greater than Bach."[70]

Such ideas, and Henry's renown, ought to have made him a magnet for composition students, but he seems to have done almost no private teaching, probably because of his travels. He was, however, a natural, informal advisor to young composers, and an inspiration to others, such as Henry Brant and fifteen-year-old Morton Gould, who used extensive Cowell-like tone clusters in his early music.[71] His intuitive faith in Ruth Crawford was one of his most astute judgments. The sudden blossoming of her composing commenced when he persuaded her that Chicago was a dead end. With his help, she came to New York in 1929, moved in with Blanche Walton,[72] and began studying with Charles Seeger, who had settled in New York. Although Seeger at first did not believe a woman could compose, her talent blossomed as he opened many creative routes for her. Eventually they married.

Another important protégé in the 1920s was George Gershwin. The story of their encounter is preserved in a 1954 letter from Henry to David Ewen, who was preparing a biography of Gershwin,[73] and in conversations a few years later as Robert Payne prepared his own book about Gershwin. Henry met Gershwin around 1927 through Ira Gershwin, the husband of Henry's childhood friend Lenore Strunsky.[74] Having loved Gershwin's shows, he was amazed to find that although he improvised so securely that it sounded like a written-down piece, Gershwin read music slowly and laboriously. Notes "really had no live meaning for him." He gave his ideas to an arranger, who created a continuous work out of them and scored it. To Henry's astonishment, he could not hear written music in his head, and "had no fundamental talent for recognizing notes as tones," though he had a fantastic ear. He said Gershwin was almost ignorant of music theory.

> He knew harmony by ear, and most of the time he was right, but he could be terribly wrong. He used to say, "I'm crazy with ideas, and don't know what to do next." He was always in a terrible hurry, and he always regarded himself as a master. He absolutely believed he could combine classical music with popular music. Once when we were arguing about the history of music, he said, "What's it all about? I'm history." He was

like that. There was tension in his music and in his voice; he was always scurrying to get the words out, always hurrying to finish one thing and get on with the next. He had tremendous gifts, but did not always know what to do with them.

Recognizing his own problems and eager to improve his skills, Gershwin first approached Varèse for instruction, but Varèse felt they were going in opposite directions.[75] Henry wrote Ewen,

> The success of the Rhapsody in Blue made [Gershwin] feel that (1) The great American music must be a combination of pop and "classical" (which meant Liszt and Chopin, etc.) (2) That he himself was the best man to undertake this and (3) That classical music could only be done well if he knew more about the formal art of writing music, and doing the whole thing himself. So, after having attained fame and wealth, he started at the very beginnings of counterpoint. I don't remember exactly the date. 1927 or so. The lessons were to be once a week, but usually something would interfere, so they were nearer once in three weeks. His fertile mind leaped all over the place; he thought the rules of counterpoint were just about the silliest things he had ever come across, and was far too annoyed with them to devote himself to perfecting the counterpoint; it was never more than 90% right. But this was because he was exasperated at the rules, not because he was incapable, of course. With no effort he rattled off the almost perfect exercise, but would get side-tracked into something using juicy 9th and altered chords that he liked better, and would insert these into the Palestrina-style motet. The whole period lasted something over two years, with many interruptions (I went to Europe in the meantime) and I don't think he ever felt that there was any value in the study.

During that same period Gershwin also had some harmony lessons with Wallingford Riegger, "with much the same result." When the Russian composer Joseph Schillinger came to the United States in 1928, Henry spoke with him about Gershwin and almost certainly introduced them. Schillinger's method appealed to Gershwin, and the counterpoint lessons ended, but Gershwin and Henry remained good friends, and Gershwin would report on his progress. He delightedly told Henry that he had written and orchestrated *An American in Paris* entirely by himself, and was "overcome with joy" by the success of *Porgy and Bess*, the real climax of his studies with Schillinger. Henry concluded, "Judging how difficult it was for him to do his own orchestration and form, and to manage complete continuity, I feel that he made an astounding achievement."[76]

Henry certainly had a full plate, but we still have not seen it all. In 1927 he also became involved with the American Section of the International Society for Contemporary Music (ISCM), agreeing to let the New Music Society act as a collecting agency for American scores to be considered for submission to the jury of ISCM's international festival, World Music Days. He also developed a relationship with E. Robert Schmitz's Pro Musica until it closed in 1932. Fortunately, a few other board invitations were transitory, because Henry seemed incapable of saying no.

Meanwhile, new music in New York was expanding again, with the Copland circle in charge. A series of concerts organized by Copland and Roger Sessions opened in April 1928 in lower Manhattan, apparently attended by Henry. His long-standing irritation at American neoclassicism emanating from France was mollified by Copland's new and very serious *Vitebsk* trio, which Henry considered a big improvement.[77] In its three years the Copland-Sessions concerts programmed music from both the Copland and Cowell circles, certainly improving relations between Copland and Henry. However, in 1929, Copland and his friends in the League of Composers announced the formation of Cos Cob Press as an East Coast counterpart to *New Music Quarterly*. Stylistically rather conservative and emphasizing Jewish composers, Cos Cob revived the internecine rivalries.[78] Nevertheless, Henry had already been offered and accepted a seat on the Board of *Modern Music*, the journal published by the League of Composers, and wrote articles for it for decades. Gradually the friction between Copland and Henry died down.

Europe, Third Installment (1929)

Discouragement after the European tour of 1926 dissipated quickly. When Henry reached a good deal with a Dutch concert management, he recommended the search for engagements and soon had a promising list of appearances. Accompanied by Harry and Olive, who had arrived in New York following the cross-country leg of their round-the-world trip, he sailed on March 18, 1929. On shipboard Henry worked on his theoretical treatise—which had already occupied him for more than a decade—although still uncertain about its value, but took time off to dance all night at a costume ball, using his long-dormant skills to dress up as an Indian.[1]

Their first destination was Ireland. Equipped with a recording machine and a list of singers and players obtained from a priest and Varian's Theosophist friend, the poet and political activist Ella Young, Henry, Harry, and Olive rented an old car and driver and set off from Cork for a trip around the southwest. When two young men in Killarney let him try their war pipes, Henry ordered a set, counting on its instruction book and advice from the pipers to get started, and Harry equipped him with a traditional piper's costume. A little mountain climbing topped off the pleasures.[2] Five years later, he used the recordings for an article on Irish traditional music.[3] Even more important, hearing Irish music performed by traditional musicians created a much stronger bond between Henry and his ancestral culture than had Varian's translations of myths or the songs Harry sang to him when he was small.

After visits to Harry's and Varian's fathers, Henry left for his concert tour while Harry and Olive stayed on. At the small hall of the Amsterdam Concertgebouw on April 2 he had a sparse but warm audience and some friendly reviewers.[4] When he described it to Blanche Walton he was already passing through Geneva on his way to Milan for Lazare Saminsky's concert-conference on American and Russian music.[5] A couple of weeks later he was in Paris to play for the Groupe d'Études Philosophiques et Scientifiques pour l'Examen des Tendances Nouvelles at the Sorbonne, which sponsored new-music performances. Near the American Express office he ran into Olive and Harry, who accompanied him as he made the rounds of Parisian contacts including the Varèses and Nadia Boulanger.[6] By late April he was at Pension Schmolke readying himself for a concert at the Sturm-Saal in the Kurfürstendamm. This time, instead of playing an endless stream of individual pieces, he used the last section of the program to give the audience a chance to re-hear the music of the first part. The effect of his experiment, which he had tried in New York, is impossible to estimate but may explain why the Berlin critics were less hostile than before. After persuading the Berlin ISCM chapter to have an American evening in the fall, he resolved to arrange more concerts in Europe, where American music was still unknown.[7]

From Berlin he went to Dresden, Prague (for a recital at the Rotary Club),[8] then back to Dresden to play for a women's Theosophical group. Olive acknowledged that membership in Halcyon repaid him with useful contacts in Europe but concluded that he would play for "anyone who would listen to his music and pay him something." Next, she and Harry accompanied him to Prague for his concert at the Society for Contemporary Music, and visits with Pospíšel and Hába. Then they returned to Berlin to prepare for one of the most amazing events of Henry's life, a trip to the Soviet Union as the first American composer and only the second American performer—Roland Hayes was the first—to be invited there.

This extraordinary adventure has been described previously, using information supplied or corrected by Sidney Cowell. Unfortunately, her failure to verify her statements against primary sources led to errors that were entirely avoidable, because Henry wrote five major magazine articles that seem consistent and convincing despite his propensity toward embellishment. The first, "Conservative Music in Radical Russia," a survey of the general condition of music in the USSR, was written immediately after the trip and published by *The New Republic*. "A Musician's Experiences in Russia—Some First-hand and Unbiased Impressions," printed in *The Churchman* in April, 1930, offers his impressions of Moscow life. It was partly recycled into "Adventures in Soviet Russia," a two-part series in *The San Franciscan* at the end of that year. A detailed account of the professional aspects of his trip appeared in May 1931 in *Musical Courier*. A fifth article, dealing only with Russian music, was first printed in the Moscow journal *Muzika I Revoliutsiia* late in 1929, and reprinted in the New York Russian-language newspaper *Russky Golos* the following February.[9] A memoir by Olive, various letters, and other documents complete the picture. The following account draws upon all sources from that time and a few of Sidney's later statements. One must constantly bear in mind Henry's predisposition to spice up his stories.

The earliest contacts with the Soviets showed Henry that he was dealing with an unconventional host. Right after his 1926 London concert, someone calling himself a consul charged with finding genuinely interesting artists invited him to play in the USSR under official auspices. Intrigued by the idea of a diplomat sent as a talent scout, Henry made all necessary arrangements. Then the entire Soviet delegation to Britain was unexpectedly sent home, and attempts to contact the consul went unanswered. This, he said, "was the first example of oscillation between unexpectedly hearty interest and utter indifference."

As improbable as the story seems, it was characteristic of those years. Amy Nelson's fascinating study of music in the early Soviet period[10] describes a musical world in a constant state of flux. The first commissar for public education, appointed in 1917, was Anatoly Lunacharsky, whom Boris Schwarz described as "the single-handed architect of this whole period of musical creativity," a cultivated nonconformist who would harness anything to serve the revolution. Factions representing traditional "classical music," new music, and proletarian interests competed for attention and support. Research institutes studied applications of electrical and electronic technology to music, new scale systems, acoustics, and many other areas where science and music intersect. The amazing career of Leon Theremin is representative of that lively time; among other things, he produced an early version of television.[11]

The struggle between the avant-gardist internationalists—the Association for Contemporary Music (known by its Russian acronym ASM)—and the Russian Association of Proletarian Musicians (RAPM) is well known, with each side split into competing subdivisions, while a third group pressed to educate the masses in the European classics. The government, insofar as it cared about music, neither repressed the avant-gardists nor particularly supported the proletarianists in the mid-1920s but focused upon raising the musical literacy of the masses. The internationalists were free to invite leading Europeans such as Berg and Schoenberg to come, and to produce *Wozzeck* in Leningrad. Henry therefore was a good candidate for an invitation and a prospective convert to communism.

Early in 1927, a trade officer whom he met in Montreal sent Henry's promotional material to the Canadian branch of the All-Soviet Society for Cultural Relations with Foreign Countries (VOKS).[12] This body, according to the Soviet Information Bureau, "was formed for the purpose of establishing closer relations between cultural and scientific bodies in the Soviet Union and those of foreign countries." A "service bureau" assisted foreigners who wanted to come for study or research. VOKS's president was Mme. Olga Davidovna Kameneva; official materials do not mention that she was Leon Trotsky's sister.[13] Finally connected to the appropriate body in Moscow, Henry attempted to contact Soviet music administrators and musicians as his 1929 tour took shape. The sole reply came from a musician who suggested that he come and give concerts—an absurd idea in a country where nobody could perform without official support.

Henry's Soviet prospects nevertheless began to interest his associates. Varèse actively promoted Soviet-American musical relations through an affiliate of

VOKS, the American Society for Cultural Relations with Russia (USSR). Its membership included "some of the most distinguished figures in arts and professions in American life." (Among its vice-presidents were Leopold Stokowski and the social reformers John Dewey and Lillian Wald.) Varèse suggested that he accompany Henry to Russia during Henry's European tour, conducting orchestral pieces; Henry would play solos.[14] Varèse believed it would be easily organized because Henry's name would be familiar to those who had originally planned to bring him.[15] Nothing came of it, nor did Louise Varèse refer to it in her biography of her husband, which terminates at just that time. Dane Rudhyar proposed to enlist the help of a friend who lived in Moscow.[16] Nicholas Slonimsky, who had become a close friend, offered to use his contacts in Russia, which he had maintained since emigrating in the early 1920s.[17] (A project to play in Moscow with Lazare Saminsky conducting was unrelated to Henry's personal negotiations.)[18] When the 1928–29 season began, nobody knew anything definite,[19] but as of December Henry expected to go.[20]

He faced great obstacles because the United States had not recognized the USSR. When he applied for a tourist visa in New York, he was informed that he would get a decision in Berlin. Eternally optimistic, he told John Varian in March (1929) that he would play in Leningrad and Moscow,[21] and wrote Blanche Walton from Geneva that he had "met the all-important man who says whether or not one plays in Russia, and he said, thumbs up! so I suppose I will play there."[22] When he got to Berlin he learned that his visa had been denied. The story was far from over, however. Dr. René Allendy, a prominent Paris psychiatrist whose wife had strong ties with the avant-garde arts world, had referred him to the USSR Embassy in Paris[23] and through it to Ernst Chain, a music-loving chemist (and later a Nobel Prize winner) connected to the USSR Embassy in Berlin, and empowered to invite innovative artists to the USSR. Because Chain was forbidden to invite conventional performers on the grounds that the Soviet Union had plenty of its own, it must have been reasonably easy for Henry to persuade him and his embassy colleagues to attend his Berlin concert. They "became wildly excited, said my music was something Russia must positively hear, and telegraphed Moscow to grant a visa and arrange concerts at once." Since the Soviets had been inviting prominent foreign architects to design very modern buildings, Henry had every reason to expect a warm welcome. Thus, at the very last moment, he found himself going east, but not alone. Olive and Harry unexpectedly announced that they had obtained visas and would accompany him. None of his published accounts allude to their presence, which, however, is documented elsewhere. According to Sidney, he was extremely irritated to have them along, sensing that it might lead to unforeseeable consequences in a land brimming with unforeseeable consequences. She also thought that his repeated assertion that he went alone reflected the fact that the Soviets did not provide him with an escort as they had done for Roland Hayes.[24]

The adventure started in the Berlin station, where the weekly Paris-Vladivostok train, the only one available, always was packed with people riding beyond Moscow. Berths or seats were out of the question; in fact, there was hardly room to stand. Appalled, Dr. Chain arranged for a private railcar. Henry began to imagine an official reception committee and being housed in state in some former Moscow palace. But he also felt guilty about the hordes of standing passengers and requested that the car be opened to all riders. Among them was *New York Times* music critic Olin Downes, who had recently trounced Henry's music. (Downes was never told that he was traveling as Henry's guest.)[25] Olive: "It seems that he and Henry had the same compartment, with all their opposing views as to modern music. We fared well on the train which was very comfortable, and the food good."[26]

At the Russian border, where incompatible rail gauges require a change of train, Henry was amazed when the porter who moved his bags refused a tip. It was a warm welcome to Russia, he wrote. The reality of Soviet trains quickly dampened his enthusiasm. In his third-class sleeper, the bed was a wooden shelf for which one could either bring bedding or rent it from the porter, who only had a thin mattress—no blankets, quilts, or pillow. Since it was cold, Henry slept on the board and used the mattress as a blanket.

Although the exact date of their arrival in the USSR is unknown, it must have been at the end of April. No official committee—or anybody else—greeted Henry. With Harry and Olive, he took one of Moscow's very few cabs to the home of Samuel Feinberg, a thirty-nine-year-old composer and piano virtuoso whom he had met through Dr. Chain. (One later account fancifully has Henry climbing into a taxi and uttering the only word that he thought the driver might understand, "Conservatory.") Foreigners were such a rarity that Feinberg was amazed to see him. After many telephone calls he learned that a concert sponsored by VOKS had been announced for May 2. Henry then visited the VOKS Music Committee, who "as a polite gesture" asked him to play for them. After whispering in a corner, they informed him that the concert was canceled because his music was far too radical for Soviet citizens.

Henry had arrived at just the wrong moment. Stalin had terminated the New Economic Policy under which the USSR had been operating, replacing it with the centralized economy of the first Five-Year Plan. A decree of May 1928 launching the Soviet Cultural Revolution had called for the proletarianization of society in general and the arts in particular.[27] The power struggle intensified, even within the Moscow Conservatory. With Anatoly Lunacharsky removed as cultural commissar, all sides began jockeying for power. The Russian Association of Proletarian Musicians competed fiercely with the new-music circles, the traditionalists, and other proletarian factions within the Moscow Conservatory and elsewhere. Henry played for the VOKS committee just as anti-modernism was being turned into a weapon in the class struggle, and any musical event could be used against any other factions.

Much more immediately troublesome, the cancellation of his performances deprived him of any claim to lodging. Feinberg graciously attempted the near impossible job of finding him accommodation, but Harry and Olive also needed to be placed. Feinberg explained that although the city's population had almost tripled since before the world war, almost no new dwellings or hotels had been built. To accommodate the crush, housing was allotted at about five people for every two rooms. He spent hours vainly telephoning every hotel and trying to locate even a space where Henry could curl up on the floor in a blanket. Since Feinberg's own cot was in his mother's room, he could not give it to Henry and sleep on the floor. Part of the difficulty was that Henry, unconnected with communism in the United States, lacked introductions that might have reassured individuals who feared consorting with foreigners.

He also had no way to obtain ration cards after being dismissed by the Music Committee. Finally, Feinberg induced a friend to share his family's supper with the dazed Henry. As the nights were mild, he did not hesitate when someone suggested he sleep on a park bench. Feinberg escorted him to a convenient bench near the Kremlin and left him there.[28] Then a woman whom the Cowells had met in New York and who knew Russia well persuaded an American journalist to release his room in the Grand Hotel. That room went to Olive and Harry, however, leaving Henry in the park.[29] His greatest fear that night was passport theft. Around midnight the porter of a hotel where he had left his "bench-location-address" fetched him and said that a guest had suddenly left, leaving a palatial room with running water at the palatial price of $18 [2010: $229].[30]

Because food at the hotel was very expensive—$2.50 [2010: $31.80] for a glass of tea and black bread—he lunched at a clean-looking restaurant across the street, ordering by pointing to an item on the menu that he could not read. Dill-pickle soup appeared, the very look of which turned his stomach. Tasting it was even worse. The waiter, furious at his refusal to eat it, dragged him outside to the menu, where Henry moved his hand as far as possible from the list of soups and pointed to something that he also did not understand. After the waiter took his soup away and brought it back with sour cream on it, the entire room watched to see what he would do. Letting it go to waste was not an option. Suddenly he was inspired to offer the soup to a ragged young man. "The crowd was not only appeased, but I became the object of admiration. I had made the great personal sacrifice of giving up this delicious and life-giving soup to one poorer than myself. I did not disillusion them as to my nobility." A diner offered to find him a wife.

A little walk on a warm May day took him down to the river, right in the center of the city. There, fully in view of one of Moscow's main streets, more than 8,000 people bathed in the nude, men in one area, women in the next, but all together in the water. A handful of people who wore bathing suits "were objects of constant curious glances and derision from the other bathers, since the only possible excuse for wearing a bathing suit in Moscow is in case of some physical deformity." Another excursion included a visit to a friend at a "butter center," a private clearing house for the butter business, which was on the edge of extinction because of government undercutting. He saw huge crowds worshiping at Lenin's body. All in all, he was impressed by some aspects of Soviet society and baffled by others.

Olive recalled Feinberg taking them to VOKS, probably for the meeting at which Henry was rejected. She was delighted to learn how to get tickets for forthcoming musical events and to be introduced to Mme. Kameneva (now the ex-head of VOKS, but still a force in the arts world) "who promised to plan many things for us, meaning of course Henry."[31] Not even the committee's rejection dampened Olive's spirits. In fact, she did not even mention it in her memoir.

Henry soon discovered that the committee's rejection was the best thing that could have happened. The word of his presence unleashed a stream of invitations to play privately for musicians. The first person to summon him was Konstantin Igumnov, a distinguished piano virtuoso and rector of the Moscow Conservatory. He does not say how he received Igumnov's invitation, but Sidney's version is worth reading even if it is fanciful. At a very early hour, she says, "a young man came by and said the Director of the Conservatory had arranged for him to play for the faculty of the conservatory, very privately and 'entirely safely'—inaudible from the street!" There is no way to know if he was still sleeping on the bench, as Sidney thought.[32]

Impressed by Henry's playing, Igumnov declared that the VOKS Committee was stodgy and overly cautious. He would back Henry and present him in concert. Such an action was, as Henry says, the equivalent of declaring musical war, because the committee was an official body whose decisions were normally final. Igumnov, however, had risen to the top of the profession, and as director of the conservatory, whose enrollment had swollen to 11,000 after private teaching was banned, he wielded authority. When he had Henry play for the faculty, his music created such a stir that he was asked to play for students. Those performances took place in relays, since there was no space sufficiently large and, if Sidney's story is accurate, isolated from hostile ears. He began at four o'clock. "After I played my first number for them, there rose from the hall an indescribable roaring and bellowing, like Niagara Falls and touch-down at a football game combined. Yells, shouts, clapping, and stamping of feet jumbled into one mighty din. The noise indicated neither approval nor disapproval, I think, but intense interest." When he had quieted the crowd and began the second piece, the noise resumed. A student delegate came forward and asked in German if Henry might play the first piece again, which he did again and again for half an hour. The session ended after four hours, when the hall was needed for another event. Students gathered around him to lament that he could not keep going. Henry wrote that he did this on three successive days, but in recalling the episode many years later said he played every day for thirty days.[33] The timing of other events suggests that "three" was a typographical error.

He realized that the students demanded encores not because they liked a piece, but because they wanted a deeper understanding of it. Many of them wrote down his pieces from memory after hearing them so many times. They were starved for new music, partly because the nonconvertible ruble prevented them from importing scores, but even more because of conflicting government policies. One group insisted that all music be immediately understood by the masses; a nobler, less conservative faction nevertheless opposed excessive individualism. As a result, young composers were discouraged from pursuing their own visions and pushed to write in a single, uniform style. At this stage, however, there still were some Russian radicals led by Aleksandr Mosolov. The conservatory itself had two competing proletarian factions; a third group existed, but outside the walls.[34] Furthermore, the government was far less focused on music than on the written word, leaving the factions to fight it out among themselves, despite the thrust of the 1928 decree mandating proletarianism.

The surprising possibilities within that convoluted world became even clearer when he got an invitation to play for the jury of the state music publisher, chaired by Nikolai Myaskovsky, a progressive. After hearing Henry's music, they immediately asked to publish "Tiger," which could never be called conservative, and "Lilt of the Reel," which would barely pass that test. Then they flabbergasted Henry by giving him advance royalties on the first 500 copies rather than asking for a subsidy, a treatment unimaginable in the West. Even stranger was the honorarium, 88 rubles. (That was about $44 [2010: $560] at the official rate.) Asked how they arrived at the number, the spokeswoman replied that their rate was 10 kopecks (5 US cents) per quarter note. (Henry later joked that he wished he had written more separate quarter notes, because each tone cluster was counted as one quarter-note event no matter how many pitches it contained.) A system that paid composers for their labor like all workers could not be all bad. As an added benefit, Soviet publications were distributed in the West by Vienna's Universal Edition, "so I will now be in that famous house as well."[35] Unable to convert the rubles to dollars, however, he arranged to be paid in scores by Soviet composers. Everything had happened very quickly. On May 5, only about a week into his trip, he wrote Becker that his music was going over "big," and would be published there, and, to his delight, released in Europe by Universal. (Universal's title page calls the Irish-style piece "Silt of the Reel.")[36]

He then played for the "State Department for the Science of Music," which he thought was doing some of the world's most important research in the field.

Although he did not describe their projects, their work on the existence of undertones impressed him.[37] Gradually he got to know researchers in acoustics, microtones, and electronics.

Finally, the VOKS Committee declared that the public concert had only been "postponed" to May 27 in the Central House of Workers' Arts (19 Herzen Street), which organized it jointly with VOKS. They called it a presentation of new acoustical experiments on the piano—not a concert—with an introductory paper by Henry. Everything about the announcement smacks of a face-saving gesture. Sure enough, trouble was brewing behind the facade. By scheduling the concert for 5 P.M., the committee bet that the audience would walk out and go home for dinner, thereby allowing the original cancellation to be declared "correct." To ensure the right outcome, it delayed the start of the concert to irritate the audience. While Henry was told that he had to await the arrival of the official who would introduce him, the audience was told that he was having an artistic tantrum. An hour later Mme. Kameneva arrived and opened the evening. According to custom, there were no printed programs but a narrator to announce each piece, in this case doing it during the applause so that no one could hear him. When his voice caused the applause to stop he refused to repeat himself. Finally, a flash photographer set off his light right behind Henry in order to blind the audience. The audience, however, knew all the tricks and stayed to the end, rewarding Henry with a tremendous ovation. Mme. Kameneva later hosted a party for Henry where he and other composers played. Caviar and sturgeon were served despite the food shortage. The Music Committee had crossed the wrong person. Mme. Kameneva, Olive said, made sure it "lost its official sanction on account of this episode."[38] Olive did not know that Kameneva herself was in trouble politically.

Olive related a few other adventures in Moscow—hearing the Persimfons, the distinguished conductorless orchestra; going to the theater and to plays and performances in factories and shops. Konstantin Kuznetsov, a distinguished music historian who spoke good English, invited them to dinner at his house, where Henry played again. Once more, the food was delicious, despite shortages. The two of them developed a good working relationship that continued over the next years. Henry also met with an ethnomusicologist—probably Victor Belaiev—who had just returned from Central Asia "where he thought he had discovered the origin of the chromatic scale."[39]

Right after Henry's concert, the Cowells took the night train to Leningrad, where a VOKS official led them to the Hotel Europa. On May 30 he played at the Institute of History of Arts for about a hundred music theorists, scientists, and critics. He also tried to arrange a performance at the Contemporary Music Association through composer Yuri Shaporin, thanks to a recommendation from Joseph Schillinger, but since concerts did not have printed programs, there is no sign of whether it took place.[40] The only extant review of the entire trip was written by Alexander Slonimsky after the Leningrad concert and translated by his brother Nicolas. Ironically, for this country that was squashing artistry to a uniform middle level, it was one of Henry's best foreign reviews.

> I went to hear Henry Cowell at the State Institute of History of Arts, in the Theatrical Laboratory, and was transported with delight. Our qualified public (members of the Musical Department) lavished compliments on him. I could not imagine that anything like that could be done to the piano . . . [He then described the techniques.] Somebody opined, learnedly and marxistically: "Industrialisation, a revolution in music." Others (musicologists, conservatively inclined) remarked: "Rebikoff, Scriabine, elementary stuff." But the direct impression was stupendous. Henry Cowell possesses a remarkable combination of romantic Californian essence and American mechanized form. The piano is treated as if it were a pig prepared for slaughter: fat and flesh, all is utilized. Why fuss with the keyboard alone? . . . But with all this Cowell discloses a fundamental gift of fresh melodic invention and a vivid pictorial sense . . .[41]

One critic called his music "the last gasp of dying democracy," the other praised his "fresh new blood."[42] While the divergence was surprising, Josef Szigeti said that conflict of critical opinion in official newspapers was familiar from his many tours there between 1924 and 1929.[43] Other reviews and clippings, including articles from *Izvestia* and *Pravda*, disappeared after being accidentally sent to the lime and cement company founded by the other Henry Cowell.[44]

Henry said almost nothing about Leningrad other than hearing some organum-like music from the Caucasus. The day after the concert, the three Cowells left for the West. According to Olive, an official who came to say good-bye promised him all expenses from a European city if he would come again to play.[45] Henry wrote Blanche Walton, "Russia was really exciting, and I had a great time. I really stirred them up greatly, I think. My concerts were the scene of wild emotional outbreaks, mostly pro, but some con."[46]

On his return from the USSR the first week of June, Henry, in rapid succession, played at the university in Bratislava, at Masaryk University in Brno (where his string quartet had just been performed), and on Brno radio, and spoke on folk music in Podobrady. The most important newspaper in Czechoslovakia, which printed his article on Irish music, now requested one on Slovak music. Ulehla proposed to publish a collection of Henry's articles translated into Czech.[47]

Olive claimed that she and Harry joined Henry at Schmolke's in time for a performance at Schoenberg's master class, which is puzzling, as we shall later see. "Henry met Stravinsky and played for him." Later they went to visit a group of English pianists studying with Schnabel. "Henry played for them to their delight, according to my notes." She does not say if she joined Harry and Henry for a visit with the Kandinskys. Henry also tried in vain to see Dr. Chain.[48] He left for Hannover on the sixteenth, on the way to Cherbourg, whence he sailed for New York on June 18;[49] Olive and Harry went on with their tour of Europe and Asia. Henry next saw them when he met their boat in San Francisco a year later.[50]

His summary of the Soviet musical world in *The New Republic* shows great political astuteness and very ambivalent feelings. He concluded that the peculiar detours and side roads in his trip resulted above all from the serious way in which Soviets treated music. In a time of wrenching transitions the arts were being turned into propaganda because the pre-revolutionary anti-modernists "succeeded, on the whole, in convincing the Soviet leaders that giving all people the opportunity to listen to musical performances is an expression of Communism in music." Musical complexity became anti-communist because it made music hard to perform and harder to appreciate. Paradoxically, the stifling of complexity had the compensatory merit that thousands learned the music of old Russia and the classics of other countries. "This, of course, is an excellent thing, and is laying a foundation of cultivated musical taste among the people." He noticed an ironic consequence, however: the new "soviet" music expressed the bourgeois feelings of the nineteenth century. To be "communistic" thus was to write the same old types of tunes. "The introduction of new musical elements would be the wicked voice of individualism. Thus, much of the new life that might have come into Russian composition through the political changes has been sidetracked into conservative channels."

The chief exception was the State Conservatory, where he found more freedom of composition than in any other institution he had ever visited. The young faculty encouraged pupils to write in a style influenced by Mussorgskii and Scriabin. Contemporary music was "more thoroughly taught in the Conservatory than in most schools in other lands" and played on official programs. Such activities, however, angered the conservatives, who tried to block change. As a result, most young composers used some contemporary sounds but did not venture past "a certain middle level. Apparently public opinion will not allow it to do so, and on the whole the composers have gone as far as they dared." Therefore, although the standard of compositional technique was high, the range of material was disturbingly uniform. Mosolov used new techniques, but, in Henry's opinion, lowered his technical standards and resorted to "childish tricks." The situation had driven potentially talented composers into other fields, such as the invention of new instruments, musical psychology, world music, and microtones.

The one kind of music that really interested Henry was made by workers in evening gatherings at which they improvised theater pieces with (improvised) musical accompaniment. The spirit of play prevented the music from being taken too seriously. It was completely unlike anything Henry had heard otherwise. Remote from the dominating pedantry, it vaguely suggested the free music of peasants singing in the fields. "This carefree and little-thought-of music is the most promising thing I see toward a real music of the new Russian workers."[51]

The relatively liberal conditions in the conservatory made sense under Igumnov's leadership, which lasted until June, when he was removed as head of the conservatory and replaced by a Party boss with little musical training.[52] The timing strongly suggests that he was being punished for having supported Henry just as Soviet policies began to change for the worse, but that may have been a coincidence. The precipitous decline of Mme. Kameneva's influence is even more telling.

16

New Musical Resources

Henry's treatise had been languishing since he published some of his theories in the "Harmonic Development in Music" articles. After a fleeting possibility in Czechoslovakia collapsed,[1] he declined Blanche Walton's offer of a publication subsidy.[2] Sensing his frustration, Olive prodded him to see if someone would publish it without a subsidy.[3] The first target, Macmillan, rejected it outright. Henry told Olive that it created "a great stir among the readers, who all favored it except the musical reader, who was so angry he fairly spluttered."[4] Henry then wrote up more of his ideas for *Modern Music* as "New Terms for New Music" (1928), which sought to clarify the murky usage of words like polytonality and polyrhythm.[5] His book thus was more than ten years old when Chávez gave it to a senior editor at Alfred Knopf,[6] who reacted positively. Negotiations dragged on, however. Finally, in early March 1929, Henry closed the deal by agreeing to buy 500 copies at a 40 percent discount and coordinate sales himself.[7]

On the boat to Europe, he touched up the manuscript and, upon returning, submitted the final version,[8] which incorporated new material gathered in the USSR.[9] Thanks to Knopf's quick work, *New Musical Resources* was soon in print, some seventeen years after its inception. Bulk purchases by Ives, Harry, and Walton fulfilled the guarantee. Henry earned $25 [2010: $325] on his private sales and expected royalties of about $200 [2010: $2,600].[10] A month after release it was in a second printing.[11] By May 1930, *New Musical Resources* was available in England;[12] at the end of 1931 Edition Adler was contemplating a German translation.[13]

The nine extant reviews, from the United States, England, France, and Italy, were generally complimentary about the ideas and their presentation. *Musical Opinion* (London) understood Henry's aim to provide "a guiding light to those who find the tendencies of contemporary music an impenetrable jungle. It may produce much impatience before it makes converts. . . . Many laymen regard these violations of their established belief as so much 'leg pulling.'"[14] Although Marion Bauer (in *Modern Music*)[15] thought some of Henry's reasoning was arbitrary or insufficiently substantiated, she was grateful that he "challenges the past

and encourages the future. He makes provocative statements, sets forth his arguments with conviction, and succeeds in stirring his readers to think, whether or
not they agree with his point of view . . . his speculation may open the way to an
extension and explanation of the harmonic, melodic, and rhythmical boundaries
of music." Voices like hers were overwhelmed, however, by general apathy. The
American Mercury wrote, "It is scarcely a tribute to our musical world that this
book has not aroused more interest."[16] Even Bauer could not have imagined its
long-term importance, which was appreciated only after the Second World War,
when some of his theories began to bear fruit. Stockhausen told Sidney that
Europeans were amazed to discover that Henry had proposed the "new ideas" of
the early 1950s so many years before.[17]

New Musical Resources was the product of Henry's will to utilize his musical
and scientific talents in order to make modern concepts comprehensible to any
intelligent reader. Unlike Schoenberg, whose primary interest was pitch relationships, Henry sought the musical equivalent of a unified field theory—"a
theory of musical relativity"—that would transcend the pervasive emphasis on
teaching music only through harmony and counterpoint.[18] He laid out ideas that
could generate future explorations, rather than explain earlier music. To emphasize the book's predictive nature, he excluded examples from existing works, no
matter how new, focusing instead upon new paths of inquiry.

His journey away from the "inspirational" environment of his childhood is all
the more impressive because he had written most of *New Musical Resources* when
he was only about twenty-two. By then, he had concluded that while "the aim of
any technique is to perfect the means of expression," a technique cannot be
formed simply through the creation of rules. Harmony, for example, contained
discrepancies between immutable rules based on an underlying science and alter-
able rules created by the taste of former eras. In Henry's mind, taste and aesthetics
were irrelevant to theoretical explorations. "It is my conviction . . . that the finest
taste and the perfect use of scientifically co-ordinated materials go together, and
that the musical resources outlined add to the possibilities of musical expression
and are therefore vital potentialities, rather than merely cold facts." He had seen
the inapplicability of old rules to new music lead some composers to reject the
need for a solid knowledge of musical materials and to use "childish crudities . . .
accompanied by absence of musical invention." Only one set of immutable laws—
the overtone series—contained explanations of past music and limitless possibilities for the future because it represented the perfect union of art and science.

All of this is found in the introduction to *New Musical Resources*. The interested reader should proceed to the book itself. We shall only take a few moments
for a brief overview of its more striking features.

Part I concerns "Tone combinations." After explaining the physical nature of
overtones, Henry offered an unusual historical view of the dominance of the

major triad. Because early instruments were not rich in overtones, he wrote, the clear audibility of the first few—the octave, fifth, fourth, and major third—made them seem like the most natural sounds. Since modern instruments allow high overtones to be heard easily, however, our sense of acceptable pitch combinations has expanded to include dissonances that follow natural overtone complexes. He maintained that when a major chord is heard simultaneously with the overtones of its three components, the sound is much more complex than the simple triad. The truth of it is obvious to any orchestrator wrestling with the conflicts of overtones that result from certain combinations of instruments.

Like some other theorists such as Schoenberg, Henry saw that music history's forward march had brought more and more overtones into use, causing composers to regard earlier, simpler overtone ratios as insipid and dull. Like Schoenberg, he assumed that that process would continue infinitely. The rebirth of triadic harmony in the late twentieth century suggests that they were oversimplifying, however.

Henry believed that the traditional classification of intervals as consonant or dissonant regardless of their registral distribution also was flawed. "Thus, the interval of a major seventh within the octave has a ratio of 8:15, whereas if it were spaced three octaves and a seventh apart, the ratio would be 1:15. Since this ratio contains no beats, but, on the contrary, the vibrations are periodically even, it is questionable whether the interval of a major seventh can be called dissonant in this spacing." [The correct wording should be "effectively no beats." A beatless ratio would be 1:16.]

Henry's knowledge of non-Western music, acoustical research in Moscow, the quarter-tone work of Hába, and the instruments invented by Leon Theremin led him to reject the quarter-tone (vibration ratio 31:30) as the next logical interval to be explored. That designation, he said, belongs to the small half-step (16:15). He surmised that the quarter-tone probably came into use because it seemed logical to cut the half-step in half. Although such intervals pose serious performance problems, Henry looked to new electrical instruments to facilitate the performance of any interval. Sliding tones, which are used commonly in Hawaiian music, and noise or other sounds from the world around us "indicate the possibility of musical systems derived otherwise than from overtones." The vastly extended sound world of the post-1945 electronic age proved him right.

Henry's perception of the complex interaction of the overtones of triads led him to propose polychords, chords based on the combined overtones of several fundamentals, which he had described years before. A triad, for example, contains three fundamentals. It would become a polychord if all three sets of overtones were turned into chord tones. He advised creating polyharmony from units that are more distantly related than the tones of a triad to avoid suggesting complex conventional harmonies.

In "Tone-Quality," he proposed creating a rational basis for tone color, which itself is governed by overtone combinations, and suggested that tone color might progress as a compositional element if it could be notated. In fact, Debussy often linked thematic recurrences to specific instruments, effectively making tone color part of the thematic structure. Post-1945 coordination of pitch, rhythm, dynamics, and articulation were a step in that direction.

Henry's ideas contain numerous inconsistencies,[19] and some naive extensions of logic, especially in the area of undertones and dissonant counterpoint. What is indisputable, however, is the richness of his thinking, his knowledge of music, and his desire to create order out of the chaos of new, rich materials.

The ideas of Part II, "Rhythm," are even more striking because rhythm had not been the subject of "theory" since the Middle Ages. Recognizing that most of his readers needed clarification about the meaning of the term, Henry attempted to formulate precise descriptions of rhythm that would unlock the imagination. Rhythmic complexity seems daunting, he wrote, only because of human limitations.

The most arresting aspects of his theories commenced with the linking of rhythm to overtones. A chord whose components vibrate in the ratio of 4:5:6 could be expressed by rhythmic values in the same ratio (a quadruplet against a quintuplet against a sextuplet). Under the rubric "Time," he called for a new notational system that would eliminate the cumbersome adjuncts needed to write nonbinary subdivisions of the whole note, such as triplet signs, which he felt inhibited rhythmic freedom. He believed that his proposed system of notating "third notes," "fifth notes," "seventh notes," "thirteenth notes," and so on, with individual signs would clarify the principle of rhythm-overtone relationships. Knowing that he would be met by skepticism, he argued that Oriental peoples and fine Western virtuosi all use rhythms more subtly than notation permits. Although Henry's notational system, with many new symbols, was too cumbersome to win support, by the early twenty-first century his ideas have drawn eager composers.

The extensive explication of his ideas needs to be read in full, for it contains the potential for his rhythmic systems to transcend all limitations of the bar line. Strangely, he does not mention the ultimate implication, which he applied in his Quartets *Romantic* and *Euphometric*—sequences such as two third-notes, followed by three fifth-notes, followed by one thirteenth note, and so on, which are difficult to notate with the traditional method. Although he claimed that motivated performers could learn to play highly complex rhythms with only fifteen minutes' daily practice for six months, "these highly engrossing rhythmical complexes could easily be cut on a player-piano roll. This would give a real reason for writing music especially for player-piano." Conlon Nancarrow, who read and reread the book, applied Henry's suggestion to an almost unimaginably complex degree in his *Rhythmic Studies* for player-piano. Henry also anticipated the sampler, proposing a device upon which pressing a single note would trigger a whole rhythmic sequence, allowing complex "rhythmic counterpoint" to be controlled by a performer. "By playing the keys with the fingers, the human element of personal expression might be retained if desired." He provided "scales of time-values" analogous to pitch scales.

Henry then applied the concepts of rhythmic counterpoint to meter. "Metrical melodies" would be sequences of meters forming a metrical analog to the sequences of tones that produce melody as it is normally defined. This concept, he proposed, would offer a welcome relief to the tediousness of hearing the same meter repeated hundreds of times, which led performers to use excessive rubato in order to blur the feeling of repetitiveness caused by metric inflexibility. Other solutions to metric boredom could be found in jazz, or in the barless writing of Satie. Attempting to suppress or disguise so powerful a force as meter was fruitless. Meter needed to be elevated to the standards of variety of other elements of music. To that end, he proposed counterpoint of meters, related mathematically to the counterpoints of overtones, melodies, and harmonies. One could also construct "metrical chords," using ratios of meters analogous to ratios of overtones and rhythms. The same principles could be extended to dynamics, form, and tempo. Although some of that total integration was realized decades later in extended serialism, many of his ideas have not been tried.

The final section of the book, chord formation, explores the potential of clusters for individual chords, in melodies, and in counterpoint. His proposed notation was finally used by many postwar composers.

The profusion of Henry's ideas leads naturally to the question of originality, which was already partially explored in Chapter 7. In his preface, Henry explained that the book was first written in 1919 with Seward's help. For unexplained reasons, he did not credit Seeger or Russell Varian with any role in the formation of his ideas. Seeger's role is, in fact, unclear. He said that discussions with Henry were so tangled that neither of them knew who originated what. He resented the omission, however, and claimed he never read the book.[20] Henry may have wished to claim all the credit for himself, but it is also possible that Olive and/or Seward were so concerned about Seeger's politics and the pervasive fear of red terror that they advised leaving out his name.[21] Henry's relationship with Seeger healed fairly quickly, however.

Russell Varian's role is also uncertain. The interchange of letters from 1916 shows that many ideas could have originated with him, but he may also have been continuing earlier discussions of Henry's thoughts. Either way, Seward may have convinced Henry to take the credit in the benign hope that it would help him establish his name and scholarly credentials. It is unlikely that Henry simply forgot Seeger and Russell. The credit to Seward himself was harmless, since he was not a musician. In the end, as David Nicholls has said,[22] it does not really matter. Wherever the ideas originated, by putting them together in coherent form, Henry could lay claim to an achievement that was monumental for a young man. By the time the book was published, however, he had largely stopped using many of his own ideas, leaving them for others to explore.

New Projects and Old (1929–1931)

After Europe, Henry's performance schedule was fairly light—a few engagements in California, then nothing until an October tour on the West Coast and in the Midwest. On September 11, 1929, however, he was hospitalized with blood poisoning caused by a neglected boil under a shoulder blade. Although he did not feel like composing, he passed the time in bed writing articles and dealing with business.[1] Mother Carrington and her students bombarded him with greeting cards; John Varian sent money because Henry had gone in without taking his checkbook.[2] Suddenly his condition deteriorated. Although the original infection in his leg and back had healed, his stitches became infected and had to be removed prematurely.[3] Then he worsened again and nearly died. The doctors had to operate several times to drain the infection and perform skin grafts; an area the size of a hand was eaten away.[4] He finally was discharged on October 25 after some six weeks in the hospital[5] and salvaged concerts in Los Angeles and Claremont, where the teenage John Cage heard him for the first time. A concert in Palo Alto on December 27 drew 1929 to a close. The beautiful stringpiano piece "The Fairy Answer" was his only composition of that entire half-year.

His performances in 1930–31 included the New York premiere of a movement of his Piano Concerto with the Conductorless Orchestra, a lecture and private recitals in Philadelphia—where he excitedly saw Schoenberg's *Die glückliche Hand*—a major series of lectures at Northwestern University, and concerts in Milwaukee, St. Paul, and Portland, Oregon. He finally reached California in May[6] and spent much of the summer lecturing and preparing a production of *The Building of Bamba*, for Carmel. In the fall he performed several times on the West Coast and in St. Paul on the way to New York. Completed compositions included *Polyphonica* for small orchestra and some piano pieces.

If "business" seemed a little slow, a rude awakening was lying in wait. The day before he was discharged from the hospital, the stock market had crashed. He did not feel the effects immediately, as previously contracted engagements held firm. Beginning in September 1930, however, almost all his public appearances were lectures. The shift toward speaking may not, however, have represented a defeat. Like Liszt nearly a century earlier, Henry knew that his hypervirtuosity distracted the public from his creative aims. Furthermore, the attacks on his concerts were extremely irritating, whereas the quality of his lectures had almost never been questioned. Terman somewhat insulated him from shrinking concert budgets by arranging lecture-recitals through psychology departments.[7]

While the dream of teaching at Stanford was a particular frustration, one institution was a natural home for his unconventional ideas—New York's New School for Social Research. Situated in cramped quarters on West 23rd Street, it had been conceived ten years before "as a reaction against the traditional academic establishment." With no entrance requirements, examinations, credits, or degrees, its courses at first were reputed to have been (in its own words) "diluted to the intelligence of those whose wits were not sharpened by grinding against conventional academic routine." The school quickly shifted its focus to "self-dependent" adult education. In 1929 its faculty of fourteen included psychiatrist Alfred Adler, poet Alfred Kreymbourg, and economist and political scientist Alvin Johnson, its co-founder and president. As it prepared to move to its dramatic new building on West 12th Street—a short walk from the house where Clarissa and Henry had once been caretakers—it formulated a systematic plan of research "organized around the problem of understanding and interpreting the contemporary social movement." Enrollment skyrocketed, but it offered no music courses[8] other than Copland's lectures on the appreciation of modern music.[9]

During a visit to New York in the winter of 1928–29, Olive, who must have known Alvin Johnson through the international-relations community, suggested that he sponsor a concert by Henry. Johnson, another unconventional product of the American West, was just the sort of person to understand him. His credentials as a man of the heartland are illustrated by a story that he told Sidney Cowell many years later. Once, when he was a child, two men on horseback appeared at his parents' Nebraska farm, seeking food for their journey. In the tradition of the plains, Mrs. Johnson prepared a meal while they took little Alvin for a horseback ride. After they departed, the Johnsons learned that the visitors were Jesse and Harry James, on the run from a recent bank robbery.[10]

Having taught at Stanford just when Henry was under Terman's and Seward's guidance,[11] he knew enough of Henry to offer him a concert, which took place on March 6, 1929, shortly before Henry left for Europe. Henry and Johnson immediately took to one another. With the ticket income, Johnson sent an apology for its meagerness and stated his wish to bring Henry back.[12] Olive was overjoyed for having accomplished what Gassner could not do.[13]

The concert may be what convinced Johnson to form a music program. According to Sidney, he interviewed both Copland and Henry with regard to how a music offering might be shaped. Copland (again according to Sidney) had conventional ideas about theory, history, composition, and similar traditional subjects. When Henry advised Johnson to do what was not done elsewhere, he got the job despite his lack of degrees.[14] As a result, the term beginning in January 1930 was suddenly packed with music, although the school still had not moved from the old building. Henry's personal contribution was a series of four ninety-minute lectures on Friday evenings, called "A World Survey of Contemporary Music." Totally unlike a conventional academic music course, its topics were "The Paradoxical Musical Situation in Russia," "Europe Proceeds Both Forward and Backward" (neoclassicism vs. the experimental vocal styles he had observed in Czechoslovakia in 1926), "Newly Discovered Oriental Principles" (the seed of Henry's world-music courses), and "American Composers Begin Breaking Apron-Strings," an elucidation of the end of American music's reliance upon the European tradition, with the assistance of Ruth Crawford, Adolph Weiss, and Dane Rudhyar.)[15] He also curated a series of contemporary-music concerts that effectively shelved the reigning dogma and presented the entire spectrum of new music.[16] Henry's lecture on world music tempted Johnson to make an appointment in comparative musicology, but offering comparative musicology without a giant like Erich von Hornbostel seemed unwise.[17]

A tour to Havana in December 1930 was five years in the making. Hunting for talented Cuban composers whose music he might publish, Henry had contacted María Muñoz de Quevedo and her husband, the publishers and editors of the new Cuban periodical *Musicalia*. They directed him to twenty-year-old Amadeo Roldán, and twenty-two-year-old Alejandro García Caturla (a pupil of Pedro Sanjuan Nortes, the Spanish conductor of the Havana Philharmonic),[18] and invited Henry to write about American composers for *Musicalia*.[19] Señora Quevedo also enlisted him to help Caturla and Roldán, which necessitated his negotiating the intense rivalries plaguing Cuban composers.[20] The connections with Henry and thus the larger new-music world stimulated the Cubans to create a Society for Contemporary Music, whose first action, María promised, would be to import Henry. Henry, in turn, made Pedro Sanjuan "selector" for the PAAC in Cuba and encouraged him to conduct something by Ives on a regular concert of the Havana Philharmonic.[21]

By April 1930, the Quevedos' Havana Society for Contemporary Music, which had been selected as the Cuban section of the ISCM, elected Henry an honorary member in recognition of his efforts on behalf of Cuban music.[22] María de Quevedo's press campaign for Henry's coming concerts showed her determination to outdo her rivals as presenters. Rivalries also extended to composition: the Caturla and Roldán supporters were at each other's throats, and Pedro Sanjuan's place in the PAAC was questioned because he was Spanish, that is, not Cuban, naturalized Cuban, or American.[23] Henry saw that he would have to be very careful not to offend anyone in Havana. In fact, his recitals, on December 23 and 26, and the

December 28 premiere of parts of his Piano Concerto with Sanjuan and the Havana Philharmonic, won over both factions. Since neither Henry nor Sanjuan had expected the audience to like the piece, they were amazed when it "stamped and roared, and yelled for a repeat of the last movement. I played 4 encores." At Henry's urging, Señor de Quevedo decided to create a journal for Latin American music similar to *New Music*.[24] Henry's "terrific time" included a trip to the "very quaint" city of Matanzas, and many private parties and receptions. His friendly relationship with the Cubans was then undermined by extreme political instability, to the point that when Slonimsky attempted to buy congas drums for Henry, he found that they were illegal because rebels in the mountains used them to send messages. Meanwhile, the first closing of the University of Havana in 300 years provoked Henry to call for support for a protest.[25] The overthrow of the dictator Gerardo Machado in 1933 only brought in others. Henry never went back, nor did he visit any other Latin American country, not even Mexico, where Chávez was increasingly influential.

The Cuban concerts return us to the Pan American Association of Composers, which had been comatose since Henry left for Europe. He tried to interest Chávez in reviving activities, now that Varèse had moved to Paris with the intention of remaining there. "Frankly," Henry told him, "while I have the greatest appreciation of Varèse's work, and consider him one of the most interesting of composers, I feel that he works so politically in an organization that it is better to try to run it without his immediate direction." He had already obtained Walton's backing for a concert of North American and Latin American music.[26]

Despite an almost empty PAAC bank account, Henry worked intensively with Ives and Slonimsky to plan a joint project with the Theatre Guild (New York), Slonimsky's Boston Chamber Orchestra, and Adolph Weiss's Pan American Ensemble. When the plan had to be abandoned,[27] Henry continued with other ideas. Weiss, who was in Berlin studying with Schoenberg, reported the collapse of a proposed ISCM concert of American music and offered to help the PAAC from there.[28]

The first PAAC concert, on April 21, 1930, at the Carnegie Chamber Hall— now the 268-seat Weill Recital Hall—had excellent songs by Ives, Ruth Crawford's powerful *Rat Riddles*, and works by Caturla, Chávez, Weisshaus, Vivian Fine, Dane Rudhyar, Gerald Strang, Henry Brant, Adolph Weiss, George Antheil, and Henry himself. While the concert cannot be described as balanced between the United States and Latin America, it was a promising beginning that made Henry even more ambitious to create major events such as a PAAC concert with the Cincinnati Symphony.[29] Funding was always on his mind, especially after misunderstandings forced him to pay $73 [2010: $953] in PAAC expenses personally. In mid-February 1931, Ives, who had not yet been hit by the Depression, committed himself to giving $200 [2010: $2,860] toward PAAC expenses and

$100 toward the European concerts that had become Ives's and Henry's greatest goal. When Harmony Ives and a friend added $110, Henry enough money to build a mechanism for further solicitation.[30]

Weiss's idea of a European project gradually expanded into a series of symphonic concerts of American music there. Arranging them from 4,000 miles away would have posed insurmountable problems without the assistance of Weiss and Ruth Crawford, who was in Berlin with a Guggenheim Fellowship and eager to help. She began with advice about local factionalism and counseled working patiently toward a "smash-up concert" the following fall, when Imre Weisshaus, who had become an apostle of American music, would be on hand to help. Since the planned demolition of the Kroll Opera might put Otto Klemperer out of work, Crawford thought (incorrectly) that he could be available to conduct for the PAAC as he had already done for the ISCM.[31] Convinced that the concerts were feasible, Henry asked Slonimsky to plan dates in Paris, obtained Blanche Walton's promise of further help, and found another patron.[32]

It was obvious that the PAAC could not consider bringing an American orchestra to Europe. Instead, a conductor supplied by the PAAC would conduct local orchestras, which had the additional benefit that European musicians would experience American music directly. On June 6, 1931, Slonimsky launched the series in Paris, conducting the Straram Orchestra in a program of singular variety: Adolph Weiss's *La Vie Americaine*, Ives's *Three Places in New England*, Ruggles's *Men and Mountains*, Roldán's ultra-Cuban *La Rebambaramba*, and the world premiere of Henry's new *Synchrony*, a tone-cluster chamber-orchestra piece. The second program contained works by Caturla, Chávez, Riegger, Salzedo, and Varèse.[33]

While Nicolas Slonimsky was prone to exaggerating, his elated report to Henry concurs with several reviews showing that Paris had paid attention, and that the success of the first concert drew more listeners to the second. Ives could enjoy being described as a real discovery, and the fourth movement of Roldán's *La Rebambaramba* had to be encored. On the other hand, Ruggles and Weiss received not a single good word. Slonimsky wrote, "Varèse proved himself an honest ally and a good fellow. He worked like a nigger to bring in a crowd for both concerts. Undoubtedly we owe at least 33 percent of the house at the second concert to his efforts. He entertains a high opinion about me as conductor too, and is trying to arrange paying dates for me in Europe. We must give more Pan-American concerts next year, and you must come to play your Concerto. This will be a sensation—I know it."[34]

Because of Slonimsky's position in Boston, the programs drew the attention of the local press. An outraged Philip Hale, the conservative critic of the *Boston Herald*, excoriated Slonimsky for conducting music by "wild-eyed anarchists," composers who, Hale asserted, were not leaders and who had never been chosen by the conductors of great American orchestras. "He thus purposed to acquaint

Parisians with contemporaneous American music . . ." Had he chosen Loeffler, Deems Taylor, or Foote, or a tasteful traditionalist with skill and some individuality, "his audience in Paris would now have a fairer idea of what Americans are doing in the art." Hale did not tell his readers that Parisians liked Slonimsky's selection. In fact, Slonimsky had acquitted himself so well that Henry henceforth took it upon himself to promote him as the ideal champion of American modernism. Ives, whose common sense was at least as valuable as his money, now urged Henry to eliminate a New York concert of the PAAC and concentrate resources on "conquering Europe."[35]

When reading through the documents of the months since Henry returned from Europe, one is hard-pressed to imagine how he could concentrate on composing. Yet he produced a dozen piano pieces, eight songs, and several orchestral works, including *Synchrony*, *Polyphonica*, and the *Irish Suite* (a concerto-like arrangement of earlier piano pieces). It was not a huge quantity for two years, but much of it is wonderful.

PART THREE

THE FRENETIC YEARS

18

Looking beyond Europe from Berlin

Some last-minute additions to *New Musical Resources* show the impact of Henry's meetings with Russian researchers. Upon returning to Berlin from Moscow, he proposed to Erich von Hornbostel and Carl Stumpf, leaders of the University of Berlin's Phonogramm-Archiv (which was essentially a world-music institute), the creation of an international network to exchange and disseminate information through centers in Moscow, Leningrad, Berlin, Paris, New York, and Stanford.[1] In New York shortly afterwards, he presented the plan at a meeting hosted by Blanche Walton and attended by Otto Kinkeldey (chief of the music division of the New York Public Library), composer/theorists Joseph Schillinger and Charles Seeger, and music theorist Joseph Yasser. Whereas twice before a group had been created and had floundered, this time it moved forward, naming itself the New York Musicological Society, with Walton as a major patron.[2] In 1934 it was reorganized as the American Musicological Society, national in scope and based in Philadelphia.

Although Henry read three papers at meetings in 1932 and 1933, he did not remain actively involved as the Society narrowed its focus to the European tradition;[3] his concept of "the science of music" embraced extra-European cultures.[4] His childhood acquaintance with Asian music influenced his compositions at least as early as the 1917 piano piece "Amiable Conversation," which was modeled on the tones of Cantonese dialect and almost certainly was one of the "lively descriptive compositions influenced by Oriental music" that he played in 1920 at St. Mark's-in-the-Bouwerie.[5] Nancy Yunghwa Rao has shown how the tonal inflections of Chinese speech then spread through Henry's music and theories.[6]

Chinese music was only a beginning, however. In the 1920s and early 30s he developed relationships with outstanding performers of non-Western music. Kitaro Tamada, an accomplished shakuhachi player who graduated from the Tokyo Agricultural College, worked as a butler in Los Angeles, sold vegetables, and became a monk,[7] provided illustrations for Henry's lectures in the Los Angeles and San Francisco regions. Unfortunately for Henry, who needed the ticket receipts, Tamada demanded that the lectures be free and exclude anyone who might have "a bad moral influence on the audience."[8] According to Sidney, after he introduced Henry to the director of a settlement house in the Asian district of San Francisco, Henry gathered players of ethnic instruments for concerts there.[9] His first documentable presentation of extra-European music was the symposium on exotic music on December 28, 1924, at St. Mark's-in-the-Bouwerie, which may have been the first fully transcultural event in the United States.[10] Two years later, he curated another symposium at the church, using performers of Hindu, Chinese, Japanese, and "Arabian" music.[11] Elliott Carter remembered hearing non-Western music for the first time at one of those events.[12]

Henry's path toward the systematic study of extra-European music probably included three other influences that he did not mention: explorations of Hindu rhythms around 1916 by Edgard Cheetham, Halcyon's music director;[13] probable conversations with Bartók about folkloric research; and his 1926 trip to the Moravian mountain village. That Moravian experience and Bartók were on his mind in two 1927 articles, "Moravian Music"[14] and "How Young Hungary Expresses Individuality," which discuss East European composers' attempt to find personally meaningful substance in their traditional music.[15] Subsequent study of the psychology of musical perception intensified his vision of other cultures contributing to Western composition. His slightly younger friend Colin McPhee may also have played a role in Henry's evolution. Sidney thought that Henry heard Balinese music in the late 1920s on recordings that McPhee had received,[16] possibly as early as 1929, but McPhee's biographer, Carol Oja, could not determine when those recordings arrived,[17] and Henry does not refer to McPhee or the recordings in his later recollection of the period.[18]

Henry's extensive performing experience with extra-European music dates from his use of American Indian thunder-sticks in *Ensemble* (1924). In 1927 he began studying the raga and tala system of North India with Sahat Lahiri, and Arabic music with an unnamed teacher. A year later he studied drumming with a Yale student who claimed to be a Ugandan prince.[19] He does not say when he began shakuhachi lessons with Tamada.

In Berlin, Hornbostel must have described his crowning achievement, a Phonogramm-Archiv containing some 22,000 cylinder recordings of music from all parts of the world. The collection was bound to interest Henry, but he could not afford to study abroad. Hoping that a grant might help the degreeless Henry win a faculty position, Terman suggested he apply to a new funder, the John Simon Guggenheim Foundation, which had awarded grants to Copland and Ruth Crawford. Henry initially inquired about support for *New Music*, which the guidelines excluded; Sidney's claim that he was rejected for a composition grant in 1927 is not substantiated by the Foundation's archive.[20] He may have decided against applying because he believed that the musical establishment would never support him. Terman's suggestion to focus upon research allowed him to side-step that problem.

On the application, Henry listed four goals: to increase his knowledge, write a book "with the aim in view of establishing a broader outlook on the music of the world as a whole," widen the field of musical materials suitable for composing, and write a symphonic work employing "materials gleaned from all musical systems." He proposed to profit from Hornbostel's assistance but not study with him formally.[21] Having no higher education to list, he supplied an impressive outline of his achievements and letters of reference from twenty-three dignitaries including musicologists Hornbostel, Seeger, Edward Dent (Cambridge University), and Konstantin Kuznetsov (Department of Music History, Moscow Conservatory); the German critic Stuckenschmidt; composers Bartók, Chávez, and Alois Hába; and Alvin Johnson (director of The New School for Social Research). Terman solicited letters from psychologists impressed by Henry's lectures on music and psychology, who would not have to comment about his music. Bartók's brief, warm letter described Henry as "one of the most serious and gifted composers of today." Seward, of course, was unstinting in his praise.[22] Terman urged the Foundation not to hold Henry's lack of formal education against him.[23] Charles Seeger, however, wrote such a negative "recommendation" that he felt obliged to add an apologetic but even more damaging cover letter, stating that "one can deplore some of [Henry's] activities without having any less high regard for his real capacity." He doubted that Henry, "ignorant" of musicological method, would undertake essential studies with Hornbostel.[24] Fortunately, the grant panel disregarded his anti-recommendation and awarded Henry a fellowship for the year beginning October 1, 1931, as a "composer of music and musicologist," with financing one third greater than his proposed budget[25] and permission to split the grant period so he could teach for the spring 1932 semester at The New School.

He summered in California and sailed from New York on September 22, 1931. Once settled into Schmolke's pension, he obtained a key to the archive, the right to borrow a phonograph and recordings and work at his lodgings, and borrowing privileges at the State Library.[26] He began with a preliminary survey of the most primitive music, from African pygmies, Pangwe (Central Africa), Tierra del Fuego, Borneo, the Solomon Islands, New Guinea, and Malacca. As Edward Dent predicted in his Guggenheim recommendation, Henry's discoveries roiled the waters of ethnomusicological research, which in Berlin focused on acoustical issues such as tuning. Henry quickly surmised that Hornbostel's team lacked sufficient knowledge of music, and that their tabulated results were faulty.[27]

He cultivated Johannes Wolf, director of the music division of the State Library, and Curt Sachs, director of the extraordinary Musical Instrument Museum, rejoicing when Sachs allowed him to play anything in the collection, "not like our Metropolitan, who refuse to open their cases! Musty old things!"[28] He spent two hours daily studying Javanese performance and theory with Raden Mas Jodjana, a distinguished young Javanese musician and nephew of the Sultan, who was living in Berlin and agreed to teach Henry once convinced of his sincerity.[29] A. F. Roemahlaiselan, a young dancer and musician, taught him the "Balinese point of view."[30] Pichu Sambamoorthy, a thirty-year-old performer and scholar from the University of Madras who was studying Western music, became a resource for Indian music.[31] Jodjana suggested that he go to Java for further study, but Henry recognized that the probability of war in Asia would preclude any studies there.[32]

Two notebooks of research plans largely compiled in Berlin in 1931 show that Seeger had underestimated Henry's awareness of investigative methods. He broke down the process systematically, including musical and nonmusical aspects, such as language and religion, and watched for mixed systems (hybrids), which Hornbostel's group considered unworthy of study. He read publications by Hornbostel and others, attended a lecture by Sambamoorthy, and heard a performance by a gamelan orchestra with dance. Subjects for articles were already racing through his mind. With $100 [2010: $1,430] from the New School's president, Alvin Johnson, and Dean Clara Mayer, he bought copies of 120 cylinders in the archive, giving the school what probably was the first collection of non-Western music in the United States.[33] Like Bartók, Henry considered his studies of other musical systems as important as composing.

Although Henry told Olive very little about his research, he supplied her with fine details of the formidable competition for his attention. Berlin and its beautiful surroundings captivated him, and he was strangely silent about the increasing political violence. Schmolke, he said, "made his life comfortable and pleasant beyond reckoning." Traditional and progressive artistic currents were all around, and not just in concert halls. Georg Schünemann, the director of the Hochschule für Musik, showed him around its advanced center for studying radio, electrical technology, and acoustics. Henry was particular impressed by its new Trautonium, an electrical instrument for which Hindemith had already composed. The conservatism of American music education became obvious and very distressing. Endless projects included performing, writing, reading proofs, and developing contacts. He also had to tend to business in the United States, such as overseeing the music curriculum and concerts at The New School and getting Ives to help with the New Music Society's nearly empty bank account.

The biggest consumer of his time was the grand project of the Pan American Association of Composers (PAAC) to present American orchestral music in Europe. A good foundation had been laid by Adolph Weiss and Ruth Crawford during their stays in Berlin, but the budget required that its scope be focused.

A single symphonic concert could consume the $1,000 [2010: $14,300] contributed by Ives. Fortunately, Weiss had succeeded in getting the well-known Berliner Funkstunde (Berlin Radio Hour) to give a full orchestra concert of American music at its own expense, with its own conductor. For Vienna, Weiss proposed beginning with a chamber orchestra concert conducted by Webern; Henry rejected the alternative of a small-scale concert performed by players from the Vienna chapter of the International Society for Contemporary Music (ISCM). Knowing that Ives wanted to abandon a proposed New York concert and put all resources into "conquering Europe,"[34] Henry accepted Weiss's suggestion and asked Webern to reserve a concert hall in Vienna.[35] As the arrangements proceeded, he assured Harry and Olive that "We will be on the map yet."[36]

Just two weeks of Henry's work on the PAAC plans shows the magnitude of the challenges. As arrangements for the Berlin concerts were falling into place, he investigated prospects in Cologne, Hamburg, Milan, Munich, Paris, and Budapest.[37] Musicians in Copenhagen and Stockholm were interested in playing PAAC compositions. Wolff & Sachs, the firm that had managed his earlier trips, solicited broadcasts at no cost to the PAAC.[38] The ground kept shifting under Henry's feet, however. A proposed Madrid concert, to be conducted by Pedro Sanjuan, crumbled in the chaos following the overthrow of the Spanish dictatorship.[39] The depreciation of the pound suggested limiting Berlin to one concert and arranging something in London, but Henry feared that English musicians would balk. Just when backers of a Berlin concert reported suffering from financial distress, Varèse wrote that money was urgently needed in Paris. (Henry did not tell him about Ives's donation, fearing it would reduce his incentive for aggressive fund-raising.)[40] Vienna then looked shaky because Webern felt the music was too difficult for his players, and hiring another orchestra might offend him.[41] It thus seemed desirable to postpone Vienna and undertake concerts in Prague and Budapest instead. Now Sanjuan surprised Henry with the news that the Madrid concert would take place after all.[42] It is a wonder that Henry could keep it straight. And that was just two weeks' worth of headaches.

In late October, Henry went to Brno, Prague, then Vienna, where he visited Alban Berg, whom he knew from 1926.

> I remember him so well, sitting on a high stool in the middle of his studio. He was writing music from the high stool, and he had each page of "Lulu," on which he was then working, separated, and in the form of garden paths through the studio, so that you walked up Page 1, Page 2, Page 3 and so on, all laid out there, so he could see them all, if he wanted to turn around and look at what he'd already written, so that he could relate the music to what he'd already done. He didn't have to remember. He looked at it. Walked all up and down. It was laid out like an English

formal garden . . . [The scores were on the floor.] . . . he took me on a personally conducted tour of "Lulu" . . . Such a good idea, I thought, and no wonder the opera is so well integrated . . . He always composed that way, yes—which I thought was very interesting. I always had such a good time going there.[43]

Henry got Blanche Walton to invite Berg to be her guest in New York, but Berg could not afford the trip.[44]

Webern's decision about conducting the PAAC concert seems to have hinged on Henry's *Sinfonietta*. Thirty years later Henry recalled their meeting.

He was extremely *difficile*. I had one evening with him, in my life, from 8 to 12—and this is perhaps the most concentrated evening I can remember. He sort of pierced you with an eye and asked questions about the meaning of each note. He said, "Why did you put this F sharp in this spot? Wouldn't it have done just as well over here?" Fortunately I did have a reason why I'd put it where I did, and this reason was acceptable. He said, "Oh, yes, I see this, this is a very good reason why you should put it there." But every single solitary note, as a composer I had to have a reason for it . . .

So by 12 o'clock we were both absolutely tired out, and I felt that I had come in contact with one of the most forceful people I'd ever seen—all about music and all about this particular score which he was going to play. There was no time for anything else, and I never saw him again. But that was a real occasion of meeting a person of tremendous fame.[45]

Henry's pace became feverish. In addition to setting up PAAC concerts, he was promoting Slonimsky's conducting career and working with Varèse on a plan for concerts in the Soviet Union.[46] Convincing Bartók's manager to allow him to play in the Paris PAAC concert was a major triumph,[47] but programming the concerts was like tiptoeing through a minefield. Unless all PAAC composers were represented, some would complain that a small inner circle was favoring itself. Henry proposed that Ruggles, Ives, and his own music be played most; Weiss and Riegger should be featured in "Teutonic" countries. Hanson's more conventional style seemed best suited to Budapest; Hanson, Rudhyar, and Harris needed careful handling; Sanjuan's music would be done in Berlin by Taube's chamber orchestra and in Madrid, along with Roldán and Caturla; Villa Lobos needed to be included somewhere. As to the others, Henry could only encourage Slonimsky to find some place to perform them.[48]

The PAAC concerts opened on November 23, 1931, to a full house in Madrid after Henry counseled against a second cancellation. Limited to four rehearsals for the entire program, Sanjuan had to drop a piece by Ives because the players could not read the parts. Furthermore, because Caturla's and Roldán's music never arrived, all the composers were from the United States,[49] with the result that a reviewer attacked the Panamericanism of the concert as "the application of the Monroe Doctrine in Norteamericano style." Of Henry's *Sinfonietta* he argued with some justice that Wagnerian romanticism underlay the modernism.[50] Henry saw the bright side. "The critics," he told Olive, "wrote an enormous amount over the concert, mixed middling as concerns praise of works, but all agreed it was the most unprecedentedly modern of any concert ever given in Madrid!"[51] It was painful to tell Ives about the fate of his piece, but Henry offered as consolation Imre Weisshaus's intention to play a movement from the "Concord" Sonata.[52]

The sold-out PAAC concert on December 2 served as the opening of Imre Weisshaus's new-music series at the Bauhaus, which had moved to Dessau after being closed by the right-wing government in Weimar.[53] While there is no record of the impression made by the music, Willi Reich reported the good reception of the concert in Vienna conducted by Webern, which took place in February.[54]

The entire PAAC enterprise helped shape Henry into an astute entrepreneur and perceptive advocate, sensitive to professional politics and public prejudices. He should have been applauded by his colleagues but, he told Sidney, the very idea of the PAAC concerts provoked "acute resistance" from a group including Varèse, who apparently was annoyed at not having been consulted first, although he was in Paris and "seemed to have given up on the PAAC entirely." Ives stood by Henry, morally and monetarily, having been spared the financial devastation that ruined Blanche Walton.[55] Now he consented to help Henry with *New Music Edition*, a periodical for orchestral scores,[56] which became affordable because the global economic collapse made engraving in Germany cheap. Moreover, new technology facilitating reproduction of holographic scores promised to lower costs. Everything encouraged optimism about the future of American modernism in Europe.[57]

19

American Interlude

Henry left Berlin just before Christmas of 1931, settling at 35 Stuyvesant Street, near St. Mark's church, in the decrepit East Village, using Walton's elegant 68th Street apartment as his professional address. Unfortunately, composing was facilitated by a precipitous decline in touring caused by the economic crisis. Unemployment had risen from 2.3 percent in 1929 to 8.9 percent in 1930, to 15.9 percent in 1931, and reached a peak of 24.9 percent in 1933.[1] The music world suffered especially terribly because of vast joblessness already induced by the introduction of the sound film, radio, and recording. Commercial concert bookings dropped by nearly a third by 1932–33; in 1933 the New York musicians' union said 80 percent of its musicians were unemployed. Nationally, in 1934, some 60 percent of formerly employed musicians were jobless despite a rising economy.[2] Furthermore, as the novelty of Henry's ideas began wearing off, he was left in the same position as his colleagues—a man of only moderate notoriety.

Fortunately, his advocates were multiplying. An undated list from these years names some ninety soloists and ensembles that had performed his music. Since most Cowell performers had close ties with him, he was elated when Stokowski unexpectedly decided to read the *Sinfonietta* with the Philadelphia Orchestra.[3] Such triumphs rarely come by chance, however. An acquaintance had asked several hundred friends and music club presidents to bombard Stokowski with requests for Henry's music.[4] Their success surpassed expectations. On April 1, 1932, Stokowski conducted *Synchrony* on an American music concert. Henry postponed his departure for California to hear this first professional performance of one of his orchestral pieces.[5]

Although Henry-the-pianist was hardly to be seen on stage, Henry-the-lecturer was talking nonstop at The New School. Before leaving for Germany in September 1931, he had brought in Seeger for music and Doris Humphrey in dance,[6] and organized an impressively varied series of twelve concerts with dance, Western music, and world music. Clara Mayer, the associate director and dean, who initially opposed Henry's ideas, happily informed him that the first two concerts were huge successes, the third looked like a sellout, and Henry deserved a hero's parade.[7] Despite the deepening Depression, The New School was in relatively good shape. To celebrate the first anniversary of the move to its new building on West Twelfth Street, it had added eight subjects, including more music.[8] Henry gave twelve Wednesday evening lectures on the appreciation of modern music, at each of which he analyzed one piece in lay terms, to equip the students to examine other modern compositions by themselves. His broadly based choice of music even included Parisian neoclassicism, though he may not have presented it dispassionately. His second series of concerts retained the breadth of the previous year but featured the juxtaposition of new and early music. He also created a workshop series presenting Ruth Crawford, Riegger, Rudhyar, Ruggles, Charles Seeger, Weiss, and unnamed others, discussing their own music. Audiences for the workshops ranged from twenty-five to a hundred, with an average of about forty.[9] His greatest innovation was a world music sampler, twelve weekly lecture-recitals comparing the musical systems of the world, with live performances of "Arabian," Balkan, Chinese, Indian, Irish, Japanese, Javanese, Mexican, Russian, Scottish, American Indian, and traditional "Hebrew" music.[10]

Although three months' work brought him only $500 [2010: $7,980], he was fortunate not to have lost his job like some colleagues. His successes brought out his worst competitiveness, however. He proudly told Olive that Johnson thought his courses made Copland's "look like kindergarten." He may have been exaggerating for Olive's sake, but there is no question that the administration supported him. In fact, the money to purchase recordings of non-Western music came from the personal funds of the president and the dean. For 1932–33, he initiated workshops in rhythm, addressing his discovery that only two American institutions devoted attention to it.[11] He constantly varied his class subjects[12] partly because his view of music kept expanding, and also to safeguard his income by providing incentives for returning students to enroll with him again.

Firmly convinced of Henry's greatness, Olive began jotting down everything that he told her on scraps of paper and in notebooks that are a major source of information about his ideas and biography. Among them are her notes on his six lectures on contemporary music at the Sutter Street YWCA in San Francisco in May 1932. Because she had no musical training, these notes confirm that Henry became a popular teacher and lecturer because he could project ideas simply and informally.

20

Berlin Again

In mid-July 1932, Henry arrived in New York and promptly had to backtrack 180 miles to a hotel where he had left his wallet with all his papers.[1] [Sidney: "A list of such incidents wd hardly be believed—London '23 (his mss), Prague (26) & Dresden (all his papers), SF on return from Asia in '57, Drugstore at 112th and Bdwy in '60."] When he got to Berlin at the end of the month, Germany had been hit very badly by the Depression. Schmolke's pension was half empty; her son had emigrated and she would have too, if it had been possible.[2] Visits from friends like Henry, the Iveses, Mrs. Terman, Adolph Weiss, and Imre Weisshaus were her sole source of cheer. Good news about performances of his music in Germany were offset by the shocking news that Sam Seward had died suddenly, age fifty-six, after a minor operation.[3] Still, work had to begin. He assigned Olive to scour Chinatown for beginners' books on playing Chinese music and on the Chinese language, which were unavailable in Berlin.[4]

The previous spring, Chávez had told Henry that the Mexican Education Ministry wanted to build a recorded archive of world music. Having already decided to form a similar collection for The New School, Henry agreed to help. Most of the commercially available discs were only arrangements of folk music, however, not the real thing. Because the Hornbostel recordings could not be purchased, he obtained permission to copy some cylinders to the new electric disc technology. Needing recording equipment, he turned to the Carl Lindstrom company, Europe's largest record pressers, where he learned about a marketing strategy concocted by Lindstrom's Odeon and Parlophone labels. Technicians sent to "many primitive places" around the world induced the local people to record their own music, and used the recordings to market windup phonographs so they could hear their own performances. It was only a business scheme; the sales force, ignorant of the musical value of the recordings, sent samples back to Berlin, where the company unloaded them cheaply.[5] For Henry, it was an amazing opportunity. A very modest outlay bought him the nucleus of collections for himself, Chávez, and The New School, and allowed him to expand the scope of his lectures on world music.[6]

In a December report to the Guggenheim Foundation, he said that he divided his day into two-hour periods (on average), working with recordings, writing up his findings, composing, and taking care of business correspondence. Despite losing a month to a bad case of flu, he had inspected nearly two hundred recordings at the archive and about fifty at Baida, a Lebanese firm that pressed records in Berlin. During a short trip to Sweden he studied Swedish and Lapp music at the University of Uppsala and heard performances by "natives of north Sweden," that is, Lapps. He began a book about world music, aiming to elucidate individual musical systems, compare them with one another and with European art music, highlight common musical principles, and indicate "such musical practices as are individual instances rather than common practice." He expected it to be unique in any language.[7] Unfortunately, renewal of the grant to complete the book in Menlo Park and conduct research in Mexico was denied on the grounds that there were too many first-rate new candidates.[8] Although Sidney claimed that Hornbostel told the Foundation that he had never seen Henry, its archive contains nothing to that effect, and Hornbostel himself had arranged for Henry to work in his room at Schmolke's. Sidney also claimed that Guggenheim secretary Henry Allen Moe later thought that the denial was one of the Foundation's great mistakes. That too cannot be substantiated.[9] In any event, Henry, lacking support to write his book, eventually abandoned the idea.

In January 1933, Henry sent the Foundation samples of the first of some thirty articles that he planned,[10] of which he apparently completed only studies of Irish, Balkan, and Icelandic music, and methodology. (An article on neoprimitivism preceded the Guggenheim fellowship.) His jottings show increasing interest in the cultures, especially Javanese, about which Prince Raden Mas Jodjana was providing indispensable information and insights. It is possible that Henry would have left more evidence of interest in the cultures had there been material on hand, but cultures were not of great interest to Hornbostel and his circle when Henry was there.[11] Understanding that his conclusions implicitly criticized the Berlin group, he refrained from writing anything while Hornbostel was alive. In a later, unpublished article entitled "Hybrid Music," Henry explained that although Hornbostel was "the world's greatest enthusiast for scientific investigation of primitive and folk music," he refused to permit his students to investigate music that was culturally mixed. Hornbostel's stubbornness caused many interactions among "primitive, folk, and cultivated music systems" to pass by without being preserved. Henry, on the other hand, felt that a thorough study of such interactions was urgently needed, having become convinced that even the music preserved on the archive's recordings might already have been hybridized. "There is very little music in the world of which one may say with certainty that it is completely indigenous to the region in which it may be found. And when, through integration, does a hybrid form cease to be hybrid? It is hard to say. Opinions differ." One of the most provocative ideas arising from his research was that "the single tone with a given pitch is not the basis of musical sound." Instead, the basic sound should be represented by a curve, which he compared to the sound of a derisive "Oh, yeah?" He also became convinced that duple rhythm is not essential in all systems of music. A rhythm of single, equally accented beats seemed perfectly satisfactory "to many simple souls."[12]

His experiences with hybrids were sometimes incredibly entertaining. He found recordings of "Yes, We Have No Bananas" in nine languages, including one in Arabic, accompanied by oud, Arabic flute, and drums. "The full realization of what the tune was didn't burst in on one until it had been going on for some time—it sounded like Arabic music. Even stranger was the version from Java, with the nasal Malayan voice, and the orchestra of gamelon instruments." He also heard "Onward Christian Soldiers" sung by Solomon Islanders. Lacking a leading tone in their pentatonic scale, they altered the tune, "and so the famous opening of the main phrase changed itself from C,C,C,C,C,B,A,B,C, etc. to C,C,C,C,C,A,G,A,C etc. These natives, so returned soldier friends now tell me, are crazy about American popular tunes, but still change them into the nearest pentatonic equivalent."[13]

He concluded that a foundation should be created to support specialized research into Western music's place in the context of world music. It would investigate the philosophical, psychological, physical, mathematical, and anthropological contexts of new Western music; primitive music of all peoples; the sociological importance of music; and music's position "in the activities of the peoples of the world."[14]

Although he pursued research seriously, his claim of spending two hours daily on business affairs undoubtedly was understated. He organized the music offerings at The New School, dealt with a Berlin publisher who wanted Harry's reminiscences of Jack London, assisted conductor Pedro Sanjuan with problems resulting from the collapse of the Cuban government, worked on a new book on American music, wrote several articles about Ives, and kept promoting Slonimsky as a conductor. The orchestral project of the Pan American Association of Composers (PAAC) was endlessly frustrating. Proposals for concerts in Poland, the USSR, and at the first Maggio Musicale Fiorentino all fell apart.[15] In fact, all his enterprises were faltering for lack of money, despite Ives's support. Because communal action seemed to offer the best prospects, Henry and Adolph Weiss planned a PAAC rental library, managed by New Music, so that composers would not have to share their tiny profits with publishers.[16]

Henry also had to supervise the New Music Society. Although no concerts took place during his absence, New Music Quarterly and the orchestral score series New Music Edition presented unrelenting challenges, among them prodding Ives to select songs for a special issue,[17] which became the superb collection

Thirty-Four Songs. Henry was extremely irritated that Cos Cob Press, the rival venture founded by Alma Wertheim and the Copland circle, also planned a volume of Ives's songs, and Ives was not in the United States to help settle who would get what. Although Cos Cob's *Seven Songs* beat Henry's *Thirty-Four Songs* by a few months, Henry's collection is much more impressive and adventurous. He followed it in 1935 with nineteen additional songs.[18]

He also jumped headlong into a new large-scale project, the Commission for International Exchange Concerts, founded in Vienna in 1930 by composers Daniel Ruyneman (Holland) and Hans Pless (Austria) to promote international interchange of repertory.[19] Their concept was simple: Country A would perform music from Country B; Country B would reciprocate.[20] The committee comprised one musician of each member-country; a country joined the Commission when one of its musicians joined the committee. When Henry became its only non-European, its other members represented Austria, England, France, Germany, Holland, and Hungary.[21] Each correspondent was to appoint fellow countrymen as advisors, who would only have a national role; the central office in Amsterdam, headed by Ruyneman, would act chiefly to resolve conflicts and keep statistics. Essentially any type of exchange was possible—whole evenings of music of another country, performances of individual pieces, or anything else that would advance the cause. No stylistic tendency was favored; in fact, the representatives were asked to cover all tendencies. The exchange partners determined for themselves who would pay expenses.[22] Viewing the exchanges as an efficient means for propagating non-European music, Henry immediately invited Chávez to represent Mexico, arranged concerts of Polish and Dutch music in the United States in exchange for concerts of American music in Warsaw and Amsterdam,[23] secured Swedish and Danish participation, and attempted to organize concerts of various nations in New York, financed by their consulates. To spread exchanges around the country Henry obtained the backing of the National Federation of Music Clubs and foresaw radio having a role in the exchanges.[24]

Despite being overloaded with work, he also became American representative of *Pro Musica*, a journal of new European compositions, published by Wilhelm Hansen in Copenhagen and unrelated to E. Robert Schmitz's American concert organization. He accepted the position assuming that, as an insider, he could prevent *Pro Musica* from competing with *New Music Quarterly*. Actually, he did not have to worry because *Pro Musica* was very conservative. Although it showed interest in printing Henry's "Sinister Resonance," Hansen discontinued it after a year.[25]

As Henry supplied his parents with a steady stream of information meant to generate publicity in the United States, Olive detected a disturbingly egocentric tone. While he had every reason to be proud of his accomplishments, concern about his self-image may explain why she criticized Slonimsky for writing an overly adulatory article about Henry. Slonimsky apologetically replied that he was incensed by seeing how little help Henry got for his gigantic tasks.[26] One can see his point. Copland's survey of American music from 1923 to 1933, in *Modern Music*, scarcely credited Henry's work.[27]

His Berlin social life flourished; every day seemed to bring him new friends. In the first month alone, he enjoyed evenings with Ernst Toch, Adolph Weiss, the director of the State Opera, the curator of the Ethnological Museum, and the painter, designer, and photographer Laszlo Moholy-Nagy. Playing bridge with Weiss was a special pleasure because no one else in Berlin knew the game.[28] No social activity quite equaled Henry's tennis games with Schoenberg, however, another priceless story fraught with contradictions. Although Henry later placed the games both in the 1920s and in 1931, his letters do not refer to Schoenberg and tennis until August 1932, when they describe very recent events, and Schoenberg only began to learn to play tennis in 1927. A letter of December 1932, thanking Weiss for introducing him to Schoenberg, also implies that they had met relatively recently. Moreover, Henry's statement that Schoenberg first learned he was a composer at the tennis court implies that Schoenberg did not come to that 1926 dinner at Schnabel's.[29]

Although the passage of time may have given the tennis story some extra flavor, Nuria Schoenberg Nono confirmed its outline as Henry described it thirty years later.[30] Henry, the Weisses, and the Schoenbergs all belonged to the Berlin Tennis Club. Because Henry and Schoenberg were equally terrible, while Mrs. Schoenberg was excellent, Henry's appearance at the club freed her from having to play with her husband. Henry says he "fed very very careful soft balls to Schoenberg which anybody could have returned, and he did return them once in a while. He was still worse than I." They were stuck with one another, however; the club required doubles matches.

Now curious about Henry, Schoenberg arranged to hear him play his music on August 26, but in the end Henry, the Schoenbergs, and the Weisses simply dined together.[31] That may have been the occasion when Schoenberg invited Henry to attend the analysis class held in his home twice a week for four hours each, attended by two music critics of daily papers—Josef Rufer and Hans Heinz Stuckenschmidt—and three unnamed composition students.[32] Henry attended regularly but did not publicize his participation for fear he would be regarded as a student.[33] Sensing that Schoenberg's methods could provide ideas for future lecturing,[34] Henry took careful notes, which regrettably vanished.[35] His 1962 description may show the effects of time upon his memory, but is worth reading.

> These were exceptionally interesting things, these classes, because these were top-flight composers who came at this time . . . undoubtedly hoping to hear from Schoenberg about his famous 12-tone row and serial music. Not at all. . . . During this whole period of four months, except

for one session, we talked about the F major String Quartet of Mozart, one string quartet, and if there's anything that anybody didn't know about how Mozart related his materials in this quartet, I'm sure I don't know who it was. . . . So Schoenberg very sweetly said, after he had had this enormous study of this thing: "Now you know how a good composer relates his material. You go and do this with yours." In the last session, he said, "I will show you how I have done it in my own case." And so he took his Chamber Symphony, Opus 9, which doesn't sound a bit like Mozart superficially, and showed where every relationship in this whole work is derived in the same way . . . that Mozart used for his. I have no doubt at all that Schoenberg was the greatest exponent of the line of German-speaking composers of this time, because I don't think anybody else in the world knew that much about Mozart.

He added that with Schoenberg dead, he felt free to reveal Schoenberg's admission that he had listened at the keyhole when a friend had his composition lessons with Brahms and called himself a "keyhole student."

As Schoenberg himself said, and I have no doubt at all that this is true, probably the greatest knowledge of classical music reposed in Brahms at this time, and so it went from Brahms to Schoenberg and from Schoenberg it was transmitted to us as students of Schoenberg.

Schoenberg finally heard Henry play on October 19. "Although I do not think he [got] a great deal out of 'Dynamic Motion,' he said it was interesting," and invited Henry to play for his class.[36] Thus Henry could tell Olive in November, "My music was praised to his class again by Schoenberg . . ."[37] (Sidney added a bit of confusion by claiming that Henry played for Schoenberg's class in the 1920s. Henry only mentions having done it in mid-October 1932; and surely that is another topic he would not have kept from Olive, or that she would have discarded.) Henry and Schoenberg also spent part of a December day together.[38] Schoenberg left an indelible impression on Cowell, who considered him the greatest living composer on the basis of his craft and his remarkable ideas.[39]

Henry only did a little performing during his second stay in Berlin. In September he played for Hornbostel, who, he said, was very excited.[40] After endless negotiations, he acquired two engagements for himself in Sweden, and a friend of Schmolke's organized a concert in Copenhagen, for which Henry had to pay the costs.[41] On October 3, at the Music History Society of the University of Uppsala, he lectured on modern music's development and scientific background, modernism in American composition, and new instruments, and played ten of his pieces. The next day he gave a similar performance for the Swedish-American Society in Stockholm, repeating it in Copenhagen on October 6. (It was during this trip that he persuaded Swedish and Danish leaders to enter the International Exchange program[42] and heard Lapp traditional music.)

His reception in Sweden and Denmark more or less repeated his earlier experiences in Central Europe. Sweden, on the musical periphery, netted him tremendous publicity and extremely good reviews. Uppsala critics talked of the real imagination, high quality, positive worth of the music, and of course his techniques.[43] Stockholm's *Dagbladed* called him "one of the most original musicians living at the present time." Denmark, where connections to the German mainstream were stronger, received him with suspicion and some hostility.[44] Copenhagen newspapers were generally negative with scattered positive comments.

By December things were humming. Chávez programmed *Synchrony* in Mexico City;[45] Edition Adler agreed to publish *Four Continuations;*[46] a PAAC concert was set for Hamburg;[47] the Berlin chapter of the International Society for Contemporary Music (ISCM) gave him a concert that was a real honor from such a cliquish group.[48] That performance took place on November 22 at the Charlottenburg home of a wealthy retailer. After Henry spoke about the extension of piano techniques and sounds and played seven pieces, Schünemann, director of the Hochschule für Music, talked about music and recordings.[49] Although semiprivate, the soirée generated a nice review in *Berliner Morgenpost;*[50] *8 Uhr Abendblatt* mentioned the projected book on comparative musicology.[51] Henry described a short sarcastic notice in the "Berlin Concerts" column of the *Münchner Neueste Nachrichten* as "a good roast."[52]

On December 1 he played "Sinister Resonance" and "Dynamic Motion" in the first of Weisshaus's contemporary music concerts at the Bauhaus, which was now in Berlin, having been expelled from Dessau by the local Nazi-controlled government. It was approximately his fifth performance since Kandinsky invited him the first time. Through the Bauhaus he became friendly with leaders of the central European avant-garde painters. Paul Klee always asked Henry to call upon him, but never came to his concerts, having little interest in music, "or anyhow music of Americans." László Moholy-Nagy and Walter Gropius, however always did, "and they claimed for my [piano] music a relationship with their ideas of architecture." Lionel Feininger also expressed interest in his music.[53] (Henry's contact with Kurt Schwitters probably took place in Vienna.)

A week after the Bauhaus concert, he played in Hamburg at a PAAC concert jointly sponsored by ISCM and the US consul. Now composers included both the PAAC old guard and Copland and Piston, whom Henry was encouraging in the hope of ending factional divisions.[54] He told Ives that it went very well, with several hundred listeners "who were very interested, although not the type that applauds very much."[55] He told Piston that the audience liked his piece best, refraining from mentioning that the critics devoted most of their energy to Henry's music, albeit tepidly. The *Hamburger Fremdenblatt* proclaimed that Henry showed how America still had some surprises for Europe.[56]

In a flurry of last-minute activity, he recorded five pieces for Hamburg Radio, which were promptly broadcast, "a great honor in Germany, not like in America."[57] On December 10 he spoke to the Deutsche Musikgesellschaft about new possibilities for the piano.[58] His last performance took place in the Neukölln district of Berlin on the 20th.[59] At some point he recorded "Banshee," "Aeolian Harp," and "Harp of Life" for Lindstrom.[60]

One of these concerts—or possibly one the previous year—was attended by Grete Sultan (1906–2005), a pianist who soon fled the Nazis, settled in New York, and became a well-known teacher and performer, especially of music by America's leading modernists such as Morton Feldman, Stefan Wolpe, and John Cage. (Cage wrote two pieces for her.) She had met Henry in 1923, when Buhlig brought him to her parents' home. At that time, Henry taught her some of his music, which she soon performed. She heard him again when he returned to Berlin in the early 1930s, and forty-five years later sent Sidney one of the few vivid descriptions of his playing at that time.

> His sound on the piano was so voluptuous, elastic, vibrating, he moved on the keyboard like a dancer—or an animal-like relaxed contact to the instrument—the piano being a harp—never a percussion-drum—Henry's sound was never harsh or hard, always open and round and ringing, even in the fastest clusters—there was the enjoyment of sound. [61]

His December letters give no clues as to whether the Nazi plurality in the November election had sunk in. He does not allude to the possibility that Hitler would be named chancellor, the possible effects of a Nazi government, or the election of Roosevelt. Yet he must have known that his Berlin management Wolff & Sachs had been boycotted well before the Nazis' accession, and that other Jewish friends anticipated trouble.[62] Asked in April 1933 if had he felt the Nazis' ascendancy, he only cited the cancellation of an international concert that he had arranged. "This the Nazi chieftain branded as 'super-Bolshevik.'" [63]

As the end of 1932 approached, it was time to go home. Schoenberg and Toch saw him off at the train to Hamburg. He sailed on December 22.

21

The End of Virtuosity

The Guggenheim Fellowship had only postponed the reckoning with the Depression's effects on Henry. He lost his New York City base when Blanche Walton, crippled by stock market losses, had to sell her West 68th Street palace and moved to a tiny apartment.[1] He had had a reasonably full calendar for 1930–31, including the tour to Cuba and orchestral appearances in New York. Then the bank crash triggered the general economic collapse. In 1933–34 he had only seven concerts, in 1934–35 even fewer, and 1935–36 hardly any; sometimes he played nothing more than one or two pieces in the context of someone else's concert. Now that he could no longer afford a clipping service, a few other engagements, especially private events with no printed program, may escape notice, but the decline of his public performing is visible in his turn away from writing piano music.

This new situation had its compensations, however. His desire to stop battling for engagements, settle down, and be taken seriously as a composer was intensifying. Moreover, abuse by too-clever journalists was turning him into a nervous performer.[2] Unfortunately, the economy forced him to change direction just as the initial shock of his music had worn off and critics began to judge it less frivolously. The trouble was that he needed sources of income but could not shed his compulsion to create labor-intensive, nonremunerative projects and involve himself in every facet of the musical world. As a result, the next four years became a whirl of activity on parallel tracks, for which a simple, linear narrative is impossible.

At The New School, Dr. Johnson empowered him to shape the entire music program, avoiding duplicating courses available elsewhere and concentrating on living composers and world music. Since there were no appropriate textbooks, the courses had to be invented. Henry's responsibilities comprised teaching about modern music and world music, and curating concerts of contemporary music and world music.[3] During the first year in the school's new building, he was the only music teacher; Copland was too busy and may have resented not being named director of music. As the student body increased, Henry added Seeger to the faculty and expanded the offering. Now anyone teaching music was invited by him, or in his absence, Seeger. Henry also was responsible for shaping the new dance courses, engaging, at Alvin Johnson's request, the leaders of modern dance—Martha Graham, Doris Humphrey, John Martin, Charles Weidman, and Mary Wigman.

Although Johnson said that if the school ever had a music department Henry would head it, The New School's enrollment policies ultimately controlled everyone's courses. When the history of music was instituted as a for-credit course, for example, it only drew six students, who gradually trickled away. When Henry returned from Europe in January 1933, his courses drew fewer students, and the school brought back Paul Rosenfeld, "who draws better, although he lectures frightfully and tells lies. I MAY not remain here next year. The opposition is great." Then, when the music history course was reconstituted as a not-for-credit course at a lower fee, about thirty-five students enrolled and the crisis passed.[4]

In September 1933 he instituted a twelve-session course in new American music including lectures and forums "led by composers of different opinions who will discuss topics relative to their work and aims." The list of participants shows the enormous expansion of American composition in little more than a decade. About the only significant missing composer was Ives, who was too ill and reclusive to participate. Arthur Berger, then a beginning music critic, recalled getting into trouble at the *Daily Mirror* for insisting on covering those events with their small audiences rather than stars at Carnegie Hall.[5]

Aiming to be all-embracing, Henry invited composers of every conceivable style. Unmentioned in the publicity material is his love of pairing composers who disliked one another's music. In May 1933, he wrote Ives, "For my series at the NS next season, I will have some very good fights. I am getting DS Smith, from Yale, and Donovan also, and DG Mason, R. Goldmark, and Hanson—all the enemies [of modernism] (and they all accepted!) to come down to the school and give their views on American music. Then at the same forum, there will be some young blood to show up their point of view! I think the fur will fly. It should be a healthy exposé."[6] Pairing his friend John J. Becker with Daniel Gregory Mason—about whom Henry had nothing good to say—was a stroke of genius. In a thank-you note, Mason hinted at flying fur in assuring Henry that he had enjoyed the stimulating evening and that he and Becker did not hold any grudges. "In fact he has been up here [Columbia] this morning and we have been having a very interesting talk." Mason saluted Henry's effort to cultivate cordiality and mutual respect founded on more intimate acquaintanceship.[7] Douglas Moore also praised Henry's opening to the conservatives. "What we need today for American composition is a little more tolerance and less back biting."[8] Some conservatives, of course, were both victims and perpetrators of the disunity.

Thanks to Hitler, New York got Erich von Hornbostel. Dismissed by the University of Berlin because his mother was Jewish, he fled to Switzerland and accepted a lectureship at The New School, where, as Johnson had hoped, his prestige reinforced the school's role in comparative musicology. His stay was brief, however. In failing health, Hornbostel moved to Cambridge, England, where he died in 1935 at the age of fifty-eight. Conditions in Germany also prompted Johnson to create a University in Exile, a German-style school within The New School. Its music faculty included Ernst Toch, who had recently begged Henry to help get him a visa,[9] and German communism's most prominent composer, Hanns Eisler, at Seeger's and almost certainly Henry's urging.[10]

The announcement of the 1934–35 composers' forums shows Henry again expanding his scope. But as low enrollment caused courses to be dropped, competition bristled. When Copland returned to The New School in 1935, Johnson found himself in the middle, especially when Copland proposed one-man concerts, to which Henry objected. Johnson agreed that one-man concerts had to be subsidized, but supported Copland when he obtained money to underwrite the concerts and backing for concerts of recorded music, correctly foreseeing an opportunity to draw an audience south of 42nd Street.[11] As even Henry admitted, Copland's presence increased enrollment generally, so that in the fall of 1935 Henry's classes were larger. This was to be his last set of forums, however; they were taken over the following year by Ashley Pettis—possibly because Henry was in California for much of the year—as single-composer evenings sponsored by the Works Progress Administration (WPA).[12] Looking back from 1962, however, Henry expressed disappointment that the Forums became individual presentations. He always had felt that disunity produced real thought.[13]

The music program looks exciting, but only the surviving class lists tell anything about the students' response. Many classes averaged about ten students, mostly women. Enrollees in Henry's 1934 class in world music included John Cage and the singers Judith Litante and Stephanie Schehatowitsch; the students for "Creative Music Today" included composers Johanna Beyer and Wallingford Riegger (the only male). In the fall of 1935, only the course in modern harmony had a majority of men, among whom was pianist Irwin Freundlich. One student in "The Theory and Practice of Rhythm" was Henry's old California acquaintance Mrs. Sidney Hawkins Robertson, whose occupation is cryptically listed as "Social Music." For those seeking grades for teaching accreditation, the amiable Henry was no soft touch. His grade sheets show many low marks; some courses had no A's or B's at all.

In an essay for the school's twentieth-anniversary book (1939), Henry described the philosophy that governed his work and that of his principal colleagues, Copland and Seeger. "Our plan was as far as I know unique. Its foundation was the study of music in its relation to life today, that is to say, to society:

and not merely to society in America, but to society the world over. Creative music was stressed, as being the important past of musical progress." Henry emphasized the importance of the study of other musical cultures, the invitations to ethnic musicians to perform, and the translation of materials into English. "Through our encouragement, the China Institute in America printed a booklet on Chinese music which is still the best compact source of information in English."

> We studied the relation of music to physics, psychology, physiology, economics and social environment; we studied the whys and wherefores of musical response and the lack of it. We studied the purposes for which music has been used by human beings during the past and the purposes for which it is being and may be used today. We studied musical elements such as rhythm and melody technically as they are used in today's music—a completely new departure so far as I know. We studied music through creating it. . . . We showed that any normal person can, through getting rid of inhibitions, create music, and that learning to play comes naturally after the creative impulse is stirred. Our work in developing a sense of fundamental rhythm through playing easy percussion instruments was carried further than anywhere else I believe . . .[14]

Toward the end of his life, a mellower Henry credited Paul Rosenfeld for breaking down personal barriers between critics and composers, and both Copland and Rosenfeld for giving marvelous classes. By then Henry had forgiven Rosenfeld's unwillingness to say anything good about his compositions.

The stimulating atmosphere at The New School did not dampen Henry's desire to settle on the West Coast. Olive—who apparently had money—was building a magnificent house at 171 San Marcos Avenue, high in San Francisco's hills, which she hoped would be Henry's base, but no full-time teaching position was on the horizon. In 1933, he began teaching part-time at Mills College's summer division, giving courses in world music, a music history course, and later rhythm courses in conjunction with Hanya Holm and her dancers.[15] His last contracts at Mills, for the spring and summer semesters of 1936, were only possible through the physical education department.[16]

Since Stanford had no plans to form a music department, Terman convinced the administration that "Music Systems of the World" was extremely interesting from the point of view of psychology and anthropology, and committed the Psychology Department to supply half of Henry's paycheck for the 1934 summer-session course.[17] Henry devoted five of the weekly classes to Music Systems of the World and five to Modern Composers,[18] cramming in an enormous amount of material, especially considering that two sessions were devoted to examinations. The list of suggested readings included major psychological studies by Carl Seashore, Paul Farnsworth, R. M. Ogden, C. P. Heinlein, and numerous others.[19] The success of the course led to reengagement for the summer of 1935.[20] Henry still had not reached his goal of establishing a true music program, however, and Seward's death early in 1934 left the psychology department his only ally.[21]

Henry then found refuge in the Department of Hygiene and Physical Education for Women, teaching rhythm for the winter quarter.[22] When his summer appointment was renewed, he again attempted to get Stanford to implement a more comprehensive music program, and enlisted important friends to write letters of support to the university's president, to no avail.[23] Fortunately, the lectureship in rhythm was repeated for the summer of 1935, though at a reduced fee.[24] At least it allowed him to work with his ideas about teaching music through initial rhythmic studies. For the winter–spring 1935–36 session, Henry created a percussion ensemble to teach rhythm and to work with dancers on the simultaneous creation of music and choreography.[25] Negotiations got to the point of an authorization for Henry to purchase a large set of instruments from many cultures,[26] but the class was canceled because the majority of interested students had already taken it.[27] His class in modern rhythm was well enrolled, however.[28] A proposal that he develop a rhythmic accompaniment for swimming strokes met an unknown fate.[29]

The situation stymied Henry because university music departments seemed extremely stodgy. In 1933, he had drafted a treatise about how to deal with music students' lack of preparation, essentially suggesting a required introduction to music for all students with professional aspirations. University music departments should emphasize the creation or intellectual development of music, not performance, for which good private teachers were available. Where there were enough dedicated performers, a conservatory might be included in a music department. He proposed a required music course for the entire student body, teaching elementary theory and both Western and non-Western music, breaking with tradition by beginning with rhythm and melody, then counterpoint, and only then getting to harmony. It would teach the psychology of music, music's ethnological importance in many cultures, and its relationship to physics, mathematics, philosophy, anthropology, and physiology. Such courses could stimulate both laymen and prospective music students.[30] Although his treatise was never published, it anticipates key features of postwar university core curricula.

Beginning in 1934, Henry also taught at the University of California in Berkeley and/or its San Francisco extension campus, again battling unsuccessfully to create a full music program. He taught world music and modern music, but even with a good enrollment did not stand to earn much. Berkeley may be where he first used the title "Music of the Peoples of the World." Although his classes were arranged to minimize his commute from Menlo Park, travel must have been terribly draining. In January 1935 he also started a children's class in creative music at an unknown location.[31] Beyond all of this, Henry may have had other teaching positions, of which one reaches us only through a brief mention in a letter to Harry and Olive—a class in rhythm at Hanya Holm's New York Wigman School of the Dance.[32] A lecture at the Juilliard Student Club on December 14, 1934, was sweet revenge, but Damrosch was no longer director.[33]

On top of everything, he still ran the New Music Society's concerts in San Francisco and a workshop that Strang had created. The overwhelming details of 1933 through 1936 paint a sad picture of an enormously gifted man shuttling among institutions, never sure of how he would pay his expenses. Still, it was an improvement over the incessant touring of earlier years, and unlike many Americans, he came home with a little money and gave others something lasting.

Henry's courses are only a small fraction of his intricate relationships with dancers, which were largely forgotten until recently.[34] Even Leta Miller's fine study of the subject says very little about the period before 1937.[35] The reason is almost certainly that Henry's dance scores were modest, not susceptible to performance without dance, and unrelated to the Americana aesthetic that made Copland's ballets central in American musical history.

From his youth, Henry was drawn to the combination of music and motion through ballroom dancing and folk dancing in Moravia and Ireland, which, in turn, stimulated his fascination with the relationship of dance and music in extra-European cultures. In Berlin he had three months of daily lessons with A. F. Roemahlaiselan, the Javanese musician and dancer.[36] In lectures on non-Western music Henry spoke about the centrality of dance in music's development.[37] His own music is filled with allusions to folk dance, especially Irish, which he considered the "main American folk-dance influence."[38]

The vivid energies of Henry's "experimental" piano pieces made them a natural magnet for "interpretive dancers" such as Yvonne Daunt, who presented an evening of dance to Henry's music at the Salon d'Automne in 1923.[39] Other interpretive dancers followed, probably not knowing that Henry did not think much of interpretive dance. The new style known as "modern dance" was a very different matter. He may have met Doris Humphrey and Charles Weidman, of the Los Angeles–based Denishawn company, through their pianist Louis Horst, who studied with Wallace Sabin in San Francisco at about the same time as Henry and became Henry's close friend.[40] Around late 1926 or 1927, Dane Rudhyar connected Henry with Ruth St. Denis in San Francisco.[41] Strong friendships with all of them were rapidly formed.

In the next few years, Henry wrote a stream of scores for dance. On February 4, 1928, as part of their second New York season, Weidman, Charles Laskey, and José Limon danced to his piano piece "Steel and Stone," played by Horst, who now was Martha Graham's music director. It is not known if Henry composed it for them or if this was the first time that Weidman used Henry's music, but many more performances followed.[42] Two months later Humphrey premiered her choreography for "The Banshee," with Henry playing and Ives in the audience. The *Herald Tribune's* dance critic wrote about "the eerie 'Banshee,' danced by Miss Humphrey, to a blood-curdling accompaniment which Mr. Henry Cowell himself drew from a tortured piano. . . ."[43] Humphrey, who danced to "The Banshee" again in October—using an unidentified pianist because Henry was in California—proposed choreographing two or three more of his pieces to make a group.[44] "Men and Machines," a piano piece, was written for another new choreographer-friend, Elsa Findlay, whose ensemble performed it with José Limon dancing.[45]

Henry got to know Martha Graham either through connections in Santa Barbara, where her family lived, or through Horst and Humphrey. Their professional collaborations began in 1930 when Humphrey and Graham decided to get an orchestral piece from Henry for their coming season.[46] The project quickly expanded into a collaborative venture synchronizing music, dance, and lighting. As Graham prepared the dance based upon Henry's sketch of the music, she became convinced of its potential greatness. Her outline seemed very similar to his, she thought, but the moods would be more defined in her dance. The ending remained unformed in her mind. She envisioned something like "a triumphant march of peace" that would lead to silence and immobility, "all illusions of distance, and expansion like ripples in pool [sic] until they are hardly discernable."[47] She liked the proposed title, "Synchrony," but although she would have preferred something programmatic, it became *Synchrony of Dance, Music and Light*. Henry completed it shortly after staying at Graham's house in Santa Barbara in August 1930.[48] She immediately sought a venue, but the best prospect, a League of Composers concert, fell through.[49] *Synchrony* is probably the piece that Henry thought the Cleveland Orchestra might perform,[50] but it was finally premiered without dance in Slonimsky's Paris concert in June 1931. The multimedia conception was never seen, and Graham never danced it.[51] Fortunately, Henry's music stands on its own legs and has had many performances.

Working on this mini-*Gesamtkunstwerk* prompted Henry to apply his knowledge of world music to the problematic relationship between dance and music. He had found that whereas primitive societies developed traditions in which dance is independent of music (normally drumming), the West never established a good balance between the two arts. The music was either useless or too "domineering." Stravinsky's ballet music was, he felt, too interesting and detailed to be serviceable. "If one watches the dance, one loses interesting musical values. If one listens to the music, the dance is not duly appreciated." When some recent choreographers eliminated music altogether, the result, he felt, tended to be dry. Groups that used percussion produced nothing but "primitivistic" choreography "adding little or nothing to the connection between the dancer and the beats, usually less rather than more interesting and varied than among primitive peoples."

Working with Graham had allowed both of them to attempt a "contrapuntal relation between the high points of interest. We worked out all the details together, ending with a complete dance and musical composition in which the music rises to its point of interest when the dance is quiescent, and then the music dies down in interest while the dance rises. In this way, neither one of the arts relied on the other, and neither is a servant of the other, but each is given its time for shining and holding the attention of the audience." In conclusion, he advocated more use of voice and percussion combined with dance, as in nearly all primitive ceremonials.[52]

Henry relationship with choreographers continued to grow in the 1930s. In September, 1931, his name appeared on the roster of *The Fortnightly*, a new, multidisciplinary San Francisco magazine, along with the photographer Ansel Adams, his childhood friend, and Louis Horst's wife Betty Horst, who was described as the "leading Pacific coast dance instructor." Henry, however, was already on the boat to Germany, writing a chamber orchestra piece for unspecified dancers.[53] Before leaving, he placed Doris Humphrey on the faculty of the New School[54] and got Gassner to manage her.[55] New collaborations were quickly being contemplated.[56] Weidman, Laskey, and Limon returned to "Steel and Stone" in 1932, now scored for ten instruments and renamed *Dance of Work*, and presented it in conjunction with *Dance of Sport*.[57] Then Graham and Weidman commissioned Henry to write music for a tour—"Graham all through Europe," Henry declared.[58] This piece may be *Heroic Dance* for four woodwinds, five strings and percussion, or alternately for solo piano; it is marked "for Martha Graham."

The Graham collaboration resumed in February 1934 with *Four Casual Developments*, choreographed to part of his *Six Casual Developments*, one of his rare pieces with a relationship to jazz. John Martin's description of the choreography as "an incomparably innocent and maidenly piece of Victorian lyricism, composed and danced entirely with tongue in cheek" also can be applied to Henry's little suite. It became a Graham repertory item, performed by Dorothy Bird, Sophie Maslow, and Anna Sokolow.[59]

In 1935 Henry began working extensively with Dresden-born Tina Flade, who had danced with Mary Wigman's group, taught at the Wigman School in Dresden, and became head of the dance department at Mills, where she and Henry taught together. Flade frequently danced to Henry's music until she left the United States in the late 1930s,[60] to Henry's great regret. He considered her the only first-rate dancer in the West.[61]

Other collaborators of the mid-1930s included Sophia Delza, for whom he composed 3 *Dances of Activity*[62] and Betty Horst. The final new collaborator of the prewar years was Hanya Holm, for whom he wrote *Salutation* (now lost) for flute, piano, and percussion, which her company performed repeatedly.[63] Various dance projects were pending in May 1936.

|| 22 ||

The New Technologies

In the spring of 1931, *Modern Music* devoted an entire issue to radio, recording, film, and electrical instruments—innovative technologies that posed serious threats as they transformed the musical world.[1] Henry, while recognizing the dangers, was already exploring their potential. His career had hardly begun when he started recording for the player-piano, which had survived the competition of cylinder and mechanical disc recording for decades and evolved into an instrument capable of nuanced reproduction. When Western Electric developed electrical recording and the loudspeaker, whose improved fidelity had enormous implications for music, manufacturers rushed to adopt the technology, rendering the player-piano obsolete. Now capable of recording any music with respectable fidelity, the industry rapidly transformed itself with tremendous consequences. The record companies' decision that successful marketing of recordings depended upon famous interpreters playing familiar music left most performers and composers at risk.

In his introduction to *Modern Music*'s technology issue, Boris de Schloezer described another possible consequence of recording: listeners might grow used to the entirely different, and narrower, spectrum of recorded sound and lose their sensitivity to the beauty of live music.[2] Henry, however, imagined composers harnessing the potential of the distinctive tone colors of recorded instruments and manipulating of balance by separate miking. Even the apparently deceased player-piano offered interesting prospects, such as using a new method of cutting player-piano rolls to produce the subtle rhythmic relationships that he had described in *New Musical Resources*.[3] Although he had long since stopped exploiting such relationships in his own music, the young composer Conlon Nancarrow, who read and reread *New Musical Resources*, eventually took Henry's ideas to their logical end in his *Rhythmic Studies* for player-piano.[4] Talking film also suggested a new frontier: one of Henry's ex-students explored a machine that allowed a composer to draw whatever "harmonic curves" he wished directly on a movie sound track, which would then be performed by running the film, producing a synthetic music unique to the medium and unperformable live.[5]

Henry also recognized recording's potential for propagating new music, bringing it to lightly populated areas where concerts were impractical, thereby helping the new languages of modernism to be absorbed,[6] if a commercial company ever showed interest. A visit to the technology department of the Berlin Hochschule, prompted him to imagine the New Music Society issuing recordings. At first, to contain costs, he planned to record only Pan American Association of Composers (PAAC) concerts live.[7] With $200 [2010: $3,190] from Ives, he decided to use a performance of *Washington's Birthday* for his first recording, following it with Riegger's *Dichotomy* and his own *Polyphonica*. Ives's gift could only pay for masters, however;[8] manufacture and distribution would have to wait. The musicians' union then derailed the plan.[9]

Shortly thereafter, Lindstrom, the German recording giant, proposed making a ten-record set of modern music, to include six American and fourteen European compositions. Since 78 rpm records could hold only about four to five minutes per twelve-inch side, doses of modernity would be small. European composers were to include Schoenberg, Hindemith, Bartók, what Henry called "the better Stravinsky," and unnamed others. Based on Henry's proposals, Lindstrom suggested that Ives and Cowell be two of the Americans. The sets, to be recorded by the Berlin Philharmonic under Hermann Scherchen,[10] would be released in the United States by Columbia Records. Eventually, however, Henry decided that it would be cheaper and simpler if New Music marketed its own products. The need was becoming steadily more apparent. In *Modern Music*'s first issue of 1933, Irving Kolodin wrote about the expansion of recordings of living composers but the almost total absence of American music.

In New York, Henry immediately rented an up-to-date, high-quality electrical recording machine that rendered Lindstrom's proposal superfluous, which was just as well, since it became impossible after Hitler was sworn in on January 30.[11] The new machine could produce and duplicate superb, durable discs. Performances could be recorded, preserved, and circulated reasonably. A double-sided record with about ten minutes of music cost fifty cents [2010: $8.41] to make. Furthermore, the manufacturer of the machine offered to help distribute the records. Henry also foresaw transferring world-music recordings that existed only on the old Edison rolls, and duplicating rare records for which only one copy existed. He proposed that Ives immediately help finance the $125 [2010: $2,100] purchase price, since a large record company was trying to buy out the manufacturer and stifle competition. When Ives immediately sent $50 [2010: $841],[12] Henry announced the founding of New Music Quarterly Recordings.[13] He planned to make the first discs within a month at a joint concert with Grainger. The New Music Society would pay for the equipment, hall, blank discs, and a fee for "young Seeger"—Charles's fourteen-year-old son, Pete—to operate the recorder.[14] At $42 [2010: $707] per side, the master was expensive for the New Music Society, but Henry did not want to wait until they had subscribers. Ives advanced $320 [2010: $5,380] to start work and involved himself in the recordings more than in any of Henry's other projects.[15]

As usual, Henry kept his mind open about which music to include. For the first two discs he proposed Weiss's *Three Songs* (with string quartet), Ruggles's *Angels*, the slow movement of Ruth Crawford's String Quartet, and, for the fourth side, either songs by Ives or Henry's own "Movement" (for string quartet). Henry wanted to capture Brant's *Angels and Devils*, for eleven flutes, while it was being rehearsed for a concert, but Ives suggested postponing it. Of Ruth Crawford's extraordinary quartet movement, he told Ives, "I think it [is] without question the best movement for quartet that any American has written, and I would rather hear it than almost anything I can think of. It is a genuine experience, and rises far above Crawfords [sic] earlier works. I would like to make the record, if only to have you hear it!"[16] Ives responded—in an almost illegible pencil-written letter graphically evoking his deteriorating health—that he had not said anything because he did not know the scores. He had thought that the policy was to record works already published and sell them in the catalogue or perhaps in a series later on, as soon as performances by large orchestras were possible. He, however, did not have strong preferences, knowing nothing about Brant or Crawford except for what Henry and his colleagues had told him— "which is that 'in time & a nice tide' they may get man size (even Miss C)." Nevertheless, he felt that "if a record cost $160 certainly you, Carl R[uggles] Weiss & Riegger come before Brant." (Henry by then had decided not to record his own music.) Having lost heavily in the stock market crash, Ives urged caution about starting the recording series alongside the two print series that they were obligated to continue. Then, unsure of himself, he attempted to reread his draft but could not decipher his own writing. "All I tried to say is that I don't know what to say— right now"—except that Henry could count on $350 [2010: $5,890] in January. This, plus $125 on December 1, might leave a little money left after engraving Ruggles's *Sun Treader*. He would shortly know how much he could contribute in the future.[17]

An arrangement providing royalties for composers and performers reflects Henry's optimism about sales. At the end of 1933 he and the recording machine left for California in Henry's aging car.[18] There he learned that the New Music Society was extremely precarious financially. Not that his personal situation was much better. A class that generated crucial income had only one student registered and would probably be canceled.[19] One can see Ives's point about concentrating resources, but Henry, not to be deterred, proceeded with recording the Crawford and Weiss pieces for the first disc[20] and deferred to Ives about Brant's *Angels and Devils*. About that, Henry's first instinct was correct. Having missed this opportunity, they never were able to record it.

The recordings' financial underpinnings remained unsecured. Riegger suggested increasing the base of professional support by recording every piece available if it met a basic standard and if the composer paid for it and contributed an additional ten dollars toward underwriting the recording of works by composers who could not afford to pay. The regular subscription series would only market music of which they were totally convinced, but all compositions would be listed in the catalogue of New Music Quarterly Recordings.[21] Henry rejected the idea, which was clearly fraught with practical and diplomatic problems.

The first brochure lists an Executive Committee comprising Henry, Editor; Martha Beck, Treasurer; John Becker, Ruth Crawford, Wallingford Riegger, and Blanche Walton. In addition to Henry and Ives, the most active participants were Charles Seeger, Weiss, Riegger, Walton, and Beck. Riegger took charge of manufacturing the discs and oversaw recording, logistics, and marketing when Henry was in California. Nevertheless, he always deferred to Henry, who in a sense was the proprietor of the project.[22] Walton and Beck kept accounts and took care of mailing. For an Honorary Board of Endorsers Henry recruited the cream of the international new-music world, from Poulenc, Nadia Boulanger, and Casella to Bartók, Berg, Schoenberg, and Webern. The Advisory Board of Composers was a cross-section of Americans and Cubans.

The recordings began as sluggishly as the national economic recovery. As of January 2, 1934, there were only thirteen new subscribers in addition to Henry's initial list. At a subscription price of $5 [2010: $84] per year, and singles at $2, it was not cheap. The immaturity of the new electrical process caused technical problems: Crawford's subtle string-quartet texture did not sound well on the average acoustic playback machine, and electric phonographs were still rare. Metal recordings were more durable than wax but had to be played with wooden needles, which were sometimes difficult to obtain. Salzedo justifiably worried about sales because the performers were not famous.

Henry nevertheless radiated enthusiasm. After concerts in Kansas City and Santa Fe he got a dozen subscribers for the records, none of whom could read music and therefore were different from *New Music Quarterly* subscribers.[23] Over the next weeks the subscriptions steadily increased.[24] Ives now was convinced. "Good for N.M.Q.R. In some nice A.D. it will do more for the USA than the N.R.A. I didn't imagine there were 70 people in the US still with $5+ for a record. You certainly had the right idea."[25] Expenses later forced the subscription up to $6.

Blanche Walton, who labored tirelessly, packing and mailing recordings and sending out brochures and review copies around the world, feared that enthusiasm far surpassed orders and could not avoid feeling that the business was run poorly by herself and her helpers.[26] She was confident that eventually it would succeed if it were run professionally, but believed she was the wrong person and gradually withdrew. The recordings were her last project with Henry. Even if she had had the strength, her finances never recovered from the 1929 crash.

Performance quality also posed problems. Attempts to record live concerts faltered because of under-rehearsed performances.[27] At the recording session of Becker's *Credo*, the chorus was badly out of tune halfway through.[28] Editing was impossible. Salzedo—just the star performer that he felt the recordings needed—wanted to record his harp solo "Inquietude," the only piece that would fit on one side of a disc, and got Lyon and Healey, the harp manufacturers, to provide funding. It was not in his repertory, however. When he began working on it, he realized that it was "hellishly difficult." He played it publicly but imperfectly, repracticed, tried again, but never managed to record it.[29]

Henry was amused when the League of Composers announced its own recording series.[30] Although he anticipated their doing it in "a more showy way than we," he doubted that they would distribute as well or have as broad a range of composers. On the other hand, he liked their idea of letting the composer choose the piece he wished to record and pay him (or, rarely, her) for the rights, so he was not accepting "a sort of charity." He thought the PAAC should adopt the idea for commissioning. New Music Quarterly Recordings could commit to publishing the pieces and finding conductors for them. The pieces could then be performed, recorded, and published—if backing could be found.[31]

Weiss—now Schoenberg's assistant in Boston—suggested combining a first-class performance name and a famous composer by inviting Lydia Hoffman-Berendt, an impressive pianist whom he knew from Berlin, to record Schoenberg's Suite Op. 25, if Schoenberg would release the recording rights.[32] Henry, however, felt that a Schoenberg recording should be handled by a standard company such as Columbia. Furthermore, he knew from experience that dealing with European copyrights could be a nightmare of endless quarterly accountings.[33]

Around the end of 1934, the commercial labels finally began opening their doors to American composers. Walter Piston withdrew his string quartet from New Music Recordings when Columbia decided to issue it,[34] and Roy Harris convinced Victor to record Ives's "The Housatonic at Stockbridge." Slonimsky advised Henry to make his own recording of the other two movements of *Three Places in New England* while the orchestra was assembled,[35] but it probably was too costly.

The change of heart at Victor and Columbia had only marginal effects on the availability of American music, however, and New Music Quarterly Recordings continued, thanks to Ives's support.[36] After lengthy negotiations, the Gramophone Shop in Manhattan took over managing the subscriptions, receiving a percentage as an incentive to publicize it.[37] The correspondence of these years yields rich detail about the planning and financing of a seemingly impossible project in impossible times.

The financial viability of recording was intimately connected with radio, which simultaneously developed into a mass medium suited to music. Four years after Russell Varian called Henry's attention to the possibility of music broadcasting, the first commercial station opened in Pittsburgh in time to cover the bitter 1920 presidential election. Music transmission, which had already been attempted in 1877 by telephone and 1906 by radio, came to the Bay Area that year when Lee de Forest established a station to broadcast the San Francisco Symphony. Entrepreneurs flocked to the technology, but quality lagged and nobody knew who would pay for it until sponsorship by advertising began in 1922, triggering radio's volcanic expansion.[38]

Henry's first known broadcast came quickly, in February 1925, when he played thunder-sticks on a program relayed from New York to the West Coast.[39] His enthusiasm increased the following year during a tour of the radio department at Mark Hambourg's Toronto conservatory, which broadcast over the station owned by the *Toronto Star*.[40] In February 1927, he heard an experimental amplification device—a radio placed inside a grand piano for better projection in a large hall.[41] Boris De Schloezer, foreseeing rapid technological evolution, predicted that in little more than a decade, phonographs and radios would be equipped with television, permitting one to watch a concert as well as listen to it.[42]

Henry's developing perception of radio's potential can be traced through his articles on music for the *Encyclopedia Americana*'s annual supplements. In his review of the year 1927, he mentioned radio only briefly, merely observing that better musicians were being used. Only two years later, radio seemed to him one of the most important forces in the musical world, since its music programming had greatly improved. He blamed radio, however, for a chain of side effects that made it more threatening than recording. His "informal" survey revealed that up to 80 percent of concerts had been eliminated due to competition from broadcasting. Fewer children studied music as parents decided that radios rendered playing an instrument unnecessary. Consumers bought radios rather than pianos, pushing three leading piano manufacturers—Chickering, Knabe, and Mason and Hamlin—into receivership. Publishers failed as sheet music sales plummeted. Phonographs without built-in radios languished on store shelves. Composers' incomes dropped as performance opportunities shrank. Henry lamented that listeners would forget (or never learn) the acoustical superiority of live performances. Furthermore, radio companies were uninterested in new music. In his survey of 1930, radio looked even more pernicious. Live concerts, he wrote, only comprised what was left over after radio and talking pictures had done their damage. Radio raised many questions of quality and the distancing of performer and audience. While Henry offered only anecdotal evidence,[43] a later historian of the first quarter-century of music broadcasting seen from the industry's vantage point, perceived the same fears.[44] Yet Henry also knew the potential power of radio for modernism: Slonimsky's performance of Henry's *Sinfonietta* was carried by forty Columbia Broadcasting affiliates.[45]

Henry knew that European radio stations, which were state- or publicly owned, were much more hospitable to new music. He played on the radio in Germany and Czechoslovakia,[46] and a Berlin station agreed to put on a symphonic concert of PAAC composers at its own expense.[47] The Berlin Hochschule had radio study rooms, and electric and acoustic research facilities.[48] German radio offered a prize for the best radio composition.[49] He surely was told about the BBC's secure funding from mandatory licenses for operating a radio, its extensive use of live performances, and its increasing propagation of new music.[50] In the United States, on the other hand, commerce was rapidly hijacking the future of radio. Using his report for the 1932 *Americana* supplement as a platform to warn of its implications, Henry described the dramatic merger of concert managements with radio corporations, which put nearly all major artists under the control of NBC or Columbia, squeezing out smaller managers and leaving almost no work for the less-than-famous. Now the only performer who mattered was completely reliable rather than creative. "Many concerts have become almost as much 'canned music' as gramophone records." Corporations were making huge profits on a limited selection of music. Attempting to share that wealth, composers simplified their styles "in a dull, unintelligent manner."

Since American networks showed no interest in American composers, noncommercial radio was the one hope. Just as Henry returned from Europe in January 1933, the new chief officer of WEVD, an independent New York station named for the socialist pioneer Eugene V. Debs,[51] decided to broaden its traditional socialist-Jewish orientation and counteract radio's trend toward commercialism by unifying its individual lectures into a Radio University. The originator and director of this "University of the Air," the Dutch-born historian Henrik Willem van Loon, assembled an impressive faculty to broadcast talks on the arts, psychology, literature, drama, and politics. Sigmund Spaeth, a well-known radio personality, pianist Harry Cumpson (the first lecturer in music at the University of Buffalo), and Henry were engaged to speak about music.[52] Feeling a little out of his element at WEVD, Henry wrote on the back of a staff photo printed in a Yiddish newspaper, "the Faculty of the U. of the Air—do you recognize your Jew-boy?"

WEVD quickly became Henry's weapon in the fight to make radio a medium for new music. Using radio programs as the American contribution to the International Exchange fortified his belief that the live concert was not the most efficient way of promulgating living composers. Furthermore, promises of reciprocity might overcome obstacles to broadcasts of American music by European stations.[53]

His first series, for the spring of 1933, at 8:15 P.M. on Saturdays,[54] promoted the International Exchange concerts with programs of Dutch, British, Hungarian, and Austrian music;[55] the Austrian show comprised Schoenberg, Webern,

Berg, and Pless. All performances were live; almost nothing had been recorded.[56] Henry then added weekly Pan American Association of Composers (PAAC) shows on American music, which were more diverse, now that Copland and Piston had joined the PAAC. When he went to California, he left the programs in the care of two young composers, Arthur Berger and Irving Fine. (Berger, who was twenty-one at the time, later recalled many of the live performances as poor.)[57] The WEVD programs inspired a California broadcaster to feature new music.[58] Henry's first West Coast radio talk used illustrations from his own music and Ives's.[59]

Radio broadcasting also dragged Henry into the maelstrom of life in 1933. He had given written permission for Stokowski to conduct a broadcast of one of his pieces, but Adler, his Berlin publisher, claimed that he owned the copyright and Henry was not authorized to grant permission. Although Adler was correct, Henry resented being deprived of the right to control performances when he had received no money in exchange for assigning the copyright to Adler, and he worried that his reputation with Stokowski and the radio station were being damaged. Ives, however, understood that Adler, a Jew, was being harassed by the Nazis. Victory in a lawsuit could bring him enough money to save his company. SESAC, the broadcast licensing organization that controlled Adler's publications in the United States, then spread rumors that Henry had made insulting— and presumably anti-Semitic—comments about Adler. Henry passed the information to Columbia, relieved that its lawyers would fight the suit.[60]

Henry's second University of the Air series, on Saturdays and Sundays at eight P.M. in the fall of 1933, contained both PAAC and Exchange programs, with music of Yugoslavia, Russia, France, Hungary, Austria, Poland, "etc."[61] The broadcasts for the Exchange program began bearing fruit at the end of the year, as the Swiss considered giving an American concert in Basel[62] and an American program on Polish radio looked definite.[63] The WEVD programs also produced a request for a live performance of new music in New York.[64] Henry soon got other personal opportunities on radio.

Considering his immersion in radio, he wrote surprisingly little about it in his *Americana* supplement article for 1933, other than noting that the virulently nationalistic government sponsors of European stations were restricting broadcasts of foreign music.[65] Nothing suggests that his pessimism about commercial radio in America had changed. The networks felt they had to serve the larger public and left niche programming to local stations, who in any case could not afford the rights for broadcasting popular music.[66]

Unfortunately, noncommercial radio could be messy. Weiss felt that the programs on WEVD should be eliminated because the station's weak signal was so prone to interference from neighboring stations that a Ruggles performance could be infected with "The Road to Mandalay." Even his excellent radio could not pick up the other good public service station, WNYC.[67] Henry nevertheless organized five Exchange series concerts on WEVD in the fall of 1934, moving the programming a little rightward to attract an audience.

Remarks in Henry's *Americana* supplement articles for 1934 and 1935 were his last public comments about radio at that time. His correspondence about radio programs also tapered off in 1935, resuming to some extent the following year when his more accessible compositions based on Irish folk music caught the attention of the commercial stations. Then his relationship with radio went quiet for many years. Despite the drawbacks of WEVD, much had been accomplished toward propagation of the tremendous expansion in American composition during the first decade of music broadcasting.

Henry's experience with film began with the silent newsreels made before his 1924 New York debut. One of them, a twenty-second short, showed him (Sidney wrote) "battering a piano with forearms, elbows, fists etc. playing something called 'Dempsey Diapason,'" a reference to the boxing champion Jack Dempsey.[68] (When it was shown on television in 1963, Henry and Sidney were startled to hear music, since commercial sound films only began tentatively in 1926. They assumed that the 1924 clip had been dubbed for television.)[69] Another newsreel crew showed up in 1925 to film Henry with his thunder-sticks—still silently.[70]

In reviewing the musical life of 1929 for the *Encyclopedia Americana* supplement, Henry said only that talking pictures, which came to life with the 1927 *Jazz Singer*, contained very little of musical importance. Exceptions included the avant-garde visual artists who had done interesting work in silent films and now were attracted to the sound movie. One example was his Bauhaus friend Laszlo Moholy-Nagy, who gave him a film of his abstract moving designs, hoping that he would provide music. (Although intrigued, Henry never got around to it.)[71] In New York he was asked to arrange music for art films to be shown at the newly opened Film Forum, but the papers contain nothing about that plan either.[72] Unlike many colleagues, he resisted the lure of Hollywood.

Finally, in 1934, an invitation to play a live prologue to Robert Flaherty's *Man of Aran*—a film about isolated settlers on an island off the coast of Ireland—excited him so much that he popped off a rare letter to Schmolke.[73] When the film opened on Broadway in October, attended by Irish traditional musicians, he expected his financial problems to be alleviated by a steady engagement playing the prologue, and planned to train an eventual replacement so he could return to California.[74] He was to be disappointed when the critics saw a preview without Henry's prologue. Contracted to play twice a day at low pay, he tried to convince himself that it would add up.[75] After a week it was over. First the prologue was removed; then the picture closed. He got one more chance at the Boston opening,[76] after which the film closed again. Never one to let an opportunity pass, he made six records of the Irish musicians' folk songs before they went home and arranged a lecture-recital for the film's traditional singer.[77]

Just as that job was collapsing Henry was drawn into a project promising serious income. An entrepreneur named Theodore Benedek promised him $10,000 [2010: $163,000] in shares and a salary as music director of his planned films of specially staged symphonic music.[78] It was a rare chance to capitalize on his experience in music, dance, and film, and work regularly with Koussevitzky, one of the few conductors who championed new music.[79] Asked by Henry to recruit a railway executive to the advisory board, Ives happily complied.[80]

Henry and Benedek developed a plan to form "Symphonic Productions," a corporation with $100,000 [2010: $1,630,000] in capital that proposed to make high-quality "shorts"—sound pictures of twenty-two minutes or less—for distribution by a company specializing in educational films. Henry wanted to create six shorts with the Boston Symphony, five of which would be synchronized with dance or a "scenic effect," filmed in Symphony Hall with superimposed shots filmed elsewhere. The dances would be choreographed by Henry's friends Martha Graham, Doris Humphrey, Charles Weidman, and others. Benedek's prospectus implies that they would record directly on sound track. But all the complex negotiations with Koussevitzky, who originally showed great interest in the enterprise, finally collapsed. Henry was convinced that he had wanted to do it, but the Boston Symphony's manager refused to let the orchestra participate.[81] Of course, Koussevitzky may simply have let his manager kill off the project.

In his summary of music in 1928 for *Encyclopedia Americana*, Henry described the work of an unnamed Russian, connecting it with a growing public interest in "the scientific, psychological and physiological fundamentals of music, and in the employment of scientific knowledge to develop new musical instruments."[82] He was talking about Lev Terman (or Termen), a Soviet engineer with a musical background, born in Russia to French parents and generally known by his French name, Léon Thérémin, or Theremin in English. After demonstrating his Aetherophon in Europe, Theremin came to the United States, where he became a star, playing in the biggest venues and drawing gigantic crowds to see his instruments, which promised to enable anyone to make music without years of technical training.[83] Circulating among the Russian emigré community, he struck up a friendship with Nicolas Slonimsky, who led him to Henry. Theremin and Henry were about thirty. As it happened, they had previously been introduced but had no language in common.[84]

Theremin does not reappear in the Cowell papers until March 1930, when the two negotiated a presentation of his instruments at The New School.[85] Wanting him to concentrate on scientific aspects of his "beat keyboard," Henry refrained from making claims for its musical value.[86] What really excited him, however, was the realization that Theremin could build a device to demonstrate complex rhythm-overtone relationships. After discussing the idea with Seeger, he presented it to Theremin, who agreed to construct it for $200 [2010: $2,610].[87] Named the Rhythmicon and always associated with Henry, it was commissioned by Slonimsky as a personal speculation, probably because Theremin's instruments were viewed as potential goldmines. When Slonimsky forgot to make the $150 down payment, Ives saved the day.

The idea of a Rhythmicon stemmed from Henry's realization that Western music had neglected rhythmic development largely because performers could not execute complex combinations.[88] Now that rhythm had more-or-less reached the limit of human capabilities, he felt that only a mechanical device could test his rhythm-pitch concepts. He imagined the Rhythmicon creating a "rhythmical melody" for use by a composer and facilitating psychological and physiological experiments with rhythm. Seeger, he said, had suggested building an instrument using newly developed electrical technology, but Henry had designed a system using a light beam and photoelectric cell. The grandfather of the idea was Russell Varian, whose conception of a mechanical instrument was entirely different. An unconfirmed source claimed that Henry's Stanford friend Paul Farnsworth had created complex cross-rhythms with player-piano rolls and phonograph discs.[89] Joseph Szigeti, who knew Theremin and his instruments, later said that Henry had "already made a crude instrument in which wheels turned and percussive sounds in various rhythms were produced and continued as long as a key was held down." Sidney thought Szigeti might have been referring to the device that Russell proposed, not knowing that Henry and Russell never had money to build it.[90]

In mid-1931, months before the Rhythmicon was completed, Henry and Theremin presented the idea at the New York Musicological Society in conjunction with Henry's lecture on *New Musical Resources*. Henry took delivery shortly after returning from Europe at the end of the year. As the time for the public unveiling in New York approached, Ives urged him to avoid raising false expectations about its musical potential. Henry, however, already imagined it as a true instrument and had almost completed *Rhythmicana* to play with Slonimsky and his Boston Chamber Orchestra. Still, he prudently announced the device as "a new electrical instrument for the purpose of producing rhythms of different systems either together or following one another."[91]

The Rhythmicon had seventeen keys, arranged in a regular sequence of black and white, unlike the irregular layout of the piano keyboard. The lowest note produced a unit of rhythm; white keys produced even divisions of it; black keys produced odd-numbered divisions up to a fifteenth of that basic pulse. Since a rhythm continued to be sounded as long as the key was depressed, any or all rhythms could be played simultaneously. The Rhythmicon therefore surpassed the two leading electrical instruments, the ThereminVox and the Trautonium, which were monophonic. Moreover, the rhythm of an individual key could be altered so that a single key could produce multiple rhythms successively, adding to the possible combinations. A tempo controller permitted acceleration and deceleration. At top speed, the pulses of the highest key merged into a sustained low pitch, as Henry had predicted in *New Musical Resources*.

Although the Rhythmicon's normal sound was a series of clicks, it could also be set to produce reiterated pitches, tuned to the overtone series, that could be varied at will. A controller could alter the audible pitch so that a fast rhythm could have a low pitch or a high pitch. The potential combinations seemed limitless. Various tone colors were also available. Henry discovered that "if one holds down all of the upper keys, owing to the different periods of the various rhythms a melody, jumping from one to another, appears to spring forth. The melody varies according to which rhythms are being played against each other." He foresaw improvements to extend rhythmic, articulative, and pitch control.[92]

The demonstration at The New School took place on January 19, 1932, with the assistance of Clara Reisenberg (better known as Clara Rockmore), the famed Theremin virtuoso.[93] In addition to the Rhythmicon, Theremin showed a fingerboard instrument with the tone of a cello and a so-called space-control instrument, probably the classic ThereminVox, on which he played Rachmaninoff's "Vocalise." Henry told Slonimsky that the demonstration aroused great interest, despite its great flaws. Worst of all, nonstandard electric current damaged the Rhythmicon's performance, making it sound like it had a cold. Ives seemed disappointed in its musical prospects, although he liked the idea.[94] *Musical America* affirmed that the Rhythmicon had excited big interest, but Henry's underlying goal went unnoticed.[95]

The Rhythmicon was demonstrated again at The New School on March 10 at 5:00 P.M., an hour selected to ensure an intimate rather than a public event.[96] Nevertheless, a large audience and many reporters—including one for *Popular Science*—came to witness Clara Reisenberg give the first public performance of Theremin's "Ether-wave Dance Platform," later called the Terpsitone, on which her choreographic movements controlled the dynamics and pitches of Gounod's "Ave Maria" and a light-show.[97] Arthur Berger, in the *Daily Mirror*, was skeptical about Henry's suggestion that the Rhythmicon could be part of an orchestra, since he was unable to envision soloists or an orchestra letting a machine dictate the rhythm.[98] The *New York Times* called the Rhythmicon demonstration "indifferent" but indicated that its development might be worth following and made the event seem attractive. "The one thing perhaps that was lacking was an electrical page turner."[99] Marc Blitzstein, in *Modern Music*, was flatly negative about the sound of all of Theremin's instruments.[100] *Musical Courier*'s headline, "More Horrors," prompted Henry to tell Olive that he guessed he was not "getting stale."[101]

Other articles appeared in newspapers in Montreal, Chicago, and San Francisco, as well as *Popular Science Monthly*, and the Leipzig-Berlin journal *Die Musik*. The Radio Research Center of the Berlin Hochschule guaranteed a demonstration if Henry could bring it with him upon his return and offered to send him one of its Trautoniums in exchange.[102] The difference in electric current, however, would have required Theremin to build a new Rhythmicon.

By the time the Rhythmicon went to San Francisco for a demonstration at the New Music Society,[103] Henry was discouraged because so few people understood why he would create a machine just to study complex rhythms. (Olive's notes imply that she did not understand it either.)[104] After the demonstration, however, he wrote Ives that the Rhythmicon had been more successful there as an instrument with musical potential.[105] *The Argonaut* predicted that some day Henry would become known as the Edison of Music, who "put forward a principle which will strongly influence the face of all future music."[106] Yet machines will be machines, as Henry soon learned. In a demonstration in San Jose, it did not work properly, forcing Harry to assist. Henry returned it to Theremin for repairs.[107]

Now Slonimsky's investment began to dribble away. In 1934, realizing that he never could bring the instrument to Boston because, in those days of unstandardized electric service, the predominant DC current required a costly converter for the AC Rhythmicon, he offered it to Henry or the New School for half the original price.[108] In the end Slonimsky sold it for $90 to Joseph Schillinger, who used it in his teaching and eventually gave it to the Smithsonian. The second Rhythmicon was stored by Henry at Stanford, where it eventually fell apart and was scrapped.[109] Like the Rhythmicon, Theremin's star also faded. He returned to the Soviet Union under mysterious conditions and was not seen again by Westerners for half a century. Only recently was it learned that he built a third Rhythmicon in Russia. [110]

23

Collapsing Dreams

By early 1933 the Pan American Association of Composers (PAAC) could boast of substantial accomplishments, including complete orchestral concerts of American music in Berlin, Vienna, Prague, Boston, and New York; individual American works performed on orchestral programs in Berlin, Frankfurt, Copenhagen, Havana, Mexico City, New York, Paris, Philadelphia, and San Francisco; and chamber concerts in New York, St. Paul, Havana, Dessau, and elsewhere. Interchanges of scores had been organized between Latin American countries and the United States and Canada; libraries of American scores, open to musicians and the public, had been established in New York and Berlin; recordings and a rental library linked to the New Music Society were planned.[1] All of this was possible because of Henry's tireless slogging, aided by Ruth Crawford, Wallingford Riegger, Adolph Weiss, and Ives's financing. Varèse's greatest contribution was his absence, which freed Henry to use the Exchange program to the PAAC's advantage.

Henry's letters about the PAAC contain a litany of problems including finances, friction with the musicians' union, and the sensitive issue of fair distribution of performances among PAAC composers, some of whom he knew could not be compared with Ives, Ruggles, Ruth Crawford, and Varèse. Latin American composers wanted greater representation but did not provide many scores. Projects abroad were at risk as dictatorships muzzled unconventional thinkers. The projected recording series of PAAC composers that Henry had been negotiating with Lindstrom was still on the fire as late as February 1933, but, as Lindstrom's representative put it, conditions in Germany were unpredictably fluid.[2] Further PAAC concerts in Germany were out of the question. Nevertheless, Henry continued to recruit new members, especially from Latin America.

Merely joining required little effort. One only had to send a large-ish work, preferably for orchestra, to any officer, who presented it at the next meeting for a vote.[3] The fate of the applicant hung on the broad-mindedness of those at the meeting. Overcoming narrow-mindedness could be challenging, especially because the subject of certain composers could bring out real unpleasantness.

"I agree with Adolph [Weiss] and Salzedo," Ruggles wrote Henry, "that it is a great mistake to have that filthy bunch of Juilliard Jews in the Pan American. They are cheap, without dignity. And with little, or no talent. That [Arthur] Berger is impossible. They will double cross you Henry—I'm sure—in every possible way. My advice is to promptly kick them out, before it is too late."[4] No wonder Copland wrote that the "feeling of camaraderie" in the new-music world was not too strong.[5]

When Weiss attacked Jewish applicants, Henry replied diplomatically that the most important criterion was the quality of the piece judged from the broadest possible standpoint. Although he admitted to a strong preconception that Jewish composers lacked "fundamental seriousness," Henry favored any exceptions to that generalization, certainly Schoenberg and Henry Brant. He felt that the League of Composers—which included a large Jewish contingent—had declined in importance because they "present so many works by minor and untalented composers, bad mixtures of style with no direction, and of more and more conventional nature. Mostly by Jews, of course." But in order to be better than the League, PAAC had to keep high standards for all. "I, as far as I am concerned, have no prejudice against any composer. . . . And the moment when the work itself, whether by Jew or Gentile, friend or foe, conservative or radical, shows something which should be given, then we, I think, must give it if it is within our power."[6] The record shows that he followed his own advice.

Henry's remarks about factionalism refer to the new-music world at large and to his concern that the PAAC function smoothly during his extended absences from New York, since he, Weiss, and Riegger did almost all the work. In April 1933, to address matters that did not require a vote, he formed an executive committee comprising Riegger, Salzedo, Weiss, and a younger composer, either Henry Brant or Jerome Moross, depending upon who was in New York.[7] The following fall, however, Varèse's return from France produced aftershocks that Henry immediately felt in California. On December 30, Salzedo demanded a copy of the PAAC constitution by air mail special delivery.[8] Shortly thereafter, with awkward timing, Varèse wrote a letter beginning with pleasantries but reminding Henry that he, Salzedo, Riegger, and Weiss had agreed on "expedient" changes. Salzedo, who increasingly looks like Varèse's lackey, would keep Henry informed.[9] When the puzzled Henry wanted to know why the constitution needed to be sent in such a rush, Salzedo replied that he had to work quickly because he traveled so much. The reality was much more threatening, however. Having concluded that a revival of the orchestra founded in 1919 for Varèse was financially impossible, and that resuscitating the International Composers' Guild, was unwise, Varèse and Salzedo wanted to reorganize the PAAC along the same lines as the Guild, under a "real working committee" with Varèse (as chairman), Salzedo, Henry, Riegger, Weiss, Julius Mattfeld (treasurer), [10] and a secretary to be selected. They planned, for April, a concert at Town Hall and a program in a theater in cooperation with Martha Graham, for which they needed Henry's proxy.[11] Varèse promised to find subscribers and backing for Henry's recording project, which he admired but thought should be much bigger.[12] At first Henry only said that Varèse and Salzedo were taking an active role in the organization, but he knew they were engineering a coup.[13] He had to accept reality, especially since he could not control events from California.

The ominous signs in the PAAC were only part of the problems that Henry was experiencing early in 1934. Weiss was urging discontinuation of the WEVD programs because he felt the station's broadcast quality was very poor and its radius very small. New Music Quarterly Recordings urgently needed more subscribers. Even Blanche Walton was losing faith in the recording enterprise.[14] The owner of The Gramophone Shop, in midtown Manhattan, who wanted to market the recordings, suggested that Henry make a MacDowell album, since he had almost no MacDowell to sell.[15] It is hard to imagine anything more distasteful to Henry, other than Varèse's and Salzedo's compliments, which barely masked their desire to take control of the recordings, as they were doing with the PAAC. Seeger warned Henry to be careful.[16]

Roldán's report that the PAAC concert in Havana was a success provided a rare moment of cheer.[17] Mid-March (1934) brought more threatening clouds. A new PAAC letterhead emphasized Varèse and eliminated Chávez and Henry as co-founders.[18] Nevertheless, Henry separated his personal feelings from his musical taste and retained Varèse's music in plans for future recordings. With no illusions about what was going on, he went straight to Ives.

> Varèse is trying to undermine any activity that I am the prime mover in, and he and Salzedo, who work together, must be watched for moves that will place them in charge of all activities, which is what they are angling for. This might be okay if they could be relied on to do a good job, but while they are very active and get some very fine results, their work is marred by constant intrigue, politics, and a very narrow and cliquish range of likes and dislikes. So I think that it is better to be careful not to permit them to take over everything! I also admit that it seems a bit too Frenchy to have all our American new music activities under their domination.[19]

Having seen Varèse and Salzedo push Becker—Henry's chief Midwestern representative and a very close friend—out of the PAAC, and fearing for New Music's recordings, Henry moved on his own. As a counterweight to the PAAC, he suggested that independent, self-governing, affiliated New Music Societies be started in Chicago by Georgia Kober, in the Minneapolis-St. Paul region by

Becker, and in Boston by Slonimsky. The total numbers would strengthen all of them. The organization would not mimic the PAAC or Pro Musica but would permit performance of some foreign works while emphasizing American music. Members would receive *New Music Quarterly* as a bonus.[20] He foresaw extending their work internationally through an organization stemming from the United States and not simply becoming a branch of a foreign organization like the International Society for Contemporary Music (ISCM).[21] His plans came to nothing, however, possibly because the others knew how much energy would be needed.

Meanwhile, the PAAC was planning to record and broadcast the April 15 Town Hall concert, an ambitious program including major works. Varèse's vaunted ability to find money turned out to be overrated, not that he was entirely at fault. The mistake was to plan something with such a big budget in such a terrible economy. With the budget for the April concerts unbalanced and Varèse unable to guarantee anything for recording it,[22] inadequate rehearsing was a foregone conclusion. Ruggles, who was in Vermont, heard that Henry's concerts at The New School, which Varèse had been bad-mouthing, were much better. "It was the same old Varèse-Salzedo racket [as] in the last year of the Guild; only more crass and bold. Varèse is using the [PAAC] to exploit himself and is double crossing everybody that gets in his way. Salzedo has always been and is his Good Man Friday." Furthermore, there was a huge deficit. The worst news, however, was Ruggles's depiction of Slonimsky's conducting as completely incompetent (although Ruggles was only reporting secondhand).[23]

If Henry took Ruggles's bitter comments with a grain of salt, he had to think again when he heard from Ives, who had missed the concert but heard negative reports about Slonimsky from Harmony and some friends. The program was too long, the singers were frightened, and all the players were nervous after rushed rehearsing. Crushed that the concert could not be recorded live, Ives urged doing something to record his piece at once, at his expense.[24]

Weiss now was completely disillusioned. He too had felt that Slonimsky was overrated, "but the most unpleasant after-taste of the concert was Varèse's egotism. When you managed the concerts we were always happy after the concerts, but with Varèse everybody else must play the little man's part and serve his personal ambition." He and Ruggles believed that Ives was sick of Varèse. Weiss confirmed that not one first-rank critic attended despite "the great Varèse's solicitations." Nor was the PAAC concert the only problem afflicting Weiss, who wanted the League and the PAAC to sponsor a concert with Schoenberg conducting, in support of needy composers everywhere, such as Webern, who had written him a depressing letter about the advance of the political right in Austria, which had cost him his Workers' Chorus.[25]

Riegger viewed the concert more moderately, although he said it was musically uneven and not superior to Henry's New School programs. On the other hand, the live broadcast had been bungled. Part of it was to go out from 9:30 to 10:00 P.M., but the first half was so long that the intermission began at 9:50, and only twenty minutes of music actually got on the air.[26] Blanche Walton felt that the program made very little impression because fashions were turning very conservative.[27]

The second PAAC concert, presented a week later at the Alvin Theater by Martha Graham and Group, had music for chamber orchestra and small ensembles, including Henry's *Four Casual Developments*, danced by Dorothy Bird, Sophie Maslow, and Anna Sokolow.[28] The dancers were a huge success,[29] but instead of Graham generating enough money to pay the bills, the PAAC was $800 [2010: $13,000] in deficit. As managers, Varèse and Salzedo seemed incompetent to Weiss.[30]

Henry now saw that years of work were seriously threatened. Cutting his losses, he let Varèse and Salzedo run the PAAC while he concentrated on recording and publishing, and maintained control at The New School.[31] In June (1934) Henry brought Ives up to date, forwarding Riegger's new fear that Varèse and Salzedo were trying to squeeze out Henry and his friends. "We still have the New School Concerts, although this year the school cannot afford to back them, and I have to make them pay for themselves."[32] Three days later Salzedo asked Henry to sign a waiver so that business could be transacted with respect to amending the PAAC constitution.[33]

Although Henry's name remained attached to the PAAC, especially for the benefit of those who had no idea what was happening, the organization gradually disappears from his correspondence. Riegger wrote in November that the PAAC had been reduced to Varèse and Salzedo.[34] Varèse finally closed it down in April 1936.[35] About all that was left of their work was a continuing radio series on WEVD, not under the PAAC name but with many of the same composers, and curated by Colin McPhee.[36]

It is unlikely that Henry, living out of New York for so much of the year, could have beaten back Varèse and Salzedo, who were formidably manipulative. To Henry's credit, his dealings with Varèse seem to have been carried out with professional grace.[37] *New Music*'s orchestral edition published *Ionisation* in 1934, at the height of the battle. And Varèse knew what he had done. Many years later he apologized to Sidney for "behaving like a bastard" to Henry.[38]

He did not just refer to the PAAC. Another episode was unfolding simultaneously in the International Exchange Concerts (IEC), for which Henry had found the perfect ally, Helen Mills, the National Federation of Music Clubs' chairwoman of International Music Relations. Immensely knowledgeable about the psychology of the clubs, some of which were obsessed with their own prestige, she eagerly took command of the domestic side of the exchanges, allowing Henry to concentrate on getting scores. Together they organized for 1933–34 at least ten exchange programs in the United States and generated a similar number of reciprocal concerts abroad. Soon, however, Mills began experiencing problems with the clubs, which either did not like the modernism of the scores or were unable to perform them.

Since the loose guidelines of the Exchange Commission permitted virtually any reciprocal action, Henry concentrated on Exchange broadcasts while Mills dealt with her constituency. Soon European factionalism began to interfere, doubtless under pressure from the Nazis and other far-rightists. The Exchange's central commission decided to let each country determine which of its composers would be represented abroad and not leave it to the foreign sponsors, whose taste might conflict with that country's desires. Unfortunately, the new policy also prevented sponsors from taking into account their audiences' taste. The clubs soon began complaining about the scores they were sent. Moreover, they correctly demanded guarantees that reciprocal concerts were taking place abroad.[39] The issue of who was paying for what also remained unresolved.

As of April 1934, Mills was getting nowhere with plans for the following season. Its dues shrinking, the Federation had no money to buy music. Unless she satisfied the conservatives, the exchanges would peter out. She proposed quietly persisting, using conservative music until more adventurous works could be inserted. For the moment Henry would have to arrange modernist exchanges without the music clubs.[40] In the fall of 1934, however, as the New Deal slowly began to resuscitate the economy, Mills thought the Federation again would have money to buy music, giving them flexibility.[41]

Foreseeing annoyance abroad, she emphasized the "reciprocal act," rather than the content. In other words, anything was better than nothing. Knowing that composers abroad would disagree, she advised against sending them printed programs, justifying the deception because the Europeans were not sending their programs to Henry. At the same time, the clubs fretted that American music was represented abroad only by modernists.[42] The internal conflict surfaced in September 1934, when the Federation's board requested statistics and evidence that music by conservative Americans was also being exported.[43] Henry's and Mills's correspondence ended about that time. At first it seemed that the Federation had pulled out, but later events suggest that she and Henry were using the telephone instead of writing.

He now had to broaden the base for exchanges by soliciting prominent figures to become unpaid regional representatives or directors, but in some areas no one showed interest and in others his contacts felt the audiences would be completely unresponsive. As to the reciprocal concerts abroad, Henry pursued the cooperation of his European comrades, who had their hands full dealing with the terrible social conflicts. Nevertheless, for the next two years Exchange activities continued.

Another danger was looming, however, hints of which can be detected on a letterhead of the Exchange Concerts that circulated in 1934, bearing as its address not The New School, as previously, but the Library of the IEC, 8 Pitt Street, New York. "Affiliated with Music Educational Film, Edgar Varese and Hedi Katz, organizers." The Concert Committee of the IEC lists Henry as chairman and Katz as librarian and corresponding secretary, quite possibly at Varèse's recommendation. A native of Budapest, Katz had studied violin in Vienna with Arnold Rosé and Carl Flesch; in New York she became director of the music school of the Henry Street Settlement House.[44] A superb administrator, she established the Exchange library, which brought in many requests for scores; had good ideas about publicizing the program; and oversaw its needs when Henry was away. A letterhead that was adopted at the beginning of 1935 displays a major restructuring, however. A "Permanent American Commission" comprised Henry (as secretary), Isadore Freed, and Varèse; an executive committee consisted of Rudolph Ganz, Howard Hanson, Wallingford Riegger, Nicolas Slonimsky, and Helen Mills.

Katz and Henry collaborated well. She pursued ambitious dreams, such as finding sponsors, organizing concerts jointly with consulates, and using educational films, presumably made by her partnership with Varèse. In early 1935, she was planning a series of ten Exchange concerts in New York amalgamating dance, film, and music from each country and also was trying to establish relations with the Japanese Foreign Office, where she had excellent connections.[45] In general, the reach of the International Exchange Concerts was growing as it was joined by more countries, most of which had only a few years left to live.

Seeing the organizational problems, Katz suggested that everything come from one person—namely, her—and from a central office that would consolidate the distribution of music, films, and other materials. She was willing to do the work if the committee would approve it for the long term.[46] It made sense to Henry, who wrote to Varèse proposing a reorganization with her at the head. Varèse entirely approved. In Katz's mind, Henry was the generator of plans,[47] but she underestimated Varèse, whose idea of reorganization included expanding his influence. A meeting on April 10, 1935, was very disturbing. Salzedo suggested that the IEC was unnecessarily duplicating the work of the ISCM and could be dispensed with. Isadore Freed replied that through the IEC, many American works could be performed, while ISCM selected only one American work per year. If ISCM would do more, however, he agreed that the IEC would be superfluous. After considerable discussion, the committee unanimously endorsed affiliation with ISCM if the aims of the IEC could be carried out. Since several members, including Salzedo and Henry, served on the ISCM board, affiliation was not far-fetched. Salzedo moved that the complete IEC committee join ISCM and attend its next meeting. Varèse, Freed, and Katz would form a subcommittee in whose hands the furthering of the original work of IEC would be placed.

The minutes conclude, "Some hesitation was expressed by the members at taking such a radical step in the absence of four members of the committee [one of whom was Henry]; but it was felt that no time ought to be lost, as the end of the season is so near."[48]

The decision to unite with ISCM was fatal. Once again Salzedo and Varèse had killed a project in which Henry had invested enormous effort—or, in this case, pushed Henry out of the project. On the final letterhead of the American chapter, from late 1935, Varèse is listed as the American representative. Unlike the case of the PAAC, Henry's correspondence registers no complaints about the coup in the IEC. His reaction could have ranged from anger at Varèse's and Salzedo's latest trick, to a feeling that the move to amalgamate with ISCM was a good idea, to relief that he no longer had to deal with the job, or even to a sense that the project was going nowhere, at least for American composers, and no longer deserved his attention. One must acknowledge Varèse's correct perception that these organizations were stalled. But they had been Henry's life, and the way they were "stolen" was reprehensible. Contrary to Ruggles's prediction, it was not the Jews who had sabotaged Henry.

Although Henry gradually abandoned the PAAC to Varèse and Salzedo,[49] he kept New Music Quarterly Recordings under his command until he turned it over to Otto Luening in 1936. Four discs were issued annually through 1939. Only one recording appeared in 1941, two or possibly three in 1942, and a final pair in 1949—which, ironically, included Varèse's "Density 21.5."

After a disastrous New Music Society concert in San Francisco in December 1935, Henry suggested that Gerald Strang organize concerts in Los Angeles, a reasonable idea since Los Angeles was becoming much larger than San Francisco and was filled with emigré intellectuals such as Schoenberg. While Strang was in favor because Los Angelenos needed to hear contemporary music, he felt that the extreme decentralization of cultural activities, the distances, the tepid interest in serious music, and the lack of performers willing to do something without a good fee would work against it. Even Schoenberg was pessimistic. Furthermore, proper financing was unlikely because the moneyed class was unlikely to budge from its established interests. With backing through a university essentially impossible, Strang suggested working cooperatively with Pro Musica—which itself was dying—and Klemperer, who had recently become music director of the Los Angeles Philharmonic.[50] Eventually they scrapped the plan.

24

American Composition or Americanist Music

Despite the conflicts, by the early 1930s Henry and his colleagues had created an atmosphere that stimulated young talents to pursue composition with striking vigor and self-confidence. That forcefulness spawned powerful rivalries, nationalist sentiments consistent with growing isolationism, and market forces intensifying the battle to define "American" music, a complex issue entangling art with patriotism.[1] A national style in a country without unified ethnic roots seemed like an oxymoron.

While American painters and writers had achieved international recognition and consequent acceptance at home, American composers remained largely unappreciated. One faction asserted that recognition required developing a wholly new style based upon American vernacular music and understandable by the larger public. Only a novel variant of musical nationalism could take into account the brief history of the United States and its ever-shifting ethnic components. A few musicians—especially Henry—asserted that compositional Americanism was completely unnecessary and virtually impossible at a high level of quality. Not all the opponents were internationalists, however. MacDowell had feared that overemphasis on programming American music could lead to a double standard. Daniel Gregory Mason doubted that any one type of folk or vernacular music could represent such a diverse country. Ives, who admired very few European composers, had vernacular music in his blood but mistrusted the pressure to define "American." Like Henry, they agreed that folk or vernacular music was useful only if composers could substantially elevate it as they absorbed it into "art" music.

Unfortunately, the cultivation of art music in the United States was still rooted in the cultural isolation of the wealthy, who reveled in the snob value of appreciating foreign classics. Such people, upon whom musical institutions depended, were unlikely to tolerate an infusion of the vernacular music of the masses. Out of deference to them, interaction between art music and American vernacular music existed only marginally. Whereas the original residents of the continent had the virtue of exoticism and were nicely tucked out of sight on reservations, the wild popularity of ragtime was especially problematic. European composers took to it more readily than their American colleagues, who were repelled by its roots in black American culture. Charles Ives, a fine ragtime player, was a brilliant exception.

The sudden growth of jazz in the early 1920s suggested another route to "American music." Copland, Roy Harris, Louis Gruenberg, Gershwin, and others rushed to fuse jazz with traditional Western music, while Blitzstein argued against concert composers' invasion of popular music.[2] The combination of jazz and classical might have been acceptable even to Henry, had not powerful voices tried to crown that fusion as the *only* "American" music, and had not European writers dismissed virtually all American music as "unauthentic" if it did not include jazz. Some of them cynically accepted Henry's music as authentically American because it evoked American hucksterism and American industrial eminence through its noisy clusters.

Because narrow definitions of "American" troubled Henry deeply, he took it upon himself to challenge European and American ignorance of American musical diversity. His first survey of the field appeared in 1927 in *Uj Föld* [New Earth], a journal about the avant-garde produced by Hungarian artists in Vienna.[3] Similar articles, translated into Czech, Russian, and Spanish, followed. By 1929, his ability to communicate complex ideas attracted editors of many professional journals and the popular press here and abroad. Soon his lectures and articles made him one of the most important spokesmen for American composers. Of course, he was not entirely altruistic; his own career required the advancement of American music—but not *Americanist* music.[4]

He often attacked jazz as a criterion for American authenticity, especially because most people knew jazz only through inferior white versions of it, and most composers used it (he reasoned) because of Paris's intoxication with it. If his earlier dismissal of jazz as the music of Negroes and Tin Pan Alley Jews seems hopelessly bigoted, it actually was a clumsy plea for authenticity. A 1930 article explained that "the idea of utilizing jazz themes is a good one, for composers racially adapted to it.... The Anglo-Saxon American has no more talent for writing or playing jazz than the European. Both of them are more than bungling at it."[5] In other words, his attitude to jazz had come to reflect the reality that what passed for jazz was often a dilution by society big bands rather than a deeply rooted product of black musicians who played it with real character.

Europeans, he kept saying, simply had to look elsewhere to find good American music. Unlike nineteenth-century Anglo-Saxon American composers who were third-rate imitators of Europeans, he wrote, now "there are a number of composers of Anglo-Saxon American blood who write music of significance, music with something to say, music which contains undefinable American feeling, music in which the distinction from European style is clear, music which necessitates the development of new materials and modes of expression." He singled out Ives as the finest of them.

In the autumn of 1930, the growth of American composition and the problem of defining it convinced Ives that a book-length survey of American composition was needed. Henry agreed, but recommended having multiple contributors. He would edit it and write an introduction.[6] The plan materialized as a volume of essays by American composers about the music of their colleagues, subsidized by Ives. The following spring Knopf agreed to publish it, then backed out, and Stanford University Press took it over. By late 1931 Henry had assembled most of the material, some of it reprinted from earlier publications. Thanks to Olive's help during his trips to Europe, proofs were ready quickly.[7] *American Composers on American Music* was available at the end of 1932.[8] It was both remarkably comprehensive and very timely, since the number of committed composers was swelling just as the deflating economy was reducing their prospects.

In his introduction Henry partly blamed the lack of information about American composition upon professional critics who understood nothing about the aims and techniques of composers and considered vitriol a laudable goal of criticism. He had sought a solution by asking composers to write about other composers, convinced that even those who lacked a polished literary style could contribute the fruits of their experience. Since he could not include everyone, he favored those with strong points of view. As a result, modernists dominated the book, but he embraced conservatives who could offer more than a recitation of textbook information. Foreign-born Americans added additional perspectives; a few Latin Americans had been invited to comment on traditional elements in their music. On the whole, he felt that the wide range of voices made the book a unique resource.

Knowing the difficulty of summarizing such a broad subject, he assembled American composers into seven groups according to what he perceived as their commonalities.

1. Those who developed "indigenous materials." Henry used the word "indigenous" to signify both the use of native materials and the development of techniques independent of European models.
2. Foreign born. Not employing a single style, they were grouped only because they brought foreign ideas to bear on American music in ways that did not suggest including them in other categories.
3. Americans influenced by modern "Teutonic music," including Schoenberg acolytes and free atonalists.
4. Adherents to French neoclassic tendencies.
5. Americans who took what they found in America and adapted it to a European style.

6. Conservatives who used European techniques without any intention to create something "American" of them.

7. Foreign-born composers who continued to write in the European fashion with no pretense to achieving anything else.

He also mentioned some very young and promising composers without allocating space for essays by or about them.

He considered the very concept of musical nationalism dangerously narrow and purposeless. "Music happily transcends political and racial boundaries and is good or bad irrespective of the nation in which it was composed." Only artistic independence could lead to music of lasting value. "Imitation cannot be expected to produce significant achievements." In order to untie American composition from the apron strings of the European heritage, national consciousness was "a present necessity for American composers," but once works of international standing had been created, "self-conscious nationalism will no longer be necessary."

In narrowing down his large list to composer-authors, Henry displayed no noticeable stylistic prejudice. He even included writers who were unsympathetic to his own music. His love of contradictory viewpoints repaid him with a few articles that criticize their subjects. Although it is not appropriate here to consider the articles individually, the table of contents shows Henry's priorities.

Carl Ruggles, by Charles Seeger
Adolph Weiss and Colin McPhee, by Wallingford Riegger
Edgar Varèse, by Henry Cowell
Aaron Copland, by Theodore Chanler
Henry Cowell, by Nicolas Slonimsky
Roy Harris, by Henry Cowell
Wallingford Riegger, by Adolph Weiss
Roger Sessions, by Nicolas Slonimsky
John J. Becker, by Henry Cowell
The Rochester Group of American Composers, by Howard Hanson
Henry Brant, by Henry Cowell
Howard Hanson, by Edward Royce
Carlos Salzedo, by Henry Cowell
Carlos Chávez, by Aaron Copland
Nicolas Slonimsky, by Henry Cowell
Ruth Crawford, by Charles Seeger
Charles Seeger, by Henry Cowell
Walter Piston, by Nicolas Slonimsky
Charles E. Ives, by Henry Cowell

In the end, Henry contributed nearly 40 percent of the book, including four new articles. Willing to sacrifice tact to honesty, he freely dismissed some compositions as unimportant. While he usually kept out of the way of his writers, he intervened in Chanler's scathing assessment of Copland with a postscript calling attention to the power of recent works such as the new *Piano Variations*. He saved until the end his extremely perceptive article about Ives. (His articles about Salzedo and Varèse predated the conflicts described in the previous chapter of this book. Amusingly, he called the almost unbearable irritation with which some listeners respond to Varèse's music a sign of its emotional power.)

For the second part of the book, he requested eleven articles on general tendencies. He pitted Roy Harris's racist view of American music against Gershwin's defense of jazz and Still's optimism about the future of black composers; he offered a touch of musical ethnology with articles by Caturla, Roldán, and Chávez about their own music. His hope that Rudhyar would produce something genuinely interesting about the influence of Oriental music unfortunately yielded only a nebulous tribute to the Asian mind. It was a stroke of genius to conclude the book with Ives's deeply moving article on the future of music, a reprint of his "Conductor's Note" for the second movement of his fourth Symphony.[9]

The Cowell papers contain relatively few reactions to the book from the composers themselves. Those whose music was not treated sympathetically may have decided to remain silent or complained in person. Henry was happy to learn that Roy Harris was not angry about Henry's criticisms.[10] A few reactions from abroad include Berg's admission that the book showed him the misguidedness of Central Europe in denying the importance of American music.[11] An official of the USSR Society for Cultural Relations with Foreign Countries (VOKS) called it a most interesting book that would help Soviet composers acquaint themselves with American modernism.[12] Reviewers in Cuba, Austria, and the United States generally praised its contributions. Occasionally it has been described as mutual back-scratching,[13] and indeed the most ticklish matter was how Henry would include himself, since it would have been peculiar to leave himself out. Slonimsky, in fact, closed his essay about Henry gracefully, simply saying that he "would not be himself if he did not follow the path of most resistance."

While *American Composers on American Music* was far from perfect, it succeeded in broadening the discussion. Unfortunately, it remained in the niche market. Through August 31, 1935, 407 copies had been sold, possibly including the hundred that Ives purchased as a form of subsidy.[14] *American Composers on American Music* soon went out of print and waited three decades to reappear.

Surveying the Larger Musical World

In addition to championing American composers, Henry wrote some fifty other articles from 1930 to 1936. Among them are his annual surveys of the year in music for the *Encyclopedia Americana* supplements, which show what he thought were the most significant developments. Although he did not mention his own name, his list of institutions serving American composers shows how much the musical world owed to him—the New Music Society of California, *New Music Quarterly*, the Pan American Association of Composers, the music program of The New School, instigating the creation of the New York Musicological Society, the International Exchange Concerts. He also had warm words for the Copland-Sessions concerts, the Conductorless Orchestra, the American chapter of the International Society for Contemporary Music (ISCM), Pro Musica, and many other groups. Traditional institutions did not attract his attention unless they showed an interest in the new tendencies, such as the American premiere of *Wozzeck* in Philadelphia. He railed against institutional stuffiness and neglect of American music, not even sparing his old supporter Henry Hadley for having brought to Tokyo only "such works as are in style thin dilutions of second-rate European models of a century ago." While he generally ignored star soloists, he perceived the importance of the American debuts of Yehudi Menuhin, Vladimir Horowitz, and Andrés Segovia. Other performers capturing his imagination included Béla Bartók, the Chinese actor Mei Lanfang who used Chinese music in his performances, the Hall Johnson Negro Choir, and young choreographers employing new music. Yet he also highlighted a program of semi-classics in Chicago that drew 115,000, reportedly the largest audience in recorded music history.

While he generally believed that the most stimulating composers were Americans, he unstintingly praised Webern and Schoenberg,[1] and singled out young Europeans who used extended vocal techniques.[2] Apart from relentlessly attacking French-based neoclassicism, however, he had little to say about other Europeans. He considered "pseudo-modern music" by composers such as Respighi, van Dieren, Pizzetti, and Cyril Scott very dangerous; their "vague and sentimen-tal" compositions would have been harmless were they not presented as "mod-ern," tricking intelligent listeners into thinking that such music represents the best in recent thought. Even worse, trusted performers appeared to accept such dilutions.[3] He was encouraged by increasing European interest in American art music and the acceptance of some American music by major European pub-lishers, but was dismayed that the ISCM passed up good American music for its annual festival in favor of Gershwin's "syrupy" *American in Paris*. Performances of non-Western music at the 1931 Colonial Exposition in Paris delighted him, although he could not attend.

His articles repeatedly lauded the merits of innovation. Often asked why one should bother listening to something new since the old masters developed such good material, he replied that the old masters used the materials so well that "it is utter folly for any composer today to try to emulate them in their own field." Modernists, he said, revere the classics, and were trying to do exactly what ear-lier composers did—develop their own styles. "Nothing of value is offered to the world by reiterating statements of the past. We wish to preserve the past in its lovely purity; not in garbled, rehashed form." Modern music expresses life today. "To go back to classical music represents an escape from the grim realities of this age, and places us back emotionally into a former page of history. . . . A full emo-tional appreciation of the possibilities of beauty and the moving power and sweep of contemporary life . . . is to be found in modern music alone."[4] Only in-novators, or those who use old materials in entirely fresh ways, will survive.[5] Raw innovation was not enough, however. He sensed the public's distrust of new music that lacked a "scientific" basis. Although he recognized the dangers in-herent in music becoming dominated by systematized, purely rational com-posing, it was increasingly becoming "the foundation of musical criticism."[6]

Henry was one of the few who argued that composers should study non-Western music and learn from its principles rather than mimicking it. Getting more details of his thinking is difficult, however. His skill at lecturing off the cuff[7] explains why, in an archive that includes unused metro tickets from the 1920s, only one of his many lectures on the subject survives from these years, and only as an outline.

Although Henry never produced the book that he proposed in his Guggenheim application, a dozen articles in these years treated topics in world music.[8] "Towards Neo-Primitivism," in *Modern Music* (1933), brings one closest to his general atti-tudes.[9] After reviewing primitivist tendencies such as Stravinsky's rhythms, he dis-missed those so-called primordial elements as another step in making music more complex. He maintained that the popular association of such music with primi-tivism results from a mistaken belief that "primitive" always means savage and wild. The time had come for a countermovement, reacting "against the over-complexity of . . . earlier modern music but not against experiment; against the sentimentality and pomp of later romantic music but not against feeling; against the supercilious formalism of a return to the particular style of some past century but not against the use of primary musical elements." These elements, he wrote, were now emerging among Russians writing for proletarian performers, using a single line and percussion accompaniment. Their music was neither major, minor, nor modal but with melodic lines using intervals suggested by the words. Vocal slides were written in; rhythm was free, direct, and frequently changing. Such music also showed a tendency to use chords percussively and for emphasis, not for harmonic purposes. "Primitive elements may of course be utilized in many ways. One may be rather literal in their use, as in the case of Soviet musicians, or one may make a sublimation of direct and primary musical materials, unhampered by ecclesiastical rules, scales or rhythms. The latter course is being followed by many of the young American composers who have recently made a bid for attention." In short, he was asking for what, years later, would be called "post-modernism."

In "The Scientific Approach to Non-European Music" (1935),[10] he surveyed the methodology used to study non-Western music and summarized the state of comparative musicology as pursued by Hornbostel, Curt Sachs, Robert Lachmann, and others. Strongly opposed to the separation of comparative musicology into separate spheres of study, he called for a broadly based approach including psychology, physiology, conditions of religion, social conditions, relation of climate and animal and vegetable life to the instruments, and so on. He concluded that the proper coordination of all branches of comparative musicology would produce "not only a correct understanding of the musics of other peoples, but also a proper perspective in which to understand our own music, and its role in relation to the other musics of the world."

Despite his pioneering work, Henry appears not to have earned a place in the history of comparative musicology, largely because he made no significant mark upon methodology and, unlike Bartók, did not publish detailed studies or volumes of transcriptions. That view is too narrow, however. He played a role in turning attention away from the study of intonation that preoccupied Hornbostel's circle toward a study of the music itself. His interest in hybrid cultures set the tone for future scholars. Most important, he helped create a climate in which the study of world music no longer was a fringe pursuit; he was one of the first composers to embed principles from other cultures into his music rather than try to re-create other cultures in a Western idiom. His campaign for a wider view of music contradicts the view that he lost his pioneering spirit after the period of innovative piano music. The 1930s were only the beginning of his lifetime of dedication to awareness of global music, which increasingly shaped his own compositions and became a widespread pursuit for subsequent generations.

26

Music and Politics

Shortly after Henry's death, Sidney described his political interest and awareness as "minimal."[1] She should have said that during the twenty-five years they were together Henry kept clear of politics. Olive was no more forthcoming. Asked if she or Henry encountered intensifying anti-Soviet feeling in the mid-1930s, she only remembered that criticisms of his trip prompted him to write about his experiences.[2] In fact, both women were completely aware of Henry's political activities. Considering the people among whom he lived as a boy and young man, he could hardly have avoided political awareness. His sympathy for the political left surfaced in Terman's 1914 interviews; the Varian household brimmed with rebelliousness; he admired the radicals he met in New York; Russell Varian was reading about communism at Stanford in 1921 and by 1931 was contemplating capitalism's inability to cope with the Depression and the probable approach of communism.[3] Seeger could not contain his own radicalism;[4] unconventional political thought abounded at The New School; the wealthy Ives was an outspoken egalitarian committed to the dignity of the common person, even as his opposition to government interference assured that he would not be sympathetic to communism.

By 1934, Henry's annual encyclopedia articles focused almost exclusively upon political and economic influences on music. Facing hard times, he wrote, American composers were being pushed into creative sterility, writing almost nothing for orchestras or opera houses, since no large organizations wanted their music. Major institutions stayed alive by giving fewer concerts, programming only well-known soloists and safe compositions, and avoiding anything unpopular. He thought federal WPA projects offered some hope, but in smaller cities they tended to be poorly conceived and executed. Players in federally sponsored orchestras were selected according to financial, not musical, criteria. The WPA's attitude toward performing American works resulted in much of poor quality. He called attention to the harm inflicted by ultranationalism and singled out a few promising communist trends.

His enthusiasm about music created by Soviet workers only hints at his deep involvement with communism, which began tentatively with the earliest invitation to play in the USSR, germinated in Moscow and Leningrad in 1929, and flowered between 1932 and 1935.[5] At first, despite reservations about the Soviet political system, he saw the country primarily as a potential market for American modernist music. He pressed to establish International Exchange programs and PAAC concerts there, and began reporting on American music for Soviet periodicals. His name as an author appeared in Moscow for the first time in *Muzika I Revolutsiya* (Music and Revolution), a highly respected, intellectually substantial Moscow journal that covered musical and political topics so broadly that its editors sometimes criticized its own articles.[6] Undeterred by bitter attacks on modernism emanating from the Russian Association of Proletarian Musicians and other "progressive" factions, undaunted by the cancellation and restoration of Henry's Moscow concert, and perhaps encouraged by Trotsky's sister's intervention, the journal published, a few months after Henry's visit, his survey of American composers, which it claimed was written "especially for the Soviet press."[7] (In fact, he recycled it from his articles for *Melos*.) An editorial introduction praised him for coming to the USSR "with the desire to open to us new creative sproutings, and familiarize our musical youth with his experiments." Although the editor castigated him for lacking class-sociological orientation, he forgave him because he provided information unknown even to their new music specialists.[8] *Muzika I Revolutsiya* commissioned another article but closed its doors before Henry could write it.[9]

The few references to the Soviet Union in his 1930 correspondence largely concern aborted efforts to establish an exchange of new music in collaboration with the New York Public Library[10] and to have *New Musical Resources* translated into Russian. Henry was surprised to learn that Georges Rimsky-Korsakov, the modernist grandson of Nikolai, promised to teach Henry's ideas at the Leningrad Conservatory.[11] Otherwise he only mentions the strong impression made by a new Soviet talkie that he had seen in Berlin, Nikolai Ekk's *Der Weg ins Leben* [The Path to Life, 1931], one of the first Soviet talkies and a depiction of the wild early Soviet days, which used a locomotive whistle "with great art."[12] The subject of the USSR then does not reappear in Henry's papers until the fall of 1931, when he tried to arrange performances through the American Russian Institute for Cultural Relations with the Soviet Union.[13]

That locomotive whistle, and Henry's lack of "class orientation," symbolize a basic dilemma: how to reconcile modernist ideas with the need to provide music for the masses suffering from the economic collapse. During his trip to the USSR, he was disturbed by the general direction of music there but encouraged by experiments with linking several composers to work communally on a piece,[14] the incorporation of cries and other primitive emotional outbursts in workers' choruses, and the use of new harmonies to express industrialization. These, however, were "the only hopeful signs in a direction that is otherwise leading into utter musical lifelessness in Russia." A new society that ignored the most up-to-date techniques could only recycle the language of the discredited bourgeoisie.[15] Yet Henry had seen Soviet communists treating musicians as respected members of society who were paid for their labor, while capitalist society let them sink if they could not swim commercially. He was not naive, however. Censorship, poor equipment, official hostility to unusual music, isolation of Soviet composers from their colleagues abroad, and other afflictions of cultural life were all too obvious.

Despite his mixed feelings, he was among the many American musicians drawn to communism when capitalism seemed to have destroyed itself. Finding a role for music in hard times was foremost in their minds. In 1931, the Seegers and Henry discussed their inability "to connect their music with the present social catastrophe."[16] Individualism counted for nothing as the concept of art for art's sake collapsed except within the enclaves of the rich.[17] In the compositional and visual arts worlds on both sides of the Atlantic, the love of extravagance yielded to neoclassicism, simplification, and communicativeness. Even the former Futurists embraced the Mussolini aesthetic of neo-Romanism. As Elliott Carter observed, the public no longer tolerated the *succès de scandale*.[18]

Judith Tick has written that in the terrible winter of 1931–1932, the Seegers became "very loyal fringe members of the Communist front."[19] Although Charles Seeger's old radicalism suggests that he brought Henry to communist organizations,[20] it seems to have been the opposite. That 1931 conversation may be the occasion when Henry urged them to join a new organization, the Pierre Degeyter Club, named for composer of the "Internationale." Formed to explore the prospects for music in the workers' movement, it was a branch of the Workers Music League, the American chapter of Moscow's official International Music Bureau (IMB).[21] Sidney remembered the club as comprising anarchists. "HC went to some meetings and is now spoken of by survivors as an ardent member, but there is no real evidence of this, only that he occasionally played for a meeting or a benefit."[22] None of it is correct. As two historians have written, the club was a "catch-all for otherwise unaffiliated radical musicians,"[23] but they were not anarchists. A true anarchist could never have tolerated the extreme centralization of the USSR. These were communists or devoted sympathizers. While there is no suggestion that Henry joined the Communist Party, he dove energetically into the Degeyter Club, the Workers Music League, and the communist movement in general. What Sidney may have preferred forgotten is thoroughly documented.

His name quickly circulated among leftists. In March 1932, he was invited to join a committee supporting a project of the American Russian Institute for Cultural Relations with the Soviet Union to send musicians to the

USSR.[24] The group, whose officers and directors included John Dewey, Leopold Stokowski, and Varèse, was by no means a mere front organization. The Soviets publicly called it an official branch of the All-Union Society for Cultural Relations with Foreign Countries (VOKS), an acronym that began quickly to play a lively role in Henry's life. While his response is unknown, it is implicit in a lecture for the Workers Music League not long afterward. "Comrade Cowell," said the invitation, "will speak on the subject: 'New Resources in Music with Relation to Proletarian Music.' Discussion will follow the talk led by Comrade Cowell. You are especially asked to bring friends interested in the technic of music."[25] Olive's notes on a similar lecture in San Francisco show that he was very clear about both the positive and negative directions of Soviet arts.[26]

Although he could not participate fully in the Degeyter Club because he spent about half the year in California, Henry's insistence on an innovative approach to proletarian music probably fueled the debates when he was in New York. Early in 1933, he, Jacob Schaefer—the leader of an important Yiddish-language workers' chorus—and Leon Charles, another leftist musician, gave a course of lectures and practical training sessions for leaders of workers' choruses and bands. The orientation of their seminar toward practical solutions for compositional challenges stimulated some participants to form the Composers' Collective of New York, which focused upon compositional and theoretical approaches to revolutionary music.[27]

The Degeyter Club's members and the twenty-four members of the Composers' Collective pursued the specific goal of creating an American version of the successful proletarian music by European composers and writers such as Kurt Weill, Hanns Eisler, and Bertolt Brecht. They were convinced that the excellent training of the group's member-composers would help them create mass song "dealing with immediate social issues, to be sung at meetings, on parades, and on picket lines."[28] Prominent figures in addition to Henry, Schaefer, and Charles included Lan Adomian (an ardent communist emigré from Ukraine), George Antheil, Marc Blitzstein, Henry Leland Clarke, Wallingford Riegger, Earl Robinson, Charles Seeger, and Elie Siegmeister. Major theoretical statements by Seeger, Siegmeister, and Blitzstein were published in communist daily papers and cultural magazines. Copland attended frequently; Eisler, a former Schoenberg student and recent refugee who was the spiritual leader of the European workers' music movement, was a guest. They continually asked one another if their products were singable and assumed that musical progressiveness equaled political progressiveness. Conventional classically derived techniques were used in new ways as they pursued a revolutionary result. Eisler's music strengthened their belief that the newest avant-garde techniques could lead to revolutionary songs comprehensible to blue-collar workers. His opinions, which followed Moscow's line, were respected because his own proletarian songs, rooted in the German march, were sung by real workers. He also turned the group against basing proletarian music on folk music, which Soviet doctrine had declared defeatist and morbid. Seeger, who knew folk music well, was particularly hostile to using it as a basis for revolutionary music. In fact, any roots in traditional music were thought counterproductive. The *Daily Worker* frequently emphasized that proletarian music should be so distinctive that it could not be imitated and would always be associated with the working masses.[29] Henry, also in the *Daily Worker*, deplored the setting of revolutionary texts with nonrevolutionary music.[30] Other correspondence shows that conventional art song—including his own 150-odd songs—no longer interested him.

The problem was that the New York group wrote unsingable workers' music. Copland's "Into the Streets, May First," which won the 1934 prize of the Workers Music League, is a good example of a fine song that only a professional can sing. Henry actually was better equipped to write usable music. Pieces like "The Vision of Oma," with its powerful marchlike character, memorable melody, and tone-cluster coloring that did not mar its accessibility, seemed like a natural bridge connecting modernism and proletarianism. He, whom Seeger called one of the real leaders of the Degeyter Club, was just what communism needed.

The New Deal's folklore projects finally changed Seeger's attitude toward folk song, and gradually folkloric songs of protest took hold, thanks to Seeger's son Pete and the Lomaxes, among others. Furthermore, Soviet policy unexpectedly veered, making folk music the new correct orientation. At that point the members of the Composers' Collective immersed themselves in folk music through analysis, using folk songs in composition, or collecting folk music. David Dunaway, a historian of the movement, concluded that the Collective's negative example of unsingable songs indirectly gave birth to a new form of popular protest songs by Woody Guthrie, Pete Seeger, and many others.[31] By that time, however, the original members of the Composers' Collective had moved on.

While the debates and struggles preoccupied the composers, Henry pursued a solid relationship with his Soviet colleagues, hoping it would lead to exposure for American modernism in the USSR. In view of the activities of modernist architects (home-grown and foreign) in Moscow and Leningrad, his hopes were by no means naïve. Indeed, he had hints that performances of American music looked possible in the early 1930s. L. Cherniavsky, VOKS's second deputy chairman, gratefully accepted a copy of *American Composers on American Music*, saying it would help circulate information about American music.[32] "More than ordinarily interested" in receiving a steady flow of information and material, he claimed to be pushing forward exchanges of music and to have interested the Moscow Conservatory in receiving American music in exchange for Henry devoting an issue of *New Music Quarterly* to Soviet composers. Henry accepted the trade, which was perfectly reasonable, but, divining that he had better not limit his contacts to VOKS, asked Cherniavsky to send a list of other possible institutions such as the libraries of the Leningrad and Kharkov conservatories and smaller institutions.[33]

He underestimated the grip of official bodies like VOKS and overestimated their candor. In fact, the true direction of Soviet musical policy was still taking root. The dismantling of old music organizations began with a decree of April 1932, replacing all existing institutions in all fields with professional unions. In October 1933, with the Composers' Union firmly installed, the British-born director of VOKS's Anglo-American Division wrote Henry that the Union would select, for a special volume of *New Music*, six or eight pieces representing contemporary trends. In exchange, Western music would be studied in a new seminar recently set up by the Moscow Conservatory.[34]

Henry and Slonimsky had become optimistic about concerts in Russia when Roosevelt recognized the USSR in 1933 and accredited Maxim Litvinov as ambassador. Slonimsky thought the PAAC might interest Litvinov's circle but did not explain why. The answer may be that Litvinov, a tough Bolshevik who survived the purges and died an apparently natural death in 1951, was also known as a high-living Bohemian with an English wife.[35] Slonimsky did not think that his own Russian origins, which had included tutoring the imperial children, would create a problem, since many Russian emigrés were again traveling in the USSR. Unfortunately, the influential emigré tenor Sergei Radamsky had told Leningrad officials that Slonimsky's concerts were "too highbrow for an average proletarian." Radamsky's unspecified connections made him someone to be reckoned with. Unfortunately, Henry, who knew him in Los Angeles,[36] felt he was very conventional, singing folk music as proletarian music. He was not entirely correct. Radamsky was with the composer on the fateful night in 1936 when Stalin attended Shostakovich's *Lady Macbeth of the Mtsensk District*. Much later, in the West, he sang in *Wozzeck*. Slonimsky contemplated bribing Radamsky with the offer of an engagement and getting Varèse to make the event an international rather than a strictly musical affair. He knew that the stamp of approval of either the American ambassador in Moscow or the Soviet ambassador in Washington could be decisive. Like his Soviet colleagues, however, Slonimsky did not guess that the decree dissolving all the old music societies, including the militant proletarian organizations, was the nucleus of a long-term plan to ensure conformity with the official line. As historians now know, Stalin had decided that the cultural bureaucrats had become too independent.[37] Henry, too, was misled by Soviet policy. He told Slonimsky that he was getting "chummy letters" that supported a future in the USSR. He had already arranged seven Exchange concerts of Soviet music in the United States, which he thought gave them leverage.[38]

Late in 1933, when Henry was marginally involved in the opening of Manhattan's Radio City, Slonimsky, erroneously presuming that Henry had good connections inside the RCA broadcasting conglomerate, hatched the "brilliant idea" of an America-to-Russia broadcast, celebrating American recognition of the Soviet Union. He would translate, announce in Russian, and conduct. It would be a PAAC event but restricted to composers of the United States.[39] Alas, Henry's connections with RCA were a figment of Slonimsky's imagination.

At the beginning of 1934, Cherniavsky sent VOKS's choices for publication in New Music, explaining that choral works were included because the medium "as a form of mass creative activity is very popular with our Soviet composers.... Unfortunately, we had no chance to include some works by Shostakovich, he having failed to send us any up to the present time." Another selection would follow, to be used for the projected concerts of Soviet music.[40] Regrettably but predictably, the scores almost entirely comprised light music and folk-song settings; an orchestral fragment by Myaskovsky seemed completely out of place. Whereas Henry normally chose what to publish, this time he was trapped. If he rejected VOKS's selection he had to give up his Soviet plans entirely. New Music Quarterly's Soviet issue was published in October 1934. An inoffensive selection, it sold well, probably because of the great interest in the USSR among musicians.[41] Even Henry's conservative friend Lazare Saminsky had come to see American and Soviet innovators as saviors in an era when European music seemed to be losing its vitality.[42]

Although Henry and Slonimsky stayed reasonably well informed about institutional structures—Slonimsky's brother was a Leningrad music critic—they were less aware of the undercurrents and apparently did not suspect that the Soviets were using them. After all the letters, nothing concrete materialized for American music in the USSR apart from the seminar at the Conservatory, which had a limited audience if it even took place. Ever hopeful, Slonimsky thought it a good sign that the Soviets considered a PAAC series at all, even though he knew that contracts in Russia were unreliable.[43]

In February 1934, Henry started a regular correspondence with Konstantin Kuznetsov (1883–1953), with whom he had dined in Moscow and who probably translated Henry's 1929 article in Muzika I Revolutsiya. A respected musicologist trained in Germany, Kuznetsov taught music history at the Moscow Conservatory, later directed its music history program, and wrote in excellent English as music critic for the Moscow Daily News, usually under the pseudonym A. Constant Smith, a literal translation of his Russian name. From time to time Kuznetsov sent Henry clippings on subjects ranging from traditional ethnic music to the great success of Shostakovich's new opera Lady MacBeth of the Mtsensk District.[44] (Stalin's visit was still two years in the future.) In March, feeling "a civic duty" to make American music known, he decided to organize a radio program of American compositions, introducing it with an article in *Sovyetskaya Muzika*, the journal of the Composers' Union. To prepare, he asked Henry to send treatises, scores, and recordings of music by Chávez, Copland, Vivian Fine, Gershwin, Ives, MacDowell, McPhee, and Henry himself. He did not want any jazz, but planned to talk about Gruenberg's and Gershwin's connections with jazz.[45]

VOKS's Cherniavsky eventually approved the radio program; repeating the request for recordings. The scarcity of material, he said, made it very difficult to make American music known, but the All-Union (that is, national) Broadcasting Board wanted information about repertory, financial conditions, and other matters. In return, Cherniavsky promised to send a dozen Soviet recordings, chiefly of folk music, and "some interesting new creations" that were about to be published in Moscow. He encouraged Henry to send information about his own activities, as they so appreciated his efforts to acquaint Americans with Soviet composers.[46]

Henry now believed that his effort to bring American music to the USSR would succeed. Little whiffs of realism can be found, however, in a letter from Kuznetsov three days after Cherniavsky's. A great supporter of Shostakovich, Kuznetsov foresaw that *Lady Macbeth* would be a turning point in his career. (How right he was!) Lev Knipper was the next coming talent. What he meant was that Knipper had recently abandoned his earlier, German-based modernism and was complying with Soviet doctrine. Turning to the broadcasting proposal, Kuznetsov doubted that Cherniavsky would object to his demonstrating American music on the air in exchange for a concert of Soviet music in the United States, "*the more as the majority of pieces to be performed are Henry Cowell's gifts.*" Cherniavsky would see this as Henry's demonstration "of a noble, self-denying work, done in his editorial, organizing, propagating, rôle. Very often—in my thoughts—I compare your 'rôle' with the part Stassov played for the young Russian music's sake. I hope the results will be as mighty (for American music—I mean)." Kuznetsov also relayed a request from the editor of *Sovyetskaya Muzika* for an article on American music. The list of preferred content shows Kuznetsov's extensive knowledge of American music even in the absence of scores.[47] Henry could only view the collegiality of such a serious historian as an excellent development.

Henry also had established contact with the International Music Bureau, which the Soviets called "the principal agit-prop cultural unit of the international Communist movement."[48] The IMB's Grigory Schneerson (1901–82) did not make the cut for an article in the *New Grove Dictionary* but is immortalized in *Baker's Biographical Dictionary*, thanks to the remarkable sleuthing of Slonimsky, who described him as an eminent Russian musicologist and critic, a graduate of the Moscow Conservatory in piano, a gifted linguist who mastered all European languages and studied Chinese, and a scathing critic of modernism.[49] Schneerson was, in most ways, the opposite of Kuznetsov.

Schneerson lamented that the IMB had had almost no contact with Henry, especially considering his association with the Pierre Degeyter Club, their affiliate. He wanted Henry to supply opinions, criticism, musical literature, back and future issues of *New Music,* and Henry's own scores. In exchange, Schneerson would send any musical material that Henry requested.[50] With his status in Moscow seeming to have turned 180 degrees since 1929, Henry acted at once. Soon Schneerson thanked "Comrade Cowell" for two parcels of new scores, reporting that some modern American music had been broadcast, though Kuznetsov's program had not yet gone out. He rejoiced in Henry's plan to produce Soviet music throughout the United States, emphasizing that performances of choruses and mass songs would be the best assets for the movement. Events gradually showed that his declaration that the IMB would help Soviet musicians to see *New Music Quarterly* should not have been taken seriously.[51]

Kuznetsov's broadcast, aired at the end of May 1934, included selections from generally tame pieces by MacDowell, Copland, Gershwin, Gruenberg, Ives, Piston, and Henry's beautiful song "Rest." The *Moscow Daily News* (probably Kuznetsov) credited Henry for organizing performances and publications of Soviet music in the United States and praised the talent and technical proficiency of American composers, who "are bound to create a grand musical art as a response to deep social and economic changes going on their country today. One can judge by the music of former years that the soil is well prepared, the crops are good and the harvest will be plentiful."[52] Once again, Henry's success looked assured.

Kuznetsov's lecture was printed in the July issue of *Sovyetskaya Muzika* alongside Henry's newest article on American music. Allocated seventeen pages and given the lead position, Henry treated almost every imaginable subject. Since the Cowell papers contain copies of the article but no translation, he may not have known about the substantial editorial deletions and changes, and that Kuznetsov appended extensive commentary, much of it critical of composers lacking the proper proletarian viewpoint. Kuznetsov had made Henry's article a forum for the official line. One should not be too hard on him, however. He had no choice.

Schneerson, meanwhile, pressed Henry to establish a Pierre Degeyter Club in San Francisco.[53] He would have known that labor trouble abounded in America, especially in California. In addition to seething union turmoil in Hollywood and vicious labor relations on the farms, William Randolph Hearst, an admirer of nazi and fascist labor policies, had fired all journalists involved in the Newspaper Guild, including Henry's old admirer Redfern Mason, the *San Francisco Examiner's* music critic.[54] Henry passed along the idea of a club to Lan Adomian, who was all for it. Schneerson had warned, however, that the Workers Music League was going to federate all the Pierre Degeyter Clubs and similar organizations.

The proposed San Francisco chapter would have to affiliate with it. Moreover, the Division of Publications of the Workers Music League would become the sole publisher of music for the Degeyter Clubs. Henry was instructed to inform the Workers Music League of any other revolutionary music activity (such as workers' choruses, bands, etc.) in San Francisco.[55]

Henry's papers contain nothing further about a San Francisco Degeyter Club nor any evidence of his next step, now that Schneerson had revealed Soviet determination to control the entire American movement. The Americans soon rebelled against its directives. Seeger had already complained that Adomian was the worst kind of dictator—overbearing and unreliable. As a result of a badly managed concert and reception for Eisler, he had been removed from the music movement.[56] Adomian's behavior, however, was not the only proof that central control had been mandated. In March 1934, Vladimir Lakond, director of the music division of Amkniga, the sole representative of the State Music Publishers in the Americas, told Henry that he was hoping to receive American music for exchange purposes but would need permission from VOKS to accept it.[57]

Such consolidation and control from abroad was not Henry's style. Nevertheless, he continued to attend the Degeyter Club when he could, spoke and played several times, and advised the Philadelphia Degeyter Club about public events.[58] Very few of his appearances can be dated, however. Because he spent very little of 1932 in New York, the meetings involving him probably took place between 1933 and 1935. Moreover, he did not restrict himself to lecturing on proletarian matters. On one occasion he experimented with playing his music without titles to see if the music itself meant something to listeners. Another time he collaborated with a Chinese modernist painter and musician in a lecture-recital on Chinese music.

By now, Olive, who was well versed in politics and especially academic politics, was becoming very concerned about the risks Henry was taking. She cannot have been pleased when one Degeyter program identified him as music editor of *New Masses*, a far-left journal. In March 1934 she urged him to consider the danger of addressing workers' and socialist groups if he wanted to continue teaching at universities.[59] The possible catastrophic effects of being considered politically undesirable may explain her evasiveness in responding to Rita Mead's question about antagonism to Henry's Soviet trip even years after Henry's death.

After mid-1934, Henry's dialogue with the Soviets shifted completely from Kuznetsov to Schneerson. In the October issue of *Sovyetskaya Muzika* Schneerson printed foreign composers' comments about the problems of writing revolutionary music. Henry's contribution, a long and very revealing letter, began with a general picture of the Degeyter Club's weekly discussions and mutual criticism as they tried to express class struggle through music. The members agreed that revolutionary works must take advantage of different modes of expression, but each composer sought a solution differently, using more or less of his or her traditional training. Most of them agreed that revolutionary music needed a simplicity "far from that which we call 'modern.'" Henry felt so strongly opposed to the Workers Music League's demand that all songs in the *Workers' Songbooks* have piano accompaniments, that he refused to submit anything; New York composers believed that music of the old type led workers backward to a petit bourgeois psychology. On the other hand, although modernist music of the "decadent school" said nothing to the worker-listener, its complex harmonies, supporting simple melodic lines of the new type, produced a great impression. In this way music could be created in which both form and innermost content are revolutionary. Henry could not imagine how revolutionary ideas could be expressed in "unrevolutionary" music.[60]

In addition to opposing the requirements of the Workers Music League, Henry now was defying Moscow's line, promulgated in the summer of 1934 by Cultural Commissar Andrei Zhdanov and Maxim Gorky. The new concept was "Socialist Realism," a political theory that art must be "uplifting." Modernism was terminated; folk art was embraced. The New York composers' goal of using modernist techniques now constituted open rebellion.

This was the context in which Schneerson wrote a few months later to tell Comrade Cowell that the IMB wanted detailed information about the Degeyter Club.[61] Early in 1935, Schneerson (who had moved to the Composers' Union) asked specifically for a brief account of Henry's "creative discussions." He agreed that "attempts to find a new revolutionary language are positive signs of the embryonic growth and development of proletarian musicians" and should embrace the widest possible circle of musicians. A creative exchange of ideas was appropriate and to be encouraged, but "all these new experiments should of necessity be tested out in every-day practise work with the masses. We cannot think of a creative revolution of artists isolated from the masses." Simply said, Henry was put on notice that his idea of new music for a new society was unacceptable.

He wanted Henry to write an article for *Sovyetskaya Muzika* outlining the basic problems faced by American composers, along with a list of works produced by "the most prominent revolutionary composers." Because the Union of Soviet Composers was very interested in "the creative work of foreign composers and in their theoretical aims," Henry should send any criticisms of Soviet composers that he encountered. "Do not keep silent for politeness. We will also send comments on American Music."[62] Effectively, Schneerson was asking Henry to spy. The increasingly doctrinaire tone of his letter implies his awareness of the repression that began after the December 1, 1934, assassination of Sergei Kirov, the head of the Communist Party in Leningrad and an opponent of Stalin. Even Maxim Gorky was under house arrest. Everyone, Schneerson included, had to be extremely careful.

In March 1935, Henry sent him another, unidentified article. Neither it nor Henry's letter is among Schneerson's correspondence in the Glinka Museum. Their existence is known only from Schneerson's response. It probably was "Kept Music," originally published the previous December in the left-wing *Panorama: A Monthly Survey of People and Ideas*. Henry's subject was the way rich society women create "kept composers" writing "kept music" by manipulating them with flattery until they produce only works that are totally acceptable because the composer's ego tends to continue along the most-praised paths. Economic considerations reinforce the composer's actions, because no composer of "serious" music can make a living from royalties and fees. The result is a pseudo-modernist style that he called "social music"—technically proficient, smooth and polished, post-Wagnerian, "with dashes of Debussy and Stravinsky for flavoring."

> It must be slightly exotic, must be emotional and waft delicately through the sex-centers, arousing sex emotions pleasurably, but not in an unseemly way. It must create a slightly drugged mood—cast a spell. It must not be intellectual, nor induce thought. It must incite no radical feelings. It must be just modern enough so that it can be called frightfully original, but it must have no experimental modern qualities—the "modernism" must be just a suggestion, and taken from the above-mentioned known models—Stravinsky or Debussy. It must be a style pleasing to those who like Wagner, Tschaikowsky, Grieg, Humperdinck, Puccini, and Debussy.

One could also be "kept" through success on Broadway, support from Big Business, success with big conductors. "But why elaborate? The society woman is the most successful and prominent of those who influence the trend of contemporary musical style into a kept style."[63] Henry himself survived thanks to his "keepers" but probably did not feel "kept" since they admired him precisely for his music's unconventionality. He nevertheless knew what happened to composers who did not play the game. Ironically, his stylistic description of "kept music" was perfectly appropriate to Socialist Realism.

Although Schneerson never printed that article, he was pleased by Henry's satire of "the odious side of American musical life." Seeing that Henry could serve his purposes, he requested more such material. That brought Schneerson to the crucial point: the absence of consistent, broadly applicable thinking about revolutionary music responding to the demands of the time.[64]

Meanwhile, Cherniavsky sent some Soviet scores by Boris Lyatoshinsky, Aleksandr Mosolov, Dmitri Kabalevsky, Igor Belza, Igor Gnessin, Nikolay Myaskovsky, Leonid Polovinkin,[65] and an unidentified "Feldman."[66] A very uneven group, it included two credible progressives, Lyatoshinsky, the father of Ukrainian modernism, and Mosolov, a star of the 1920s Russian avant-garde. Although the others were now making their peace with anti-modernist ideology, VOKS still seemed to have a slightly open mind, at least for export.

In the fall of 1935, Schneerson requested a report on the New Music Society's San Francisco concert of May 29, with music by Davidenko, Myaskovsky, Mosolov, Shostakovich, and Veprik.[67] He said it would help a Composers' Union committee's quest for a "veritable Soviet style." The masses needed to be reached; national traditions of the ethnic groups had to be encouraged. (In fact, those traditions were being relentlessly squashed by Russianization.) "Democratic tendencies" in opera could be heard in Shostakovich's *Lady Macbeth* and Shaporin's *The Decembrists*. The committee's list of foreigners who saw music as they did (Erwin Schulhoff, Eisler, Stefan Wolpe, Copland, and many others)[68] did not include Henry, thanks to his doctrinal errors. If Henry suspected that the USSR was moving toward enforced anti-modernism, toward artificial "ethnic music," toward that dimly defined "Socialist Realism," he may have been relieved in October when Schneerson told him that one of his string quartets would be displayed in an exhibition of modern music at the Union. (He did not specify the exhibition's tone.) Although Henry still had not sent a detailed article on the Pierre Degeyter Club, Schneerson acknowledged another article that Henry had enclosed with the quartet and told him it would appear in *Sovyetskaya Muzika*.[69]

That article sits, unpublished, in Schneerson's files at the Glinka Museum. It was derived from "'Useful' Music," printed in *New Masses* in October 1935. Here Henry, under his proletarian pseudonym "Eric Clayton," explained how music can bind groups together for a common purpose, as armies and churches had known for centuries. He began by reiterating his controversial stance about modernism in revolutionary music, urging a tolerance for experimentation because of its untapped potential and uncertain results. He then recounted a personal example of the usefulness of music. The San Francisco dock strike began in May 1934. When conditions deteriorated, strike breakers were brought in. After hired thugs tried to break the strike and two dockers died, rioting erupted which gradually expanded into a general strike. On July 5, Governor Merriam called in the National Guard. Henry wrote,

> During the longshoremen's strike in San Francisco a young composer, Eric Clayton, wandered down to the waterfront. There were little scattered bunches of pickets. There were too few to cover the entire waterfront and they were knotted into little unconnected groups. They had been standing there a long time and the morale was not very strong. Police were waiting to bring scabs through. It would have been easy. There was an inactive crowd of curious spectators, numbering many hundreds, perhaps thousands. Clayton did not have any song in mind

that would fit. But he went to one of the little picket groups and after gaining its confidence by a few words, he persuaded the members to try starting a song, although none of them had ever done anything of the sort. Clayton had to make up the song as he went along, words and music. He hummed a tune, then sang it over, thought of words for it. He taught the tune by singing it over and over. (No one knew that it was being improvised.) It grew and took form. It was simple but original. It was vital to the point of electrifying those who sang it. As soon as it was learned, one of the pickets of the first group went over and taught it to the second group; in this way it spread all up and down the line. It changed the pickets from stragglers to a solidified single unit, strengthened their purpose. The crowd was also swayed. It changed from curiosity seekers to sympathizers. It took up the song. The crowd bunched together and formed a solid phalanx. The police would have had to bring the scabs through the crowd, even before meeting the pickets. It would have been so bloody that they were afraid to try it.

And they didn't bring the scabs in.

Music had been put to use.[70]

Henry enclosed the melody. Unfortunately, it has vanished from Schneerson's files.

Although Schneerson's intentions are unknown, the article may have died for reasons beyond his control. *Sovyetskaya Muzika* suddenly found itself having to dedicate its pages to an urgent matter, the turning point in Shostakovich's career. In January 1936, Stalin, a passionate music lover, attended *Lady Macbeth of the Mtsensk District*—about which Kuznetsov had been so enthusiastic—and hated it. No matter that the opera attacked the corrupt bourgeois society of the late Tsarist period and was extremely successful. The new path had been declared and dissent was harmful to the health. Doubtless Stalin's love of traditional music partly shaped his view of modern opera, but that grumpy operagoer could enforce his taste. On January 28, 1936, *Pravda* printed "Muddle Instead of Music," a vicious attack on the opera. The next few issues of *Sovyetskaya Muzika* were filled with statements enthusiastically supporting the new line—the always-optimistic, always-comprehensible Socialist Realism. The tone of those pledges could not have been more different from the proclamations of support for the all-embracing Composer's Union almost four years earlier. The Union, after all, had much to recommend it on the surface—apartments, a restaurant, library, concert hall, and other perks. Now the composers were absolutely desperate to affirm their loyalty to national policy, for it was finally clear that the Union structure facilitated political control. Although Stalin had been slaughtering his opponents in the Kremlin for several years, the purge of millions of "saboteurs" now embraced everyone. The attack on internationally admired Shostakovich was a signal that no one was safe.

In his next letter, however, Schneerson sounds unruffled. Henry had sent an article on the physical basis for new music, almost certainly "The Scientific Approach to Non-European Music," an impressive piece that was mentioned in the previous chapter. Schneerson wrote Henry that he assumed it would provoke a controversy but that their common aims would result in their jointly furthering their common cause. Its lack of ideological underpinnings, however, made it unpublishable and unsafe for Schneerson to keep in his files.[71]

"Why Modern Composers?" which Henry wrote for the March 1936 newsletter of the Philadelphia Degeyter Club, also caused trouble. He answered his headlined question by stating that modern composers are necessary "for purposes for which no old music is suited." Music written merely to sound pretty did not deal with today's reality. Music today could express today's realities clearly and uncompromisingly, and stimulate listeners to act against oppressive conditions. Neither classical music nor pretty, sentimental modern music would suffice.[72]

When Schneerson saw it, he exploded.[73] As the errors of the Philadelphians, Henry, and others persisted and spread around the United States, the more important it was for them to be expunged. He attacked Henry's idea of music reflecting the disagreeableness of the time, accusing him of blotting out the entire heritage of classical music, which the Soviets now decided should be used to elevate the taste of the proletariat. He agreed that the contemporary revolution required a new musical language, but considered the ideas of American modernists antiquated and inapplicable. The culture of the bourgeois had promoted "the decadent methods and ways of atonal and polytonal music, methods refuting the foundations of our musical language, negating the emotional and democratic character of music." Using such music to educate the proletariat had to fail. "The comrades who consider the ideas expressed by com. Henry Cowell very 'revolutionary'—are mistaken. Com. Cowell, despite his definite political sympathies and his connexion with the workers' musical movement, is in [that] respect influenced by decadent tendencies typical for [sic] the contemporary music of the bourgeoisie, but foreign to us." American communists had to reject those ideas at once. The Soviets would enforce uniformity in the arts worldwide.

Schneerson did not foresee that Soviet ideology was about to shift again, this time in the direction of folk music.[74] And he had not anticipated the Composers' Collective's secession from the Degeyter Club in 1935. American musicians were increasingly turning their backs on the USSR's policies as Roosevelt's programs took root, easing the musicians' plight, and the United States began its long recovery.[75] Schneerson's article "The Changing Course of Soviet Music," published by *Modern Music* in 1936, seems like a desperate attempt to retain the flock.[76]

Of Henry's Soviet story, the last, surprising chapter concerns his response to the banning of *Lady Macbeth*, printed in *Sovyetskaya Muzika* in September 1936 but definitely written the previous spring. He began by criticizing Shostakovich, not for sins in the opera (which Henry was unlikely to have known) but for wasting his talent in imitating old forms and falling prey to the influence of lightweight Parisian music. However, Henry repeated his insistence about the need for Socialist music to embrace modern ideas, justifying them as starting a three-stage process. Audiences become discontented upon hearing contemporary music "of the type Stravinsky-Schoenberg-Bartok," and lose their "narrowminded peace of mind. This is almost the sole goal of my journal 'New Music.'" In the second stage, people realize that such music does not offer a way out "and are then ready to accept the simple music of the working mass, music of socialist realism." In the third stage, people thirst for a higher form of music taking from the old and the new. This new music conserves everything from the past that is useful for the new creativity. He concluded, "I often run into the ridiculous tendency to reject new openings and call them bourgeois, for this reason—that they were at first used in bourgeois music. Physical phenomena are neither bourgeois nor anything else. It is indispensable to work untiringly toward clarifying questions ... independent of which goals they served earlier."

Although some of that seems to come from a different Henry, it is consistent with his conviction that music was about sound, nothing else. His ideas were so dangerously critical of Soviet policy, however, that it is astounding to find the letter printed so late in 1936. The wily Schneerson covered his tracks with comments that were gentle but politically safe. While lauding Henry's many services to the USSR and communism he cautioned that his ideas were hardly persuasive and in part pretentious and formalistic.[77] It appears that he now terminated his contact with Henry. I can only say "it appears," because virtually no letters *to* Henry from anyone survive from July 1936 to June 1940. Schneerson's file, however, contains a carbon or secretarial duplicate of every letter he wrote to Henry that is also preserved in the Cowell papers. There are no carbons of further letters. Everything suggests that continued contact with a rebel like Henry had become mortally dangerous.

A coda: In February, 1936, Adomian's application for a visa to conduct one or two broadcast programs of American music in Moscow was rejected. The grand exchange was over.[78] Fortunately, the musical world was regarded as relatively innocuous by the Stalin government and suffered proportionately fewer casualties during the purges than the writers, painters, and, of course, the politicians. Trotsky's sister Olga Kameneva, the former chairwoman of VOKS who had saved the day for Henry in 1929, was imprisoned along with all the other associates of her brother. Her sons were shot in the mid-1930s; she perished in 1941, in a mass execution of political prisoners.[79]

27

Henry and His Circle

In these years of professional frustration, Henry could count on the support of a devoted inner circle, first among whom was Ives. It had taken only a few years for them to progress from colleagues to close companions, almost father and son, in constant contact by mail and telephone, their visits limited only by Henry's schedule and Ives's poor health. The sincerity of Henry's devotion is evident in his correspondence, which shows his determination to bring Ives's music to the widest audience. Henry, in turn, treasured Ives's generosity, moral support, and invaluable insights about the art and business of music. In 1932, convinced that Ives's day was approaching, he told Olive to keep all documentation about the progress of his music.[1]

For Ives, Henry's support was a rare relief from artistic isolation. Concerning suspicions that Henry encouraged him to backdate his scores in order to establish the primacy of his ideas, there is no definite answer. They are very likely to have discussed the dates, and Henry would have encouraged Ives if he felt that redating was appropriate. No evidence implies a concerted effort, however. Nor is there any reason to suspect Ives of exploiting Henry. His letters show him deeply moved by Henry's enthusiasm and energy, and impressed by his ideas for the profession. Extremely aware of Henry's precarious personal finances, Ives found ways to help him without injuring his pride. Since The New School paid its faculty on a per-student basis, he contributed scholarships to Henry's courses, knowing that the money would reach him and simultaneously help needy students.[2] Bulk purchases of Henry's books assured their publication without seeming like an outright gift. When Stokowski declined to conduct a score of Henry's because of the licensing fee, Ives insisted on paying it.[3] His confidence in Henry was so strong that in 1932 he proposed establishing a trust for new music, administered by Henry. He would bequeath $30,000 (2010: $479,000) to his wife, Harmony, to guarantee her comfort after his death, with the understanding that she would leave the residue to Henry for a fund to aid experimental composers.[4]

Unfortunately, Ives's worsening health gradually undermined their contact. His hand shook so badly that his daughter Edie or his wife Harmony had to write what he dictated or paraphrase his words.[5] One of his last handwritten letters, around 1935, must have upset Henry badly. "Dear Henry," he wrote,

> Am just getting out of one of those g—d—slumps and haven't been able to write—or do anything much. I guess music and I are parting company—can't see it—can't hear it most of the time—eyes & ears . . . it makes me—wild—it's the creator's fault—not mine!—is that right? Now I'll shut up this woe-talk! Keep well—. . . of that no advice! Will write a betta letta soon. The enclosed just for the general fund or whatever you think best.
>   love to you from all of us
>   ever yours
>   C.E.I.[6]

When Ives's health and his extended trips abroad increasingly prevented him from immersing himself deeply in the details of Henry's projects, Henry could turn to other confidants—principally Nicolas Slonimsky, Adolph Weiss, Wallingford Riegger, John Becker, and Charles Seeger. Henry and Slonimsky enjoyed a long-lasting friendship, deep yet informal, epitomized by letters mixing serious business with amusing verbal games. Weiss became a close friend during the Berlin days and continued in the United States, especially at the bridge table. Despite some reservations about John J. Becker's music, Henry was a loyal ally. Becker reciprocated by getting Henry performances in the Midwest and working hard for the New Music Society and Pan American Association of Composers. Years later, his widow found on his copy of Ives's *Essays before a Sonata* her husband's note that Henry "did more for American composers, more than any other American."[7]

Some friendships were much more challenging, however. Carl Ruggles loved and respected Henry but bristled with prejudices, insecurities, and relentless self-promotion that cost him many friends. They had seen each other as often as possible until Ruggles and his family moved to rural Vermont in 1924, after which they depended upon the mail and occasional visits, one of which has become part of music history's lore. When Henry arrived at the Ruggles's farm,

> [Ruggles] was sitting at the old piano, singing a single tone at the top of his raucous composer's voice, and banging a single chord at intervals over and over. He refused to be interrupted in this pursuit, and after an hour or so, I insisted on knowing what the idea was. "I'm trying over this damned chord," said he, "to see whether it still sounds superb after

so many hearings." "Oh," I said tritely, "time will surely tell whether the chord has lasting value." "The hell with time!" Carl replied. "I'll give this chord the test of time right now. If I find I still like it after trying it over several thousand times, it'll stand the test of time, all right!"[8]

Charles Seeger could be extremely moody and cantankerous, but was also a loyal ally and forgave Henry for the missing credit in *New Musical Resources*. Any residue of their original teacher-student relationship had vanished, especially in the passionate atmosphere of the communist movement. How could Seeger not have been grateful that Henry pressured him into meeting Ruth Crawford, published her music—he was to be her only publisher—and paid her the enormous compliment of launching New Music Quarterly Recordings with the slow movement of her string quartet?

Remarks by Ives and other members of Henry's circle show that the difficulties of working with Varèse were not a figment of his imagination. Henry was admired for behaving as diplomatically as possible, writing positively about his music,[9] and publishing *Ionisation*.[10] He was cordial even when he completely distrusted Varèse. It would be interesting to know Varèse's view of their friction, but Louise Varèse either knew nothing or opted for silence in writing her husband's biography.

The friction between Henry and Copland was sometimes overt, sometimes subtle. Ethnicity, personality, and pure competitiveness all were issues. Henry was not alone, however, in perceiving that Copland wanted to be crowned leader of American music. While Henry was happy to praise Copland's music after hearing the trio *Vitebsk*, Copland stuck by his belief that Henry was more an inventor than a composer.[11] Their friction was exacerbated by Henry's appointment as director of music at The New School and Copland's creation of Cos Cob Press, a competitor for New Music, but gradually they coexisted rather than competing, in part because Henry was so determined to reduce factionalism in the new music community. (Composer-conductor Eugene Goossens told him he deserved a medal for that initiative.)[12] Their involvement with the political left finally eased earlier resentments.

Henry's international life changed as the situation in Europe deteriorated. When Schoenberg, Toch, and others immigrated, he helped them build a new professional life.[13] Almost as soon as Schoenberg settled in Los Angeles, Henry invited him to conduct *Pierrot Lunaire* on a New Music Society concert in San Francisco. Berg died in 1936; Webern disappeared from Henry's life and was killed in 1945, a decade before Henry returned to Europe. Henry's relationship with Bartók remained warm, but there are no references to him in the 1930s. (Letters from Bartók in the 1940s have disappeared.)[14] After 1936, Henry's Russian friends became inaccessible.

Of his new friends in these years, the most important are Percy Grainger, John Cage, and Lou Harrison. Grainger and Henry may have met as early as 1916 or 1919,[15] when Grainger was a star and Henry a novice fifteen years his junior. Their first verifiable contact took place at a concert in Henry's New School series in January 1933. Grainger, now chairman of New York University's music department, followed up immediately with an extremely complimentary letter.[16] They quickly discovered their many common interests and strikingly similar backgrounds. Both of them had spent their early childhoods in frontier towns—Grainger in Melbourne, Henry in Menlo Park. Their mothers aggressively nurtured their sons in their own image and had to cope with problematic husbands. They dressed their little boys in fancy clothes with a strong feminine cast, and while such attire was common in the late nineteenth century, the "Little Lord Fauntleroy look," as Grainger biographer John Bird calls it, provoked bullying of Grainger by bigger, older boys, as it had for Henry. They had huge vocabularies as children, were passionate long-distance hikers, made their names as prodigy pianists, and—as we shall soon learn—had mothers who tried to control their love lives.[17]

No wonder their meeting spawned a lasting friendship and the first of many joint projects—playing Henry's "The Harp of Life" as a piano duet with Grainger taking the single notes and chords and Henry the clusters. Grainger immediately promised to subscribe to *New Music Quarterly*,[18] study Henry's techniques, and play his pieces.[19] They began helping one another to find engagements, shared ideas about primitive music, and contemplated endless projects until the Graingers left for Australia.[20] Unlike so many stars who made easy promises, Grainger added Henry's piano music to his active repertory.

Whereas Grainger was fifteen years older than Henry, Cage and Harrison were respectively fifteen and twenty years younger and began as Henry's mentees and students; it was Henry who introduced them to one another. The best source about their early relationship is Rita Mead's 1975 interviews of them. Verification of Cage's responses is almost impossible, however; only a handful of letters remain because he and Henry spoke on the telephone and saw one another frequently.[21] Mead's interview, combined with Leta Miller's superb study of the Cowell-Cage connection, and a few other sources such as statements by Henry and Sidney, make possible the following account.

As a student at Pomona College from 1928 to 1930, Cage was fascinated to see Henry in recital for the first time.[22] After Cage dropped out of Pomona he began studying composition with Richard Buhlig, who was the most accomplished musician he knew of. In 1933, when Cage was twenty-one, Buhlig told him that he had nothing more to teach him and advised sending Henry some music in the hope that he would publish it.[23] At that time, Henry recalled, Cage "was writing strange little piano pieces with an unusual sense of the sound-interest created by odd tonal combinations. Then as now the music showed little desire to move about actively; it rather depended on very slight and subtle changes for its elaboration."[24]

Henry declined to publish anything, perceiving that Cage had not yet found his own voice. Nevertheless, he put Cage's Sonata for Clarinet on a New Music Society Workshop program in San Francisco, to which Cage hitchhiked.[25] He recalled the venue as a living room barely larger than the piano; the workshops did not have audiences. Finding the clarinetist unprepared, he played the piece on the piano. Ray Green, who, at twenty-five, was only four years older than Cage, remembered the event as an embarrassment; Gerald Strang (Cage's contemporary) said they rolled their eyes. When asked if the incident indicated serious deficiencies in New Music Society performances, Strang remembered the clarinetist as a good man and thought the score might have had problems.[26] Alfred Frankenstein, however, said that the New Music Society performance standards left something to be desired. In any event, the workshop helped bring Cage into contact with Henry.

Cage did not tell Mead whether Henry was at that workshop or, if not, when they first met. He could have attended Henry's lectures on world music at the Sutter Street (San Francisco) YWCA or his talk about developing an American national music. Henry thought it was around 1932, but it must have been at least 1933, the year of the Clarinet Sonata. They hit it off so well that Cage began to tell Henry his problems, which at that time were primarily financial. He soon announced proudly that he had gone on to a more systematic kind of writing.[27] In the 1933–34 season, Cage studied dissonant counterpoint with Henry in California and they wrote linked articles on modernity for the Oceano publication Dune Forum. Henry did not shrink from disagreeing with his young friend.

He advised Cage, who was experimenting with his own version of the twelve-tone method, to study with Schoenberg, but knowing that Cage was not ready, suggested preparing himself by working in New York with Schoenberg's former assistant, Adolph Weiss. He also offered Cage one of the scholarships at The New School that Ives had funded. Sidney—still Sidney Robertson— whose early connections with the California new music circle can surface unexpectedly, was among a group who saw Cage off when he left for New York in the fall of 1934. Having no money, he had decided to hitchhike and walk between rides. Sidney remembered him standing by the roadside until being picked up by a small truck, "leaving his cheerful smile afloat behind him on the sunny California air." Later she learned he was leaving with only three dollars in his pocket until a friend gave him twenty dollars more.[28] When Rita Mead asked Cage why he had not stayed in California, Cage surprisingly contradicted conventional explanations that Californians enjoyed escaping European influence, and underlined Henry's dilemma. California, he told Mead, was not a good environment for experimentation. One had to be in New York. Everything concerned making connections.

One could apply for a Guggenheim until blue in the face, he said, and never get one without knowing someone in New York. To some extent, Henry agreed.

In New York, Cage assisted Henry and took his classes in modern harmony, contemporary music, and Oriental and folk music at The New School.[29] Henry felt that Cage's work on rhythmic form, percussion music, and the musical systems of other peoples "enlarged and enriched [him]."[30] After a full day of Henry's classes and a lesson with Weiss, Cage spent the evening playing bridge with them and Mrs. Weiss. He claimed to have copied a book on rhythm by Henry. To Mead's question of whether he meant *New Musical Resources*, Cage responded that Henry had written a whole book on rhythm. "I'm so careless with things; I think I've since given it to someone and I don't know whom." Henry apparently never completed the book, however. All that is left of it is a set of elaborate sketches. Although Cage might have lost the only copy, Henry never mentioned the book in letters after his initial reference to it in 1937 as a future project.

When Weiss went to Europe on tour and Henry also was about to leave New York, Cage decided to go with him to California. Henry did most of the driving, but Cage took over occasionally, alarming Henry by driving all over the road if no one was coming toward them. Cage thought the trip took seven to ten days, including stops for illicit liquor in counties that remained dry after the recent repeal of Prohibition. In the diners they would compete to see who could complete counterpoint exercises fastest. Henry told Sidney that one of the annoyances on the drive was the jukeboxes in every diner. He remarked to Cage that it would be a pleasure to put in a penny and get five minutes of silence, thus apparently planting the seed for 4'33" (1952). To my question about it, Cage replied that he did not know, he did not "cultivate his memory."

By now Cage and Henry had become very close. Leta Miller has shown how the interaction between them played a decisive role in shaping Cage's thinking then and in the future. Henry's influence is felt in the prepared-piano, Cage's organizational methods for percussion pieces, the use of found objects, aleatoric concepts, and other techniques and ideas. Cage, in fact, attributed his essential development to Henry's encouragement. Whereas Buhlig was completely fixated on old music, Cage and Henry would always end up in utter agreement. Above all, "what characterized [Henry] in the early '30s was his devotion to other people's music. He almost never mentioned his own music."[31]

Lou Harrison, who also came under Henry's influence in the early 1930s, gave Rita Mead an even more vivid description of his role as a mentor and teacher (although Sidney questioned Harrison's reliability as a witness).[32] As a teenager he discovered *New Musical Resources* in the library at Redwood City, where his family lived briefly, and read *American Composers on American Music*. After moving to San Francisco in 1934, he enrolled in Henry's University of California

Extension course on world music. Although Lou was not yet seventeen, Henry, the first composer he ever met, gave him a part scholarship as monitor of the class and agreed to look at his compositions.[33] After their first conversation about Harrison's music, which took place in Olive's house and opened a long friendship with Olive and Harry, Harrison asked Henry to his own home, though he was apprehensive because his parents had no cultural background. He underestimated Henry, however. When his father began talking about automobiles, Henry, who had just completed a transcontinental drive with a diesel engine, had plenty to say. The evening was a great success.

That dinner was Harrison's first experience with Henry's ability to talk extensively about subjects other than music. On another occasion, he held forth about world population statistics. Harrison felt that part of his charm was his gift for the blarney. (Charles Seeger said that Henry was a stunning conversationalist even as a teenager.)[34] Henry, recalled Harrison, could make anything he was interested in seem like heaven, but he backed his charm with knowledge and enthusiasm, spinning tales and making suggestions having nothing to do with composing, such as which liquor was best to drink in each season. Life with him was always fun, as, for example, when Henry's car would not go forward, so they went up San Francisco's hills in reverse.[35]

Harrison learned some of Henry's music right away and took lessons from him intermittently for about a year. Henry occasionally made inscrutable remarks to his students, but that was just part of the "affectionate and jolly relations" they had with him.[36] Although Henry promoted Schoenberg's music, he opposed using or imitating systems devised by others and discouraged Harrison from writing twelve-tone music. They did not talk about aesthetics. If Harrison brought something up, Henry would agree, but Harrison felt that technical insights were what he really liked to offer. Harrison attributed to Henry many of the ideas he put into his own *Music Primer*. Asked by Rita Mead whether he felt Henry was a "man with a mission," Harrison replied, "Never. . . . Always one had the sense that it was fun, and that he was so interested in all these things, that he wanted to direct you to the same joy, constantly, in fact; that was one of his things."

Harrison also had a fair amount to say about Henry as a pianist, apparently referring to those early days. He played idiosyncratically, treating rhythm very freely despite his elaborate notation, and often made last-minute changes. "But mostly Henry played them straight. Well, as straight as he ever played them." Henry sometimes found his own music difficult, but his technique "was very good for what he did, and charming . . . In fact [Henry's] were the best piano concerts I've ever been to."

Harrison told Mead that Henry's influence centered on the idea of newness, of coming up with ideas, rather than the ideas themselves, but he recognized the impact of particular ideas, such as proposing the overtone series as the basis for music long before Harry Partch. Henry's concept of percussion instruments was especially important for Harrison, as it was for Cage. Once Henry got them going, "all of us were haunting junk shops, and automobile dismemberment yards . . . finding everything we could." Henry's unique idea was of "post-industrial junk music," similar to putting found objects into paintings and collages. Henry's frustration with the Rhythmicon, however, made him advise against attempting to create new electrical instruments.

Asked if he thought Henry felt isolated from the musical community in Menlo Park, Harrison doubted it, since he had so many musician-friends. And thanks to Henry, the group in California never felt isolated, because when he came back from New York he brought so many ideas with him. Above all, Henry was not just a teacher but a friend who helped one move forward. He was unusual in being able to get along with and enjoy many different kinds of people. Harrison thought Henry was one of the main people to give American music "peer group communication."

28

A Doomed Romance

Considering the richness of Henry's friendships, the reader may wonder why Elsa Schmolke, Henry's Berlin landlady, has deserved so much mention in this book. Although she made Henry, the Iveses, and many other musicians comfortable in her pension, she was, after all, just a landlady.

In fact, her relationship with Henry was exceptionally noteworthy.[1] The first hint of something special is found in a letter to him after he returned home from Berlin in 1926. "Haben Sie keine Zeit für mich? [Have you no time for me?]," she lamented because he had not written.[2] A year later, when he hinted that he might appear at Christmas, she responded with nothing less than a love letter, now using *Du*, the personal form of address.[3] He could not go, however, and silence reigned until February 1928, when she sent a snapshot and virtually begged him to write and send some music.[4] He finally returned to her pension in 1929, bringing along Olive and Harry, but his letters do not refer to her again until November 1931, during the first Guggenheim sojourn, when he told Olive, "Schmolke, who makes my life here comfortable and pleasant beyond reckoning, sends hearty greetings to you, and love to Harry (characteristically)."[5]

In addition to making life pleasant, Schmolke tried to smooth Henry's rough edges. After his departure in late 1931, she wrote Olive, ". . . You had better not call Henry 'Heinrich' as I always did here, if he was not really behaving well, for example, not washing his hands, etc. He has grown so 'fein' that you will hardly recognize him, almost as 'fein' as Harry, I say, almost!" She signed it "Your rival, Elsa."[6]

Henry came back in the summer of 1932 for the second part of his Guggenheim fellowship; "Schmoelchen is her usual self," he told Olive.[7] He shortly sent a picture postcard to Ives, another recent guest, signed jointly with Elsa.[8] Schmolke now was in the thick of Henry's life, dealing with a proof, a title page, and payments for music engraving. Hornbostel was on her mind, but it is not clear whether she refers to him emigrating or Henry coming back to Berlin as his assistant. She was in a better mood; business had improved and she was redecorating.[9] Henry's cabled answer (of unknown content) provoked another impassioned letter.[10]

When, in early 1934, Henry wrote her about the *Man of Aran* movie engagement, she responded that she had sent him some cakes. If they missed the boat, he would have to wait a long time, but hopefully not as long as she waited for his letters. She looked forward to the 1936 Berlin Olympics, when the enlarged Zoo railway station would bring many foreign spectators, but she said nothing about political conditions in Germany.[11]

Suddenly the real picture came into focus: Schmolke was going to America. Mitzi Weiss (Adolph's wife)—who knew the Berlin situation well—tipped off Blanche Walton, who told Henry that she expected to be invited to the wedding but wondered where they would live, considering the developments in Germany and the likelihood that Austria would be swallowed up.[12] Clarence pressed him to introduce her to the Iowa family and looked forward to Henry enjoying the warm home life that marriage can bring.[13]

After a few months of trying desperately to learn some English,[14] Schmolke embarked on the month-long sail to San Francisco. She and Henry planned to spend two weeks there and take a month or more to explore the country by car on their way East.[15] They arrived in New York in late September;[16] by mid-October she was back with her family near Berlin.[17] Something had gone wrong. In February 1935 she complained that Henry had not even sent a telegram on her birthday and was making her ill because he wrote so rarely. There was talk about some money he had lent her; she would gladly help him with the problem of his aging car but one could not send money.[18] A year later she wrote again, mostly to complain about the infrequency of his letters. It is possible that other letters have disappeared or that censorship stopped them. There are also many reasons he might not have written.[19] A postcard in June 1936[20] from a holiday resort is her last preserved letter in this series. She wrote him in the late 1930s, but her letters are among the lost correspondence from the four years beginning June 1936.

Although Elsa Schmolke undeniably played a powerful role in Henry's drama, hardly anything is known of her life. Born at Forst, about sixty miles southwest of Berlin, she was about seven years older than he.[21] Photos show her as pleasant looking, a large, somewhat overweight hausfrau type.[22] Sidney was interested to learn more because many people knew that Henry and Elsa were having an affair, and even more knew that they expected to marry.[23] Her curiosity must have been piqued when a neighbor declined to translate Schmolke's letters on the grounds that they were mostly love letters.[24] Henry kept silent, but when Sidney, after Henry's death, asked Olive about the "sad, beautiful love affair" she opened an old sore.

> The very mention of her name brought back Harry's and my horror of her connection with Henry. You will be surprised when I describe her. She was a large stocky, peasant type of woman who kept a pension. . . .

We assumed he was having an affair with her, but he *never* admitted it to us, which I resented. A kind of jolly . . . type of person. She never confided in us any feeling she had for Henry. There was never any evident affection between them in our presence.

When Henry could not get a visa for her to stay in America, Olive explained, Schmolke went home, "to our relief and delight!" As far as Olive and Harry were concerned, "she did not suit him in any *shape, manner,* or *form,* as to the world he was entering. She would have been out of place, very much so far, in every respect. Furthermore, he always wanted children. She certainly could not have supplied him with children—or anything else—he most needed. I don't think she spoke English. She probably evidently did fall in love with him, if she is like so many Germans, still romanticising over it. Why under heavens is she taking it out on you?"[25]

Inferring that Olive—who did not know that Schmolke was long dead—had her own axes to grind, Sidney sought corroboration from a friend of Schmolke's, who confirmed Olive's description, though from a more positive point of view. Schmolke, as Sidney relates their chat, was "very simple, uneducated really 'without any culture' but very good-hearted and kind & looked after people—made them comfortable—& let them stay on without paying often—both artists & musicians. Very concerned about everyone's likes & dislikes, v. good food & lots of it." But she was not "a companion for a great musician."[26] None of them were aware that, based on various hints in her letters, Schmolke had a love of music, possibly skill as a proofreader, and enough business sense to run a pension and help Henry with his work in Berlin.

In the end, any intentions he may have had were terminated by world affairs. Without a visa she could not stay, and for him, living under the Nazis was not an option.

Compositions of 1929–1936

Despite his frenetic activity, Henry completed some seventy pieces in the 1930s, of which about 20 percent are lost. Piano music, his former medium of choice, declined to about half of his output and was almost entirely written before 1932, when his public performing began its precipitous decline. Among those pieces is the eerie "Sinister Resonance," which is largely built out of piano-string harmonics. After 1932, the piano pieces became simpler, more folkloric in style, deliberately not innovative. Simple melodiousness became his hallmark and was beautifully applied in fifteen art songs or proletarian songs. He did not completely shelve his modernist ideas, however. In the beautiful "Sunset" and "Rest," set to words by Wallingford Riegger's daughter Catherine, he seamlessly interwove extended piano techniques with gripping vocal lines.

No longer needing new virtuoso solos, Henry explored chamber music, larger forms, and music for dance. His predominantly conservative techniques did not mean that he had lost his innovative edge. Freshness came as he applied his growing knowledge of world music to his own composing. The octet *Ostinato Pianissimo* is one of the most durable percussion works of that time, rivaling Varèse's *Ionisation*. It is not, however, aggressively "modernist," like *Ionisation*, but gentle in character, thanks to its Indian roots, which include the prominent role of a jalatarang (set of tuned bowls). Non-Western musical traditions probably explain another landmark of the 1930s, the *Mosaic Quartet*. Because Henry left it to the players to decide upon the order of the movements, it is arguably the earliest "open form" composition other than the dice-game pieces of the late eighteenth century.[1]

Lou Harrison thought that one of Henry's most influential pieces was the lost stage work *I Fanati*, with texts by Ralph Waldo Emerson and a cast of forty. The drama was communicated through songs, recitative, and piano music, but its core was a series of *ostinati* played by five percussionists placed in a box that amplified the sound. Harrison thought Henry took his idea from the similar amplification boxes used in *kabuki* theater. Delicate sounds from instruments such as crystal goblets could be heard throughout the space, thanks to the resonator.[2]

In the two and one-half years from 1934 to the spring of 1936, Henry began and abandoned several pieces for large ensemble; completed a *Suite for Small Orchestra*, a Reel, some songs, *Seven Associated Movements* for violin and piano, the "Mosaic" Quartet, a few piano pieces in the Irish style, and some dance pieces for piano or for small ensemble, most of which are lost. He seems a little at sea, swamped by the miscellany of his life, and apparently uncertain where he was heading composition-ally. It is evident, however, that simplification was foremost in his mind.

In a vivid, thoughtful portrait of Henry, written in 1940 but applicable to the Henry of the mid-thirties, Seeger said he could think of no composer whose music was more difficult to evaluate. Henry's "prodigious naivete" was so subtle that one often did not know whether he was laughing at himself or entirely serious. Critics could not tell whether they were being teased. Seeger felt that Henry's background in "an extreme western America scarcely out of its pioneer era" left him with no sense of, and thus no respect for, musical traditions as cultural reality. To Henry music was not communication—it was a tabula rasa "in which there are infinite possibilities of combination—so why not try them?" Seeger thought his attitude perfectly represented old-style progressive education, in which a child was taught to regard the world as his toy, to be discovered and explored. Thus he wrote music not according to rules but through an instinct for exploration. In Seeger's experi-ence Henry almost completely disregarded scholarly techniques, yet fought for his views and sometimes won. "He often startles a student with the sudden way he will see the end of a laborious piece of research, not by doing the spade work or by knowing of the spade work of others, but by clear common-sense and imagination."

Seeger thought Henry perversely avoided sincerity, depth, high emotions, lofty thought. His music seemed "calculatedly shallow," possibly—but not demonstrably—tongue-in-cheek. "Cowell's music is not unconventional in any conventional way. It is unconventionally unconventional, which is an entirely dif-ferent kind of thing. It is this that the academicians have found most fault with, I think." Henry's integrity was unquestionable, but "there is no veneration in him." Veneration, to Seeger, was the ultimate criterion of "orthodox professionalism." He thought that Henry's attitudes were extraordinarily healthy and necessary, especially in an era of over-emphasized subjectivity. He felt that Henry's explora-tion of new resources was imperatively demanded; his music clearly heralded the new. And so far no one had followed his paths.

In mid-career, Henry had "done enough idol-smashing to warrant broadening his field," wrote Seeger, who hoped he would "devote to the half of his field he has so far ignored the fearless thinking and penetrating vision he has employed in his former narrow field, and above all, that he will bring the two together on a higher plane, as it were, even inducing some of the emotional and intellectual 'fever' he has so studiously avoided, thus graduating from the prodigy into the mature artist."[3]

Lou Harrison, however, may have been closer to the mark. Henry, he said, wanted the world to remember that making music should be fun.

Thirty-Nine

When Henry celebrated his thirty-ninth birthday on March 11, 1936, his cheerful public demeanor disguised a difficult life. Some very close friends—Samuel Seward, Mother Carrington, Edna Smith, John Varian—were dead; Blanche Walton was impoverished; Ives's health was precarious; Jaime de Angulo's eccentricities had become unmanageable; Varèse and Salzedo had turned into enemies; friends in Europe faced mortal risks. The economic collapse had destroyed his performing career; his financial status was very shaky; his projects were largely defunct; another prospect for marriage had proven impossible. As the security of a proper academic position eluded him, he consumed his time in ad hoc lectures and part-time classes. Unrelenting activity may also account for the proofreading errors that Wiley Hitchcock discovered in the *New Music* editions of Ives's songs.[1] His perpetual unkemptness implied a man who either who was totally focused on his work, or severely distracted by some alarming circumstances.

At the same time, other aspects of his life had greatly improved. Henry's new closeness with Harry, and Ives's fatherly affection, may have balanced his diminishing bonds with the Halcyon community. Longtime friends like Cary de Angulo, Judy Brown, Lewis Terman, and half-brother Clarence and family, as well as others who went unrecorded, were always there for him. New friendships with Cage, Harrison, and Grainger were solid and rewarding. Tension with Copland had been reduced almost to the point of friendship. California retained enough of its youthfulness that his address remained simply "Henry Cowell, Menlo Park." He knew that in fifteen years he had truly moved a few mountains, and the press finally recognized what he had done for American music. In 1933, even the once-skeptical Paul Rosenfeld wrote glowingly, "Where'er he lights, in Los Angeles, Leningrad or any point between, concerts of the new and unplayed works of live American composers spring up like flowers about the feet of Flora." After enumerating Henry's accomplishments and admitting that "a number of his . . . compositions have considerable weight," he praised Henry's work to get "many new, daring and revolutionary scores" published and printed, giving "steady encouragement to those with something individual in them to express."[2]

Henry's reluctance to reveal much about how he saw himself forces us to rely upon a handful of other witnesses, chiefly Olive, who doggedly attempted to probe his depths. About the only thing she learned is that he would not allow anything to interfere with his work and could collaborate with almost anyone who had a real contribution to make musically. He knew instinctively how to handle colleagues without depending upon them personally.

In addition to Cage and Harrison, a few other colleagues help flesh out this picture. Gerald Strang, about twenty when he met Henry in the early 1930s, thought Henry was inefficient in how he conducted his business but compensated for it with his excellent entrepreneurship. He could get others to work, did not bother those who had taken on tasks, and always responded to letters. Unlike Varèse, Henry never felt he had to be a dictator. He would be on hand to do what was needed—to organize and manage a concert, conduct if needed, promote events, raise money.[3]

Dorothy Blaney, a violinist with the New Music Society, whom Sidney located in the early 1970s, remembered the period differently. Henry was so devoted to his personal projects that he "didn't mind using himself up and all his friends likewise" to advance them. She emphasized, however, that he never promoted his personal glory. He also did not care at all about personal possessions. "Henry did wonders in fostering talent, giving it a hearing, getting music in print and encouraging—that, I imagine, was the best of all. Not many people were paying attention."[4] Sidney told Blaney that she already knew him in the '30s, "but rather distantly, though I went to his concerts and lectures and so on, and he did get so he would recognize me when we met! But he seemed always to me a very isolated person. . . ."[5]

When twenty-year-old Lehman Engel met Henry around 1930, he found him "extremely self-effacing," full of energy, and extremely generous in promoting the younger generation. Engel remembered Ives's "tremendous regard and respect for Cowell." Henry was never depressed, always very up and energetic, eager to do things mostly for others. Clearly not knowing Henry's attitude to French neoclassicism, Engel said that he never spoke negatively about people or their music. "Or anything. He was almost in that respect saintly."[6]

FOUR ENDLESS YEARS

31

Life Stops

On May 23, 1936, Henry was arrested on a morals charge.

Curiosity and speculation about Henry's collision with the law were fueled by Sidney Cowell's unwillingness to cooperate with researchers.[1] Concerned that he might be remembered for nothing else, she was determined that the story emerge only in the context of a full biography. Skeptics were not persuaded by the parallel she drew to Gesualdo, who seems better known as a murderer than as one of the finest composers of the later Renaissance–early Baroque. Her insistence that Henry did not want to be a martyr for gay rights only inflamed the issue. This protectiveness implied either that the Cowell papers harbor dark secrets or that she purged it of incriminating documents. What has become public is the product of Michael Hicks's impressive research using materials that were beyond her control, that is, not in the Cowell papers.[2] His account inevitably had to miss some very important elements. Leta Miller and Rob Collins have recounted the effects of Henry's prison years on his relationship with Ives.[3] Unfortunately, old rumors still fly.

Sidney Cowell, whom I knew for many years as remarkably forthright and open, was a serious, skilled researcher who compulsively sought information about every aspect of her husband's life in order to provide the biographer with the best possible resources. Although one cannot prove that she was always honest or that she did not purge the collection, the amount of documentation about the prison years is staggering and not entirely complimentary. After reading every word, I found no holes in the story, no apparent discrepancies. One component is gone, however. Although Sidney contacted anyone she knew to have been in touch with him and obtained copies or originals of the letters he wrote to them, the many letters that Henry received in prison—as well as all other documents in his possession—had to be left behind when he was released. They should have been returned to him at the end of his sentence, but apparently no one tried to get them, and when Sidney contacted the prison authorities after

Henry's death, his papers had long since been discarded. A few letters survived because they were sent to Olive's address. Since visitors could not pass anything to inmates, Olive retained them and either summarized them in her correspondence with Henry or told him about them on visiting days. In the end, the missing letters may not have cost the story much, in view of what exists.

I have endeavored to put to rest any suspicions of a cover-up by telling this story in great detail. I hope I may be forgiven for sharing it at such length.

Over the years, Henry enjoyed helping the disadvantaged young people of Menlo Park, many of whom he had known since their birth, treating them like family, corresponding with them, and giving them Christmas parties when he was home for the holidays. As they grew up, he took them on camping trips and expeditions, bringing along wholesome food and teaching the older ones how to cook. In 1931, he allowed some of them to build a swimming pool behind his house, where they liked to gather. The boys swam in the nude on Monday through Saturday; girls swam in suits on Sundays; four older boys enforced the rules. Writing about it in a 1932 essay called "Henry and Children," Olive expressed great happiness about his fatherly treatment of all the kids. Of course, there were occasional problems, as can be seen in a petition a large number of them sent Henry, pleading for the banishment of one boy.[4] It thus seemed natural when in early May 1936, a high school advisor requested Henry's input about one boy's problems; Henry knew them so well.[5] He did not know that a relative of a seventeen-year-old member of the swimming group had lodged a complaint against him. After questioning by the police, Henry pleaded guilty to engaging in oral sex with the young man. On the surface the story is a tragic reminder of the days when consensual sex was not private. It was not so simple, however.

The complaint form, dated May 21, 1936, stated that an official responsible for youth welfare, Francis J. Robinson, accused Henry of the felony violation of section 288a of the Penal Code of California—that in the township he did "then and there wilfully, unlawfully and feloniously copulate his mouth with the sexual organ of another male, to wit, Malin Cheney." Understanding that law is crucial to grasping what happened to Henry. Section 288a stated that "any person participating in the act of copulating the mouth of one person with the sexual organ of another" was punishable by imprisonment in the state prison for a term not exceeding fifteen years. The law did not specify homosexual acts and was a 1921 amendment to a 1915 law that included heterosexual behavior: "The acts technically known as fellatio and cunnilingus are hereby declared to be felonies and any person convicted of the commission of either thereof shall be punished by imprisonment in the state prison for not more than fifteen years." That version had been judged unconstitutional because it had not been published in English; apparently the common Latin terms were judged incomprehensible. Neither the 1915 version nor its successor contains stipulations about gender, force, seduction, consensuality, or age of the participants. In both versions, any and all participants were in violation.[6]

The news of Henry's arrest immediately circulated. Brief notices in the *Palo Alto Times* and Carmel's *The Californian* only stated that he had been arrested on a morals charge involving a seventeen-year-old (who was legally an adult). In the East, similarly brief items appeared in the *New York Times* and the *World Telegram*.[7] Other articles published outside the Bay Area may have gone unnoticed; the Cowell archive has neither copies nor allusions in letters. Henry's old friend Alfred Frankenstein, the *Chronicle*'s music critic, was appalled, as were many other friends and colleagues. Frankenstein knew people who thought Henry had it coming to him—in some cases more because he had allowed himself to be caught than because of the activity itself.[8] Subsequent events may have obscured the fact that even heterosexual oral sex was a violation. Homosexuality was not a requirement of guilt, nor was Henry charged with being homosexual.

After rushing to see him in the Redwood City lockup, Frankenstein asked his colleagues not to sensationalize the affair. He succeeded in burying the story on an inside page of the *Chronicle*, but, as he later told Sidney, for the *Call-Bulletin* he had to get a rabbi friend to ask congregants who were major advertisers to "put the screws on." Rabbi Reichert had tried to work with the managing editor of the *Examiner* "and had been told to roll his hoop."[9] That was an understatement. Hearst's *Examiner* knew that sex crimes sold papers. The arrest of a famous musician, a teacher at Stanford, Berkeley, and Mills, was made to order. Two days after the arrest the *Examiner* ran a front-page banner headline: "Morals Charges Jail Noted S.F. Composer." The story was positioned in the center of the front page, with its continuation accompanied by two photos. One, nearly a quarter-page, showed Henry behind bars in Redwood City; the other, almost as large, showed him playing the piano during a half-hour farewell improvisation. Instead of saying that the sole complaint referred to a seventeen-year-old, that is, not a minor, the *Examiner* claimed that Henry confessed to improper relations with twenty-four boys between the ages of ten and seventeen over a period of four years. The vagueness of "improper relations" ignited rumors of seduction or force on a massive scale. The newspaper added that when San Mateo County authorities went to Henry's house to question him "they found the house occupied by three young boys who were awaiting the musician's return. They told the authorities that six others had been given money and the loan of his automobile earlier in the evening and had gone to San Francisco to skate." The *Examiner* did not caution that such an arrangement might have been completely innocent. The article made Henry seem evil—especially because it said that the matter had been called to the attention of the county juvenile officer by a relative of a former student at Redwood

City High School, that is, Malin Cheney. Seeing that it was not a juvenile matter, the Juvenile Officer passed the information to Officer Robinson, whom he advised to investigate "queer things" alleged to be going on at the Cowell home. The *Examiner* said that Henry first denied the charges, then admitted them and gave "intimate details" of what went on, showing snapshots taken in the house and in the swimming pool. He reportedly said that above all he wanted to protect the reputation of the boys. "No use dragging them through it all." According to the *Examiner*, he did not attempt to raise bail or hire a lawyer and waited to speak with his father. The sheriff reportedly was surprised by Henry's calm and felt no need for a suicide watch. This account implied that Henry was oblivious to the "evil" of which he had pleaded guilty. A concluding recitation of Henry's career and accomplishments could have made him appear even more warped.

Something had happened, but not what the *Examiner* claimed. Actually Henry had given the names of about twenty-five neighborhood boys who used his swimming pool but were not involved in the episode. Having obtained the list, the *Examiner* made it seem that a large group of boys had taken part in homosexual behavior.[10] The story about not engaging a lawyer was initially correct; Henry confessed without benefit of legal counsel. According to Sidney, Mrs. Veblen and others had long since convinced him that lawyers "just take your money & do nothing." Sidney said that because his statement and confession were made without legal advice, the district attorney tried to stop the prosecution, presumably fearing it would be thrown out in court.[11] Eventually we shall see how she learned this, as well as the district attorney's other reason.

The *Examiner*'s lurid story paled in comparison with a journalistic drama that opened on June 6 with the first of six articles in the San Francisco weekly *Newsletter and Wasp*, calling for Henry's death and for vigilantes to attack his family and supporters. It even assailed the "Worst" [= Hearst] papers for backing Henry, which is far-fetched to say the least. Even a few excerpts show why Henry became terrified of the California press.

> As gangrenous a character as the world has ever produced; a parasite of a fimetarious nature; a slimy snake in man's clothing, is the moron, Henry Dixon Cowell.

> Cowell, creator of a hell for honest, intelligent and fair-minded citizens, has been biographically written of by the "Worst" press. There is nothing this putrid press will stop at. There is no subject too low for it to handle. The moment this egotistical, rat-eyed degenerate was arrested, the chords of this decayed press began to throw out its fetid music; its photographers immediately began to limn the features of this pudgy, inadequate excuse for a musician and a man.

The well-wishers of Cowell should be publicized and then given a reception by a vigilance committee.

There is an international moron atmosphere [in the jail] also, that adds
to the situation. Orientals who, probably, are of the same moral fiber as
Cowell, visit and condole with him.

The vapid faced Cowell, like the slimy snail he is, will try to avoid the hard
labor that is his due, in San Quentin. The News Letter will, in the interest
of the people of San Mateo County, try and see to it that he pays his penalty properly and that Frank Sykes' Parole Board will not, conveniently,
turn this murderer of children's morals loose. It will take fifteen years, at
hard labor, to cure this mad moron of his filthy weakness. Every effort by
the law and by his own father should be made to keep him the full length
of time. . . . The "rough men" of the penitentiary, he professes to dislike so
much, may batter a few manly ideas into his rotted skull. He will have
surprises in store for him. He is going to no elysian rendezvous.[12]

Actually, the editors had nothing against Henry personally. They had come to
the jail with an offer to supervise public relations for him in exchange for a substantial fee. Not recognizing attempted blackmail, Henry demurred. As it happened,
the "journalists" were already under observation and were shortly arrested and
convicted in a similar case.[13] But it was too late to help Henry. The *Examiner* and
the *Newsletter and Wasp* fueled the assumption that he was a dangerous criminal
engaging in wholesale sex with very young boys.

Olive and Harry were horrified. She had already wondered about Henry's sex
life but he had avoided discussing it. (Their correspondence suggests that he was
finding her overbearing and intrusive.) They knew that he was hanging around
with the boys and letting them swim at his place. The boys seemed to be having
such a good time when Henry was with them "acting like a father we thought." In
retrospect she realized that since the girls and boys came to the pool on different
days, "sex play among the boys was more or less inevitable. We thought that in
his love for children he was just sublimating his sex interests mostly." What was
worse, Henry's letter said he did not realize the legal ramifications of his behavior. Why, she wondered, did his friends who knew the law, or his doctor friends,
not warn him? Charles Seeger and Blanche Walton had also worried that Henry
was engaged in risky behavior and Seeger later said that he warned Henry the
previous year that the gatherings at the swimming pool were dangerous.[14] Olive
had also been concerned about other psychological problems, especially his inability to be neat and clean, and was on the verge of approaching Terman about
getting psychiatric help when the disaster struck.[15] Thirty years later she told

Sidney that although in her youth she had read six of Havelock Ellis's books on sex, she had not read his work on homosexuality and was absolutely ignorant about the subject.[16]

Feeling incapable of evaluating Henry objectively, Olive engaged Ernst Wolff, a distinguished German-born and German-trained psychiatrist, to consult with the family. Because she had very deep feelings about Henry from the first time they met, she also wanted Wolff to shed light on her relationship with him, "what it is and what it should be. . . . I have always felt that I had a great responsibility toward him, and I have tried my best to fulfil it, without too much success! Henry swamps anyone who wants to help him with so many things to do, that the more personal things can easily be lost sight of."[17] Ray Green, a composer friend, thought that Henry did not realize how dangerous young people can be when they start fantasizing and making up stories.[18]

In the county jail, Henry was bombarded by letters offering unconditional support, laced here and there with tactful reproaches. Some friends had worried that he was headed for trouble but sweetly attributed his "aberration" to his genius. Elizabeth Moss, his old sponsor, was one of a handful who accepted some of the blame for not having warned him about his conduct.[19] Cage assured him of his friendship and expressed his faith in Henry's strength.[20] Seward's young daughter never forgot the expression on her mother's face when she read about the arrest in the *Palo Alto Times*. Mrs. Seward telephoned Lewis Terman and went to see Henry, the first of her many visits.[21] Johanna Beyer, a German-born composer eleven years Henry's senior, who had taken his classes at the New School and fallen in love with him, offered herself in marriage. Slonimsky attempted to boost Henry's morale by referring to a case in Boston in which sexual charges against a radical writer turned out to be false and had been motivated by the desire to destroy him.[22]

Henry's friend Pierce Williams could not have agreed more. A social worker, experienced government administrator, and West Coast agent for the Roosevelt administration's Federal Emergency Relief Organization, he had just extricated himself from a vicious legal battle masterminded by California politicians who wanted to grab relief funds to build political patronage.[23] Having seen how that near-hijacking had been fed by the press, Williams knew that Henry faced a very serious problem, especially because of the *Examiner's* awful photos. He hoped that once the community's "sadistic desire to see an alleged culprit suffer" died down, the matter would quietly disappear. He warned, however, that it was very easy to frame a person and that a defense can sometimes be almost impossible. "It is sufficient that he was known to be friendly with boys, etc., etc." He advised Harry and Olive to lay low and avoid reporters.[24] One of Olive's colleagues told her not to come to work for any reason because of the gossiping.[25]

Henry's calm was deceptive. He dreaded the real possibility that the shock would destroy Ives. He was right to worry. Ives's physical and mental health were both deteriorating, and almost anything could send him into a tirade that touched off serious heart problems. Henry, who decided to be silent, asked Olive to write Harmony Ives if he should be imprisoned and request her to tell her husband as she saw fit.[26] Slonimsky assured Henry that Ives never read the papers; even Slonimsky himself had missed the article and learned about it from a journalist two weeks later.[27] Charles Ives may not have known, but that was only because his wife kept him in the dark for a while. On July 3, however, Harmony Ives wrote Charlotte Ruggles a letter that has become a staple in the history of Cowell-Ives relations.

> Dear Mrs. Ruggles,
>   Have you heard this hideous thing about Henry Cowell—that he has been guilty of Oscar Wilde practices—a crime in California, must stand trial & probably receive a long sentence? Mr. Becker wrote me—fearing to write Charlie whom I shall not tell until I have confirmation. John Becker heard it by chance in Chicago a week ago & said he was told it had been in the papers. If true I think it is the saddest thing in our experience. I had no inkling of this defect, had you? I shouldn't have been surprised to have found Henry's standards of relations between men & women different from ours tho' I knew of nothing. The pity of this!—of course it is a disease—"a quirk of nature," as Mr. Becker said—Do you know anything?—Mr. Becker said he understood he was out on bail. . . . I am dreading this disclosure to Charlie—it is the only secret I've ever had from him. John Becker wrote as having no doubt of the fact but I can't bring myself to believe it.[28]

Henry was especially gratified to receive, a week after his arrest, a note from his former New School student Sidney Hawkins Robertson. Until she learned of the arrest through her boss, Charles Seeger, she had not known that Henry had been Seeger's protégé at Berkeley and that they all had friends in common such as Jaime de Angulo. Her psychiatric training with Jung kept her mind open.[29] The warm letter speaks volumes about both Seeger and her. While the salutation was a trace formal, her tone is that of a friend.

> Dear Henry Cowell: I wish you could have heard Seeger cussing you out affectionately these past days! I'm sure you know you couldn't have a more staunch and loyal friend. He interrupts his work two or three times a day to add another to his particular likings of you—which I keep assuring him isn't at all necessary because I can think up a number of my own! But it is very funny because Seeger is fundamentally rather

a gentle soul and he succeeds in making these explosive lists of your virtues sound like a special sort of profanity. He's listing his particular grudges against the world, so to speak. If you wanted to be really kind to your friends you'd think up something for us to do on your behalf. Of course you know you could ask Seeger to do literally anything at all. And may I say the same for myself?[30]

All help was welcome for a future entailing anything from probation to fifteen years behind bars. At best he would soon be in action again; at the worst, he had to ensure that the music he had published and recorded would not be lost and that his projects would continue without him. Most of the burden fell upon Olive and to some extent Harry. They had to assemble all the manuscripts by *New Music* composers that were in Lou Harrison's possession and store them at their home.[31] Henry organized general business and financial matters for her to supervise, such as depositing checks from Ives.[32] Fearing that he might banished from the Menlo Park region, he told her to put the house, car, and piano up for sale. The piano was in any case unsatisfactory because the layout of the frame and strings was wrong for his music, he said. His percussion instruments had to be collected from Mills College and elsewhere, and housed. Olive and Harry needed power of attorney so they could manage his affairs. If they needed to raise money for him, Gassner owed him $100 [2010: $1,570], and Clarence, $300. The woman who had bought the Halcyon house bequeathed to him by Ellen Veblen owed him the final payment of $100.00, but its value had probably declined by at least that much and she was too poor to make up the difference.[33] Ives needed to be informed that *New Music* had been placed in the hands of Gerald Strang, Dene Denny, and Martha Beck Carragan. Riegger had already agreed to curate New Music Quarterly Recordings. They had to notify Eastern friends like Ruggles, Judy and Armitt Brown, and Blanche Walton. Henry advised describing the nature of the offense in the most vague and general terms; Becker had to be assured that he had never behaved improperly with his children. Other than Becker, the only other person in the East whom he had informed was The New School's Alvin Johnson, whose connection with Stanford assured that he would get wind of the episode. He hoped that Johnson would reserve judgment until he could tell him his side of the story. Olive needed to type his official letters of resignation from the summer faculties of Stanford and Mills College, get Henry's signature, and send them in. Any delay could lead to his being dismissed, which would be far worse.[34] (It is well to remember that he had pleaded guilty. There would be no trial; "innocent until proven guilty" was an irrelevant concept, as was acquittal.)

Johnson was a true liberal, in the best sense of the word—an editor of the *New Republic* and author of a stinging attack on American anti-Semitism.

His reaction was mostly comforting, but he was in an awkward position. Because of Henry's association with the school, clipping agencies were feeding him news. He tried to keep "an open mind and hope that the evolution of the case will not produce so much adverse publicity as to damage our common enterprise here at the School too seriously. Of course that is the least of my concerns. My main concern is that a good friend and sincere artist has been laid by the heels. Eventually, I know, the situation will work itself out and you will be at creative work again."[35] Because Johnson was reluctant to authorize the usual concerts and lectures until Henry could commit himself to them, Henry risked losing invaluable employment unless he were released immediately.

Henry's letters make him seem cool and collected, just as he appeared to his visitors. Considering that childhood incident of being locked in a closet, one can only wonder how he felt behind bars. A letter to Harry and Olive shows something of what was roaring under the surface. Communicating in private was increasingly difficult and, he feared, might be almost impossible if he were committed to prison or a hospital. He understood the likelihood of a prison sentence and the possibility of drawing a cell mate who would try to force him to have sex. In that event, Olive was to request that he be placed with old men or in some other situation that would lessen the risk. If committed to Agnew State Mental Hospital, friends should be informed that he was found ill. If he ended up in a penitentiary, he recommended stating that he was ill and should have been hospitalized.[36]

Henry's notes, probably written the day of or after his arrest,[37] confirm that he told Olive and Harry not to hire a lawyer unless they were convinced that he could really accomplish something. He saw no point in repudiating his confession, which "was given after the district attorney's office showed me a long list of names, dates, and facts, all correct. All in their possession already. At present, enough boys would testify against me to make conviction a certainty." He may have feared that they would testify that the sex act was not by mutual consent if they were threatened with prosecution as accessories. The healthiest course, he felt, was cooperation, with the aim of trying to get the charge reduced to a misdemeanor. By cooperation he meant a plea bargain, a relatively new but increasingly common process that gave prosecutors a conviction without the risk of an unsuccessful trial.

Cooperation would also increase the prospects for avoiding "any line of action which might lead to inquery [*sic*] about illegal acts committed out of this County, and for which I might therefore be brought to trial elsewhere, either now or later." We shall see in due course what specifically worried him. Referring to the possibility of transferring the case from the local to the state authorities, which was under discussion, he added that at the State Superior Court "we will probably have to rely upon my pleading guilty and throwing myself on the Judge's mercy." Because the only possible justification for mercy was Henry's general character, he wanted Olive to assemble information about his life. He asked Olive and Harry not to incur the great expense of trying to get him out on bond.

Olive and Harry brushed aside Henry's feelings about lawyers. According to Sidney, whose antagonism to Olive and Harry frequently taints her comments, and who was not in the West at the time, "Olive & Harry went around horrifying friends & asking loudly for 'the name of a lawyer with political influence' since they had learned a lawyer was necessary. Duncan [Oneal] of San Jose was rec[ommended]. He had one conversation with Olive, apparently, who told him how important his political connections would be! He never talked to Henry, but sent an assistant to the hearing who only saw HC for the first & last time for about 15 minutes before the hearing."[38]

Her attack on Oneal, dating from thirty-seven years later, was very wrong. The well-connected son of a prominent Santa Clara lawyer, he was probably a good choice.[39] Olive may have kept him away from Henry, however, fearing that Henry's attitude toward lawyers could be destructive. Another set of notes shows that Henry came to his senses and sought Oneal's advice. He needed to know what answer to give if old matters were made public; whether he could refer questions to the lawyer or doctors, or whether he must answer; whether he should answer questions which would involve others not connected with the particular offense. If questions were asked whose answers Henry did not wish to become public, he hoped Oneal could get his answers sealed. Assuming that he might be forbidden to enter San Mateo County, he wanted to know whether he would be allowed to use railways or highways that passed through it. If he were allowed to go to the East Coast, with whom could he stay in New York? Finally, "In case D.A. tries to throw doubt on my statements concerning my women loves, shall I submit Elsa's letters, and is there any way they can be given so her name can be withheld?" He was already thinking about emigrating to Mexico.[40]

Amidst the simmering Red Scare his political past had to remain hidden. Knowing that friends like Lilly Popper would try to enlist radical organizations to "raise some sort of fuss," he asked Frankenstein to watch the radical press and warn them about the danger to Henry.[41] His instinct was correct. The virulently anti-communist Hearst papers might make the connection and fan the flames they had ignited. False rumors that he was set up by anti-communists persist to this day.

Once he concluded that the only reasonable defense was an honest accounting of those aspects of his life that led him to such an act, he wrote out a detailed autobiography for Dr. Wolff, the psychiatrist retained by Olive. It is the earliest document alluding to anything other than his heterosexual relationships.

A sobering antidote to his mother's history of their lives and to the placid Henry of his correspondence, it exposes the demons hammering away at his jocular surface.

The statement begins with familiar details of his early life, but in a new perspective. His personalized education with Clarissa left him with "no social contact with other children, such as one obtains in school; on the other hand, I remained afraid of other children and had very few companions; no lasting ones. I did not play games with others, nor did I ever enter any sports." Some of this simply does not ring true. Unless Mrs. Kiefer's recollections of the Toyon Club were completely imagined, Henry must have been couching his statement to strengthen his argument of social maladjustment. He was indisputably close to Evelyn Wells, the Varian boys and the other young Halcyonites such as George Harrison, and the Liberty sisters. In 1912, he told Terman that he had always had intimate female and male friends, although he lacked the time to maintain those relationships.

His sexual history began with an orgasm at twelve, after which he began masturbating. He masturbated through his teens but thought it was neither more nor less than all boys do and was always by himself. "The ideology during masturbation was of girls." At seventeen he fell in love with a girl of the same age. After "long gazings" he mustered the courage to ask her to dance. Although entirely innocent, the incident aroused Clarissa. "She mentioned sex to me for the first time, with more vehemence than I had ever observed in her before; she denounced as utterly foolish that a man should ever in thought, word or deed have anything to do with the person of a woman." Henry inferred from her outburst that his desires marked him as unutterably wicked. Clarissa explained the physiology of sexual relations but insisted that the sole purpose of sex was to bring children into the world. Since artificial insemination was possible, contact among the organs was no longer necessary. Henry came to believe that artificial insemination was the way in which "all 'good' people begot young." He attributed her reaction to her strict religious upbringing but does not say if he inferred that her attitude drove away her two husbands. Because [he claimed] Clarissa was virtually his only companion, her views sufficed to keep him away from girls. Unable to have social contact with them without sexual desire, and convinced that such desire was depraved, he avoided such contacts altogether. "This loyalty to my mother's wishes was greatly enhanced by her illness, and finally her death just before I was 19." As with all the women to whom he later referred, the identity of the young woman who provoked Clarissa's outburst remained hidden. It was not Evelyn Wells, who was four years younger and definitely a close female friend.

The year after Clarissa died he had his first experience of sex with others: mutual masturbation in bed together with several young fellows his own age. He did not think it was wicked because no one had ever told him so, but realized that he should not discuss it with others. This lasted until induction into the army, at age twenty. In fifteen months in the army he had no sex experience. "Whores did not interest me, and I lost any desire to be with men."

After leaving the army, he fell in love and became engaged [to Edna Smith]. He never felt any concern about sex at that point; he thought that "at 23–25" he had outgrown his mother's ideas on the subject. In any event, Edna's belief in premarital chastity had rendered thoughts about sex moot for the moment. The shock of her sudden death caused him to turn away from women, but being "highly over-wrought," he needed an outlet and again engaged in mutual masturbation with male friends, some old, some new. This took place at Halcyon and lasted a short time until older relatives of the friends discovered it. After a discussion they all parted on good terms; as he says elsewhere, there was no thought of prosecution. Halcyon being Halcyon, that discussion centered on mystical religious concepts. "Worded unclearly and setting forth opposing Catholic, New Thought and Theosophical ideas rather than dealing with the physical facts," it did not help him. This may be the event in another county to which he alluded. It partly explains why he rarely went to Halcyon after the early '30s.

In 1923 he met an unnamed woman in Europe, that is, Elsa Schmolke. When he returned there in 1926 they began having normal and very gratifying sexual relations, the first for him. (Schmolke herself believed she had cured him of his "weakness" but never found the courage to speak with him about it.)[42] They planned marriage but found that she would have to wait seven to nine years on the regular immigration quota. Ultimately, although Henry was still fond of Schmolke, he was sure it was all for the best. "She is 7 years older than I, has an unattractive form, now feels pain instead of pleasure in sex relations and worst of all cannot bear children. My paternal love of children is too strong and too sincere for any childless marriage to be a success with me."

He then described the construction of the swimming pool just before he left for Europe in the summer of 1931, its development into a neighborhood hangout, the camping trips, and his expeditions taking the boys to shows. He said that he loved the local boys "with a sincere paternal affection" and grew fond of their friends.

One day, around the time he realized he could not marry Schmolke (presumably after her 1934 visit), he came into the swimming pool dressing rooms and found two of the boys copulating with their mouths and four others masturbating together. "The sight unstabilized me and made me again wish to duplicate the experiences of my youth." He said he did not consciously seek it, but on a camping trip when he was sleeping with one of the boys, his passion got the best of him, and broke down the last barriers. In January 1936, he saw three of the younger ones (he thought about twelve to fourteen years old) masturbating together "and later was unable to resist the temptation to handle their parts." This event awakened him to his loss of self-control, as did a growing affection for a young woman of twenty-nine. He had taken her out a few times, and found less and less sexual satisfaction with the boys. (Olive said that the woman was a friend of hers and Harry's. It was not Johanna Beyer, who would have been about forty-eight.)[43] The mood at the pool had also changed. Henry said, "To aggravate matters, the boys took it for granted more and more that I would take them to shows until they demanded it (one group or another) nearly every night—they wanted my car at all times and some of them began borrowing small sums of money— the beginnings perhaps of blackmail. Also I felt that in some quarters I was being blamed because some of them learned to smoke, drink, pilfer and take girls out over night, although I combated these things with them at all times." He therefore planned to discontinue the life, by talking it over amicably with each young man, and run the pool only for little children, not lending his car or having anyone stay overnight. He planned to marry and give up the house. He regretted that it ended with enmity, but could never go back to homosexual practice. He wanted to marry and build his own family.[44]

This frank, if self-serving, account partly validates the *Examiner*'s story; some under-age children had been involved in some aspect of the affair. Henry does not say whether he engaged in oral sex with anyone other than the young man whose relative turned him in, but he certainly did not want any details to come out in court. He only spoke of it because this account was intended to prepare Dr. Wolff for the probation hearing, and was hardly likely to bring up matters that could turn into more charges. In that regard it should be recalled that Section 288a only prohibited oral sex and did not refer to mutual masturbation. He could have been charged with corrupting a minor, but no one lodged a complaint. With all the publicity, the lack of other complaints implies that no other felonious incidents had taken place, no one wanted to press charges, other potential complainants feared prosecution and/or publicity, or that a plea bargain was struck.

A plea bargain had one hidden advantage. Among the boys who would have been dragged through the mud were sons of Henry's friend Daniel Sullivan, the assistant district attorney.[45] There would have been hell to pay if the newspapers got wind of that connection. It is therefore entirely possible that a plea bargain was arranged with Sullivan's "encouragement." Indeed, the absence of this potentially explosive fact in the *Examiner* suggests that the reporter did not have the names of all the boys, chose to suppress the information, or did not make the connection since Sullivan is a common surname. Furthermore, other homosexual experiences remained hidden. In addition to the incident at Halcyon, there may have been at least three partners: Leo Linder, Billy Justema—a young artist from whom he received very suggestive letters—and, Sidney thought, an unidentified black man. Sidney knew that the affair with Linder ended badly.

When she tried to elicit some information from Justema, he only described Henry as a cheerful, passionate lover.[46]

With guilt not a question, the overriding goal was to avoid imprisonment. Seeger counseled against an insanity plea. It was used too often, and with the same battle plan: not guilty, charges dropped, temporary commitment to a hospital. It always meant the same thing to the public: "guilty but influential."[47]

At some point, probably quite early, everyone accepted the idea of shifting the case from the municipal court to the state court. Many years later Olive said that Terman and other important people persuaded Oneal to change the venue because one of them had influence with the judge and could get the charge dismissed. She thought that if it had remained in local hands, he might have escaped with a few months, but the change of venue was the fatal mistake that got the *Examiner* onto the case, inflaming the public. Her analysis cannot be right, however. The *Examiner*'s story must have been written almost immediately after the arrest since it went to press the next day. Oneal was not engaged until later.[48]

One way or another, the case ended up in the hands of the state authorities. A week after the arrest Henry proposed a resolution of the affair that refers to state penitentiaries or hospitals, offering assurances of nonrepetition in the event of probation, parole, or release from Agnew or another hospital, or from a short prison term. He proposed remaining with his parents or a hired attendant until it was determined to be no longer necessary, or until he married "in which case my wife would act in the capacity of keeper." Some form of guardianship would prevent him from meeting boys or youths alone. He would never visit Menlo Park, and would live at a great enough distance to ensure lack of contact with the old group. (So much for his dream of a Stanford faculty appointment.) He did not consider himself homosexual but could hardly have said otherwise. He believed he was victim of a disturbed and distraught emotional condition—he was terribly overworked and financially insecure—and that he could be cured with the aid of doctors, psychiatrists, and/or psychologists. He said he never *planned* to have sex with a boy; all of those experiences occurred by chance. He did not attempt to stop because his acts became a habit and he never thought them through carefully. He now knew that if he repeated the offense he would be jailed for a long time.[49]

Thus far the story follows a reasonable line. Yet one must also address Sidney's 1988 claim that Henry took the advice of the arresting officer to falsely plead guilty to spare the neighborhood children from being investigated. "Around 1938 the District Attorney who had prosecuted the case learned that the accusation brought against Henry . . . was untrue; it was a threat which the boy, with an older friend, hoped would scare Henry into surrendering his red Stutz automobile, which the two of them coveted . . . HC was bisexual to a degree, but no pederast." He was never accused of molesting children, but since young men were commonly referred to as boys at that time, false inferences were easily made.[50] Since she was in the thick of it within two years of his arrest and had plenty of access to Henry later as his wife, there is no reason on the face of it why this account might not be true, and offers another explanation of why Henry told people not to believe what they read. If so, it doubles the tragedy. But there is no way to prove it.

Olive suggested to Lilly Popper that Henry's position was aggravated by false stories told by the other boys. Of course, she may have been trying to encourage Lilly to stand by him; or she may have been deluding herself.[51] Sidney's story of a totally false confession seems improbable, though the incident about the car is consistent with Henry's comments about the soured atmosphere. Henry's own notes on the case suggest that he confessed because he feared that the earlier incident at Halcyon would be used against his attempt to be let off on probation. In the end, it did not really matter. Since Henry had pleaded guilty, his fate was going to be determined by factors that might not necessarily include truth.

32

The Hearing

During the nearly three weeks that Henry spent behind bars in the San Mateo County Jail, in Redwood City, he marshaled his energies to compose the splendid string quartet that he called the "United," and *Dance Forms*.[1] Finally, on Monday afternoon, July 6, Judge Maxwell McNutt convened a hearing in Superior Court at Redwood City. He had three options: release Henry on probation, commit him to Agnew State Hospital, or send him to San Quentin for the mandated sentence of one to fifteen years. In the third instance, at the end of one year the Board of Prison Terms and Paroles would set the length of the term and determine eligibility for parole.

In his history of prison sentencing,[2] David Rothman showed that the entire system of probation, indeterminate sentencing, and parole, a victory of late-nineteenth-century reformers, was fraught with complications and failures. Probation, the first step in possible rehabilitation, was especially controversial because it allowed felons a chance to reform but exposed society to the possibility of further offenses. Every incident of recidivism—especially by sexual offenders— undermined the public's trust. Furthermore, probation officers were too few, often incompetent and/or underpaid, and unable to manage gigantic caseloads. Nevertheless, some politicians liked probation because it kept the prison population small enough to render expensive new prisons unnecessary, and prosecutors used it as an incentive for plea bargaining. Conflicts of the various interests were particularly intense in sex crimes, which inflamed the public's virulent fear of immigrant criminals. Twenty-first-century readers tempted to tut-tut the moral climate of that era need to remember that the puzzle of sexual offenders still has not been satisfactorily solved.

Since probation had become reasonably commonplace, Henry had some reason to think that his appeal would succeed if his history touched a sympathetic ear. He would have to rely upon his lawyer Oneal, whose conduct does not suggest the negligence of which Sidney later accused him, beginning with the fact that he, not an assistant, participated in the hearing. Oneal called two defense witnesses.[3] The first was Dr. Wolff, the psychiatrist engaged to consult with Olive and Henry. Although Section 288a prohibited oral sex without reference to sexual orientation, and the charge was not homosexuality, Wolff must have perceived that it was generally understood to concern homosexuality. With homophobia rampant, the overriding goal was to convince Judge McNutt that Henry was not truly homosexual.

Under direct examination by Oneal, Wolff argued that Henry's homosexual experiences only resulted from "an arrested or temporarily fixated psycho-sexual development," not from an underlying homosexual nature. He based this opinion on the fact that in a true homosexual "there is no attraction to the other sex, that all contacts with the other sex are repugnant, that erotic dreams are only of men, that sex gratification is not connected with the ideation of women, those are the main things." None of those characteristics were present in Henry, Wolff continued, illustrating his point with a chart of Henry's complete sexual history. He felt that the budding relationship demolished by Clarissa was probably the greatest tragedy, for it left long-lasting scars. The cause was Clarissa's abnormal attention to her son, which he explained using Henry's account. Each period of mutual masturbation was characterized by extreme psychic disturbances— Clarissa's death, the engagement to and accidental death of Edna Smith, and the marriage plans with Schmolke that were thwarted by the immigration laws. When Oneal asked if he thought that Henry could repair his arrested development, Wolff replied affirmatively. If he were truly homosexual, he would not be able to adjust. As evidence that Henry was not truly homosexual, he cited the absence of sexual relationships of any sort while Henry was in the army, where homosexuality was rampant. He recommended medical treatment, because imprisonment would aggravate the sexual problems. Descriptions of prisons at this time concur that they were hotbeds of vicious homosexual behavior and that the chances of a newcomer being spared involuntary sex were very small.[4]

Oneal's second witness, Dr. E. W. Mullen, the medical superintendent of Agnew State Hospital, agreed that Henry was not a true homosexual, but rather bisexual and subject to "a psychic influence which causes his tendency to be homosexual." Mullen believed that Clarissa's reaction to his interest in the young woman, and her attitude toward artificial insemination, could have damaged the transition to ordinary adult sexual life. He also believed that Henry could now make that transition with help.

Dr. Mullen's prescription for recovery was more social than psychiatric— finding a woman with similar interests and marrying. Prison was only an option if the court's intent was to punish rather than to help. Imprisonment would be the most severe punishment imaginable; Henry would be at the mercy of homosexuals who would ruin the rest of his life. Although Mullen felt that Henry was only likely to serve a year, he would then face a very difficult adjustment to normal adult life. The intermittence of episodes of mutual masturbation convinced him that homosexuality was not the path that Henry really wanted, as proven by his avoidance of homosexuality in the army and his affair with Schmolke. When Oneal asked whether he stayed away from homosexuality in the army because officers were present, Mullen said no, that homosexuality is "notorious" in the army and navy, and officers cannot be around the men all the time. He felt, however, that Henry should leave Menlo Park, where there would be hard feelings.

Such testimony, coming from both a distinguished San Francisco pediatric psychiatrist and the chief medical officer of the state mental hospital, seems persuasive. But the deputy district attorney, Louis Dematteis, was no amateur. His cross-examination got Wolff to acknowledge that his testimony about Henry's history was based entirely on information given him by the defendant and his family and that he had undertaken no independent investigation. Dematteis then trapped Wolff by asking him to prove that the homosexual episodes were intermittent. Wolff had to admit that he could not say definitely because he was not present. After Judge McNutt asked whether the deviations were voluntary if he was not a true homosexual, Dematteis forced Wolff to admit that he could not guarantee that Henry could control his old passions. Dematteis concluded by asking if Wolff had been retained by the Cowell family, to which the answer was yes. On redirect examination, Oneal attempted to rescue the situation by getting Wolff to state that he had been retained to help Henry, not with a mind to testifying.

As much as he tried, Dematteis could not shake Dr. Mullen's assessment that Henry could make the needed adjustment, even at age thirty-nine. Dematteis pointed out, however, that after the 1922 Halcyon episode of mutual masturbation, Henry promised to desist in order to avoid prosecution but later relapsed. Dematteis then tried to get Mullen to admit that since all the known episodes of mutual masturbation occurred with sixteen- or seventeen-year-olds, Henry's restraint on other occasions may simply have resulted from the absence of suitable young men. Mullen, however, pointed out that the relapse did not explain his abstinence in Germany, where plenty of young men were around. When Dematteis reminded Mullen that they did not know what occurred in Germany, Mullen retorted that while he was not there, he had no reason to believe that Henry was lying. Quite the contrary; Henry had been extremely forthcoming. Dematteis then asked if Henry was sane. Mullen said that he was not insane, but also not "normal," in that his behavior was different from the average behavior one might find if a thousand people taken at random were assessed. Dematteis concluded by trying to get Mullen to agree that imprisonment would not harm Henry more than anyone else, but Mullen would not budge.

After cross-examination, Henry seemed to have an even chance for probation. At least Mullen held firm. Now one other person had to weigh in—Francis Robinson, the probation officer. His statement, somewhat puzzlingly, is not preserved in the court file, probably because he did not appear at the hearing but gave his opinion to Judge McNutt in writing. (Olive obtained a copy months later.) Robinson cautioned that although Henry had never been arrested before, he had been involved in a similar offense at Oceano (Halcyon) in 1922, but for unknown reasons, no legal action was taken.[5] (The "unknown reason" left unmentioned.was the mediation that had resolved the matter.) Robinson concluded, "As a result of my investigation and because of the large number of children involved in the case, and also because of a similar act, which occurred on the previous occasion, I recommend at this time, Your Honor, that probation be denied."

Judge McNutt concluded the hearing saying that Robinson and the court both had a duty to protect children. He therefore accepted Robinson's recommendation and ruled against probation. McNutt also denied being hard-hearted or punitive. He faced a serious dilemma. "The law does not leave to Mr. Robinson and me any method of supervising the lives of the homosexuals or any persons who have psychopathic sexual tendencies. If, upon examination by psychiatrists and other scientists at San Quentin, they believe that treatment can be given, they will be very loathe to deny that treatment." Although the law under which he was charged did not so much as mention homosexuality, it was the question around which the decision revolved. Furthermore, because Henry admitted guilt, Judge McNutt could not consider acquittal.

Henry was then told to make a statement to Dematteis, most of which summarizes his life, education, and profession. In conclusion he reiterated his interest in marrying Elsa Schmolke, and revealed that he had gone to Washington to see a senator, whom his brother Clarence knew, to determine if there were any way to get Elsa into the country so they could marry. Henry also repeated that the seriousness of his acts had eluded him completely.[6]

The court record includes no mention that the other participant in the sexual act should also have been arrested. There is also no evidence of an episode related by Sidney, who said that when Judge McNutt asked who would take responsibility for Henry if he were put on probation, Harry failed to answer because he was gabbing in the back of the room and Oneal failed to keep him alert to the hearings.[7] This story was repeated in a 1977 interview with Virgil Thomson, who might have heard it from Sidney, who was not present at the hearing.[8] According to the court record, the question was never asked.

In McNutt's view, the tragedy was the lack of any mechanism for supervision, without which he had to reject probation and send Henry to San Quentin. He did not refer to the enormous pressure on the judicial system resulting from violent sex crimes, including a recent rape and murder of a little girl, or evidence that probation officers could be dangerously negligent. Letting Henry loose could have caused a major uproar. The *Examiner*, having fed the story to the public, had a vested interested in making sure he was punished.[9]

33

Arriving and Adjusting

The First Summer

Back in his cell, Henry concluded that the chances of parole after a year were very slender without his friends' help. Their silence no longer served any purpose, although any statements from the radical circle would be very dangerous. Olive, however, showed better sense in advising Slonimsky against fanning the opposition.[1] After again urging Becker not to believe what he heard, Henry ended his letter simply: "I go perhaps today to San Quentin."[2] In fact, departure was postponed. It is difficult to imagine what went through his mind as he spent yet another night waiting. The *Newsletter and Wasp's* final onslaught was still to come. The last known communication from the county jail is a postcard Henry dashed off to Slonimsky on July 8, as he was about to leave for the prison, reminding him that every scrap of mail was a lifeline.[3] On that very day, Schmolke, horrified by Henry's news, wrote to affirm her love and her hope that when everything was over he would come to Germany and try to forget the past.[4] (Her letter survives because she mailed it to Olive.) The *Examiner* reported the sentence on July 9 with a strangely brief notice and a large photo of Henry crossing the Bay in suit, tie, and handcuffs.

Henry's pre-prison fear of being forbidden to write was unfounded, but the daily limit of a single two-page letter prevented him from staying in touch with his friends and maintaining his professional activities. Because there was no limit on incoming letters, he received so many that he could not even thank most correspondents for their good wishes and news. His first letter, to Harry and Olive, began with the unfamiliar salutation "Dear Mother and Father" because the rules prohibited writing to "unknown" people, that is, anyone who had not first written to him. He said nothing about the look of the prison, a gray mass on a peninsula northeast of the Golden Gate Bridge. It was all-male; women had been moved out in 1927. Most of the first day was devoted to being photographed, giving his medical history, and learning about duties and regulations. Like all prisons, San Quentin kept its inmates busy at menial jobs.

He had been temporarily assigned to a morning sweeping detail until a full-time job was organized.

Olive and Harry were probably relieved by the lack of alarming news. They did not know that he refrained from describing the reality of San Quentin. California had the country's second-worst penal system. What this meant can be found in the memoirs of Dr. Leo Stanley, the chief medical officer of San Quentin, and Clinton Duffy, who became warden shortly after Henry was released, when the revelation of brutal conditions led to the dismissal of Warden Court Smith.

We cannot expect Duffy to have said whether Warden Smith was a bad man or a bad administrator. Duffy seems like a good man in a bad situation. He knew San Quentin, having grown up in it as a guard's son. Whereas conditions usually improved only when it served the interests of the penal staff, Duffy tried to ease tensions by helping the prisoners. Dr. Stanley, whose autobiography—by a bizarre turn of fate—was co-authored by Evelyn Wells, was a different type. His incessant use of "I" suggests egocentricity, but he was on the defensive because of the uproar about conditions in the prison during his last two years. Stanley felt he was the most hated man there, blamed for everything.[5] The disturbing objectivity with which he relates some hair-raising episodes makes him a good, if seemingly cold-hearted witness.

Dr. Stanley believed that the worst experience for new prisoners was the journey there and the first days behind bars. After they were "in" for a week or so, they adjusted and probably found it was not as bad as they feared.[6] In fact, it was worse, as Stanley himself wrote. Tuberculosis was widespread. Two thirds of the inmates admitted to one, two, or even three venereal infections. Another 15 percent may have developed a venereal sore at some time. Twenty percent were "feeble-minded." There were huge problems of drugs and drink. And San Quentin did not even have the very worst types: repeat offenders went to the fortress-like Folsom prison.

According to Stanley, arrival was relatively innocuous. The medical department examined each prisoner thoroughly after arrival, studying his personal history, habits, family tendencies, medical condition, and other information and from time to time tabulated and analyzed these data. Duffy, however, described a typical prisoner's shock and desire to escape when coming in, stripped of civilian clothes, "and forced to stand naked and ashamed while impassive guards examine his body for hidden weapons, drugs, or other contraband," or later, upon hearing thousands of locks turning.[7] Prisoners were addressed by number, not name. Court Smith, the warden in Henry's time, ordered that all prisoners be clean shaven, which may have improved the atmosphere. Duffy eliminated head shaving and sloppy prison clothes with numbers. He does not say what happened to the practice of calling the men by numbers, but it is hard to imagine how the guards could know so many prisoners by name. Henry did not mention that they showered in dirty saltwater pumped from San Francisco Bay. Soon after taking over, Duffy installed freshwater showers.

In Henry's time, San Quentin seemed to Stanley and Duffy a powder keg ready to explode, jammed with 6,000 men in a space designed for half as many. The US attorney general described his inspection tour as "the most depressing experience of my life."[8] In 1934 it had looked like a riot would occur at any time.[9] The following year a group kidnapped the entire Parole Board and nearly killed Warden Holohan during a breakout attempt.[10] Part of Holohan's legacy was a gas chamber, installed in 1934 because hangings were so gruesome.[11] He was shortly replaced by Court Smith.

According to Dr. Stanley, complaints of ill treatment were unfounded. Duffy, however, wrote that San Quentin "had a reputation as one of the most primitive penitentiaries in the world."[12] Complainers could be whipped. Prisoners who crossed the guards could be forced to stand in a nine-inch circle for hours and be flogged if they moved or talked. Turning in a poor piece of jute cloth or wise-cracking with a guard was enough to send one to a horrifying dungeon without light, bed, toilet, or ventilation, with bare walls, a damp floor to sleep on, and occasional servings of bread and water.[13]

Stanley called letter writing one of the chief prison pastimes. He did not mention the complex regulations that had to be mastered, or the unpleasant penalties in the rules. Mail could not be sent to or received from other prisons, county jails, or former inmates—whether paroled or discharged—or their relatives. Prisoners could not correspond with anyone with whom they were not personally acquainted. Letters to an alias were delayed. Inmates could not advertise for correspondents. Standard magazines and newspapers published outside California could only be received by subscription and direct shipment from the publisher. Used magazines, newspapers, or clippings were prohibited. Prisoners could not ask their friends or relatives to send money, stamps, or additional articles to other inmates. Subject to inspection and approval, inmates could receive, by mail only, white cotton handkerchiefs, socks, neckties, scarfs, belts, suspenders, toothbrushes, cigarette holders, pipes, fountain pens, mechanical pencils, and safety razors using double-edged blades. (Single-edged blades were perfect weapons.)

In reality, the prison was filled with contraband—drugs, alcohol, weapons, poison, knockout drops, cigars, candy—all ingeniously smuggled in. Shortly after the breakup of a counterfeiting ring in the prison, huge amounts of contraband were uncovered. Duffy found many prison rules irrational. Until he opened a canteen in 1941, a prisoner had to gamble, fight, or steal to get what he wanted or needed. If caught, he could be whipped or thrown in the dungeon for having cigarettes, candy bars, cookies, fruit juice, postage stamps, toothpaste, or soap. Duffy also eliminated a ban on subscriptions to local papers.[14]

Henry's first needs were his safety razor and blades, his leather belt, fountain pen, and typewriter.[15] His prison number (59182) was his mailbox number and needed to be included in the address. The belt had to be made from a single strap. (Presumably a belt made of two straps sewn together could be broken up and converted into a long strip useful as a weapon, a tool for suicide, etc.) He soon learned the custom of getting small valuable objects such as pens or watches to be used as bribes "against various kinds of meanness or cruelty from the other prisoners." Requests for gifts had to be mumbled; prisoners were forbidden to utter them.[16] He could not sign over his "soldier's bonus check" and use the proceeds to repay money he owed Olive and Harry because all money received for a prisoner had to be held for him at the prison.

Proven personal acquaintances could visit once every twenty-eight days. They could not give anything to or receive anything from an inmate, or speak with any other inmate. If any prison regulation were violated, the visitor would be barred from returning. Relatives or friends could come on weekdays for up to one hour between 9 A.M. and 3 P.M. Immediate family could visit with inmates on Sundays or holidays from 9 A.M. to 2 P.M.[17] There was no limit to the number of different persons who would be admitted.[18]

On the second day, still awaiting a work assignment, Henry was given short jobs such as sweeping and filing rust from metal furniture. In addition to undergoing the medical examination, he had been tested by the Education Department. Knowing that his parents would worry, he wrote, "The food is good, and well-varied. This noon we had spaghetti, and cottage-cheese; this evening I disposed of a quarter of a delicious watermelon! So you will see that you need not worry about me—I am absolutely alright. I think of you constantly, and we will be together in spirit until such time as we may again visit in the flesh."[19] The full menu—which Henry sent a few months later—would not get any stars, but looks tolerable. Henry wrote that servings were generous and seconds could usually be had. Special holidays brought special meals.[20] After Dr. Wolff—his first visitor—advised adding milk, cheese, tomato juice or fresh tomatoes, and fresh vegetables to his diet, Henry could get canned milk and cheese, but tomatoes in any form or fresh vegetables could not be obtained except for what was cooked into the "good and plentiful" stews.

In his pleasantries about food, Henry was either not entirely forthcoming or still unaware of reality. A close look at the menu shows many areas of culinary flexibility, such as meatballs. Observers said that the food was often inedible— rancid, putrid, foul-smelling. The most serious source of unrest, it caused a riot in 1937, which fortunately did not produce the bloodshed of a similar disturbance in 1912.[21] Henry never mentioned the riot or the four armed guards on catwalks above the mess hall who were known to start shooting if they suspected an impending problem.[22] Dr. Stanley, however, defended the food, although he pointed out that butter was only provided in the hospital or for the condemned.[23]

Sundays were special days, with a more elaborate lunch (though no supper), a band concert, and visits with family. Because it was customary to wear a tie, Henry asked Olive to send something conservative.[24] Olive must have been pleased that he was taking care of himself. The sight of frighteningly tough prisoners wearing neckties over their prison uniforms would be amusing if the circumstances were not so awful.

Sidney, who became a regular visitor, felt the cell block resembled a series of "zoo cages piled one on another—6 to 10 layers, or maybe more, I forget. A footpath for guards ran outside each layer. Cells were adjacent along very long corridors; the side of the cell facing the walkway was open, protected by heavy iron bars, leaving each prisoner visible to the guards—and everybody audible to everybody else."[25] Henry's new home, Cell 1841, was about four feet by eight feet, "modern and clean—light and airy," he said, with a comfortable bed, a sink, toilet, stool, and electric light. A window gave him a view of the bay, obscured by a heavy screen; the lights of Berkeley could be seen dimly in the distance. From a spot near the dining hall he could see Mt. Tamalpais. Henry's cell mate, doing time for passing bad checks, seemed clean and orderly, amiable, in his forties, with a wife and grown daughter in the East. Henry felt lucky to have drawn him. He knew about victimization of sex offenders and could be sure that rumors would circulate. Stanley and Duffy describe vicious attacks on homosexuals— fights, knifings, thefts, murders. When Duffy separated out homosexuals he eliminated 90 percent of the sexual violence in the prison.[26]

Henry's relief about his cell mate may be one of the few honest statements about what he was seeing. His reiterated call for Harry and Olive to find calm and peace suggests that he was painting a bright picture so as not to get the dangerous reputation of a malcontent. Censors read every line of every incoming and outgoing letter, and Henry surely was warned about what could happen to complainers.[27]

In this grim environment, the Education Department was the pride of San Quentin and one of the largest in the country. Its two-hour comprehensive achievement test showed Henry the strengths and weaknesses of his peculiar education. He thought he came out fairly well in spelling, grammar, and definition of words; moderately in history, literature, and geography. Arithmetic was poor; having had no conventional training, he lacked a systematic approach to solving problems and could answer the questions by instantly devising a method of his own—that is, the easiest questions. He had to skip the others. The test had a word that he had never heard: "'elemessary'—do you know it?" he asked Olive and Harry. "There were groans of despair on the part of those taking the test when they heard it—not one of us had ever heard of it! Nor could we, of course, define it."[28] (Nor apparently can the Oxford English Dictionary or other dictionaries, where the word does not appear.) Later he learned that his IQ was ranked at 120, brought lower by his poor command of mathematics. "Of course, it is not an intelligence test, it is mostly a test of knowledge acquired. Doctors here concurred with Dr. Wolff in pronouncing me physically fit. The dentist gave my teeth a clean bill of slate [*sic*]."[29]

Locked in his cell that night he wrote Olive and Harry again, mailing it on the next day's quota. He had had a surprise summons from the secretary of Jewish activities. Still wet and in boots from the scrubbing detail, he rushed to the office "to assure him that he was making a grave error in supposing that any Irishman would ever permit himself to be taken for a Hebrew—when he came out and informed me that he had heard I played—would I play for a program he had arranged." Henry agreed and asked when. The answer was, instantly! He had to play for about 150 young Jewish inmates. They "applauded my 'Reel' so enthusiastically that I played 'the Tides' and then 'Jig.' I really played dreadfully, what with never touching a piano for so long, but it seemd to 'get over' anyway." He was told that he would be asked to play on other programs. Unfortunately he had no piano on which to practice. The one in the band room next door to his cell was "so poor that the keys stand out in every direction!" Whatever the quality, the performance earned him some credit among the inmates.

He could hear the band practicing while he was writing and would get to hear them play the next day at their weekly Sunday noontime concert. (Duffy said that the band played louder on nights when a break was being planned.)[30]

> The band personnel, as a whole, seems to represent a high grade of inmate, so I am making some of them my companions to meals, and at such other times as they are free at the same time as I. I have been able to give them helpful suggestions about their tone, chords, and other musical matters. And by being with them when in "The Yard," I am protected from association with the riff-raff—one cannot, needless to say, be too careful about one's associates here. And it would take a better judge than I to tell, always, from the face at the first, what sort of man is next to me![31]

Another understatement. Duffy described the yard as "a concrete quadrangle larger than a football field, formed by three cell blocks and the huge mess hall. Thousands of men swarmed over the stone flats, shifting and turning to loosen the press of bodies, men doing nothing, men going nowhere." When he dared to walk alone among the prisoners in the yard, something no other warden had done, he imagined that there were "no less than two hundred knives, daggers, blackjacks, or other hidden weapons somewhere in those thousands of pockets and sleeves."[32]

Reading Henry's letters, one wonders if he perceived the irony that after working so hard with little pay all those years he finally did not have to worry about his next meal. His next extant letter, to Slonimsky a week after arrival, reveals his real worries. Afraid that his music might be boycotted or forgotten, he urged Slonimsky to find performers for it. Copland's inclusion of a piece at Yaddo was a rare bright spot. He planned to compose but did not know if he could send music out or take it when he was discharged. Moreover, now that a job had been assigned, the prospects for composing shrank. To his surprise, San Quentin seemed to be an improvement over the jail in Redwood City. "The food is better, and one is not confined in so small a place—there is at least activity."[33]

Like almost all new prisoners, Henry was assigned to the jute mill, which kept the men busy—idleness in prison is dangerous—and softened them up. Nearly half the 6,000 inmates worked there, many of them "spooling"—transferring jute used to make sacks from small spools to large spools. Each one had to operate twenty spools, which whirred deafeningly. Henry marveled at the skill needed to operate the machine. He did not mind the jute mill at all; he found it "a genuine experience." That was fortunate, since the work could have hurt his hands, and mistakes such as making bad cloth or loafing were punished harshly. Duffy wrote that "there were always three gun guards suspended like uneasy tightrope walkers over the heads of the prisoners. In the nerve-racking clatter of the looms inmates were quite apt to make some gesture that could be misinterpreted, and the strain on them and the gun guards was unbelievable."[34] By the time Henry was back in his cell, he was exhausted from eight hours of work.

By mid-August he still had heard nothing from either Charles or Harmony Ives, whose silence gnawed at him.[35] Since he knew it was unlike them to turn against him, he assumed that Ives was very ill.[36] He was right about Ives's health and wrong about their attitude. Had he seen Harmony's reply to a letter from Charlotte Ruggles he would have understood that his admired stoicism, his insistence on not worrying anyone, had been misinterpreted.

> Dear Mrs. Ruggles,
>   Thank you for writing. In the mail with your letter was one from Henry addressed to me which contained a letter to be given to Charlie if I saw fit. It was a strange letter—admitting his commission of the offense but with no *suggestion* of contrition—there was in fact, a spirit of bravado it seemed to me—his "spirit was undaunted" (stock phrase) & he is "absolutely contented." Is he contented with *himself* do you suppose? Anyway, I told Charlie & he & I feel just as you do. A thing more abhorrent to Charlie's nature couldn't be found. We think these things are too much condoned. He will never willingly see Henry again—he *can't*—he doesn't want to hear of the thing—The shock used him up &

he hasn't had a long breath since I told him but he will get used to it—
isn't it almost shocking the things we "get used to"? He said characteristically "I thought he was a man & he's nothing by a g—da—sap!"

I can't write any more—the letter from Henry was largely about the
carrying on of New Music—He has planned it all out as you of course
know—He said Mr. Ruggles & Mr. Luening (?) wanted to do it from
Bennington but Strang is to do it & Henry's name left on. We want to
see New Music go on . . .[37]

Trying as always to prevent his friends from pitying him, he told Blanche Walton that he intended to profit from the experience as much as possible. In addition to composing, he planned to take a University of California extension course
in Spanish and perhaps other subjects if he could concentrate. Forms of human
nature that he had never encountered—especially depravity—continued to astonish him. "But it is all an amazing human experience, and I believe that a greater
richness of human understanding is bound to result from it."[38]

Walton, however, also misinterpreted Henry's emphasis on the positive.
Having deluded herself into thinking he was innocent, she was, like some other
good friends, crushed that he did not attempt to deny or excuse his conduct.
Now she had to adjust to "the horror that has happened for while I knew Henry
was sexually abnormal I had no idea it had taken such a terrible form."[39] Surely
one incident of consensual oral sex would hardly have fallen under the rubric of
"horror." Regrettably, the *Examiner's* story of crowds of children was making the
rounds. Indeed, the image of Henry as a pederast persists even now, since a long
sentence for one incident of consensual oral sex seems implausible. Judy Brown
was also mystified that Henry had pleaded guilty when he kept assuring her that
the rumors were unfounded. And if they had no basis, why did he get one to fifteen years? Nevertheless, she still wanted to help him and promised to send a
monthly check for $10 [2010: $157] and start a fund so he would have money
when he was freed.[40] Alvin Johnson also remained loyal, despite a sentence that
seemed so damning.[41] He might have been shocked by two leaflets advertising
pornographic literature that were sent to Henry in early August and intercepted
by Olive. None of it seems like Henry's style; the merchants probably got his
name from some mailing list. Ironically, the brochures could have been used as
proof of heterosexuality.[42]

Corresponding required learning more and more regulations. Envelopes that
Olive sent had been destroyed as contraband. Writing paper was forbidden; only
typing paper could be used. Letters longer than two pages were delayed by the
censors. He asked Olive and Harry to thank those who had written since he
would not be able to reply for a long time. Incredulous that some friends thought
he did not want to hear from them, he asked Popper to encourage them but warn

them to put the return address on the outside and not send stamped return envelopes or clippings, only snapshots. Sending nothing was preferable, since any
enclosures invited the prying eyes of censors. Olive's incorrigible habit of typing
her name rather than signing it to verify her identity also attracted the censors. As
letters poured in, Henry was happy to learn that Strang, Weiss, Rudhyar, William
Grant Still, and others had formed the hoped-for branch of the New Music
Society in Los Angeles; he hoped Weiss would also keep the Society going in San
Francisco. Strang was doing well with *New Music Quarterly*.

He was very grateful that Weiss sent news to Schmolke. Henry had written
her at once when he was arrested and twice subsequently, though only from the
Redwood City jail, not from San Quentin because of the quota imposed on
inmate correspondence. He repeated to Weiss much of what he had told Wolff
about their relationship, and though he might have been deliberately imaginative in his depositions, he had no reason to lie to Weiss, who was a friend of
Schmolke and would have known a lie if he saw one.[43] Johanna Beyer's passionate letters were not helpful: her unfortunate habit of putting her return
address as "Sunny Hades" was guaranteed to arouse suspicion.[44] The letters
about Henry that she sent to Olive seemed pathetic in their passionate nature.

Gradually he had better news to report. He was making good grades in Spanish and was amused to be getting grades rather than giving them. His skill at
spooling was improving. He had finished a march for the prison band called *Reel
Irish*, copied parts, shown it to the leader, and thought it would get a reading
soon. If it were programmed, he hoped that Olive and Harry could come; Sunday
band concerts were held outside the walls at midday for the benefit of the community. Ever the publicist, he asked them to tell friends who lived in the north
Bay area. "I think many of them would like to hear it, as it is really an excellent
organization."[45]

After about a month, Henry made the curious discovery that prisoners had
ordered *New Musical Resources* and *American Composers on American Music*
more than a dozen times under a lending agreement with the state library at
Sacramento. The band leader (a prisoner) knew all the details about Henry from
Slonimsky's article in *American Composers on American Music*. Henry was
impressed by the library and its users.

> The class of books ordered seems rather high to me. Lots of non-fiction.
> There is much serious study in the attempt to rehabilitate. You [Slonim-
> sky] asked whether the prisoners were of the type portrayed in the
> movies—I must frankly say that I haven't seen one! On the surface,
> they impress one as being a rather rough and ready, good-natured
> group, something like army men. It is only when one becomes better
> acquainted with them, that their lack of feeling for ethical behavior

becomes evident. In a group of about fifteen or so, one will find one or two who really do have a strong or stronger moral sense; ten or twelve who seem to be rather childish, good-natured morons; and one or two really "tough eggs," bad men of whom one has to be careful. I cannot convey to you how extraordinary is the experience of being thrown in with such a motley crew. The whole thing is really an experience which, if not too protracted, one would not wish to have missed.

Henry was pleased to have developed some skills in the mill. "To operate a whole machine is the goal; I can now operate my half with ease, and could probably take on the whole machine for a limited time, if necessity arose, and provided I was not fed a great many tangled spools." Still too tired in the evening to do much serious composing, he had completed a conventional band arrangement of someone else's composition and hoped to master band arranging, potentially a real asset. Hearing the band had convinced him that there was a future for those who composed serious band music rather than the insipid arrangements and simple marches that formed the current repertory.[46]

After Olive paid her first visit late in July, she decided to seek the help of Dr. Alfred Adler, the distinguished Austrian-emigré psychiatrist, through a friend of Henry who had studied with him. Since Adler had taught at the New School, he might have heard of Henry. She thought that if Drs. Adler, Stanley, and Wolff were favorable, it might be possible to get Henry into a state hospital. Alfred Frankenstein also was contacting important people. Olive imagined the Parole Board fixing the sentence at somewhere between three and seven years, half of which might be paroled.[47]

Adler, his wife, Dr. Wolff, and Dr. Schmidt, the San Quentin psychiatrist, quickly convened a surprise meeting with Henry, who told Olive that he was unprepared for "such a weighty conference. The results of it were quite too complex to be written in detail; I must be able to discuss them. And something has come up which makes it necessary to discuss it at once; the sooner the better." Because the rules kept Olive from returning for four weeks, he hoped she could get one of several people to come right away: "Helen," Alfred [Frankenstein], "Evelyn," or any of some others that she had mentioned during their visit that day.[48] There is no further indication of what was so urgent, but it probably related to Olive's hope of getting him transferred to a hospital. "Evelyn" almost certainly was Evelyn Wells, now a well-known journalist; the unidentified "Helen" may have been Henry's friend Helen Mills from the National Federation of Music Clubs.[49]

After the conference Wolff wrote a letter of assessment reiterating the basic elements of his court testimony, emphasizing his conclusion that Henry could achieve emotional maturity, have a normal sex life, and not repeat the offense if he were released on probation at once.[50] Adler, however, disagreed about Henry's potential to be "cured." Only psychiatric care could reveal the inner causes of his behavior, and success could not be guaranteed.[51]

August brought a visit from Georgia Kober,[52] a gift of $5 [2010: $78.70] from Riegger, which made Henry very uncomfortable since Riegger was poor,[53] and news that Stokowski wished to perform *Reel*.[54] By the middle of the month Henry had sold his membership in Halcyon.[55] When Strang came to San Quentin on August 28 he found Henry thinner but in good health. The hard work seemed to have benefited him physically. Having not yet received Adler's report, Henry described a consensus that he was "normal except for a readily curable sexual neurosis which is all but cured already." What remained was a means of getting him treatment. Unfortunately, Strang had to tell him that Harmony Ives had not even mentioned his name while assuring Strang of her husband's continuing support for *New Music Quarterly*.[56] The good news was a scheduled performance of the *United Quartet*.

On September 1, Henry summarized his strictly regulated life: awaken at 5.30, clean the cell, make his bed, eat, and go to work at the jute mill by about 6:45. He worked on a spooling machine until 3:45 P.M., with time off for lunch. After supper, locked in his cell, he could write or study. He still was too tired to do much concentrated creative work. After thirteen months he would be eligible for other jobs, some of which were less tiring. He had played twice for the inmates, both times gratified by "a stirring ovation, although the crowd here is very rapid in booing anything it doesn't like." Such performances were welcome because they were his only opportunity to play a piano. He got perhaps ten minutes in advance to practice.[57] According to Sidney, the one hour daily that prisoners had for their own affairs had to include everything—composing, practicing, writing, conversing with the cell mate, whom Henry had first suspected of being there to entrap him into further criminality. It was very difficult to concentrate since that recreation hour allowed all the band members to play their instruments—a bedlam of every sound, especially accordions, trumpets, guitars.[58]

By the end of the summer Henry had settled into his new life and saved gloom for a few trusted friends.[59] When Lilly Popper imagined him despairing of life without nature he countered with a description of the garden near the main gate, "one of the best I have ever seen anywhere. I am not able to be at that part of the grounds every day, but often have duties which take me there.... The dahlias this summer were breath-taking, really. And every day, after eating, there is a nice garden strip that one walks by." Rather than dwell on the shortage of creative time, he emphasized the possibility of accomplishing something on weekends and storing up plans for the future.[60]

Rereading letters expressing Henry's determination to profit from imprisonment reminded Sidney of a potentially disastrous attempt at self-improvement in the jute mill. Having spent years training himself to play difficult simultaneous rhythms, practicing even on the subway, Henry adapted the physical movements required by the jute machine as exercises in irregular rhythms. His jerky gestures quickly attracted attention, which is the last thing a prisoner wants. Co-workers began questioning his sanity; supervisors could report him for inexplicable behavior. Eventually he stopped. Says Sidney, "I don't think it ever occurred to him that he was producing thread of very uneven thickness!"[61] He did not tell her about the potential punishment for producing poor cloth.[62]

Dr. Stanley remarked that the prisoners read newspapers incessantly and analyzed everything.[63] Henry's lifeline was the *New York Times*.[64] The authorities preferred the *Christian Science Monitor*, however. In it Henry found an article about him by Slonimsky, which made the rounds and gave him a good reputation among the inmates, who became easier to deal with. He urged Slonimsky to get its editors to commission an article from him, either about practical solutions to problems in writing for concert dance, or the dismal state of music education for children.[65] He could do them easily from prison because they had been on his mind for a long time.

Of news from "outside," the threat of war in Europe occupied his thoughts most. He worried about Olive's plan to go there for a desperately needed break and was frustrated by being unable to help his endangered European friends. Even writing on their behalf was impossible; sending a visa recommendation with a San Quentin return address would not be wise. In one case Harry wrote the letter and mailed it from home.[66] Correspondence from abroad also was vexing. Olive had received numerous letters from Henry's friends in other countries but could neither enclose them in her letters nor give them to him during a visit. Unidentified correspondents were a problem even if they held distinguished faculty positions.[67] Slonimsky, who was all too familiar with censorship from his youth in Russia, decided to be cautious about sending him some remarks from the USSR that praised Henry's evolution toward understanding music as a social force.[68]

As time passed, describing daily life over and over became terribly boring, since almost nothing varied. Tiny changes that were inconsequential to outsiders— such as getting onions—were extremely significant to prisoners. When the routine changed for a few days because the spoolers were ahead of their quota, he got an extra forty-five minutes for himself. That was the level of news.

With no limit on the number of visitors, he asked his friends to encourage everyone to come and provide respite from the mill. Even if many of them arrived on the same day, there was no problem because visitors, like spooling, kept the inmates occupied.[69] Visitors were struck by Henry's placidity, acceptance, and determination to make the best of his lot. If he complained that his hands could be ruined by the spooling machine, no one mentioned it.[70] Of course, he was always conscious of the dangers that could befall complainers, but occasionally his armor showed signs of wear and tear, because he did not harbor false hopes of a short stay.[71]

By the fall, he had achieved a kind of celebrity. Two September performances earned him more ovations, winning over the cynics. He sensed that his performances might have helped keep inmates from creating difficulties for him, since bothering a prison celebrity could earn a roughneck some serious enemies.[72] To maintain his skill, however, he needed to practice. The quest for a piano led him to Dr. H. A. Shuder, the only professional in the Education Department, whose fifty-odd teachers were inmates.[73] Shuder quickly invited Henry to give a course in music appreciation for laymen beginning in October (1936).[74] By mid-September, enrollment had nearly reached the limit of ninety. Although Henry had to sacrifice his free time because he could only teach on weekends, when it did not interfere with the routine at the mill, he believed he could contribute to the inmates' education and rehabilitation.[75] He therefore asked Olive and Harry not to come at the lecture time "for it does seem a shame not to give my one lecture a week; of course, in a matter of that or no visit, I would always prefer the visit." He also accepted Shuder's invitation to write about the place of music in education for the Department's magazine.[76]

The strong enrollment for his course prompted Shuder to propose a second class, on advanced harmony and theory. Although it would eat further into his free time, Henry welcomed the opportunity to sustain his former career. Teaching was not just altruistic, however. He foresaw that Shuder would be consulted about the suitability of any proposed job, should parole become possible. As it happened, the second class could not be scheduled, but when Olive proposed that Shuder get Henry transferred to the Education Department he promised to cooperate.[77] He then suggested a Sunday class about Henry's travels abroad. Having never taught anything other than music, Henry accepted at once, appreciating the opportunity to broaden his experience.

The sacrifice of more time was a good investment. Even before the first course began, Shuder got Henry a permit to practice on the Education Department's piano on Labor Day, when the mill was closed. A real practice period was a rarity, and any snippet of time vanished when fog kept the inmates locked up. The fog could be nasty in many respects. Duffy described it as sometimes so heavy that they felt they could bottle it; they had to feel their way around and anything could happen—riots, murder, breakouts.[78] On holidays, Henry might get extra time to practice, fog willing. On Thanksgiving (1936), the fog, regrettably, was uncooperative.[79] He sensed some degeneration in his technique but no memory problems. One solution was to get a mini-piano for the cell, paid for by the sale of his piano. His cell mate did not mind, but first Olive needed to get permission, which Warden Smith declined to grant because only small instruments were permitted in cells.[80]

When a new prisoner was assigned to help him in the mill, Henry felt less tired and better able to work in the evening.[81] His end-of-summer project was *How They Take It: Prison Moods*, a stylistically conventional suite for band, portraying types of characters among the inmates. The first movement suggested the braggart; the second, the self-pitier; the third, the "wise-cracking Irishman"; the fourth, the religious fanatic; the last, "the happy-go-lucky duet-singing Mexican."[82] Although he first thought to keep quiet about it, the suite attracted the press on both coasts after a performance in the weekly concert outside the walls.[83] The San Francisco *Call-Bulletin* said it was a huge success, earning him many admirers on both sides of the wall. The score, presumably left behind upon Henry's release, has disappeared.[84]

The reviews of *How They Take It* eased his fear of being forgotten, as did some requests to write or compose for "outside." In accepting a commission he risked wasting his time, however, since it could only be sent out with Warden Smith's permission, and Smith could be expected to withhold authorization without seeing the finished product. The problem first arose in September 1936, when Alois Hába asked him to write about American music for the Czech periodical *Přítomnost* [The Present]. Luckily Warden Smith authorized exporting the article when it was still only half-finished.[85] Encouraged, he wrote an article on the relationship between music and concert dance and began a book on melodic construction, which he felt he could manage in little bits because he knew the subject well.[86] Gradually the warden got used to his requests and allowed him to export freely.[87]

In that first winter Henry devoted his free time to addressing the weaknesses in his education. An English grammar book borrowed from the Education Department was not just intended to correct his writing, however. Although his letters, typed straight off with no time for editing, show that his earlier weaknesses were ameliorated, he had something larger in mind. "I hope to be able, eventually, to detect the parts of speech, and master its other intricacies. With all the talk of a grammer [sic] of music, no one has ever applied to the tones of melody, the same analysis of their functions as is in grammar applied to words. And this is just what I have been working on, in my melodic book," a major study of the art of melody-writing, to which we shall return in Chapter 37.

By late January 1937, he had finished the four University Extension courses in Spanish with three A's and one B+. In March, immersed in sixth-level Spanish, he proudly read a letter from the Uruguayan musicologist Francisco Curt Lange with almost no assistance from the dictionary. He also squeezed in a little work on French.[88]

With so little free time, and access to a good library, it is no wonder that he told Beyer that he did not need books. He must have said something similar to Grainger, who preferred to send books about their mutual interests, such as the origins of music, the arts among the Celtic and English peoples, the distribution of certain streams of culture, and significant new compositions.[89] Henry was excited when Slonimsky gave him a subscription to the science fiction monthly *Astounding Stories*.[90] "I do not have as much enjoyment from anything else I have here!" he replied. "Have received two issues so far. Even this afternoon, by means of it, I was taken beyond the planet Pluto! Think of it! I do pity those who must stay in either Boston or Maine, or any such places, not going on any spaceliners!"[91]

Dr. Stanley called the Christmas season hell for the prisoners. In addition to magnifying feelings of loneliness, it produced an outpouring of regulations. Although family snapshots were not challenged, commercial photos brought scrutiny that delayed letters.[92] Regulations were relaxed to permit any number of Christmas cards, though there were restrictions on the types of envelopes.[93] A revised list of permissible and impermissible packages was issued.[94] Henry received two welcome gifts, one of them a letter from Ruggles, "and I am very happy for it, because I hoped he would not follow the policy of a pained silence." It remained, however, Ruggles's only letter. The other gift was the weather: the fog stayed home so Henry could practice and play for the inmates.[95] More conventional Christmas presents included neckties, two books, and a collection of Beethoven's letters whose sender was unknown. He was informed that a box of candy had been confiscated, leaving him in the awkward position of not knowing whom to thank. Later he learned that it came from his very early piano teacher, Elizabeth Bates. (He gave it to an orphanage.) John J. Becker, one of Henry's earliest visitors, wanted to send money, but Henry preferred a collection of classical piano pieces appropriate for concerts for the inmates. They needed to be relatively easy because Henry would not be able to practice them.[96] The final seasonal "gift" was a flu epidemic so severe that a quarantine looked possible.[97]

A brief slowdown in mill activities early in 1937 gave him time to attend some classes, but by the beginning of February the schedule was back to normal. By then he had started a new project, studying Japanese with a "curious but intelligent little old Japanese man," a prisoner teaching in the Education Department.[98] Soon Olive was dispatched to find a set of Japanese readers and a writing brush. He was learning about fifty words a week and could form simple sentences, but now needed to take the course because the structure was so complex. He was happy that imprisonment finally gave him an opportunity to study an Asian language.[99]

Most of his circle stuck by him. Judy Brown sent money monthly despite her own financial problems.[100] Tamada, the shakuhachi player, visited every twenty-eight days like clockwork and gave him lessons in the visiting room, probably confining himself to instructions about breathing.[101] In the fall of 1936, Sidney Robertson had moved to San Francisco and now became another regular visitor. She recalled that she would not have gone to see Henry at first had the Seegers not insisted. "I would not have felt I knew him well enough to prevent his feeling like an exhibit in the zoo."[102] Years later, she still remembered the experience of visiting San Quentin. After parking the car she entered guarded gates and walked up a long driveway bordered by beautiful flowers. Inmates working there were ordered never to look up. At an entry post next to a huge barred gate, she filled out the application blank, which a guard took and went off to fetch Henry. She had to run a gauntlet of guards who would snicker, mutter about Henry not being interested in women, or whisper exaggeratedly behind their hands; they assumed that only a lesbian would be interested in a purported homosexual. In the visitors' room were a few chairs and a guard who would indicate the "guichet" in the wall. When Henry arrived, the mood lifted. He immediately wanted to discuss her folklore recordings. As the months dragged by he would talk factually about applications for parole or about the difficulty in writing enough letters, asking her (and other visitors) to write a letter for him. He never complained.

Letters and visitors brought worries about his friends and his stepmother Henrietta, who was in failing health and completely alone. His fear of being forgotten persisted, but performances of his music continued; he clearly was not being boycotted. Georgia Kober played one of Henry's pieces three times for President Roosevelt at the president's request; he remembered Edwin Hughes playing it for him. (Hughes had said that Roosevelt had asked for it specifically.)[103] *Six Casual Developments* was added by popular request to a program at Yaddo devoted to composers in attendance.[104] Stokowski personally wrote Henry to confirm that he planned to study *Reel* in rehearsal with a mind to performing it; eventually he visited Henry.[105] Howard Hanson also wanted to see *Reel* for possible programming at the Hollywood Bowl. (Since they must be referring to *Reel Irish*, which Lichtenwanger says was lost, it can be presumed that Henry was not allowed to send it out and it disappeared with his other prison papers.)[106] Edwin Hughes was still playing his music and giving it to his pupils.[107] Henry's songs also got some exposure. In May 1937, he decided to apply for a composition prize offered by the New York Philharmonic.[108] The *United Quartet* was played twice in mid-1937. When Slonimsky sent an article that mentioned Henry, he replied, "It is professionally important for me to keep my halo polished, and I hope that some performances of my music can be scraped together for next season."[109]

The break with Ives was an unrelenting misery. Henry longed to know that he was not in awful health. "Not hearing is torture," he told Slonimsky, "because as you know, I regard Ives the same as a father; no one who has ever known him could ever fail to be very [much] attached to him."[110] Then Henry's car became the mediator. Considering his chronic financial problems, it is a mystery how he afforded the superb Stutz that reportedly drove Malin Cheney to attempt blackmail. In fact, Ives had advanced $400 [2010: $6,028] in exchange for which

Henry worked for him. Now that the car was to be sold, Henry wanted to return the money. Knowing that Ives would not accept it, he asked Olive to send it out of the proceeds from selling the car, and tell Ives that she knew Henry owed it to him.[111] When 1937 began and the car was still unsold, Henry told her to send the money anyway and explain that she saw that debt in the accounts and was acting with power of attorney.[112] This she did; and Ives returned the letter, noting on it that Henry owed him nothing.[113] In addition, Harmony informed Olive that Charles had denied that even a cent was owed him and explained that Ives never wrote Henry because he was unwell and did not know what to say or do.[114] Henry then wrote him a short note of thanks, uncertain whether he had done the right thing.[115] The car, and Henry's house, were finally sold in April.[116]

Although a tentative line of communication had been established, by late May 1937, Henry still had not heard directly from Ives. Then, not a day after he lamented to Becker that "none of them have showed any sign of life,"[117] he received a letter in Ives's shaky handwriting, which said approximately the same thing that Harmony had written to Olive. "His writing was very bad," Henry told Olive, "and he said he cannot see or hear music anymore. He must be in a dreadful condition, and it is heart-rending to look at the tell-tale scrawl."[118] It was better than nothing, but Henry seems to have suspected that Harmony was shielding her husband and not reading him his letters. Accordingly, he sent a message to him through Clifton Furness, a mutual friend and member of the faculty of the New England Conservatory.[119] Among other things, he would have told Ives that he had introduced his music to the prisoner-musicians, the most advanced of whom were in a "great tether over Ives," since Henry lectured them about *Washington's Birthday*, using a score he could import because printed music was not contraband. "They were mystified," he told Slonimsky, "but highly interested."[120]

Blanche Walton was displaying almost as much hostility as Harmony Ives. Judy Brown explained, however, that Walton was easily swayed by others but still loved him.[121] Then Walton's visit to San Quentin set things aright—except that she told him about Ruggles's attitude. Henry concluded that Ruggles and other friends had formed a judgment based on "a certain Western clipping," and asked Luening to help spread the truth,[122] which he agreed to do, assuring Henry that he, his wife, and their friends would take the court record as the facts. "In any case, your work on behalf of American Music has been so valuable that many of us want to keep your influence alive until you can fan it yourself."[123] A surprise letter from Aaron Copland gave Henry some hope that the whole mess might cement their once-rocky relationship. After sharing Copland's happiness about his reception in Mexico, he suggested, perhaps disingenuously, that it was good to be away from the New School for a while. "Too much of one thing done too long doesn't do." He was impressed by Copland's plan to write a high school opera. "Your phrase 'gebrauchsmusik with a difference' seems to hit the nail on the head. If music isn't of use, it is useless!" *Gebrauchsmusik* had gotten itself a bad name by "a sort of smartalekyness, coupled often with lack of workmanship and idea. And these things are certainly not essential to the term, nor the sort of music it COULD represent." He hoped Copland would support Strang in his administration of *New Music* and help counteract some of the more "vicious and untrue tales" about his "misdemeanors."[124]

By this time, Henry had been in prison for nearly a year. Some people still had not been informed, partly because he could not write everyone, partly because there was no point in spreading the word indiscriminately. He absolutely did not want his nephew Edwin Davidson (Clarence's son, in Des Moines) to know. Edwin had always been very attached to Henry; his warm letters contrast vividly with Clarence's awkward, stilted writing.[125] Learning about San Quentin, however, could make the whole family feel disgraced.

On July 5, 1937, Henry's job in the jute mill ended with a transfer to the Education Department. Instead of spooling he would give harmony classes three times a week, elementary music three times weekly with an extra class on Sunday, his class on foreign travels, and a general music appreciation course. The new schedule allowed him time to take the class in Japanese and ten minutes at the piano every morning just before 8 A.M., if no one else wanted to use it. He had a desk at which he could do his own work, but because the desks were uncomfortably close together, he used his free time in the office to study or write letters and left composing or writing articles for the evening in his cell. In the next weeks he also finished writing a correspondence course in elementary music for beginners, to be used by inmates who could not come to classes and did the homework in their cells.[126]

Among the unwelcome news that summer was Gershwin's sudden death. Henry wrote Slonimsky that he "enjoyed him, and although his music always seemed horridly gushing to me, I recognized its vitality, and believe that he would have improved consistantly [*sic*], as he was doing to the end."[127]

From the very beginning Henry had done his best to keep the New Music Society and its projects alive. Even in prison, he remained the key to the future of the enterprises, marshaling loyalists who were willing to expend something like his energy. His powers to inspire were limited by the ban on receiving carbons of letters, which prevented him from keeping track of affairs. Stripped of civil rights, he could not enter into binding agreements. Manuscript music needed for editorial choices was contraband. Even a relatively remote connection with *New Music* was hobbled by the quota on letter writing. As most of his colleagues were in the East, they could not visit him. He therefore decided to replace himself with an Editorial Board and set up regional sections to seek submissions and ensure *New Music's* nationwide reach. The sections would weed out scores and send the best ones to the Board, similar to the ISCM's selection process for World Music Days. Ives's failing eyesight ruled him out; Ruggles "would simply turn down all the scores, and ask to have the publication discontinued, as he would find nothing suitable!"[128] He advised keeping the New Music Society's California address, with Strang as central coordinator. Henry would not (and could not legally) have executive powers, but he would make suggestions, which could be disregarded. Thanks to that plan, *New Music Quarterly* continued to publish regularly. With Henry no longer in charge, his compositions could be included as special editions or in the recording series.

Just before going to prison Henry had signed a contract for Columbia Records to take over the recordings. Almost at once, the artistic management of Columbia changed radically and the deal fell through, convincing Henry that New Music Quarterly Recordings was more important than ever. When the volunteer successor to Blanche Walton dropped out, leaving no one to ship the records, Henry urged Luening to see if Bennington College, where he taught, could take it over, as Luening had once proposed for the publications.[129] The college's president suggested turning it over to the school's cooperative store, which Luening approved.[130] That plan worked reasonably well. Recordings came out four times a year through 1939, after which they faltered and appeared only sporadically. The California concerts ended when Adolph Weiss unexpectedly moved to New York and Henry could not think of a competent replacement. Unable to suppress his annoyance at the lack of advance notice, all he could do was encourage Weiss to work with Luening and Riegger to raise the recordings to a very high level of works, performances, and circulation.[131]

To Luening he offered one editorial suggestion, applicable to the periodical and the recordings: they should continue to be "all-inclusive—favoring no one style or tendency in selections, and avoiding any cliqueishness [sic]." He continued to interest himself in the details, offering suggestions whenever he could write and pushing Luening to visit stores that might stock the records, as Henry had always done.[132] When Luening reported that Bennington would have to skip a January recording, Henry strongly cautioned that omitting a scheduled release could cause the subscribers to lose faith in the project.[133] Riegger was probably too tactful to tell him that he should consider himself lucky that Bennington agreed to take over the records under Luening's guidance, since no one else was prepared to help.[134]

34

The Second Day of Reckoning

As the spring of 1937 turned to summer, the Board of Prison Terms and Paroles had to determine Henry's sentence. Unfortunately for him, the system had major flaws. Indeterminate sentencing was conceived as an inducement to good behavior and endorsed by prison authorities as a tool for controlling inmates.[1] At the end of one year, the Board could choose to discharge a prisoner for time served, sentence him to the maximum, give him anything in between, or release him on parole. Paradoxically, parole, the prospect of which was also intended to induce good behavior, could lead to a prisoner's serving the maximum term because parole is effectively imprisonment outside the walls. For example, whereas a defined sentence of ten years kept an inmate in prison for ten years, a sentence of "up to fifteen years" could lead to a shorter term behind bars but a full fifteen years of reports to a parole officer, travel restrictions, and lost civil rights, including a ban on signing contracts and other impediments.

Even worse, prison reformers who created the systems of indeterminate sentencing and parole did not anticipate that the minimum and maximum terms prescribed by law would become an outline whose details would be filled in later by the Parole Board. As in many states, the California Board of Prison Terms and Paroles comprised three citizens named by the governor. A federal study published in 1939 found that nationally most Board members were political appointees with scanty qualifications and no legal training. In Henry's time, the California Board comprised a San Francisco contractor, a Sacramento banker, and a Stockton lawyer and professional Legionnaire.[2] A prisoner's fate was thus entirely in the hands of the administrative branch and its appointees, who might or might not have been qualified. The judicial branch, which was presumed to be thoroughly familiar with the evidence, was completely excluded from the process.

It was also misleading to presume that the Board acted on the recommendations submitted to it, even if they came from the judge or the prosecutor. Board members rarely devoted time to each case and frequently were incapable of responding fairly to a parole petition—if they even read the supporting material. Because parole was usually granted after an instinctive estimate of whether the prisoner could do well in society, white middle-class convicts were favored. Non-whites, recent immigrants, and members of the lower classes tended to be out of luck. Arbitrariness was common; parole was often granted because an inmate seemed like a good fellow. In one documented case, a man got out because a Parole Board member thought he had a nice body. Even the rare Board that did its job well had to take into account public sensitivities, especially in sexual cases. Furthermore, an attempt to apply pressure on the Board through political connections could backfire by triggering the hostility of one or more Board members.[3]

Aware that thorough preparation was critical, Henry, his parents, and his friends began laying the foundation right after he was jailed. Alvin Johnson's brother, a judge, warned that a minimum term was very unlikely and that Henry's friends probably underestimated the challenges. He felt it very important to get the right man, preferably a lawyer, to lead the effort.[4] Duncan Oneal, Henry's first lawyer, was not appropriate. Johnson's brother suggested a former US district attorney in San Francisco, who might have been considered but was not engaged. Another friend considered it imperative to have a lawyer in good standing with the prison administration, with expertise in the political situation of the last few years, personal acquaintance with the members of the Board, and maximum political power regardless of his ability. Olive's final choice was (John) Douglas Short, from San Francisco. He is said to have been recommended by Sidney Robertson, who had excellent connections and may have known that Short's wife had studied with Henry about twenty years before.[5]

What Henry could expect is suggested by a study of sentencing undertaken by Short. A compilation of sentences imposed upon thirty-seven violators of California sexual laws (including rape, incest, and sodomy), 1900–1923, showed that the longest was ten years; most were about six to eight years. A compilation of sentences imposed on and served by 1,147 prisoners in twenty-seven prisons in twenty-one states for sodomy, sex perversion, lewd and lascivious conduct, but not rape or assault with a deadly weapon, showed that California's sentences were the longest of all, averaging approximately eight years four months at Folsom (which held many recidivists) and four years nine months at San Quentin— two to eight times as long as in other states. The sentences meted out and served in California were higher for those sexual offenses than for robbery or assault with a deadly weapon to rob, kill, or rape.[6] Warden Duffy later confirmed the incredible disparity of sentencing nationwide.[7]

Because the Board was sensitive to public opinion, the *Examiner*'s screaming headlines about Henry lengthened the odds. Nothing arouses the emotions like sex crimes, and California had its share of rapes and murders. While Henry's offense was not in that league, one could not count on the Board to discriminate. A letter from Lilly Popper renewed Henry's fear that radical friends might speak up and add anti-communists to his antagonists in the press, oblivious to the risk of exposing the Board to public pressure.[8] Slonimsky understood the danger, however. In sending a packet of translations of articles about Henry from *Sovyetskaya Muzika* he warned Olive to tell no one about them other than Henry.[9]

Even the slight chance of being released or paroled made Henry nervous about survival outside. Not knowing the rules, he suffered from exaggerated fears. A suitable job might influence the Board to take a chance on him, but what job could he get? He thought that teaching could be denied to a parolee on a morals charge. Even if Johnson invited him back to The New School, the job might be forbidden because classes were in the evening and parole regulations could require him to be home early. Performing would also be almost impossible because of restrictions on travel—if anyone engaged a paroled felon for a concert. Composing was not a stable job in the Parole Board's mind. Feeling boxed in, he asked Chávez to see if anything were possible in Mexico.[10] Seeger suggested finding a job collecting folk material, unaware that ex-convicts were ineligible for government work and that parole rules prohibited crossing state lines without permission each time.[11]

Lilly Popper offered him a job at her little school and her hand in marriage.[12] Though profoundly appreciative, Henry emphasized the uselessness of both ideas. The only job of high enough stature to influence the Board would be at The New School, if the authorities did not bar him from teaching.[13] Like Schmolke, Popper did not realize that marriage entails a contract, which Henry could not sign until his sentence was up whether inside or outside on parole. He thought (incorrectly) that the regulations specifically prohibited marriage. At any rate, her communist connections put her and her school off limits. Schmolke's solution was to send money now and provide him with a home and care upon release. Henry was grateful, but the personal and the penal were so entangled that he needed a German-speaking friend to help him explain the American parole system, which was a mystery to Europeans.[14] Schmolke had to be told that he might not be able to go to Germany for fourteen years. Even if they waited, he could not live there permanently; he would have to work steadily in the United States to get by, and he was sure "that there would be no final happiness if she were to come here." He was deeply touched, but stopped writing her because he did not want to encourage her falsely.[15]

Because of Henry's extensive connections, he had to approach the Board very delicately. Short felt, however, that a letter-writing campaign emphasizing his good qualities was appropriate.[16] Olive, who kept abreast of every detail of the case and sent Short endless suggestions about strategy, amassed eighty-eight testimonials from composers including Schoenberg, conductors as well known as

Koussevitzky and Stokowski, dancers including Martha Graham, figures in the arts such as Ansel Adams, professors, businessmen, and even the eccentric grandson of former president Chester Allan Arthur. The lineup was so impressive that Short worried about antagonizing the Board.

Conspicuously but unsurprisingly absent from the list are Ives, Ruggles, and Varèse. Blanche Walton, who was renowned for open-mindedness, told Olive that she could not bring herself to write. She would state that Henry is a genius, but nothing more. If her letter could provoke a negative reaction, Olive should destroy it. Walton concluded that she would have to do the same even if it were her own son. Olive did not send the Board the letter, which sits in the Cowell papers with its stamped envelope.[17]

At the beginning of 1937, Olive solicited the advice of Daniel Sullivan, the assistant district attorney in Redwood City whose boys had played at Henry's house. Although he was not involved in the case, he advised Olive to get the file, in which she finally saw the report of the officer who recommended that Judge McNutt deny Henry probation on the basis of an inaccurate account of the incident at Halcyon.[18] When Olive suggested tracking down information indicating that there had been no prosecution because no one felt a crime had been committed, Henry told her to do nothing until he had asked Wolff or Harry about possible negative effects resulting from the reputation of Halcyon's residents, who were regarded as hopeless eccentrics capable of any sort of loose behavior.[19] Elizabeth Moss, Henry's old friend and sponsor, also warned that any statements by the people of Halcyon could draw reporters at once. "They have been so misunderstood and harassed by evil thinkers—paying their penalty I suppose for *living* a little in advance."[20]

Another matter demanding silence was Elsa Schmolke. Although their affair should have helped establish his prospects for heterosexual adjustment, Henry realized that their cross-country trip could expose him to prosecution under the Mann Act, a federal law directed against white slavery that forbade interstate travel for immoral purposes.[21]

A new channel of support opened when the prison's Jewish chaplain heard about the case from a friend and told Henry he would do anything he could. Statements by the Jewish and Catholic chaplains, the doctor, and some unnamed supporters could make a difference. Even the Christian Science advisor became involved.[22] Henry felt that a review of the case being prepared by Short should go to all interested parties, including the judge, who might be asked for an opinion but had heard nothing about Henry's character at the hearing. He did not suggest sending the review to the Father Divine Peace Mission of Oakland, from whom he received an unsolicited postcard, addressed to Henry Cowell, esq. Distinguished Musician, Stanford University and Mills College, c/o San Quentin. It began, "You are not unique among troubles." Henry was amused that the card gave 20 W. 115th Street, New York, as "the address of 'God Almighty.'"[23]

It is already clear that Sidney, years later, was completely wrong to complain that Douglas Short did nothing. He kept up the momentum, compiling numerous analyses of the case. In February 1937, he perked up on hearing that Governor Merriam had criticized excessive sentences and prison overcrowding, but unfortunately the governor's remarks had not been preserved.[24] Terman gave Short an expert opinion focusing on the dozens of mental tests he had administered, Henry's vast accomplishments, and the unlikelihood of his ever being guilty of "a delinquency."[25] Short also got authorization to quote to the Board a statement from Judge McNutt supporting parole on the condition that Henry would devote himself to his music, stay away from his former environment, and be carefully supervised.[26]

In April the Board notified Henry that he would come up sometime in July and invited letters of recommendation and information about his life. The secretary to the Board had already written to references and former employers whose names Henry had given when he entered the prison. Where the application form asked for his attorney, Henry wrote Short's name, relegating Oneal to a parenthesis. He decided not to make a personal statement. Since it was mandatory to name his employers on the form, he offered Johnson, Terman, Gassner, and James Mundstock, who directed a dance school. He omitted the universities where he had taught, preferring that they not be contacted.[27]

As part of the process of documentation, Henry prepared a list of his creative work behind bars. Meant to substantiate his worthiness for leniency, it demonstrates how much he crowded into his precious free time. In Redwood Jail he wrote the *United Quartet*. In San Quentin he wrote ten pieces, of which the first four, for wind band, had to be left in the prison and were lost. *Vocalise*, for soprano Ethel Luening, flutist Otto Luening, and a pianist, is probably the best known of them. The others, for chamber groups, beginning pianists, and voice with small orchestra, are rarely heard. Four other compositions of these months are not on Henry's list. He completed four literary works—the textbook on melodic construction (eventually entitled *The Nature of Melody*), which actually was not completed for another few months, an article on music in education for the San Quentin educational journal, "Music in America Today" for the Prague magazine *Přítomnost*, and "Music and the Dance" for *Dance Observer*, January 1937. At the time they were preparing for the sentencing determination, he was writing an article on music education for the official musical bulletin of the Uruguayan Ministry of Education.

Henry suddenly heard that the Board was trying to clear its calendar to prepare for vacation. An early summons now seemed possible.[28] Unfortunately, the Board had recently meted out very severe sentences in similar cases, one of them twenty years. The fifteen-year maximum prescribed by Section 288a would be bad enough.[29] Henry's politically savvy friend Pierce Williams cautioned that the worst thing would be if any sexual cases got in the newspapers and put the Board on the defensive.[30] In other words, the matter was beyond anyone's control because the issue was not simply Henry's case.

When Short discovered that the Halcyon incident could not be suppressed because the secretary to the Board had referred to it, he wrote the Board that the incident had been mentioned by the probation officer at the original hearing solely on the authority of a single letter in the district attorney's file from a resident of Oceano [Halcyon]. Its true nature and amicable disposal had never been mentioned.[31] Taking no chances, he explained it to a Board member personally.[32]

June concluded without movement. On July 6—a year after he arrived—just as Henry began full-time work in the Department of Education, the impressive reach of Cowell contacts again became apparent. Collectively, Olive (a political scientist), Sidney (the daughter of a well-connected family and a former teacher at an elite boarding school whose students came from influential families), Pierce Williams, and Douglas Short (as well as possible others left unidentified) seemed to know everyone who was to be known. Someone now brought into the picture a prominent lawyer from Carmel who knew Fred Esola, the Board member from San Francisco. After convoluted maneuvers to call in some political favors, Esola suddenly seemed to be on Henry's side. An article in a San Francisco newspaper also strengthened their hand by arguing for the need to discriminate among offenses and solicit medical opinion about each one. Prisons now had staff psychiatrists, it said, but hard-headed members of the Parole Board often ignored their findings. The fear of public disapproval that haunted the authorities prevented valuable experiments from being tried.

Better ammunition for Henry could not have been invented. Short sent the article to the Board members with a note saying that this was the point he tried to make when they were kind enough to permit him to discuss the case with them. He reminded them that all the psychiatrists concurred that Henry was cured or curable and should be paroled.[33] Unfortunately, clipped to the Cowells' copy of that article is a short item from an unidentified, undated newspaper reporting that the Board of the California Parent-Teachers Association voted to lobby for more drastic penalties against those found guilty of sex crimes.

At this point a fan wrote to Henry, fortunately via Olive, who kept the letter. Next to nothing is known about Helen Hope Page except that she lived in a big house in Oakdale, California, with a dog and cat, had a connection with a Stockton newspaper, and was a friend of Carl Sandburg. Her age is unknown. Page began with lovely declarations of admiration. She only wanted to offer moral support and friendship in a time of trial. "You've made a lasting contribution to the meager pile of fine things humans have built. Those for whom you have composed will always be in your debt and will always have a deep sense of gratitude." The letter would not have merited mention here were it not for her concluding wish that if he were to be paroled in August, he would come to see her. "This may all seem very odd—But it is a gesture of both friendship and understanding. I know you have many friends who are deserving of your time and energy. However you have a host of friends about whom you know nothing. I wish you would count me as one."[34] How she knew about the parole hearing would not be revealed for another year, namely, that as a resident of Oakdale, she was a friend of David Bush, a member of the Board. Henry now had allies with excellent connections to two of the three Board members.[35]

On Wednesday, August 11, Henry learned that he would go before the Board within the next few days. Olive could find out the result by enquiring ten days later. Henry hoped that a secretary could be engaged to address notifications to absolutely everyone, to be paid from his general account. The wording should make clear the doctors' opinion of future possibilities and also something to clarify the case. "People who are unfamiliar with the customary procedure here are going to be violently shocked, and I fear will believe anything and everything."[36]

At 5:00 on Friday the 13th he went to the Board room for a typical hearing:[37] a formal atmosphere, few questions asked, no new information requested, only five minutes expended. Henry's brief answers were mostly met by silence. The Board gave not the slightest hint of its disposition. Afterward he ate and lingered a while in the yard, where he "saw the late afternoon sun for the first time since last summer, which was very pleasant."[38] Then he learned what his influential allies had accomplished. The next day he passed along the news to Olive that his sentence had been set at fifteen years with no parole consideration until half the sentence was served. If he got full credit for "good time"—something which was never guaranteed—half-time would be four years and eight months. "I had been waiting all evening for the notification, and now it is just time to go to bed, so I'll stop; I feel quite comfortable, however, not a bit upset, since I was afraid that something of the sort would happen, as you know, and so was set for it! With love to you both, and endless appreciation of the great efforts you have made to prevent this from happening, Henry."[39]

35

Living with It

He now faced fourteen more years in San Quentin, ineligible for parole until 1944 at the earliest. With time off for good behavior he could apply in 1941. Duncan Oneal, his first lawyer, was shocked by the outcome, but cannot be blamed.[1] Lilly Popper again had to be instructed that public protests were both futile and dangerous.[2] Henry tried to comfort Olive with a prediction that he would be in for another year but "the full pound of flesh will [not] be exacted."

Just after the bad news arrived, the *San Francisco Chronicle* reinforced his argument that public hysteria about sex crimes prevented the authorities from discriminating among offenses. "Women Rap Release of Sex Criminals" reported a drive for mandatory permanent institutionalization of criminals convicted of rape, pitting those wanting to treat sex offenders as criminals against those supporting psychiatric treatment for the least violent offenders.[3] One wonders, however, if the proponents of psychiatric care foresaw the potential for a nonjudicial sentence to life in a mental hospital. The *San Francisco News* urged that sex offenders not be sent to prisons, where they are at great risk of being dragged down even further—precisely the danger that Dr. Mullen had predicted in Henry's original hearing in Redwood City.[4] Such arguments seemed to mean nothing to the larger public, as they still do not. In our time, the registering of released sex criminals requires a delicate balance between community feelings, prospects of recurrence, civil liberties, and the permanent staining of the lives of the accused, many of whom are later exonerated by DNA evidence. Some post-imprisonment rehabilitation programs have become vehicles for long-term or permanent detention of those upon whom society is unwilling to take a chance. Only the details have changed since Henry's day.

Henry thus was trapped by the law's refusal to differentiate among degrees of aberrant behavior. Furthermore, another legal question refused to go away: both participants had broken the law but only Henry was prosecuted. Olive claimed that he accepted a plea bargain to prevent further prosecutions but the authorities broke their agreement, probably fearing the wrath of the press. Now, with the case in the hands of the Board of Prison Terms and Paroles, the police and courts were powerless.

Henry's supportive friends were thoroughly shocked. Of course, homosexuals among them, like Copland, could easily empathize. Lou Harrison said that the "prevailing lack of balanced perception in the great mass was never so wholly apparent to me before."[5] Slonimsky, who was not at all sympathetic to homosexuality[6] and viewed the case through a filter more political than sexual, doubted that Henry could ever get paroled "in a state which keeps Mooney in jail, which is bent on persecution of free thinkers." He was referring to labor activist Thomas Mooney (1882–1942), who had been convicted of murder in connection with bombings in San Francisco and sentenced to death two decades earlier. Widespread outrage and confessions of perjury at the trial caused the death sentence to be commuted to life in prison, but Mooney still was behind bars despite the probability of a seriously defective trial. Slonimsky thought that Massachusetts was no better, but knowledgeable friends thought Henry would have been liable to six months or a year at most in Massachusetts. Slonimsky, like Olive, felt that Henry had mistakenly trusted officials who promised him a lighter sentence if he would confess.[7] Georgia Kober, a Chicagoan closely acquainted with California, declined to dismiss the problem as uniquely Californian. Illinois seemed to her "even more violent regarding [the] parole system, and also the very offense Henry was sentenced for—but, 15 years!! it is heartbreaking to even think of that.... As you know, my dear [Olive], I love Henry very dearly, always have from the day I met him."[8] Alvin Johnson also saw the sentence as part of "the present hysteria," and admired the courage with which Henry was trying to salvage the long years.[9] Judy Brown called his attitude "magnificent."[10]

The case resonated deeply in Grainger. In his characteristic exclusionist language, he placed Henry among the highest class of human, who works toward progress and cannot be judged by the standards of the lower classes. Contemptuous of "normal" humans, who lack purity of motivation, Grainger predicted that people oriented toward progress would have to unite against those of the "lower orders." He feared that his mother's suicide resulted from either the murmurings about their "unnatural" relationship, or her self-torture over Grainger's own sexual peculiarities. (Actually, the chief cause of Rose Grainger's mental illness was syphilis, contracted from Grainger's father.) Grainger said (probably correctly) that he would have been imprisoned many times were he judged by his inferiors. Humanity would sink were it not for the geniuses who were pursued by the common folk.[11]

Henry did not permit himself such extreme moodiness. Nor was he likely to agree with Grainger. Two days after he learned his fate, Olive found him "in remarkable condition.... He had steeled himself for such an outcome and indeed we all had been working on the assumption that this would happen, unless we could exert political influence."[12] Other visitors remarked on his placidity or stoicism, but some worried that he had capitulated to the situation. Henry explained himself simply: he could choose between giving up or making the most of his time. He would plan for long-term creative activities such as writing little pieces of music and working on further books about music theory, now that the melody book was almost finished. To deal with the brevity of work periods, he wanted to develop large-scale compositions built from a lot of very short movements.[13]

His placidity was deceptive. "Words, particularly those which I must choose for dealing with this subject, are regrettably cold and inadequate. I wish I could do better with them." He needed his friends to write as often as possible; letters "help very much in facing a situation which cannot be pretended to be any too pleasant."[14] Henry's letter informing Blanche Walton is especially touching because Olive would not have told him that she declined to support parole. He asked only that people write him rather than send gifts[15] and insisted that his music be played only for its merits, not out of sympathy.[16]

The long sentence stimulated a few people to revise their attitudes. Henry was very surprised by a "splendid and warm" message from Ives, delivered by Ives's friend Clifton Furness. It now seemed that Harmony was hostile but Charles sympathetic. Charles, however, was unable to write directly because of his near-blindness.[17] Since flare-ups were basic to his personality, his original hostility may have been short-lived, but with Harmony sheltering him, it was impossible to know. She certainly had to filter news out of concern for his health. As to Ruggles—one letter, then silence.[18] Assertions that Ruggles briefly broke from Henry, or that he remained loyal and wrote regularly to him, are quite wrong.[19] John Kirkpatrick thought that Ruggles would not react as badly as the Iveses,[20] but Ruggles abandoned Henry more decisively than just about anyone.

Blanche Walton finally grasped the implications of her blanket condemnation of sexual offenders.[21] After seeing Henry behind bars and absorbing the reality of what he faced, she gave him outright some securities that she had lent him with the understanding that he would use the interest and return the bonds to her estate at her death. Henry was extremely grateful because he anticipated a huge struggle to earn a living after release. He told Olive that the sooner this grim reality was faced, the better.[22]

Reopening the case was impossible. The only options were petitioning for early parole or attempting to get him transferred to a hospital. The latter was extremely dangerous, since he could end up there longer than in prison. There was talk of people with "friends" who might move on Henry's behalf. They discussed a proposed statistical study of sex offenders in San Quentin, similar to one that had led to the segregation of such prisoners in New York State.[23] (Warden Duffy implemented segregation with great success, but by then Henry was gone.) Henry discouraged hiring experts because of the expense.[24] Olive proposed putting pressure on Governor Merriam, but Henry doubted that he could dare to do anything because of public opinion.[25]

Daily reality was the mindless routine of prison life. His new job made little difference to his practicing—which was limited to Sundays from 7:35 to 7:55 A.M., if weather permitted—and he resigned himself to never playing again, knowing that even in the best case, as a public performer he would have to cope with the stigma of San Quentin. Then, after a good practice session on Labor Day, 1937, showed that his playing was just a little rusty, he felt more cheerful.[26] Although creative work was exasperatingly slow, he was determined to press forward and asked friends for stimuli in the form of requests for music. He didn't care if his pieces seemed unworthy. The main thing was not to get stale.[27]

There is no reason to believe that the simplified music Henry wrote after San Quentin was caused by discouragement in prison. Many factors, including the communist days, had convinced him that simplicity with depth was preferable to complexity. San Quentin, however, forced him to rethink his methods. He had always composed in his mind but relied upon a piano to try novel ideas. Without that, new pianistic techniques were out of the question. Because he habitually confirmed his ideas by playing through pieces at the piano, he lost confidence that what he wrote would work properly.[28] Furthermore, time limitations forced him to compose in short units. Simplicity had many merits, but in such a situation simplicity could lead to triviality. Returning to an earlier exchange, he told Copland, "I think we are in entire agreement as to trends toward simplicity, but a simplicity in which all of our best training and ability is preserved. That's the real rub. It's a matter requiring the greatest technique and ability to do this. I find best for me the idea of attaining simplicity by unifying seemingly complex elements, and using them so that they seem simple, rather than cutting out all complex elements altogether; but there are many ways of attaining the result."[29] Endlessly curious to hear his new works to see if he had imagined them correctly, he also craved sincere criticism but was not sure whose opinion to seek.[30]

Despite the limitations, Henry tried to stay involved with the professional world. In October 1937, he sent an a cappella chorus to Columbia Records' competition—the first time he ever entered a competition.[31] Reports of performances cheered him. When Alfred Wallenstein showed continuing interest in his compositions, Henry offered to write one-minute pieces for full orchestra, to be used for filling time in Wallenstein's semi-weekly nationwide broadcasts.[32] He was heartened to learn that more string quartets were taking up his music, more conductors were requesting his scores, and Martha Graham revived one of their dance pieces.[33]

The biggest supplier of moral and professional support and feedback was Grainger, who decided that Henry was the perfect composer to help him upgrade the repertory for symphonic wind ensemble. Henry eagerly accepted Grainger's requests for new pieces, telling him to make any changes necessary. To complement a new Reel he composed a lament (Keen), for which he used the Gaelic spelling *Caoine*. After an exasperating struggle it was completed in October 1937. He told Grainger that the arrangement was very Gaelic in style, simple, with original melodies and plain chords. "If you think it is worth trying to do something with, go ahead, since you were so good as to offer to act as agent for it. If you don't think it worth while, don't bother, nor feel obligated in any way."[34] (In the summer of 1938 he added a hornpipe and called the three pieces *Celtic Set*. This time he was able to export the music, and Schirmer published it in 1941.)

At the beginning of 1938, Grainger finally could plan a visit to San Quentin.[35] Because he was coming from the East Coast he was granted a visit of more than one hour, which was good because they had a lot to discuss, including Grainger's projects in world music and electrical instruments. The most important subject, however, was Grainger's suggestion that Henry, if granted parole, could work as his secretary and live with him and his wife in their house at White Plains, just north of New York City. A job and a home with a person of great renown might be decisive in another bid for parole.[36]

Dealing with Grainger was never easy, however. Sidney, who knew him slightly through the folk-music field, corresponded with him for a year before he finally arrived on March 31, 1938.[37] It was a most peculiar experience. He insisted on traveling by slow trains and wrote postcards as soon as he alighted. Henry got her to drive Grainger to the prison, neither of them knowing that he was so phobic about cars that the very idea of riding with an unknown driver terrified him. At first Grainger thought it was not so bad to be in jail; Henry would have time to compose. Sidney set him straight.[38]

Shortly before receiving Grainger, Henry got a new, mild-mannered cell mate, but a few days later he was gone. The temporary peace was salutary; Henry had not been alone for a minute in nearly two years.[39] In addition to teaching and trying to practice and compose, he was still studying Japanese and practicing shakuhachi with Tamada's guidance. In his cell he now had a phonograph, which he could play during "music hour," when all inmates were allowed to practice or listen to music. The musical isolation was terrible: he knew about broadcasts of his compositions, but prisoners were not allowed radios.

Working in the Education Department kept some of his talents sharp.[40] Although endless grading of papers was tedious, he became convinced that there was "great and important" work to be done in preparing the men to be good citizens. At first his energies were splintered among giving his own courses, grading English papers, helping design a course in economics, and writing a course in the fundamentals of music. Paul Farnsworth, the Stanford psychologist, sent some music texts, which Henry tried to get adopted by the Education Department. Obtaining clearance for the slightest change in any aspect of life was, however, very difficult.

Teaching brought special challenges. The classes had to be purely theoretical because the lack of soundproofing precluded playing instruments in the classroom. Smaller instruments could be used in the cells and on the weekend in specified prison yards where the inmates could apply what they were learning. There was no class singing or other group singing. Henry hoped to organize whatever constructive musical activities would be permitted. His students were inmates whose work left them some time to come to classes. At first he had some 200 men in classes limited to 40 per group; by the first session of 1938 the total had grown to some 300, mostly Mexican. The crowds were unwieldy, however; he later tried to reduce enrollment to about 200. Other inmates, who could not attend classes because of their work assignment or because they were confined to their cells, studied "by correspondence." Those numbers gradually doubled from about 75 to about 150 per term. (A term lasted about four months.) Knowing nothing about Mexican music other than the works of Chávez, Henry was startled by the Mexicans' musicality. Many of them wanted to compose, and they produced melodies, which Henry harmonized and laboriously taught them to sing. After a few months he was made director of the department's music offering. Later he was invited to extend his activities to the prison hospital.[41]

He decided that access to recorded music would be beneficial to everyone including himself. First, however, he needed more needles for his little windup machine, which was not suitable for public performance. Then a shipment of records from Harry—Bach, *Tristan*, Palestrina—was rejected as contraband. When the Education Department finally got a phonograph in early 1938, Henry and his boss Dr. Shuder organized monthly concerts of recorded music. Maintaining the concerts was a real job, however, because of shifting rules about importing records. Under changes instituted around the time Henry got the phonograph, previously permissible objects became contraband even if sent directly from shops. Books, musical instruments, socks, phonograph needles, typewriters, and typewriter ribbons were all affected. There was no explanation of the ban on foreign recordings, or why only Victor, Columbia, and Brunswick records were acceptable. A violin sent to Henry by a friend was already on its way, unfortunately. He had to wait weeks until permission to receive it was granted.[42] That violin was for Henry's personal use; he had decided to add it to his studies of shakuhachi, flute, Spanish, and Japanese. While he was not the great virtuoso that Harry had always hoped for, he wrote tiny trios for strings, which he and two other prisoners enjoyed playing for about twenty minutes on

Sunday mornings. He also played the piano in chamber music with a cellist and singer.[43] He was happy to be busy all the time, but life was made more complicated in April, when a new schedule required inmates to be in bed from 9 P.M. to 7:30 A.M., leaving one hour less for his own work.

At the beginning of 1938 he had also started a daily one-hour class in musicianship for members of the band, which he used to iron out performance details and strengthen his own knowledge of band instruments. As a consequence, he received a band card and technically became a member. The class then developed into an extra rehearsal that he conducted. When the band leader, violinist John Hendricks, told him that they played like different men under Henry's baton, he felt really pleased, although it was sometimes hard to detect the improvement. Soon he was named concertmaster.[44] Being respected by Hendricks was in every way a good thing. A murderer in for life, he was a member of the prison elite and, according to Henry (as told to Sidney), he was actually a good man and protected Henry against sexual assault.[45] Henry began working harder on the flute in April 1938, temporarily suspending shakuhachi and violin. For months he described his playing as very bad, but it gradually improved enough that he could sit in on band rehearsals under Hendricks. Many of the musicians were very dull-witted, he said, and none were really talented, but he felt he gained a better feeling for the reality of music's place in society by having actual contact with a cross-section of people who were interested in it without being gifted. He also discovered some excellent Arkansas country fiddlers playing in a distinctive style related to Irish and Scotch tunes.[46] The human side of life there, he told Copland, was overpowering.[47] It is fair to say that Henry was no longer just putting on a good face; he had become deeply immersed in the prison's culture.

He soon began rehearsing the band in more difficult music, beginning with the last movement of Tchaikovsky's fourth symphony.[48] By the summer, Hendricks, having seen what Henry got the players to accomplish, raised his sights and ordered the score of *Also sprach Zarathustra* with the idea that Henry would make a band arrangement of it. "Should I recover from the effect of this, I shall deserve a medal!"[49] (Presumably copyright infringement was not an issue in San Quentin.) Even before the score arrived, the band was rehearsing the prelude to Act II of *Lohengrin*, *Pictures at an Exhibition*, and the overture to *The Flying Dutchman*.[50] That summer Henry got permission to play with the band, wear its bright blue and red uniform, and join the Sunday performances outside the walls. (His flute playing, he said, was not bad in the slow parts.) It was a great pleasure to be able to see Treasure Island and the Bay Bridge, which, like the Golden Gate, had opened since Henry was imprisoned.[51]

His impact upon the band's repertory is visible in programs from before and after he began improving the repertory. A typical pre-Henry concert:

KELER-BELA: *Rakoczy* Overture

WARREN: "Popular: 'You're an Education'"

March

Intermission

The Serenaders, presenting songs of yesterday and today. Jack Healey,
    tenor; Art Crowe, accordion; Al Ellis, guitar.

March

WALLACE: Selection from *Maritana*

GORDON: "Sweet as a Song'"

ROBIN: "Thanks for the Memory'"

March

THEME SONG: "Time On My Hands" [Vincent Youmans]

A program for which Henry was guest conductor included similar lightweight pieces but also the overture to *Don Giovanni* and four pieces by Henry himself. Still, with all the sophisticated additions, the inmates needed music commensurate with their backgrounds. In July 1938, for example, the band gave a program of Stephen Foster's music combined with a lecture on his work. Henry liked "the old tunes," but some of them seemed commonplace, like "de-natured versions of things that colored folks did much better."[52]

As the end of the second year approached, Henry's supporters continued to press for his parole. In a discouraging conversation, Shuder informed Dr. Wolff that the Parole Board operated under a mandatory resolution, approved by the US attorney general, to keep sex offenders behind bars for their entire time. Shuder felt that the only way to get Henry out was to ask David Bush, the chairman of the Parole Board, to reopen the case, and that approaching Governor Merriam was still useless. Dr. Wolff decided to get three national psychiatric authorities to examine Henry during the forthcoming national meeting of the American Psychiatric Association in San Francisco; Helen Hope Page would ask Board member Bush if he would reopen the case should the authorities report favorably.[53] Henry and his lawyer Douglas Short decided to argue that medical advice was not correctly reported to the Board at the 1937 sentencing hearing. In preparation, Short petitioned to obtain confidential reports that had been presented to the Board at that time.[54]

Meanwhile, Grainger, having become nervous about why Henry ended up in prison, asked Helen Hope Page to confirm what Henry told him. He seems to have wondered if the original article in the *Examiner* might have been accurate. She assured him that there was a single offense, magnified out of proportion because of Henry's prominence. Page, who was trying to maximize momentum by unifying all the efforts on his behalf, added that Grainger's letters awed Bush.[55] Grainger relaxed.

The Psychiatric Association's convention gave Dr. Wolff the opportunity to approach one of the leading prison reformers, Dr. Adolf Meyer, the head of psychiatrics at Johns Hopkins Hospital in Baltimore.[56] Meyer's pledge to help added real weight to Henry's side. In mid-June 1938, Wolff brought to San Quentin Meyer's young associate, Dr. Joseph Wortis, a thirty-two-year-old researcher working with Meyer and Havelock Ellis on the problems of homosexuality. They were cordially received by the prison authorities, interviewed Henry, discussed the case with Dr. Schmidt, the prison psychiatrist, and Wortis, and reported to Meyer that the Board had been erroneously informed "that Cowell was a socially dangerous homosexual, and . . . had previously been involved in a similar offense." He enclosed three expert opinions (from Drs. Mullen, Terman, and Wolff) that the second point had been grossly misrepresented. Wortis's report would form the basis of Meyer's expert opinion.[57]

Then Terman was devastated when Bush told him that he could only reconsider the case if it were definitely recommended by the prison's medical department. Nevertheless, Terman pressed forward, hoping to familiarize Drs. Stanley and Schmidt with the case, and Meyer agreed to write a statement to serve as the basis of the appeal to the Board. Henry, who only a week earlier had doubted the power of psychiatric testimony, now felt encouraged that Bush had expressed some small will to reconsider.[58]

Regrettably, Henry's first instinct was correct. All of that last maneuvering was a waste of time because David Bush had deceived Terman. The Board had already denied Henry's request for reconsideration at its meeting of June 17–18. Short was not informed until nearly a week later.[59] Henry said nothing when he wrote Olive and Harry on July 7. He either had not been notified or chose not to ruin their holiday in Europe.

36

Living with It (Continued)

The challenge of the new rules is graphically illustrated by Henry's letters, which faded almost into invisibility until he finally was allowed a new typewriter ribbon. Incoming letters were plentiful: when the writing quota was suspended for Christmas 1938, Henry requested 175 cheap Christmas cards because nearly 300 people had written to him—many of them repeatedly—although fortunately not all of them needed replies. Christmas cards were only an exception to the rules, however. Writing on plain paper would classify the communication as a normal letter subject to the quota.[1]

Visitors are only known from references in letters because Henry had to surrender his personal list on departure. Regulars included Harry and Olive, Kitaro Tamada, Ernst Wolff, and Alfred Frankenstein. Lou Harrison said that he had some composition lessons when he visited. Sidney Robertson sweetly told Henry not to waste a precious letter on her since she would return to the prison on schedule.[2] In a warm, if still slightly formal letter of August 1938, Henry thanked her for coming so faithfully. "The visits have been very stimulating for me; no one else who comes here . . . has the same interests."[3] In March 1939 he celebrated St. Patrick's Day by writing her after enjoying "a royal dinner of corned beef and cabbage, the annual Irish treat!"[4] Other visitors of note included Evelyn Wells; choreographers Martha Graham and Hanya Holm; conductors Henry Swoboda one of the Goldman Band directors (probably Richard Franko); composers Carlos Chávez, Lou Harrison, Douglas Moore, William Grant Still and his wife Verna Arvey, and even Varèse, who was gentlemanly despite his utter lack of sympathy for Henry's plight. (Milton Babbitt said that when he and Varèse happened to pass the Cowells' Greenwich Village apartment, Varèse called Henry "that fucking pederast—but what do you expect from a country that would elect Roosevelt?")[5] A band concert brought many friends. On August 29, 1939, Bonnie Bird, the choreographer and former Graham star, was his 200th visitor.[6] He knew that the flow of visitors was in part a byproduct of the migration of artists to Los Angeles, but his pleasure was tempered by the fear that even if he were paroled, he would never be allowed to go there.[7]

Many friends and colleagues—including Schoenberg—pitched in to keep his "outer" life going. Blanche Walton copied some of the scores that he was able to export; Johanna Magdalena Beyer, acting as his manager, sought a publisher for the melody book.[8] Richard Franko Goldman persistently encouraged him to compose for band. Graham and the other choreographers stayed in touch. It was obvious, however, that he did not have universal sympathy; Ruggles was not the only "friend" to write once and no more.

As conditions worsened in Europe, Henry worried increasingly about his friends there. Harry's and Olive's letters from their extensive 1938 trip were stimulating, but their brief comments about witnessing the German annexation of Austria and its effects on their Jewish friends made Henry's own problems look minor.[9] When Szigeti wrote that he and Bartók would tour America again in the 1939–40 season, Henry sensed that they might never return to Hungary.[10] The Nazi invasion of Poland upset him so much that he could not work properly.[11]

In the fall of 1938 he formed a chamber ensemble that began with two violins, viola, and flute and grew to flute, clarinet, four violins, viola, and bass. He wrote a piece for them every week, and the group also attracted his better composition students. One ensemble member, Raul Pereira, was the first professional musician to enter after Henry. He had studied with Joachim in Berlin around the beginning of the century and was "full of old tradition, yet not too much worried over modern music." Since they hoped to play concerts together, Henry asked his friends and Olive to send some standard repertory. As usual, there was no hurry; Pereira would be around for a while. Sidney thought he was the murderer who protected Henry, but he was in for writing bad checks.[12] The actual protector must have been the other violinist, band conductor Hendricks.

That season—1938–39—was full of music. For Armistice Day (November 11), commemorating the end of the Great War, Henry was asked to create a program devoted to the history of military music. Although he had no idea where to find repertory, he was determined to do it.[13] Two days after Thanksgiving he was master of ceremonies for the musical portion of a program celebrating Leif Erikson, although the only Norse composer was Grieg.[14] The student composition concert took place in late December, with an audience of nearly 500.[15] Sometime that winter he and Pereira gave what Henry thought was the first program ever in San Quentin that was entirely made of good music— Beethoven's F-major Sonata, Handel's in A major, and a Bach Suite. All earlier programs had interspersed some classical music among the popular, but prisoners who enjoyed classical music wanted uncompromising programs.[16] Henry and Pereira decided to give a similar concert in March, with the Bach a-minor

Violin Concerto, a solo violin Sonata, and a Loure, followed by some small works including a new piece by Henry. By then he was leading daily band rehearsals of the *Egmont* and *Don Giovanni* overtures, and excerpts from Wagner. He also was having fun writing for his instrumental ensemble, which had swollen to a small orchestra of six violins, viola, cello, bass, flute, some clarinets, horn, trumpet, and tuba. The prisoners' passion for music continued to astonish him.

In June 1939, probably with an eye to a parole hearing, Henry compiled statistics on his first two years of teaching. In addition to 1,547 students who had registered for classwork, he had another 343 elementary correspondence students, and 59 University Extension students studying harmony by correspondence, for a total of 1,949 registrations. He already had had another 150 students before joining the Education Department. By the end of 1939 the total had risen to about 2,500 (some of whom may have repeated courses or taken more than one).[17] His load now consisted of classes of elementary music, intermediate music, harmony, composition, musicianship, history of music, and chamber music ensembles, for a total of twenty-two class hours. In addition, he spent three hours per week supervising other teachers and seven and one-half hours rehearsing with the band as a flutist, attended a teachers' training class and a special teachers' meeting, each one hour weekly, and a Japanese class four days per week.[18]

The smaller classes included thirty-nine students of harmony and nineteen of composition—mostly "rank beginners."[19] He wrote an intermediate harmony course to fit in with the elementary and advanced courses that the correspondence division of the Education Department already used.[20] In March 1939, after nearly two years' teaching in the Education Department, he received a state certificate authorizing him to present classes in elementary and advanced music, valid in the San Quentin Department of Education. His previous teaching probably violated some requirement for certification, not that it mattered much under the circumstances.[21]

Little repertory projects continued. In the spring of 1939 he arranged Chopin's A-major Nocturne for the prison band and wrote a minuet for the chamber ensemble. The orchestra pieces had to be almost conventional—though slightly less conventional than the band pieces. He was now rehearsing an excerpt from *Rheingold*.[22] At the end of April he conducted the entire band rehearsal including the *William Tell* Overture and Weber's *Euryanthe* Overture. He was also writing a hornpipe for his little orchestra, using the experience to improve his symphonic works.[23] The group, for which he was writing weekly, now consisted of seven violins, viola, cello, flute (Henry himself), two clarinets, horn, trumpet, and bass tuba. One clarinetist could also play saxophone. It was a fluid formation: the former double-bass player had been released and the violist was expected to leave soon. Henry was practicing saxophone three days a week and planned to start learning a brass instrument. His shakuhachi playing continued to improve, but he had almost nothing good to say about himself as a flutist.[24]

Prisoners have been known to say that they like to sleep because it helps their "time" go by. Henry, on the other hand, used any free time for new projects. In the summer of 1939, he began writing short pieces for each instrument represented in his ensembles.[25] He took up the clarinet, "not that I shall ever play it well, but one writes so much better for an instrument that one knows a little personally."[26] Now he was arranging Bach chorales for a brass choir that he rehearsed three times a week.[27] One August day he dashed off a Haydnesque trio for flute, oboe, and clarinet in fifteen minutes, including copying parts. Then a horn player came along, so he added a part for him.[28] As a result of his labors, when Warden Court Smith called together all the bandsmen to praise their work, he singled out Henry, who was surprised that Smith could pick him out of a crowd. Surely, he thought, this would act in his favor in the event of another parole hearing.[29]

In September 1939, he was once again alone in his cell. It should have helped his composing, but under a new schedule the lights went out so soon after lockup that Henry feared his output would lessen.[30] Although he still worried that the search for simplicity could lead to the commonplace, he planned to copy his newest pieces and send them to Goldman, hoping he might at least rehearse them.[31] He took modest pride in the volume of what he had accomplished and liked *Celtic Set* when he finally heard it on the radio. Otherwise he thought much of his work was mediocre. His morale rose in October when he conducted rehearsals of his own band pieces. By then he had also become librarian of the band's rather good collection of scores and parts.[32]

In fact, prison life had facilitated his return to the endless activity that characterized his life outside, but since he did not have to waste a second earning a living, most of his activity was creative. He continued to take an interest in *New Music* and the recordings, but apart from offering occasional advice, does not seem to have played much of a role. Unable to receive the recordings, he asked Luening to have them sent to Shuder. They would become the prison's property, but Henry could use them, and was eager to hear the one with his own music. When the records finally arrived he was impressed by the musical and technical level, and very moved to hear for the first time his own oboe and piano piece *Three Ostinati with Chorales*, which he had composed at the end of his Year I in San Quentin.[33]

After December 1939, general news disappears from Henry's letters to the family. The next parole application dominated everything. There is no reason to suppose that his daily life changed otherwise.

|| 37 ||

The Melody Book and Other Ideas

Henry's search for simplicity with meaning also found a voice in two major theoretical writings of the San Quentin years. Just as *New Musical Resources* provided underpinnings for his early radical compositions and food for future thought, *The Nature of Melody* provides a context for Henry's later music and teaching. Had it been published, it might have become as much an icon of postmodernism as *New Musical Resources* is for ultra-modernism. Yet apart from Nancy Yunhwa Rao's studies of the book's relations to Henry's interest in world music,[1] almost nothing has been written about its many other interesting aspects.

Henry began writing it primarily to keep his mind honed behind bars. While some useful books or scores may have been available through the prison library, fragmented working time made extended research impossible. It is therefore reasonable to assume that he worked almost entirely with memories of his experiences and studies. Finished in 1937, after only a year of work, *The Nature of Melody* is an impressive accomplishment, especially for someone employed full-time in a prison jute mill.[2]

He soon imagined it as a textbook and doubtless hoped it would eventually add to his income. When Warden Smith granted permission to export it, Johanna Beyer set out to find a publisher. Carl Fischer was interested but doubted that a market existed. Beyer then proposed a pre-subscription and Grainger offered to donate to its publication costs. Ives, who in earlier times enabled many publications, could not be approached. Henry suggested obtaining advance orders from schools, starting with allies like Walter Piston (at Harvard), Richard Donovan (Yale), and Rudolf Ganz (Chicago Musical College).[3] Despite Beyer's persistence, trying to sell such a book would have been challenging even in a healthy economy. Henry eventually gave up on it. Its three copies sit in the Cowell archive.

The subject of pure melody had been on his mind at least since he learned how other cultures made music without polyphony. Gradually he concluded that Western music needed to relearn the art of thinking in melody, as opposed to thinking in harmony. The idea of writing a textbook on the subject and a projected study of rhythm (which he drafted but never completed) also resulted from his disillusionment with music education, which had neglected both skills. Before San Quentin he had begun teaching rhythm and melody at several schools. In the 1933 article "Towards Neo-Primitivism," he envisioned music built on a non-harmonic basis, in which melody and rhythm would dominate.

The Nature of Melody was conceived for anyone who could read notes and recognize intervals, and organized as a textbook for schools and conservatories, to be complemented by *The Well Tempered Clavier* Book I. He envisioned a complete refashioning of music theory, which he must have applied in his San Quentin classes. The study of harmony was too long and over-technical for the student who did not intend to be a professional, he felt, and too archaic for the professional. Henry saw no good solution without radical changes, because teaching fully about harmony deprived melody and rhythm of sufficient time. When melody-writing was taught, it tended to be too rigid and limited by the poor training of teachers. Harmony-teaching itself was unsatisfactory, primarily because it was a remnant of the days "when the aim was not to know facts about harmony"— that is, its relationship to the overtone series—"but to know the conventions of 'good taste' as recommended by famous and skilled musicians." Furthermore, he perceived that educators ignored the fact that rhythm and melody are much more fundamental elements of music than harmony, which was developed "by slow degrees through the combining of melodies. The sounds which they formed when combined gradually became identified as chords to those familiar with them; still later the idea of trying to form an art of combining the chords one after the other into a system of formal harmony was developed." Harmony, therefore, had to be seen as a product of melody and melodic combinations, not their generator. The student "was expected to combine melodies when he did not know how to construct a melody in the first place." Henry advised applying the concept of gestalt psychology to the study of creative music.

Although the rules of harmony were said to be systematic, he considered them rules of taste, some of them retained from ancient times for forgotten reasons, such as the ban on consecutive fifths, which, he wrote, occur always and naturally as the second and third overtones. The concept of discord was also outmoded. Books on modern harmony contented themselves with pointing out some new chords, doing little more than naming them. He concluded that the only real reason for the study of harmony is to show how it was studied in the past.

A chapter called "The Value of Knowledge" effectively recounts Henry's evolution toward composing more systematically. For the great composers of the past, what counted was the exactness of handling materials so every note had a place in the scheme of things. Composers of the highest order knew such relationships so well that they did not have to think them out. The same skill, he wrote, is required no matter what the style, and training must begin with melody-writing. The then-current method of teaching it began with the prejudice, inherited from the Romantic age, that a melody was "received" by inspiration and was not a product of study. Henry's own survey of instruction methods led him to conclude that no satisfactory approach to melody-writing existed. He suggested defining melody broadly as "any organized succession of sounds." Instead of giving rules, he proposed surveying the most familiar ways of making melodies, asking students to develop them, analyzing melodies in old masters, and only then suggesting free creative work. He would avoid value judgments and favor no school of composition, hoping to lead the student to discover what is impractical or produces "very unrelated results."

In "Some General Melodic Considerations," he tied together many phases of his own self-education. Pondering how melody evolved as a means of expression relating to speech, he drew upon his work in Berlin listening to music of primitive peoples. His friendship with Terman, Farnsworth, and other academic psychologists enabled him to refer to psychological studies showing that "when a listener is really following a melody, his vocal cords flex and unflex in such a way that if he used them he would be singing the melody." That suggested why a melody filled with great leaps could cause the listener to lose the thread, "being unable to follow it with the vocal cords." Becoming at least temporarily confused, the listener would probably reject the melody as displeasing or uninteresting. Janáček's process of notating the rise and fall of speech in situations of emotional stress and using such speech-melodies in his operas struck Henry as a truly creative application of the physical-psychological realities.

He also was intrigued by the apparent role in melodic formation played by the neume, a medieval notational convention according to which several melody notes were written as one character. (Either he found some source in the prison library or had an impressive memory of the names and details of different types of neumes.) Although neumes are normally the stuff of courses on medieval notation, Henry saw them as melodic units, successions of tones that are naturally sung in one breath. "A neume, therefore, is to a group of horizontal, or successive tones what harmony is to a group of vertical or simultaneous tones: Namely, the organization into a unit." While that construct had disappeared in favor of melody as a succession of individual tones, a little "psychological self-experimentation" showed the ease of hearing groups of tones. The meaning of the term "motive" may more or less equal that of neume, he added. Lou Harrison credited Henry's idea of the neume (which Harrison called the "melodicle") as opening him up to new worlds of musical thought.[4]

Much of the remainder of *The Nature of Melody* comprises detailed instructions and exercises aiming to free melodic composition from old baggage of culture and taste, so that it could be studied with the detachment that leads to true compositional control. Melody would be like language, but without being tied to specific culturally imposed meanings and preferences. Our preferences, Henry proposed, are one of the most interesting branches of psychology, but the subject was still not well enough understood to permit making many statements about it. It was certain that the hearing, mental, and nervous systems "form a physiological-psychical compound which is 'conditioned' by its experience." The nature of that experience forms the basis of likes and dislikes. As a result, he concluded, we shall always tend to reject something entirely new.

The Nature of Melody, a storehouse of provocative ideas about music, the history of music, and music education, deserves to be available. It is a pity that Henry never completed the book on rhythm, about which he surely had a lot to say. The timing of events suggests that it fell victim to Henry's responsibilities in San Quentin's classrooms, his desire to write music for both sides of the walls, and his absorption with getting paroled.

In addition to *The Nature of Melody*, Henry completed nine published articles and at least a few others for the Education Department's journal.[5] By far the most intriguing one is "Relating Music and Concert Dance,"[6] published by Louis Horst, in which he returned to the perplexing question of uniting music and choreography. A visit from a good friend and colleague, the German choreographer/dancer Tina Flade, catalyzed this exploration of ideas that led to a new concept of the composer and the composition.

After a brief account of the intertwining of dance and music since the earliest days and its decline after being banned from Christian liturgy, Henry reached his starting point. He observed that modern ideas, including dance without music, dance to percussion only, and attempts to write music at the same time the dance is "invented," helped turn dance away from its frivolous mode of technical display, in which motions represented beats in the music. Reversing the tradition, some choreographers were creating dances for which music was composed afterward. These valid and promising directions still did very little toward assuring the dual development of music and choreography. In dance with percussion, the danger was "an inexpert attempt to revive a primitive ceremonial, usually with a bit of sophisticated tinsel thrown in." In general, the extremes of rigid form and formlessness remained serious obstacles to the simultaneous gestation of dance and music.

His proposed solution lay in a novel kind of music in which the performers engage in the process of creation, transcending the traditional options found in *basso continuo*, cadenzas, and melodic ornamentation. He had taken a first step in that direction with the 1913 *Sonate Progressive*, which allowed for reshaping and expanding movements, and the *Mosaic* Quartet (1935), in which the string players decide upon the order of movements. He doubtless also knew about the use of stock melodies that could be recombined in many ways by musicians playing for silent films, and saw precedents in the improvisatory forms of some non-European musical cultures. *Random Round* (ca. 1912–15), Percy Grainger's experiment with controlled group improvisation that attempted to combine the communal improvisation of South Sea Islanders with Western art music, was a possible cure for the stagnation of Western music.

Henry named his idea "Elastic Form," calling its relationship to older concepts of form the same as the relationship between ancient and modern conceptions of the universe. The ancients considered the stars' positions as fixed, whereas we now regard galaxies, stars, and all other bodies as in motion and in relation to one another. Form would be fluid and could be given many embodiments by the choreographer and, by extension, the players. Elastic Form entailed creating a group of melodic phrases, each of which could be expanded or contracted by lengthening or shortening certain key tones. He recommended that the composer supply all the different versions. Each of those "sentences" should be constructed so that it could function as a self-contained block usable before or after any other "sentence," or repeated, either identically or varied, if expansion of a part of the dance was desired. His study of English grammar and structure had led him to the idea that "each section should be so constructed that it may be used in the same way as suggested for sentences; that is, as well as being capable of being long or short, owing to how many repeats are employed in the sentences, it must be able to be repeated or not repeated, owing to the circumstances." Sentences and sections had to be arranged so that they could be shuffled and not always appear the same order. "If not all orders are practical, the composer may indicate which ones may be used." He also incorporated flexibility of orchestration. The length of the work and its instrumentation could thus be as variable as desired. It would be easily adaptable to the "changes and freedoms so essential to the dancer's creation." Elastic Form therefore amounted to a complete revolution in the Western ideas of a "composition" and a composer.

Louis Horst, who published the article, would have brought it to Martha Graham's attention just as she was thinking about creating a piece relating to the Spanish Civil War. When they visited Henry on April 9, 1937, she asked him to write her a sarabande, a stately dance of Spanish origin. According to Sidney— who was already seeing Henry regularly—Graham moved around the visitors' room showing him what she wanted while he took notes and the guards and other visitors watched with astonishment.[7] Henry needed to know if sarabandes observed regular sixteen-bar phrases but, having no access to them, asked Olive to find Louis Horst's article on the subject.[8] Since he could not see Graham's choreography as it developed, Elastic Form was the perfect tool. He used it to compose a sarabande for oboe, clarinet, and percussion. The first section was eight measures long, the second, twelve measures, but various means of dovetailing them ensured that either section could be as long or as short as Graham needed. To do it, he devised numerous junction points in the phrases, conceived so that an acceptable melody would always result. Graham was happy, and requested another movement, which Henry called "Canto Hondo." She either used both or just the Sarabande for the dance "Immediate Tragedy," which she premiered at Bennington College on July 30, 1937.[9] Norman Lloyd, who participated in shaping the music, said the process took about an hour, and the total effect was complete unity—"as though dancer and composer had been in the closest communication."[10] José Limón described the premiere as a tremendous event, with the entire audience roaring, "clapping, stamping, whistling, and yelling. I remember being too benumbed by emotion to applaud." He could never understand why Graham never danced it in future years.[11] The newer movement, "Canto Hondo," was used for Graham's dance "Deep Song," premiered in New York on December 19 of that year. In fact, the music was lost for decades until "Canto Hondo" was discovered behind a desk in the Graham offices in 2003. The Sarabande was never found.[12] Most regrettably, Henry's imprisonment prevented him from propagating Elastic Form. The concept became "open form" in the postwar years, but Henry's role was forgotten.

Henry's articles, books, and compositions of the San Quentin period reveal his intense desire to restore to music-making qualities of usefulness, simplicity, practicality, melodiousness, and just plain fun. To be fully renewed, music had to be an active experience. His work teaching children and prisoners, and experiences like that confrontation during the San Francisco dock strike, taught him that a revival was possible. His challenge as a composer was to infuse this simplicity with substance, integrity, and perfection of materials. Rather than dampening Henry's creativity, San Quentin seemed to be providing him with new incentives for innovating and new outlets for his musicality.

38

Toward the Exit

Another attempt at parole began immediately after the 1938 rejection. Douglas Short felt they absolutely needed to win over Dr. Stanley, the prison doctor, who had some ideas that were unconventional, to say the least. Although he had serious doubts about medical treatment of criminality, he did not hesitate to subject prisoners to experimentation. Believing that the anti-social behavior of disfigured men originated in their ugliness, he taught himself plastic surgery to aid them. Extremely interested in glandular malfunctions, he experimented with testicle implants for sexual deviants. He believed in using sterilization, which was legal in California, to halt the transmission of criminality. Convinced that certain people had to be kept out of society, he urged sending them to asylums when their terms expired. He had dictatorial tendencies, blamed the New Deal for society's problems, and was contemptuous of "alienists, women's clubs, and the usual gallery of the overly sentimental."[1]

Bringing Dr. Stanley around would not be easy. He had advised a Board member that Henry was "a bad bet for parole, all these cases are alike, they only get worse," thereby disregarding the opinions of psychiatric and psychological specialists, who unanimously supported parole. San Quentin's psychiatrist Dr. Schmidt, who seems like a completely different sort of person, hoped that Dr. Stanley might accept a favorable statement from someone as renowned as Johns Hopkins' Dr. Meyer, but he could not predict how Stanley would react to Meyer's emphasis on treatment instead of punishment.

To prepare the way, Short sent Meyer all the documents and results of his own research, explaining that no evidence had been taken at the original hearing because Henry refused to defend himself, and that Henry probably could not have been convicted if he had stood up for his rights, especially as he was not accused of seduction.[2] Henry observed the maneuvers closely, fearing that like Alfred Adler, Meyer might conclude that he was homosexual. Meyer's agreement to cooperate brought great relief.[3]

Helen Hope Page, one of the most clear-sighted members of Henry's team, thought that Board member Bush's attitude made the psychiatric approach useless. In a long letter to Wolff, she explained that David Bush had already deceived Terman and was convinced Henry was a confirmed menace to society. If, however, the November gubernatorial election brought in a Democrat, the Board would be reconstituted and Bush would be gone. Page had even talked briefly with the Democratic candidate, Culbert Olson, who said he would immediately remove Bush and would favor parole and release. Furthermore, even if Governor Merriam were reelected, Bush might be removed, as Merriam had debts to repay and Bush could no longer deliver votes.

The enormous range of Page's contacts makes the mystery of her identity even more exasperating. She had asked Martha Graham to speak with Mrs. Henry Morgenthau, an intimate friend of Mrs. Roosevelt, and request presidential intervention. She also asked an unnamed musician to whom Henry referred her—almost certainly Edwin Hughes—to try to see the president or play for him and get his support. She recruited the influential Catholic priest of San Quentin and got the unequivocal support of Dr. Edward Twitchell, a professor of neuropsychiatry at the University of California Medical School. His official story would be that he had developed an interest in Henry's situation. Personal connections (i.e., Mrs. Page) were not to be invoked. Page related all this to Wolff with an admonition to keep silent and destroy her letter, which could damage her if word got back to Oakdale and Bush heard about it. Wolff should bring all her news to Henry personally; she could not put it in a letter, which would be read by censors. She has not seen Henry in a long time; her letter implies serious health problems.[4] Fortunately, Wolff disobeyed and bequeathed to posterity this crucial chapter of the story.

Page's strategy worked. Dr. Twitchell must have convinced Dr. Stanley that Henry no longer should be considered a menace to society, and that he—Stanley—could look favorably up on parole. Apparently Page and Wolff also had discussed looking beyond parole to a pardon. Wolff, however, warned her that any pardon through a newly elected governor or through President Roosevelt should be deferred until after June 1939, when the three-year statute of limitations expired, lest officials in Redwood County interfere or generate harmful publicity.[5]

Dr. Wortis's "expert opinion without remuneration" restated that no minors were involved in the charge, there was no aggressive behavior—and no attempt to apprehend the other participant. He refrained from confiding his belief that homosexuality was part of a wide spectrum of sexual possibilities and not subject to "treatment"—an unusual attitude certainly not shared by members of the Parole Board.[6] After recapitulating the argument about the Halcyon incident and the false reports in the press, Wortis alluded to another, unspecified element that called for investigation, by which he may have meant the intimations of blackmail with intent to obtain Henry's car, which surfaced around this time.

Dr. Stanley was now on Henry's side but it was unclear whether he accepted Meyer's opinion that such cases needed to be individualized. If so, Wortis felt Stanley would recommend clemency and medical supervision after release, precisely the step that Judge McNutt could not legally take. The Parole Board's dangerous ability to act on its own thus could also produce remedies not provided by the law.[7] By that time Drs. Stanley and Meyer had established a good professional dialogue. Stanley conferred at length with Henry and sent Meyer documents including a study of sexuality in prisoners.[8] Meyer, in response, emphasized that Henry had suffered a very severe punishment, especially in comparison to the youngster who had turned him in. He requested Stanley to forward his opinion to the relevant authorities and to advise him if he was overlooking any points of California law.

Meyer's statement summarizes advanced attitudes toward homosexuality in the late 1930s, although his description of homosexuality was a little less modern than Wortis's. In short, one could not choose to be homosexual, nor could one alter it any more than one's complexion. As long as active homosexuals caused no harm, they could be referred to properly trained agencies for help. Meyer agreed that Henry was not "a confirmed and exclusive homosexual, but one with homosexual preponderance, partly through frustration of his heterosexual leanings and intentions and partly through the temptation of persisting prevalence of homosexual promiscuity." He too was bothered by the fact that none of the other men had been questioned.[9] Yet those of Henry's supporters who believed that consensual sex among adults of the same gender was not a psychological malfunction could not have said so publicly. And we must bear in mind that the original charge was not homosexuality.

Despite those favorable developments, the chances of parole were nil unless Henry lined up a job. After Grainger's 1938 proposal that Henry become his secretary, the subject went dormant, probably because the Graingers expected to spend a long time in Australia. Reading Grainger's account of a voyage to Samoa made Henry think of enlisting Alvin Johnson's aid to find sponsorship for recording folk music abroad. Grainger's story of his trip to Bogotá also got Henry to consider being paroled to South America, a rather unlikely possibility.[10]

Only one of Grainger's replies to Henry—from Melbourne, in October 1938—is preserved; he must have sent it to Olive. He began with an offer to help Henry to get a "'Guggenheimer" Fellowship; the "Guggenheimers" had a Norwegian secretary, and Norwegians, he said, are sensible. Of course, Henry would have to learn Samoan. Much more significantly, Grainger—who must have assumed that he and his wife would soon return from Australia—repeated his offer that Henry first live with them in their White Plains, New York, house, where he had many Samoan and other Polynesian bibles, dictionaries, and collections of folklore. The two could study Polynesian languages together and Henry could notate Grainger's Rarotongan and Maori recordings. He could live rent free and receive a small salary for acting as Grainger's secretary, with flexible responsibilities, including organizing his messy library, notating folk music, and other tasks that might arise. Grainger had a lot of jobs that would be really helpful, if Henry agreed only to accept tasks that he really liked. He waxed near-ecstatic about the life they all would share. Even if Henry wished to marry, it would not disrupt the plan; their house was big enough for all.[11] He volunteered to write David Bush, if it would not seem "unduly interfering."

Henry was deeply moved. Here was the first sign that he could survive outside of prison. Grainger was the only person to offer to help him, apart from Schmolke, Popper, and Beyer, whose marriage proposals did not fulfill the requirement of a job with a salary. Grainger's stimulating and feasible plan addressed all his concerns and might get a positive reaction since Henry's whereabouts, company, and responsibilities would be known to the authorities. He was sure that he would enjoy the work but insisted that Percy be completely frank, should the arrangement end up unsatisfying to him. Once Henry had a good parole record it would be easier to find an acceptable alternative. He was full of excitement about what could be learned if he could get to Polynesia, but he told Grainger not to waste his time writing David Bush.

After learning that Wolff also liked Grainger's offer, Henry put them in touch.[12] By the time they met, in late January 1939, a crucial milestone had been passed: the inauguration of Culbert Olson, the Democrat who defeated Governor Merriam in the November election. In a 1979 memoir, Carey McWilliams, a state official under Olson and later, as editor of The Nation, one of the country's most important and outspoken radical journalists, described Olson as a good man, whose first act was to pardon Tom Mooney, the labor activist who had served twenty years for a crime he did not commit.[13] Another of Olson's earliest acts was to revamp the Board of Prison Terms and Paroles under a new chairman, John Gee Clark, a Los Angeles lawyer, the state's director of penology, a fine person, and Olson's right-hand man.[14] Clark was immediately flooded with complaints about the penal system and got Governor Olson to act. Clinton Duffy's appointment to replace Court Smith as Warden of San Quentin in July 1940 had long-lasting positive consequences.[15]

Translating Olson's liberalism into a parole for Henry was another matter. Further consideration of his case remained postponed until March 1941, when he would have served nearly five years, and the secretary to the Parole Board saw no reason to expect any change in status.[16] He, however, was a civil servant, a holdover from the Merriam-era Board. Dr. Twitchell thought that the secretary still adhered to a rigid policy against parole adopted by the Parole Board during

Governor Merriam's term, although that policy was intended to curb a plague of offenses against underage girls.[17] (Duffy wrote about a man committed to San Quentin for lewd and lascivious behavior after patting a little girl on the leg while seated next to her at a soda fountain.)[18] Dr. Twitchell told Dr. Stanley that keeping Henry imprisoned would neither aid his reform nor improve public security. The world should not lose "this rare genius," and the work awaiting him in New York was the best possible therapy.[19] By then, Stanley's thinking had changed so completely that he urged Twitchell to write Warden Smith, who would present his letter to the Board. Stanley was also impressed by a visit from Grainger.[20] In this promising atmosphere, Henry cautioned Olive not to rock the boat with any personal initiatives.[21]

On his forty-second birthday, March 11, 1939, Henry received a splendid greeting that showed Shuder, the director of the Education Department, could be counted on. "There are no words adequate to express my appreciation of your fine service to me and to the men. If I thought that you were made up a little bit more of the spirit of the missionary, I would suggest that your participation here was in keeping with a high purpose as I am sure that it is assisting a noble cause. Let me thank you once again most sincerely for your many contributions, for your refinement of spirit, and for the fine example which you are."[22] How Henry managed to take that note with him is a mystery. It seems doubtful that Shuder would have mailed it to him in care of Olive.

Then Henry's letters imply that the process had ground to a halt. Hardly a word is said other than a comment in May 1939 that he thought the case might come up in the fall.[23] He had good reason to hope so, and even better reasons to keep silent. Behind the scenes, activity was intense. Olive had spoken with Carey McWilliams, who happened to be a friend, proving that her network was the equal of anyone's. McWilliams's aggressive pursuit of the rights of agricultural laborers had brought him into a very close relationship with the new governor, who appointed him director of the Division of Immigration and Housing to give him an official base for that battle. A tireless combatant for justice, McWilliams immediately saw that Henry "had foolishly pleaded guilty to a morals charge which should never have been filed."[24] He brought in his friends John Gee Clark, the new Parole Board chairman, and State Senator Robert Kenny, another liberal who, as state attorney general in the 1940s would aggressively defend the rights of interned Japanese Americans. All three of them were so powerful that their names had to be kept out of public view, lest the press get wind of it and stir up trouble. In addition, at the June meeting of the American Psychiatric Association, material provided by Wolff led to statements asking legislators and Parole Board members to consider the best psychiatric opinions in cases like Henry's.[25] Now that the old guard was out of power, there was a chance that their call might be heard. In early July 1939, Henry urged Short to apply immediately for a rehearing lest they miss the deadline.[26]

The Board approved a request for reconsideration, placing Henry's name on the November 1939 Regular Parole Calendar. In a guarded comment to his parents, Henry wrote, "I am wondering now whether this favorable action was a result of the new or the old order of things? I have had no sign of the new yet. I wonder if you would not be good enough to tell Dr. W[ortis] and D[ouglas].S[short]. about this, and give them my thanks for all that they have done on my behalf." There was plenty of time to discuss the details, he said, but there was no new supporting material. The question of soliciting statements from Halcyon remained open.[27] It was even conceivable that he could be out in time for Christmas, but he could not leave the prison until Grainger had been investigated.[28] If the inquiry uncovered Grainger's peculiar heterosexual practices, such as flagellation, their plan would be dead.

The parole application was a factory for paperwork. New information had to be gathered. Grainger had to file a guarantee to employ Henry at $42 [2010: $659] per month plus board and lodging.[29] A psychiatric advisor had to be engaged. Although a Manhattan-based doctor would be cumbersome because of restrictions on travel for parolees—White Plains, where the Graingers lived, is a separate city, a northern suburb—Meyer favored Wortis, now a psychiatric research associate at Bellevue Hospital in Manhattan.[30] Wortis assented, and his fellowship for sex research meant that remuneration was a minor consideration.[31] In preparation, Henry asked Olive to collect the addresses of his friends, as he would be forbidden to bring out his address book.[32]

By the time the hearing came up in the second week of November, everyone was convinced of its success. Seeking to protect the Board from backlash if they voted to parole, Short had Grainger write the Board that he anticipated transferring his work to Australia and would bring Henry along.[33] On November 16, Henry appeared before a two-man Board. This time, instead of being rejected, his application was not acted upon. "No action" was good, however. Although his next official appearance before the Board would take place in March 1941, he could initiate another attempt at reconsideration earlier, since this attempt had not been "rejected." Unsurprised, Henry suggested that "McW" [McWilliams] talk it over with "C" [John Gee Clark] at the nearest opportunity.[34] They immediately started pressing for reconsideration.[35] More letter writing was organized, and the psychiatrists resumed their campaign to convince the authorities that Henry was no risk, despite the futility of earlier psychiatric support.

At Olive's request Henry prepared an updated report on his activities. Reading it makes one wonder if the Parole Board wanted to keep him in prison to preserve the excellence of the music program. In addition to having taught more than 2,700 students to date, he had established systems for the loan of music, books on music, and musical instruments to deserving students. Impressive enrollments suggest that his classes were decisive in giving San Quentin the nation's highest percentage of inmates participating in education courses.[36] In his capacity as official band arranger he had completed about fifteen large arrangements for full band as well as individual parts as needed. For the past two years he had conducted five band rehearsals a week. As band librarian, he issued and collected music, and supervised a group of copyists and band men who were studying arranging and assisted him in creating arrangements. In addition to his official work, he listed one completed book, fourteen articles, and about sixty compositions ranging from large symphonic pieces to small chamber works and single movements for symphonic band. Some pieces now had publishers and a few had been performed on the outside.

Henry's case was put on the April 1940 docket and again deferred. Olive, who did not have to worry about prying eyes, dared to write Grainger that the chairman of the Board, John Gee Clark, was "absolutely favorable"—something that she had kept secret for months—and now counted on getting another Board member to vote with him.[37]

A letter to Sidney in early April best summarizes Henry's state of mind. He was surprised but grateful that only one newspaper review mentioned that a piece was written in prison. He was not worried about it, however: his relationships with people would change, but he felt he could cope with the mention of San Quentin. He did not intend to start public work immediately but hoped that in the future it would not be entirely curbed. He agreed with her that later is better; it was time to stay as quiet as possible. Above all, he needed a rest, after which he would re-enter society gradually."I think that no one knows better than I that nothing can be taken for granted, and that the whole matter is one which may or may not bring any results."[38]

The November failure had taken its toll on Olive, however. When Henry saw her in April she was visibly suffering from severe stress.[39] A couple of days later she told Short that she was dropping all connection with the work being done for Henry.[40] She appreciated Wolff's keeping her informed, but "the fact is, I have put the entire case entirely *out of my mind*, and simply *never* give it a thought. I not only can not do anything, I do not even want to *hear* or *read* anything about the case."[41] That outburst could be ignored. A lot of correspondence had to be channeled through her.

With the hearing imminent, Wolff urged Meyer to ask the members of the Board to go beyond parole and commute—shorten—Henry's sentence so that he could enter a normal personal life with the possibility of marriage.[42] Terman, who had credibility because of his 1918 study of San Quentin prisoners' mental state,[43] was granted forty-five minutes with the Board, in which he focused on Grainger's offer of the perfect job, rather than on psychology. He also reminded the Board that California's sentences were now far heavier than was previously customary even in California, and two to three times as heavy as the maximum permitted in a majority of states. The four years that Henry had served equaled six years with one third off for good behavior. The demands of justice therefore had been met.[44] He did not, however, leave the argument at that. In a separate statement Terman stated that in tests of sexuality given before the offense was committed, Henry ranked well within the normal range for men and was unlike the 140 known homosexuals whom he had tested. He was slightly more effeminate than the average man, but no more so than the average artist or musician.[45] Terman's meeting rekindled Olive's enthusiasm. She imagined him as a character in an old painting "where the learned doctor makes a plea for justice before some mob in the middle ages!"[46]

Among the forty people who wrote to the Board was Ives, whose credibility stemmed from his success in the insurance industry. He affirmed Henry's honesty, reliability, and capacity for work. Henry had been sufficiently punished.[47]

For a short time it seemed that the people of Halcyon would also raise their voices, but in the end only the librarian dared. Her covering letter said that Henry's supporters were still afraid to speak.[48] Grainger, meanwhile, talked with the deputy director of the Probation Department of Westchester County and found him very cooperative. His earlier proposal to take Henry to Australia was now in question because of the likelihood of war in the Far East.[49] (Considering the restrictions on travel by parolees, a proposal that Henry leave the country might have had a negative effect on the Board.)

A few days before the hearing, Shuder pointed out a serious flaw in the tactics. The sheer mass of data and statements risked provoking the Board to refuse to review the case. Warden Smith, having become another sympathizer, suggested compiling a summary, which Sidney asked Douglas Short to do. Short's reply that he didn't have time and would assign it to secretarial help shocked Sidney because the material was confidential. She and Wolff worked for a few hours that evening and made a summary; Wolff continued all night. Sidney claimed that the incident confirmed Henry's opinion that they had been paying Short $50 [2010: $777] a month to do nothing. Later she learned that Short had not only worked very hard for him but had been trying to persuade the legislature to modify the law on sex cases.[50] She should have known that legal staff often work with confidential statements.

McWilliams also induced his friend Senator Kenny to write an extremely supportive letter, which doubtless was fed to him by McWilliams himself.[51] Kenny, however, was too late. On May 6, the Board voted for the parole. The terms show that the end of Henry's prison ordeal, like his release from the army, would take time. Parole took effect on June 8, but the sentence, with credit for good behavior, would not expire until December 8, 1945. In other words, he had not gotten a reduction in his sentence, but a credit for a third of the total. He would be serving his sentence outside the walls for another five and one-half years.

Ten Commandments would govern his life outside:

1. Change place of employment or residence, or leave the county of employment or residence, only with permission.
2. Civil rights are still suspended. Do not enter into any contract, engage in business, or marry without written consent of Board of Prison Terms and Paroles. Do not drive or operate a car, truck, motorcycle or airplane, without written permission of parole officer.
3. Do not carry a weapon. It is a felony.
4. Do not think about money or other property in the custody of the Warden, or jointly controlled by the parolee and the Warden. It will remain in the Warden's custody until discharge from parole unless the Warden and the State Parole Officer rule otherwise.
5. Do not associate, correspond or make contact with any present or former inmate of the penal institutions of California, and be in the company of any ex-convict from any state without permission.
6. Do not enter any public place where liquor is sold or given away for the purpose of indulging in its use. Do not engage in public speaking without permission.
7. Break the rules on pain of returning to prison.
8. Report to the parole officer on the first day of every month.
9. (The standard requirement that the parolee support his minor children and dependents was moot.)
10. Do not forget that the instructions of the State Parole Officer are law.[52]

Most of Henry's fears turned out to be unfounded. Chairman John Gee Clark assured Johanna Beyer, who was effectively Henry's manager, that the Parole Board would not prevent him from teaching, lecturing on music, or performing. Permission to drive would be granted unless there were a good reason to the contrary. Permission to marry and to leave his district could also be granted. (Beyer still hoped he would marry her.) Board Chairman Clark doubted that any parole restrictions would greatly affect his work and knew that the Board would cooperate to ensure his rehabilitation.[53]

Congratulatory letters and telegrams poured in. McWilliams told Olive that when they applied for commutation of the sentence he would happily speak to the governor.[54] Quite appropriately, if coincidentally, Henry had just put on an Easter concert with a new piece that depicted the Resurrection.[55] The opening of the gates still awaited the investigation of Grainger and authorization of his proposed job, however.

Nothing would be simple, starting with Henry's travel arrangements. The Parole Board would decide his route, buy his ticket, and make sure that he went that way. It was not even certain that they would send him by train.[56] Sidney claimed that the parole specified that he was to live outside of California,[57] but such a restriction does not appear on the parole document and seems a little unlikely, since supervision became more complex if a parolee were in another state. She may have been thinking of the arrangement with Grainger that sealed the agreement. There was, in any event, every reason for Henry to leave California, where newspapers remained a threat. Indeed, Grainger immediately learned what he had potentially gotten himself into. On May 8, only two days after the Board meeting, the White Plains *Evening Dispatch* ran a brief article stating that a freed convict would be working for a local musician. (Its claim that his term had been cut from fifteen to three and one-half years was as wrong as the idea that he had been "freed.") Although he was not named, Grainger was upset. Henry apologized profusely, promising to keep his route secret.[58] Detecting Grainger's nervousness, he agreed that press interviews should be avoided. If cornered, he should make a statement that only appears to say something. "The main thing is to make the statement say absolutely nothing!" He liked Grainger's idea of keeping his presence unknown for a day or two, when the news value would have worn off, and did not believe there would be any press interest once the actual move was over. Henry promised that he would not let his presence interfere with the Graingers' lives. Whatever the White Plains parole officer said could be believed; he doubted that there would be any special instructions from the California Parole Board. The most likely requirement would be regular sessions with Dr. Wortis, whom Henry knew only from one meeting at San Quentin. Should Grainger hear of any special requests that seemed to pose problems, he recommended contacting Douglas Short, who would discuss the matter with the parole officer in San Francisco.[59]

In early June the investigation of Grainger's job offer still had not been completed. To speed it along, Shuder spontaneously recommended Henry to the Eastern Parole Officer. Transportation arrangements kept changing. Only a week or so before he was scheduled to be released Henry still did not know whether he would be sent by train or bus, or, if by train, via the northern route to Grand Central Terminal or the more southerly route to Weehawken, New Jersey, and then by ferry to New York.[60]

The days leading up to the end were filled with music. On June 2 he and Pereira gave a violin and piano recital dedicated to Shuder, with music by Brahms, Gossec, Grieg, Kreisler, Mozart, Schumann, and Cowell.[61] On June 9, the day after he should have been let out, Henry conducted the band in two complete concerts, which Harry, Olive, Ray Green, and Lou Harrison attended. Henry was delighted by how well the prisoners played the greatly simplified music.[62] The next day he thanked Sidney for bringing his friends out for the concerts. "I shall miss our visits! They have been a very enriching experience to me, and I thank you for them, as well as for all the many things you have done for me, and are doing."[63] He continued to wait through the end of June. At least the end was definite, if not quite in sight.

Henry's exit brought Carey McWilliams almost as much pleasure and relief as it did the Cowells.

It took months of patient negotiation—the Hearst press had a vested interest in his conviction—and the aid of John Gee Clark, director of the Department of Penology, and State Senator Robert W. Kenny, both friends of mine, to bring about Cowell's release on parole. Incredible as it sounds today, he had served three and a half years [actually four] of a fifteen-year sentence before we were able to secure his release. Nothing in my term of service gave me greater pleasure or more lasting satisfaction. In a letter dated July 7, 1940, Cowell wrote to say that his release was "due in much part to your most appreciated efforts on my behalf"; years later I received his personal thanks in New York.[64]

PART FIVE

LIFE RESUMES

39

The First Six Months

Henry left San Quentin at the end of June. He was not allowed to make a detour to visit Becker in Minnesota en route but managed to meet Georgia Kober while changing trains in Chicago.[1] On one train he ran into Arthur Berger, who noticed that he could not go to the bar car.[2] To Henry's relief, no reporters showed up when he arrived in New York.[3] The Graingers gave him a beautiful room and advised him to relax until he felt up to working. A month later a White Plains reporter found him, but instead of making life awkward for the Graingers, he wrote an innocuous feature with no mention of San Quentin. When a *New York Times* reporter tried to bring up the subject, Henry persuaded him to let it rest.[4]

Not even his letters to Dr. Wortis reveal how Henry felt to be out of prison after four years. Wolff's assessment that he always hid his problems behind a positive façade seemed validated when, almost immediately after release, he suffered a gastrointestinal upset, without being conscious of its probable emotional cause.[5] Wortis, however, decided to concentrate on rehabilitation rather than dwell on personal problems.[6] In fact, since he believed that homosexuality and bisexuality were natural states rather than disorders, "treatment" of Henry was irrelevant, and he never attempted it with Henry.[7]

Henry may not have missed much about San Quentin, but his absence was felt immediately. Shuder, the director of education, said he would always remember him "as one of the happiest men that it has been my good fortune to meet," and told a friend that life at San Quentin seemed dull without him.[8] Yet although a small, warm world could develop within San Quentin's forbidding perimeter, contact with inmates or released prisoners was forbidden to parolees.

Henry knew that he had been released from custody but was not free. Failure to comply with regulations or to file a monthly report could lead to unpleasantness for all. He could travel without clearance only within Westchester County; New York City was off limits except on business, and then only with a permit that required listing every destination. Since he had no idea how many permits he would be granted, he had to be judicious about reunions with friends. The

resulting sense of isolation was magnified because the Graingers had no telephone. He was relieved that his parole officer, William Edelstein, was based in
downtown Manhattan and unlikely to snoop around. Fortunately, Edelstein
turned out to be eager for Henry to resume his professional life.[9] More than half
a century later, Wortis still remembered Edelstein as extremely nice and helpful,
trapped to some extent in the regulations he had to follow.[10] Like all conscientious parole officers, Edelstein also knew that misjudgment of a parolee could
have disastrous consequences.

Offers of kindness, help, and advice were legion. Clarence wanted to help him
financially despite his own straits; Judy Brown continued her monthly gifts; Sidney Robertson, still in California, reported regularly about his friends and kept
her eye on the press.[11] Ruggles, Ives, Varèse, and Salzedo were not heard from.[12]

The parole restrictions did not discriminate between financial and moral
violations. Forbidden to sign contracts, engage in any business of his own, solicit funds without special permission, or have an official role in any organization that disbursed money, Henry could not resume leadership of the New
Music Society. Strang was doing a good job with the Society itself, but Henry
bowed to Slonimsky's urgings and took back the leadership of the periodical and
recordings. He decided not to dismantle the committee system and reduce the
decision-making power of the two editorial boards, but stipulated that he would
do nothing other than make editorial decisions with the board. In fact, he was
forbidden to do otherwise. Business matters were handed over to the American
Music Center, which had opened the previous year.[13] Nevertheless, he was soon
struggling with *New Music Quarterly*'s huge problems. Because investment losses
forced Ives to halve his support, streamlining operations was urgent. Perceiving
the formidable logistical problems of getting a nationwide board to approve manuscripts, Henry proposed that he reject utterly unsuitable compositions without
circulating them. Eager to give the composers a little income, he suggested emphasizing single sales and sharing receipts annually among the composers. He
wanted to expand the base by placing South Americans on the advisory board,
enlisting young composers as endorsers, and establishing promotional committees in many cities to ensure that retailers stocked the music and that local colleges, conservatories, and libraries subscribed. He deliberately diluted his own
power to prepare to hand everything over to a younger generation.[14]

While he began to withdraw from *New Music Quarterly*, his participatory
instinct soon had him in the thick of activities with the League of Composers,
including writing for *Modern Music* until just before its demise in 1946. The Pan
American Association of Composers seemed to be beyond salvaging, however.
Its account still held a few hundred dollars, but Julius Mattfeld, the treasurer, had
no idea what could be done with it because Salzedo was very opposed to doing
anything and Varèse was silent. Henry told Becker, "Doesn't it beat anything! It

lies idle for years, but activity is opposed!" When Varèse promised to talk it over with Salzedo, Riegger and Mattfeld, Henry concluded that he had "plans for that dough" and gave up. The PAAC was never heard from again. Becker suggested starting a new Latin American organization, but the murder of García Caturla on November 12 cost Henry a crucial Cuban ally.[15]

In mid-August Henry finally wrote Ives. Harmony's reply does not seem unfriendly but contained much bad news. Ives had been unwell for a year and was in "a low state." To reduce the heart attacks, the doctor insisted that he be peaceful. He could no longer participate in planning New Music's publications and recordings but would continue his support at the current level. She conveyed his good wishes to Henry and the Graingers, and gratitude for the Graingers' kindness.[16] Whatever she really felt, her husband's diabetes, heart problems, cataracts, and fragile nerves gave her good reasons for concern. At the same time, she was who she was—an old-fashioned New England gentlewoman who would not have approved of homosexual relations no matter how mild.[17]

To establish a mature social life, Henry had to meet women, which, in turn, required surmounting multiple obstacles—parole restrictions that kept him from social events in New York, the expense of the train, and Grainger's expanding list of projects.[18] Not that he had to hunt for women; Lilly Popper offered sex therapy to cure his "problem," assuring him of her extreme flexibility in choosing sexual partners.[19] Olive, who thought Beyer's passion was pathetic, had already tried to make her see the light and worried that Henry actually might love her.[20] He, meanwhile, recognized Beyer's devotion and occasionally took her to performances to avoid crushing her completely. This approach both encouraged and frustrated her. Later that summer, mired in poverty and unrecognized by the New York avant-gardists, she began to suffer from a thus-far undiagnosed illness that gradually affected her mind.

Henry rejoiced upon reconnecting with Henrietta, who had returned from France and lived in solitude and poverty across the Hudson in Fort Lee, New Jersey, because she refused to use her substantial assets, which, he told Harry and Olive, included "an incredible piece of property [in the Bronx] . . . it is as wild as nature . . . wild woods. It might be in the middle of the wildest part of Borneo, not a trace of signs of man . . ." She was as chaotic as her real estate, complaining but refusing any help. When travel restrictions relaxed he visited her weekly at her home.[21]

Olive made herself Henry's tireless social advisor and cheerleader. If he would get new clothes, women would chase him around. "(I remember that one even landed in your house in Menlo—she may have paid her fare across the country for all I know to get to you). At least you will have some fun; and fun is an Irishman's middle name. You are at least half Irish, which makes you at least half as good as your father when it comes to the fair sex, and that is something."[22] At the end of August he accompanied the Graingers to his first post-partum party, wearing a new suit provided by Olive.[23] A month later, universal admiration of that suit still had not translated into unmarried women. Olive counseled patience and persistence. Every young woman who had heard him play or met him in any way had a crush on him. "No telling how many have died of a broken heart because they did not meet you!!" He had to take the initiative.[24]

Grainger, Henry's most important musical advocate, arranged his first public appearance, six weeks after release, at the summer session of the Ernest Williams School of Music, near Woodstock, New York, where Henry played his piano pieces and conducted the premiere of Part I of *Ancient Desert Drone* and two movements from *Celtic Set*, and Grainger performed some of his own music.[25] Henry then got his publishers' authorization to arrange for piano and orchestra "Tides," "Harp of Life," "Reel," and "Exaltation," which he would perform with Grainger conducting. Grainger committed himself to playing Henry's piano pieces on every recital in the coming season and induced him to arrange *Celtic Set* for piano solo and for two pianos.[26] They appeared jointly again in September for a crowd of 1,200 in Port Chester, New York,[27] and in December at a concert by the opera star Marjorie Lawrence, a benefit for Bundles for Britain, at which both of them played guitar in Grainger's arrangement of a Danish folk song. Henry said it was the first time he ever held a guitar in his hands, and that he did "phenomenally badly" with the three chords he had learned.[28]

Grainger's performances of Henry's piano music got off to a rocky start in October. For the stringpiano piece "Aeolian Harp" he had invented some kind of pedal scheme that he soon abandoned.[29] When he attempted another performance in Racine, Wisconsin, he suddenly discovered that it cannot be played on Baldwin pianos, even if transposed, because of the layout of the frame.[30] Grainger delightedly reported to Henry that a crowd of Detroit schoolchildren liked "Aeolian Harp" and "Lilt of the Reel" better than his own "Country Gardens" arrangement. He then decided to promote Henry's pieces to local teachers, confident that they would sell as well as "Turkey in the Straw." He admitted to playing them very badly but believed that one learned a piece best by performing it publicly.[31] Sidney emphasized that Grainger was not feigning modesty. He played Henry's music for many years, requesting coachings whenever possible, but really did not understand them and just banged away at the tone clusters.[32]

Grainger's desire for a new Cowell piece led to "Mice Lament," for voice and stringpiano, written late in 1940 for his wife Ella to perform with him. They were delighted by the "scratching, nibbling sounds of the finger-mandolining, & the small, frail sounds of the finger-tapping."[33] Yet for all Grainger's wonderful effects on Henry's morale, their living arrangement had to be kept as brief as possible. The job was hard on Grainger's wallet and the menial tasks—including cataloguing his library and sending out scores to interested parties—drained

Henry's energy. Although the longevity of government jobs could not be trusted, Seeger looked for something better for Henry in Washington. Dr. Wortis was enthusiastic and Edelstein, the parole officer, authorized a visit to the capital to investigate federally supported folklore research. The trip, at the end of 1940, was not encouraging, however. Harold Spivacke, chief of the music division of the Library of Congress, told Seeger that he was sympathetic but unwilling to jeopardize his own position by hiring a paroled felon and would not even meet Henry. It was, nevertheless, a nice vacation, allowing Henry to see the Lomaxes and Seegers and Sidney Robertson, who had returned from California and cheerfully drove him around. Afterward, she sent a long, good-humored letter about his habit of dressing in rumpled, unmatching, tattered, western-style clothing.[34]

Washington held out one glimmer of hope, thanks to Seeger's resignation as head of the WPA folk-music project in favor of a job at the Pan American Union. If Sidney were approved to replace him, she would request a temporary appointment for Henry as her assistant. That would not be for months, however, and in the end she did not get the job. Seeger's new job seemed durable, but for the moment he was allowed only one assistant, who had to be Latin American. Until he could rewrite the project to add a post, he could only pay Henry as an occasional consultant. Although far from ideal, any short-term job would keep Henry on the scene in case rising international tension led to more work. For example, a project was being planned that would counteract successful Nazi propaganda by showing foreign groups that their cultures were respected in the United States. Its probable director was undisturbed by Henry's history.[35] The catch was that all those jobs entailed travel, that is, innumerable parole clearances for at least five more years. Furthermore, hiring a paroled felon was risky business for any Washington official, especially if Henry's radical past became known.

Because everything underlined his need to get paid for composing, Henry quickly resumed the frustrating chore of soliciting performances. At least he now had a reasonable portfolio of orchestral music that could produce substantial royalties if he could tempt major conductors to perform some of it. Slonimsky had faith in Henry's ability to write in an understandable idiom,[36] probably not imagining that Henry's "understandable idiom" might undermine his status among his old admirers.

A few conductors were unafraid of Henry's past. The band conductor Richard Franko Goldman helped Henry develop a relationship with G. Schirmer.[37] Fabien Sevitzky, conductor of the Indianapolis Symphony, got him a commission for an orchestral overture to open the new auditorium at Purdue University; its main theme became the university's alma mater. Sevitzky then got him another commission for an overture for Indiana State University.[38] Leopold

Stokowski, however, was truly a hero. After abruptly altering a program to fit a piece by Henry into an approaching concert at Lewisohn Stadium, New York's famous summer venue,[39] he engaged him as soloist for the planned South American tour of his All-American Youth Orchestra, taking a gigantic risk that a reporter might combine the phrases "Youth Orchestra" and "sex offender."[40] Miraculously, neither Stokowski's invitation nor Grainger's collaborations with Henry awakened the press, which might have perked up at the potential benefits of combining rumors of Grainger's strange sexual practices with Henry's troubles. Henry's story was looking refreshingly stale. He did not take part in that tour, however; obtaining permission to leave the country so soon would have been impossible.

A month after getting out of prison he had heard from his old manager, William Gassner. Although he would have understood the limitations to Henry's prospects as a traveling performer, he was extremely optimistic about his chances of making a living in radio, theater, and film. Having encountered interest in Henry's work at Columbia Broadcasting and the Labor Stage Theater (a project of the International Ladies' Garment Workers' Union), Gassner consulted with Parole Officer Edelstein, who had no personal objection to Henry's working with the Labor Stage but had to consult his superiors.[41] Gassner also put Henry in touch with conductor Leonard de Paur, who became an advocate for his choral music.[42]

Henry's original fame, based on his solo piano music, no longer brought him advantages because he rarely played publicly. In any event, under any management he would have had to wait at least one season for engagements to materialize. In September he could not contain his frustration. "It is highly unfortunate that I now, in the years when I should be at the height of my earning powers, should be so nearly down and out financially." Illness could have brought disaster. Dentistry alone cost him more than half a month's salary from Grainger. Wortis did not charge him for counseling; a German Jewish refugee doctor offered him free medical attention and gave him vitamins to compensate for deficiencies accumulated in prison. Henry economized on everything to build a reserve for professional investments, such as paying to record broadcasts of his music or continuing to employ Beyer as a personal assistant. At the end of the summer, having no offers of fee-paying lectures or concerts, he could only depend upon Grainger's salary and Judy Brown's monthly checks for regular income.[43] Then Edelstein gave him the right to go to New York without any pre-clearance, permitting him to teach a once-weekly course at The New School.[44]

With Elastic Form a natural asset for scoring movies, Henry unsuccessfully attempted to penetrate Hollywood.[45] It is odd to see him participating in a written symposium about film music, since he had never worked in the industry as a composer,[46] and even stranger that he wrote about film music as if he had experience. As usual, he had no shortage of ideas, the most interesting of which was to write scores utilizing special miking or combining separate tracks in re-recording.

By the end of 1940, Henry's prospects for entering the rarified world of musical commerce seemed bright enough for him to enlist Olive to oversee his royalty income. He took seriously Grainger's advice to get a lot of pieces into print, each of which would bring in a small amount but collectively could harvest substantial royalties, and Schirmer accepted the right of first refusal on anything he wrote.[47] Nevertheless, royalties and performance rights never exceeded a few hundred dollars a year until the end of World War II.[48]

40

First Turning Point

As time passed, Henry's hunt for a better job intensified. Although Officer Edelstein either did not know or did not care that the Graingers were away most of the time, that arrangement was developing severe problems—increasing friction with Ella, Percy's financial pinch, and the nature of Henry's responsibilities, which now included shoveling snow.[1] Even if something materialized, delays were inevitable because any change required the authorities to investigate a new guarantor of parole. Percy urged Henry not to rush into anything that would require changing parole officers, since continuity of supervision could speed the easing of restrictions.[2] When Governor Olson recommended sweeping changes in California's penal system, Henry imagined possible benefits for his case,[3] but nothing tangible transpired.

Edelstein facilitated Henry's public appearances but did not have much to facilitate. A February 1941 engagement at Columbia University gave Gassner visions of Henry speaking on the radio to a mass audience, like the famous music wit Alec Templeton, but with more subtlety and dignity. With his excellent material, Henry could present modern music so that the nonmusician would enjoy it. Gassner suggested arranging a popular dance band number for orchestra, leaving the melody accessible but orchestrating it "in a burlesque of ultra modern dissonance." It was a great idea, perfectly suited to Henry,[4] but his good friends continued to worry about backlash and could not produce more than an occasional lecture. Moreover, Henry shied away from imposing on his friends, to spare them the embarrassment of admitting their fears.

Teaching prospects improved slightly. He got two courses at The New School—"The Science of Musical Sound" and "Creative Music in America." Lilly Popper engaged him for ten lectures at the Metropolitan Music School, but it was so broke that it could only guarantee a percentage of the meager proceeds. Despite the risks of being associated with a far-left institution, Henry accepted her tiny offer and other little jobs as an investment toward a better position. Following Grainger's advice to act on his own behalf, he pushed for a government job and commissions to compose but knew that he could consume himself with miscellany.[5]

Having not forgotten the better moments of his prison years, he sent news to Shuder and offered to advise him about the prisoners' education. Henry's triumphs, in turn, delighted Shuder. Pleased to hear that pieces written in jail were being played, he was gratified to think he might have contributed modestly to Henry's achievements. "The Music Department in San Quentin is not a Music Department without Henry Cowell. It was his and without him it just isn't. There will never be another who can take your place."[6] Shuder was sweet, but the program, having collapsed when Henry left, now had the potential to grow under the new Warden, Clinton Duffy, who had recently replaced Court Smith. Duffy turned to a San Quentin guard with fourteen years' experience in commercial music to design America's first prison conservatory, with classrooms for practical instruction in a remodeled former tuberculosis ward. He had gotten some promises of pianos and had a thirty-member glee club, which sounded fairly good after only eight rehearsals. Recalling Henry's offer to find secondhand brass, wind, and string instruments, Shuder assured him that his help would never be forgotten by the prisoners and himself.[7] Although Henry's former inmate-students could not express their gratitude directly because of the ban on contact with parolees, one of them, recently freed, offered to continue copying parts for Henry as he had done in prison. Laundering his response through Sidney, Henry replied that he would pay him for having copied *Pastorale and Fiddler's Delight* if he ever got a penny from Stokowski for it. He may have risked communicating with him because he had the only score of *Danza Latina*, one of Henry's prison products, which Schirmer wanted to publish.[8] It was foolhardy: even indirect contact could have returned Henry to San Quentin.

When the courses at The New School started in February 1941, Henry's were just large enough not to be canceled.[9] The Metropolitan Music School course also opened with only a handful of students.[10] Everything was a struggle. The dancer Martha Hill invited him to give a summer course at Bennington; Henry could not accept it without permission, which took time; Bennington needed an answer at once; the parole bureaucracy preferred to procrastinate.[11] Olive urged Wortis to get the parole relaxed so Henry could find a "real" job, but Henry thought Edelstein was doing everything he could. His only hope was a better Board of Prison Terms and Paroles. He suggested that someone sound out the chairman of the Board, John Gee Clark, about whether a commutation (reduction) of his sentence was possible without waiting until the remaining unsympathetic board member was gone.[12]

The delicacy of Henry's position became obvious in mid-March when the Grainger house was burgled. Not much was taken, but Grainger's manager, the next-door neighbor, decided against filing a police report since Henry might become a suspect. Henry agreed, "as the police have a way of suspecting anyone in my position of anything and everything irrespective."[13]

Tension with the Graingers steadily increased that spring. Henry did not get along with Ella, and Percy was so peculiar that living with him was very stressful. Yet Percy flatly refused to entertain Henry's proposal to move somewhere nearby. Edelstein, sympathetic to Henry's plight, agreed to let him live as a freelancer if someone would sign the monthly report, but he could not guarantee that the California parole authorities would approve, and they had the last word.[14] In March, Alvin Johnson said he would be the parole sponsor if needed.[15]

In addition, Henry had to face a serious predicament about Johanna Magdalena Beyer. Grateful for her efforts but unable to bear her affection, he urged her to go her own way, make decisions exclusively based on her needs, and remember that he could not afford to pay her to assist him because he had almost no money. Their relationship did not have long to go, however. Her mental and physical condition plummeted and she died in 1944 at fifty-five of amyotrophic lateral sclerosis (ALS—"Lou Gehrig's Disease").

A report on his activities in the six months since San Quentin shows why he needed to find another job if he had any hope of resuming his career. As Grainger's secretary, he had copied parts, created orchestra scores from parts, shipped and received Grainger's music, and kept track of rentals; conducted rehearsals of Grainger's music, repaired and sent out folkloric instruments, learned to play various new instruments for performances with Grainger; photographed, developed, and printed music and letters and other documents for the Grainger Museum in Melbourne, organized Percy's music library, catalogued music and records, advised Grainger about orchestration, and other endless tasks. Nevertheless, he wrote six articles, composed, taught at the New School, gave some lectures, and secured some performances of his music.[16]

He was also immersed in several organizations as editor of New Music Quarterly, chairman of the Executive Board of New Music Quarterly Recordings, a member of two League of Composers committees, and a member of the board of the American Composers Alliance. In short, he was back to his old frantic self. And where did it leave him? A progress report to Olive on March 31, 1941, shows much and little. At that time his freelance work brought in $50–$60 [2010: $740–$888] extra per month; his total receipts for March were $111 [$1,640]. Still, he managed to save up $175 [$2,590] toward leaner times (i.e., the summer) and had about $400 [$5,920] in a savings bank. Private teaching brought in about $30 [$444] a month if everyone took a lesson; Erick Hawkins and Hanya Holm still owed him money. So he thought he did not absolutely have to have Percy's $41.66 [$617] a month, but Grainger would insist on paying him until July no matter how much he earned. (In fact, the parole terms required Grainger to pay him.) He thought he could survive for five or six months with no earnings in the worst case.[17] Sidney assured him that job possibilities in Washington were still brewing.

The need to leave the Graingers intensified when they returned in April (1941) from their travels. One symptom is Henry's handwritten letters. Even typing in the Graingers' cellar was impossible because Percy wanted to be free to dash in whenever he felt like it. Otherwise, he told Sidney, things were normal— "just a certain exaggeration of former tendencies. I do my own cooking, independent of their mealtime; I still order my own groceries—use cellar bathroom (it's very good now!) and do not feel free to practice at all, of course. It is a problem because I have to perform on recorders and pipes etc. for Erick Hawkins on April 20."[18]

When he tried to follow Sidney's suggestion of discussing Ella's complaints, Ella exploded. Another time, when he told her that he was leaving for town and would return in the evening, "she fairly screamed at me 'do anything you want, but don't bother me about it—I don't want to know what you do.' Yet I feel sure that she would have felt it a lack on my part if I went out and no one knew when I was expected back!" Percy posed no problems and Henry did not want to complain about Ella, which would be "very indelicate, as well as useless. And when I ask him about what he wants me to do (in household habits) he always suggests the things that I know bother Ella—so when I say that perhaps she would be bothered (which I did) he says 'Oh, no—I'm sure not'!" To keep the peace, Henry arranged to type and practice two or three days a week in the apartment of a friend who was out all day.[19] Dr. Wortis advised him to stick it out until July or whenever he got a job. A forthcoming trip to see Sidney eased his discomfort. She had proposed camping in the South, but the parole office needed to know his exact location, which was impossible in the mountains. Nevertheless, he hoped that they could "have a wonderful evening drive through them."[20]

That April was full of bad news. Instead of enlarging the staff to include Henry, Bennington expected to cut existing faculty.[21] Boston University College of Music passed him over for another candidate.[22] He pursued Gassner's idea for radio shows through personal connections at WOR and CBS, only to get refusals, and he doubted that anything would come of an impending dinner with an NBC executive. Dr. Wortis now thought of applying for inactive parole, that is, getting all restrictions lifted. The parole would remain on the books, however. Olive decided to propose it privately to John Gee Clark, the chairman of California's parole board.[23] In late April the issue became urgent when Stokowski invited Henry to be soloist for a tour with his All-American Youth Orchestra beginning in less than three weeks and including concerts in California, where Henry dared not perform. He also feared that his playing was too insecure for such important engagements, since Ella prevented him from practicing.[24] To complicate his life further, Grainger could not consider extending their agreement beyond June even if Henry wanted to stay, because the war abroad and an ongoing royalties dispute between ASCAP and broadcasters had cut badly into his income.

In May, Wortis requested John Gee Clark to have parole restrictions lifted and informed him that the New York authorities promised to recommend commutation of sentence or inactive parole if they were approached by the Californians, but they could not write unless written to. Henry simultaneously asked Olive to get Clark's advice about limitations to freedom of motion that hampered his professional activity.[25] Grainger wrote Clark and the New York parole authorities, testifying to Henry's work and behavior in the year since he left prison, and explaining his own need to eliminate the expense of employing him.[26] Just then, Stokowski's manager confirmed Henry's appearances with the All American Youth Orchestra beginning only six days later in Atlantic City and moving on to Connecticut, Rhode Island, and Massachusetts. All the conditions had changed, however. Instead of the original proposal of $100 [2010: $1,480] per week plus expenses, they offered transportation costs only and $15 [2010: $222] to cover the cost of parts for Ancient Desert Drone. Henry would come away with excellent exposure, nothing more.[27]

To everyone's delight and relief, Grainger's tribute persuaded John Gee Clark to instruct California's Chief Parole Officer to lift unnecessary restrictions and to take up with the Board the restoration of his civil rights so that he could become fully professional again.[28] Wortis agreed to be supervisor.[29] Henry had already changed his permanent address to the American Music Center and notified Grainger, who was away, that he would move out on July 1.[30] Even Grainger's cordiality was beginning to fade under domestic pressure. In a letter redolent with eccentricity, he told Henry that he was jittery, and the constant interruptions of the telephone—they had finally gotten one—caused by having a composer as famous as Henry around, were too much for him. He begged Henry not to think him unfriendly. He was grateful for his work, but got stupidly addled and needed to be left alone.[31] Henry responded that he had applied for a job with Seeger in Washington and assured Grainger that if the new job were not yet ready, Edelstein would sign the parole paper beginning July 1, so that Percy's assistance would be unnecessary.[32]

Despite the trials of life with the Graingers, Henry could look back on a reasonably productive year. His catalogue lists twenty-three compositions and two alternate orchestrations, of which a third is known only through listings in Henry's own register of compositions. The survivors include his first collaboration with Sidney, a setting for soprano-alto-tenor-bass chorus of a tune she had collected during fieldwork. There are two songs on poems by Ella Grainger, dance works for Marianne Tuyl and Sophie Delza (both lost), and Trickster Coyote for Erick Hawkins. All seven of the piano pieces are lost, implying that Henry did not value them highly. More surprising is the number of large-ensemble pieces—the commissions from Fabien Sevitzky; *Shipshape Overture; Four Irish Tales*, for piano and orchestra, which are orchestrations of four solo piano pieces requested by Stokowski for Henry to play with the All-American Youth Orchestra; two band pieces; and incidental music for a production of *King Lear* by the emigré German director Erwin Piscator.

Henry also managed a respectable amount of writing, primarily about music, childhood education in music, and dance. "Drums Along the Pacific" (in *Modern Music*) surveyed the extraordinary interest in percussion music that had developed on the Pacific coast in the previous two years, thanks to Cage, Harrison, Ray Green, Strang, "Meyer" [probably Beyer], William Russell, and Cubans Ardévol, Caturla, and Roldán.[33] In "New Sounds for the Dance" (for Horst's influential *Dance Observer*), he returned to fundamental issues in combining music with choreography, this time proposing that the refined elegance of orchestral instruments caused problems of compatibility that might be solved by using more "awkward" tone colors. While the result would be incomplete musically, such tones could be used in connection with dance, where it was preferable that the music not feel too complete. Most percussion instruments, he said, have the asset (when used for dance) that their tones are never perfect enough, that is, not focused on one pitch. Dance could complete them and utilize their rhythmic incisiveness. "The more purely melodic an instrument is, the less rhythmic. Accentuation brings in the element of noise-sound as opposed to pure tone. The more noise-sounds which are used on the melodic instruments, therefore, the more rhythmically biting they become." He had had good success with such sounds in composing the score for *Trickster Coyote*,[34] about which *Dance Observer* wrote, "Henry Cowell's music, with its outrageous squawks from an instrument reported on the best of authority to be a Chinese oboe, is one of the best dance scores written in years." Martha Graham was reported to have said, after attending a rehearsal, that she was intrigued by its "primal," rather than "primitive," character.[35] In "Creating a Dance: Form and Composition," Henry attacked the common practice of using improvisation to teach dance, which resulted—he asserted—in most concert dances having "no form, from the standpoint of other more precise arts." To improve choreography, he urged the development of dance notation[36] and advised choreographers to study formal procedures in music.

In mid-July the California Board restored his civil rights, allowed him to travel, and offered him "inactive parole," supervised by Wortis rather than the New York parole officers. Once New York signed off on it, he would be free to do as he chose. New York's agreement was not a foregone conclusion, however. Wortis had not realized that state law did not provide for "inactive parole." Henry therefore might have to choose between remaining under the New York parole regulations or relocating to a state that accepted California's inactive parole.[37] With his status unsettled all summer he still needed approval to go to Washington at the end of August. And even if inactive parole were approved, he still bore the stigma of being a paroled felon.[38] In November, California finally notified him that he had been removed from the jurisdiction of the New York State Division of Parole and placed under Wortis's sole supervision. He had to send a card when he needed to leave New York City but could operate an automobile and get a license if he carried insurance.[39]

Clarissa Cowell, ca. 1870.

Harry Cowell lecturing, ca. 1900.

Henry Cowell with violin, November 1902.

Clarissa Cowell, ca. 1893.

Henry Cowell at his Aunt Jenny's ranch, ca. 1907–9.

Henry Cowell playing the piano, ca. 1913.

Henry Cowell and
Clarissa Cowell, ca. 1914.

Ellen Veblen, storytelling for neighborhood children, ca. 1910.

John Varian, ca. 1916.

Charles Seeger, ca. 1930.

Henry Cowell with flower baskets at Palo Alto station, ca. 1911.

Elsa Schmolke, ca. 1930.

Nicolas Slonimsky, ca. 1932?

Henry Cowell and
Sidney Robertson Cowell
on their wedding day,
September 27, 1941.

John Cage, ca. 1945.

Olive, Harry, and
Henry Cowell in the
Cowell House, San
Francisco. Photo by
Childress Braun.

Lou Harrison, ca. 1935–40.

The Cowell house, Shady, New York. Photo by Sean Hartnett.

Henry and Harry
Cowell, summer
1940.

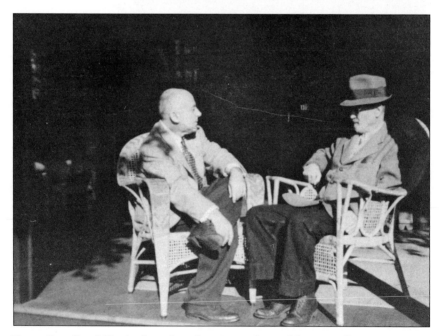

Henry Cowell and Charles Ives, the only existing photo of them together, ca. 1950?

Henry Cowell and Carl Ruggles, 1950s.

Henry Cowell demonstrating shakuhachi to Edgard Varèse, 1950s.

Henry Cowell
feeding a chimpanzee,
Singapore, 1957.

Henry Cowell at Shady, ca. 1958–59, with cats. Photo by Sidney Cowell.

Henry and Sidney Cowell, ca. 1958. Photo by David Linton.

Spontaneous birthday party birthday party for Cowell, March 1, 1957, Colombo, Ceylon [Sri Lanka].

Henry Cowell, 1959.
Photo by Sidney
Cowell.

Henry Cowell, 1965. Photo by Sidney Cowell.

41

Problem Solved

While Henry was telling Olive that his search for a woman was going nowhere, an excellent candidate was already on hand, Sidney Hawkins Robertson, a native of San Francisco born in 1903 to a reasonably prosperous family.[1] When her parents moved to Dayton, Ohio, she stayed in Menlo Park, attending Castilleja School, an academically oriented boarding school. Although she already had remote connections with Henry as another member of Terman's study group of extremely gifted children, and had met the Sewards through Terman, her first encounter with Henry took place around 1916 or 1917, when she was about thirteen and a freshman at Castilleja. This was the occasion when Elizabeth Bates, the teacher who supervised her piano practice, took her to play for Henry, hoping she would get the idea of asking her parents to aid him. She only vaguely recalled the occasion; Henry's personality left no impression on her. "Although he loved children I was not enough of a child still to appeal to him, probably." Her comment that he probably showed his "usual" reserve with strangers seems at odds with almost every other description of him.

During that same spring (either 1916 or 1917), she heard him perform for the first time but did not realize that he was the "famous musician" for whom she had played. "Like most people in those days," she wrote, "I probably found the intensity with which he dashed at the keyboard comic; but I would never have laughed aloud, and I was probably so absorbed with the effort to keep a straight face that I failed to remember much about the music. I had great respect for him, by contagion from college professors like the Sewards and the Termans; but like many people I seem to have found it impossible to listen to the music itself."

At fourteen she transferred to a public polytechnic high school in Dayton, having decided briefly and misguidedly to be an engineer. She was admitted to Stanford within its quota for women, spent her sophomore year at a lycée in Tours, and returned to receive her BA in 1924, majoring in "Romantic" Languages. Just before graduation from Stanford, she married Kenneth Robertson.

They spent 1924–25 in Paris, she at the École Normale de Musique, studying with Alfred Cortot and Charles Koechlin. (She was among the students singing Fauré's Requiem at his grand funeral.) Then the couple took Carl Jung's graduate seminars on analytic psychology in London and Zürich. By an odd coincidence, upon returning to Palo Alto, they lived in the house that Ellen Veblen had built after she and Thorstein Veblen separated, the very house in which Henry had spent a lot of time as a boy. Sidney continued her musical education at the San Francisco Conservatory and in summer programs at Mills College and Berkeley, adding Ernest Bloch and Harold Bauer to her splendid array of teachers. She also devoted two summers to the study of English folk music and folk dance. In 1926, after a brief period as secretary to Stanford's Geology Department, she joined the faculty of the experimental Peninsula School of Creative Education in Menlo Park and later chaired its music program. That job ended in 1932 when the Depression devastated the school.

During her time at the Peninsula School, her interest in Henry's ideas led to their next encounter, which she felt was the beginning of a really personal acquaintance. A number of bathtubs left from the building's previous incarnation as a Catholic boarding school were no longer needed because the Peninsula School was a day school. Just after Henry returned from a European tour, Sidney learned that he was adding running water to his house and might love to have "one of the perfectly enormous bathtubs which were awaiting the junk man in the school's back yard." Wondering if he would play a concert in exchange for a bathtub, she sent him a note—he had no telephone—and he responded, in essence, that he would be right there! A week later he played for faculty, children, and some parents.[2] The headmistress recalled that the parents, like much of the community, considered him an eccentric and laughed at his innovations, but "the children responded with immediate comprehension. He fascinated them by opening the lid of the grand piano and playing 'The Banshee' on the strings. Indeed, he himself was like a little Irish leprechaun—slight of figure, quick-moving, and whimsical. He had translucent blue eyes and a mysterious smile, and there seemed to be something primitive but ages old in wisdom about him."[3] In August 1930, Sidney attended the performance of *The Building of Bamba,* and heard Henry play in Palo Alto several times. At one house concert they spoke briefly, the first conversation she remembered.

When the Depression hit the Peninsula School and Sidney lost her job, she had no backup because her parents' finances had collapsed even earlier. She had already separated amicably from Robertson and in 1933 divorced him "much against his will."[4] At first she stayed in California, attending Henry's world-music lectures in Carmel twice. Miscellaneous jobs followed until she bridled at the stifling world of wealthy California art lovers and craved the excitement of the East. For 1935–36 she got a job at the Henry Street Settlement in New York and took Henry's course a third time at the New School, where she renewed her acquaintance with John Cage, a fellow student. The New School may be where she met Charles Seeger, although she already knew a lot of his Bay Area friends.[5]

Seeger got her a job in the music section of the Resettlement Administration in Washington. Her principal duty was to record folk music of communities that had been relocated from the Oklahoma Dust Bowl to the far West, so that recreation leaders could be properly trained to work with the displaced, distressed communities. In the course of her work she traveled several hundred thousand miles and made several hundred recordings, which were deposited in the Archive of American Folksong at the Library of Congress. Her recordings were the first ever done in seven or eight states, notably in the Ozarks, where she became an authority on the music. Eventually she collaborated with Alan Lomax in compiling a bibliography of regional folk song.[6]

Around the time Henry was jailed, she moved back to California because of health problems in New York and began visiting him faithfully every twenty-eight days. Sometime in 1938 or 1939, under a WPA project sponsored by the Library of Congress, she collected and edited folk music "to show what the WPA could do with folk music in a single state." This may be the project he enjoyed discussing during her visits to San Quentin. After he was paroled they corresponded and looked forward to seeing one another if she came East. As of late August 1940, she had no job and was living at her family's fig ranch near Fresno.[7] In the fall she moved to Washington, DC, to become a consultant in folk music for the music division of the Pan American Union, which Seeger headed.[8]

During a November 1940 trip to New York, she offered to come to White Plains to see Henry. His response shows that their friendship was moving to greater intimacy and that his gregariousness was hiding internal battles.

> My sense of personal contact develops slowly. I don't have immediate personal impressions of people, and so of course, don't show feelings that are not there. This doesn't mean that I am coldly against such personal developments, but that I await their natural, not over-stimulated and hurried development. It is also probably true, although it is not conscious, that since no very intimate personal contacts ever turned out well for me I am unconsciously inclined to fear them somewhat. But if this is so, it is very far down deep. Perhaps I can never be the one to make the start in the development of close personal relations, I should perhaps have unconscious fear of it. And although I don't feel any embarrassment on account of the SQ factor, yet it probably gives me still more timidity. It is certainly true now that people exaggerate the probable meaning of every minute thing I do or seem to suggest, and impute motives to my actions that I certainly do not knowingly have.[9]

They met at least once in the next ten days. Then the Seegers' invitation to spend Christmas in Silver Spring meant they could be together again. Hoping for some sustained time with Henry, Sidney proposed exploring the Maryland and Virginia countryside.[10] Henry, however, feared that adding another destination could make Officer Edelstein nervous. Seeger therefore issued an official invitation for Henry to examine Grainger's folk music recordings at the Library of Congress, adding that the holiday season would be ideal because he (Seeger) would have free time to help him. He also offered to introduce Henry to people at the Library with a view toward a job.[11]

While they were waiting for clearance, Henry and Sidney had an exchange about the sensitive issue of Henry visiting a family that had young children.[12] Then Sidney, now confident of her friendship with Henry, revealed something she had always kept to herself—the loss of one son to pneumonia when he was not quite three, and a second son who was born prematurely and lived only two months. "Some things one never gets over, really . . ."[13]

After commiserating over the loss of the babies, Henry described another touchy situation: an acquaintance wanted him to provide his young children with a musical education.

> I am unfortunately always somewhat aware of the fact that I have to be careful in my relations with [the children], and I can't do freely all the things that would be quite natural under other circumstances, such as undertake their entire care, while I was in the apartment, thus releasing their nurse for the hour, etc. The latter is always in the apartment, although of course not necessarily in the room, and everything is quite open, so I don't think there is any danger of my being considered too little chaperoned there. I have discussed my relation with children with Dr. Wortis, and he is all for my having as natural a relation there as possible. On my part, I don't propose to let constraint enter into my relationships with children, any more than can be avoided. There is no use in my meeting any at all, if I were forced to erect a barrier in my relations with them that would be utterly incomprehensible to the child, and would most certainly be felt. So what I shall do is to take reasonable precautions not to be left entirely alone in the house with them, but otherwise I don't try to be restrained. All of this sounds more self-conscious than it really is—I don't have it too much in mind all the time. I simply will not wreck all my human relationships by going about having to put on an attitude all the time![14]

Edelstein finally cleared the trip to Washington,[15] which was the occasion upon which Harold Spivacke would not even meet with Henry. In fact, the prospects of finding work in Washington were dimming generally; WPA money for white-collar jobs was almost certainly going to be diverted to national defense. In March (1941), when Sidney lost her own job,[16] she proposed the first of many collaborations with Henry—writing accompaniments and introductions to folk songs from the West.[17] Henry began immediately.[18] Then he enlisted her as an intermediary to deal with the former San Quentin inmate who wanted to be paid for copying music.[19] Soon he was signing his letters "Love, Henry," and sought parole permission so they could travel together in the South. With his departure from the Graingers almost at hand, he rented an apartment at 16 Seventh Avenue South, in Greenwich Village, and bought a used Steinway.[20] When the Bennington summer school job finally came through, Henry accepted it, but lamented that it would deprive him of time with Sidney.[21] Even worse, she thought she might have to return to California because she was still unemployed.

Henry does not say what happened next. After his death, when Sidney left no word unwritten, she added confusion to what looked like a straightforward love story. She said that when she told him about an offer to be Ernest Bloch's assistant in Oregon, Henry said, "If you want to help a composer, you'd better marry me and help me!" She, however, was in love with a brilliant and attractive man with whom she had made folk song expeditions into the mountains. A recovering alcoholic and a widower, he was interested in her, but she, having supported her first husband, was not eager to do so again. Nevertheless, she brushed off Henry's remark, but he persisted. When he insisted that she must love him or she would not have encouraged him, she agreed to marry him, knowing she was not in love with him, but also aware that he interested her, "his mind, his projects, his way of looking at things. This I did not say, and I let him act out whatever demonstrativeness he felt necessary for years."

Of course, she said, Henry interpreted her hesitation as evidence that she believed he was still homosexual, so he sent her to Drs. Wortis and Meyer for assurance, which they gave her.

> I would never knowingly have married a homosexual, and I accepted all this at face value. A little less concern for Henry and more for myself might have led me to inquire into the reason why I really did not find Henry physically attractive. But given my only half-abandoned feeling for the earlier affair, I avoided any inquiry into my own feelings and based my acceptance on Henry's absolute determination . . . and the reasonableness everybody was given to in the matter.

The tone of her story conflicts strangely with the intimacy of the letters they exchanged in 1940 and 1941. When asked how this could be, she told me that she felt grouchy about Henry for some years after his death, but really loved him. Clearly she was at least as complicated as he.

While she was running from one psychiatrist to another—she thought she had also gone to Alfred Adler, forgetting that he had died five years before—Henry told the parole authorities that he was needed in Washington at the end of August.[22] Sidney's name is next found in a September 8 letter to Harry and Olive announcing their engagement.[23] Later he told them about her background, her wish to raise a family, her "remarkable social grace in all classes of human relations ... We have been unusually free from constraint in our discussions of our own relationship and future, and I feel that our understanding and deep love is a very mature one." Wortis was delighted, and he was sure Terman would be also, especially as she was another of his "genius children."[24]

Permission to marry was required because New York had not yet agreed to the relaxation of parole authorized by California. Sidney luckily had landed a job as a researcher for the State Department Committee on Inter-American Music. Henry confided to Grainger, however, that life was rough. Stokowski would only pay him $25 [2010: $370] for two concerts with the New York Philharmonic. He had no other prospects for paying engagements, and no orchestral works had been accepted for performance. Nevertheless, he thought they could cope, barring unforeseen circumstances should war break out.[25]

Immediately after mailing that letter to Grainger, he learned that he had been hired by the Pan American Union (PAU). Founded in 1889–90 as the Commercial Bureau of the American Republics, and renamed in 1910, the PAU sought to further international cooperation through the exchange of technical and non-technical information. Later subsidiary councils advanced economic, social, juridical, and cultural relations. (Since 1970 it has been called the General Secretariat of the Organization of American States.) Seeger, its new head of music, had succeeded in finding money to bring in Henry.[26] PAU chairman Nelson Rockefeller's tardiness in approving the appointment[27] was more than a bureaucratic nuisance, however. Henry had given Grainger notice that he would leave on July 1 but the required parole permission was stalled until Rockefeller signed the papers. Needless to say, Rockefeller could not be told why time was of the essence. When Henry's job was finalized in mid-August, he proposed to Sidney.

Feeling more secure because of the job, he told the Iveses about their engagement.[28] Charles Ives replied at once through Harmony, in a letter that once was considered a sudden reconciliation but actually was the conclusion of a gradual thaw, for Henry and Harmony had been corresponding since April in response to his offer to help organize Ives's manuscripts.

Dear Henry -

It was great to hear your good news—

Our kindest wishes to you both—May the marriage bring a happiness which will last thro' to the end of eternity & then on.

We take great pleasure in enclosing our wedding present—for we cant [*sic*] enclose a Book-case or a sofa—& then Mrs. Cowell can select something for the family home which wont [*sic*] be a duplicate. That problem we learned of by recent experience—Edie at her wedding received about 20 flower pots & not one salt sellar.

We will write Mr. [Harold] Spivacke [regarding his desire to have some of Ives's music for the Library of Congress]—There are some of the old copies around somewhere—although some are probably lost— When we get back to N.Y. next winter we hope to see you both.

Again our kindest wishes to you & Miss Robertson now & forever.

Chas. E. Ives

Congratulations & greetings—

H.T.I. [29]

Ives's pathetically shaky signature is a vivid reminder of why Harmony's reluctance to speak of Henry was not just homophobia. Overjoyed, Henry replied with thanks for their present and the hope that they would let him introduce Sidney.[30]

Permission for the marriage came very quickly from the New York authorities, though California dithered. Hoping to avoid provoking unpleasant backlash, they had Sidney's biological mother announce the wedding in her own name. They married on September 27 at the Seegers' house in Thurmont, Maryland, and installed themselves in their New York apartment, a very small, cramped space with a tiny bedroom and large living room, one closet and one cupboard, and stuffed with piles of records and music. It held a big desk, a seven-foot Steinway, and, Sidney told her stepmother, "a big davenport, it only just fails to look corded. All the walls are cream color & there is Chinese matting all over the floor—living room has 2 north windows, bedroom & bath each one south & kitchen 1 north, so we are light enough."[31] It was, however, only their town apartment. They had found a little dream house at Shady, on the edge of Woodstock, New York. The purchase of that cottage was in part Henry's acknowledgment that he would never return to California permanently. Shady was the chief Cowell residence until Sidney's death in 1995.[32]

Five days after the wedding Henry left for Chicago on Pan American Union business, stopping to see Clarence and family on the way.[33] When he got back, he had sold-out performances with Stokowski and the New York Philharmonic at Carnegie Hall, which got excellent press. Sidney, meanwhile, was beginning to perceive the meaning of being married to Henry. "Henry has the most extraordinary collection of friends" she wrote home. "He gets letters from Stoki & Bela Bartok & Schoenberg, Bloch & Ernst Bacon and Radiana Pazmor . . . and Alfred Harcourt (of Harcourt Brace) and endless interesting refugees from all over Europe."[34]

Their joy was tempered by Henry's fear that a newspaper might mention their marriage and link San Quentin to him, especially since Sidney's mother was the only person in her family who knew about his imprisonment.[35] Anticipating that Olive might be uncontrollably exuberant, Sidney spelled out the reason for restraint: over-advertising of the marriage would surely give the impression of a marriage arranged "with a view to the public impression."[36] That suspicion persists even now, nearly three quarters of a century later. Yet the affection in their correspondence unquestionably speaks of a loving union. Even before the wedding, Seeger thought Henry had become noticeably richer, warmer, more quiet, more natural.[37] Whatever motivated Sidney to overcome her reservations, she would not have stooped to marrying him to provide cover for his past.

Henry's position at the Pan American Union, Chief Music Consultant, was to last five months at $200 [2010: $2,960] a month. He divided his time between Washington and New York to retain his classes at the New School. The title "consultant" underlines the impermanence of the post, but two renewals of funding kept him secure through the fall of 1942.[38] The combination of the job and Henry's impending marriage prompted Wortis to drop a hint with California authorities about a pardon, which was essential for him to work in Washington.

He directed a project to select and edit compositions from Latin American countries for possible publication in the United States. When he arrived at the PAU, radio networks and orchestras were programming many pieces, some of them acquired by American publishers even though a lot were mediocre. Furthermore, Latin American musicians resented the careless proofreading and unauthorized reprints stemming from confusion about copyright law. In revenge, some South American publishers were pirating copyrighted North American music. The Editorial Project for Latin American Music was the PAU's attempt to correct the situation. Four consultants—Pedro Sanjuan, the Spanish-born Cuban conductor and composer, Henry's longtime friend; Luis Heitor Correa de Azevedo, a distinguished Brazilian musicologist; Richard Franko Goldman; and Henry—examined, collected, and classified all available Latin American music in the library of the PAU, the Library of Congress, the Music Division of the New York Public Library, the libraries of the Navy, Army, and Marine Bands in Washington, and some private collections.[39]

They concentrated first on music suitable for public schools, conferring with Henry's contacts at the Music Educators National Conference (MENC). Out of some four thousand Latin American pieces, they chose about 150 that MENC thought had potential for educational use, which is to say, large-scale sales. After consultations with the composers and publishers, those compositions were recommended to prominent American publishers, who agreed to publish music by some twenty Latin American composers. Henry and his colleagues gradually realized that for daily life, music was much more important to Latin Americans than to "Norteamericanos." Proud of their music, Latin Americans wanted it to be accepted and liked in the United States, unlike "North Americans," who did not care whether their music was understood in Latin America. It was, however, a product by which Latin Americans judged the culture of the United States. In some respects, Henry finally could further the goals of the defunct Pan American Association of Composers.

Now that the Cowells were employed, they decided to begin a family immediately, hoping for twins when Sidney quickly became pregnant. Difficulties began to arise almost at once, forcing her to spend most of her time in bed. At the end of May (1942), the pregnancy ended, leaving Sidney with serious phlebitis. They nevertheless tried again, without success, and an application to adopt was rejected.[40] Decades later, Sidney learned that incompatible blood types were the culprit. It may also have been true in her first marriage, when she lost two babies. Apart from the obvious tragedy—Henry had wanted five children[41]—her pregnancy also revealed what he faced even posthumously. When I interviewed Nicholas Slonimsky in 1989, he cautioned me to be careful about what Sidney told me. Why, he said, she claimed to have lost a baby by Henry, but "We know he couldn't do that!" I remained silent, but when I gave him the evidence, he was astonished. If that was true of Slonimsky, who knew both Cowells well, it is no wonder that the prison story refused to go away. In July 1942, Sidney had to keep warning Olive about loose talk because Seeger was too timid to defend Henry should there be problems. Sidney also felt she had to protect Henry from having to tell his whole story to everyone he met. He acted casually but was very sensitive about being affronted.[42] Olive, unfortunately, began to see Sidney as controlling rather than cautious.

That July, just as Henry learned that his work at the Pan American Union would last only six more months,[43] the State Department approved a project for the distribution of American music in Latin America that would give him another year's work. This time his employer would be The New School, acting as administrator.[44] In this project, the Music Educators National Conference and the Pan American Union selected pieces to be sent to Latin America. Loan libraries of scores and recordings by North American composers were created in all the republics of Central and South America. For Henry they replaced the defunct International Exchange Concerts, allowing him to send music in both directions, although performance was only a side issue. According to Sidney, he ultimately inspected several thousand compositions. His mid-1940s report—which contains essential material for any study of inter-American musical relations at that time—said that the Project sent out $10,572.36 [2010: $141,000] worth of musical materials, in packets valued from $244.78 [2010: $3,270] to Honduras to $1,164.10 [2010: $15,600] to Brazil. Styles spanned the entire range from conservative to experimental. They were restricted to printed material, to the regret of Henry, who knew that many unpublished pieces would have been valuable.[45]

Seeger said that the most important aim was to create a Spanish equivalent of the standard contract. "The Latin American composers had been skinned by the Americans until it was known throughout Latin America that it was a skin game." That became a big joke at a party for Mexican composers hosted by Ralph Peer, the president of International Music Publishers. Someone said of Mrs. Peer's beautiful fur coat that she came "with the skins of the Mexican composers on her back." But Seeger added that Peer was very nice about the contract and ready to do what was right.[46]

The inter-American projects seem extremely selfless, a wonderful sign of American generosity. Seeger knew the real incentive, however. After the United States entered the war in December 1941, Germany and Italy, capitalizing on Latin American resentment of the United States, intensified their search for bomber bases. Establishing American cultural credentials in the face of Axis propaganda was urgent.[47] Exactly how much the music programs contributed to world events is unknown, but the Axis influence in Latin America was kept in check.

42

End of an Era

Dramatis Personae

Joseph Brennan: San Francisco-based Supervising Parole Officer on Interstate Matters

John Gee Clark: Judge in Los Angeles, formerly Chairman of the Board of Prison Terms and Paroles

Gilbert Ferrell: San Mateo County District Attorney

Maxwell McNutt: Sentencing judge at Henry's 1936 hearing

Carey McWilliams: Close aide to Governor Culbert Olson

Stanley Mosk: Executive Secretary to Governor Culbert Olson

Culbert Olson: Governor of California

Daniel Sullivan: Assistant District Attorney, San Mateo County, and friend of Henry

Earl Warren: Attorney General of California and Governor-Elect

Paul Yarwood: Secretary of the Advisory Pardons Board

Sidney's battle for Henry's pardon has been tainted by accusations that she manipulated information to whitewash the case. In fact, her 1973 account of the pardon process is corroborated by voluminous documents, which she may have consulted to refresh her memory, and a letter to an old friend written a few months after the pardon was granted.[1] Only the events of the final two days are not described in letters to Henry, for reasons that will be seen. A few minor errors are easily corrected.

She, however, may not have understood the true implications of a pardon, which is not a proclamation of innocence. Acceptance of a pardon amounts to admission of guilt; otherwise, one would not have to be pardoned. In fact, offers of pardon are sometimes declined because the accused is unwilling to admit guilt. Nevertheless, it terminates imprisonment or parole, restores civil rights, and returns the pardoned felon to society.

In Henry's case, guilt was not an issue. The question of whether he falsely pleaded guilty was not even raised. It would have been distracting and could have jeopardized his cause. The issues were (a) whether such infractions should be felonies; (b) whether the other participant should also have been prosecuted, as California law demanded; (c) whether imprisonment was an appropriate response to the infraction; and (d) whether a sentence of fifteen years suited the offense.

Applying for a pardon, an idea first floated by Olive, Henry, Carey McWilliams, and Wortis while Henry was still in San Quentin, was impossible until the relaxation of parole restrictions. Once Henry was hired by the government, obtaining a pardon became extremely important lest he be a target for blackmail. Furthermore, any new federal position might require vetting that could uncover his background. On December 7, 1941, what had been important became urgent. With the United States at war and many jobs unrelated to defense likely to be eliminated, a prison record could render Henry unemployable just when he needed flexibility. Sidney decided a pardon was worth the almost super-human effort required.

A nice note of wedding congratulations from John Gee Clark suggested that he might be a good ally, but he soon left the chairmanship of the parole board to become a Superior Court judge in Los Angeles. With Henry employed, a feeler was put out in June 1942 to Joseph Brennan, the San Francisco-based Supervising Parole Officer on Interstate Matters, who coordinated Henry's parole with the New York authorities. He responded noncommittally but not negatively.[2]

The process was extremely arduous. Applications had to be accompanied by statements evaluating the merits of the petition, from the judge, district attorney, members of the jury who tried the case (moot for Henry since there was no trial), and the sheriff who investigated it. Henry could not do it himself because he had to work.

On November 3, 1942, Governor Olson was defeated in his reelection bid by a Republican hard-liner, the former state attorney general Earl Warren. Now remembered as a powerful liberal force in the Supreme Court and as the chairman of the commission that investigated the assassination of President Kennedy, as attorney general he breathed not a whiff of liberalism. Furthermore, he declared that his first act would be to fire Carey McWilliams, the defender of workers' rights and the Cowells' powerful ally. (In fact, McWilliams, like all ap-pointees, would have resigned when the governorship changed.) Because exec-utive clemency was connected to the Christmas season, missing the 1942 deadline would force them to wait a year, during which Henry would not only lose job opportunities in Washington, but these jobs might dry up. Furthermore, a pardon had the best chance when the issuing governor was leaving office and would not have to pay a political price. In 1943 they would have to deal with Warren as an incumbent. Sidney's connections within the California Democratic Party and with other influential friends—some of them parents of her former pupils at the Peninsula School[3]—could bring her into direct contact with Governor Olson. McWilliams must have been one of the names in her mind, but although he had offered in 1940 to help with the pardon, his name does not appear anywhere in Sidney's reports to Henry.

Unfortunately for Sidney, stubborn complications from the miscarriage included infected varicose veins in her legs. Although she was still supposed to spend hours lying with her feet elevated, she decided it was now or never, and she set off on short notice, colliding immediately with wartime travel conditions in which civilian passengers were a low priority.[4] Strangely, her first letter, from Berkeley the day after the election, is either misdated or suggests that she anticipated Olson's defeat and left before the vote. Knowing that the current editor of the *Palo Alto Times* had been incensed about what happened to Henry, she immediately asked the business manager of the paper and its affiliates to suppress publicity. Quietness would help the governor because grants of clemency—especially in sexual cases—can provoke nasty reactions. She hoped the editor could instruct her about the political situation in San Mateo County, where Henry was arrested and charged.

The rest of her first letter hints at the complexity of the process, though she was not yet aware of just how difficult it would be.[5] To begin with, she needed a good typist to make multiple copies of a statement of reasons for requesting a pardon, which she had to give to people who might write supporting letters. She then asked Grainger, Stokowski, and "Martha" [Graham] to write Governor Olson's secretary. Next, she needed influential people to accompany her when she called on the sheriff. Among them were the Tylers, wealthy San Mateo County residents "of impeccable antecedents" who were very close to Governor Olson. Although she did not know the Tylers well, she knew that the case "outraged them" and they would arrange for her to see the governor if she had trouble.

She then went to Los Angeles, shopping for "essential equipment"—a good hat—before seeing Judge John Gee Clark, who was friendly and gave her a thorough briefing. She had to call on each official in the case: Judge McNutt, Sheriff McGrath, Probation Officer Robinson, District Attorney Ferrell,[6] Interstate Parole Supervisor Brennan, and half a dozen others whose names she had never heard before. They would write the State Advisory Pardons Board, which would issue its recommendation to the governor, who had to hear their advice although he was not compelled to follow it. The Board consisted of the lieutenant governor as chairman, Earl Warren (in his capacity as outgoing attorney general), and another three or four people whom she saw but did not name. She asked the (unidentified) brother of Olson's campaign manager, whom she had known in Palo Alto and Washington for years, to write the governor; she picked up the letters personally because she was squeezing into a few weeks a procedure that usually took months or years, running from one person to another while barely recovered from the infection in her leg. Success hung on her stamina, the swift postal service of that era, and the telephone.

Her meeting with Joseph Brennan, the supervising parole officer, seemed oddly casual. Since he required a personal statement about the reasons for the application and its timing, she drafted something and got Henry's approval. She had been advised not to file the application through a lawyer since the Pardon Board wanted to get the "feel" of the applicant. Therefore, without consulting anyone, she based her request first on the principle that a pardon would agree with the recommendation of doctors and thus with a recent requirement that courts take into account psychiatric recommendations in sex cases.[7] She also explained the problem of Henry's obtaining any federal job,[8] incorporated his suggested emphasis that his work in the war effort was hampered because he could not travel outside the United States, and added that he earned much less money than he would if he had the proper title of manager.[9] Her formal phrasing, however, led Brennan to assume it had been done by a lawyer. When she said that she and Henry had written it themselves, he said that officials paid more attention to applications that were "funny." She did not change her draft, however.

When Henry examined the application papers sent by Brennan and considered the rule about serving notice on the San Mateo County District Attorney, he advised Sidney to see Assistant District Attorney Dan Sullivan instead. Although Sullivan had not worked in the criminal section, he was Henry's friend. Henry thought Sullivan might be able to sign the papers by himself to minimize publicity and could advise her about approaching Maxwell McNutt, the judge at the original hearing, who also had to provide a statement. At least there were no jurors to track down. To address the requirement for new facts, Henry suggested using the recent opinions of Drs. Wortis and Meyer that his case should have been handled medically. If Sidney agreed, Wortis would be asked for a simple opinion that Henry should have been treated medically, that he was cured, leading a normal life, and was not a menace. After reminding her that he did not trust lawyers, Henry urged her to find Duncan Oneal and consult with Judge Clark to be sure everything was in order.[10]

Sidney was living in a hotel in San Francisco, communicating only with people directly concerned with the pardon and trying to recline with her feet elevated for several hours a day when she was not going from one interview to another. During a trip to Menlo Park she passed by Henry's old house, now refurbished and painted, the pool empty, artichokes running wild. She didn't care for the way the area was getting filled up with little houses. "I felt so strongly today that we have both outgrown all this part of the world that Palo Alto & Menlo are definitely *past* for me & I think probably for you," she wrote Henry. "I'll always love this country, the form of the hills & the wonderful light—but I'm satisfied not to be living here."[11]

To her astonishment, no one objected to the request for a pardon.[12] Finally Sidney summoned up the courage to approach Gilbert Ferrell, the district attorney. At first he was away, so she spoke with Daniel Sullivan, his assistant, who described Ferrell as a real saint whose help was assured. Sullivan, she wrote in 1973, had some eleven sons who had played "over the years . . . on the 'Cowell baseball team' (which used Henry's open lot for their games and his shed to store things)." He said he had questioned the boys closely and concluded that nothing much had ever happened and that Henry had never approached the boys but joined in a few times "'in what was going on anyway.' . . . The Sullivan boys had separately come to the conclusion, which their father came to share, that the complaint was made in revenge when Henry ignored for many months the demands that he give his Stutz car to two relatively older boys who were not really part of the local group and lived many miles away." Sullivan confirmed that Henry had refused a lawyer and insisted on defending himself. Recognizing the obvious danger, he had brought in an attorney, but when Henry was told that the lawyer was sent by the prosecutor's office, he refused help. Henry (said Sullivan) thought that all he had to do was explain things and he would be released. Sidney's conversation with Sullivan reinforced her faith in Henry's truthfulness.

When she returned, Ferrell, the district attorney, declared that he had been looking for several years for a family member, without whom he could not initiate remedial action. (Presumably it would have been indiscreet to contact Henry through the parole board.) Ferrell confirmed that the storm of publicity made it even harder for him to render true justice. He was the one who noticed that the couple who published a "sort of gossip sheet" and attempted to blackmail Henry had been to the jail previously, offering to "help" inmates. Her report of that conversation was the first time Henry learned that the two had been arrested. He had continued to worry about them when he was paroled.

Ferrell told her that the whole case got out of control because Henry would not accept legal help, "so that the law got caught up in a series of obligatory moves nobody really intended—and that the setting of the maximum sentence for the offense had never occurred before or since and was, he felt, due to a couple of other and quite different sex cases that had made everybody nervous." He supported the pardon wholeheartedly and was puzzled that it had never been requested before. "Mr. Sullivan sat by at the beginning of my interview, smiling benignly at evidence that sustained his claim to sainthood, or saintliness, I guess I mean, for [the D.A.], who was certainly the oddest looking man, for a saint; he had a broken nose and very knobbly face and two cauliflower ears; he was once a prize fighter."[13]

Her next heroic efforts, omitted in her later memoir, fill her enormous November 16 letter to Henry. After eight hours on the train she arrived in Los Angeles, where she and Judge John Gee Clark had "the best possible" talk on November 15. He told her that Governor Olson's Advisory Pardons Board was an enormous improvement over its predecessors, and he referred all applications to it.[14] Clark agreed that the case was not criminal but medical, but warned that two Board members, and possibly the governor himself, would have difficulty swallowing that. He advised her to emphasize that originally the case had not been recognized as medical. Now that that status had been proven, criminal liability was an unfair burden. This approach might persuade the recalcitrants. Judge Clark assured her that the chairman of the Advisory Pardons Board was "a fine person and will be helpful." Like Brennan, he advised against using a lawyer. Clark was so convinced about the pardon that he offered to do anything, including talking to the governor.

Sidney was content to have to wait around until the end of the week; it allowed her to get off her legs. Henry now needed to get documents and copies of Alvin Johnson's strong letter to Governor Olson. She planned to wait to see the governor until mid-December, when he would have the documents. In the meantime, she wanted to amass some "big sticks" to prevent publicity . . . "if I can locate the right sort of sticks in the county. I wonder whom a Sheriff is under obligation to???" Publicity could break out when the incoming Warren administration changed the Board, but she thought the newspapers would be too consumed with Christmas to bother much about the application. Nevertheless, she told Henry to ask to New York critics Virgil Thomson and Olin Downes to monitor the newspapers there as Alfred Frankenstein was doing in San Francisco.

Judge Clark then urged an all-out, immediate effort, but had contradictory thoughts about the next steps. After first telling Sidney to try to get the Board of Prison Terms and Paroles to recommend the pardon, he concurred with Henry's idea that the need for a pardon was so obvious that the Board should not be approached. Then, after warning that pardons usually follow the expiration of the sentence, he suggested getting the Paroles Board to commute the sentence with a recommendation for a pardon and promised to solicit the opinion of the chairman of the Advisory Pardons Board. Finally they agreed to aim at both the Paroles Board and the governor in case the Advisory Pardons Board failed them. Sidney was ready to see all of them. "I have a new black hat which is better than the red one for calling on Governors, et al. and you've no idea what a morale raiser it is to be so obviously a lady that courtroom attendants give you special consideration—undoubtedly thanks to the poise contributed by the new hat. It's very plain but extremely smart and becoming."[15]

Clark urged her to see his successor as chairman of the Board of Prison Terms and Paroles, and Stanley Mosk, the governor's secretary in charge of pardons, who were expected shortly in Los Angeles. When neither one appeared, Sidney took the fast train to Sacramento to find them. For the next several weeks she rushed from place to place, sending and receiving documents, encouragement, discouragement, and strategic advice. Told to get letters from famous people, she thought Grainger, Martha Graham, Stokowski, Dr. Johnson, and a certain Dr. Mozer would suffice, but added more targets.[16]

To prepare her for the struggle against publicity, Alfred Frankenstein got the managing editor of the *Chronicle* to explain how news is circulated. (By now she realized that Frankenstein was a supremely good person who would help in any way he could.) She was encouraged to learn that with the election finished, pardons were less of an issue, and the press rarely bothered about pardons to parolees. The wire services, he said, should be kept in the dark, however, something that was almost impossible. Sidney warned Henry that if a pardon looked likely, he should leave town and change the phone to an unlisted number. If the newspapers had trouble getting information, they would drop it.

Just before Thanksgiving she went to Parole Supervisor Brennan, whose assistant said that if the pardon failed, he would apply for termination of parole after the New Year. Max Radin—a renowned professor of law at Berkeley, writer on issues concerning pardon,[17] a good friend, and a key figure in her negotiations—told her that the Pardons Board was purely advisory. If the governor wanted to act, he would. She also discovered that friends of friends in Menlo were intimate with the governor and would make sure she could see him.[18]

On Thanksgiving Day, Sidney was back in Menlo Park. With so much contradictory advice it is no wonder that this supremely rational woman wrote Henry a long letter largely about omens—a black cat outside Judge Clark's office, a rainbow seen on the way to Pasadena, and bluebirds in Menlo Park the day she left to meet Max Radin and Brennan. "Today's black cat will serve me in good stead, perhaps, when I get the DA's signature in Redwood tomorrow." She was conferring with the governor's secretary, Stanley Mosk, in Sacramento on Tuesday, and would see the governor when he returned from the East. Sullivan, the assistant district attorney, had told her that the statement of reasons for pardon on the application was excellent. "The only person I *have* to get anything from is the DA. The other 2 people are consulted by the Pardons Board *if* the Governor asks that Board's opinion. I'm skipping the Sheriff but will see Judge McNutt tomorrow and ask him to write the Governor direct."[19]

She then went to Redwood City to get the district attorney's signature on the papers, which she planned to take to Governor Olson's office in Sacramento early the next week. Judge McNutt, who had sent Henry to jail, claimed that he had been instrumental in getting him a parole and that the parole board had met in his office "because they were 'scared of the thing' and wanted to go over it on the spot." (Sidney didn't believe him.) He didn't tell her openly that he would support a pardon but muttered something encouraging. Sullivan told Sidney that she could refer the governor to him.[20] A few days later Judge Clark informed her that he would soon talk to the governor about worthy clemency petitions.[21]

At the beginning of December, Paul Yarwood, the secretary of the Advisory Pardons Board, gave Sidney three letters of inquiry, addressed to the judge, the sheriff, and the district attorney, for her to deliver in person. Judge McNutt took it "with a mutter that was not unfriendly—but you can't be sure what he will do." In the absence of the district attorney she gave the letter to Sullivan, who again confirmed the decisive role of the press in Henry's sentence. She was slightly relieved to learn that the Board's actions were reported to all newspapers and wire services, but only the name, county, and number of the statute were given. No commentaries; no addresses. She thought that if there were a lot of names, it might not be noticed, but she still wanted Henry to make himself and his closest associates invisible. "I finally went shaking in my boots to see the Sheriff who was very friendly, wrote on the bottom of Yarwood's letter: 'I should be in favor of a pardon' & signed it with flourishes like that XIVth cent. music ms."[22]

Then Sidney discovered by chance that they were about to miss the final meeting of the Advisory Pardons Board, scheduled for December 10. Facing an early deadline for submissions she needed a stenographer to make eight copies of the material virtually instantly. She thought it barely possible that the governor would have acted without the Board if they had missed the meeting or if Yarwood, the Board's secretary, had not permitted her to file at the last instant. "Part of the initial trouble was that Yarwood was worn down by the nitwit who preceded me." She concluded, "Such a funny thing happened to me as I got into the hotel . . . [She told a story of a soldier and a very young wife insisting on a room with a double bed]. I could do with a double bed myself tonight, sweetheart. . . ."[23]

Later the same day, in pain again, she saw Mosk, the governor's secretary, and heard him request the Board to bring up the case out of turn. She would shortly see the lieutenant governor, who served as Board chairman. She also was told that if the Board recommends pardon, the governor signs automatically. On the 11th she would hear their decision, and if it were negative, Mosk would set up an appointment with the governor. Mosk thought it was borderline—but he had never seen a district attorney endorse a pardon. He added that the governor's office issues no publicity but the press comes to the Board meetings.[24] Henry rented a room in Greenwich Village. There was no sign of "the wicked reporters."[25] He shortly disappeared to Boston.

Despite the excellent prospects, the Board did not recommend the pardon, believing that "he should complete his fifteen-year term which will expire [with credits] December 8, 1945, and then permit some period of time to elapse thereafter enabling subject to demonstrate complete rehabilitation."[26] They recommended denial "without prejudice." Sidney persuaded Mosk to try for an appointment with Governor Olson on December 18, two days after he returned to Sacramento, and cancelled her return ticket to New York. "Don't be discouraged—I ain't."[27] In another letter, however, begun before she got the bad news, she admitted to being very frightened. Once she heard the decision, she resumed writing in a better frame of mind. Although granting the pardon could make life difficult for the governor, he did not have much to lose politically, since he had been voted out of office. She planned to ask Sullivan to go with her to the governor and repeat what he had told her about the effect of publicity at the time of the sentencing, explain the Board's position, and show that if there had been a reasonable sentence, conditions for favorable consideration would have been met. Sullivan agreed to her plan. At the very least she thought he would win commutation (shortening of the sentence) after January 1. To her delight, the county officials were all on her side, the only exception being the probation officer, Robinson, who was never approached, "& fortunately no one is likely to think of him."[28] In a sweet love letter, she confessed to feeling a little down and could only trust to fate. She was infinitely proud of the way Henry was taking it.[29]

Sidney went to Sacramento on Thursday, December 17.[30] When she saw Stanley Mosk the following Monday, he tried to dissuade her from letting Sullivan come in person, recommending that he write or wire instead. "I explained that since what he was going to say was an implicit attack on a San Mat. Co. Judge I di n't think he would do that—but anyhow I tried unsuccessfully to stop him—Sullivan . . ." She could not decide whether the governor's absence with a "cold" meant he would have time to read the petition or that Mosk did not want to tell her that the governor was going to deny the pardon. Sullivan had already arrived; she went off to find him and have a great steak dinner.[31]

Just after Christmas, Sidney wrote Henry that the news was neither good nor bad. Mosk, in fact, had not told her that the governor was not reading Henry's file. Sullivan then spent two hours persuading Mosk to remove the file from the negative stack and add it to the two hundred which could still be considered. Mosk finally decided that Sidney and Sullivan should see the governor. Sullivan, however, was under extreme pressure to get back to his job. Sidney was completely disheartened.

> If it is as hard as this to get the Gov. to give a few minutes to the case after all the people who have written, etc. & the entirely favorable lie of the land, then it is really impossible to get past the Governor's prejudice & I don't feel I'm smart enough to accomplish that, though I shall try. I do feel terribly low in my mind tonight. The Governor has n't touched an exec. clemency case since April! which sounds as though he were afraid of them.

She cancelled her reservations again and got a seat for the New Year's holiday. But her money was running very low.[32]

No letter to Henry gives the details of the next days because Sidney telephoned him when it was over. Some of the story is contained in an April 1943 letter to a friend.[33] For the rest, we must rely on her 1973 recollections. Governor Olson at first felt he could not reasonably pardon Henry, because the recommendation against clemency was too strong. She therefore decided to play her last, and strongest card—to get her friend Walter Packard to telephone him.[34] A soil scientist and influential member of the Roosevelt administration, Packard, we now learn, was the previously unidentified brother of Olson's campaign manager. His call changed the atmosphere. On Christmas Eve she was summoned to the governor's mansion, met by the governor's sister (or daughter, she wasn't sure), offered tea, and taken on a tour of the house.

> When the Governor was finally free, he looked over the brief papers I handed him and said kindly: "Well, it does seem to me this is something we can do!" I made the idiotic reply: "You'll be giving us a very happy Christmas, Governor!" This emerged from the depths of self-consciousness and some memory of some old-fashioned novel, I think. Governor Olson quite properly made an impatient gesture at me, and said seriously: "I suppose you understand these things better than I do: Can you guarantee that Mr. Cowell will never give trouble again?" I had recovered my wits, and said: "Governor, I am confident that he never will, but at the same time who can answer wholly for any human being for the rest of his life? All I am asking is that you take the same chance I have taken." He looked at me a moment very seriously, nodded, and said to Mosk: "I'll sign the papers at once and we'll mail them wherever you say." I said to HC in NYC, and 3 days later this was done.

The pardon, dated December 28, 1942, cited Sheriff McGrath's and Judge McNutt's recommendations, Seeger's urging that Henry be employable by the government in a regular capacity rather than as a "consultant" (a term designating casual or occasional employment); character recommendations from Stokowski, Edwin Franko Goldman, Percy Grainger, and others; and medical information that Henry was cured of the urge that had led to the abuse.[35] Mosk's cover letter ended, "May we urge that you at all times conduct yourself in a manner that will reflect only credit upon this act of clemency by the Governor."[36]

On leaving the governor's mansion she suggested to Mosk that "avoidance of publicity was in everybody's interest, and a journalist friend had suggested that this could be held to a minimum if the information was released to a newspaper in some small town where there were no wire services." Apparently he agreed.

The *Palo Alto Times* only had a brief article; Frankenstein asked his colleagues in San Francisco to monitor the announcement and ask their news editors to "give Cowell a chance.'" Nothing appeared in the East. In fact, to keep the newspapers quiet, almost no one was told about the pardon, although some possible benefits to Henry's reputation were thereby sacrificed.

Sidney departed without seeing anyone other than her mother and Dr. Wolff, whom she credited with accomplishing "the major part of whatever was sensibly done for Henry." To protect everyone involved—especially Walter Packard—she put nothing in writing about how the pardon was obtained until 1973, when just about everyone had died except Stanley Mosk and Alfred Frankenstein. This chapter's narrative is the first account of the whole episode.

In concluding her story, Sidney reflected on the effect of the pardon. Getting off parole meant the end of Henry's visits to Edelstein, "who often questioned him about his sexual life, to Henry's indignation. Henry told me, also, that his name was on the roster of the precinct in which he lived and a couple of times a policeman on the beat stopped him and warned him roughly that he was 'being watched.' All this, of course, stopped." Henry never overcame some of his fears, however, "not having understood much if anything about the law to begin with." He now could vote, but never did for fear of being challenged. Many friends said he never talked about being in jail but remained afraid of appearing publicly in California. When in 1945 he signed an exclusive agreement with a new manager, he excluded California from her territory, claiming that he had an extensive personal network there. But in fact he would not take engagements in that state out of fear of the press.[37] Lawyers whom Sidney consulted affirmed that he could have answered "no" if asked whether he had ever been arrested or convicted of a felony, but apparently that advice was not correct. In May 1943, Governor Warren signed into law a provision that pardoned felons could, after a period of time of moral living, apply for a certificate of rehabilitation, which removed the stain of a conviction. This new option was partly intended to let men clear their records so they could serve in the war. Although the period of waiting time for those discharged from prison before May 13, 1943, was shortened, there is no evidence that the Cowells ever applied for rehabilitation, and no references in any documents proving that they were aware of the new statute. It may therefore be presumed that he had to answer "yes" to the question of prior convictions, and then could mention the pardon as a mitigating factor. Currently, California—and other states—provide for expungement, with the same effect.[38] Sidney's lawyers might have been thinking of full presidential pardons, in which case the charges have automatically disappeared since the 1860s. In any case, she said Henry would never answer "no," and he may have been right to fear doing so. As a result, she said, he never applied for a full-time university appointment, "at Columbia, for instance, where he was always a Visiting Lecturer and then an

Adjunct Professor, at half the regular salary, because he would not put a job application through the mill." She also doubted that Douglas Moore would have supported it—an opinion independently offered by Moore's colleague and friend Jack Beeson.[39] Moore told Sidney that he worried for several years and was surprised not to have any complaints from parents about Henry's presence in the music department. "[Moore's] helping hand . . . deserves the more credit, I think, since he was so apprehensive." Henry's fears suggest that he never got his papers back from San Quentin because he felt safer keeping his distance.

She also thought that it was largely as a result of the involvement of the American Psychiatric Association that California law for sexual offenses was modified to require the court to consider the recommendations of psychiatrists.[40] Eventually she learned that Douglas Short, whom she had considered useless as a lawyer, worked assiduously for the change. (She may not have known that section 288a, the law of which he was in violation, was subsequently modified so that it now applies only to sexual acts with minors.) In concluding her story, Sidney said that she never was able to get confirmation of District Attorney Ferrell's statement that Henry was innocent of the offense as charged, and decided to drop the matter.

So it was finally over. Judge Clark, very pleased, congratulated Henry on the pardon, and Sidney for her extraordinary work.[41] She found out over the years that Wortis considered Henry's recovery one of his finest triumphs, thinking not about having treated him (which he did not do) but of his role in the parole and pardon struggles and his friendship with and encouragement of Henry, which helped get Henry through such awful times.[42] Sidney knew, however, that all the arguments in Henry's favor, all the support of influential people, the change in the law—none of it would have won the pardon had Walter Packard not intervened and gotten Governor Olson to think about the case.

43

The War Effort

As it happened, the pardon was granted just in time. Shortly after 1942 turned into 1943, Henry and Sidney attended the Washington wedding of her friend Bess Lomax, the daughter of John Lomax and sister of Alan Lomax, the distinguished folk-culture specialists. Bess told them that her employer, the Office of War Information (OWI), was hiring. Thanks to the pardon, Henry was eligible. Shortly after meeting with OWI's heads of music,[1] he had the job, for which he worked primarily out of its New York branch near Carnegie Hall. As expected, he also traveled a lot.[2] Needing to supplement the modest salary of $25.50 [2010: $321] a week after taxes,[3] he continued with the State Department–New School's Latin-American Distribution Project until it ended late that summer,[4] served as an occasional consultant for the Pan American Union until the end of the war, and taught at the New School. Since June 1942 he had also been giving workshops at the Mills School, a New York institution that educated female nursery, kindergarten, and primary teachers.[5] He now turned that job over to Sidney, whose qualifications were at least as good as his. Even without it, he was again forced to spread himself very thin.

The OWI was a new version of the Foreign Intelligence Service, created in 1941 to combat Nazi propaganda. Renamed when the United States entered the war, it was directed to coordinate the wartime message. Its radio arm, the Voice of America, had only begun work two months before Henry joined the agency. From the outset, a conflict raged between two factions. An idealist group wanted to disseminate only the truth about the United States and emphasize its aspirations for universal freedom and security. Their opponents, who included President Roosevelt, were determined to win the war by any means, including bending the truth and employing questionable tactics such as convenient alliances with a North African French colonial leader who had been a Vichy supporter, and with "former" dedicated fascists jockeying for power after Mussolini was deposed in the summer of 1943. Malodorous as were such collaborations, the idealists also made some disastrous mistakes, such as calling the Italian king "a little moron" on the air. Ultimately they were forced out of OWI, leaving it to concentrate upon military propaganda and psychological warfare, a job at which it excelled.[6]

One might imagine the music section filled with idealists who had to evacuate when the internal battle came to a head. Actually, they were barely affected, since their work was straightforward and apolitical—programming music that would attract listeners and keep them tuned in for political messages. The selection of music was conditioned largely by the broadcast technology, which included shortwave from abroad, longwave from ships or territory unoccupied by the enemy, and "outpost" transmissions from clandestine stations within enemy territory. The main broadcasting unit, the Voice of America, was sent recordings for longwave transmission into enemy territory in Europe and Africa. Shortwave was not a good medium for music however; reception is unreliable and marred by interference, and underground receiving stations could not waste a second listening to music. They needed news quickly, because the longer a receiver was in use, the greater was the risk of discovery. Nevertheless, some music was broadcast or smuggled to outpost stations.[7] The number of transmissions was staggering. Shortwave programs were sent out from many studios simultaneously day and night, covering the globe. Some 25,000 pieces of music were sent out worldwide in addition to the massive stock needed for Western Europe.[8]

At the time Henry joined, the music staff faced serious issues of quality. Technicians were broadcasting music they liked rather than music that would do the job. Careless programming had already provoked destructive responses from enemy stations. When, for example, OWI broadcast an American version of the German song "Tannenbaum," the Nazis used it as evidence that Americans did not have their own culture.[9] Bess Lomax Hawes said that Henry was brought in because his knowledge of world music enabled him to find music that both represented the United States well and attracted listeners.[10]

As associate music editor, Henry first supervised OWI's library of music for broadcasts to Continental Europe. As the war progressed, he supervised selection of music for other countries, which, by early 1944, included much of North Africa and the Middle East. He also filled requests from the San Francisco office for material suitable for India and occupied countries in Asia and the South Seas, helped the foreign-language desks of OWI select local and American music for transmission to their respective countries, wrote program notes for translation into various languages, and drafted label copy for the records. All of this required him to keep abreast of events in many countries and read all reports by the heads of OWI foreign desks. He could not possibly have been unaware of politics, as Sidney claimed.

The OWI record library had to be expanded continually. When its music stockpile was inadequate, Henry obtained material from commercial and private sources, but some pieces had to be specially recorded or composed, such as his arrangement of "Yankee Doodle," which became the call sign of the Voice of America. The demands varied considerably. Most of what was needed was readily available, including good American performances of Italian operas and other works by Italian composers, popular Italian artists singing folk songs and pop songs, and ecclesiastical and other early Italian music. The Balkans were much more difficult because each ethnic group had different requirements.[11] Henry and Hawes fought to keep the "language desks" (the staff handling propaganda for particular areas) from distorting the United States' reputation. According to Hawes, Henry excelled at negotiations with the desks because he knew both the overseas and the American points of view. Occasionally there were angry discussions with a national representative working at a language desk, such as a South African who insisted that no black or jazz-related music be transmitted.[12]

Unfortunately, the whole prewar European record-pressing industry had been centered in Berlin. With factories like Lindstrom in the enemy camp, new facilities had to be built from scratch. A pressing facility set up in Greece was wiped out in the Nazi invasion, and North African countries urged OWI to press records of their indigenous music in the United States. Henry solved the North African problem in Brooklyn, contracting with a firm from which he had been buying Arabic records and instruments since the mid-1930s.[13]

One State Department request for special materials turned out to be challenging and very entertaining. The Shah of Iran, having decided to improve the muscularity of his army, asked the State Department to prepare a series of recordings for physical exercises. The job was given to Henry, who had studied Iranian folk music. He composed short pieces to be recorded with instructions for touching one's toes and other exercises, arranged them for string quartet and Hammond organ, and hired musicians from the New York union. They also needed a speaker to call out exercise instructions in colloquial Farsi. Finding no one in the United States, they finally imported two Iranians from Canada, both of them so frail that the staff had to take great care not to lose such precious assets. Because they had poor rhythm and counted in Farsi too irregularly to align with the music, Henry decided to have one of them count and the other do the exercises; he conducted the musicians. The one doing the exercises then would get tired and need to be revived. Bess Lomax Hawes remembered the recording taking about two days, as the "tough" union musicians looked more and more fed up, but the album turned out well because "Henry used exquisite taste." The State Department was very pleased. "So was the Shah," added Sidney, who thought it would have been more constructive to feed the soldiers better.[14]

The exercise music—an odd sequel to that unrealized 1935 plan to create music for swimming strokes at Stanford—did not make it into the catalogue of

Henry's music. Other known pieces composed for wartime broadcasts were *This Is America, 1943*, a fanfare for brass; *Improvisation on a Persian Mode*, for orchestra; and "Theme for Arabia." His signature music for the Persian-desk broadcasts was used daily for more than two years.[15] Henry also created some short programs about individual American composers including a fifteen-minute show about Ives. Making a program was only the first step, however; it had to be accepted for broadcast. In December 1943, when the Ives show was certified for transmission in Europe and the Middle East—with other locations pending—the war gave Ives one of his earliest opportunities to be heard nearly worldwide. It did nothing for him domestically because OWI programs could not be aired in the United States.

In February 1944, a *Time* Magazine story, "Hoosegow Harmony," reported another wartime radio series—"San Quentin on the Air," broadcast coast-to-coast and by shortwave to American troops abroad. John Hendricks, serving his life sentence, was still conducting. Apparently the new prison conservatory was effective, because there were twenty-two players and a twenty-six-inmate glee club. When a producer suggested using simpler arrangements, he was told that they did not want to sound like "a bunch of lop-eared cons." They needed a drummer, but assumed one would turn up.[16] The theme song "Time on My Hands" was gone, having been purchased by a watch company. Henry does not say whether he had a hand in arranging the prison's broadcasts to the troops. It is fair to guess that he kept clear of it.

Shortly afterward, Henry was put in charge of music for East Asian broadcasts.[17] One of his first acts was to get a naval unit close to Japan to record Japanese popular music from broadcasts on Japanese radio. The OWI then inserted American commentary in Japanese to show that Americans knew and loved their music, and broadcast it back.[18] At about the same time, when Sidney went west for an extended period to care for her ailing stepmother, she and Henry decided to induce OWI's San Francisco office to request him on short-term loan so that he could advise them on Asian music and inspect their record library. (Since he would not be performing, he did not worry about coming to California.)[19] The agreement was finalized right on D-Day, June 6, 1944.[20] After the summer he returned to New York and went to San Francisco for OWI in December, his last official trip,[21] but he continued to consult with the San Francisco group by telephone.[22] Fortunately, General MacArthur, the supreme commander for the Asian war, who had once distrusted propaganda warfare, gradually recognized its utility.[23] Otherwise, funding might have vanished and Henry's expertise in Asian culture would have been wasted.

Despite Henry's impressive accomplishments,[24] further professional advancement was blocked because he lacked Civil Service status. Quite possibly he never applied for it to avoid discussing his past. Therefore, when, according to

Hawes, he should have been appointed head of the OWI music department, the job went to Daniel Saidenberg, a young conductor, and Henry became "Senior Music Editor," which was supposed to be a promotion.[25]

In the early spring of 1945, with the war far from over, Henry suddenly resigned. A gracious on-the-record letter from John K. Fairbank, acting deputy director for the Far East, praised his speed and efficiency.[26] The truth was that Henry had been fired without warning and told to empty his desk. He told Bess Lomax Hawes that it was some kind of security check problem. She was mystified; she knew he should have been made director. Henry never told her that when Seeger learned of the probable promotion, he cautioned Henry's superiors, who summarily discharged him. Seeger explained that since he himself was working for the government and had recommended Henry, a scandal could also cost him dearly. While Sidney understood Seeger's perpetual nervousness about his own political past, Henry, in fact, had told OWI's administration about his background. "Once [Seeger] undertook to consider it a risk, and to mention it out loud, they felt they had no choice."[27]

As it happened, he got out just in time. In August, as the nuclear bombings abruptly brought the war to an end, the office was in chaos, its future uncertain. Since no one knew how long it would survive, planning was impossible.[28] It was assumed that OWI would be dissolved and absorbed into the State Department, which, Bess said, was "hovering . . . like crows over the corpse."[29] In November, the office was struggling to stay alive. When Roy Harris took over from McPhee, who had replaced Saidenberg, strategic errors abounded, especially the revival of the discredited idea that OWI should propagate American taste. Sidney felt that Harris acted "against all common sense: the operation was only intended to attract listeners. Anybody with any experience in the U.S. government knew that you could n't talk about activities in music, nor in art, without upsetting Congressmen; it was necessary to be inconspicuous and to have a very clear useful war aim. . . ."[30] Harris was soon dismissed, and President Truman finally abolished the OWI. The Voice of America was revived in 1947 to fight the Cold War.[31]

With the termination of OWI, the music archive was marked for destruction, but the staff refused to oversee the death of their irreplaceable holdings. Bess Lomax Hawes thought she had successfully negotiated the transfer of the archive to the Library of Congress,[32] but OWI's scores and recordings actually went to libraries at the United States Information Service's centers in London, Paris, Bern, and Rome.[33] Excellent reference facilities, the libraries lasted well into the 1980s, when they were gradually eliminated as security measures meant to combat German and Italian terrorists led to the exclusion of the general public from embassies and consulates.

Despite the war and the demands of his OWI job, and his supplementary positions, Henry continued many of his customary activities, albeit on a very reduced level. His few public performances included a recital at the Juilliard Summer School and an appearance as guest artist on Szigeti's Town Hall recital.[34] Still a composer-performer with visual appeal, he made his first television appearance on January 19, 1945, in Schenectady, New York.[35] Miscellaneous engagements included a pleasant, informal East-West evening at the White House arranged by Pearl Buck at the invitation of Eleanor Roosevelt. Henry had been asked to organize the Chinese musicians for two plays by proletarian writers, but Ms. Buck spoke for so long that only one of them could be performed. A guest encouraged one Chinese musician who never got to play to sound a few notes so he could say he had performed at the White House. The evening ended badly when a pickpocket at Union Station lifted Henry's cash, train tickets, and Ives's checks for *New Music*.[36]

44

Old Friendships Renewed

With San Quentin in the past, the war over, and the OWI job finished, it is a good time to pause and examine how Henry's friendships had come through. Some of his oldest friends were gone. Georgia Kober had died in 1942, Bartók and Webern in September 1945. Kitaro Tamada, his shakuhachi teacher, alive but trapped in the Owens Valley, California, detention camp for Japanese-Americans, wrote regularly. Weisshaus, on the run from the Nazis, seemed to have vanished in the USSR. The chief survivor among Henry's most distinguished European friends was Schoenberg.[1] Henry found that he had not lost the confidence of old friends like the Seegers, Alvin Johnson, Judy and Armitt Brown, Cary de Angulo, and Terman. Relations with Copland and Varèse had steadily improved. The disturbances in Henry's relationship with the Graingers had been resolved when he moved out of their house.

To Henry's relief, Harmony Ives's reservations about him were overcome, in part by her deep affection and respect for Sidney. The Cowells' relationship with the Ives family was rapidly becoming more important than ever to them. As Ives's health deteriorated, it was urgent that someone deal with his music and get it to the public. Manuscripts needed to be organized, edited, and published, but despite Ives's cooperation, the process could be extremely frustrating. The first project, to prepare the *Robert Browning Overture* for publication, is a good example. Henry cleaned up errors and ambiguities in the messy manuscript, but Ives could not find some missing pages and authorized him to fill in the gaps. After five months of work, which Ives approved despite his poor eyesight, the missing pages materialized, rendering Henry's labors useless. He declined Ives's offer to pay him.[2]

Henry's plan to publish the third Violin Sonata in an edition by Sol Babitz and Ingolf Dahl brought more aggravation. After Dahl declined to copy it, it was sent to a professional, who charged $200 [2010: $2,520]. Fearing that this was too much to ask of Ives, Henry offered to pay three quarters of it from *New Music Quarterly*'s production budget, since Ives had already committed himself to paying for that volume in its entirety.[3] Ives responded (via Harmony): "You wont [sic] be a celebrated musician unless you learn to send out bills—ask Wally Damrosch, Josy Hoffman, Vicky Herbert—et al. So enclosed is in payment of your unsent bill for your fine work & help—if this is not enough, more will be sent!—A ba koi!"[4] Then he sent the postdated monthly checks for New Music, apologizing that because he had not been at all well, he "can't attend to nothin."[5] Despite the professional copying, the Violin Sonata puttered along for seven more years.

Henry's efforts to get Ives's music performed brought profound frustration. Artur Rodzinski was particularly disappointing. In June 1943, he requested all available movements of the Holidays Symphony, implying that he would perform them with the New York Philharmonic. Henry complied, but Rodzinski did nothing. Next, he asked for the Fourth Symphony, but again did nothing.[6] Henry then got Lou Harrison to convert Ives's World War I song "They Are There" into a "war march" for orchestra and chorus, apparently at Rodzinski's request. A recorded performance would have been perfect for OWI, but Harrison was in no psychological condition to follow through. Henry did the job but asked Ives to send his fee to the very needy Harrison.[7] In September, "War Song" was ready for Rodzinski, who did not even perform it as an encore.[8]

The many false promises of performances were so distressing that Henry and Elliott Carter proposed to assemble an informal committee of musician-friends who would try to get Ives's music to more performers.[9] Harmony unexpectedly replied that they thought the plan "most kind & generous." Ives had experienced a major change of heart, repudiating his past professional reclusiveness as more and more people told him to exert himself for his music. Harmony had convinced him not to object, hoping that it would not give Henry and Carter too much trouble.[10] As Ives's seventieth birthday (October 20, 1944) neared and Henry's Ives program was being transmitted worldwide by OWI, the two of them organized a celebration, but Ives, again unwell, had been advised not to see anyone.[11]

Henry could now see that the rupture with Ives had partly been caused by his physical and emotional fragility. Although Ruggles had no such excuse, Henry had such high regard for his talent that he could not hold a grudge. By 1943, they were back to their old form. Ruggles himself had not changed; insecurities and prejudices did not prevent him from accepting the friendship of those who could help him, and Henry's was no exception.[12] In the spring of 1945 the New Music Society gave a party in his honor. Despite the old hostility between Ruggles and Varèse, Louise Varèse was the hostess; Lou Harrison handled all arrangements; John Kirkpatrick played Ruggles's piano music for the guests, who included many good composers and painters. Henry spoke lovingly about their long relationship, characterizing Ruggles with good humor. "Ruggles has always been far from reluctant to make public his dislike for other composers. His reasons for this are always good, from his point of view. . . ." He studies scores very thoroughly, Henry said, and there is no appeal from his judgment: "Ruggles is not really conceited; he thinks his own music is the best only because no one else writes according to his standards. He is quick to call attention to positive values as he sees them." Yet his brusqueness had made him some very good friends. To conclude, Henry told the story about Ruggles putting a new chord to the test of time.[13] Ruggles was beside himself. "I tried to get you on the phone 3 times, You and Sid must have been away. It was a magnificent reception; one of the most significant events of my life, and I can't find words to express to you my deep appreciation for all you have done for me, both past and present."[14] He seems to have forgotten having rejected Henry in his time of greatest need.

The Cowells' relationship with Lou Harrison became more and more complex. When Harrison moved to New York in 1943, he was a troubled twenty-six-year-old[15] to whom the Cowells gave emotional support and advice to consult with Dr. Wortis. Henry also found copying and editing jobs for Harrison, and almost certainly is the one who steered him to Virgil Thomson, who engaged him as a stringer for the *Herald Tribune*. Regrettably, Harrison's mental state was too fragile for such an exposed job. Before long he was hospitalized with a nervous breakdown, pouring his heart out to Henry and especially Sidney, who seems to have become a substitute mother.[16] Once Lou was functioning again, Henry helped him withdraw from music criticism by getting him jobs to do for Ives.[17] An excellent idea, it gave Ives another champion and led to Harrison's conducting the 1947 world premiere of the Third Symphony, the first complete performance of any Ives symphony. Ives stayed away for fear he would be laughed at, but it won him the Pulitzer Prize.[18]

Ives, Ruggles, Grainger, and Harrison are the friends about whom most is known in the early 1940s; Cage was very close to both Cowells, but their friendship is poorly documented. All three said they telephoned or saw one other frequently,[19] and Cage and Sidney remained close until his death.

When a man becomes as busy and famous as Henry Cowell, one cannot help wondering if he bothered about his oldest friends. One example is Evelyn Wells. The lack of letters suggests that he had relegated her to history, but a chance remark in the 1970s reveals that he visited her and her family whenever he was in San Francisco; Sidney described Henry and Evelyn as lifelong friends. In the later 1950s, when Wells had moved to Dobbs Ferry, New York, not far from the Cowells, they spent a lot of time together. After Henry's death, Wells and Sidney remained close friends. Jaime de Angulo, who disappeared from the correspondence in the 1910s, also must have been in touch, because a handful of letters from the 1940s do not imply that relations had lapsed for twenty years, and he gave the Cowells a parcel of land on his ranch in exchange for their helping solve some problems of water supply. Although there are very few letters between Riegger and Henry after 1940, Riegger considered Henry his closest friend. His appointment books indicate regular contact by phone and at many social events, especially bridge games.[20] Adolph Weiss also fills the pages of letters in the 1920s and 1930s, but is scarcely mentioned later. Yet when he was in New York he often joined the Cowells in playing bridge. Other bridge regulars included the Greissles—Schoenberg's in-laws—and Cage. John J. Becker, who had never lost faith in Henry, was in close contact.

It seems that most people had welcomed Henry back with open arms. Paul Farnsworth felt that more publicity of the pardon would have helped, but he did not believe that Henry had fewer real friends as a result.[21]

45

Figs

In April 1945, Henry completed the periodic follow-up form for Terman's gifted program, irritated at its one-size-fits-all questions, which did not take into account his unusual history. For the question about education, he answered, "You have nothing low enough listed here. Never got to high school." For employment he wrote, "many jobs, musical." His income had risen from about $1,400 [2010: $20,700] in 1941 to about $4,927 [2010: $61,000] in 1944. Allowing for inflation, it was about double its pre-prison level, also adjusted. He described his physical condition since 1940 as good. Asked if he has had any tendency "toward emotional disturbances, nervousness, worry, special anxiety, or nervous breakdown in recent years," he answered with a firm NO. Sidney disagreed. Nervousness, worry, and special anxiety definitely described his feelings about earning a living, developing security for the future, and the thought of his past. The pardon had not improved his prospects for a full-time teaching position, although Henry's courses constituted 60 percent of the New School's music offering.

That spring Sidney went to California again to care for her stepmother. After spending the rest of the semester teaching and composing, Henry went west, where they planned to spend most of their time.[1] It was not that he had decided he could re-start his public career there. In fact, he had accepted a job working on the fig ranch near Fresno owned by Sidney's father, C. A. Hawkins, with whom he had developed an excellent rapport.[2] Hawkins was about to lose his ranch manager and wanted Henry to succeed him. In March, as Henry and Sidney were contemplating their future, Hawkins sweetened it with an interest in the business. Henry would be expected to do anything Hawkins and the manager thought he could handle, including buying ranch supplies, repairing harvesting materials, operating a dehydrator during the harvest, driving a truck in the orchards to deliver the harvest boxes, scouting for additional labor, helping to harvest and sell the crop, finding trucks to haul fertilizer and rationed gasoline to run them, writing government reports.[3] Although it was worlds away from Henry's usual life, the income was steady, he and Sidney would be together, and he would have peace to compose.[4]

Ranch life was hardly idyllic. Almost immediately upon arrival, Henry had to arrange testing for crop infestations, price all manner of plumbing equipment, deal with fruit buyers, investigate leasing of prefabricated building units, and so forth. It is no wonder that Sidney worried about the job being too open-ended.[5] Yet he took the work in stride, telling Lou Harrison that he was being creative while raising a million figs a year.[6] And the musical world was never far by mail and telephone. A presentation of Henry's music at Fresno State College in September (1945) must have been his first public appearance in California since 1936.[7] The atmosphere was good for composing. In November, he wrote Richard Franko Goldman that he was testing figs and writing band pieces.[8]

Although he did not complain about the hard work, it had its effects. During the first summer on the ranch, Henry's heart began racing, thumping, and keeping him awake. The condition was diagnosed as auricular fibrillation, which some doctors thought was nervous while others ascribed it to physical damage to the heart, possibly from chorea, possibly from conditions in San Quentin. His doctor told him to avoid physical or nervous strain and rest daily, believing that the damage might have no effect for years.[9] Henry's condition gradually improved until the irregular beats disappeared and he was taken off digitalis.[10] Over the next year, however, the symptoms returned and he was put back on medication.[11]

The Cowells stayed at the ranch until the middle of January 1946,[12] when Henry was committed to teach at the New School. They returned to Fresno in April,[13] remaining through the fall. During their cross-country drives there were some odd moments. Once, finding themselves in the emptiness of Nevada with no place to stay, they camped on what turned out to be Kennecott Mining property. A guard who roused them—apparently a Swede—recalled Henry's 1932 appearance in either Uppsala or Stockholm and invited them to stay on his lawn instead.[14]

Sidney described the ranch routine to Harmony Ives in the summer of 1947.

> I wish you could see Henry slip off to the little trailer standing under a fig tree which he has appropriated for his office, very early in the morning, to spend a couple ... [of hours] before the work of the day thickens. Then from nine to five or so he earns a living, and does his own music late in the afternoon and after supper. Lately his business activities have consisted of making the arrangements for harvesting, cleaning, sacking and selling the 15-acre bean crop. Figs come along later. He gets letters with the letterhead: "John Simmons, Bean Seller" and "Tom Joyce, Bean Buyer." As the annual bean crop is comparatively small and soon over, these gentlemen must have an assortment of letterheads—peaches, raisins, olives, nuts, figs, all come along later, each briefly and intensively.[15]

Henry felt the summer of 1946 was especially productive. His career advanced, thanks to his strengthening relationships with conductors like Koussevitzky and Richard Franko Goldman. He toured a little and got good reviews; a nationwide broadcast brought his music to his Iowa relatives for the first time. During the two years split between the ranch and New York, Henry produced a quantity of music that looks impressive at first glance, but much of it is occasional pieces for family events and piano pieces for beginners. There are also many choral works, some songs, and a few chamber pieces. He completed an Overture for two orchestras, for the summer music camp at Interlochen, Michigan, and his Fourth Symphony, for Koussevitzky and the Boston Symphony. Many pieces from these years are incomplete. The Sonata for Violin and Piano and the *Hymn and Fuguing Tune* No. 7 for viola and piano are about the only compositions still played reasonably often. In New York, on March 11, 1947, Henry was given a grand fiftieth birthday party, which Ives could not attend, although Harmony expected to be there. It looked like Richard Franko Goldman would write a biography of him.[16]

In October 1947, Henry and Sidney spent their sixth wedding anniversary in Yosemite, hiking, picnicking, and dealing with bears.[17] Then they left the ranch for the last time. Sidney felt that her father never got used to Henry's absence, although Henry continued to help from the East by dealing with food brokers about pricing the figs.[18]

Despite the bright signs, the combination of his legal and political histories weighed heavily. He constantly had to fend off his radical friends, who were potentially more dangerous than ever as fears of communism heated up. When the young composer Conlon Nancarrow spent a few hours with Henry in 1947 he did not see his celebrated cheerfulness.

> I had never met him before, so I don't know how he was originally. But the impression I got was that he was a terrified person, with a feeling that "they're going to get him." He may have had that all his life, but I don't think so; I think it had to do with that [jail] experience. And of course, after that, politically, he kept his mouth completely shut. He had been radical politically, too, before. It's quite a sad case.[19]

‖ 46 ‖

A Settled Life

Henry now spent nine years constantly busy but, for the first time, without spectacular adventures. His economic position improved as the flood of veterans transformed the world of education and brought new teaching opportunities, all of them, alas, part-time and time-consuming. At The New School he gave three or four courses each term,[1] ranging from "pre-elementary" theory (how to read notes), to advanced theory and a survey of modern music.[2] Although he was paid per student, he did not shrink from driving away potential enrollees by grading severely, sometimes giving nothing higher than a C.[3]

In his surveys of new music, invited guests presenting their own music gave his students a feeling for the vastness of new composition. In 1952 alone they included Alan Hovhaness, Douglas Moore, Virgil Thomson, Elliott Carter, Morton Feldman, Christian Wolff, Pierre Boulez—who was advertised as France's "most hissed" composer—and John Cage and his experimental group. (Sidney said that after attending the premiere of Cage's 4'33" in August 1952, Henry "gravely asked John for permission to compose a set of variations on themes from this piece, and John graciously gave it."[4] That impressive group of composers was by no means the outer limit of his eclecticism, however. A 1953 summer course for laymen, "The Nature of Music," emphasized current events, country and city folk music, jazz, ragtime, rhumba, bop, and more. Henry also participated in New School symposia involving composers, writers, visual artists, dancers, and art and literary critics.[5] Among his students was Burt Bacharach.

On November 16, 1953, The New School celebrated Henry's twenty-fifth year with a major retrospective concert. Selecting Douglas Moore to preside was itself a salute to Henry's ecumenical spirit. Dean Clara Mayer, who had originally been skeptical about his ideas, declared that he and music at The New School had always been synonymous. A list of the composers whom Henry had invited to the school over the years included just about every name of consequence except Ives, who almost certainly declined more than once. In the concert, Henry played percussion in two movements from *Set of Five* and concluded with a small piano group.

If Henry's open-mindedness to conservatives had ever been intended as a political investment, it never paid off. As chairman of Columbia's music department, Douglas Moore could have offered him a post but would have had to convince tough administrators to appoint someone whose highest degree was a third-grade certificate. Furthermore, he remained nervous about Henry's history.[6] Fortunately, Columbia's School of General Studies—which primarily serves adults—could engage teachers who were not Columbia professors. In 1948, Willard Rhodes, an ethnomusicologist who also chaired the General Studies music program, engaged Henry as an adjunct,[7] a rank that paid only $700 [2010: $6,340] for two courses, which could be canceled for insufficient enrollment. It carried no benefits, but was better than nothing. He taught composition and advanced composition in the evening to accommodate working students, and joined the summer session faculty in 1954. This part-time association with Columbia lasted until mandatory retirement in 1965.

In addition to his commitments at The New School and Columbia, in 1951 Henry accepted a massive teaching schedule at the Peabody Conservatory in Baltimore, committing himself to sixteen hours weekly, spread over four days, with classes in music literature, advanced solfège, and pedagogical principles; private lessons in composition, counterpoint, harmony, and orchestration; lectures on related subjects; and counseling students. Out of a salary of $5,600 [2010: $47,000], he had to pay for travel and rent a place to live. Clearly happy with his work, Peabody broke precedent and raised his salary for his second year.[8] Despite the load, he enjoyed his trips to Baltimore, which included regular meals with Hugo Weisgall and his family and singing in Weisgall's chorus. He loved relaxing at the small bar of the Hotel Stafford, which was run by an ex-magician. In addition to magician-colleagues who liked to discuss their repertory, it attracted potentates including Spiro Agnew, later governor of Maryland and eventually the disgraced vice-president to Richard Nixon.[9]

Henry's composition students at Peabody included the Canadian pianist Anton Kuerti and Stuart Feder, later a noted psychiatrist and author of a psychological biography of Ives. About twenty-one at the time, Feder had been studying with Nicholas Nabokov, whose treatment of students he found abusive. Upon learning that Henry had been hired, he switched to him and left one of the most detailed descriptions of Henry's teaching.

In contrast to Nabokov, Feder wrote, Henry was unassuming, straightforward, and naturally friendly. He gauged people only by their interest in music. If one could think of music as a thing in itself, separate from one's self, one was treated more as Henry's colleague than his student. Feder especially liked Henry's attitude that his students already knew something that should be cultivated, as opposed to condescendingly allowing them to profit from his lofty experience. As they worked through exercises in dissonant counterpoint, he was struck by how Henry taught principles rather than a system that could turn into dogma. Feder described himself as the sort of person who would have liked a textbook or similar material, but Henry, as far as he could recall, never recommended a single article. In their private lessons, they relaxed at a couple of student desks. The only time Henry went to the piano was to show him how to play the string-piano pieces "Aeolian Harp" and "Banshee." He often spoke about Ives and Ruggles but never about himself in the same breath.

He would read Feder's scores very thoroughly, rarely making suggestions or changes; he once commented that Feder would be surprised by what a passage would sound like, but did not encourage him to make any changes. Feder later realized that Henry heard everything when he read a score; he himself only imagined music with a piano tone. His experience with Henry helped him get his bearings and convinced him to leave music. Sidney told him that Henry believed one should not be a composer if one could think of being anything else.[10]

As if teaching at The New School and Columbia were not enough, beginning in 1949, Henry also gave a once-weekly course at Adelphi College, in Garden City, Long Island, which he enjoyed despite the travel because his seven students all were serious and had solid foundations.[11] He also collaborated with Juana de Laban of the Adelphi Dance Department—whose father devised a dance-notation system, something Henry had called for years earlier[12]—and with the college's Children's Theater. Although he resigned when he joined Peabody's faculty,[13] he continued to participate occasionally in collaboration with Hanya Holm and Louis Horst.[14]

Of course, with so much teaching, touring was next to impossible. That he did much at all can be attributed to the postwar boom, the broadening of American interest in the arts, the increasing ease of air travel, and his energetic new manager, Erminie Kahn, who worked with him for the rest of his life. Since her main income came from a public-relations job with a Latin American banana-boat company, she could afford to be scrupulously fair, raising Henry's fees, consolidating engagements to lower travel costs, and accepting no money unless she had actually procured the engagement.[15] Public events included a brief appearance on a CBS network television show, for which, to his great joy, he was paid.[16] He recorded his piano music for the Circle label, finishing the project in the summer of 1956. No longer able to play the very difficult solos, such as "Tiger," he had them dubbed off his old record.[17]

The Circle recording was later reissued by Folkways as part of Henry's long collaboration with Moses Asch, whom he had met through OWI. Asch had founded Folkways in 1947 primarily to promote high-quality jazz, but had begun collecting world music before the war. Using his own collection and copies of recordings that Henry had obtained in Berlin, he issued LP sets of world music entitled "Music of the World's Peoples," with liner notes by Henry. Asch remembered him as "a small laughing human being that . . . always was creative. . . . I never had enough of him."[18] Henry's last Folkways project, on Czechoslovak music, was left unfinished at his death.

As the stain of San Quentin faded, Henry got increasing invitations to be the featured composer at festivals and guest speaker at concerts and other special occasions in his honor. In 1951, upon election to the National Institute of Arts and Letters, he proudly informed Harry that he now had a respectable son.[19] Two years later, Wilmington College, a Quaker school in Ohio, awarded him an honorary doctorate, his first academic qualification. "It was very much fun being made a doctor," he told Olive, "and I now have a beautiful green, pink and white hood!" [20] Sidney wrote a friend, "When Henry was given an honorary Mus. D. degree . . . I was entertained to discover that there are Quakers still living who are n't sure they approve of music. One such lady whipped down the receiving line like a ship in full sail, shaking hands wordlessly with Henry but recovering her voice as she reached me: 'I suppose music *does* have a place, does n't it!' she said to me with a large graciousness, and passed on."[21]

The year 1954 brought two more honors—a Cowell Week at Stanford and an appearance on Edward R. Murrow's popular nationwide radio show *This I Believe*. The invitation to contribute to Murrow's program was a beautiful testimonial to his accomplishments, because other participants included some of the most prominent figures in political, intellectual, and artistic life, such as former president Truman, as well as ordinary folk. Henry probably was a bit satisfied that the invitees did not include Aaron Copland. Murrow's staff surely was wary of the fact that Copland had been summoned before Washington's communist hunters.

After beginning with a lovely statement of why he is a composer, Henry proceeded to his moral beliefs, which included a view of the USSR that represented either a rethinking of his earlier ideas or a need to reinforce himself against possible resurfacing of his past.

> My belief is that the Golden Rule is the supreme guide in human relations. I do not believe that any race or people is better or worse than any other.
>
> I believe that each human being should have the liberty to be an individual, and that everyone who wins the right to act in his own way must, in return to society, behave ethically.
>
> I used to be almost totally uninterested in politics; but it becomes increasingly clear to me that ethical individualism cannot flourish under radically extreme political conditions. Thus I abhor communism, under which individualism is impossible and expression of liberal

thought is punishable; and I abhor its right-wing counterpart under which innocent liberals fear persecution and reprisals of various sorts if they express their sincere ideas for the betterment of the government.

My own belief is in a regard for individual rights according to the letter and spirit of the United States Constitution. This I fight for by creating music which I hope will reach and touch all who listen so that they will be thereby encouraged to behave according to their own highest possibilities. Unexpected inner response to the power of music dedicated to human integrity might reach dictators more easily than an atom bomb.

In any event I believe that a truly devoted musical work acts to humanize the behavior of all hearers who allow it to penetrate their innermost being.

This is why I am a composer.[22]

Stanford's Cowell week comprised a concert of his piano and chamber music played by students (with Henry playing a few easier pieces), a workshop on student compositions, his "Autobiography of a Composer" lecture, a talk on extra-European music, a concert by the university orchestra and chorus, and a performance of *A Curse and a Blessing* by the Stanford band. Henry considered Stanford's festival a vindication of his life work.

As if to prove Sidney's point that Henry was regarded seriously as a composer despite a certain isolation within the profession, his music was taken up by more and more major conductors, and newer compositions entered the repertory of major orchestras. As radio performances rendered him reasonably "profitable," his publishers released most of his new orchestral and band pieces right away and without subsidy. Critics generally responded positively; Marjorie Fisher, music editor of the *San Francisco News*, who had written about Henry in her novice days, observed that what scandalized the press in the 1920s no longer raised an eyebrow.[23] Some reviewers felt, however, that his later compositions seemed disturbingly similar.[24]

Henry reduced his organizational work but did not eliminate it entirely. He had stayed with the New Music Society until 1945, gradually handing over leadership to younger people so he could devote more time to composing. The withdrawal of his energy was a powerful blow, however. The recordings lasted only until 1949; after Ives's support ended on January 1, 1955 (the January following his death), *New Music Quarterly* petered out, and closed three years later.

Quite surprisingly, the International Exchange Concerts reappeared as European cultural life began to revive. Daniel Ruyneman, still in charge after so many years, envisioned a bigger program than ever, with the collaboration of radio, conservatories, and universities. The only new feature was an attempt to involve

Latin Americans. Ironically, Ruyneman asked Henry to solicit the former sabo-
teur Varèse for the American board.[25] After 1950 the Exchange Concerts disappeared from Henry's correspondence.

As a member of the Executive Board of the League of Composers, Henry
tried to expand its work, urging that it extend its repertory to conservative
music, experimental music, and music for dance. He proposed League radio
concerts, more recordings (to replace New Music Recordings), an improved educational program, aggressive efforts to gain the cooperation of conductors, an
extension of the League to Latin America, and exchange concerts with groups
elsewhere in the country, as a kind of domestic version of the international exchanges.[26] He remained with the League until it dissolved in September 1954 by
merging with the New York chapter of the International Society for Contemporary Music (ISCM). He also continued to energetically for Broadcast Music,
Inc. (BMI) and the American Composers Alliance, of which he was president
from 1951 to 1955.

Henry appears to have been as placid as ever, but his and Sidney's serious
health problems were forcing change upon him. In 1951, he required an operation and long recuperation after doctors realized that his back pain was caused
by a ruptured disc, and his heart flutters seemed to forecast bigger trouble. Sidney spent a lot of 1952 in California dealing with her arthritis and cancer.[27]

The realities of mortality became apparent in January 1954 when Harry, a few
weeks before his eighty-eighth birthday, suffered a heart attack and died the following afternoon, after two decades of declining health. He and Olive had been
married for thirty-one years. Shipments of his clothing from Olive began to
alarm Henry. "It is fine that our own relationship has grown—I am delighted.
However, I feel that it is our own, and I hope you wont [*sic*]try to put me in Harry's shoes—it might result in some psychological confusion!"[28]

Henry's relationship with Sidney gave him the stability he needed to compose. The only problems that show up in their correspondence are the annoyances of daily life, such as finding decent, inexpensive housing in New York
during the teaching season. After only a month in a reasonably acceptable apartment at 169 West 104th Street, they had to vacate because the area was being
cleared for a huge low-income housing development. The frustrating search for
space probably accounts for a dream in which Henry visited an old apartment
and found that it had two enormous new bedrooms, a second-story front porch,
and a back porch looking out on a beautiful country meadow with a huge tree.[29]

Like so much in Henry's life, however, the evidence can be reinterpreted
depending upon whether one reads the family correspondence or Sidney's statements. In their letters one sees a close, loving relationship, filled with affection,
deep trust, and abundant shared interests. Once again, however, a statement by
Sidney some time after Henry's death overturns that well-documented picture.

After eight or nine years of marriage, she concluded that "there was a limit to what should be expected of me, and Henry and I lived thereafter as friends." Presumably she meant that sexual relations had ended. Although she had not the slightest idea of leaving him, he was so upset by the thought of her separating that he was overwhelmed by "all his embarrassment, shame, deep, deep distress at the public position his arrest had put him in" and temporarily lost the "poise and dignity with which he had always faced the world when he left SQ."

When I asked her to characterize their marriage, she told me a few anecdotes, implying that she did not want to say more. Three days later she apologized.

> I turned anecdotal, whereas what you needed to know was, would I call it a good marriage? The answer is yes, decidedly so, although like most marriages it could be quirky and unexpected. Its strength went beyond a middle aged love affair to a dependable friendship. We had many interests in common, and I never tired [of] the surprises produced by Henry's original mind. . . . And he was endlessly obliging if you asked a favor, if you could put what you wanted into words. He was not good at anticipating requests, but he liked to establish a domestic routine or two, and we had morning coffee together, with cat or cats, come hell or high water. We laughed at the same things, except that I could laugh at myself and he couldn't: he definitely did not care to be teased, which surprised me, and I had to learn better.[30]

With Sidney, however, nothing is easily dismissed. In a later statement about their relationship, she wrote that tremendous tension, resulting from his assumption that she would help him in his work, came to a head around 1948. Apart from all of the energy he required and, to her frustration, could match, she had to sacrifice her own goals and skills. "I had become increasingly the subservient and all-forgiving mother, and a servant, a slave, besides, and I simply could not stand it any longer." Unable to see why she could be bored by having to reshape his ideas, he was deeply offended, as one might expect of someone who could not laugh at himself. Even worse, she could not explain lucidly why one thing or another made her uncomfortable. "Anything I did n't want to do, or asked him not to do, was interpreted as a criticism, and he once informed me that he had *never* been able to take criticism, and did n't see why he should, since his intentions were always the very best!" She felt that the root of the problem was his conviction that "he *had* learned; he *knew*." Gradually she saw that the attacks on his music and the years of imprisonment had forced him to consider attacks on his dignity and pride as irrelevant. She saw that he was not about to change.

As his "so-unbelievably strong identification" with her began to totter, he became very critical, but instead of criticizing her directly, he would announce his displeasure in the company of others. "This did n't happen often, or I might really have left him; also I was more overcome with astonishment than with annoyance, I could n't imagine the gentle Henry. . . . But of course he had a ruthless and very aggressive side too." She would examine whether she really was at fault, but by the time she knew if the problem was Henry's, she could no longer feel angry or resentful. "Discussion was impossible. . . . He could argue rings around me, intellectually, for one thing; and could move from point to distant point, away from the core of the matter, so fast I could only laugh at his skill and my helplessness."

She eventually realized that such behavior arose whenever she "claimed the right to *feeling* differently from him about anything." But she also accepted some blame because she had married him "without the profound feeling of emotional dependence on him through which he might (but I don't really think so) have matured emotionally more than he did." He had no tolerance toward what she called the foibles of women; "let them be ever so little ineffectual or irrational and he was poised to attack at once." Strangely, her success at helping him in his work made him intolerant otherwise and "prevented his developing this adult compassion and tenderness." She does not seem to have perceived that on some level, he considered her an equal and thus ineligible for foibles.

She began having terrible nightmares and "occasional hallucinations of being buried in ordure as I walked along the street." After the second time, she made an appointment with a Jungian analyst in New York. That doctor was not quite right, however. A lesbian, on hearing of Henry's background, she wanted him to come to her also. The two of them then ganged up on Sidney, arguing that it was wrong to insist on cleanliness of clothes, the lack of which came from his desire to spare his sick mother doing laundry. In retrospect the experience seemed hilarious.

Later she added a note to her statement.

> It used to surprise me that Henry's music could express so much more warmth and feeling than he as a person could. . . . When I understood how unconscious were the sources of his music I came to see an unconscious development toward emotional maturity was brought about by time, esp. after the S.Q. experience in which pain & grief, others' as well as his own, seem to have become real to him for the first time. But this remained in his music and did not reach his relationships—at least not with me nor with anyone else so far as I observed. This is why his remark "As a man I suppose I am mostly music" rang in my ear with so clear a bell-like tone, of absolute clarity and truth as one rarely achieves about one's self in life.[31]

It is very difficult to know what to make of all this. Sidney herself was not an easy person, and her complexity is not mitigated by the fact that such an enormously gifted woman belonged to a generation in which the role of wifely helpmate was generally accepted. For a woman with her talents, Henry's demands were difficult. She would have needed more strength to resist them early, although, as she said, resistance was made difficult because Henry wanted help for laudable projects.

Considering Henry's sensitivity about San Quentin, his acceptance of some public appearances in California at first seems heartening. It, too, was deceptive. In 1947 he was extremely upset about receiving a letter with the San Quentin return address and feared that if rumors started, they could threaten everything he had accomplished. When Sidney wrote about it to Douglas Short—his old lawyer, who now worked at San Quentin—he was surprised and distressed. If he, Short said, had to live with such tension, he would prefer to take Sidney's suggestion and dig potatoes away from the public eye.[32]

The other danger, Henry's political history, came not just from his old radical friends. As the anti-communism of the 1940s mutated into the McCarthyist hysteria of the 1950s, blacklisting was in full force in all of the arts. John Copley's frighteningly detailed 1956 report on its effects in radio, television, and film[33] was unfortunately not followed by an examination of the classical music world, where blacklisting also existed. Henry's lifelong radical friends still did not comprehend why they should keep quiet about him. They persisted in believing, entirely without substance, that he had been framed as part of an anti-communist witch hunt.[34] He certainly was not being oversensitive about their unwanted attention; even his short exchange of letters with the Russian composer Reinhold Glière, in 1943, could now have worked against him. Despite his involvement with communism and the Soviet Union in the 1930s, Henry had passed security clearances for the OWI job after an FBI security check that noted his arrest, parole, and pardon.[34] Unlike Copland, he was never called up by the House Un-American Activities Committee (HUAC) or Senator McCarthy, despite a 1953 speech by William Grant Still, an old friend and almost a protégé, naming Henry as a communist sympathizer.[36] (It would be interesting to know whether Henry's name appeared in HUAC's Appendix IX, a huge list of alleged communists that was ordered destroyed because it violated civil rights. I have been unable to locate any of the few surviving copies.) Coincidentally, the Soviets had attacked Henry in 1948 during the renewed offensive against modernism that is best remembered for the assault on Shostakovich and Prokofiev. A hilarious cartoon of Henry destroying a piano by playing it while standing on his hands on the keyboard was published in *Sovietskaya Muzika* in 1948.[37] As to why Izrail Nyestyev and Grigory Schneerson singled him for other assaults, one can speculate that they did not know how much his music had changed, they believed he was useful to their efforts to enforce the new cultural policy, [38] or they needed to renew their own credentials as true believers. Indeed, they did.

In 1949, Nestyev and Schneerson, consummate organization men, were attacked during the campaign against Jewish musicologists,[39] and Henry and Copland were singled out again as formalists in a prominent Ukrainian newspaper.[40]

The Soviet attacks can also be viewed, somewhat perversely, as signs of Henry's renown. All his honors renewed Olive's desire to secure his place in history. In the 1930s she already had thought of honoring him by establishing a foundation to further his ideas, but San Quentin and the war intervened. When his music began having a life of its own, she, Henry, Sidney, and Harry decided that the fund would support, past his lifetime, his characteristic open-mindedness and generosity toward fellow-composers. The articles and declaration of trust, signed in 1949, sum up Henry's lifelong attitude: "The benefits of the Foundation should not be confined to exponents of any single type of new art music, since it is a fundamental element of its purpose that it is never possible to detect in advance which new elements will be important in making a permanent contribution, for the future, to the art of music. . . ."[41]

After Henry and Ives spent a Sunday together, Ives said he would alter his will and leave $10,000 [2010: $90,600] to the Cowell Foundation, hoping that more money would come if his fortunes held. Ives intended to leave another $40,000 for musical purposes, for which Henry expected to be an administrator.[42] Henry and Sidney also willed their estate to the fund. Problems arose after Harry died, when confusion about the deed to the Cowell house held up the probate of his will.[43] In Olive's hands, everything became more complex as she tried to figure out how to further Henry's activities in a way that would be profitable to him rather than to the Cowell Foundation. Apart from questions of legality, it meant that the foundation might be activated only after his death.[44] It had been assumed from the beginning that Olive's beautiful and valuable house would be a principal asset, but she concluded it was best to keep the house separate and continue giving Henry some of the proceeds of renting it out.[45]

On May 19, 1954, Ives joined Arnold Schoenberg (1951) and Ruth Crawford Seeger (1953) on the lengthening list of Henry's departed colleagues. In a few months, he had lost his father and father-figure. To deal with Ives's bequest to the foundation, he sent all the information about it to Ives's son-in-law, George Tyler, explaining what he knew of Ives's intentions.[46] It turned out that the will did not mention the Cowell Foundation. Tyler thought Harmony might leave something to it, but that depended upon what was left when she died.[47] At this point, the Cowell Foundation was not looking like a reliable mechanism for projecting Henry's legacy into the future. The complexities were unrelenting, and Sidney was stuck with the work.[48]

‖ 47 ‖

Simplicity

By 1945, Henry's music had completed the transition away from modernism. He often argued that fun had to be restored to music-making, an idea encouraged by his experiences teaching at San Quentin and working with children. He enjoyed writing for children or amateurs, sometimes using folk tunes that Sidney had collected. Overall, his portfolio shows that although he wrote in many styles, he still considered simplification-with-substance his goal. He also warned against simplicity becoming a mere reaction against complexity rather than a firmly grounded conviction.

His new approach is perhaps most powerfully expressed in the eighteen *Hymns and Fuguing Tunes*, a series that he began just after leaving San Quentin and stretched almost to the end of his life. Each one contains a slow, solemn movement paired with a brisk, dance-like companion, both of them extremely contrapuntal, in a style rooted in uniquely rural American music of the eighteenth century. The idea of composing "modern compositions" in this eighteenth-century style germinated when Sidney showed him publications by hymn compilers William Walker (1809–75), from Spartanburg, South Carolina, and Lewis Edson (1748–1820), a composer who lived in Mink Hollow—now called Shady—New York, the village in which the Cowells made their home. Their tunebooks *Southern Harmony* (1835) and *The Social Harmonist* (1801) brought back memories of midwestern country singing from Henry's childhood. For the Goldman Band's 1944 premiere of a band arrangement of the first *Hymn and Fuguing Tune*,[1] he acknowledged his indebtedness to William Walker and William Billings, adding that "the early style is not exactly imitated, nor are any of the tunes and melodies taken from these early masters. Rather, I asked myself the question, What would have happened in America if this fine, serious early style had developed?" (It had been suppressed by the nineteenth-century Protestant church establishment.) "[This work], which uses old modes [and] open chords . . . is a modern version of this style." Using as a model the discarded culture of eighteenth-century music is another instance of Henry's search for new paths and simplicity by combining contrasting cultures.[2]

The Hymns and Fuguing Tunes have been among his greatest successes. After a 1949 performance by the Boston Symphony of *Hymn and Fuguing Tune No. 2*, for string orchestra, Virgil Thomson, wrote "It sings; it soars; it leaps with joy. And it is full of great seriousness and a great dignity. . . . Myself, I should have preferred it longer. Certainly I was sorry when it ended, because it had made music all the way through."[3] This remarkable series was the subject of a major article by Wayne Shirley,[4] who concluded that ten of Henry's symphonies also have a relationship to the hymn and fuguing tune concept. The eighteen pieces remain one of the finest assertions of an Americanism rooted in music history and theory rather than in patriotic folklorism. Grateful for Sidney's introduction to the tunebooks, in 1944 Henry dedicated the entire series to her, irrespective of how many he eventually wrote or what instrumentations he used.

A musically minor but personally significant manifestation of simplicity and good fun began in 1941 when Henry wrote a little piece for Sidney celebrating their first Christmas together. Eventually he presented her with dozens of such tidbits to mark her birthday, their anniversary, or Christmas. The scoring of many of them for two recorders evokes a homey image of the Cowells trying them out in the living room at Shady. Together with similar pieces for friends—including some very early pieces for Ellen Veblen—and special events, these miniatures comprise some 10 percent of the nearly one thousand listings in the Cowell catalogue. The best of the miniatures could make good teaching pieces for children or beginners.

Although some of his old admirers were having trouble with Henry's new directions, in 1946 *Modern Music* decided to honor him with a composer portrait. The Cowells first tried to persuade Ruth Crawford Seeger to do the job because they felt that "only a Seeger" could do it right. Sidney's long letter of July 1 summarizes how they saw his place in the musical world. Out of her characteristically elegant but rambling prose, one central idea can be abstracted: in the professional music world, he was thought of as everything but a composer. His colleagues still subscribed to Aaron Copland's decades-old statement that Henry was an inventor, not a composer, despite the fact that Koussevitzky and other important conductors championed him. And if that were not annoying enough, other important spokesmen, such as Harold Spivacke, chief of the music division of the Library of Congress, felt that any discerning person should respect him above all for his knowledge of world music. Sidney said that Martha Graham told him that she thought Henry's music was the best she had ever had, but when it came time to commissioning scores, everyone argued for Copland, leaving her no choice because she was not paying for the commissions. In short, despite his undeniable acceptance by the public, he still felt isolated. Ruth Crawford Seeger declined Sidney's request, however, and a beautiful article by Edwin Gerschefski—emphasizing the contrasts of styles, the multiple musical personae that, if taken as a whole, make Henry's music so distinctive—was printed in what turned out to be *Modern Music*'s farewell.[5] That issue also included Richard Franko Goldman's "A New Day for Band Music," which highlighted Henry's importance to wind-ensemble repertory.[6] Clearly, despite the Cowells' concerns, the new simplicity that cost him some old admirers was winning him many supporters just when the early radical piano pieces were finding a new audience among young listeners.

The rapid advancement of Henry's acceptance in the larger musical world is best measured by the increasing number of commissioned pieces, especially for orchestra. Between 1952 and 1956, Henry produced seven symphonies, the *Variations for Orchestra*, and numerous works for instrumental or vocal soloists with orchestra. Almost all of them were commissioned by prominent conductors, including Leopold Stokowski, and quickly recorded. He also completed many full-sized chamber pieces, for varied and often unconventional ensembles—clarinet quintet; clarinet choir; brass and organ; violin and stringpiano; saxophone quartet; trumpet quartet with muted piano; violin, piano, and percussion; flute, oboe, cello, and harpsichord; and violin and harpsichord. For conventional ensembles there are only two string quartets and a duo for cello and piano. The mixed quality of these pieces implies that Henry accepted too many commissions because of his persistent concern about an adequate income. Some of them are still played, but others, like his wind-band, choral, and vocal compositions, are only now being rediscovered.

One of his biggest projects was the opera *O'Higgins of Chile*, commissioned by the Alice M. Ditson Fund of Columbia University. The story is based on the life of a half-Chilean, half-Irish adventurer who so impressed the king of Spain that he was appointed viceroy of Peru and later led the colonists' rebellion against Spain. Unfortunately, when General Eisenhower decided to run for president in 1952, Henry worried that the opera would be construed as an unacceptable, unintended criticism of military men entering politics. It was never orchestrated, and although some excerpts have been heard with piano, the entire opera sits on the shelf.[7]

Henry's interest in simplicity transcended his dispositions as a composer. Sidney's work as a scholar, combined with Henry's previous experiences with communist policy, drew his attention back to the role of folk music in society. In a wartime speech to the Music Teachers National Association, Henry called folk music "music of the people, as democracy is government of the people." Cultivated music, he said, grew largely out of conditions in the aristocracy or church, but folk music was for all people to join in and make up anew. Whereas in nondemocratic countries folk music often expressed either oppression or the hope of escaping it, in a democracy, folk music often expressed thankfulness for freedom; tragedy usually concerns unhappiness in love. The growing interest in such music, Henry correctly observed, was helping to destroy the barriers between folk, popular, and classical. He believed that once democratic people came to realize the valuable qualities of their own folk music, they would take a vivid interest in the folk music of other peoples "and find in it a remarkable means of communication, of penetrating to the feelings of an otherwise foreign group." He expressed some disdain for popular music that only catered to the mass mind, but praised Copland for using "both country tunes and city jazz rhythms in serious symphonic works."

In a jointly written article for *Modern Music*, the Cowells decried a fatal confluence of folk and popular—the disappearance of real country music as film and radio promoted an artificial version passing for folk song under the classification of "hill-billy." In their natural state, performers of country music had an audience of friends and neighbors who were interested in the tune and the story. "Personality, as a sophisticated performing artist understands it, counts for little in the rural tradition." When transplanted to a stage, country singers had to alter their performance to project their songs to audiences unfamiliar with the tradition. Subtlety of style, the Cowells argued, disappears when the music goes into an urban stage.[8]

In a 1942 article about the USSR's ambivalent attitude to folk music,[9] he praised the communists' efforts toward creating a uniquely proletarian style. He seemed unaware, however, that, in a curious parallel to the replacement of authentic American folk music by commercialized approximations, the Soviets had dropped their efforts to create a uniquely proletarian style, mandating instead the creation of concertified folk song and folk dance, using them as a tool to crush the non-Russian cultures of their country.

48

Collaborations and an Ives Biography

During those mornings in the ranch trailer, Henry worked on his most important collaboration with Sidney, a biography of Ives. Although it has been supplanted by more recent studies, the Cowells' book retains the unique qualities of a history written for the average reader by people who knew the subject intimately. The idea was born in 1946 when Gorham Munson, the trade book editor for Prentice Hall, proposed it to Henry. "Henry," says Sidney, "phoned from their meeting to ask if I would help and if I had any idea how many hours it would take me to type a book of 300 pages. Responding literally I made a hasty calculation on my fingers and heard Henry turn from the telephone to say that he could deliver the book in three months. (More experienced heads intervened and the contract was for two years.)"

According to her, the Iveses, although extremely grateful, were at first reluctant to consent, but felt that if a book had to be written, Henry should do it. Ives's poor health threatened to restrict their discussions, however, and responses to questions frequently were delayed.[1] Henry decided to use two or three pieces as a vehicle to discuss Ives's ideas, wrote the section on the music quickly, and started talking with Ives about his life. Both Iveses, Sidney said, were "imbued with the New Englander's personal reticence, and Henry found that no matter what he asked, Mr. Ives replied at length about something else." He soon decided it was a waste of time and asked Sidney to try. "I hesitated, but not enough, and I found myself gradually embroiled in Mr. Ives's search through his memory and his papers." Requests for reminiscences went out to many people who knew him.

Having completed his part of the job, Henry went on to other matters and left the biographical work to Sidney.[2] Ives's health kept intervening, however. In the fall of 1948 Harmony delayed her replies to Sidney's questions because he was hospitalized. Later, when Harmony read parts of the draft to him, he suggested changes, to which she added her own thoughts. Meanwhile, publication problems emerged. Soon after the contract was signed, Munson left Prentice Hall, but the Cowells were assured that his colleague Henry James, Jr., still stood behind the book. When the new editor demanded an exciting biography, which he proposed calling something like "Lust for Life,"[3] the Cowells returned the advance, feeling confident because they knew that Schirmer's Nathan Broder had been disappointed not to get the book. Schirmer first accepted it and sent a contract in 1951,[4] but Gustav Schirmer then rejected it because Ives was not a Schirmer composer. Broder then approached Oxford University Press, which took it over on the condition that the book be more substantial, thereby adding to Sidney's work.

Meanwhile, Sidney continued her research, fascinated by the interactions of Ives's business, economic, political, philosophical, and musical interests. Unearthing biographical information was difficult because Harmony prohibited interviews with family members and worried that her husband would not like the book. Sidney now saw that he wanted "a record in print of 'the progress of the music toward the Universal and its acceptance by the Majority Mind,' which he expected would be documented entirely by the favorable progress perceptible in printed reviews of his scores." In other words, he did not want to tell the story of his life. Later he changed his mind and gave her unsorted material, most of which was intended to refute negative or inaccurate remarks already in print. Throughout the gestation of the book, he and Harmony bombarded Sidney with corrections. Some of Ives's responses to her questions reinforce suspicions that he and Harmony tailored the information to help shape the portrait they wanted painted.[5] Of course, when the Iveses sent revisions, the Cowells could not have told him if they suspected he was manipulating them, but they left no hints that they were suspicious. Indeed, there is no way to know if the theories of manipulation are true.

While Henry and Sidney were still in the early stages of research, *New Yorker* had wanted to publish a profile of Ives, but Harmony, mistrustful of the magazine, worried that her husband "would not do himself justice." At first she asked Henry to write his opinion on a separate piece of paper, in case she felt reluctant to read it to Ives, but then told him to just say what he wanted.[6] Henry must have encouraged the profile, because the author, Bernard Herrmann's wife Lucille Fletcher, went ahead with it. Eventually *New Yorker* canceled it because Fletcher and her editor realized that it upset Ives and threatened his health. (There is, however, another side to that story. A note on a letter from Harmony says that the *New Yorker* profile died when Oxford University Press would not let the Cowells' book be used as a source.)[7] Fletcher's draft contained most of the extant boyhood history, which she had obtained in an interview with Ives's brother Moss a week before he died. Yet instead of blocking the draft, Ives astonished Fletcher by giving it to Sidney with permission to use it.[8]

As the biography neared publication, more problems arose. The process of selecting illustrations was derailed when Harmony denied consent to use any photo of herself. "I didn't know Mr. Ives had given Henry the picture—he was a bad boy. Thank goodness it got no further." When the book was ready for simultaneous release in England and the United States, Ives unexpectedly raised new objections. Harmony's propriety made Sidney fear that she would be disturbed by the use of the present tense and by some of the personal details such as Ives helping the servant wash the dishes. She explained to Harmony that they wanted "to give the feeling of the great and simple human being that Mr. Ives was, and in terms accessible to the average man, to whom the book as a whole is addressed, not just to musicians." They needed to indicate the importance of the composer's wife to understanding the composer. House-hold details also helped the reader understand how many-sided he was.[9]

Ives never saw the book; he died shortly before it was published. His daughter Edie, delighted with it, sent Sidney a truly beautiful appreciation. "You have both indeed accomplished in a masterly fashion the most difficult achievement of giving a comprehensive & faithful portrait of a complex, diversified personal-ity that nevertheless had as its firm base such direct, loving simplicity."[10]

Although the Cowells' book clearly was an "authorized biography," their careful and thorough research fortified their aim of presenting Ives to the larger musical world and stimulated the recording, publishing, and performing of his music. The book and the publications of Ives's compositions occupied a huge chunk of Sidney's and Henry's lives and continued to pursue Sidney after Henry's death.

In addition to the Ives book, between 1940 and 1955 some two hundred articles appeared under Henry's name—reviews of New York musical events in *Musical Quarterly's* "Current Chronicle"; book reviews and articles on many subjects for journals, collections of essays, and *Collier's Encyclopedia;*[11] and frequent contri-butions to *Modern Music*. It is difficult to imagine how someone teaching and composing as much as Henry could possibly turn out prose in such quantity. The truth is that he couldn't have. A few articles co-signed by Sidney are the tip of a peculiar iceberg. In "The Cowells and the Written Word,"[12] she explained with wry humor and in amusing detail the extensive collaboration that began soon after they were married. Henry, she said, admired Roy Harris's wife Johanna, who ran a complex household that included some live-in copyists, raised a family, and performed some of Harris's piano and chamber music. Since Sidney, unlike Johanna Harris, was not a professional pianist, it seemed senseless to try to learn Henry's techniques, and although she was willing to copy scores and parts, her slowness made Henry impatient. She could type, however. "So the typewriter took me from copyist and secretary to amanuensis, editor, co-author, and (twice) to ghostwriter." She became his fourth editor, following Seward, who worked on *New Musical Resources*; Olive, who helped with *American Com-posers on American Music*; and Minna Lederman, who edited his articles for *Mod-ern Music*. When the news got out that she was working with him on reviews, some composers tried to influence her by making sure she was aware of admiring comments about their music. This, she said, was especially a problem with Copland's friends.

Sidney admired Lederman's ability to "relax the intense concentration of Henry's writing imperceptibly, so that the best elements of his style were kept in place." Of her own work, Sidney said that anyone could detect "the more expansive rhythms that frame Henry's succinct ideas after I had been at work on a piece." He demanded extreme concentration from his listeners and readers because he spoke and wrote "directly, concisely, and simply." Unlike Sidney, he would jump from an idea to contradictions, paradoxes, and contrasts that intrigued him. He proceeded similarly in his music, she felt, rather than employing logical development.

She avoided any idea that did not originate with him and any possible distortion of the text, "only trying to translate the spoken phrase as it came so tersely from Henry into a more relaxed written form on the page." He was grateful, and editors offered more and more commissions for articles. His reviews of this period, however, were so clearly thought out that they rarely needed her "assistance." She would never sign her name unless joint authorship had been expressly requested, except for two reviews of books that he had no time to read, which she signed in his name. By the time she wrote this account of their work, she had come to believe that ghostwriting was idiotic. "I suppose I did this partly because, like Mrs. Ives, I had been brought up to believe that there was something a little vulgar about having one's name appear in print." In fact, she left her own name off her own first major article, obligating the editor—who had not noticed the omission—to send a correction slip with every copy. She also wrote, without attribution, brief introductions to some of Henry's scores.

Gradually, she said, Henry began to assume that she had all his thoughts in her own head. This became a problem because the demand for articles grew just as he wanted to preserve more time for composing. He began to rely "recklessly" on her supposed familiarity with the subjects. Although he usually knew better, when he was approached in 1954, shortly after they finished the Ives biography, to write a book about Palestrina, he signed the contract "without the slightest intention of writing the book himself. The fact that this was a composer and a period that I knew practically nothing about, and for which there was little primary material in this country, never crossed his mind. He didn't get around to mentioning this contract to me for several weeks, either. He said he thought I might need a little rest after the Ives book." And he could not understand why she declined to do the Palestrina book. From her point of view, there was no question of taking it on after seven years of working on the Ives biography, in which she had never intended to be involved from the beginning.

‖ 49 ‖

Europe Again

After the war, the United States began to send American artists abroad to talk about their work in an effort to repair the damage Nazi propaganda had inflicted upon America's reputation. Henry, who was known from his years with the Office of War Information (OWI), was a good asset, for he could stimulate the revival of Germany's musical life by informing musicians about modernist activities during the Nazi blackout. Sidney thought he made a trip in the late 1940s that was kept very brief because cultural life was still "in far too great disarray for anybody much to be interested in cultural news from outside Germany." The Cowell papers contain no trace of this trip, for which she probably got the date wrong. She might have been thinking of a proposal to send him around 1950, but their health problems and deaths in her family ruled out any travel.[1]

Meanwhile, increasing tension with the USSR led to the founding of the United States Information Agency (USIA) in 1953. That name was used by the parent agency, based in Washington; its activities only took place abroad, under the name United States Information Service (USIS). Fortunately, USIS's ardent anti-communists believed in the potency of "truth," which included putting the best products of the arts before European audiences. The vehicle for presentations was the network of America Houses or American Centers, at which USIS showcased the country's multifaceted culture. The America Houses operated in Europe until the end of communism diminished the incentive to maintain them. Elsewhere, some American Centers still function.

When it seemed likely that Henry would be invited to the 1955 World Music Days in Baden-Baden sponsored by the International Society for Contemporary Music (ISCM), Adolph Weiss suggested that he lecture at America Houses.[2] In April, William Glock, the festival's British chairman, issued a formal invitation but could only offer £5 or £6 in compensation.[3] By May, however, the participation of the USIS made the trip feasible. Henry would play in London on June 7, represent the American Composers Alliance at the ISCM festival June 17–21, possibly go to Vienna, and sail back on June 28. Looking forward to the adventure but ignoring his own unstable health, he imagined making new contacts leading to more tours.[4]

Although a major tour was impossible because of Henry's teaching schedule, USIS added events up to the last moment. The short trip became a month abroad, from May 30 to July 4,[5] with stops planned for Shannon, London, Paris, Vienna, Munich, Frankfurt, Copenhagen, and Oslo. Although Sidney accompanied him to Shannon, she remained in Ireland to record folksingers and arranged to meet him in Copenhagen.

In London, Henry gave a concert that stretched to two hours by audience demand.[6] After a brief stop in Paris, he went to Munich and Vienna—the projected Frankfurt event never took place—where, as a result of the American occupation, he found he hardly needed his German.[7] The sheer quantity of music in Vienna astonished him—two or three times as much as in Paris or London, including a lot of new music. One day he shared a box with the president of Austria at a morning concert of 900 children who sang "quite dissonant music very well,"[8] and heard Strauss's *Arabella* that night at the Staatsoper. Stokowski had departed, but Ormandy had just arrived with the Philadelphia Orchestra, bringing, to Henry's disappointment, only the conservative Norman Dello Joio as the representative of American music.[9] In Grinzing, Henry "climbed about a bit and walked along Beethoven's pathway by the brook," he told Sidney. "There were singing birds everywhere, and while many twittered and made indistinct sounds, there were many that had startlingly clear short themes, like our Beethoven bird only with a different tone-quality. . . . I wrote down as many as I could of the tunes and will show you." Of all people, the Russian tenor Radamsky, who had been an obstacle to concerts of American music in the USSR in the 1930s, was in town.[10]

World Music Days in Baden-Baden was extremely exciting. It seemed like every European composer who mattered—and many Americans—were there. Henry heard "all *very* modern music. Lots of valuable contacts made, and new music styles studied. I am not trying to compose, myself! Too much going on."[11] He was happy that people knew his name, and not surprised that they did not know his recent music. There was no chance to play records for anyone, however, because everyone was too busy making contacts.[12] They heard an electronic piece by Stockhausen "so full of beeps and bloops that there were titters from the audience which was supposedly inured to atonal music." Fortunately, he and composer Douglas Mackinnon suppressed their laughter, because when Stockhausen bowed he turned out to be the man sitting in front of them. Some chuckles must have greeted the sight of Mackinnon taking Henry to concerts on the back of his Vespa.[13]

After Baden-Baden Henry linked up with Sidney in Denmark.[14] The last stop was Oslo, where she stayed for the International Folk Music Council meeting.[15] Henry arrived in New York on July 4 after a smooth voyage that included a sighting of icebergs.[16]

PART VI

WORLD TRAVELER

50

The Big Trip

After Henry's 1955 routine physical, his doctor told Sidney that "with great care and good luck" he might last another two years. Since back problems prevented him from running, lifting, or putting similar strains on his heart, she saw no reason to tell him to be careful and kept the news to herself, avoiding saying anything that could arouse Olive's suspicions. One person who needed to know was Oliver Daniel, the director of the Concert Division of BMI (Broadcast Music Inc.), who had founded that division and CRI (Composers' Recordings, Inc.) the previous year. In addition to administering the concert division, he undertook to promote certain composers, especially Henry. While Erminie Kahn looked for speaking and playing engagements, Daniel took charge of getting Henry's music in front of conductors. Informed of his condition by Sidney, Daniel arranged for BMI to give him an annual guarantee of $3,000 [2010: $24,400] against broadcast rights and $2,000 against publishing rights, which enabled the Cowells finally to live on the proceeds from his music. Broadcasting, which once had seemed so threatening to live music, thus became a crucial part of Henry's income.[1] As Sidney and Daniel hoped, the contract relieved and relaxed Henry. After the spring semester of 1956, he resigned from Peabody, leaving Columbia and The New School his only employers. On March 11, The New School saluted his fifty-ninth birthday with a "Music Day," celebrating his focus on active participation rather than passive listening.

Having decided to preserve Henry's vitality by keeping his world lively and unchanged, Sidney proposed that they finally organize the year-long trip to Asia that they had been discussing, so he could hear live performances of the music to which he had devoted so much of his life, and she could explore Asian folk music. BMI's advance and money from Henry's share of the rental of Olive's house were a good but inadequate start. Then a fortuitous conversation in Beirut between the composer Anis Fuleihan and John Marshall, Associate Director for the Humanities at the Rockefeller Foundation, changed the prospects. John D. Rockefeller II, who had come to see Asia as a critical Cold War battlefield, had been advocating programs to support projects in agriculture and population studies and had just added cultural support to the foundation's agenda. To advance the Rockefeller Foundation's interest in improving local programs in the arts and humanities, Marshall wanted a leading American musician to appraise the situation of music in many Asian cities. When Fuleihan mentioned the Cowells' plans, Marshall realized he might have found the ideal person— someone competent in Western and non-Western music.

Marshall realized that he, Chadbourne Gilpatric, the assistant director for the Humanities, and Charles Burton Fahs, the director of the Division of the Humanities, could "buy" parts of the Cowells' trip for their areas of interest by commissioning Henry to report about topics of interest, and Sidney to report about folk cultures. Marshall wanted Henry for the Middle East; Gilpatric would send him through India and East Pakistan; and they assumed that Fahs (who was then abroad) would want him for Indonesia, the Philippines, and Japan.[2] Fahs, an orientalist and later a professor at Claremont and Pomona Colleges, particularly valued Henry's knowledge of extra-European music and hybrids of Eastern and Western. When he expressed his desire to develop a good comparative-music program in a leading American school, Henry offered to propose it at Columbia after their trip.

It was already mid-April 1956, and preparations had to advance rapidly. In only two months Sidney would be recording folk music for the BBC in Ireland, where Henry would join her after teaching at summer school. They planned brief visits to London, Rome, Vienna, and somewhere in Germany, arriving in mid-September in Athens, the starting point for their year in Asia. A tentative itinerary included Turkey, Lebanon, other unspecified places in the Middle East, then Iran, Pakistan, India, Burma, Hong Kong, the Philippines, and Japan. By keeping the schedule flexible they could insert Java, Bali, and other locations that might unexpectedly look desirable. Henry formally proposed to examine the preservation of folk music and fine-art music, the penetration of Western music, and the hybrids that were being developed, including the philosophies surrounding them, as well as training in music theory and performance. Sidney wanted to record folk music and observe how other cultures introduced music to children. The Cowells hoped to hear as much music as possible and meet musicians of all types.[3] The Rockefeller staff also requested reports on musical life and institutions such as orchestras and schools to help them and others plan meaningful support.

As they pondered the itinerary, Gilpatric pressed for two to three months in India and Pakistan alone, since, to his knowledge, no American composer with real qualifications had ever been there to study the music in its context. Fahs recommended a week in Korea, where interest in Western music was high and the court orchestra played some of Asia's most ancient music. On the other hand, the Philippines had weak traditional music and only a few "modestly competent" Western-style composers. He thought a few days each in Malaya and Thailand would be useful. Bali struck Gilpatric as the only place in Indonesia where music was truly alive. A month in Japan would be a good ending. Marshall offered a per diem of $25 [2010: $200], travel commencing in Istanbul and ending in Japan, and an honorarium of $1,000 [2010: $8,000] for the reports, which the Cowells could use freely without having to credit the Rockefeller Foundation.

Despite dangerous tension in the Middle East, the plan went forward.[4] When Fahs suggested giving the Cowells a small fund to purchase instruments and musical materials,[5] Henry decided that the rental money from Olive's house would allow them to buy more instruments. A gift from Harmony Ives saluting Henry's and Sidney's work for her late husband was added to the pot.[6] The total grant itself was $9,600 [2010: $77,000], for use through December 31, 1957.[7] The Rockefeller staff foresaw considerable consequences for Asian music in the United States because of Henry's reputation, especially if the trip fortified interest in an ethnomusicology program at Columbia, where opposition within the music department was powerful.

Endless paperwork included up to eight copies of mountains of documents for visa applications, all of which had to be typed separately. Many visas were difficult to obtain; some would expire before the Cowells even arrived.[8] Henry obtained a letter of credentials from Columbia president Grayson Kirk, which emphasized their competence in non-Western music and Sidney's interest in childhood education.[9] The Library of Congress testified to her work as a scholarly, noncommercial folk song collector.[10] In addition to declarations that no money would be earned in the host countries, they needed certification that they were both Christians, that is, not Jewish. Although extremely reluctant to prove his non-Jewishness to get a Syrian visa, Henry had no option, given his wish to spend time studying Arabic music outside Damascus. They were amused that the declaration of Protestantism was engineered by Clara Mayer, the Jewish dean of The New School.[11]

By mid-May, the trip had acquired two more partners—the State Department and USIS.[12] Although it is not known how or when the State Department learned of their travel plans, USIS effectively became Henry's manager, organizing speaking engagements alongside the Rockefeller-sponsored research. In preparation, the agency shipped his recordings to all the European and Asian cities where he might lecture.[13] When the State Department initiated discussions about inserting a project in Iran within the Cowell's time in India, Marshall approved Henry's request to add it to his itinerary,[14] but Henry declined to spend six months there, which would have limited their other travels.[15] The State Department and John Marshall persuaded him to agree to two months, although

Marshall worried that their work could be compromised if they were associated with the government. Henry was especially happy that the Iranian government had specifically requested him. Since Sidney had already left for Ireland, a discussion with her was impossible. He nervously wrote her that he would be working for Iranian radio and that the government grant was for him to write music, "music, of course, with some relation to Persian needs. It gives a chance to live quietly in one spot for enough time to compose—what we had planned, but which rather disappeared in the face of the Rockefeller [grant]." Unfortunately, it upended their careful arrangements to avoid certain places when the weather was at its worst.

The government's grant was confirmed at $700 [2010: $5,620] per month, a per diem, and plane fares for him to and from Madras.[16] Although Marshall was happy to get a report from Iran at government expense, Washington's involvement split the Rockefeller staff. Marshall believed that government connections were not a problem in the Middle East, but Gilpatric felt they could be a liability in South Asia and the Far East,[17] where the concept of "Third World" as a descriptor of countries that avoided alliances with the United States (and the USSR) was taken very seriously.[18]

Wanting to exploit Henry's diplomatic assets, USIS cabled its offices throughout Europe and Asia, offering him for lectures on American music, lecture-recitals, and conducting. He was described as one of the best-known American composers, a musicologist with wide interests, particularly in the field of Oriental music, and a brilliant speaker who could lecture in German if required. While his talks would concern American music, he could slant lectures to suit the area that he visited. Responses varied.[19] USIS-Burma declined to use Henry because the Burmese lacked interest in classical forms of American music. Ignoring Henry's stated qualifications, they asked for a renowned American composer who was interested in Oriental music.[20] On the other hand, the Public Affairs Officer in Dacca, East Pakistan, wanted Henry precisely because the region had had so little contact with Western classical music. He guaranteed that Henry would hear plenty of native music and liked the idea of conferences with small groups, though lectures could be arranged in Dacca and their six branch centers.[21] The problems created by inserting Tehran into the schedule show up in the eager response of the embassy in Manila, which anticipated a receptive but small audience, since Henry's visit now would coincide with school vacations.[22]

The very fact that the State Department and USIS had arranged a tour for a composer should have delighted Henry as a sign of the evolution of American music. He saw it differently, however. Says Sidney: "Asked by US Ambassador Taft in Dublin in 1956 whether he thought the State Dept. idea of sending composers around to meet composers in other countries worked well, HC said he thought it would be better to send music (or records) than people. I thought this was more revealing about HC than about the program!"[23]

With Sidney in Ireland, Henry had to undertake tasks utterly unsuited to his cardiac condition—subletting their New York apartment and finding an occupant for the house at Shady. It may account for another circulatory episode in early July, when his doctor was on vacation.[24] A month before departure, everything was still up in the air. The woman who was to sublet the apartment backed out when her roommate had a nervous breakdown. The crucial cat sitter had not been found. Henry was on the verge of abandoning subletting and giving notice on the New York apartment when the Columbia music department's administrative assistant found two reliable young women to rent it. Then he had to move himself and a lot of furniture to Shady to make room for them. When the deal to rent Shady fell through he had to "park the cats" and close up the house. A cat sitter finally materialized four days before departure.[25] Sidney gave him the excellent advice to get a thorough cardiogram, medical records for his back operations, and a lot of gout medicine before leaving.[26] On the eve of departure, Henry sent the Rockefeller Foundation the final itinerary:

August 19–30: Galway, Ireland
August 31–September 6: Dublin
September 7–14: London
September 15–October 6: c/o US Embassy, Bonn (a mail drop for his
    European lecture circuit)
October 7–21: Istanbul
October 21–28: Ankara
October 28–November 3: Beirut
November 3–10: Syria and Jordan
November 10–24: Cairo
November 24–30: Alexandria
December 2–9: Karachi
December 10–23: Delhi
December 23–30: Madras
December 31, 1956–February 28, 1957: Tehran
March 1–April 1: Delhi, Calcutta, and Benares
April 2–13: Dacca, East Pakistan
April 15–21: Rangoon
April 22–May 1: Bangkok
May 2–5: Singapore
May 6–20: Jakarta and Bali
May 21–June 3: Manila
June 4–10: Hong Kong

June 11: Tokyo with a possible side trip to South Korea.
Approximately September 1–December 31, 1957—Departure for home
    and four months to write reports.[27]

On August 19, Sidney met Henry at Shannon Airport. He had arrived for a
year on the road "with *26 lbs. of blank music paper, one* pair of pyjamas, 1 ½ prs.
socks and only the pants of his one warm suit."[28] After some resting in Shannon
and a visit to the Aran Islands, Henry spoke at the Ireland-America Society in
Dublin, the Music Association of Ireland,[29] and the Royal Irish Academy. A
fourth talk, sponsored by the US Embassy, was extensively reviewed and warmly
received, probably because Henry declared that the greatest influence on American music was Irish and blamed the backwardness of American musical development on the persistence of (English) pilgrim prejudices against the art.[30]

The Public Affairs Officer at the US Embassy in Bonn, F. Lee Fairley, an avid
amateur cellist who graduated from the Eastman School of Music and was
knowledgeable about modern music in Germany,[31] arranged for Henry to talk at
the America Houses in Hamburg, Berlin, Cologne, Darmstadt, Stuttgart,
Freiburg, and Munich. To stimulate discussion, professionals, students, critics,
and personalities in local musical life were invited. The State Department's inability to pay for Sidney's expenses did not bother her. Strongly prejudiced
against Germany, she had refused to go with Henry in 1955, but this time first
decided to give it a try, then changed her mind and went ahead to Athens.[32]
Henry stopped in Amsterdam to see Olive, forgot his coat there, and began the
German tour in Hamburg on September 17.[33] He was surprised to find many
recordings of his modernist circle in all the America Houses—two or three
times as many as in the London embassy—and in constant use.[34]

Berlin was very upsetting. His old neighborhood had been bombed to bits;
Pension Schmolke was a weedy lot. Henry probably did not attempt to find Elsa.
Unencumbered by concerts or lectures, he met with Philipp Jarnach, Boris
Blacher, Benjamin Britten, and Hans Heinz Stuckenschmidt. Apart from Josef
Rufer, his old friends were gone, dead or had emigrated. Although his music was
being played here, he was glad to leave for Cologne, where the new-music world
was extremely lively.[35]

After a talk and some performing in Wuppertal,[36] Henry returned to Cologne
to inspect the electronic-music department of WDR (West German Broadcasting), and heard "the tapiest tape music yet—some of it done by drawing the
vibration lines." [37] From Stuttgart on September 27 he wrote Sidney (who was
unwell in Athens) that he felt fine after a "nice cozy session with about sixteen
people last night, and a ½ hour broadcast over the American Forces Radio here
and rebroadcast over Frankfurt." Stuttgart's press bestowed the praise that had
been denied him in prewar Germany.[38]

He said next to nothing about Darmstadt, but Freiburg, the only city he visited that had not been ruined in the war, completely charmed him, as did the view from 3,800 feet up in the Schwarzwald, with the Swiss Alps in view beyond the Rhine valley. In one packed day he saw the folk-record collection, held a radio interview, and gave a lecture-recital at America House. A critic warmly observed that what was met with hoots and whistles in the 1920s had become the foundation of electronic music.[39] The new enthusiasm for modern ideas was nothing short of astounding.[40]

Henry joined Sidney in Istanbul on October 11. Turkey's peculiar position between East and West, modern and traditional, struck them immediately. So did the fact that his connection with the Rockefeller Foundation was known, thanks to their hotel reservation and letters of introduction. He could no longer count on getting disinterested, objective answers to his inquiries about local musical needs. Musicians and administrators began their "laments and begging" at once. After a week of meetings, one obvious need was for instruments if there were to be new generations of musicians. He advised the Rockefeller Foundation to channel aid through the conservatory, although assistance to the Istanbul orchestra would help international understanding. Every step had to be taken carefully, lest traditional musicians protest that Westerners were hijacking Turkish culture. They would not have been entirely wrong. The Rockefeller grant officers' interest in indigenous music could easily seem like benevolent cultural colonialism. Henry addressed that problem in his lectures by emphasizing the need to retain one's roots and not assume that only the new and modern is worthy of attention. He urged the Turks to be proud of their culture's prospects as a world resource. Gradually he learned that powerful figures in the musical community clashed over whether traditional Turkish music should receive funding. Marshall was impressed, having failed to untangle the roots of the conflict.[41] The Rockefeller Foundation had only enhanced its understanding, however; solutions were not apparent.

Eager to hear contemporary Turkish music, Sidney and Henry visited Ahmed Adnan Saygun, Turkey's leading composer and Bartók's guide when he collected folk song there. At Saygun's home they heard a string quartet by Ilhan Usmanbas, a thirty-four-year-old composer who had studied in the United States and received a Fromm Foundation commission, and Saygun's own oratorio *Yunus Emre*, which Henry called "magnificent."[42] Stokowski's performance of it in New York two years later is likely to have come on Henry's recommendation.

Sidney's reports and letters contain colorful accounts of their daily experiences, such as their trip to Edirne, Broussa, and a couple of other small towns with USIS stations and next-to-no foreigners.

The driver had been personal bodyguard to Ataturk and at the latter's death reported to the US Ambassador, saying that a job with him would be the nearest thing to the one he had had: his dignity would allow nothing less. He was a picturesque brigand-type, whose wide connections everywhere we went somewhat impeded travel, as he had to find a place in which to get into his uniform at the entrance to each village and then spend a couple of hours over tea, fully expecting us to be content in a tea house too. Usually he did not turn up when expected so I would go looking for him, with not a word of the language but so foreign that it was easy for villagers to make the connection and they always produced him. A trip planned for four days took ten, but we would n't have missed it.

The drive to Edirne included a stop to see dancing and hear drumming and singing by Gypsies whose dancing bear staggered around with a drum in its paws, asking for coins. "Our driver . . . took the position that gypsies are backward people and he was embarrassed to be seen with them on the road; he dissociated himself from our dusty friends and protested to our Turkish interpreter at allowing us to stop."[43]

Unfortunately, these memorable experiences paled before world events. International tensions resulting from the Egyptian nationalization of the Suez Canal in July boiled over on October 31 as Israel, France, and Britain attacked the Canal while the USSR was distracted by the revolution in Hungary. Henry had left for Beirut on October 30; Sidney, stuck in the Istanbul Hilton with the flu, had intended to meet him in Aleppo, Syria, on Sunday, November 4. Then Aleppo was put under martial law after a plane with Algerian rebel leaders was seized. Henry wrote from Beirut on November 1 that she should wait at least overnight before deciding whether to come. In fact, Beirut's airport was closed to civilian traffic while officials were evacuated from all over the Middle East. The embassy thought it might be open in a couple of days, but it might be impossible to fly to India over Iraq.[44]

Henry spent a week in Beirut at the upscale Bristol Hotel while Sidney rested in Istanbul, assuming that he could not accomplish much. Because he did not keep elaborate notes, her Rockefeller report says very little about his activities there, which actually had been reasonably fruitful. The details are found in a report to Washington filed by Ambassador Heath, who was impressed by Henry's effortless skill at making friends with everyone he met. Just after arriving on October 30, he lectured at the American University of Beirut to an enthusiastic audience of some two hundred. Not knowing normal attendance statistics for new music, the ambassador attributed the "low" turnout to world tension and to the lack of an admission charge, since Lebanese assumed that free events were inferior. That night, the Public Affairs Officer hosted a dinner with prominent members of the Lebanese musical community. The next day Henry gave an interview on Radio Lebanon and an hour-long evening lecture at Jeunesses Musicales. He spent much of Thursday, November 1, with Anis Fuleihan until his evening speech at the conservatory. On Friday and Saturday, the embassy took him to assorted official social events honoring the tour of the American Ballet Theatre. After the weekend there was a dinner party with performances of folk dances and music. World events were right at hand, however: Henry's hotel was crowded with Americans evacuated from around the Middle East. Extremely disturbed to see the evacuees' children left on their own, with no school or plans, he offered to perform exclusively for them and devoted the last part of his recital to showing the children how to pluck the piano strings. Totally charmed by Henry's rapport with the children and their parents, Ambassador Heath requested recordings and publicity materials so he could capitalize on the interest he had generated.[45]

On Sunday, November 4, while the West was distracted in Egypt, the Soviet Union invaded Hungary to put down the revolution. Fortunately, the attack did not worsen the travel situation in the Middle East, which could hardly have been a greater mess. Henry finally got to Istanbul and settled with Sidney into the luxurious Hilton.[46] With American passports now invalid for Israel, Syria, Jordan, and Egypt, they reluctantly canceled all plans for the Arab countries. Sidney glumly wrote her grandfather that although Henry's talks on the influence of Asian music on American music were very good and timely propaganda, the 5,000 pamphlets in Arabic describing his appearances, which had been distributed around Damascus and Aleppo, were useless. She thought they might spend a few more weeks in Turkey, where the mood was more heartbroken than angry, "since the Moslems make a point of not being like the backwards Arabs."[47]

Iran, I

With the Arab world off limits, the Cowells' next destination was Tehran, where a different brand of politics would have to be mastered. Iran had become an Anglo-American venture in August 1953, when Mohammed Reza Shah Pahlavi was returned to the throne after a coup engineered by the US Central Intelligence Agency and Britain's MI6 deposed the popularly elected government of Moham-med Mossadegh. When the Shah's planned modernization of his kingdom antag-onized his conservative subjects, he responded with brutal repression, with long-term consequences that are all too familiar. In 1956, however, the Shah's dream was in its infancy and the United States happily nourished it.

The Department (i.e., Ministry) of Fine Arts played a major role in the Shah's program. Its director, Mehrdad Pahlbod, a violinist and brother-in-law of the Shah,[1] recognized that in a large, primarily rural country, whoever had the radio had the country.[2] Attracting and keeping the audience was the job of music. How to do it was the question. Competing interests included enthusiasts for Western popular music and classical music; a mixture of Persians, Kurds, Azeris, and other ethnic traditionalists who wanted their own music; and religious ultracon-servatives who believed music was sinful. The radio and the Fine Arts Depart-ment competed for support because the radio wanted hybrid music mixing Western and Iranian styles, and Pahlbod, backed by the Shah, wanted to strengthen traditional music and raise the social level of its musicians, some of whom were opium addicts and drinkers. Both Pahlbod and the Shah felt that the improvement of traditional music was contingent on bringing a higher level of society to appreciate and play it.

To accomplish this, Pahlbod had to convince better families that music itself was not to blame for the condition of musicians. The Shah was so keen on music that he invited musicians to dine with him.

Unfortunately, Iranians, especially in the volatile northwest, were abandon-ing the official radio in droves, tuning instead to a popular station in Baku, Soviet Azerbaijan. C. Robert Payne, the extremely cultivated Public Affairs Officer of the US Embassy, became a close partner in the effort to retrieve the lost audience. Payne, who grew close to the Cowells, eventually provided Sidney with a detailed account of the circumstances that led the American government to recruit Henry.[3] With Payne's encouragement, Sidney obtained the complete correspondence from the Department of State. The accuracy of Payne's story was confirmed by Pahlbod, who had befriended him.[4]

Payne knew that music on Iranian radio was dismal. Since the finest musicians were concentrated in the radio orchestra and the college orchestra that functioned as a national symphony, the obvious solution was to have the orchestras record for the radio. He also perceived great rivalries operating to the detriment of traditional music. Played only by small ethnic groups, it had no function in the larger Iranian culture, but the radio needed to attract those communities. As in Turkey, Western classical music was only approached from the "French outlook"—a concept that neither Payne nor the Cowells define, but one that certainly excluded cultural hybrids. Henry usually equated "French" with "superficial."

Pahlbod and his colleagues wanted someone who could put the orchestras together, encourage composers and arrangers, and serve as a talent scout to identify the best areas for developing music. He had to be an outsider with a fine reputation, who would not be resented and whose ideas would be implemented, "a patient saint"—Payne's words—who could stay long enough to be effective and prepare the way for his successors. As he filed the request, he knew that the State Department would think he was out of his mind for dreaming that one person could do everything. In fact, a Persian had already suggested Henry, saying he was well known in Iran because (Payne wrote) "during the war they were greeted the first thing in the morning and the last thing at night with a composition which Henry had composed for Iran." He was referring to *Improvisation on a Persian Mode*, an orchestral piece that Henry wrote for the Persian desk of the OWI in 1943 and that was broadcast either on Voice of America or Iranian radio. (Pahlbod, who was very young at the time, did not remember it.) Payne learned that the Shah, who had been in his early twenties during the war, also liked Henry's music for military calisthenics. (He kept it in use at least as late as the 1960s.) The more Payne thought about it, the more he realized that Henry was the perfect person to retrieve lost listeners. Since the State Department already knew Henry, Payne's request was answered with uncharacteristic speed.[5]

A year earlier, an Iranian senator also had suggested that both Iranian music and the United States would profit if an American composer would study traditional Persian music and apply Western techniques to it in his own music. Henry was interested in the challenge, since Iranian traditional music, which uses voices and instruments in unison, would be extremely difficult to hybridize with polyphonic Western music. Iran's European-trained composers had doomed their attempted fusions by imposing harmonies and polyphony upon the traditional melodies. Furthermore, it might not improve listenership, since the average

Iranian had no more interest in hybrids than in Iranian traditional professional music. Such people preferred the fine performances of unadorned folk music broadcast from Baku. Henry would have to initiate a process of gradual change.[6]

This was the situation in July, when he was interviewed by the chiefs of the Music Branch of USIS and the Cultural Specialists program, both of whom felt he was ideal. The specialist's grant was awarded, and the embassy was asked to provide examples of Persian melodies, information about Iranian folk music, and a list of the instruments available for broadcasts and performances. (The reader should note that "Iranian" refers to all the inhabitants of the country, whereas "Persian" refers to the dominant, Farsi-speaking ethnic community.) Henry also offered to lecture on American music and on the influence of Oriental music upon it, give lecture-recitals, and conduct as needed.[7] By mid-September, when he was still in Germany, the Persian melodies had arrived, but when he started composing arrangements, he found that his future boss at Iranian radio had written the melodies, supplying the complete tune, "evidently hoping it will come out on regular V-I cadences, but it doesn't!!" he told Sidney.[8]

In mid-November, the Suez war had ended but flights were still so unpredictable that the Cowells had to keep their suitcases packed and ready. They suddenly got seats and left Istanbul the evening of November 14, arriving in Tehran at 6 A.M. the next morning. The post-Suez plan kept them there through late February with the exception of a side trip to the Madras Music Festival in late December. After Iran they would return to India and try to reach Pakistan before the hot, pre-monsoon weather of March and April.

Knowing she would have to file the reports, Sidney kept exhaustive diaries of their stay in Tehran, which, thanks to her excellent eye, capture the details and absurdities of life. Although one can only sample it here, her travelogue is irresistible, beginning with their arrival at Tehran Airport, where they enlisted a "vague and perhaps drugged young man" to find them a taxi. Afterward he asked for a note on hotel stationery that he could use to charge Pan American Airways for his services. They later realized that it was a perfect introduction to the wheeling and dealing lying ahead. Their first priority was to find reasonably priced accommodation in a very expensive city, ideally near the radio station, since the 5,000-foot altitude could be unwelcoming to Henry's heart.

Payne immediately started the introductions, with Pahlbod at the top of the list. Dinner parties were a way of life. Sidney: "Here we are knee deep in Iranian senators, princes & assorted ambassadors & are to meet the Shah & his pretty Queen soon—I hope not before I have lost 10 lbs. & can get into my clothes. (I have lost at least 50 lbs. in the last year—the same 10 lbs. 5 times.)"[9] The main topics of conversation were the policies of President Eisenhower—who had just been reelected—Britain's actions in Suez, and Iran's ethnic conflicts.

Soon Senator Hedjazi, a handsome man of about fifty, who spoke excellent English and wrote fiction and essays, came calling. (Pahlbod thought he was probably the senator who proposed Henry for the job.) His government car took them to the beautiful home of the eighty-ish-year-old Mochir Shardar (Shardhar or Chardhar), the director of music at the radio and "grand old man of music," who spoke only Farsi and some French. Belatedly recognized as Iran's most distinguished composer, Shardar wrote in mixed style, of which the Western part resembled music of the 1890s. It was he who had sent the three Persian tunes to Henry, but the project to make arrangements of Persian tunes had been hatched by USIS's radio technician, "who thought that all you need to do is arrange something and you have 'modern music.'" Henry realized that Shardar knew nothing of modern radio needs. Yet Shardar, like Senator Hedjazi and Pahlbod, understood the political context of the Cowells' trip, namely, that the tension between the Americans and the British over Suez could tempt the USSR to start a war and immediately occupy Iran. Iranians had to have confidence in their alliance with the United States.[10]

Odd obstacles to Henry's work arose at once. As a courtesy, he was assigned the use of the radio director's luxurious office, but only from 4 to 8 P.M., when all the radio staff had gone home and transacting any business was impossible. Furthermore, Fridays were holidays, Saturday was a half-day, and Sunday was the Western Sabbath. Payne had to delicately ask the undersecretary to the Prime Minister for Parliamentary Affairs to provide a simpler office for Henry so that he could be more productive. Knowing that rivalries undermined the soil upon which they were treading, Payne also solicited the undersecretary's advice about a solution to the problem that very few of the Radio Tehran Orchestra's players could read music, tactfully proposing that Henry work instead with the Tehran Symphony.[11] Without Payne's expertise, almost anything could have derailed Henry's efforts.

Pahlbod himself was another potential problem. Alarmed by a newspaper's incorrect report that the Cowells "had come 'to make Iranian music known in America,'" he declared that he had prohibited the export of Iranian music until it could be presented by Iranians. The Cowells understood that Pahlbod wanted control over Iranian music. If provoked, he could restrict their work disastrously.[12] Yet paradoxically, the "elegant, cultivated, English-speaking" Roman Catholic Pahlbod, who feared Westernization of Iranian music, also oversaw a conservatory of Western music, whose composition students he urged to use Persian themes in Western-style music.[13] His possessiveness was not directed at Henry personally; he had only met him once or twice and felt no need to help him because Payne was taking such good care of him. The real cause was persistent annoyance that the Persian tunes used by Rimsky-Korsakov in *Scheherazade* had become known as "Russian." The Iranians wanted to prevent further cultural robbery.[14] The Cowells quickly learned that Iranians and Turks considered Americans novices at hating Russia.

On the fourth day, when Henry and Sidney finally recovered from their sleepless night on the plane, they started exploring Tehran and began to sense what a different world they had come to. On their first walk, on a Friday afternoon, they were struck by an atmosphere of tension in the streets, which they learned was tied to the recent declaration making narcotics illegal. Other than in foreign quarters or near a school, they saw very few women in European dress, whereas schoolchildren wore French-style uniforms. The street sounds were endlessly fascinating. Sidney was especially amused by "an ostinato of a vendor of socks" that went on all day. When they drove to the Elburg foothills, they were relieved that their driver was more cautious than most Tehran taxi drivers, who drove carefully only if paid more since careful driving took longer and cost them trips. On other outings they saw extremely ancient artifacts at Rey and the late Shah's magnificent tomb. They quickly started Farsi lessons.

Everything was stimulating except driving and eating. They had had shots against typhus, typhoid, and yellow fever; plague and cholera shots were due shortly, and an embassy staff member briefed them about health.[15] Intestinal problems nevertheless commenced at once. Henry had already been attacked—he felt sure he was going to die "and then wished [he] would." The hazards of eating were also a long-term investment, however. Since acquiring a reasonable immunity would take about three months, during which they could expect to be ill frequently, they began to regret planning only about that much time in Iran, because by the time they could be active all day for more than three consecutive days, they would be leaving. After their "Iranian miseries," however, they had no more problems for the entire trip.

The natural world delighted them despite their discomfort. Innumerable birds fed at their window. The beautiful rim of mountains, clearly visible in those pre-smog days, and the gardens everywhere were a delight. The dry air helped them recover from colds. Henry worried that Sidney would tell Persian friends that she was dying for a camel ride, which his back would not have tolerated. They eagerly dived into local life, constantly encountering problems in making arrangements because of what she called the Iranian sense of reality (or lack of it). They became masters at tempering extreme irritation with a recognition of the culture from which the irritants sprang. A good sense of humor was essential, especially when trying to find their way around the city. "House numbers were chosen by numerologists, with no concern for mathematical sequence."

American Thanksgiving was celebrated on November 22 at an embassy official's home, without Iranians, whose presence would have kept bacon from the salad dressing or wine from the thirsty. The Cowells were the "ranking civilians"; most of the American guests were oil men or construction engineers, who paid them great attention.[16]

Payne promised them that when they came back from Madras he would send them to the other USIS centers around the country. Sidney wryly noted that that was the reward for their enthusiasm for Turkish small towns and what USIS in Turkey considered their unusual adaptability. "Since we walk little, sleep much, feel stiff and full of aches, and seem to ourselves very decrepit, this opinion really does not flatter other travelling Americans. But we propose to take advantage of our reputation even if it is spurious and to maintain the illusion as long as we can."[17]

The world of music seemed "almost surreal." The small audience for Western music largely comprised wealthy titled people, many of whom had been exposed to music in France. A weekly program of recorded Western music was curated by an Iranian from the USIS Radio Department. In contrast, from every shop blared American hit tunes and "a dreadful lot of non-hit parade stuff that seems to have been dumped by commercial distributors." Radio Tehran's twelve-man orchestra blended Persian and Western instruments. Its piano was tuned to include some quarter-tones, which Henry saw as a fetish that accommodated neither Eastern nor Western music, and drove all live music to be written in a special hybrid style. Outside Tehran, Western music existed almost exclusively in the rare performances arranged by USIS.

Complex cultural-political problems also affected Sidney's work. Recording or photographing on the streets was illegal and dangerous. A widespread but inaccurate story held that the American ambassador had been stoned to death in 1922 by a crowd angered when he took pictures in the streets. In the countryside Sidney wore a chador, pretended to be Iranian, and followed the rules, but her miniature tape recorder fit under her chador, and as long as she was escorted by Iranians, she had no problems. An attempt to record some Iranian traditional professional music at the conservatory had to be scuttled, however, when Pahlbod got nervous. A copy of a tape of a virtuoso performance done for USIS arrived containing rubbish—"the Iranian technician at USIS having been unable to reconcile himself to having that 'backward' old traditional stuff let out of Iran to damage his country's reputation!" Four years later she was still trying to get tapes of that music.[18] Not just a foreigner but a woman, Sidney already had had bouts with Islamic fanaticism. In Istanbul, some women had flown into a rage when she put her unclean Christian money into a collection box. Now she found peasants equally frightened by foreigners and literate Iranians, but made some "mud hut friends" with the help of a friendly and fearless young guide. She recorded some beautiful street vendors' songs by going out really early.

At the radio station, Henry was provided with disc recordings and tapes of Iranian music and broadcasts, from which he hoped to decipher an age-old debate about the function of quarter-tones in Iranian music. At the end of November, he worked on a suite based on Persian song and dance styles that could be taught by rote to the orchestra of Persian instruments, whose players had learned Western notation but did not use it. Then he wanted to arrange Persian melodies for Western instruments, using them for suites incorporating whatever Persian elements seemed appropriate. Two of them were to be recorded in New York and sent back for the radio's use.

By December 18, when they left for Madras, he had also listened to live performances of Iranian folk music from many ethnic groups including Azeris, Armenians, Kurds, Lurs, Turkmens, and Baluchistanis; orchestral rehearsals of compositions by young Iranian composers, in Persian style, but with Westernized instrumentation and compositional influence; and a rehearsal and concert of the Tehran Symphony Orchestra. All of this became the nucleus of a four-movement suite for small orchestra in Iranian style called *Persian Set*, in which he preserved his relationship with Pahlbod by carefully avoiding authentic Persian melodies. He also produced two arrangements of melodies by Shardar for small orchestra and chorus, at a level suitable for the Iranian Radio Orchestra, and began an annotated list of American composers and recordings of their works in the USIS Library, adding commentary advising the radio staff of USIS about how to use them.

Although he deferred making elaborate recommendations until the end of their second stay in Tehran, Henry already had suggestions, which required improved cooperation between the radio and Pahlbod's Fine Arts Department. The Radio Orchestra needed to get rid of some terrible musicians and find a proper conductor; the current man led from the violin. He advised getting good American-made arrangements for the orchestra and having it play Western music and music composed by Iranians in Western style. Broadcasting needed to differentiate more strongly between programs of pure traditional art music and pure folk music in Iranian style, since many Persians avoided Radio Iran because the traditional and folk styles were always corrupted.[19] Implementing these changes promised to require a lot of work after he returned from Madras.

India

The Rockefeller staff's advice that the Cowells attend the Madras Music Festival no matter how much travel was required[1] must have resonated on December 20 as they endlessly waited at Tehran airport while fog in Britain kept planes on the ground. An overnight stay in Karachi was necessary, complete with border checks.[2] The next day they flew to Delhi and had to go through customs again, a process still new to the locals who remembered British India as one country a decade earlier. On the approach to Madras, an hour of circling provided an endless view of the gorgeous coastal beaches. Finally settled in their hotel, they were cheered up by birds that flew into their room through windows with split bamboo screens instead of glass.[3] To save time for her fieldwork and their tourism, Sidney decided that long letters to her sister would substitute for a diary. Unfortunately, her sister later shared them with friends, who discarded them,[4] with the result that the rest of the Cowells' world tour can only be pieced together from Sidney's rough notes, a few other letters, and the reports to the Rockefeller Foundation.

The United States had sent its first ambassador to India nine years earlier, just before independence and partition. Gradually consulates opened in major cities, so that by the time of the Cowells' visit the American diplomatic presence could be helpful in many parts of the country. Although USIS was not funding any part of the Cowells' trip but the Tehran segments, it arranged Henry's schedule and made an invaluable contact for him with Narayana Menon, a British-educated, Madras-based composer, comparative musicologist, and Yeats scholar who was rising to the top of All India Radio.[5] Henry's other important and enduring link to India was C. Harold Tufty, the Public Affairs Officer at the consulate in Madras. Interviewed in 1977, Tufty said that at the time of the Cowells' visit almost no Americans—particularly of Henry's prominence—were around. Despite the fact that Henry was not a government employee, Tufty had been asked to help him however he could, and in fact was invaluable, because it never occurred to the Cowells that merely attending the festival was not a foregone conclusion from the Indian side. Months earlier, Henry had inquired about getting tickets. After several silent weeks, "a quite chilly formal note" stated that admission was $60 [2010: $481].

Because they doubted that Indians could pay so much, the tone of the letter led them to conclude that they were not wanted. With help from the State Department (that is, Tufty) and the Rockefeller Foundation, however, they finally obtained their tickets. At the first two concerts, Indian skepticism about their presence suggested that they were caught in the middle of some local squabble. Then they learned that skepticism was normal: in the world of Indian traditional professional music, only peers were deemed to have earned the right to listen. People of lesser musical cultivation were not encouraged to attend concerts of the highest quality. Inconvenient and perhaps condescending to some, this attitude had the virtue of eliminating the distance between performer and audience so familiar in the West. The Cowells therefore had to prove that they were of the suitable "rank" to hear the music. Tufty's many introductions to musicians helped greatly.

For Henry, proof was no problem. Attending the Madras Music Festival was the culmination of his three decades' experience with Indian music, beginning with his boyhood acquaintance with exiles playing in San Francisco, and the Indian musicians he included in his first presentation of non-Western music at St. Marks-in-the-Bouwerie in 1924.[6] Three years later he commenced theoretical studies with Sarat Lahiri, a Bengali virtuoso and exiled activist living in New York.[7] In Berlin he studied Karnatic (South Indian) theory with Pichu Sambamoorthy. Fortunately, Sidney's comparatively rudimentary acquaintance with Indian musical systems also earned her the Indians' respect.[8]

Festival performances, held in a big tent, lasted ten to twelve hours a day. The concerts drew more than a thousand listeners, and fifty to a hundred people attended scholarly meetings and participated in lively discussions.[9] Tufty remembered with delight how Henry could follow the intricate rhythms, nodding his head with the flow. The Cowells, along with the audience, kept time by tapping and making complex hand motions governed by the type of beat. (Tufty thought it resembled an odd chorus line.) Henry said his attention was held "by the rhythmic and melodic variety, and the time passed quickly...."[10] Newspapers praised the Cowells' endurance.[11]

At the meetings, hybrid music was the subject of heated discussion because so many Indians felt that Western and Eastern should be kept apart. The festival musicians, for example, complained about an orchestra playing hybrid music that was broadcast from Delhi on All India Radio. The Cowells also saw that the high standards of Indian music were not carried over to Western music. There was little systematic education in Western music in Madras; private piano teachers served foreign residents, while the climate rapidly destroyed pianos. The music-loving Maharajah of Mysore attempted to correct the situation by importing one piano after another, with the humidity claiming twenty-six of them before he gave up.

In addition to listening to discussions, Henry gave a morning lecture-demonstration on "The Influence of Oriental on American Music" for the Expert Committee of the Madras Music Academy, using illustrations of hybrid music by McPhee, Hovhaness, P. C. Chow (a Chinese composer living in the United States), Cage, Harrison, and Peggy Glanville-Hicks. Responding to a questioner, he said it was too early to know whether the influence of Asian music on American was good or bad, and lamented the lack of teachers of Indian music in America.[12] (Sidney suggested that the most important thing the Music Academy could do, apart from maintaining its superb quality, was to produce English-language materials.)[13] Henry urged composers drawing from both cultures to appreciate their equality of sophistication.[14] Indians who thought his open-mindedness represented an important current in American culture needed to be corrected, however; Henry had found that Cage and Harrison were about the only Western musicians who understood his interest in Eastern music.[15] (Apparently he forgot McPhee.) Ravi Shankar's American tour that year changed the situation on a scale that was beyond Henry's reach.

By the end of the Festival, Henry's empathetic style and patient listening made such an impression that the Indians presented him to the audience as an honored guest. A very elderly and famous flute player then played something as a tribute to both Cowells. To their dismay, the theme for his improvisation was a famous but dull popular American song of the beginning of the century, "which moves along chord lines so that he could never get his improvisation off the ground, and the whole performance seemed to us childishly vulgar and pathetic." Many apologies followed.[16] Tufty felt that the warmth accorded the Cowells was symptomatic of the great difference between Indian hostility to the United States as a country and its high regard for individual Americans.[17]

The strong respect of Indians for purity in their music was one sign that their musical culture had achieved an extraordinarily high level—certainly much higher than Iran's. As a result, when Henry looked for talented young musicians who could be considered for Rockefeller fellowships, he found them uninterested in learning about Western music. He therefore recommended instead that the Foundation bring Dr. Sambamoorthy to give a course in Indian music in America, where there was "no authentic source of knowledge of the world's most complex melodic and rhythmic system."[18]

Tufty and the Cowells had long discussions of East and West, problems of communication, similarities, and areas of common interest, which he thought helped Henry develop his *Madras* Symphony (No. 13), in which he wanted to fuse cultures without sinking into exoticism, a difficult challenge considering the gulf between those cultures. Tufty then managed to get an embassy grant to support making parts for the symphony.[19]

Thanks to Menon, Henry conducted a radio interview and supplied informal commentary for a half-hour show about his recorded music,[20] for which he was surprised to be paid $60 [2010: $481]. Having agreed not to earn any money, he and Sidney proposed donating it to the Music Academy for use as a prize, only to discover that the acceptance of gifts was no more automatic than the granting of tickets to the festival. A special board meeting had to approve even such a small sum. Menon explained that wealthy Indians, wanting to accrue prestige by donating to the academy, often demanded a voice in programming, choosing artists, and other decisions. He thought, however, that a gift made "with love" might be accepted. In response to Henry's proposal of a prize for drumming, Dr. Venkataraman Raghavan, a renowned Sanskrit scholar and musicologist, suggested focusing on the neglected south Indian *mridangam*. Once the gift was accepted, USIS provided a cup, upon which the names of recipients of the Cowell prize would be engraved. The Cowells later sent recordings of Western music, with the stipulation that the purchase price in rupees be added to the prize money. Later, the performance fees for Henry's thirteenth symphony, the *Madras* Symphony, were also contributed to the endowment.[21] As a result, the prize is still awarded.

Henry's comportment and graciousness were put to good use in their encounter with Jayachamaraja Wodeyar Bahadur (1919–74), the last Maharajah of Mysore, a powerful figure in British India and one of only a few maharajahs allowed to retain their property because of their previous generosity. A great music lover, Mysore had studied at the Guildhall School in London, became a Nikolai Medtner fan, started a Medtner Society, underwrote publication of his complete works, and funded some recordings. According to Sidney, Stokowski had recommended that the maharajah grant the Cowells an audience when he came to Madras to visit the provincial governor. Since Mysore had a standing order with European and American record companies to send him every recording of twentieth-century music that was issued—all of which he played— he was extremely well informed about new music, and told Henry that he felt American composers, in the last five or six years, had become technically and musically better than Europeans. "He want[ed] me to give that message from a neutral country."[22] When Henry and Sidney gave him recordings of Henry's music, Sidney was amused by "the shyness with which this elegant potentate hesitantly asked: Would Henry mind autographing the records for him? and at his boyish pleasure when this was done." They subsequently met him in New York three or four times. "He would have liked a real talk about music with Henry I am sure but the formal occasions always prevented [it]."[23]

Sidney called the week in Madras a huge success, "the most extraordinary musical experience [Henry] ever had, and the most completely enveloping . . . his supreme experience of music. Nothing he had ever heard seemed to reach the heights that these performances did."[24] Their experience in Madras also taught them a political lesson. The idea that the Public Affairs Office of an embassy is there to "sell" American culture had to fade. Visitors made a much greater impact by showing that they were there to learn, not to teach. Tufty encouraged that attitude and remained a good friend of the Cowells.[25]

Iran, II

On New Year's Day the Cowells returned to Tehran to complete the remaining forty days of their State Department grant.[1] Sidney's reports say very little about Henry's work, which probably did not measurably change. Their travel experiences blossomed, however, as the eagerness to have Henry lecture at other posts, such as Tabriz, in the Azeri region of northwestern Iran, was shared by both the USIS and the Iranian government. The center of Kurdish nationalism and Soviet influence in Iran, Tabriz was an important place to polish the American image. Impassable roads and closed airstrips made going there in winter almost impossible, however. The same was true of Meshed, the Holy City of Shiite Islam, in the east. Several planned trips in both directions were canceled because of bad weather and obligations in Tehran, which multiplied as their stay neared the end. An attempt to get to Kerman was also thwarted by weather and landed them in Karachi. Fortunately, their Pakistani visas were still valid.[2]

They only succeeded in reaching Isfahan and Abadan, the oil refinery town, whose Iranian-American Club requested Henry, with the encouragement of the American consul and the new USIS office. The journey required a two-day stopover in Isfahan, at that time the only place in Iran where non-Muslims could enter working mosques. Because the experienced US consul had relations with the local leader, the few minutes the Cowells spent with him immeasurably enhanced their status. They visited a famous old Armenian center nearby, enduring what Sidney called "a depressingly Christians-are-always-despised-here view of the place" from the guide. The next day they spent an hour at two of the mosques in the main square with a "less huffily Christian" guide. Fearless (or perhaps reckless) as usual, Sidney went alone to the bazaar, where Iranian men came to her defense when she was criticized for not wearing the chador. Henry suffered an attack of gout, but an English doctor was able to postpone the worst until after his talk in Abadan.

On the way to Abadan, the pilot took them off course to see the archaeological site at Susa, a detour that required passing over mountains at least 17,000 feet high in the unpressurized plane. Henry felt extremely ill, although Sidney did not realize it until later. Abadan itself, a town of 260,000, had been created by the oil industry near the head of the Persian Gulf to serve the world's then-largest oil refinery at the Shatt al Arab, on the border with Iraq. They stayed comfortably in the Iranian-American clubhouse, "observed at a chilly distance by its mostly English members." (She combated their sense of superiority by pointing out that American clubs were the first Western clubs to welcome cultivated natives as guests.)[3] Henry spoke twice, illustrating his music from recordings. The second lecture was at the Naft [Oil] Club, where Sidney was pleased that the many men who felt "dragooned into coming" came away feeling they had had a good time.[4] The USIS had prepared the ground by getting the radio to broadcast Henry's Symphony No. 5. She, however, had great difficulty recording folk music there because the fearsome police kept foreigners away from all but the modern parts of town.[5]

From Abadan they went south to Persepolis and Shiraz, where four inches of snow paralyzed the city. Unable to leave until the airport could reopen, they found local instrumentalists and dancers to perform for them. When the weather improved they returned to Tehran, where on February 6, Henry, still suffering badly from gout, gave his autobiographical talk in the USIS auditorium.[6] Various odd experiences during their last days included fulfilling a request from the head of the Ladies' Committee of the Joint Distribution Committee—the international agency serving the Jewish poor—to record the sound of new flush toilets and play it for their colleagues in New York who had raised the money for them.[7] Then it was time for the Cowells to leave Iran. The biggest disappointment of their entire stay was their inability to get a recording of Henry's OWI-period music for military calesthenics.[8]

C. Robert Payne, sharing his memories with Sidney twenty years later, felt Henry "accomplish[ed] wonders. He had patience, credibility, a sense of humor and an ability to recognize talent, spotted problems, solved them, and convinced the Iranians that it was their idea. Only an outsider could have done it. Those who didn't want any change went along because Henry convinced them change was the best thing for them individually but to achieve it they had to be part of the team. Those in charge were enthusiastic and approved everything because, even though they didn't for the most part know the first thing about music and things musical, they saw and heard improvement in the situation." He thought that the officials wanted Henry to succeed because the Shah was behind it. "Henry gave the symphony new direction and interests. He uncovered artistry which had been dormant. He made the classicists conscious of the fact [that] they had some national music which could be developed and popularized. Composers and arrangers were born—perhaps with limited talent but with unlimited possibilities."[9]

In 1994, when I asked Mehrdad Pahlbod for his recollections of that time, he felt that his policy of musical isolation was the "misguided impulse of youth."[10] He thought, however, that he had succeeded in elevating some musicians, especially Tehrani, the phenomenal zarb (Persian drum) virtuoso who began playing when a zarbist was considered a low-level musician who had given up all hope of prestige.[11] Despite his position in a court bent on modernizing, Pahlbod had always wanted more energy to be invested in traditional Iranian music.

54

Change of Plans

For the main phase of the Cowells' visit to India, the Rockefeller staff made arrangements of half a week to half a month in Karachi, Delhi, Bombay, Calcutta, and East Pakistan (now Bangladesh), where they hoped to visit Dacca and up to four more cities despite a prediction of rugged travel.[1] Henry's first public lecture was scheduled for February 15 in Karachi, sponsored by the Arts Council of Pakistan and the US Educational Exchange Program.[2]

Sidney, having decided to make one more attempt to see Kerman, got off the plane there while Henry continued to Karachi. Since previous attempts had been aborted because of bad weather in the valley, which is surrounded on three sides by mountains up to 16,000 feet, she could not forget being warned that "once you get [to Kerman], you may not be able to leave." This time she got through and had indescribable adventures, including getting caught in the middle of a squabble between a local potentate, the governor, the shah, and the American consul.[3] As a result of the stopover, she arrived in Karachi a little too late for Henry's talk but caught the post-performance party at the home of the Public Affairs Officer, where Henry drank a lot of martinis and was unusually sick all night. The next morning, it was clear that something else was wrong. The doctor arranged to get him to a hospital; ironically, there was no room for an invalid at the house of the Public Affairs Officer because a big party in Henry's honor was to take place that night.

At the Seventh Day Adventist Hospital, he was diagnosed with a mild but debilitating stroke. In retrospect, Sidney recognized warnings. He had arrived in Ireland with "startlingly blue" lips and needed to rest for three days before moving on. In the process of leaving Iran, Henry seemed "fantastically apprehensive about everything." She thought his terrible sickness on the unpressurized, high-altitude flight from Isfahan to Abadan might also have been something much worse than normal airsickness.[4]

She set up a cot by the window of his hospital room—standard procedure in Pakistan, where relatives were expected to help with the nursing. The admitting physician found his blood pressure high, his speech thick and hesitant, his right extremities weak, but his reflexes normal. Although his symptoms were slightly easing, she was told that he might not survive.[5] The few Americans on the hospital staff "sang Rock of Ages & other appropriate hymns outside our door nightly—not that Henry noticed." The word quickly spread around the American colony, drawing a flood of visitors, some well-wishing, some morbidly curious.

A moderately large hospital, with a school of health care, it did an extraordinary job, although conditions were, in Sidney's words, "very Kipling." Someone next door cooked for an invalid, much to the nurses' annoyance. The morning call for prayer was followed by figures kneeling outside every room. Sidney was asked if the male doctors might examine her mastectomy scar, something they had never been allowed to do. The caste system operated within the staff, which was bloated to spread employment. Despite the exotic atmosphere, after ten tense days Henry left the hospital to have a seafood dinner with friends. In the middle of the night he felt nauseated, began vomiting, and about two hours later developed diarrhea. His symptoms persisted for nearly a month, but the doctor pronounced him fit to travel and finally discharged him on March 6, on vasodilating and gout medication. He had recovered all motion and his speech, but remained weak and in danger. The doctors advised him to wait a few weeks before working and to avoid overexertion and pressure.[6] He spent two more weeks in bed, his problems compounded by gout.[7]

Sidney notified the State Department, USIS, and the Rockefeller Foundation and canceled his engagements to perform or lecture. "But Henry was busily planning to carry out these assignments, and much annoyed with me for cancelling anything, he had never failed to do what he'd undertaken, ever in his life!" She told the Rockefeller Foundation to halt remittances until it could consider terminating the project, and requested confidentiality. Friends would be told "casually" that he had been unwell and they had changed plans to avoid hot weather. Tehran's notorious difficulties for Westerners would be an adequate explanation.[8] They had managed to accomplish a little in Karachi, but had felt "encapsulated" in the American colony more than anywhere else and had had very little contact with Pakistanis. The cancellation of their visit to East Pakistan was especially disappointing since USIS had planned talks at six satellite centers, which, in combination with Sidney's contacts in folk-music circles, would have helped them understand the country.[9]

Having decided to get Henry onto a cruise ship where no one would bother him, she booked them on a handsome new, fully air-conditioned ship with good food and service,[10] stopping at Bombay (Mumbai), Colombo, and Jakarta, and leaving them at Singapore on March 17. After a few days they would fly to Bangkok, stay for two weeks, and go directly to Tokyo for two or three months. The doctor approved flying on big pressurized planes—which were not yet in general use—and recommended avoiding hot weather.[11] They relaxed a bit when the Rockefeller Foundation opted not to change the terms of their grant.[12] USIS stations were told that Henry would pass through but not make public appearances.[13] The staff in Indonesia offered to help him hear gamelan music.[14]

The ship departed on March 7.[15] Henry's future depended upon enforced rest, but even limited shore time permitted some adventures. During two days at Bombay they met Victor Paranjoti, a composer-conductor who wanted to perform Henry's music. Later they realized that had they stayed in Bombay as originally scheduled they would have gotten involved in USIS's plan to have Henry help create an orchestra for the Goans and thereby irrevocably estranged Paranjoti. Henry's illness preserved their fine relationship and got him performances in Bombay.[16]

In Colombo, Ceylon (Sri Lanka), the USIS librarian cheerfully told them that her husband had heard Henry play at a Chicago home in the 1920s. She introduced them to the head of the Government School of Music and Dance, "who interrupted his examination week schedule so that his teachers could give Henry a demonstration of Sinhalese music. . . . It was Henry's sixtieth birthday and they made a very gay and warm and flattering fuss." Then the Cowells took a long, cool drive along the coast "to a fishing village with a beautiful rest house, where a dignified character in conventional collarless nightshirt, dhoti, celluloid comb and top knot fed us the best fresh pineapple imaginable and reverently offered us the opportunity to sit in the very same chairs as the Duke and Duchess of Kent! and brought us his testimonials to read."[17]

Then political turmoil again impinged upon their plans. They were first cautioned that Bali and Java had to be avoided because unrest had turned violent. The musical disappointment was relatively minor, however, since gamelan music was available in the United States on recordings.[18] Nevertheless, the captain decided to take the ship to Indonesia anyway, to the Cowells' relief, for USIS had already got Henry's old teacher Prince Jodhjana to arrange for his brother's gamelan to come to Jogjakarta and perform specially for Henry on board the ship during its three-day stopover. Suddenly Indonesian President Sukarno declared martial law and a state of siege. The ship bypassed Jogjakarta and went directly to Singapore,[19] where the Cowells had a wonderful time despite its profoundly colonial atmosphere. Determined to experience something of the tropics, they spent "a lovely afternoon and part of an evening listening to a Chinese opera in the open air—lovely audience to watch too!" At the botanical gardens hundreds of wild monkeys ate out of visitors' hands. Shopping was a must: they bought Indian saris, cotton fabric, Thai silk sarongs, an Iranian scarf, Singapore flutes, and a book on Malayan social behavior.

Even in such a short time they got a little sense of Singapore's musical life. Henry felt well enough to visit the conductor of the city's Western-style symphony orchestra and junior symphony, and met Zubir Said, a good composer, whose music struck them as the best hybrid of their entire trip. Said is probably the same "delightful man" who, Sidney said, "had been interested all his life in folk and primitive music but had no idea that anyone else in the world shared this interest, so he was ecstatic when I asked if he could find me some authentic musicians." He corralled a bride, groom, a male friend, and some food vendors from the streets. An "officious Malay character from USIS" insisted on running the tape recorder that she had borrowed and deciding what would be sung, until Sidney laid down the law.[20]

Bangkok, where they arrived on March 19, still gave the magnificent impression of low, ancient buildings and picturesque canals, which were soon to be filled in as the city became bloated. "The streets were filled with Buddhist priests. After relaxing boat rides, Henry was feeling better and sought out music." Everything had to take place very early in the morning or very late; at other times, oppressive heat kept them in their "more-or-less air-cooled room," which looked out on layers of rooftops with "delicate squiggles on their corners." [21]

In a letter to Olive, Henry used his activities to excuse his long silence, but he probably waited until his handwriting was completely repaired lest she suspect something was amiss. "In Bangkok," he told her, "we were particularly fortunate in hearing several groups of Thai musicians, including the official group maintained by the King . . . and a group of players and dancers who went into a temple to do ritualistic music and dance. I examined and tried out many instruments, including many Burmese gongs. This music is not known much in the U.S., so I feel especially rewarded."[22] Thai music flourished, but the foreigner had to search for it. Native popular music mixed with pseudo-Broadway arrangements was more pervasive than in any country they had visited—even the king wrote some—but they detected very little interest in hybrids with classical Western music,[23] and even less interest in Western classical music itself.

Although Henry made no public appearances, he was the subject of a large feature in Bangkok *World*, which described a collection of Thai instruments that cluttered their room—gongs, of many types, cymbals, drums, etc.[24] Henry explained that to his knowledge these would be the first Thai instruments in the United States and expressed interest in unique Thai adaptations of American popular tunes, a style that kept changing as new American tunes invaded. "He seemed to feel real regret at having to [go] off and leave this fascinating subject unexplored."[25]

At the end of March, Henry still wanted to visit Korea if a pressurized plane were available,[26] and to see a friend at the American Embassy in Cambodia. Ultimately, they skipped both and flew early to Hong Kong, where wonderful April weather was a great relief. Henry was strong enough to request that the Public Affairs Officer organize a luncheon with musicians, teachers, composers, and officials of music organizations, and get him and Sidney tickets for traditional Chinese theater. Later they visited some musicians in their homes and recorded interviews for Radio Hong Kong.[27] His health seemed to be holding steady, but after a blood test, Sidney was handed more Demerol and a hypodermic for emergencies because the doctor feared that another stroke was imminent. Luckily nothing happened. On April 14 they left by boat for a brief holiday in Macao organized by the American Consulate,[28] which had arranged a meeting with Dr. Pedro Lobo, a mixed Chinese-Portuguese whose black-market wealth had bought him "literally all the business life of [Macao]." He had retired, although he still owned the local airline, waterworks, steamship company, two hospitals, and a hotel, proceeds from which he channeled to Mao. Otherwise, he liked to compose in what Sidney called "good if conventional [style] . . . a sort of Muzak music," a potpourri of Gilbert and Sullivan and many other warhorses.[29] As a composer, Lobo had an enviable position. When the local radio station did not play enough of his music, he bought it, and later added the rival radio station to his collection. Now only his music was heard. "A composer's dream," Sidney said. Henry was the only other composer he had ever met.

They ended up in one of Lobo's hospitals, however, two early victims of the Hong Kong flu. This time Henry was hit only lightly, but Sidney was so sick everyone thought she would succumb. Their return to Hong Kong after two weeks brought more amusement. They now learned that the boat to Macao was such a common route for defectors to the Soviet Union that when the Cowells had not returned to their hotel as expected, their mail was not forwarded but returned to the senders marked "Gone to Macao."[30]

In their few remaining days in Hong Kong, they shopped and had Henry fitted for two tailored suits. Concerts by the Korean Symphony Orchestra and Classical Dancers gave them a little view of Korea, which was no longer on their travel list. On May 1 they left for Japan.[31]

Their Tokyo hotel room and its furnishings were so small that "we felt as if we'd had Alice's enlargening cake fed us on the plane." The wash basins reached just above their knees, toilets were a foot off the floor.[32] Through the Rockefeller Foundation they got a much better room at International House, in Minato-ku, with views of a beautiful, peaceful old garden that more than compensated for its inconvenient location. Henry's health held firm; the local Seventh Day Adventist hospital did blood tests only to check the effects of his anti-coagulant.[33] In the mornings he worked on a second commission from the Louisville Orchestra (a rare honor),[34] for which he wrote a piece powerfully influenced by the music he was hearing in Japan, eventually entitled *Ongaku* ("music"). He was completing a shorter piece, *Music for Orchestra 1957*, for Dorati and the Minneapolis Symphony, and proceeding nicely with the *Madras Symphony*.[35] After a siesta in the early afternoon, the Cowells went to the theater, paid visits, and heard music, including a rehearsal of the court musicians, many temple performances of *gagaku*, and performances on shakuhachi and old secular instruments.³⁶ Henry was delighted to hear the shō, a mouth organ that produces sustained tone clusters.

Tokyo's complex musical life brought two surprises. It resembled that of European countries, including high educational standards and six major orchestras of the level of second-string American orchestras; and many Japanese were familiar with Henry's music through broadcasts and recordings. Henry assembled a list of about thirty-five major composers of serious, Western-type music, including two of the leaders of the developing avant-garde, his ex-student Toshi Ichiyanagi and Toshiro Mayuzumi.³⁷

Although he was not soliciting appearances, he used interviews in two newspapers and on the radio to talk about his disappointment at hearing no symphonic works that drew on Japanese tradition. A transcript of a translation into English of the Japanese version of his remarks quotes him as saying, "I don't like to see the world where all the musics will become similar or same. I hope therefore that each country in Asia will develop her inherent art and will not perform only European musics. For there are enough rooms in the world to accommodate various kinds of musics. . . . It is not desirable to imitate."³⁸

A trip to Kyoto for the Hollyhock (Aoi) Festival threatened to be a mistake because of crowding and sporadic railway strikes, but everything turned out well. They stayed for five days in a Japanese inn and saw a parade whose participants were in antique dress, and beautiful floats with traditional musicians. Sidney loved the bowing of serving people in Japanese inns. "We bow back gracelessly and end up by bumping into things."³⁹ They spent mid-June visiting the little islands Takematsu, Matsuyama, Miyazima, and Iwakuni, returning via Osaka.⁴⁰

The top social engagement was the elegant marriage of koto virtuoso Shinichi Yuize to another young koto player.⁴¹ A charming group picture features Henry and Sidney in the front row surrounded by the clans. They were invited to a preview of a Firefly Viewing, with movie actresses, speeches, food at Western cloth-covered tables with paper flowers, and wire cages filled with thousands of fireflies. "Two of the cages, about a foot square and 18 inches high, were set aside for the dozens of photographers from newspapers, television, and just plain people with cameras. They were diligently flash-gunning the poor fireflies, and I would love to know the result! Funniest of all were the television people who turned their floodlights onto the cages and then couldn't tell if the fireflies were 'firing' or not." In the garden of the restaurant stood a magnificent ancient pine tree, "its trunk curved and stretched to frame a famous view of Fuji over the city of Tokyo—invisible in the mist when we were there." A 1,200-year-old pagoda, one of the oldest wooden structures in Japan, had been moved into the garden.⁴²

Henry told Olive, with evident satisfaction and no reference to the stroke, that he would continue his new Japanese diet—"not more than two drinks per day, no butter, about an egg per week, all-lean meat, and not too much of it, more fish. No salt added to anything. It is not drastic, but I am sure you would find it an improvement."

Shopping provided endlessly entertaining examples of Japanese English as they amassed chests, boxes, scrolls, souvenirs and gifts, furniture and paintings, small articles of cotton, clocks, paper, pottery, stone lanterns, kano tigers, five cotton "Happy Coats," an old woodblock print from Kyoto, two chairs and an arm seat, cloth material, a new "Shuro" (hemp-palm curtain), and male and female kimonos.[43]

It was now time to go home, however. Henry did not say anything about what he felt he had accomplished; his reports only enumerate his activities and observations. There is some evidence that he didn't think he had done much. Elaine Fry, his contact at the State Department, thought he was just being modest, however. The people at the State Department loved to pick his brain, and he would pick theirs about what was going on abroad. "I know . . . he was very effective that way as a person-to-person individual, because he was so warm and lovable." All the posts wished they could get more like him, she said.[44]

Sidney's final impression of Japan: "dear Grandfather: Please smile and save . . . stewardess on Japan Air Lines announced arrival at Tokyo and added brightly, 'We hope you have enjoyed your fright. Please remember about forgetting everything.'"[45]

A New Radicalism, 1957–1961

Following a brief interlude to enjoy "orchids and volcanos" in Honolulu and visits with friends in San Francisco and Palo Alto, the Cowells arrived in New York. A year had passed since the grand tour began. Henry seemed fine, but a doctor warned Sidney to keep his life very quiet because he could not live much longer.[1] That prognosis was tested the following May, when Henry, alone at Shady, bent to pick up his shoes and lost consciousness. After a couple of minutes he awoke on the floor, having lost a lot of blood from his nose. On the way to the hospital at Kingston, New York, he repeatedly vomited, again expelling blood. The electrocardial report was "abnormal consistent with left ventricular hypertrophy, myocardial disease and digitalis effect."[2] The doctor concluded that it was not a stroke, but could not assign another cause. Henceforth Henry carried his doctor's information and a letter stating his condition and medications in case of emergency.[3] If he developed a new outlook on mortality, he probably only confided in Sidney and possibly not entirely to her. That may explain why she did not know that in November 1959, when she was at Shady, he was admitted to St. Luke's Hospital, near Columbia University. When she saw the documents years later, she could not tell whether he had gone for tests or had another incident.[4]

Fortunately, his health stabilized, no small achievement for a man who had had a spinal operation and suffered from an unreliable heart and severe gout. Keeping his life calm would be challenging, as Sidney had seen in Karachi when he resented her canceling his engagements. At least he was no longer running around performing his most strenuous piano pieces. He traveled to lecture, attend performances of his music, and participate in professional events, but his schedule was infinitely lighter than in the old days. BMI's guarantee provided a floor to his income, and other sources were reasonably good. In fact, his income from teaching was only one third of the gross, which included distributions from BMI, ACA (the American Composers Alliance), and Associated Music Publishers, and some income from Sidney's parents' estate. They also benefited from tax deductions, as they donated his music manuscripts to the Library of Congress.

The BMI guarantee finally allowed him to devote most of his energy to composing. In the four years between his return from Asia and his next trip abroad, in the spring of 1961, he composed twenty-four substantial pieces and an equal number of tiny birthday, anniversary, wedding, Christmas, and similar occasional pieces for Sidney and their friends. Only one piece was left incomplete, an unusually small percentage.

His great achievement in these four years is a large body of orchestral music—three symphonies; concertante pieces featuring accordion, percussion, and two violas; and four other orchestral works. Some of it, late Cowell at its very best, enjoyed many performances before falling into neglect as his old champions left the podium. Because this music is accessible on first hearing, it has been used as evidence that Henry had rejected his adventurous past, with inferences that he had been "broken" in prison. These pieces can hardly be disposed of as conservative, however. To begin with, most of his later music was conceived as pure melody, a concept alien to the thinking of both the avant-garde and the adherents to the Western harmonic tradition. While all the orchestral works have very startling qualities, *Ongaku* and the *Madras* Symphony are as unconventional as his wildest early piano pieces. Intimately drawing upon the principles of two of the world's most elaborate musical cultures, they exemplify the hybridization that Henry sought in Asia. The title *Ongaku* translates as "music," but he used it more generally to highlight the influence of Japanese music on his piece. Japanese modes, rhythms, and forms that he heard at rehearsals and performances of traditional music all were employed "as felt by a westerner," he said, but without quoting any melodies. He based the first movement on his impressions of *gagaku*, a music that particularly interested him because it uses the shō, the Japanese mouth organ whose secundal chords correspond to Henry's tone clusters. The second movement was based on the feeling of *sanyoku,* a more modern music for instrumental trio.[5] In his program note, Henry admitted that it was "rather brash for him to write his impressions of Japanese music for Western orchestra as a neophyte, but the desire to do so [came] from an inner urge based on long love of and association with this sort of music." *Ongaku*'s resistance to forward motion has proven extremely provocative to Western listeners.

Brian Silver's analysis of the *Madras* Symphony shows that Henry adhered to principles of musical development drawn from India, exploiting facets that are compatible with Western procedures, including changes of pitch-groupings that function like modulations. His use of a tabla and jalatarang (tuned bowls) as solo instruments years before Takemitsu's *November Steps* should have put his mixture of Western and Asian instruments into the history books. Unfortunately, the *Madras* Symphony has rarely been played and never recorded. After the Madras premiere, Indian writers expressed pride that their music, so long ignored by Westerners, could inspire and inform a Western symphonic composer. An Indian diplomat who attended a performance of the symphony in New York in 2010 was especially struck by its lack of sentimentality or excessive preoccupation with sounding "Indian," and impressed by Henry's incorporation of the "energetic" aspect of Indian music as opposed to the timeless and meditative aspects that so often mark the music of orientalists.[6]

His chamber and solo music of these years also has many unusual features, beginning with their instrumentation. The most unusually scored is the beautiful *Homage to Iran*, the publication of which obscures its true significance. Although published for violin and piano duo, Henry conceived it for piano, violin, and Persian drum, probably zarb. According to Sidney, he intended the drum part to be improvised. C. F. Peters, however, guessing that classical musicians would resist improvising, insisted that the drum part (in the first and third movements) be fully written out and transferred to the pianist, who simulates the drum by muting the strings with the fingers, a practical solution that greatly diminishes Henry's innovativeness.[7] Like his earlier *Persian Set*—which uses Persian drum and tar (the long-necked lute)—*Homage to Iran* contains no Iranian tunes, although its modes link it to Persian classical music and make it a true hybrid.

Another hybrid from those years has a curious history. In 1957, a few months after Malaya (now Malaysia) left the British Commonwealth, the new government opened a worldwide competition for an anthem, but rejected all 514 entries. They then invited Britten, Walton, Menotti, the Cowells' Singaporean friend Zubir Said, and Henry to submit entries. Not knowing that Said had been invited, the Cowells inferred that the Malayan government felt only an outsider could write an anthem acceptable to the country's mutually antagonistic ethnic groups. Henry, therefore, created a tune based "on melodic forms common to several of the peoples of Malaya, on the theory that the government meant what it said about the integration of peoples, political equality, common aims, etc." None of the entries were accepted. Henry was surprised to be paid fifty guineas (fifty pounds, fifty shillings in the old system, now £52.50) for his time [2010: £911 pounds, approximately $1,600].[8] Zubir Said later wrote the Singaporean anthem when the island became independent of Malaya.

This charming story lacked its most interesting component, the anthem itself, of which the Cowell papers contain only a sketch.[9] Fortunately, a pencil copy turned up unexpectedly in a small spiral notebook at the Sacher Foundation in Basel, which had acquired the book as part of a collection without realizing what it was.[10] Henry had created what looks like the perfect anthem for a Southeast Asian country—a tune and a four-part "harmonization" that are both entirely pentatonic. The Cowells eventually learned, however, that his setting was considered too Chinese and insufficiently Malay. In the end, the government adapted a popular song released in Australia in the 1930s, which, in the Cowells' opinion, was "neither Malayan nor Chinese nor anything else identifiable—and perhaps this is better after all!"[11]

Henry again tried to achieve some commercial success with a seven-move-ment orchestral piece, *Characters*, for Alexander Semmler, a friend at CBS who wanted to use it as background music. Sidney was unsurprised by its failure. "HC having never heard a soap opera or listened to radio or TV except for his own performances, [and] having been to 3 movies since 1941, he had a 1920 notion of the sort of 'characters' for which music could now be used."[12]

Most of his music was eagerly embraced. Commissions and performances by major orchestras and conductors abounded; recordings and broadcasts yielded substantial income. (Chamber and solo pieces generated almost no money un-less they were broadcast.) Although his music no longer attracted the tabloids, Henry continued to be newsworthy. *Time*, which allotted very little space to music, highlighted him repeatedly. When Dorati and the Minneapolis Sym-phony Orchestra (now the Minnesota Orchestra) played *Music for Orchestra 1957* and *Persian Set*, it ran a feature entitled "Bad Boy at 60," with a photo cap-tioned "Still Battling with Kid Knabe" and anecdotes of riots, Persian calis-thenics, the Malay anthem fiasco, the drumming prize at the Madras Academy, the aborted plan to announce Henry's arrival in Damascus with leaflets dusted over the city by low-flying planes.[13] San Quentin disappeared from the news, though not from the Cowell mythology. Controversy abounded: conservative critics claimed him as a convert to their values, while progressives accused him of playing it safe.

Henry, in fact, had offered a new challenge for commentators and analysts. It was easy to damn or praise serial, aleatoric, and electronic music, but not so simple to find words for a composer who defied categorization. Although his music's accessibility was greatly appreciated in an epoch preoccupied with inno-vation and dogma, it had neither the quasi-romantic drama of Roy Harris's or William Schuman's, nor the Americanism of Copland's. In an era of larger-than-life composers, accusations of paleness were to be expected, though many lis-teners did not grasp that compositions drawing upon non-Western cultures need different ears, since those cultures do not use dramatic contrast in their music.

Composer-pianist Yehudi Wyner described how Henry's music drew him in by its simplicity, by the fact that it makes no apologies for itself. He thought its greatest characteristic was its surface naïveté, the fact that it is not music with an easily identifiable character, not concerned with external drama or striking themes, or astonishing color. Inevitably, even when there was something naïve, there was also something that grew in depth. He compared Henry's later music to a continuous letter from a very open-hearted man who was unafraid to say what he was really thinking.[14]

In his warm appraisal of Henry's music for *Musical Quarterly*, Hugo Weisgall attacked the accusation that Henry had no recognizable personal style. Hailing his goal of composing however each compositional challenge required, and rebutting a recurring criticism, Weisgall called Henry's refusal to create a single compositional persona the thread uniting his music and the most enduring mark of his ever-rebellious personality.[15]

Ironically, just when his recent, more ingratiating compositions were finding an audience, his previously vilified early piano music was embraced as an icon of modernism. Glowing reviews of Henry's CRI piano recording were an incredible vindication. Pieces like "The Banshee" were called fresh, alive, and pioneering, heralding the sound-world of *musique concrète. Time* saw no disconnect between early and later Henry. "If the once-daring innovations sound tame to modern ears, they nevertheless provide an intriguing reminder of the experiments that led Henry Cowell, 60, to some of the most vital U.S. symphonic work of his generation."[16] Reviewing the recording of Henry's Seventh Symphony for *American Record Guide*, "J.L." wrote, "I like everything of Cowell that I know, to tell the truth. What other composer of our time writes with such lack of conceit, such directness?" He pointed out that cheerfulness—a musical quality that was swamped by the *Innerlichkeit* of the nineteenth century—could be hard to take seriously.[17] As Richard French, an exceptionally serious writer, put it, "Cowell has never recovered from the fun of finding himself a composer, and I hope he never does."[18]

Henry's compositional productivity and the BMI guarantee now allowed him to reject most requests for articles other than his regular reviews of new music and recordings for *Musical Quarterly*. In part he was conserving his energy, but the truth is that Sidney refused to continue her quasi-ghostwriting.[19] His one major project was an exploration of regional versus universal music, which he never completed. Distressed by the apparent triumph of twelve-tone music among young composers, Henry intended to write about the "facelessness" of serial music, but eventually discarded the idea. His main noncompositional activity was teaching. As adjunct professor at Columbia's School of General Studies, he normally taught Introductory Composition, Music of the World's Peoples, and one or more sections of an introduction to music required of all undergraduates. The minuscule extant information about his classes in those years includes his class list for the 1957–58 composition course, of which two of the four students—Nicolas Roussakis and Philip Corner—went on to considerable careers.[20] Henry's colleague Jack Beeson thought that his lack of degrees was only a partial explanation of why he was never offered a full-time position. The department chairman, Douglas Moore, Beeson said, had always been too afraid of Henry's prison record to risk it.[21] By 1960, San Quentin did not worry Moore's successor, William Mitchell. Henry, however, declined offers to increase his course load, obviously enjoying having time to compose. As mandatory retirement loomed, a real job became a fantasy of the past.

Sidney was apprehensive about his traveling to lecture, but decided it fell under her rubric of "things to make Henry's last days enjoyable." Much in demand, he was even invited for (and declined) extended residencies as distant as Hawaii and South Africa. The usual topics were his life as a musician, music education, and aspects of the interaction of Western and Asian music. While he did not consider himself a true ethnomusicologist, he was one of the principal spokesmen for defining music as broadly as possible and learning from other cultures.

Since board memberships did not entail lifting heavy boxes, they also were risk-free enhancements of his life. As vice-president of Stokowski's Contemporary Music Society, his work extended his lifetime goals of presenting performances of new music, commissioning, encouraging young composers, reviving important neglected music, promoting broadcasting and recording of contemporary music, making available contemporary music from all over the world, ensuring friendly relations with existing composers' organizations everywhere, and helping the United States become "the leader in the contemporary cultural and educational developments of life" here.[22]

He was especially devoted to the Asia Society, which had been incorporated in June 1956 to realize John D. Rockefeller II's dream of promoting mutual understanding between Asia and the West while avoiding political issues. Paul Sherbet, the director of USIS programs in South India when the Cowells were there, became the Asia Society's executive director at the end of 1956[23] and quickly brought in Henry. When William Kay Archer, a specialist in world music, persuaded the Asia Society to fund the Society for Asian Music in order to bring Asian music to Western listeners, Henry became its first board chairman.[24]

Other board memberships included Composers Recordings, Inc. (CRI), the American Composers Alliance, the Composers Forum, and the Eva Gauthier Society for Contemporary Song. Passionate about Stokowski's American Symphony Orchestra, Henry served on its score-reading and long-range planning committees and participated in the summer workshops that gave composers unique opportunities to hear their music. He especially enjoyed serving on BMI's juries for its student-composer awards. Considering his early ambivalence about jazz, it is surprising to find Henry on the Advisory Council of the Newport Jazz Festival, but in the intervening years, jazz itself had evolved into a major force in new music. These were only his most important involvements, however. Sponsoring committees, review panels, educational organizations, conferences—everyone seemed to want Henry's name on their stationery.

He carefully avoided foreign political entanglements, however, steering clear of contact with the Soviet Union other than attending dinners honoring Shostakovich and other Soviet composers during their 1959 visit to the United States. In contrast, he maintained connections with the American government, especially in relation to Asia. State Department personnel had become good friends and passed Henry along to their successors as they rotated out of Asian postings; Iranian and Indian officials remembered him fondly. Performances of the *Madras Symphony* in India and *Persian Set* in Iran added to his legacies there. A visit with Mehrdad Pahlbod in New York made Sidney realize that a "peculiar Asian combination of superiority and inferiority" leads Asians to assume that the United States foists off third-rate people on the "unsuspecting Oriental."[25] Pahlbod confirmed that he had underrated Henry because he assumed that anyone who had the time to come to Iran could not have been important.[26]

An unnamed Iranian composer promoting his own interests ended up triggering the creation of another service to composers involving Henry. In 1958, the chief of the Music Branch of USIA solicited Henry's advice about the perennial problem of foreign composers who wanted USIA's assistance in promoting their works. While not wanting to promote foreigners at the expense of American composers, the agency also did not want to overlook a foreign composer of rare talent. Henry and the USIA decided to establish a small committee to examine submissions by such composers, restricting it at first to the Near and Far East and not publicizing it to avoid being flooded. The Contemporary Music Society administered it as an "Oriental Music Reading Committee." Henry selected an evaluation team of three musicians, based on their broad tastes rather than their experience with Asian music.[27] The first composer to be assisted was Toshiro Mayuzumi, one of Japan's most promising talents.[28]

Relations with India also continued almost without interruption, at first with regard to the drumming prize and the March 1959 Indian premiere of the *Madras* Symphony by Thomas Scherman and the Little Orchestra Society. In June, the chief of USIS in Delhi, acting at the suggestion of Harold Tufty, Henry's friend at USIS in Madras, asked Henry to write something for the coming *mela* (agricultural fair). Henry decided on a piece in two movements, one in Indian style that might be heard at a *mela* and one in American folk style as heard at an American country fair. USIS provided him with recordings of *mela* music, suggesting that he use half a dozen simple, flexible tunes that could be hummed or sung by everyone and could be extracted and arranged simply for additional use elsewhere. Henry, however, avoided copyright issues by writing his own melodies, using modes common to both cultures, and mixing Western and Indian instruments.[29]

All that activity makes one wonder whether Henry still had time for his old friends. Because many of them ceased to write, a few lines in an unexpected letter make one realize how much of daily life defies detection. Such revelations increased as Sidney tried to put his legacy in order before it was too late. His old Halcyon connections are a case in point. It is natural to assume that his misadventure there cost him friendships, yet a brief 1959 exchange between Henry and Aileen Harrison, John Varian's elderly sister-in-law, shows that when Henry and Sidney visited with his Halcyon friend George Harrison, a physicist at MIT, they were shocked to learn of the death of Russell Varian, whom they had recently seen.[30] Other letters from Halcyonites confirm that connections had never been broken.

Terman was always there for him. In August 1956, now seventy-nine years old, he warmly recalled a day in the Redwood City (jail) "when you told me you would do your best to 'pick up the pieces.' And how you have succeeded! You have built the pieces into a structure that may be as grand as anything you could have wrought if the tragedy had not occurred. Perhaps it only made you try the harder."[31] It was their last communication; Terman died five months later. The Gifted Children follow-up continued, however. Henry's 1960 update reveals how he saw himself at age sixty-three. He was still guarded about his feelings, claiming to have no tendencies toward nervousness, worry, anxieties, nervous breakdown, or special problems with regard to sex. (The response about anxieties was flatly untrue.) He described himself as a moderate drinker; his chief avocational interest was bridge. Asked about changes since the age of forty, he responded (to multiple-choice questions) that he had experienced the greatest changes in the categories of excellence in work, recognition of accomplishments, and further vocational advancement; "somewhat more" change in financial gain. Over the last five years his ambition to achieve had "increased somewhat." Asked about frequency of voting, he checked "never," adding "Inadvisable for reason you know (all parties split)." This, too, was disingenuous: Sidney said that he never voted out of an irrational fear that his past would surface. He described his party leanings as northern Democratic, his economic attitudes as average— "liberal, but not radical." He only joined professional clubs; work was his source of greatest satisfaction.[32]

Olive, of course, was a constant for Henry and Sidney, but their relationship with her is truly inscrutable. Sidney may have been right that Olive considered her a threat, but Olive tells the story a little differently. "As long as we were using our minds, all went well, but we could not relate emotionally. Just very different personalities, which no one could help. . . . We three Cowells were all introverts, perhaps that explains why we got along so well. Any differences, any sarcastic remarks from Sidney would be ignored by me. I treasured harmony, as did Harry and Henry. Henry and Sidney got along well; I never witnessed any friction between them. Anyone could live with Henry. Sidney mellowed very much as a consequence of living with Henry."[33] Olive, however, was deceiving herself. Their friction is unmistakable in the ongoing saga of the Cowell Foundation. When Olive decided to use it to sponsor concerts she overstepped the mark. Henry thought her choice of performers was entirely inappropriate and quietly terminated the Foundation, which had always seemed tainted by Olive's ambitions.[34]

56

Asia Again

In November 1960, Nicolas Nabokov, secretary general of the Congress for Cultural Freedom, invited Henry to a week-long conference in Tokyo, the opening event of an "East-West Music Encounter" that would continue with three weeks of concerts by some of the world's most prominent traditional musicians and Western classical artists.[1] An event of global stature that was not to be missed, it posed a problem for Sidney. Knowing that the festival could not afford to bring her, she worried about Henry going alone but could not urge him to stay home without revealing the fragility of his health. Then UNESCO asked him to speak in Tehran at an international symposium on "the preservation of traditional forms of the learned and popular music of the Orient and the Occident."[2] Henry accepted both invitations, setting aside a few days in Hong Kong to relax midway. Since her policy of keeping him active seemed effective—the first warning about his imminent demise was six years in the past—it was pointless to intervene.

Theodore Wertime, C. Robert Payne's successor as Public Affairs Officer in Tehran, was especially happy that Henry was coming because someone of his stature and experience was badly needed. According to Wertime, Iranian musical life had made such progress since 1956 that it resembled Japan's, with less traditional music and more nineteenth-century Western music. But although the embassy might be able to contribute toward the presentation of Henry's music, he doubted that the orchestra or any other musical group could play it.[3]

Even the visit of a composer presented political opportunities. Sidney prepared presentation copies of Henry's music and informed Wertime that the queen, who was said to be interested in Western music, might welcome a score of Henry's Symphony No. 11. Washington then suggested having some copies arrive late to give Wertime an excuse to distribute them personally to interested parties and cement his relationships. Henry was advised to bring pieces that ensured his not being taken for an American composer of "Iranian music," that is, by Pahlbod.

The trip was just the type to make Sidney anxious. Henry arrived in Tehran on April 1 after eleven hours' flying and five hours of stopovers. "Thank you for your lovely little love notes sprinkled about! I love you too!" he wrote Sidney, who was relieved that he got a lot of rest on the plane but would have preferred that he had remembered to bring his speech. The next day he left on a private trip to Tabriz, which had been thwarted by winter weather in 1957.[4] After a smooth ride through magnificent Iranian mountain and desert scenery, he was met by the province's governor-general and the American consul, William Eagleton, a thirty-five-year-old diplomat already in the twelfth year of what became a distinguished career. Henry gave a private lecture at the US Consulate, a public lecture at the Tabriz Conservatory, and heard Persian musicians in Eagleton's home.

The governor, whom Henry described as a "grand old man," had ordered Radio Tabriz to give him tapes of local music, hoping that Folkways would issue them. Since the Azeris' Turkic culture is very different from Persian culture, Henry thought he had something unusual until he discovered that the performers were radio musicians playing in a popularized style that would not have interested Folkways. The handful of local musicians that could be found had been spoiled by Persian music to such an extent that the Turkic roots were nearly gone. In any case, Sidney wondered all along if he would succeed in exporting any tapes. "Between the difficulties of getting tapes out of Iran (with Iranian music) and then into the US (unless performed within the US by Musicians' Union members!) and the normal hazards of package transmission, such undertakings rarely come to any good end."

Numerous social events included lunch with Senator Hedjazi, his acquaintance from 1956, whose influence was all the greater now that his brother headed the Iranian army. He also visited another acquaintance from the 1956–57 trip, William Archer, the scholar who organized the Society for Asian Music and later edited the Tehran conference's proceedings. Henry felt well in "colorful and quaint" Tabriz, except for the absence of toilet paper, towels, or hot water, which could be provided for foreigners only upon request.[5]

He was back in Tehran on April 6. The weather was perfect—"Pansys [sic] all in bloom—white blossoms on fruit trees and magnolias are starting—weather mild—no coat needed," but he learned that Riegger had just died. Then he went to a grand reception at the magnificent Golestan Palace.[6] The next day, the queen opened the conference with ample speeches and a concert featuring Shinichi Yuize, the Japanese koto virtuoso. It was a good opportunity to see old acquaintances, including a Columbia University composition student representing Ghana (J. H. Kwabena Nketia), Adnun Saygun of Turkey, other people he and Sidney knew from 1956, and Pahlbod, who struck Henry as unusually friendly. Marius Schneider, who had succeeded Hornbostel in Berlin, told Henry that the communists had found and taken the Hornbostel cylinders, although they had deteriorated beyond recognition. Shardar, "old and trembly" but friendly and still head of music at the radio, told him proudly that the four stations of 1956 had grown to more than eighty, and television was available.

Contrary to Wertime's fear, Henry's *Hymn and Fuguing Tune No. 2* was performed by the Tehran Symphony, conducted by Virgil Thomson, replacing Heshmat Sanjari, the regular conductor. Sanjari, who said he planned to conduct *Persian Set* after Henry's departure, was a product of the Shah's modernization—a violinist and conducting student of Hans Swarowsky at the Vienna Music Academy. His father had been a famous tar player.[7]

Although Henry customarily spoke off the cuff, he had to read his conference address because the talks were to be published, and possibly because strokes had impeded his improvising. As a result, the Tehran speech is one of very few that is completely preserved. It is, in many respects, his finest articulation of how composers in general and Henry in particular dealt with the multiplicity of the world's musics, a subject that hardly existed before he talked about it.

Almost every speaker explored aspects of traditional music and/or its interaction with Western music. Henry, the only Western contributor, elucidated the compositional process in a culture that emphasizes the final product instead of the process of music-making. He began his speech, entitled rather generally "The Composer's World,"[8] by differentiating himself from his conference colleagues. ". . . I am a composer, not a musicologist. So I am more concerned with the future of musical traditions than I am with their past." To learn where traditions can lead rather than where and how they originated, he had devoted vast amounts of time to studying non-European musical systems, having assumed from his youth that a composer in the twentieth century should know the many musical "inheritances," not just the French and German. He attributed his outlook to having grown up in the United States: because the country is situated midway between Europe and Asia, it seemed natural to stretch his mind "beyond the limitations of European traditions, and welcome the infinite variety and vitality of the human imagination as it has expressed itself in the music of the world." Having spent decades unable to understand what makes American music "American," he finally understood it as the product of a nation to whom shaking off traditions is the natural course of life.

Each continent, however, has a host of its own musical traditions, forming a "great sea of musical imagination [that] seemed to me my natural inheritance. . . ." Having accepted that it is a fact of life, he had to discover "how may one learn to live in the whole world of music—to live and to create." Because he had the good fortune to hear so many kinds of music as a child, he gradually saw that the basic elements of music are always the same but have developed differently.

At the end of his teen years, he focused upon creating systematic approaches to and explanations of modernism, even referring briefly to non-Western systems. Since he had already decided that nineteenth-century harmonies were tiresome and old-fashioned, he was open to new possibilities that grew out of natural and acoustic phenomena, but soon was writing music that was impossible to perform. As a consequence, he abandoned the complex rhythmic and metric possibilities proposed in *New Musical Resources*, leaving them to others to develop when the time was right. Gradually undertaking the systematic study of other cultures, he became aware that one cannot learn the thousands of traditions individually. Ideas could be grouped, however, so that composers could study and understand any type of music that was interesting. "The limitations of his music will then be due only to his own capacity for absorption and use of new ideas; they will not be imposed by the past."

When he then studied rhythm and melody in other musical traditions, he realized that Westerners had not subjected rhythm to the same level of orderly study as harmony. He needed Oriental teachers. "I was not planning to write Oriental music, of course, partly because I do not think a Westerner can completely abandon the multi-level music which is so impressive a part of music in the 20th century." To transcend the rudimentary Western ideas of melody and rhythm, he turned to Indian, Indonesian, and Japanese teachers and to the Hornbostel cylinders.

Eventually he understood that all musical experience, East and West, came from long undisturbed traditions. Composers made music "out of an unconscious experience of organized sound which had developed so gradually into an integrated style" that conscious activity and a total experience of music combined almost effortlessly. But sometimes a shock, a collision of cultures, rendered the "unconscious practice conscious and available for study." A composer then could extend the results of the collision forward to create "fresh integrations." To do this, he had to reject aspects of a new culture that were unsuitable "either because of the artist's limitations or because the elements are so distant from the composer's own culture as to be beyond integration." He saw that Hornbostel's circle was wrong to avoid studying hybrids, because they thereby missed the transformative collisions.

Returning to the multiplicity of musics worth studying, he recalled once having feared that commercial pressures eventually would lead to a single worldwide style—"a dreadful prospect." Then he realized that the effort to establish one dominant style of art music (emanating from Schoenberg and Vienna) did not result in music that sounded the same no matter who composed it. "Neither commercial popular music nor dodecaphonic 'internationalism' have been able in 50 years to reduce the world's music to monotony . . . The process of musical change and hybridization continues, and it is pointless to lament the changes in tradition."

He suggested that the great twentieth-century thinkers such as Einstein, the Curies, and Freud "struggled to formulate complex concepts that they had first perceived and begun to use intuitively." Composers always must accomplish the same thing: "bring unconscious traditions under conscious control." Obliquely criticizing Pahlbod, he warned that old traditions can no longer be transmitted orally within a protected culture. Today's currents had to be considered. He doubted that the elaborate structures of Indian music could have been achieved if the Indians had been isolated from other cultures. The pressure to assimilate or reject refines the underlying tradition and brings it to the level of consciousness, whether people migrate or their music migrates. Remembering, perhaps, his confrontational forums of the 1930s, he concluded his introductory remarks by saying, "Faced with great contrast and variety, the human spirit is forced to *think*, not only to *feel*. . . . Thought is a technique for examining, accepting or rejecting, and then recombining ideas."

He then explained the art of composing, so familiar to Westerners but foreign to an audience for whom composing, in the Western sense, does not exist. Although his specific comments need no mention here, they explain why he resisted rewriting compositions. The complex combination of logic and instinct, he said, requires that there be free interplay between the conscious and the unconscious. Composers must study their material so thoroughly that the unconscious can come into play. Creativity is "'an act of faith.' . . . One must trust one's self, and be unaffectedly willing to be whatever one is at the moment of creativity." Once that moment passed, the composer risked letting the rational side take control and losing the unaffectedness of trust. Everyone needed to understand the difference between popular composers, who write for the moment, and composers of fine-art music, who write "out of some inner compulsion that is a law unto itself, so they are often quite incapable of conforming to the immediate expectations of other people, most of whom tend to prefer what they have heard before." Such composers cannot be sure that any one will care, but must cultivate their gardens and "render thanks for the many beautiful living things in music that have been preserved . . . by the efforts of men and women like [the participants in the conference.]" If the composer works at the depths of the unconscious, with the many tools assimilated from the conscious, the music, "however national, [will] be more than national, so that [the composer] is able to speak freely, as man and artist, in personal accents but of universal things."

Just before leaving Tehran on April 11, he wrote Sidney that everything had gone well, with "lots of talk with friends, many lectures, mostly boring and repetitious. 12-tone row not mentioned—electronic music also not. There was a talk on acoustics and taped music as applied to faithful quality on microphones." Newspapers printed no more than the usual errors, such as saying that he had collected Persian folk music to use in *Persian Set*. He was able to correct that with Pahlbod.[9] He felt that the conference was a milestone for Iran and a modest victory for those opposed to Pahlbod's attempt to isolate Iran's music until a modern Iranian school of composition could compete successfully with Western music without copying it.[10]

The next day he was in Hong Kong for his rest stop. "Such lovely little notes from you! I love you, and wouldn't dream of being married to anyone else, either!" His simple missions were to get fitted for new clothes and have Sidney's sandals copied. He enjoyed the sight of the bay full of junks and ships, skyscrapers sprouting along the waterfront, tall new apartment buildings under construction on the hills.[11] In fact, he was witnessing the beginning of the end for traditional Asia. He was shepherded around by a friend from his visit in 1957, Maple Quon, a Canadian-born writer who edited Hong Kong's main music journal and was the leading local music critic. Through her, he got to hear unfamiliar music from north China and ate constantly, thanks to Quon and her very wealthy friends. A Peabody graduate who was head of serious music at Radio Hong Kong had him record a fifteen-minute interview, a half-hour program on Oriental influence in America, and short comments about some of his music.[12] Among the products of four press interviews was a large feature in the Hong Kong *Standard*'s Sunday magazine, in which Henry predicted the inevitable integration of Eastern and Western music.[13]

He now proceeded to the East-West Music Encounter, whose purposes were "to deepen the mutual understanding between the musical cultures of the Eastern and Western World and to develop a greater degree of cooperation between Asia and the West in the field of music," simultaneously celebrating the dedication of the Tokyo Metropolitan Festival Hall, which honored the five-hundredth anniversary of the founding of the city. The opening ceremony represented the stated aims by pairing a sample of *gagaku* with Gabrieli's *Sonata Pian e Forte*. The week's talks and seminars were followed by a spectacular array of performances. From the Eastern tradition there was *noh*, Indian and Thai music and dance, a program entitled "Classical Music and Dance of Japan," a recital by Indian soloists, an event oddly entitled "Contemporary Japanese Traditional Music," *kabuki*, and a performance of "Oriental Music and Dance." Western music was represented by the Royal Ballet, Japan Philharmonic, two concerts by the New York Philharmonic, the Toho Conservatory Orchestra, Ensemble Européen de Musique de Chambre (conducted by Bruno Maderna), two concerts by the Juilliard String Quartet (including music by Elliott Carter and Leon Kirchner), two concerts by New York's Pro Musica Antiqua, Gruppo Polifonico di RAI, the Modern Jazz Quartet, and recitals by Isaac Stern, Hermann Prey, and Zinka Milanov. In addition to Henry, prominent individual participants were Luciano Berio, Boris Blacher, Elliott Carter, Gottfried von Einem, Alfred Frankenstein, William Glock (the BBC's Controller of Music), Bruno Maderna, Colin McPhee, Isaac Stern, Josef Tal, Virgil Thomson, Iannis Xenakis, Shinichi Yuize, and various historians. Many of them were old friends of Henry.[14]

The great expenses of this all-star event were met by governmental support from many countries, UNESCO, and private sponsors including the Asia, Catherwood, Farfield, Ford, and Rockefeller foundations. Curiosity about the Congress for Cultural Freedom's role led me straight to the Web site of the Central Intelligence Agency, which revealed what almost no one knew in 1961—the Congress for Cultural Freedom, the Catherwood Foundation, the Farfield Foundation, and the Asia Foundation were CIA fronts or conduits. The truth finally came out in 1967. Even now, fifty years later, Japanese musicians and arts administrators indicated that they preferred not to think about the East-West Music Encounter.[15]

The CIA's involvement[16] was triggered by a 1949 conference of pro-Stalinist intellectuals at New York's Waldorf-Astoria Hotel, who gathered to press for greater friendship with the Soviet leader. Among them was Shostakovich, who was brought over to praise freedom in the USSR. Horrified anti-Stalinists, many of them Russian émigrés, met in Berlin the following year to discuss how to combat the strong leftward drift of European intellectuals. Having decided that the best course was to show how the arts and letters flourish in free societies, they created the Congress for Cultural Freedom, based in Paris and directed by composer Nicolas Nabokov.

Their strategy captured the attention of the newly born Central Intelligence Agency, which had already become convinced that foreign intellectuals could be lured away from communism if they learned that America's best visual artists, writers, and performing artists were living manifestations of cultural freedom. The CIA quickly created secret links with Nabokov's group. Within the CIA, the program was controlled by highly cultivated graduates of the same Eastern prep schools and universities, a white, Anglo-Saxon, Protestant elite that formed the nucleus of the agency and later rose to the top ranks of politics. At first, the CIA funded these activities with inventive bookkeeping, such as filtering Marshall Plan money through dummy foundations, some of which also channeled contributions of rich individuals who supported the cultural effort. The old-boy network also enabled the CIA to work intimately with giant foundations such as Ford without being discovered. Secrecy was not a game: exposure of the CIA would have poisoned the plan, which, artistically at least, was beyond reproach.

The CIA's sponsorship of the East-West Music Encounter is certain. Its success at co-opting unsuspecting donors and legitimate foundations then suggested taking a second look at the Cowells' 1956–57 world tour, which obviously fulfilled the goals of the cultural Cold War. The situation at the Rockefeller Foundation is unclear, however. Henry's grant officers all had backgrounds in intelligence. John Marshall had been with the Foreign Broadcast Information Service, a unit of the CIA; Charles Fahs had served with the CIA from its inception in 1947 until he went to the Rockefeller Foundation two years later; and

Chadbourne Gilpatric's wartime background in the Office of Strategic Services (OSS) gave him close connections at the CIA, which employed many OSS veterans. Moreover, John D. Rockefeller II's son Nelson was immersed in the intelligence world. The senior Rockefeller, however, who was always wary of being tainted by connections with propagandists, mistrusted the CIA, which had tried to infiltrate the foundation. He knew that any suspicion of government involvement would sabotage his foundation's work, especially in Asia, where anti-Americanism was extremely strong. Rockefeller thus was unlikely to have cooperated knowingly with the CIA. In fact, at about the time of the Cowells' trip, he was considering founding the Asia Society to promote understanding with Asia because the Asia Foundation was correctly suspected of being a propaganda unit and indeed was funded by the CIA.[17] Nevertheless, it is equally improbable that he was unaware of his departmental chiefs' connections with the agency. As Frances Stonor Saunders emphasized in *The Cultural Cold War*, getting to the truth often boils down to the question of who knew what, and almost all the people involved claimed to have known nothing. The fact that so many board members and foundation executives came from the same class as the CIA's top administration has prevented the issue from going away.

Intelligence missteps, such as the 1962 Bay of Pigs mess, badly tainted the CIA's reputation, but in the cultural program the agency and its friends effectively were the United States' first—if secret—Ministry of Arts. Resisting imitating the USSR, the program's leaders did not dictate cultural norms; less interference made free expression a stronger product. Its finer accomplishments included covertly sponsoring the Boston Symphony's European tour of 1952, which established American musicianship as world-class. Jackson Pollock and other Abstract Expressionists got their start in Europe through the CIA's programs. The respected British intellectual journal *Encounter* was founded and funded by the CIA. The State Department ought to have been able to accomplish the same goal, but the old battle between projecting "truth" and dishing out propaganda also raged there. Its admirable cultural efforts were attacked by congressmen who insisted that modernism disguised a Soviet plot and that the State Department was riddled with communists. As Frances Stonor Saunders vividly shows, congressional anti-communism drove the cultural Cold War underground, where only the CIA could wage it.[18]

While it is impossible to know whether the Cowells' world tour was indirectly sponsored by the CIA, Henry was a perfect example of what the CIA sought: a former communist sympathizer who symbolized American artistic freedom. Senator McCarthy might not have agreed about Henry's fitness, but Henry had remained below McCarthy's radar. A security check by the FBI, undertaken to clear Henry for his State Department activities in 1956–57, explains why. Despite Henry's background with political radicalism that had included

writing for *The Daily Worker,* the FBI found no identifiable derogatory information about Henry or Sidney with regard to security.[19]

Henry's Tokyo speech is the only complete version of his lecture entitled "Oriental Influence on Western Music," but there is no way to know how much it re-
sembles his many off-the-cuff talks on this subject.[20] His speech expanded his
idea that an influence from one culture can only be adopted and assimilated effectively enough to survive in the recipient culture if the recipient culture is
ready for it. Readiness requires a clear relationship between the two cultures in
the area where the borrowing is to take place. By examining Western music history in this light, one can explain previous types of borrowings, the absence of
more frequent borrowings, and why only some borrowings have lasting consequences. In other words, the techniques that he applied to studying non-Western music and hybrids could also be applied to Western music itself.

He believed that the history of Western music was the opposite of an East-West
Music Encounter. It was, in effect, a divorce rather than a marriage. "Western
music escaped from the East, and as it hurried westward it was subjected to a
series of selections and simplifications, both in Greece and, several hundred years
later, in Rome. Thereafter it began a long development back toward complexity
again, but this time in a new direction of its own. It is in the development of techniques for handling many simultaneous musical levels . . . that the West has made
its great contribution to the music of the world." The West's trajectory, however,
sacrificed melodic and rhythmic subtlety, which continued to develop elsewhere.
It could not match the sophistication of melody and rhythm in the art-music traditions of India, China, Japan, Persia, and the Arab world, despite the fact that, as
Greek theory demonstrates, elaborate melodic and rhythmic systems were part of
the Western inheritance. He attributed the split to Pope Gregory's determination
that Christian Europe's music be based on the diatonic modes. Once that decision
had been made, the church's monopoly on literacy guaranteed that the subsequent history of Western music would grow from those seventh-century decisions.
Polyphony evolved within the modal system, but later was distilled to major and
minor scales, which allow transposition, modulations, the tempered system, en-
largement of instrumental groups, and so on. The grand tradition of symphonic
music did not require rhythmic or melodic evolution on a large scale because
polyphonic complexity was an adequate framework for development. Western
culture thus was not ready for the outside influence of Asian melody and rhythm.

Its unreadiness for outside influence is demonstrated by the first obvious example of a collision with an extra-European culture—"Turkish" music, an eighteenth-century fad that could hardly be described as Turkish and for good
reason. "Our composers in those days were intoxicated by the possibilities
within their own music, and they had no attention to spare for anything else as

long as Western styles had within themselves so much capacity for growth." The West considered all other musics primitive and monotonous; Easterners not trained to listen contrapuntally tended to judge Western music in similar terms. Western music only became ready for Oriental influence when Western symphonic styles began losing vitality in the late nineteenth century.

The way toward a more open attitude was prepared by the fragmentation of styles in the late nineteenth and early twentieth centuries. "Experiment, as always, owed its first vitality to the tendency to react against various things that had been done too long." Reactions against the old system produced the serial idea, new systems for organizing dissonance, a search for new sounds, new rhythmic forms, and more. Then composers gradually looked at other cultures. Debussy, the first composer receptive to the Orient, used the whole-tone scale derived from *slendro* tuning, and transmuted gong-groups into sound blocks. Bartók, however, was the first composer to think systematically about musical materials from outside his traditional training and to create a systematic music theory based thereupon. Even though he had never studied classical Turkish music theory, he found his own systematic organization, "creating forms of his own to fit into obvious gaps, much in the way an old language is reconstituted." The beauty of Bartók's music was that its organization was Western, although its modes and rhythms often were not. He could apply Western principles of voice-leading to modes new to the West, and pour Near Eastern modes into the mold of sonata form and other Western forms, instead of clinging to major and minor keys.

The next stage was for Western composers to study Eastern techniques and Eastern materials, learning to distinguish among the many Eastern styles. "I must apologize for bringing myself into the narrative at this point, but I have not been able to learn of any Western composer who studied several Eastern musical traditions from within, with Eastern teachers, before I did." He had to do it on his own, because very little music of the East was heard in the United States, and no organized study of it had been made. When in 1932 he began his New School courses on the "Musical Systems of the World" and "Primitive and Folk Music of the World," the range of receptivity was obvious. Some people sat through them three or four times; others thought he was wasting his effort.

He emphasized that his studies of extra-European music were all directed from the composer's viewpoint. "I approached all this music as a composer, and everything I learned I tried to use. So one may find in my music Eastern materials developed in Western ways, or in Eastern ways, but always with Western instruments and involving polyphony and harmony in various degrees, because I am of course primarily a Western composer." At the time of this speech, he already could name other composers—McPhee, Hovhaness, Chou Wen-Chung, Cage, and Harrison—who had taken that leap. He concluded that it is virtually impossible to carry forward any single aspect of music without arriving at something from another culture. The situation had changed so much that in New York in recent months "orientalism" had replaced Schoenbergism or Stravinskyism in getting the blame for anything strange in a new work.

Henry's Tokyo speech was also emblematic of his life. Although he lived in the whole world of music, his compositional interest in extra-European music was limited to the music of Asia, early Americans with their distinctive harmonic system, and Irish folk song. His letters from Berlin said nothing of studying Latin American music; his interest in African music—as a composer—waned. In retrospect, his natural point of convergence with the variegated music of Asia had been established by his peculiar childhood in San Francisco and by the extreme sophistication of Asian music.

Henry felt that the content of the Tokyo talks was better than that at the Tehran symposium, despite the oddity that the Asian speakers promoted Western music and the Westerners promoted Eastern music. At the end of the conference, a small group including an Indian and a BBC representative gathered in Lou Harrison's room to listen to each other's tapes. "So many have become good friends—we are thrown a great deal together." The next day all the participants were given an expense-paid trip to Nikko National Park,[21] after which they were on their own. It was time to shop, especially for a camera suitable to Sidney's blossoming photographic artistry. Shopping also confronted him with another Cold War problem. He had bought a Chinese instrument in Hong Kong, but could only import it if he could prove that it was not made on the mainland. Maple Quon, the Hong Kong journalist, suggested saying that it was given to him by oriental musicians in Japan, because there was no way to certify its origin or age. Since the bamboo was from Laos, he would not be lying when he said it did not originate in China. He had to count on the ignorance of the inspectors.[22]

During the festival, Henry was very disappointed about the fate of his own music. A program to be presented by the embassy's American Center, with music by Henry, Ives, Carter, and Andrew Imbrie, was canceled because it conflicted with a farewell reception.[23] Even worse was the New York Philharmonic's cancellation of *Ongaku*, because the fault was Henry's. When he showed Leonard Bernstein a piece by Toshiro Mayuzumi,[24] Bernstein dropped *Ongaku* in its favor. When the word got around Tokyo, Henry became "the hero who has given up his performance so that the N.Y. Phil. may play a Japanese work,"[25] a strange remake of the incident in a Moscow restaurant thirty-two years before, when he caused a sensation by giving his (inedible) soup to a poor young fellow. Despite having lost a performance, he was happy about Mayuzumi's piece, which he called "a real stunner, brilliant for orchestra," conducted very well by Bernstein's twenty-six-year-old assistant, Seiji Ozawa. After the second Philharmonic concert, on May 2, which included two pieces by Ives, the American Embassy gave a reception to end the festival. The apologetic Bernstein promised to play *Ongaku* later (which he did not). Mayuzumi was "very abject" because his work had displaced Henry's.[26]

A few days after the end of the Encounter, Henry was still having a stimulating time. There was a tape-playing session including music by Lou Harrison, Thomson, Vanraj Bhatia (India), and Ikuma Dan (Japan); lunch with Edwin Reischauer, the new American ambassador; a performance by a shakuhachi player; a very good, dissonant piece by Yuize for nine kotos, with Yuize as soloist; and an excellent concert of modern music for Japanese instruments. He went to the theater of the Imperial Palace to hear *gagaku* "and the world's largest drums—very impressive"; then *kabuki*. He started a koto duo for Yuize and his three-year-old son, a rondo in which the kotos were retuned for each presentation of the main theme.[27]

It seemed to Henry that the director of the American Center had no interest in arranging events for the composers,[28] but it was director E. J. Findlay who made the post-festival weeks productive and enjoyable. At a primary school Henry addressed more than 1,100 children who had never seen an American, and heard "very perfect" performances of Handel and Frescobaldi by fifth graders. As part of his talk he gave the children a freshly composed marching tune, which they later sang on the radio.[29] Afterward he spoke for two hours to twenty-seven music education supervisors from Tokyo, substituting for Sidney, the original invitee. Next, he spent two days at Ueno-Gakuen College, lecturing about world music and his own music, a day each at Nakashima koto school and Kaikan University in Osaka, and, finally, two days at the Music Circle in Kobe-Fujita. Dinners and parties abounded without any effect upon Henry's health. At the end, Findlay thanked him for his "many kindnesses and for all that you did in Japan to win the cultural cold war."[30] Indeed.

57

Years of Honor, 1961–1963

In mid-May, after six weeks abroad, Henry and Sidney reunited in Seattle, visited Olive and Bay Area friends, and adjourned to their property on Jaime de Angulo's former ranch. Some fourteen years had passed since their last substantial stay in California and twenty-one years since San Quentin. Olive, still dreaming of bringing him back permanently, proposed pushing for a faculty position at her school, San Francisco State College. Henry's past continued to haunt him, however. "[It] would be embarrassing both to me and to college officials who might like to have me but would not want to stir things up; and I am not sure but what something might get stirred up if I came as a faculty member. One letter to some yellow newspaper would set the thing off, and undo the remarkable silence in which I have been able to accomplish so much. I could, I am sure, retire to S.F. if I wished, but fear a college position there."[1]

Among the achievements of that remarkable silence—which, to be sure, did not exclude whispering about him—was a marriage whose finest qualities must have been enhanced by their ample periods of separation when he traveled to lecture or went to New York to teach and she remained at Shady or went to California to see her family. Sidney, however, could not call her life her own despite her retirement from ghostwriting. Abundant other Cowell business and a certain amount of caregiving restricted her efforts to pursue photography. Henry agreed that calm was more likely if Olive were kept in the dark about his health, since she could be very annoying. He does not appear to have imagined Sidney's real motivation, her fear that if Olive knew the truth, she might inform Henry about his fragility and wreck his fighting spirit. Sidney's secretiveness unfortunately increased the tension between the two women.

From Henry's point of view, the biggest disappointment of their marriage was their failure to produce the children he longed for. His closest American relative, Clarence, had died in 1953 after years of unemployment and sadness; Clarence's children loved their Uncle Henry dearly but were also adrift. Henry had better luck with his family in Britain and Ireland. In 1961, he renewed his relationship with his Scottish cousin Maureen Kershaw, the first European Cowell to cross the Atlantic since Harry and Dick emigrated three quarters of a century earlier.[2] The Cowell name was also passed along as the middle name of his godchildren, the sons of Frank Wigglesworth, John Becker, and Henry's former student Roland Wiggins (at one time John Coltrane's teacher).[3] Henry and Sidney's immediate family was their cats, who live on in Sidney's beautiful photos of Henry composing with Pepper or Strawberry snuggled in his arm.

Although his old friends were almost family, they were going rapidly. Becker, Riegger, Grainger, and Sigurd Varian all died in 1961, Wesley Kuhnle the following year,[4] McPhee in 1964. Fortunately, Henry's friendly chattiness, long experience, and position as an elder statesman, and Sidney's warmth and no-nonsense intelligence virtually ensured that they would continue to make new friends, among whom Yehudi Wyner and his wife, Susan Davenny, were particularly close as neighbors in the Shady area.

With miscellaneous commitments continuing to shrink, Henry's compositional productivity continued to increase. In the less than two years between his return from Japan and his next trip to Europe (1963), he completed his sixteenth symphony, the *Icelandic*; three shorter orchestral pieces; concertos for flute and harp, for koto, and for harmonica; five chamber works, and several songs. While on the surface the melody-driven style typical of his later music sometimes seems tame, the best pieces are still packed with musical adventures. In the *Icelandic* Symphony, for example, Henry used the basic property of Icelandic "double-singing," with its parallel fifths and cross-relations, as a tool to steer his material toward a kind of atonality and then back again. The "atonal" section, suggesting a vocal ensemble that can't quite find the right notes, disproves the truism that atonality and humor are incompatible. Henry's Koto Concerto, the first by a Western composer, predates by some five years Takemitsu's *November Steps*. The striking 1962 Harmonica Concerto, for John Sebastian, is the opposite of a display piece. It is derived from the *gagaku* movement of *Ongaku*, with the harmonica evoking but not mimicking the shō.

Assessment of Henry's status as a composer is much more difficult in this period than in earlier years. The quantity of reviews declined as radio and television began pushing newspapers out of business. Furthermore, now that his earlier radical music seemed less outrageous, more musical and natural, performances became less newsworthy. Recent pieces sometimes were called fresh and exciting, sometimes not extremely interesting, but almost always suitable for the general audience. Unfortunately, in the climate of the 1960s, a bigger insult is difficult to imagine. Alfred Frankenstein, who previously had defended Henry against assaults on ultramodernism, now rebutted attacks on his postmodernism. Of the Symphony No. 15 he wrote, "The work as a whole is one of the strongest, most eloquent, and powerful in Cowell's huge list, and is a crushing reply to those who would write him off as one of the conservative elder statesmen of modern American music."[5]

The frequency of commissions and performances of major works implies financial success as a composer. At a 1962 conference about establishing a government arts agency, Henry broke a taboo by revealing the truth, complete with numbers, and horrifying the successful author James Michener, who said that a writer with a tenth of Henry's skill could make $150,000 [2010: $1,080,000] a year. After reporting Henry's remark that Ruggles gave up composing to paint because he was so poor, the *New York Post* said, "Cowell is considered one of this country's most financially successful composers. A gentle, somewhat timid little man whose conversation is as restless as his hands, Cowell may lament present conditions, but he hastens to add that there is a vast improvement over what once existed."[6]

Henry continued to teach at Columbia, but The New School's old, familial atmosphere was vanishing. Alvin Johnson, president emeritus since 1945, was in poor health.[7] After Dean and Associate Director Clara Mayer was forced into retirement in 1959, the new administration adopted policies that seemed to the faculty to be undermining The New School as a center of adult education.[8] Even the concerts retreated from the innovativeness that Henry had established. He finally resigned at the end of the 1962–63 school year, turning over his responsibilities to Frank Wigglesworth, whom he had brought in to cover his classes during the trip to Tehran and Tokyo.

While Henry was still in Tokyo, Allen McHose, dean of the summer session at Eastman, proposed that he replace Bernard Rogers. Although Sidney was torn between keeping him active and preventing him from pushing himself too hard, Henry accepted the offer to give three composition classes, each meeting five times weekly, and participate in the Theory and Composition Workshop. In the workshop, he lectured on secundal harmony, the raga system of tonality, and tonal versus atonal music, whereas his colleagues talked about various new books on theory, research studies for teachers of diction or sightsinging, directing of orchestration toward new styles, and similar matters.[9] In general, the summer was peaceful; Henry said he actually did very little, at least in the later weeks when his students were busy copying their pieces. He began work on a concerto for flute, harp, and orchestra and recorded comments about his compositions for a broadcast on a "Tribute to Cowell Day."[10] McHose reinvited Henry for 1962 with an even less arduous schedule implying that Sidney had cautioned against overworking him. A speech that summer expanded into an illuminating article on teaching, "Freedom for Young Composers," which emphasized the importance of Eastman's excellent readings of students' compositions.[11]

The summer session was a welcome respite from old, lingering projects. Although *New Music* ceased independent publication in 1953, the Board still existed in the early 1960s, largely to accept or reject pieces for publication by Merion Music. The list of Henry's services to other boards and committees seems endless, but the Board of the Society for Asian Music—of which he was chairman—continued to be his favorite preoccupation, placing him in contact with major performers of non-Western music and important actors in the East-West movement, such as Yehudi Menuhin and Ravi Shankar.[12]

Fielding inquiries about Ives matters was the inevitable price of the Cowells' biography, which was already some eight years old. The most pressing Ives business concerned John Kirkpatrick's project to assemble Ives's and Becker's correspondence with Henry on behalf of the Cowell and Ives archives, and Kirkpatrick's search for missing pages from Ives's autobiographical memos, which turned up among the material that the Iveses had given the Cowells for their biography. In inspecting the papers, Henry and Sidney saw that Harmony and Edie had not always written what Ives asked them to, a matter with special relevance to the San Quentin years.[13]

In short, Sidney did not have to worry about Henry sitting on the sidelines, and he had plenty of time to compose. Furthermore, his status in the musical world was recognized by a series of major honors. The election of John Kennedy as president ushered in a new era of respect for culture, as the Cowells learned when an invitation arrived for the Kennedy/Johnson inauguration and gala in January 1961, which they declined because of the expense.[14] In November, however, they accepted an invitation to a white-tie dinner and concert at the White House, honoring the governor of Puerto Rico.

The Cowells were amused when their arrival in a taxi caused a stir; everyone else came in a limousine, including the Elliott Carters, Roy Harrisses, and Alan Hovhanesses. At the end of the evening, an attendant was amazed when Henry and Sidney asked that a taxi be called. It was clear that a new era had dawned. "During the FDR administration," Sidney recalled, "there might well have been limousine-with-chauffeur arrivals but there would also have been arrivals in taxis and on foot for the same occasions. Actually, except for my very high-heeled shoes, we would have walked both ways."[15]

> We felt highly complimented [wrote Sidney] to be asked to dinner there for the first time; hitherto we have come in later. Everything was beautifully done, with great formal elaboration but in beautiful taste—fanfares, flags, Marine Band, Army Orchestra, and so on—and the most sophisticated and delicate French food imaginable. The Kennedys were friendliness and dignity combined in the nicest way. Henry sat by a long-time fan of his whose name he never learned. . . . The occasion was in honor of the Gov. of Puerto Rico and Mrs. Muñoz Marin, and as Casals had offered to play (for the first time since the Spanish War, in the US) the whole affair was turned into a compliment toward US achievement in music, primarily, with a dozen or so composers, 4 or 5

orchestra conductors, chairmen of symphony boards of major orchestras, a few chief contributors, and a number of editors and commentators. Result: incredible amounts of front page publicity for American creative achievements in music, very nice thing, with expression of national obligation to musicians, indebtedness, I mean, from Kennedy, compliments to P.R., all easily and gracefully and simply expressed. It's incredibly valuable to have a cultivated man able to use words in this meaningful way, without affectation, in his position.

Casals was so fine, and so little showed his age, hardly at all in the music, a wonderful privilege to hear him after so many years . . . Henry looked extremely handsome, as always, in his wh. tie and tails; formal dress is so becoming to him, unexpectedly enough.[16]

It was thrilling to see fifteen composers, Ormandy, Stokowski, and Bernstein among the guests. A performance by Pablo Casals, Alexander Schneider, and Mieczyslaw Horszowski—playing Mendelssohn, Schumann, and Couperin arrangements—reinforced the president's words in support of music, but the absence of a note of American music, or a single American-born performer, made the presence of American composers among the guests even more surprising.[17] Henry caused a stir a few weeks later when *Life* quoted him saying that more is due to composers. He responded—hoping for a published correction—that he was simply pointing out America's lack of the honors, orders, and titles given in other countries. Rather than meaning to suggest that more is due to composers, "I felt that the occasion was a gala coming-of-age party for creative music in America that was no less serious and important for being so festive and gracious."[18] *Life*, however, decided to drop the matter.

C. Robert Payne was disappointed in another way, having imagined Henry at the center of the evening. He and USIA had wanted to arrange something special for him, but it fell through. "In any event I know that you know how we in the Agency appreciate all you have done for our country. I had just hoped that we could have added our insignificant word to the tribute being paid to you by the White House. Sorry I missed."[19]

In fact, another honor was on the way. Hugo Weisgall had proposed a major salute to Henry's sixty-fifth birthday (March 11, 1962) and the fiftieth anniversary of his first professional appearance. Although Sidney first thought Weisgall might have reacted to rumors of a sixty-fifth birthday celebration for Virgil Thomson on November 25, 1961, it is equally likely that the convenient confluence of the anniversary and Henry's birthday prompted the thought that he might not make it to seventy. The organizing group chaired by Weisgall included Juilliard's president William Schuman; the Cowells' banker-composer friend Avery Claflin; William Mitchell, chairman of the music department at Columbia; Douglas

Moore, the previous Columbia chairman; Otto Luening, Virgil Thomson, Nicolas Slonimsky, and Varèse. Schuman and Juilliard's Dean Mark Schubart proposed a one-man concert, only the fourth that the school had ever given. (The other honorees were Bloch, Hindemith, and Copland.) Juilliard accepted cosponsorship with Columbia University's Alice M. Ditson Fund, the American Composers Alliance, and the Contemporary Music Society, with Juilliard paying about half the cost. Its contribution was all the more touching because Henry had had no connection with the school other than his expulsion from it. BMI produced a handsome jubilee booklet. There was talk of celebrating the occasion with a new CRI recording of Henry's string quartets and *Homage to Iran*. On the same day, the Louisville Orchestra was scheduled to release its recording of Symphony No. 15 and publisher Frederick Ungar was reissuing *American Composers on American Music*.[20] *Musical America* and *Musical Courier* planned stories focusing on Henry's influence on European and Asian composers.[21]

Henry agreed to play four early piano pieces including "The Tides of Manaunaun," which, it was stated, he performed on his first public concert, March 12, 1912. The problem was that the Cowells could find almost no evidence of what happened at the Pacific Musical Society on February 28, 1912, when he played one piece, and no evidence of "The Tides" having been played anywhere in March 1912. They concluded that the 1912 performance could not be considered a debut, nor could the performance of "The Tides of Manaunaun" be confirmed. Henry was probably confusing it with his first reviewed concert, on March 5, 1914, which also did not include "Tides," but it was too late to change the jubilee. As Sidney said, they had to bluff it.[22] The date of his professional debut remains wrong in the literature about Henry.

By the time March came around, the jubilee had expanded to a Manhattanwide celebration, including a party for 300 guests sponsored by Columbia University and Associated Music Publishers; an exhibition at the New York Public Library; a luncheon at The New School honoring his contribution to music education and cultural understanding during three decades on its faculty; and a concert of Asian music at Asia Society, celebrating Henry's role there. In the Sunday *Times*, a big feature article by chief music critic Harold Schonberg recounted Henry's history and aesthetics, with photos from the 1920s and a now-famous picture of Henry with one of the Cowell cats.[23] Robert W. Dowling, Cultural Executive of the City of New York, acting on behalf of the City (and with greetings from Governor Nelson Rockefeller) gave him a book, *The Face of New York*.[24] The Asia Society presented a scroll and a recorded song from his 1,200 "adopted Japanese grandchildren," the Tokyo boys and girls for whom he wrote a march in 1961. The concert featured Dorothy Maynor singing "How Old Is Song," with Henry accompanying; Henry, playing a group of piano works; and Jorge Mester conducting *Hymn and Fuguing Tune No. 2*, *Sinfonietta*, and the Symphony No. 7.

So many tributes required a huge amount of work, especially by Sidney. The celebration at the Asia Society was extremely problematic. Combining players from Turkey and Iran threatened to provoke diplomatic problems because the three "Turkish" performers, who were claimed by the Turks because of their fame, were ethnic Armenians. Only one of them said he was Turkish; the others said they were Iranian. The Cowells anticipated difficulties from the Iranian government because the men's music was not "what we fear that Iranians will be proudest to be represented by," wrote Sidney, "it is too close to folk music . . . and as a heap o' Consuls-General and UN and US Ambassadors from Asia seem to be coming, we are all a shade nervous."[25]

The Juilliard event treated Henry as a real celebrity. Weisgall read a telegram from President Kennedy[26] and the greeting from Governor Rockefeller, which had praised Henry's work as "an interpreter of Asiatic music."[27] Other well-wishers included Ellsworth Bunker, who had been ambassador to India when the Cowells were there and was now on the board of The New School; Congressman William Fitts Ryan; New York Mayor Robert Wagner; Martha Graham; Henry's old parole psychiatrist Dr. Joseph Wortis and his wife; the Mills College club; Savilla Millis Simons, the general secretary of the national YWCA, an old friend of Ellen Veblen, and apparently the wife of a man who once held the pedals for "The Banshee;"[28] and countless colleagues. Shinichi Yuize hailed Henry's pioneering vision of the Western tradition as only part of the greatness of the world's music, calling him the first to do it. "This seemed wildly eccentric and even ridiculous to your Western colleagues for many years, but it is now recognized that you were right to say that you wished 'to live in the whole world of music' and that you are truly the first world-citizen of music." Henry responded with a restatement of the ideals he expressed in Tehran and Tokyo.[29]

Scarcely was the jubilee over when honors recommenced. In 1963, Henry was inducted into the National Institute of Arts and Letters and awarded his second honorary doctorate, by Monmouth College, in Illinois.

With all that fuss, it was appropriate for Henry to be interviewed by the Columbia Oral History Program. The choice of interviewer was just right. Beate Gordon had grown up in Japan, wrote the clause on women's rights in the postwar Japanese constitution, and later headed the performing arts department at the Japan Society and Asia Society. The timing suggests that Sidney had quietly expressed doubts about Henry's longevity.

The Cold War Again

In August 1961, as East Berliners fled to West Berlin by the thousands daily, the East German authorities walled in their portion of the city. With West Berlin isolated deep inside East Germany and likely to wither away, only massive subsidies prevented it from being depopulated. As part of the effort to attract "immigrants" to West Berlin from elsewhere in the Federal Republic, the Bonn government underwrote a brilliant cultural life in the former capital. Successive American administrations had already ensured a strong American presence in Berlin's musical world through institutions like RIAS (Radio in the American Sector), which had a fine orchestra and excellent music programming. In 1962, Nicolas Nabokov was appointed Adviser on International Cultural Affairs to the Berlin Senate. Nabokov, apparently no longer interested in the CIA-sponsored activities of the previous decade, was eager to reenergize Berlin's cultural life.[1]

When the Berlin Senate decided to produce a huge music festival in the spring of 1963, and the United States' Berlin Mission guaranteed American participants all costs other than international travel, Henry could consider accepting Nabokov's invitation. Despite Sidney's distaste for Germany and the extra costs that they would incur if she went, her fears about his health required her to consider the trip seriously.[2]

His condition was difficult to assess. After at least one health problem in 1961, major events seemed to subside. Sidney suspected that he had had minor strokes, but never knew for sure. One doctor had said he was so unlikely to survive for more than a few months that he might as well enjoy them, and eight years had passed since another doctor had pronounced Henry on the brink of death. Sidney was determined to keep him from turning into an invalid. He had mentioned several times "how lucky he thought Adlai Stevenson was, to drop dead without warning in the midst of his diplomatic activities." Henry was told that many people have small strokes and function fine. Since he recovered quickly, he never thought much about it. Determined to sustain his confidence in the future, Sidney suppressed thoughts of death in his presence. Keeping him focused on work was never a problem: he composed even when hospitalized despite being so

uneasy that he wanted Sidney within reach so he could hold her hand. She sometimes stayed in the hospital with him nearly twenty-four hours a day.

When Henry decided to participate in the Berlin festival, Sidney told the
State Department only that his frail health would limit him to one activity a day,
scheduled so that he could rest for several hours in the afternoon and retire early.
Doctors approved his giving live demonstrations, but would not let him play the
difficult early tone-cluster pieces.[3] Henry offered the festival either the world
premiere of his Harmonica Concerto with John Sebastian as soloist, the European premiere of his Symphony No. 15, or the European premiere of his nascent
sixteenth symphony, which would be based on ideas from traditional Icelandic
music. Since William Strickland, the newly appointed conductor of the Iceland
Symphony Orchestra, planned to invite Henry to the world premiere of the
Symphony No. 16 in April in Reykjavik, the Berlin trip could be efficiently connected.[4] When a successful concert with the RIAS orchestra led to Strickland's
immediate reengagement, he proposed bringing Henry to RIAS and performing
major works like the *Variations for Orchestra*, Percussion Concerto, and Harmonica Concerto.[5] In this way, a good-sized tour began taking shape.

The Iceland project moved forward, unhindered by the country's refusal to
follow the American political line. Or rather, it almost certainly moved forward
because of Iceland's annoying independence. For where should one fight the
Cold War if not on an island straddling strategic sea routes? When Henry proposed dedicating his symphony to Vilhjámur Stefansson, the late great Icelan-
dic-American explorer, the American ambassador enthusiastically asked the
State Department to send Henry for the premiere. When Strickland mentioned
Henry's wish to meet with Icelandic composers, the embassy applied for money
to underwrite copying the parts, increasing the likelihood of a recording, and
suggested he begin the trip with ten days of lecturing at the conservatory and
meeting informally with Icelandic musicians and composers before going to
Berlin.[6] Although the Berlin Senate unexpectedly decided to devote its festival
to opera, making Henry's participation unnecessary, the State Department,
which still wanted to use him, requested a "European Pool Grant" and circularized the American embassies throughout Europe, hoping that some of them
could use him, preferably with Strickland.[7]

Confirmation of the State Department grant required a security investigation.
The State Department had been accused of harboring communists, and rising
international tension added to the need for thorough housekeeping. Eerily attached to the security report is the disclaimer, familiar to everyone caught up in
the blacklisting scandal, that the information was supplied solely as an aid to an
inquiry or investigation, and the subject was not to be regarded "as positively
identified by the Commission with either the persons or the organizations
named in the request," since the identity of the person and the credibility of the

information had not been established or verified. Furthermore, the mention of an organization was not to be taken as a characterization by the commission of either the nature or purpose of such an organization. It was pernicious nonsense, a breach of civil rights posing as a declaration of fairness. Once such an "unverified" listing became known, the subject was presumed guilty of communist sympathies or worse and added to the blacklists that supposedly did not exist but ruined countless lives. Only if the subject could prove his or her innocence was the problem solved, though often the stain on the person's reputation was indelible. Henry had managed to get through the worst of the period without being blacklisted or called to testify, but accusations of far-left sympathies in the 1930s were well grounded, and he still was afraid the press could link his leftist past with San Quentin. The discoveries of the investigators are therefore of special interest, and underline the haste with which the security report needed for the 1943 OWI job had been done.

The new report alleged that Henry was among the signers of a pledge sponsored by the League of Professional Groups for Foster and Ford, reading in part, that the signers "pledge our support in the national elections to the Communist Party and its candidates, William Z. Foster and James W. Ford and call upon all educators, writers, engineers, social workers, artists . . . to join us in this move and form Foster and Ford Committees thruout the country." The source: *The Daily Worker*, September 14, 1932. The report said that Henry signed the same pledge as it appeared in an election pamphlet of the following October. Although it seems unlike Henry to have signed such a pledge, an allegation that he signed a call for a Dance Congress and Festival to be held in the spring of 1940 had to have been spurious, since Henry was in prison at the time, desperate to hide any connections with the political left, and certainly unable to receive or export such a petition. As often happened, someone else must have signed his name, assuming he would be sympathetic. In this case, the "someone else" may have been Marc Blitzstein, who apparently did it at least once before.[8] The Joint Committee for a Dance Congress and Festival was described as "a Communist-front organization" but the Dance Congress petition was not called a security risk.

The second security item, based on information that surfaced during the 1947 House Un-American Activities Committee hearings that led to Hanns Eisler's deportation, cited Eisler's praise for Henry's progressive ideas, alluded to Henry's role in the workers' musical movement in San Francisco, and referred to an article in *Sovyetskaya Muzika* praising the Pierre Degeyter Club and Henry's role in it. The remaining references in the report concern Lilly Popper's Metropolitan Music School, about which the House Un-American Activities Committee's 1957 annual report stated that its hearings "showed clearly that the Metropolitan Music School is controlled by Communists. . . . Twenty-four identified Communists have been on the faculty of the school." Yet his activities for the Composers' Collective, his articles in *The Daily Worker*, and his regular contact with Moscow cultural authorities went unnoticed. The security report form stated that the provision of this information was not to be considered as clearance or nonclearance.[9]

Although some statements could have been construed as incriminating, they did not sabotage the American Specialists Program grant. It could have been wrecked by the timing, however. The grant was not confirmed until March 1, and Henry did not receive notification for another week—only seven days before departure. He was told that cuts in the State Department's program budget—the result of congressional intimidation—precluded a briefing in Washington, but that he, a veteran specialist, did not need it.[10]

Since the embassies in Germany, France, and Sweden had decided to join the project, the final schedule of transportation now was settled: departure, March 14; a week in Iceland; a few days in Paris; and roughly four days each in Berlin and Stockholm. Then back to New York, with intermediate stops in London and Copenhagen. Bonn—the site of the American Embassy in those days when the town was capital of the German Federal Republic—was just a jumping-off point; the embassy had scheduled him to give his "Autobiography of a Composer" talk at America Houses in Hannover and Hamburg. Out of respect of Sidney's wishes for a light schedule, no other sessions were planned, although nothing ever deterred Henry from meeting his colleagues.[11] Then everything began to unravel. Henry gave Sidney the flu, forcing her to join him late in Iceland. Paris canceled because of scheduling problems. Luxembourg—which Strickland had pursued[12]—requested to use the vacant Paris slot, but subsequently canceled for lack of preparatory time. The tour thus was reduced to Iceland, Germany, and Sweden. Henry added a week's vacation with his Scottish relatives, returning around April 17 in time to give a talk in upstate New York.[13]

Initially, Sidney had been relieved that she could not afford to go with Henry, because on such trips she rarely got to see what interested her, and when they visited Henry's composer-friends she got stuck in small talk with their wives rather than listening to the men as she preferred. She also thought Henry was getting tired of her ministrations and eager to take care of himself, as he had done in Asia in 1961. A week before departure, however, Henry's doctor and his wife came for a visit, took one look at him, "and when they found I was not going along, [he and his wife] conferred a moment, then took me aside and told me they had $1,000 [2010: $7,120] they did n't need and they wanted me to take it and accompany Henry, he looked very ill and should n't go alone. What friends, what friends! I accepted with little demur, as I was concerned too, and the obligation lay the more lightly on my soul because I really did n't want to go and had been looking forward to staying home!" And, she added, he "never had any idea of the amount of surveillance and concern that surrounded him. By that time he was accustomed to resting every afternoon and he seems not to have noticed that this was unusual in travelling dignitaries and required some special arrangements. He was supposed to rest, so he just did!"

Everything was fine for Henry in Iceland. Sidney, however, was saddled with arranging an exhibition about him and typing a large-print version of Henry's Berlin address, first in English, then in German. They did manage some tourism outside Reykjavik, such as seeing the site of the ancient Icelandic parliament. As the result of his radio talk about world music, the University of Iceland invited him to spend a year lecturing on world music and told the Cowells that if support were found, it would add music to the curriculum and name the first Chair for him.[14] Strickland later said the Iceland reviews had been mixed, but the one in the politically radical newspaper was the best, probably because of the folk elements in the symphony. Henry was caught in the trap of many 1960s composers, Strickland added: critics were German-trained and probably thought his music was not sufficiently atonal. A lot of people went out of their way to express pleasure, especially young listeners.

The plan to record the new symphony in Iceland took CRI (Composers Recordings Inc.) completely by surprise. Nobody at the company knew anything about the orchestra, the recording facilities, or the engineers.[15] In the end, however, they were delighted.[16]

Next came Germany. In Hannover, America House planned three free events over two days—a lecture about Henry, Henry's own talk, and a recorded-music hour featuring his seventh symphony.[17] His notes for the European talks verify that in a single lecture he covered a huge spectrum of American music, almost all of which would have been new to his listeners. In Hamburg his lecture provoked two hours of discussion over coffee.[18] The four surviving reviews testify to the huge change in the climate of new music since Henry's early tours. His originality made a big impression upon audiences described as engaged and fascinated. While there were some reservations about whether he had minimized the development of a personal style, the critics were persuaded that he could not be dismissed as an eclectic.

In Berlin he was booked to attend Strickland's recording sessions of the *Variations for Orchestra* and *Synchrony* with the RIAS orchestra, give a lecture on styles in American music at America House, repeat it in German on RIAS, and receive the keys to Berlin in recognition of his long connection with new music in Germany.[19] At dinner after the first orchestral rehearsal, however, he felt so unwell that a young army doctor immediately put him in the US Army hospital. Sidney remembered Strickland's extreme kindness and support. "He was going to take me back to the hotel but the hospital offered me a bed across the hall, and Henry said 'Please stay!' when I asked him."[20]

After an initial diagnosis of a heart attack, the doctors determined that he was suffering from digitalis poisoning resulting from the failure to reduce his dosage after his cardiologist had raised it.[21] It was the first of a series of medical or surgical mishaps caused by Henry's concerned doctors or by bad luck. With his heart failing, his blood pressure had dropped very low and his pulse become alarmingly slow; he was very near death.[22] Sidney left their hotel, the very traditional Bristol Hotel Kempinski, where she was "refused service in the dining room at noon because I was unescorted by a gentleman!" and moved into the American Officers' Club, where the German manager harassed her by complaining daily that she was not supposed to be there without her husband, despite knowing her husband was in the hospital. The fact that she had been assigned a VIP suite irritated him further. She told him to complain to the embassy.[23]

Henry revived well enough to have visitors. "[Boris Blacher and Nicholas Nabokov] stood by the bedside and I remember so well Blacher's look of compassion as he looked down on Henry who looked very shrunken in a big bed." Having got used to being given no consideration or attention by German men, Sidney was surprised when Blacher took her arm and spoke of plans for Henry and his music when he felt better. He said, "'I wish your husband could know how he has been regarded by many of us in Germany: We felt it was he who made music *move* in Germany, as the Schoenberg school had never been able to manage. . . .'"[24]

Eventually he was pronounced well enough to record his autobiographical talk for RIAS, but it was too late for him to practice RIAS's German version, and no studios were available. It was decided, therefore, that he would tape it in the Voice of America's New York studio. All other engagements in Berlin were dropped. (Fortunately, RIAS certified that he had fulfilled his duties in Berlin; otherwise, reimbursements might have been due the State Department.)[25] Sidney also canceled the Stockholm trip, which the US embassy there had arranged as for a true dignitary.[26] As soon as Henry could travel, he and Sidney flew to Glasgow and Dublin to see the Cowell families, and to Reykjavik, taking a tiny holiday there on Icelandic Airways' two-day tourist package. With Henry on leave from Columbia for the rest of the semester, they proceeded straight to Shady. Strickland's recording of the *Icelandic* Symphony was edited by early May, to the pleasure not only of Strickland but even CRI. It quickly attracted attention in the northern United States and Canada, where there were large concentrations of Icelandic immigrants. CRI also released the *Variations for Orchestra*, with Strickland conducting the Polish National Radio Orchestra.

Among Henry's papers is the RIAS lecture, the only written-out version of his "Autobiography of a Composer." Even without a surviving version of the early talks, a few comparative observations are possible. His account of the first half of his life probably had not changed much over the years, although it may have become more colorful. It recapitulates what we know about his early life and music, although without the comedy that made his live lectures so entertaining. It also clarifies his route to and retreat from some discoveries, especially the realization that his rhythmic ideas could not be executed by humans. Addressing those who wondered how he could have pursued such ideas, he said that the circle around his parents—he named Jack London and Mary Austin—transmitted ideas partly coming from Ralph Waldo Emerson, "who urged young men in America to stand on their *own* feet, and speak for their *own* world." Such ideas turned his attention to the sound of the world around him. "It never entered my mind to tune out any of the sounds of nature and people, nor to exclude *any* of the many different kinds of music that fell on my ears."

One of the biggest differences between the RIAS autobiography and its ancestors is that Henry no longer was an outsider. Instead of being scorned as a radical, now he was being described as an eclectic, a word he abhorred. "Eclecticism is a placing side by side of several unrelated things. My music is the opposite of this, because I believe that the Art of Music is a single world-wide art, an art which has simply developed the same elements differently, in different combinations, and to different degrees in different parts of the world." Because music can be made from many elementary materials, he chose whatever appealed to him, "combining them however I liked at any given moment, and deriving from them a work having its own forms and techniques of writing. . . . My hope . . . is to create in each work a fresh integration of musical materials that can be shown to be related in a fundamental way even though they may have developed at a distance from one another."

The other obvious difference is that in the early days, all he had for demonstrations was his piano music, which would have branded him as a radical, even in tamer pieces like "Aeolian Harp" or "The Tides of Manaunaun." In 1963, armed with recordings, he could show his evolution with a *Hymn and Fuguing Tune* and describe how his acquaintance with Asian music prompted him to write *Ostinato pianissimo*, pieces so user-friendly that they would have distressed his circle in the radical days.

Radical modernism was a thing of the past, as was the pioneer world of new music in which he had become who he was. But new radicalisms were now flourishing, and as always, Henry was interested. In the Columbia Oral History interview, he praised the work of Luening and Ussachevsky at the Columbia-Princeton Electronic Music Center, and Henk Badings in Holland, but felt the field was a baby. At the other extreme, Cage's newest ideas intrigued him. Asked if he felt those composers were doing the right thing or going too far, he said, "I think that they are experimenting with something, and I think that they, to my knowledge, have not yet arrived at a point where you could say that this was great music.

I think that it could easily become great music in the hands of great men. This is always a prerequisite."

Nothing, however, underlines the transformation of the American arts world so much as two recent developments that made Henry very happy—Governor Rockefeller's encouragement of public funding (which was formalized in 1965 as the New York State Council on the Arts), and Washington's tentative steps toward a federal arts agency.

‖ 59 ‖

Home Again, 1963–1964

Having taken a leave from Columbia for the rest of the term, Henry spent several months at Shady composing and resting until it was time for Eastman's summer session. He drove there by himself, to the dismay of Sidney, who thought he looked increasingly fragile. A lighter schedule that left the morning clear for composing promised a low stress level, but a doctor was available in case of trouble. Henry quickly dispensed with residual business from Europe, reading and approving the script of "Autobiography of a Composer," which he was to record in New York for RIAS. With ample time for composing, he selected images of the Creator translated from Russian as the text for an oratorio commissioned by Stetson University, and finished a concerto version of *Air and Scherzo*, which Sigurd Rascher was going to premiere shortly and play in Europe. In the evenings Henry taped radio shows on Ives, Schoenberg, Bartók, oriental music, and his own symphonies.[1]

Apart from scraping the side of a neighboring car in a parking lot, Henry had no disasters to report. After spending the July 4 holiday at Shady, he returned to Eastman safely. A generally fine summer included good news about forthcoming publications and warm reviews of Folkways' recording of his piano music, but also the sadness of Blanche Walton's death at ninety-one. New summer suits made him look "*very* elegant" he told Olive. After seeing him, however, Sidney felt so worried that she urged BMI to replace him on a forthcoming panel that would have required traveling.[2] Her instincts were right, as she says in her 1973 summary of Henry's health history. On the morning of July 26, 1963, he walked into the Eastman music office unable to speak. A penciled note said that he had been confused since the previous night, his words were jumbled, writing was difficult. He feared he might have had a stroke and needed a doctor. Sidney raced to the Albany airport, managed to get a flight to Rochester, and was greeted by the wife of the director of the summer session, who said, "He's still alive," which shocked Sidney, since she had not "entertained an alternative." His speech returned, but real communication followed very gradually. After some time he could remember the names of objects and write without problems. Gradually the complete paralysis of his right side began to recede. She thought that the damage might have been confined to the speech centers, "which never behaved again with their customary readiness; but as Henry habitually talked slowly and a bit carefully, this was not noticeable."

Then, during a test, part of a catheter broke off, necessitating abdominal surgery to extract it. Considering the state of his heart and circulatory system, it was miraculous that he survived. Sidney was astonished when the doctor, obviously oblivious to their ages, assured her that cosmetic surgery could improve the look of the abdominal scar. Henry thought the test that led to the broken catheter had been done by a student; Sidney's doctor said it was inexcusable. Knowing that the hospital was nervous about legal action, she forced them not to charge for the surgery. When Henry was released about a month later they drove home slowly because the scar was still painful. His mind was doing well, however. Some weeks later he provided by memory a list of corrections to proofs that he had read, astonishing everyone by giving page, line, and measure numbers as if he were looking at the score.[3]

When they returned to Manhattan for Columbia's fall semester, they had to keep silent about the latest stroke lest his employers and colleagues worry that he could collapse at any time. Henry wanted to resume teaching but still had trouble remembering words, as after the first stroke in Karachi. "So we made a game of recalling a word, and Henry loved to think of the one I was groping for, triumphantly. He was competitive to the last degree, concealed though this often was, and he just loved to be able to succeed with words where I could n't. Which no wonder, after all his struggle to retrieve the connection between mind and speech."

Nevertheless, Henry had complete faith in his ability to carry on. Sidney, less confident, talked to William Mitchell, the Columbia music department chairman, who worked out an arrangement whereby a faculty member or even Sidney herself would fill in if he didn't feel up to teaching. The first priority was to lighten his load, which was not strenuous intellectually—just "Music of the World's Peoples" and two sections of the required introduction to music.[4] Thinking it would be good to know whether his trouble finding words was affecting his teaching, Sidney enlisted Ernest Bloch's daughter Suzanne, who was attending Henry's classes, to report back. Everything seemed fine, she said, although he would go off in an unexpected direction because of some peculiar word association in response to questions from students, but nobody minded. Bloch found him as interesting, striking, and original as always. By the end of the fall semester his speech was almost normal.[5]

On the other hand, he did not always remember appointments. Once or twice, having been cooped up between the apartment and the classroom, he decided to go out to dinner, having forgotten that he was to meet Sidney. She had no idea where he had gone, and when various lookouts she used ("a phar-macist, photographer, Puerto Rican grocery man, P[uerto]R[ican] barber—on the route between Columbia . . . and our apt.") had not seen him, she called the police. Inquiries at hospitals and police stations turned up nothing. "Eventually Henry made his rather unsteady way home without incident except for the years taken off my life by imagining horrors. Once he had gone to the Blue Ribbon (a bar on West 44th Street) where he had been known for years; a great fuss was made over him and he had a fine time. The other time he went down to the Village . . . looking for Romany Marie's and old friends there; but she had long since shut up shop and he had a very bad dinner, he said, elsewhere. Fortunately he took taxis both ways! He might easily have decided to econo-mize by taking the subway, with all those stairs." (A policeman told her that if he had collapsed in the subway, he might not have been found for hours.) Another time Otto Luening picked him up in a cab in a blizzard and brought him home. Sidney tried very hard to prevent Henry from noticing how carefully she tracked him, but his glee over his "escapes" on a few occasions suggests that she was not successful.

Olive, traveling in the Far East, could not snoop. Keeping their letters to her unrevealing, the Cowells described their busy social calendar and business mat-ters. Indeed, letters of that autumn say very little about the essence of Henry's life or his feelings. Life was reasonably quiet and he was composing productively. Commissions, performances, and recordings abounded. He was constantly sought after for advice and asked to lend his hand in important service functions, the newest of which was the Fulbright music panel. All this could be told to Olive. Slightly—but only slightly—more revealing are his letters to Sidney, who was in California for a few weeks. Phrases like "If I feel good after the afternoon nap I'll go to Asia House to hear Bhatia on Indian music" remind us that his health was always an issue.[6]

Sidney was due back from California in mid-November 1963, just in time for the premiere of the Percussion Concerto. For Thanksgiving they went to Shady, where Hal Tufty, the former Public Affairs Officer in Madras and now director of the Peace Corps in French West Africa, joined them. The assassination of President Kennedy a few days earlier had hit hard. Henry immediately wrote *Gravely and Vigorously*, for cello solo, in Kennedy's memory. Originally conceived to be *Hymn and Fuguing Tune No. 17*, it was not given a number at his publisher's suggestion. The next—and final—*Hymn and Fuguing Tune* (for the unforget-table duo of soprano saxophone and contrabass saxophone) was numbered eighteen.[7] Then he unveiled more proof that he was still his old self—*26 Simul-taneous Mosaics*, for violin, clarinet, cello, piano, and percussion, which takes the principle of Elastic Form further than ever. In the *Mosaic* Quartet, the players could arrange the movements as they saw fit. In *Sarabande*, the phrases could be cut and pasted, lengthened or shortened, as Martha Graham saw fit. In *26 Simul-taneous Mosaics*, each player has five or six little pieces that can be played in any order and as many times as desired, with repeats and reprises of da capos at will. No coordination among players is attempted. Ample silence between move-ments cleanses the atmosphere of clutter. Although dedicated to Oliver Daniel, it seems to be a musical greeting to John Cage, whose pursuit of music freed from personal taste—an extreme form of Henry's desire to compose without the burden of an imposed tradition—intrigued and amused Henry.

That fall (1963), Elsa Schmolke died, and Imre Weisshaus surfaced after thirty years. His long letter came as an incredible shock, because Weisshaus's disappearance had mystified everyone. His story summarized the collapse of so much that Henry had known. Having left Hungary in 1930 for relatively lib-eral Germany, Weisshaus fought Hitler until the reckoning came three years later: in 1930 imprisoned by the Brownshirts, he was forced to watch SS men burn his music as a prelude to shooting him. Fortunately, they were drunk and he escaped to Paris with nothing. Ferociously determined to fight, he took part in the Spanish civil war, where his mass songs were popular among Republi-cans; joined the French propaganda ministry in 1939; and fled south when the Germans invaded. Just before the liberation the Gestapo emptied his Paris flat. Eventually he learned that thirty-three members of his family had been killed by the Nazis. Almost worse, he said, was the postwar discovery that those with whom he fought—the Left—were just as bad as the Right. Having lost all his illusions, he withdrew from his familiar world. His bitterness was finally miti-gated as he saw that he had been right about Stalin's murderousness. In a post-script he added that he had consigned his old name to the rubbish and now was known only as Paul Arma.[8]

When the fall term ended, Henry and Sidney returned to Shady. On Christ-mas he wrote his British family that he felt better if he was careful and avoided stairs. He had time to compose, but the paperwork of his exciting life consumed all available space at Shady. "Sidney," he told them, "is doing a grim job of getting all my old manuscripts and letters to the N.Y. Public Library."[9] She was not just clearing space, however. She could hardly avoid thinking about the near future. When in January he went to Miami to hear Sevitzky conduct the premiere of the *Concerto Grosso*, they arranged to have him met at the airport (after midnight) by a doctor, who agreed to send a specialist if needed. Henry said he felt fine; there was not a single step anywhere. He would have radio and TV interviews, a rehearsal, and "no parties!"[10]

After Columbia's second semester began, the good professional news contin-ued. USIA was showing around the new recording of *Homage to Iran*; Pierre Salinger and Pablo Casals sent notes of thanks for the Kennedy memorial piece; the complete 1916 *Quartet Euphometric* and the second movement of *Quartet*

Romantic were finally going to be played. (The first movement of *Quartet Roman-tic* was still considered unperformable by humans and not premiered until 1978.) The New York musicians' union gave him an Honorary Membership—"this means I have all privileges, but do not have to pay any dues!"[11]

In March he resigned from the American Composers Alliance, with which he had been linked as a member and officer since its beginning. It was sad, but he faced the problem that when he was forced to retire from Columbia in a year, he would get no pension because he was only an adjunct. If he did not resign now from ACA and take BMI's offer of an exclusive four-year contract for radio and TV rights, he might risk getting a worse deal.[12]

His life now seemed like a very relaxed version of business as usual. Plans were complete for another summer at Eastman, a project at Dartmouth's Hop-kins Center for the Creative Arts, more recordings, and a little traveling to hear a few performances and speak. The Rockefeller Foundation asked him to consult about music departments, focusing on creative activities. Columbia had reen-gaged him for 1964–65 with a raise for his final year. [13] Thanks to the successful concealment of his poor health, he was offered a one-year appointment at the Chicago Music College, which he declined.[14]

Finally came June and the end of the school year. Lukas Foss had requested a piece for Buffalo, and when Henry decided he could not complete one in time, Foss programmed the *26 Simultaneous Mosaics* as the opening piece of Evenings for New Music, a renowned feature of his new Center for Creative and Perform-ing Arts at the State University of New York at Buffalo. Considering the prevail-ing opinion that Henry had turned conservative, it was a great compliment. In fact, the "conservative" Henry had just completed *In Memory of Nehru* for var-ious possible duets of Indian and Western instruments. The next project was his nineteenth symphony, one of the few pieces from the later years for which he had no commission.[15]

He and Sidney planned to spend four weeks in Shady, then the summer ses-sion in Rochester and three days at Dartmouth in August, returning to Shady for some peaceful weeks until Columbia reopened. A photo in the Kingston *Daily Freeman*, taken just before he left for Eastman, shows Henry looking consider-ably aged. The occasion was a celebration of his service to the Kingston-area community. When the time came to present the award, Henry had to be carried by the catering staff.[16]

60

Finale

In 1973 Sidney spent four weeks writing an account of Henry's health history. Her narrative of the final eighteen months is virtually the only source for the end of his story.

As the 1964 Eastman summer session approached, Sidney arranged to work at the Rochester Institute of Technology so she could keep watch on him while preparing a forthcoming show of her photography. The summer was productive for both of them and there were no health crises despite the heat. With a light load, he had ample time to compose. Luckily, they were not affected by severe rioting concentrated in Rochester's black-dominated district.[1] In August, Dartmouth held an all-Cowell concert and conference, where Henry played, lectured, and worked with composition students.[2]

Now, however, he began to have trouble urinating. Sidney put him in Brooklyn Jewish Hospital, where her friend and physician Mort Rosenfeld could watch out for him. He was discovered to have a five-inch rectal tumor that seemed likely to be malignant and had to be removed. They were amazed that in all his hospitalizations it had never been discovered. Sidney had told the doctor who had taken charge of Henry in the late 1950s that there had been bleeding, but was told it was just hemorrhoids. Now, she said, everyone felt bad, and no one took the blame. Columbia gave Henry a paid medical leave of absence for the fall semester.[3] Unfortunately, that was just when Shinichi Yuize came to Columbia on a guest fellowship at the ethnomusicology program that Henry and the Rockefeller Foundation had encouraged.

Sidney and Dr. Rosenfeld decided to tell Henry only that he had polyps. Cancer had killed Clarissa and filled his maternal family history, and Henry, as Sidney put it, was not eager to talk of death. When another doctor disagreed with them, she had to be sure that Henry was never alone, lest that doctor take it upon himself to reveal the truth. She went back to the Rosenfelds' and played the piano for an hour, practicing Bach fugues to enter "into the world where fear and death are not." It was now October 5. To complicate matters, an operation had to be put off because Henry was discovered to have a rare blood type; the hospital had no supply of it and the New York City blood bank too little for a major oper-ation. That evening Henry busily composed while they waited eighteen hours for the blood and rescheduled the surgery.[4]

Two weeks later, Sidney wrote Olive that he had been operated on for kidney stones and would be discharged in about ten days. It was not the worst possible operation, she said, "but at 67 such things can't be dismissed lightly either. He has immense resilience, they have been quite astonished at his progress. . . ." Henry was in good spirits but complained of tiredness and inability to concen-trate on proofreading, partly because of the medications.[5] If Olive had thought about it, she might have suspected that such a recuperation from a kidney stone operation was improbable.

The surgeon initially had said he could not operate because the malignancy had engulfed too much of the Henry's innards. After Dr. Rosenfeld prevailed upon him to try, the surgeon agreed to go ahead, although he knew that Henry would never be free of the terrible pain that would start up almost at once. (Sid-ney suspected that Rosenfeld hoped Henry's heart might fail on the operating table and save him later agonies.) This was to be the first of five operations, the others to combat emergencies caused by the tumor's damage. Many exceptions were made to rules because at each operation no one thought he would survive. Sidney explained all those operations to Olive as polyp removal. She also had to explain the colostomy to Henry, however. Unlike the doctors, she had no com-punctions about lying and told him it was necessary to allow healing after re-moval of the polyps. "Poor Henry said: 'I suppose they'll put it all back as before later on!' I said, 'Oh yes, if they feel it is worth the trouble: you've had quite a lot of surgery by now, after all, and you may decide you want to take a vacation from it.' Turning the conversation to what I knew he feared, I said, 'One good thing: there was not a sign of cancer.' 'Oh,' said Henry, 'I'm glad to hear that. One always wonders, of course.'" After that, she recalled, she never heard him express either apprehension about or interest in what was happening. When his unhappy, de-voted doctor tried to explain something to him, Henry told him, "'I don't want to hear details, because I don't really understand them anyway. *You just go ahead and make me well!*' Under the circumstances this injunction was almost more than poor Dr. C[astleman] could take."

Medical care comes at a price, and not a good one for the Cowells. Round-the-clock nurses for nearly three months at almost $100 a week [2010: $703] were not covered by their insurance, nor were the doctors, but nobody ever sent a really large bill. Hospital expenses were met by Blue Cross and the Jewish Fed-eration, which treated the Cowells as if they were Jewish. She does not explain why, and appears not to have noticed the irony after all the old implications about Henry and anti-Semitism. "There were so few gentiles in the hospital that I was sometimes asked abruptly by strangers in the hall: 'What are you doing here?' understandably enough." She was determined not to let anyone know that money was a problem. The administrator of the National Institute of Arts and Letters felt that Henry spent so much energy raising money to help others that Sidney should apply for assistance. She declined with thanks.[6]

Just before Christmas (1964), Dr. Castleman felt Henry was getting too dependent upon nurses and wanted to send him home where he would have to do more for himself. In a sense, Sidney was prepared, because Dr. Rosenfeld had asked that some hospital regulations be set aside so that nurses could train her in techniques she might need. She was very pleased until she realized that she would have to do everything, such as deal with the matter of a bed. Through Dr. Rosenfeld they got an old hospital bed with a crank to raise it, which should have made life easier for Sidney, because hospital beds are constructed high to ease the work of nurses. Unfortunately, Henry insisted on urinating standing up and could not get down without her help. To Dr. Castleman's annoyance, Sidney finally got another nurse, who refused to touch Henry when he got serum hepatitis, leaving her with more work.

They still spent time in their New York apartment on West 111th Street, five blocks south of Columbia's music department, for Henry's Columbia colleagues William Mitchell and Willard Rhodes agreed with Sidney that he should try to teach if he wanted to. They arranged the simplest possible schedule and kept replacements on hand. She wrote, "He was supposed to take walks by the time the new semester started, but I'm under the impression that I, or somebody, met his classes for a couple of weeks before he was able to get so far. . . . Sometimes I walked up Broadway to meet him, but he always objected to this, he hated the feeling of being watched or looked after. (His Columbia colleague Otto [Luening] said: 'Henry was a real pro & always completed what he undertook. Those last months were heroic.')"

Other activities were almost nonexistent. In October (1964), he was given an award by a music school primarily serving the black community in Brooklyn, but Alan Hovhaness accepted the citation on his behalf.[7] Sidney and Henry declined the invitation to the Johnson-Humphrey inauguration on January 20, 1965, and could not attend most performances of his music, even the Philadelphia Orchestra's premiere of his Koto Concerto, but he knew of its success and of subsequent performances in Tokyo and Seattle. In March, he wrote Lan Adomian a perfectly clear if somewhat shaky letter, mentioning that he had started his twentieth symphony, although the previous three had still not been performed.[8] His New York circle may have thought everything was all right because he still was active. On April 1, he played at a Contemporary Music Society concert at the Guggenheim Museum; a month later he was given the Laurel Leaf Award of the American Composers Alliance for distinguished service to American music. He managed to finish his full teaching period before mandatory retirement at the end of the semester following his sixty-eighth birthday. On

June 1, 1965, the Cowells left New York for good. The Shady house had been rebuilt so he could live on the ground floor. Henry seemed to believe that if he avoided climbing stairs he would live forever.

At this point in her narrative Sidney commented that it was April 5, 1973; she had been writing since March 12. She might have had to catch her breath, knowing that a letter he wrote two days before they moved back to Shady would be his last.

June 2, Sidney's birthday, was celebrated with friends. On the way home Henry said he didn't feel well. The next morning he had to be taken to the hospital with another stroke. His left side was paralyzed, his face slightly twisted to one side, and he had trouble articulating and talking. When he seemed to be improving, Sidney went home, only to learn why his temperature should have been taken in the armpit rather than orally, as an apprentice nurse had done. He had bitten the thermometer into three pieces and swallowed them along with the mercury. One piece was stuck, and if it didn't turn lengthwise an operation would be necessary. At the last moment it turned and was expelled.

Improvement came gradually. His face straightened out and the leg paralysis improved enough so that he could almost balance with a walker, but endless physiotherapy did nothing for his left arm. When he learned it was June 15 and despaired of missing their laurel tree in blossom, Sidney hired an ambulance and a couple of men to take him home to see it. His mind seemed clear but he could only get enough breath to utter a single syllable at a time. It took several months of speech therapy until he could sound almost normal for a few sentences. But on that trip to see the laurel "he absolutely floored all 3 of us by giving [the] botanical names to a whole series of shrubs and flowers that we passed—. . . some mental channel from his boyhood activated unexpectedly."

That was his final hospitalization. In the nine and one-half years since Henry's doctor predicted the worst, he was in the hospital thirteen times, of which two were for tests. The other eleven times, Sidney was told that she should not expect him to survive. She was so successful in keeping the truth from Henry that one doctor was convinced that she had no clue as to the seriousness of his condition until Dr. Rosenfeld set him straight. She developed euphemisms and lies for the outside world, fearing that the release of the truth could reach Henry and destroy his hopes.

Dr. Castleman had told her even before this last stroke that only a rather small portion of Henry's brain was still usable. In midsummer he informed her that if he had another stroke, he would be "to all intents and purposes feeble-minded!" (Castleman, she thought, believed that the worst possible news was reassuring.) Sidney replied that Henry was certainly not feeble-minded, or at least she never thought he was. When Dr. Castleman drove to Shady to see "this phenomenon who had survived with mind intact after at least 6 strokes . . . Henry sat in a stuporous state the whole time . . . and had n't a word to say! . . . [He] was often in a stupor, or very torpid, seeming half asleep and entirely unresponsive, anyhow; but there were also periods when he seemed fairly [aware and responsive], except for the difficulty of bringing out the sounds of the words he wanted to say. . . ." Some facial paralysis persisted, however. After the last stroke he could no longer smile except a little bit with his eyes. Previously he had recovered quickly, but this time, as recovery eluded him, he burst out in distress. "'Why maybe I can't play the piano any more!'"

Funds from the National Institute of Arts and Letters got him a better hospital bed. Sidney hired a wonderful nurse who was obsessed with laundering. When the therapist finally said there was no more to be done for his arm, and Sidney asked for therapy to continue, she was told she could certainly do it herself. That meant creating pain—by stretching the arm—to stimulate the nerves. Sidney knew she could not do that. Henry was expected to go out for walks once or twice a day, which was possible because she had planned the renovations with future strokes in mind, but the wheelchair ramp had not been completed.

Their neighbor, composer-pianist Yehudi Wyner, helped her try (unsuccessfully) to get Henry to work on his twentieth symphony, for which he had projected a fifth movement. Wyner came almost every afternoon, and to everyone's surprise Henry showed some signs that he looked forward to his visits, when they would listen to recordings together. "This is one of the brotherly services, of which we both had so many from many people, that stands out by the impossibility of ever adequately acknowledging it: it was a sensitive, subtle, warm and supportive thing that could not have been better for Henry." She understood, however, that the visits were an enormous strain on Wyner, who never showed it in any way. Wyner, in turn, was impressed with Sidney's disciplined and unsentimental constructiveness, and her refusal to waste time on useless pity. He and Henry could not really converse; on some days Henry could barely talk and Wyner could hardly understand him. It was a heartbreaking contrast to the days before Henry became so ill, when they would visit happily and pleasantly chat about real estate, community affairs, local musical history, and rarely about music itself. He thought Henry was childlike, with fantastic recall. On the surface he seemed to harbor and cultivate the simplest thoughts, unburdened by academicism and intellectualism. "It was a very different kind of intelligence; it was an intelligence that somehow struck me as being much more closely related to a much more ancient type of knowledge that would be the product of an oral tradition. Somehow he'd be much more in the nature of a tribal guru . . . who simply had everything in his head; he didn't need to read or study scores, or commentaries, or analyses, and so on and so forth, in order to somehow mobilize his own intelligence."

Unfortunately, Wyner innocently let slip among New York friends that Henry was dying of cancer, but it did not seem to matter because the few people who might "penetrate their seclusion"—Seeger, Luening, Weisgall—could be trusted not to let Henry know. In any case, she had no idea what Henry would have understood. They had almost no visitors other than Wyner; it was too exhausting. After Charles Seeger came he told Sidney in distress, "'My Henry has gone—he no longer has his old smile!'—I assured Charlie it would come back, doubtful though I knew this to be of course."

Days were busy and tiring, between his bath, physical therapy, and walks. In the afternoon Sidney would spend a couple of hours with him even if Wyner had been there; he often asked to hear one or another recording, especially his fourth symphony, which he said was the one "in which he felt he had been most successful in doing what he intended." She read *Huckleberry Finn* aloud every day. "As with small children I was inclined to feel that it was the sense of having my full attention that was important to him and that he did n't often really follow the story. But he certainly liked the idea and if I was slow to get started he always asked for it."

They took a couple of little trips. On August 8 his *Trio in Nine Short Movements*, which he had completed in the hospital just before the previous Christmas, was premiered in the Maverick Concerts, not far from their home. At the rehearsal Sidney sat with Henry to relay what she believed he was trying to say. In September they went to Lincoln Center to hear his *Ultima Actio* sung by the University of Puerto Rico chorus. A wheelchair was provided to take him to an accessible part of the balcony at Philharmonic Hall (now Avery Fisher Hall). Then Henry insisted on going to the Chelsea Hotel on West 23rd Street in the hope of seeing Virgil Thomson, who was away, as it happened. He had to walk to the elevator, followed by Sidney carrying a chair so that he could rest every few steps. When he fell, twice, Sidney, with no one to assist her, could barely pick him up. Arrangements were made for him to go to Nashville for the October 18 premiere of his Symphony No. 19, but when Oliver Daniel learned that the town was expected to be mobbed with a Grand Ole Op'ry reunion, he decided that the jaunt was impossible. Sidney was relieved, but knew that Henry would not be able to understand what had happened and would be disappointed.

Sidney: "To save one more bit of work on Henry's person he agreed it would be fun to grow a beard and mustache. Both were white, of course, and very becoming; and pleasant as his face grew sharper-pointed, quite softening in effect. He was hard to recognize, actually, except for his domed head and his brilliantly blue eyes."

Between coming back from Eastman in the summer of 1964 and the big 1965 stroke, he had written profusely, including *Zapados Sonidos* for tap dancer and chorus, the Koto Concerto No. 2, for Shinichi Yuize, *Twilight in Texas*, for studio orchestra (commissioned by Eastern Airlines for a commercial), and Symphony No. 19, which he dedicated "to the Doctors and Nurses of Brooklyn Jewish Hospital, without Whom This Music Would Never Have Been Written." Work on Symphony No. 20 was ended by the June stroke. There are several occasional miniatures, mostly for Sidney, and early sketches for his Symphony No. 21, but composing was almost over. In July he nearly broke her heart expressing his desire to get back to writing music. "He settled at the table, his useless left arm on a pillow shared often by a cat—one or both cats always sat with him when he settled to write music. He wrote some brief melodies for various friends, Hugo [Weisgall] among them I remember, very dissonant and very brief. One of these did n't suit him when I played it back on the piano, but he could n't remember what he had intended. He wrote sketches at first, then whole pages of score, absolutely involved and lost in what he was doing, with concentration of an unbelievable intensity after such a stroke . . . and the score pages are on the whole logical and reasonable music, but once he turned the page he could not remember what had gone before, so each page is as of a quite different piece. He seemed happier doing this than anything else, as always before; his eyes shone with enthusiasm often." He sketched four little pieces—in July a birthday and an anniversary greeting for Sidney and a little tune for his friend and banker Avery Claflin, and on September 22, his last musical utterance, a little piece for Charles Seeger. Erminie Kahn, who had not been told about his true condition, was still booking engagements. Henry correctly feared that his difficulty speaking would prevent further lecturing, however. For a while another doctor encouraged them to send him for therapy at the Rusk Institute. When Sidney wondered whether it was worth doing since Henry's situation seemed hopeless, the doctor responded that if one is on the side of life, one does everything possible, even if it is against all hope. At the last moment, however, Henry was too exhausted to go, unable even to sit up. Then a speech therapist in Saugerties was able to help the breathing, and Henry got a bit stronger, but further trips to New York were impossible. In their old Pontiac they went for drives, when he would doze or go blank.

Olive telephoned, wondering why she hadn't heard from him. When Sidney refused to wake him, and Olive made a date to phone again, Sidney and Henry practiced a conversation, which was possible because Olive's conversations were completely predictable. All went exactly as anticipated, to Sidney's great amusement. Olive recalled it well: "I was with Charles Seeger two or three days on my way to Mexico in 1965. . . . I arranged before I got out of the country to phone [Henry]. I well remember how feeble his voice was. Sidney told me he had a hard time trying to figure out what to say to me, which showed of course his mental state."[9]

At the suggestion of friends, Sidney arranged sham games of bridge, which Henry could no longer play. One player made Henry a little rack, similar to a piano's music rack, where the cards were held by a rubber band so he could slip them in and out with one hand. Each session was the same—dinner, then cards. Henry's very sensitive partner would coach him as to what card he should have played and change his cards. At first his concentration was good, but it rapidly deteriorated. Finally they knew—"maybe also even Henry, one can never know," that the games were finished. She does not say if she told him that Varèse died on November 6.

Early in December, Paul Farnsworth, the Stanford psychology professor, received a letter from Henry requesting access to Terman's papers for Hugo Weisgall and Theodore Strongin in their capacity as Henry's biographers.[10] Farnsworth gave the authorization, unaware that the letter was from Sidney. Henry had not written a letter since May 30 and could not even have dictated this one.

With strokes, life can persist no matter how awful the conditions. Cancer was another matter. Henry's doctor and Sidney agreed to do nothing to preserve life, hoping that he would die quietly before the cancer became really painful. All his systems were operating badly and his body was filled with strong poisons. The oncologist found it hard to resign himself to doing nothing, even though he knew it was best. In November, Henry looked fine, as if he could live another few months, which alarmed Sidney because she knew that the metastases were rapidly spreading and likely to cause pain very soon. On December 8, however, a doctor gave him two or three more days at most.

That day, Henry learned that he had been given the Thorne Music Fund Honorary Award, whose previous recipients were Ben Weber, Lou Harrison, and Stefan Wolpe.[11] Later Sidney described to Francis Thorne how "he glowed over it, though by that time only his eyes were expressive. It was his last word from the world outside our home, and I am so grateful that it was a friendly and appreciative one." She decided to use the money to pay for prints of the microfilm of Henry's music manuscripts that the New York Public Library was making before sending the originals to the Library of Congress.[12]

On December 9, Vivian Fine and her husband came for dinner. She held Henry's hand with incredible sweetness "and he looked up at her with what seemed to me real pleasure but also a kind of puzzled effort to understand something unexpressed. She said: 'Dear Henry! it's been a long time, hasn't it, a long long time.' That was all, but a lovely smiling end to friends for him." After they left Henry said he felt "awfully sick!" Sidney reassured him and offered a sleeping pill. "He said he had no pain—perhaps the stroke dulled the nerves; but I could hope really not." Later he made a gesture toward the phonograph. She played the Fourth Symphony for him and he dropped off to sleep.

Sidney now concluded her account.

> In the morning he seemed unseeing, mostly, though when a huge and brilliant red cardinal came to the feeder outside the window within his view, he sought me with his eyes and with the eyes alone made a sort of gesture to me to look, so that I did with an exclamation of pleasure in

the vibrant creature. Our last human exchange, faint but unmistakable. His mouth was very dry so about 10:15 I sent [the nurse] . . . into the village to get some glycerin to moisten his lips and mouth, as I had been taught when my father was dying. . . . I later learned she went in the other direction first to see her dogs, so that in all she was gone about 2 hours—I was so very grateful for her delinquency as it left me alone, with the 2 cats, during Henry's last moments.

Before she left, Pepper [the cat] had jumped up on Henry's bed and burrowed under Henry's right hand, normally responsive but not now. . . . Henry's eyes were always very sensitive to light, he had very thin lids and could never sleep in daylight, and I had installed white nylon curtains, very full ones, across the row of windows on the [southeast], behind the head of his bed. The sun came out brilliantly (for December) so I drew the curtains, which enveloped Henry's head in a lovely glow of soft white light; he looked radiant, the back light outlining his tonsure of white curls and the edges of his beard. His hand in Pepper's fur looked very frail.

The curtains drawn, I looked about for anything else I could do, and then noticed his respiration was very rapid and shallow; so I knew the end was very near. I sat down beside the bed and took his left hand in mine; Strawberry, the big red cat, pleased as ever to feel sure his family would stay put and provide a lap for a while, jumped up to purr on my knees, and went to sleep. Henry's breathing continued another 10 minutes, perhaps, before I could be quite sure it had stopped, which it did absolutely gently and unnoticeably, in that beautifully diffused sunny light. When I leaned forward to test the pulse at his temple, Strawberry was affronted and ran off. Perhaps feeling the family was too quiet, he proceeded to jump into the bathtub and chase his tail round and round in a bumpy rucktious kitten fashion most unsuitable to his age. This of course provided the comedy that always comes along with tragedy in the world. I was hardly surprised. I felt entirely quiet and happy that H. had left without the period of pain from the malignancy we all so much dreaded for him. I went into the kitchen to phone the doctor, who had to call back, and told me he was at least an hour away. I had already taken a shot of brandy between phone calls; he told me to take another. It's remarkably settling to the emotions. He said he would come as soon as he could, and that I should phone some friends to come stay with me. He had a shot of comedy en route, himself, for he was stopped for speeding and the officer said to his explanation that he was en route to a dying man, "Well all right; but that man had better die!"

Before phoning anybody I decided we would have a farewell of our own, as Henry emphatically wished no services. So I played his Fourth Symphony and sat beside him, the cats nearby again.

When the doctor came he found her euphoric—she "felt so triumphant at having won the race with the pain. Also relieved for myself I am sure, because I had reached several ends to my tether, on and off, and wasn't sure how many more I could count on." Henry had lived for almost ten years to the day from his doctor's first warning.

More than seven years had passed since that final December 10. "There remain to be told many funny or warming incidents of consolation gifts and messages but this is all I promised myself before I leave for Italy on Monday. So will have to do for now." She put down her pen.

61

Who Was Henry Cowell?

During his entire adult life and after his death, Henry's colleagues and friends overwhelmingly spoke of him in glowing terms—warm, generous, charming amusing, lovable, friendly, open-minded, insightful, devoid of greed and professional jealousy, impervious to criticism, a lover of social drinking, cooking, playing cards, a true lover of nature and avid "host" to the animals whose territory he and Sidney shared in Shady. Bess Lomax Hawes even remembered him as elegant in his tastes and dress.[1] Gerald Strang called him an extraordinary entrepreneur who found people to help him with his projects and turned them loose, in contrast to Varèse, who always kept total control over his associates.[2] John Cage crowned him the "open sesame for new music in America."[3] Dr. Joseph Wortis, his psychiatric consultant during parole, never heard him run down anyone, a quality that he found rare among the many artistic people he knew. Wortis was amazed by his strength, especially as he continued to compose while dying.[4]

Of course, such a wholly positive view is too good to be true. Indeed, a few contra-indications emerge from the mass of praise. Several people described him as messy, disorganized, so focused that he forgot the people around him. Gerald Strang also considered him inefficient in managing his projects, though in the same breath he said everyone could always count on an immediate response to a letter, suggesting at least efficiency of communication.[5] (Henry's business correspondence does not suggest negligent or careless management, but appearances can be deceiving.) A good friend in Woodstock praised his tolerance, adding that his tolerance ended when it came to music. (She does not say whether he was intolerant of particular styles or of lack of sufficient creative commitment.) His broadmindedness was too much for her on the occasion when Henry walked out of a meeting of the National Institute of Arts and Letters after it rejected Ezra Pound for membership. "Henry looked on him solely as a poet and had no interest in politics or whether this guy was a Jew-baiting Fascist traitor. My position was that such a person could not possibly be a good poet."[6] Charles Seeger said he never learned whether Henry had any deep emotions. "I have my serious doubts that he ever had a passionate love affair or was capable of it." Sidney, knew about the devastation wrought by the death of Edna Smith, and one of Henry's early male lovers remembered him precisely by his passionateness.[7] She thought Seeger was projecting; people had expressed the same doubts about Seeger himself.

Seeger also wondered if his guilelessness might have been a façade. "Henry had a marvelous sense of humor and could laugh off anything," but when he laughed at the abusiveness of music critics, Seeger couldn't tell if he was hurt or not. And he did not laugh off San Quentin. Seeger decided not to bring up the subject ever again after Henry told him that "he was building the wall that nobody could look over."[8] That "wall" explains a lot about the inability of Henry's friends to find flaws in him.

There is good reason to believe that he always had had a wall around him, though it must have been higher and more impregnable after he was imprisoned. It may explain why Hugo Weissgall thought Henry was the most isolated person he had ever met.[9] "Walls" would explain some of the peculiarities of the earlier years. He learned early not to complain, since he was aware of his mother's struggles, their poverty, and her illness. A "wall" may also account for the gap between the braveness that Evelyn Wells admired and the panic she detected beneath his surface. He joked about his highest degree being a third grade certificate until he got an honorary doctorate, but if he had any complaints that his unusual education gave him no qualifications for academic jobs, he generally kept them to himself and perhaps his family. His diplomatic treatment of Copland and Varèse can be seen as a normal act for someone who preferred not to stir up trouble. His apparent placidity in San Quentin was not simply fear of the complainer's fate, or refusal to be pitied, but another product of long years of refusing to succumb to his worries. In the last years he also tucked his medical problems behind his wall. His friend "Pete" (Mrs. James) Turnbull, who lived near the Cowells in the country, said that Henry mentioned his health problems only once, but unforgettably. "One evening he faced me with tears and announced that he would never be able to play the piano again." She tried telling him that this did not prevent him from composing and others could play his beautiful music, but "he was in a deep funk . . . and it wasn't too long after that he died."[10] His wall, however, was also marvelous isolation against distractions and suggests how he could compose amidst his hectic life.

Occasionally his competitive side emerged, in the way he relished Leginska praising him above Ornstein, and Ornstein praising him above Levitzki, and in his desire to outdo Cos Cob Press. Competitiveness and perhaps jealousy seems uncomfortably close to the surface in Henry's irritation at the Copland circle's pressure to make Copland the undisputed leader of American music; his rivalry with Paul Rosenfeld and Copland at The New School; or his decision to become

American representative of the Danish journal *Pro Musica* to prevent it from competing with *New Music Quarterly*.

An even less perfect Henry emerges in Sidney's recollections. When she was not trying to analyze him, she could only praise him as a wonderful man and a great companion. Although at one time she considered leaving him, she recognized and treasured the depth of their intellectual and emotional kinship. When she wrote about particularly problematic issues, however, the complexity of Henry's inner life emerged, colored by her early psychological training and magnified by the intensity of her memories. Despite possible distortions, her reflections are essential to any attempt to grasp who Henry was beneath his genial exterior.

After he died, Sidney finally wrote about her thoughts on the most intimate and controversial side of Henry's personality, his sexuality. She felt that the sex drive was not of much interest to him "except that he was convinced that its release was necessary to his health. He was always shy with girls or women, always impersonal and detached: they appealed to him, if at all, through their minds if they had any. Otherwise he often found them incredibly silly. This was of course a holdover from the attitude of his early teens. Several older friends thought he should meet girls and arranged this, and Henry was always agreeable about it, but never followed it up." When he needed sex, he looked for a sexual object, "but he always seemed to me incompletely involved with whichever sex—though of course I never was on sufficiently intimate terms with him to know about this before we married." She thought he probably agreed with his mother that the demands of sexual partners used up energy best saved for music.[11] Her description of him as "impersonal and detached" should be interpreted as referring to his sexuality, however, and his attraction to women with active minds hardly seems like a defect.

He might not have shown jealousy or intolerance to his colleagues, but he was very jealous of Sidney's old friends and had an "old-fashioned attitude" about her being alone with men. She would get "talked about," he fretted. Her annoyance is understandable, considering how his history provoked so much gossip when they got married.[12] Old-fashionedness seems completely at odds with his reputation as a California rebel, but may be one reason why the Iveses felt so comfortable with him and were so shocked by his arrest.

Henry's and Sidney's biggest conflicts arose from his tendency to exploit what she could contribute to his professional life. Nor was this new. Evelyn Wells's description of their youthful closeness suggests that they were a natural couple, but as much as she loved him, she told Sidney, "I knew I was lucky that we didn't live in the same town or I'd have had no life of my own, I was so useful to him."[13] Olive, too, felt (and allowed herself to be) exploited. Fortunately, everyone, including Sidney, attributed his exploitative nature not to egotism but to his dedication to music in all its meanings. Enlisting others to promote projects for the general advancement of American composers was difficult to criticize.

Rightly or wrongly, Sidney blamed Harry's defective fathering for many of Henry's peculiarities. "Henry had always a kind of obsession about doing generous things for a whole series of youngsters whom he mentioned frequently as 'fatherless boys'; this of course had to do with his own fatherlessness: Harry was 'no kind of a father' and Henry had no filial feeling for him; [Harry] had no paternal, warm protective feeling toward Henry at all, but only tried to drive him in the direction of the greatest applause and the greatest possible name-dropping position for him, Harry. So a 'fatherless boy' was a very personal thing to Henry."[14] She thought that he did some things that were not absolutely essential because he was constantly looking for applause from Harry. For some years, his relationship with Ives made up for Harry's failings, but even this was ruptured. She didn't think he wrote music for the public's approval. "If he wrote *music* for anybody but himself, it was for the performers & their approval."[15] Yet "he was curiously impervious to compliments: I think he valued them but he gave me the impression he did not really believe them to be true." She attributed that to his experience with Harry[16] but may not have realized the possible effects of being forced to defend his ideas, especially in the early days when the very legitimacy of his music was constantly questioned. She also noticed that Henry drew a sense of triumph from his lecture-performances, perhaps suggesting some hidden feeling of educational inferiority.

Another of his peculiarities was his attitude toward money and possessions. Although he was not greedy, his early poverty—Sidney thought—made him fearful that money would run out, whereas her childhood had taught her that something would always turn up.[17] He did not seem to her to understand the concept of rent, [18] but perhaps an inability to understand ownership is more to the point. He would give things away—his scores, someone else's record player—without much thought.

In short, Henry was a much more difficult man than his colleagues knew, because that high, durable wall succeeded in keeping his complexities and contradictions from the public eye. Yet what Sidney considered his biggest flaw—exploiting others—was also difficult for her to condemn completely. A man intensely motivated to leave something behind in exchange for the space he occupied in life, he might trample on some of those closest to him, but never with malice. Made of music, he put himself and everyone around him into its service.

Epilogue

Henry was cremated and his ashes were scattered in an unidentified place, without any ceremony. Sidney took a friend's advice not to attend. Olive, in Mexico, was contacted through the State Department.[1] For days, the Shady mailbox was bursting with letters of condolence.

Although Sidney had loved Henry, after twenty-four years of being Mrs. Cowell, almost half of which required her to be his caregiver, his last breath liberated her to fulfill the promise of her own talents. The world, however, bombarded her with requests having to do with him. Her annoyance permeates her 1967 response to "Curley" (Oxford University Press's Carroll Bowen, the editor of the Cowells' Ives book), one of several editors who had approached her about writing a biography of Henry.[2] Upon rereading her letter to Bowen, she was so struck by the ease with which her grumpiness could be misinterpreted that she extracted a promise not to use it in her lifetime.

She told him that in the year and a half since Henry died she had been practicing the piano for hours a day, "practicing hard, which I love to do, with no idea of making music except for myself. . . . Henry always objected to any music, any sound, in the house except his own, naturally enough, I suppose; but I've been surprised to find how much I missed it." The idea of writing a biography of him irritated her deeply. She had a lot of nice things to tell about him, but someone else could do it. After the war she had begun gathering material for a biography, but Henry diverted her to seven years of writing the Ives book. Then she spent more years sorting Henry's and Ives's papers, and was "bored to death with composers! . . . If after another 20 years I could be expected to be competent to write a book, why maybe!"

She said that other possible biographers either had no money or "they belong to *les boys* who couldn't be expected to resist the temptation to make a martyr of Henry. . . ." There would be a book, and she'd complain, or think she'd have done it better, but handling Henry's every demand for twenty-four years was enough. "After his death, my arthritis, migraine and ulcer all disappeared! and that is a 'sign' if I ever saw one, that all this preoccupation with Henry is not for me any longer. Nothing I now do is of the slightest importance except to me, and I find that a fine thing! He really exploited me till I was quite used up." Henry never could understand why she could not keep up with his demands. The reason, as Sidney was a little too modest to say outright, was probably that she fulfilled them so well that he found more for her to do. "So! people are the way they are, and Henry was a wonderful human being as well as a great figure in music— so I am convinced. But if this is true it will be clear without my hand at the helm of his posthumous reputation. This is not, I feel a role for wives. . . . This sounds as if I were protesting too much, but it's not that, I'm just arguing over again with all the people who have or have had plans for me and my energies and time."[3]

Her annoyance did not last. After Hugo Weisgall failed to produce a book, she intensified her labors, drafting her "memoir of Henry" up to his first trip to Europe. She was much too close to the subject, however, having been not only Henry's wife but also a product of the same California in which he grew up. As she surrendered to the compulsion to include more and more detail, she began to doubt her own accuracy. Ultimately she failed to go further, and what she wrote is barely usable. In the process, however, she commissioned invaluable interviews with many of Henry's aging friends and colleagues. She also did the hoped-for biographer the questionable favor of writing depositions and dictating tapes about every imaginable aspect of his life and career, which she then edited, causing incredible confusion, redundancy, and self-contradiction. As Henry's name and music gradually fell out of the repertory, she became even more driven to secure his place in history, which seemed irrevocably stained by his imprisonment. Rather than hide that terrible chapter, she wanted it balanced by the story of a man whose greatness she believed in, despite the demands he made upon her.

To Sidney, his music was the most important part of that legacy, and that is as it should be. In trying to show his significance, however, she became obsessed with demonstrating the multifariousness of his influence. On dozens of small pieces of paper she wrote the name of every composer who seemed to use his techniques. The obvious cases are clear: Cage and Harrison attributed much of their development to him; Bartók and Berg are supposed to have asked his permission to use clusters, but never used the peculiarly Cowellian techniques. Morton Gould, as a boy, applied Henry's clusters to his own pieces.[4]

George Crumb's music illustrates the elusiveness of Sidney's quest. The influence of Henry's stringpiano seems obvious, but Crumb said that by around 1962, when he began writing in his now-famous style, he had never heard any music by Cowell (or Cage), and only years later learned that there had been some recordings, which had not circulated to Colorado, his home at the time. Furthermore, he said, the scores themselves reveal the sound of the Cowell world only to those who have heard it before. Everything people knew was by word of mouth. Cowell's indirect influence was definitely important to him, he added.[5] In short, one can only guess who was inspired directly by Henry's music and who drew upon what was in the air.

Doubtless much of what was and still is in the air is the direct or indirect result of Henry's work. The list of the seeds he planted is very long indeed. He was one of the first composers, along with Varèse, to explore sounds that transcended the twelve-pitch Western chromatic scale, making "noise" a valid element of music. *New Musical Resources'* call to use pure overtones as the basis for music had a bearing on the work of Harry Partch (who read the book with great interest) and anticipated by some three-quarters of a century the ideas of spectral composers (who almost certainly did not know of it). Henry's example stimulated composers to explore unconventional performance techniques. His Elastic Form antedated the open structures that permeated the music of many postwar New York and European avant-gardists and undermined the old philosophy that a composer should always dictate the final shape of a piece. (He wanted musicians to have some fun making a piece their own.) His attitude that composers should invent their own systems of composition helped shape Cage and Harrison, and is now characteristic of many composers. As one of the first to combine non-Western instruments, using their own characteristic languages, with Western instruments and compositional techniques, Henry showed the vast potential of cultural hybridizing, which he promulgated through composing, teaching, and writing. His idea that music and dance should develop simultaneously had a brief but powerful effect on Martha Graham, and started Cage and Merce Cunningham on the road to making pieces in which the music and dance had no relationship at all. The effect of the boundless ideas in *New Musical Resources* is difficult to measure, but Conlon Nancarrow was one composer who attributed to that book his most important idea—using the player-piano to bring to life unperformable rhythm-pitch combinations.[6] Henry's efforts to upgrade the repertory for wind band helped bring a marginal medium into the mainstream. If it seems like a lot for one life to accomplish, one must bear in mind that Henry often hatched ideas, worked with them until he felt satisfied, and turned them loose for others to exploit.

All this is true whatever one concludes about the quality of Henry's music. Most readers will not even be able to begin to judge it because only a tiny fraction of his nearly 1,000 pieces is known. His orchestral music was performed and broadcast so frequently that, long after Henry's death, Sidney could still live on the royalties, but once the original conductors died or retired, it largely disappeared from concert programs. The same is true of his vocal and choral music and most of his chamber music, so that the general repertory was left without much more than a few percussion ensemble pieces and some of the early solo piano pieces. That process alone left the public with a one-sided view of a remarkably multifaceted composer. The timing was wrong: the *Hymns and Fuguing Tunes* and symphonies, which speak so beautifully to the general audience, were born just when opinion makers rejected simplicity and guilelessness. In that context, Lukas Foss's commission of a new piece for his predominantly avant-garde concert series in Buffalo was a tribute from one multisided composer to his role model. The unusual early piano pieces, which remain exciting nearly a century later, have become curiosities of twentieth-century history. Gradually, however, more of his music is reclaiming its place as old ideologies fade. Festivals of his music now are more than occasional events; knowledgeable musicians hearing works like the *Madras* Symphony or the Harmonica Concerto, are amazed that he wrote such music. The biggest surprise, as Henry Cowell's music and ideas become better known, is that his dedication to world music constituted far more of his creative life than his more celebrated ultramodernism. Yet it is equally true that his insistent exploration of new ideas, his refusal to create a single compositional persona, had their liabilities. Such multisided minds also can sometimes produce music that does not seem fully ripened.

Perhaps the most extensive and least tangible product of Henry's life is the vast world of American composition. Schoenberg once said that if he had not been Schoenberg, someone else would have to have been. The same is true of Henry Cowell. Even when he was still the consummate ultramodernist, he helped any American composer who pursued a personal vision, no matter what the style, as long as he detected quality and commitment. In that way, he helped define American music as an art with many streams, of which "Americanism" was only one. The composers published in *New Music* or featured in *American Composers on American Music*, such as Ives, Ruggles, and Ruth Crawford Seeger, might have gone unnoticed for years if not for Henry's faith in them. By persuading the nearly-defeated Ives to let him publish his music, by inducing performers to play it, and by producing—thanks largely to Sidney— the first biography of him, he performed a rescue operation whose consequences, one hopes, will be felt far into the future. Bringing Ruth Crawford and Henry Brant to New York helped save them from an unstimulating obscurity.[7] His friendship with Lou Harrison and John Cage helped fortify their visions at a crucial moment in their development. Of course, not all the composers whom Henry respected could fulfill their early promise, but, as *American Composers on American Music* demonstrated, Henry had a good sense of those who had great potential.[8]

His influence as an educator is literally immeasurable because so few of his students have spoken about him. Of the young composers and other musicians at Peabody, Columbia, Eastman, and The New School; the innumerable amateurs at The New School and Columbia; the children at Adelphi College; the dancers in California; and the thousands of prisoners at San Quentin to whose lives Henry's classes brought a bit of humanity, one may guess that it is the last group upon which Henry's influence was most powerful.

Although he is not remembered as an ethnomusicologist, he was the first person to bring world music to a broad public through lecturing, writing, broadcasting, and recording. He probably helped overcome resistance to ethnomusicology at Columbia, though he had failed to embed it in the New York Musicological Society. He left his mark in India through the drumming prize, which is still being awarded half a century later. Above all, he helped make transethnicity a central feature of American experimental music.[9]

In pondering how to draw Henry Cowell's story to a close, I was reminded of a question posed by the biographer Carol Oja. After getting to know Henry Cowell so intimately, did I still like him? Most definitely. Whatever his dysfunctions, whatever discomforts he caused Sidney, his honesty, dedication, generosity, and above all his infinite love of music merit only the highest admiration. Even Sidney admitted that he did not turn her and others into his "slaves" for personal gain but to help him develop his and his colleagues' talents. He suffered greatly but refused to be pitied. He thought of himself as a man made of music, but he was also a man made of ideas and action. Full of fun, and a lover of life, he intended to get the most out of it and bring the most to it. His finest gift was his music at its best.

Sidney's immense sacrifices for and devotion to Henry earned her the last word. Explaining to Charles Seeger why the melody Henry wrote for him, his last composition, has no final bar-line, she said,[10] "It is as complete as Henry intended it. He liked always to leave room for more, so that he often failed to put a double bar at the end of a piece. Of course, he knew that he was, or had been, very ill; but with life as with music, I do not think he really expected the end of anything."

NOTES

All materials are in the Henry Cowell papers, New York Public Library for the Performing Arts JPB 00-03, unless otherwise specified.

Abbreviations

BW	Blanche Walton
CEI	Charles Ives
Clarissa Materials	Clarissa Cowell, "Material for a Biography," Cowell papers. Published in *American Music* (Spring 2009): 1–59. Pagination in this book refers to the original.
CUOHROC	Reminiscences of Henry Cowell, October 16 and December 17, 1962, in the Columbia University Oral History Research Office Collection
EV	Ellen Veblen
Harry	Harry Cowell
HC	Henry Cowell
H&O	Harry and Olive Thompson Cowell
JdA	Jaime de Angulo
JOV	John O. Varian
JS	Joel Sachs
NS	Nicholas Slonimsky
NYPLFPA	New York Public Library for the Performing Arts
Olive	Olive Thompson Cowell
PG	Percy Grainger
RF	Rockefeller Foundation
RV	Russell Varian
SR	Sidney Robertson, later Sidney Robertson Cowell
SRC	Sidney Robertson Cowell, Sidney Cowell
SRC, Memoir	A memoir of HC, drafted by SRC, in the possession of JS
Walling Papers	Anna Strunsky Walling, largely unpaginated essay about Henry Cowell written for 1962 Cowell jubilee. Anna Strunsky Walling papers, Yale University Library, Department of Manuscripts and Special Archives

Chapter 1

1. SRC, Memoir, I, 1.
2. Clarence erroneously calls her father Stephen.
3. HC to Douglas Williams, 1/11/63.
4. Hicks, *Bohemian*, 13.
5. SRC learned the name Eddyville; SRC to Paul Averich, 6/29/79.
6. SRC to Clarence Weaver, 11/30/74.
7. SRC, Memoir I,7; SRC to Paul Averich, 6/29/79.
8. HC to Harry and Olive, 12/20/53: Clarence died in 1953, aged eighty-two.
9. HC told Olive, 5/21/35.
10. See Evelyn Wells, *Champagne Days of San Francisco*, passim.
11. Hicks, *Bohemian*, chapter 1.
12. Paul Avrich to SRC, 6/11/79.
13. *Liberty*, 9/3/1892, 2–4.
14. *Irish and Anglo Irish Pedigrees*, 616–29, Addenda, No. 243.
15. Hicks, *Bohemian*, 11.
16. Clarissa Materials; additional information assembled by SRC and Olive.
17. Hicks, *Bohemian*, 10–11. Hicks's other reasons for his departure do not seem correct.
18. Olive, "My life with [the] Cowells." Undated. Olive Cowell papers, NYPLFPA JPG 99–3; Olive, biographical outline of Harry's life.
19. SRC, Memoir I, 19.
20. HC interviewed by Beate Gordon, 10/16/62, CUOHROC, 1.
21. Clarence Weaver, "About Henry Cowell and the Temple at Halcyon." Transcript of tape dictated December 1974.
22. Hicks, *Bohemian*, 15.
23. HC interviewed by Beate Gordon, 10/16/62.
24. SRC to C. Robert Payne, 8/26/82.
25. SRC, Memoir I, 3.
26. Transcript of tape by Clarence Weaver, 1976.
27. See Preface concerning currency values.
28. Loan documents.
29. Hicks, *Bohemian*, passim.

Chapter 2

1. Clarissa Materials.
2. Ibid.
3. SRC, Memoir II, 14.
4. Walling papers, unnumbered page.
5. SRC, Memoir, II, 3.
6. Walling papers, 4–5.
7. SRC, Memoir II, 6.
8. SRC, Memoir II, 7.
9. SRC, Statements and Narratives, 10/63, pencil, on sheets from a spiral notebook.
10. Walling papers, unnumbered page.
11. Harry to HC, 01/09/01–3/13/01.
12. Walling papers, 3.
13. Ibid., unnumbered; Hicks, *Bohemian*, 19.
14. HC interviewed by Beate Gordon, 12/17/62. CUOHROC, 67.
15. SRC, Statements and Narratives, 10/1963, pencil, on sheets from a spiral notebook.
16. SRC to Evelyn Wells, 7/18/75.
17. Harry to HC, 5/23/06.
18. Walling papers: correspondence with Harry and Olive.
19. SRC, Statements and Narratives,10/63. The date Henry gives cannot be right; Clarissa and Harry were already divorced.
20. SRC, Memoir, II, 9.
21. SRC, information about the divorce. The decree is lost.
22. Jennie Dixon to SRC, 8/7/05.
23. Ibid.
24. Mary Dixon Clark to Clarissa, 12/22/04.
25. Frank L. Beach, "The Transformation of California," 1–5.
26. Unidentified article from a local newspaper about the Joulies' piano.
27. Mrs. Charles Harkins to SRC, 3/11/1997.
28. Clarissa Cowell, "The Free School System," *American Journal of Politics*, 10/1893.
29. SRC, Memoir II, 17.
30. Ibid., verified in Walling papers, unnumbered page.
31. Ibid.
32. HC, "How and Why I Compose," an address to the annual Conference of the

National Committee on Art Education, 5/6/60, at the Museum of Modern Art. This, a reprint of a 1953 interview, is HC's most comprehensive account of these years.

33. Mrs. Henry Holmes to Clarissa, 11/11/03; Henry Holmes to Clarissa, 11/15/03.

34. SRC, Memoir, II, 15.

35. SRC, Memoir II, 14.

36. Hicks, *Bohemian*, 17.

37. SRC, Statements and Narratives, 10/63.

38. SRC, Memoir, II, 11–12.

39. HC, "How and Why I Compose."

40. Ibid.

41. Lewis Terman, notes on a dinner with HC, 3/1/17. See Chapter 6.

42. Beach, "The Transformation of California," 178–79.

43. SRC Memoir, II, 21; III, 1–11.

Chapter 3

1. Various letters between HC and Harry.

2. Harry to HC, 6/20/06.

3. SRC, Memoir III, 1, 4–5.

4. SRC, Memoir III, 4.

5. SRC, Memoir III, 6.

6. HC to Harry, undated.

7. SRC, Memoir III 9, and Clarissa Materials: 82.

8. In his discussion of Henry's education, Terman refers to the attack of chorea taking place four years earlier than in Clarissa's account, though it is conceivable that the attack in the Midwest was not the first. SRC (Memoir, III, 8) thought it damaged his heart permanently.

9. Evelyn Wells, statements to SRC, ca. 1970–71.

10. SRC, Memoir III, 7.

11. Clarissa Materials, 99.

12. Harry to HC, 12/24/07.

13. Clarissa Materials, 85.

14. Harry to Clarissa, 6/13/08.

15. Harry to Clarissa, 4/12/08.

16. Harry to Clarissa, 8/21/08.

17. SRC, Memoir, III, 12.

18. HC interviewed by Beate Gordon, 12/17/62. CUOHROC, 63.

19. Clara to Harry, transcript, undated, with 1907 suggested. More likely date: September, 1908.

20. HC, "The Process of Musical Creation," offprint from the *American Journal of Psychology* 37 (4/26): 233–36.

21. SRC, Memoir III, 16.

22. HC to Harry, 10/11/07. Misdated by HC; it should be 1908.

23. *Who's Who* to Clarissa, 08/25/09.

24. HC to Harry, 5/5/09.

25. Evelyn Wells, "Re Henry": Wells learned it from Ellen Veblen.

26. Sidney thought Henry must have known all these details because of Clarissa's unwillingness to conceal anything from him. SRC, corrections to Oliver Daniel's 1974 *Stereo Review* article.

27. HC to Harry 8/8/09.

28. SRC, Memoir, III, 24–25.

29. HC to Harry, 7/25/10.

30. HC to Clarissa, 10/13/10.

Chapter 4

1. See Chapter 1.

2. 1965 account assembled by Sidney, largely dictated by HC and filled out with documents from the family papers.

3. Clarissa Materials, 102.

4. SRC, Memoir, IV, 5.

5. Jean Seward Uppman, conversation with JS, 1995.

6. HC to Harry, 7/23/11.

7. HC to Harry, 7/29/11.

8 Described by Mrs. Kiefer, in Mrs. Charles Hackins to SRC, 3/11/97.

9. HC to Harry 1/28/12, 4/8/12.

10. HC, "A Conservative Interprets the Modern," *Saturday Review* 26/5 1/30/43; Hicks, "Cowell's Clusters."

11. Thanks to Michelle Gott for information about Blind Tom.

12. Tape made by Jean Seward Uppman, early 1960s.

13. HC to Harry, 7/16/12.

14. Transcript of taped deposition by Clarence Weaver, 1976. Information about Davidson from D. Varian, *Inventor*, 35.

15. Hicks seems wrong in saying that the cluster came from "milkmaid's grip."

16. Terman sent the information in 1942 at SRC's request.

17. Terman, *Intelligence*, 250.

18. "Bio Bits 1970s." Because anti-Irish sentiment was weaker in California than in the Northeast, Sidney correctly inferred that they were New Englanders.

19. Punctuation and orthographical errors are HC's.

20. Information about Henry Cowell from writings by Laurie MacDougall, www.santacruzpl.org/history/people/cowell; and www.parks.ca.gov [7/25/07].

21. Labeled by Terman *"What I think about Socialism* Henry, 2/22/12." It is less an essay than Terman's transcript of, or notes on, Henry's remarks.

22. Frederick Emmons Terman to SRC, 5/21/76. Terman, 1900–1982, an electronics engineer, was head of the Department of Electrical Engineering and later Provost of Stanford.

23. SRC, Memoir VII, 13; HC interviewed by Beate Gordon, 12/17/62. CUOHROC, 78.

24. HC to Harry 1/28/12, 4/8/12.

25. Terman, *Intelligence*, 249.

26. SRC, Memoir, IV, 16.

27. HC to Harry, 5/11/12, 7/8/12.

28. At SRC's request, Edith Partridge Harkins told her story to Mrs. Kiefer in 1977.

29. See Chapter 2.

30. SRC, Memoir IV, 16.

31. Clarissa Materials, 106–7.

32. SRC, Memoir V, 11.

33. "The Joulie Piano." It was a Jacob Zech grand square rosewood piano with two pedals, built in San Francisco around 1860 and purchased by the Joulies around the turn of the century.

34. Clarissa Materials: 106–7. HC's 1965 account to SRC adds to the confusion, perhaps because he was then extremely ill. He placed the purchase a year earlier,

spending $60 and getting piano lessons from a Mrs. Boyland in exchange for gardening.

Chapter 5

1. Duffus, *Innocents*, 143 ff.

2. Evelyn Wells, statements about her friendship with HC.

3. Clarissa Materials, 102.

4. SRC, Memoir, V, 4.

5. Clarissa Materials, 109.

6. *Caramel Pine Cone*, 16/35, 8/29/30.

7. Clarissa Materials, 111.

8. SRC, Memoir, VII, 7; Clarissa to Henry, undated, from this period. Re: TB, SRC's commentary written on Evelyn Wells's letters.

9. SRC, Memoir, V, 8.

10. Information about John Varian is drawn from Dorothy Varian, *The Inventor and the Pilot (Russell and Sigurd Varian)*.

11. Photocopy from unspecified journal, probably the *Temple Artisan*. Marked 4/1904.

12. Russell, 1898–1959; Sigurd, 1901–1961. The story of the bikes has been attributed to Henry, in a somewhat tangled correspondence between SRC, Dorothy Varian—Russell's widow—and Anne Hadden, the librarian of Palo Alto, in 1976.

13. Probably Lichtenwanger No. 24.

14. Frederick Whitney, "How the Poet and the Composer Met." *The Troubadour*, 3/8, July 1931. (John Varian memorial issue.)

15. Clarence Weaver, transcript of taped recollections, 1974.

16. SRC, Memoir IV, 12.

17. See also Wells, *Champagne Days*.

18. Biographical information from Gui de Angulo, *The Old Coyote of Big Sur*.

19. SRC, Memoir VI, 6.

20. Gui must have been relaying Jaime's or Cary's words, since she had not yet been born at the time.

21. Gui de Angulo, *Big Sur and the Oranges of Hieronymus Bosch*. [no location]: New Directions, 1957, 347 ff.

22. Clarissa Materials, 108.

23. The location was pinpointed by Sidney in a letter to Robert Sherman, 6/4/72; copy in JS possession. Thanks to Robert Sherman. Some letters refer to Henry's property as being in Santa Lucia, which is farther south.

24. JdA to HC, 6/6/14.

25. JdA to HC, 2/15/13.

26. JdA to HC, 12/4/13.

27. JdA to HC, 2/20/14.

28. JdA to HC, 9/5/13, 9/29/13.

29. JdA to HC, 12/4/13.

30. JdA to HC, 7/2/14.

31. "Pacific Musical Society's Anniversary." *Pacific Coast Musical Review*, 21/23 (9/3/12): 5.

32. SRC, Memoir VII, 1.

33. Clarissa Materials, 111.

34. JdA to HC, 6/1/14.

35. Olive's commentary, from small loose-leaf sheets. "En route to Carmel, May 1932." On Judy Brown, SRC, Memoir VII, 3. SRC to Olive, 3/18/66.

36. Copy of letter from HC to "'Peter,'" i.e., Amy Seward, 09/18/32. She was the widow of Samuel Seward, who died of an embolism following a minor operation. HC was in Berlin, writing from Schmolke's. Jean Seward Uppman, their daughter, told me in 1995 that her father never had much money.

37. At the time of Seward's death in 1932, Sidney had a job at the home of Seward's brother in Pebble Beach, Carmel district. (SRC, statement beginning "Surviving written records.")

38. Ibid. confirms Jean Uppman's comment that there is virtually no correspondence left. Mrs. Uppman said that the only papers that remained from her father were the Hoover years correspondence. (Conversation with JS, 6/8/98.)

39. SRC, Memoir VII, 2–3, apparently based on conversations with Amy Seward.

40. Lewis M. Terman to S.S. Seward Jr., 1/10/[14].

41. Seward, report about HC's progress and the fund, 10/14.

42. Cary de Angulo, Menlo Park, to Clarissa, 1/16/14.

43. Elizabeth E. Bates, to SRC, 5/8/66.

44. Julius Rehn Weber, Berkeley, to S.S. Seward Jr, 3/1/14.

45. Ana Cora Winchell, unidentified SF paper, possibly *SF Chronicle*, based on type style. Marked [by SRC?] 1913 or 1914. A photostat is marked 3/6/14.

46. Redfern Mason, "Work of Merit at Concert of Local Society," San Francisco *Examiner*. A photostat has clipped to it the date 3/14.

47. Evelyn Wells, "Re: Henry Cowell," 3/14/67.

48. Seward report, 10/14.

49. SRC, Memoir VII, 17.

50. HC to Clarissa, 8/10/14. HC interviewed by Beate Gordon, 12/17/62. CUOHROC, 68.

51. HC to Clarissa, 8/10/14.

52. SRC, Memoir VI, 12.

53. Mrs. Mary Elizabeth Lloyd to HC, 9/18/40 enclosing obituary of "Mother" Carrie L. Carrington from Monterey newspaper, name incomplete. On the payment, Mother Carrington to HC, undated, just before Weisshaus played in California.

54. SRC, Memoir VI, 13–14, 16.

55. HC interviewed by Beate Gordon, 12/17/62. CUOHROC, 61.

56. HC and/or SRC, "Lessons with the Boston Symphony." Typescript.

57. Business card, "Mr. Henry Cowell. Piano—Voice—Harmony. Menlo Park." A reference, in letter of 12/24/15. On the pay: SRC, Memoir VII, 8.

58. Undated program, "Recital given by the pupils of Mrs. Henriette Cowell. Accompanist Mr. Frederick Maurer Jr."

59. Christabel Elliott to Clarissa, 04/06/15.

60. Ibid.

61. SRC, Statements and Narratives, 10/1963.

62. SRC, Memoir VII, 4.

63. See Tick, *Ruth Crawford Seeger*, passim., on Charles Seeger's psychological problems.

64. The following is based on Seeger's "Henry Cowell," *Magazine of Art*, May 1940; Seeger interviewed by Andrea Olmstead, 7/7/77; and statement by Seeger to Board of Prison Terms and Paroles, 5/4/36.

65. HC: "What Should Composers Study," *Peabody Notes*, fall, 1952.

66. Seeger, statement to Board of Prison Terms and Paroles 5/4/36. This is not confirmed anywhere else.

67. Born 1880, according to University of California Berkeley Web site http://texts.cdlib.org.

68. Dorothea Jensen to Lewis Terman, 12/9/26.

69. Seeger, statement to Board of Prison Terms and Paroles, 5/4/36.

70. Dorothea Jensen to Lewis Terman, 12/9/26.

71. Seeger, *Studies in Musicology*, II, 3.

72. Obituary of Walter Spalding, with note by SRC. Spalding later taught Douglas Moore and Virgil Thomson at Harvard.

73. Seeger, *Studies in Musicology*, II, 9, 19ff.

74. Charles Seeger interviewed by Rita Mead, 11/17/74.

75. Charles Seeger interviewed by Andrea Olmstead, 7/7/77.

76. Tick, *Ruth Crawford Seeger*, 115, says it was over his opposition to the war, and that he returned to New York in 1918.

Chapter 6

1. Evelyn Wells, "Re: Henry Cowell," 3/14/67.

2. Legal documents, 9/29/37, concerning Clarissa's will and its settlement.

3. Biographical material assembled by SRC in conversations with HC, dated 5/65.

4. SRC, Memoir VIII, 1–2. She would have learned this from Henry and Evelyn; she did not know Henry's mother.

5. SRC, Memoir VIII, 3–4.

6. Dorothy Varian, *Inventor*, 48 ff.

7. George Harrison interviewed by Dorothy Varian, 6/26/62. Although Harrison's memory was very faulty, his estimate of the high number of intelligent parents and children at Halcyon seems accurate.

8. See D. Varian, *Inventor*, 35.

9. Steven Johnson, "HC and Halcyon."

10. Copy of pages from the *Temple Artisan*, 87–91; no year given, 1916 or early 1917 from context.

11. RV to "Florence" from Halcyon. On it a note in pen, "Coast trail trip Rus Sig Henry Cowell Mr Wolf." Stanford, Green Library Special Collections. Russell Varian papers.

12. EV to Ellen Wells, 10/2/16.

13. HC to Harry, 10/15/16.

14. HC to EV, 10/17/16.

15. Seward Jr. to HC, 10/14/16.

16. HC to EV, 10/17/16.

17. Application dated 9/12/16. Halcyon archive.

18. HC to EV, 10/20/16.

19. Brochure, "About the Temple of the People," 1990s.

20. Pamphlet, "Musical Principles of the Work of the Builders." Undated.

21. Duffus, *Innocents*, 143.

22. Clarence Weaver, "About Henry Cowell and the Temple at Halcyon." Transcript of tape dictated December 1974.

23. See D. Varian, *Inventor*, 54.

24. JOV to HC, 10/26/16 (postmark date). Original in Stanford, Green Library Special Collections.

25. Harvard 1895. Thanks to Mary Saunders, Harvard Club of New York.

26. Letters folder 393. HC to EV, 10/27/16 (postmark date). He enclosed an eleven-bar melody for her.

27. Susan Dakin to HC, 10/31/16; Sigismund Stojowski to HC, 11/2/16.

28. Susan Dakin to HC, 10/31/16, 11/8/16.

29. EV to HC, 10/23/16.

30. HC to EV, postmark date 11/7/16. Evelyn Wells to SRC, 3/24/79: "You can see we were a closely knit trio in those days and H did nothing but encourage us both. *He was always kind.*"

31. Seeger to HC, 11/4/16.

32. EV to Evelyn Wells, 11/9/16.

33. The absence of references to Lola in later correspondence suggests that she either moved away or died. Halcyon's Guardian

34. was unable to identify the girls (email, Eleanor Shumway to JS, 9/12/11).

34. Agnes and Lola Liberty to HC, 11/5/16.

35. HC to EV, 11/18/16.

36. HC to EV, 11/18/16.

37. HC to EV, 11/22/16. Michael Hicks, *Bohemian*, 75, does not indicate why he thought this statement refers to the rich students, or on what basis he determined that the Institute's students were rich.

38. Note at the Juilliard School Archive. Thanks to Laura Drake and Jennifer Dahmer, archivists. HC (recollections, about 1945, to SRC) later said that the chorale trick was played on Maidley Richardson. The incident took place early in 1916–17. He erroneously says it took place after the army.

39. George Martin, *The Damrosch Dynasty*, 228–29.

40. Blank beige folder, Terman, "Notes on Henry. March 1, 1917."

41. Damrosch to HC, 2/4/21.

42. Maxwell Anderson to HC, 1/27/17.

43. Seeger to HC, 12/16/16. Seeger mistakenly thought he had not been in the East in 1916.

44. Agnes Liberty to HC, 1/9/17.

45. HC to EV, 11/22/16.

46. HC to EV, 11/18/16.

47. Terman, "Notes on Henry. March 1, 1917."

48. Ornstein to HC, 2/13/17.

49. Victor Wittgenstein, letter of introduction to Ornstein, 11/18/16.

50. Elizabeth Moss to HC, 9/27/17, may refer to a proposed meeting with Ornstein in California. There is no evidence of whether it took place.

51. SRC, "Leo Ornstein, HC and Tone Clusters," 12/17/87. Sidney thought that the San Jose concert took place before he went to New York, though it is possible that HC had been taken by Terman to hear him before leaving for New York. There is no evidence that they met before the concert in late 1917.

52. SRC, Memoir VIII, 24–25. SRC incorrectly refers to Edna as "adolescent."

53. *Daily Palo Alto Times*, 9/2/12.

54. SRC, typescript relating her history with HC: SRC Memoir IX, 1–2.

55. Lewis M. Terman, "Notes on Henry. March 1, 1917." Copy of holograph.

56. Ibid.

57. Ibid.

58. San Francisco *Examiner*, dated, probably incorrectly, in pencil 3/25.

59. SRC, Memoir VIII, 9.

60. See Lichtenwanger for a full discussion.

61. *Temple Artisan*, 8/17/17, 214–19.

62. SRC, Memoir VIII, 13.

63. Clarence Weaver, transcript of tapes made in in 1974 and 1976. Weaver was at Stanford 1917–25. Henry dated "Exultation" 1921.

64. Anna Snyder to HC, 11/21/17.

Chapter 7

1. Their brother Eric was too young, had other interests, and does not figure in the story at all; nothing is known of Franklin Wolff's interest in music.

2. D. Varian, *Inventor*, 41–45.

3. Ibid., 56.

4. Russell's letters are marked "October? 1916," probably by SRC; The surviving document is a retyped version by SRC who noted that the original is in pencil.

5. HC to RV, 12/11/16.

6. RV to HC, 12/18/16, with *The Electrical Experimenter*, December 1916, 561–62.

7. D. Varian, *Inventor*, 57.

8. HC, "Melody, Harmony and Counterpoint"—Miscellaneous holograph sheets with ideas, paragraphs, charts, etc. of the concepts that went, on the whole, into *New Musical Resources*.

9. SRC, Memoir VIII, 17.

10. See introduction to C. F. Peters publication of Quartets *Romantic* and *Euphometric*.

11. Further, see Bruce Saylor, "The Tempering of Henry Cowell's 'Dissonant Counterpoint.'"

12. SRC, Memoir IX, 13.

13. SRC, Memoir VIII, 18–20.

Chapter 8

1. Unnamed paper, undated clipping, "Local Musician to Enter Service."

2. See Hicks, *Bohemian*, chapter 4.

3. SRC, Memoir, IX, 17.

4. Discharge certificate. The comment about volunteering for the medical corps is related in Olive, "Henry's experiences in the army," 7/4/32.

5. Evelyn Wells, to SRC postmarked 3/14/67; Evelyn Wells to SRC, 10/28/83.

6. Henry's recollections, about those times, told to SRC shortly before his death. Folder "US Army," notes by SRC, undated, on note paper of "The Hanover Inn & Motor Lodge," ca. May 1965.

7. HC to Harry, 3/12/18, 3/19/18.

8. SRC, Memoir IX, 18.

9. Based on information provided by Jean Seward Uppman, conversations with JS, 1995.

10. Ibid.

11. On Camp Crane, www.defrance.org/articles/Camp_Crane.htm, from Ann Wlazelek, "Army's Camp Crane Remembered at Fairgrounds." She cites as her source Wendall Phillips, a former commander. More detail on this in Hicks, *Bohemian*.

12. Told to Olive by HC, and Olive, "Henry's Experiences in the Army," 7/4/32.

13. Charles Seeger interviewed by Andrea Olmstead, 7/7/77.

14. Hicks, *Bohemian*, 93.

15. See Ziffrin, *Ruggles*, 54–55.

16. HC to Harry, undated, spring 1918. HC turns up in Ruggles correspondence for the first time on March 15. See Ziffrin, *Ruggles*, 55, 57.

17. Folder "US Army," discharge certificate.

18. From Sidney's transcription of HC's oral memoirs; HC to Harry 6/17/18, 7/2/18.

19. SRC, Memoir IX, 18.

20. Olive notes on conversations with HC, ca. 1932?

21. Folder "Misc 1940–49," Theodore G. Otto to HC, 3/19/41.

22. HC to Harry 6/17/18, 7/2/18.

23. "Camp Crane Boys at the Grand Now," from newspaper in either Allentown or Wilkes-Barre.

24. Evelyn Wells, "Re Henry Cowell," ca. 1967.

25. According to Olive's notes on conversations with HC.

26. HC to EV, undated.

27. HC to EV, 1/6/19 (dated, apparently, from postmark). Stanford, Green Library, Special Collections, Varian papers.

28. SRC's transcription of HC's recollections, ca. 1965. She added in the margin: On visits to NYC during short leaves from Allentown HC heard concerts and met Ruggles.

29. HC to Harry, undated.

30. HC to EV, 2/2/19. She was sending him $19.50 a month for the rent of his piano, but he told her not to send it now; there was nothing on which to spend it.

31. Folder "US Army": HC to Harry from Fort Ontario, undated.

32. HC to EV, 2/2/19.

33. Seeger to Newton D. Maker, Secretary of War, Washington, DC.

34. EV to HC, 2/27/19.

35. HC to Harry, 4/2/19.

36. The discharge certificate was signed at Fort Ontario three days later and authorized 5/16/19.

37. JOV to HC, undated. Stanford, Green Library Special Collections.

Chapter 9

1. David Nicholls, in his excellent preface to the reissue of Cowell's *New Musical Resources*, shows that the final version contains most of the material of a draft probably completed in 1919. Some material was added in 1929.

2. Lichtenwanger, 50.

3. Date on the Cowell papers copy: 6/19/19, in pencil; could not be verified. Lichtenwanger, #213/1, accepted it as legitimate.

4. HC interviewed by Beate Gordon, 12/17/62.

5. HC, "Statements and Narratives," with footnote by SRC. Carbon of a typescript by HC. Undated.

6. HC to EV, 10/12/19.

7. Told to Harry and EV, 12/4/19.

8. HC to EV, 10/27/19, 10/31/19.

9. HC to Harry, 11/16/19.

10. HC to EV, 11/16/19, 11/21/19.

11. HC to EV, 10/20/19.

12. HC to EV, 11/16/19, 11/21/19.

13. HC to EV, 11/16/19.

14. HC to Harry 11/19/19. Bartlett's sunniness is apparent in his reports to the reunion books of his Harvard Class of 1895.

15. Lichtenwanger; completed 12/1919.

16. HC to Harry, 11/19/18 and HC to EV 11/21/19.

17. HC to Harry, undated.

18. HC to EV 11/27/19.

19. Announced in the program of 11/29/19.

20. Stanford, Green Library Special Collections. Russell Varian papers. Box 7, Folder 2, passim.

21. HC to EV, 1/4/20.

22. HC to EV, 1/13/20.

23. HC to EV, 1/13/20.

24. From a flyer produced by Knopf for *New Musical Resources*; the copy is marked January 1930. The school was a descendant of the Metropolitan Conservatory (founded 1886) that became the Metropolitan College of Music in 1891, the American Institute of Applied Music in 1900, and failed around 1940.

25. Folder "N." HC to "Dr. Eddy," 2/25/48. Woodman had been head of the Metropolitan Conservatory's organ department from 1989 to 1898; possibly he still had an affiliation in the 1920s. Verified in HC's Guggenheim application; see chapter 18.

26. HC interviewed by Beate Gordon, 12/17/62. CUOHROC, 78.

27. HC to EV, 2/28/20.

28. Woodman to HC, 3/1/20; HC to EV, 3/2/20.

29. HC to EV, 2/28/20.

30. Clarence Davidson to HC, ca. 2/28/20.

31. HC to EV, 3/15/20, 3/29/20, 4/7/20; RV to HC, 4/15/20; HC to Harry, 4/30/20; HC to EV, 3/29/20.

32. The announcement is in program files.

33. Rev. William Norman Guthrie to HC, 5/6/20.

34. EV to HC, 5/18/20.

35. Program and advertisement (in the press folders). The city is identified in pen.

36. 9/13/20, a recital by eighteen-year-old Albert King.

37. Copy in JS's possession.

38. Armitt and Judy Brown to HC, 9/2/20; SRC conversation with JS, 1989.

39. RV to his parents, 10/25/20. Stanford, Green Library, Special Collections, Varian papers.

40. *Palo Alto Times* (the date October 1920 in pencil).

41. Obituary, *Musical Times*, 104/1492 (April 1963), 278.

42. *Palo Alto Times* 10/27/20, 11/4/20.

43. Attribution to the *Chronicle* and approximate date in pencil.

44. RV to his parents, 11/12/20. Stanford, Green Library, Special Collections, Varian papers.

45. San Jose *Evening News*, 11/10/20.

46. *San Francisco Examiner*, 11/8/20.

47. *San Francisco Chronicle*, 11/8/20.

48. San Jose *Evening News*, 11/10/20.

49. *San Francisco Call and Post*, "Cowell's Concert Proves Another Sensation."

50. Congratulatory postcard signed "C."

51. Duffus to HC, 11/29/20.

52. HC to EV, 2/10/21.

53. Three-part series. *The Freeman*, 3/55 (3/30/21), 63–65; 3/56 (4/6/21), 85–87; 3/57 (4/13/21), 111–13.

54. Ray Brown, "Development in Harmony Writer's Topic," *San Francisco Chronicle*, 5/15/21.

55. RV to his parents, 3/14/21. Stanford, Green Library Special Collections. Russell Varian papers.

56. HC to EV, 5/5/21.

57. "Henry Cowell, Composer, Plays at Flower Show," *Bay and Valley News*, Halcyon, 5/18/21.

58. *Family Letter*, 5/15/21; Josephine Chang, "Henry Cowell as Piano Pedagogue."

59. HC to Harry, 8/9/20, 9/30/20.

60. There are no financial records from this time, but considering the low admission charges and the relative infrequency of his appearances, he could not have netted much, and he said numerous times that he earned very little.

61. Carbon of Seward to Edna Smith, 10/31/21, informing her Edna that Henry could be reached in New York through Dr. F. H. Bartlett, 19 E. 72nd St.

62. Armitt Brown to HC, 12/4/21.

63. HC's recollections, written around 1945 for SRC.

64. *Family Letter*, 3/21/22.

65. HC interviewed by Beate Gordon, 12/17/62. CUOHROC, 72.

66. Ziffrin, *Ruggles*, 75–76.

67. Flier/program "A Concert for Villagers." Promotional flier for Vermont, a contralto.

68. *The Greenwich Villager*, 4/15/23.

69. Seward to HC, 4/23/22.

70. JOV to HC, undated. Original in Stanford, Green Library, Special Collections, Varian papers. SRC's suggested date 1917 is unverifiable.

71. SRC, Memoir IX, 21.

72. Birthdate from Columbia University; thanks to registrar John Carter. Hicks's erroneous statement that she was the same age as Henry stems from the *New York Times* report of her death.

73. De Angulo, *Old Coyote*, 155.

74. Ibid., 125.

75. Information from Colleen Mallet, Vassar Registrar's office, 7/8/2003, and Columbia Registrar John Carter, 7/15/03.

76. *New York Times*, 4/16/22; *Herald Tribune*, 4/16/22.

77. SRC, Memoir IX, 29–30.

78. SRC, Memoir IX, 28.

79. SRC, Memoir IX, 29.

80. SRC, Memoir IX, 26–27.

81. SRC, Memoir IX, 27.

82. Seward to HC 4/23/22; Walling papers, unnumbered.

83. Jean Seward Uppman, conversation with JS, 1995. Only the Hoover materials remain.

84. HC's recollections, written around 1945 for SRC.

85. New York *Globe and Commercial Advertiser*, 5/12/22. The complete program is in *Musical America*, 11/20/22.

86. "La Guardia Discusses Music at Mail Concert," *Evening Mail*, 6/17/22.

87. *Denver Express*, 7/7/22.

88. *Rocky Mountain News*, 7/2/22.

89. Typescript of a review from an unnamed Greenwich newspaper, 7/13/22: Major Arthur de Bles, "'Last Word' In Music Delights. First Performance of Work by American Genius at Mrs. Seton's Yesterday."

90. Typed transcript, unnamed paper, 7/13/22.

91. *New York Times*, 7/12/22.

92. Ziffrin, *Ruggles*, 59–60.

93. Undated clipping.

94. *Palo Alto Times*, 7/15/22.

95. Date of concert not known; no program survived.

96. "Family Letter," 2/21/22.

97. SRC to William Mayer, 1/8/75.

98. *San Francisco Call*, undated copy.

99. *Musical Leader*, 11/16/22.

100. HC to Harry, 11/22/22.

101. *Pasadena News*, 11/15/22.

102. *Holly Leaves*, 11/17/22.

103. *Hollywood News*, 11/21/22.

104. *Hollywood Citizen*, 11/22/22; *Holly Leaves*, 11/24/22.

105. HC to Harry, undated.

106. The brochure lacks information about its origin.

107. *San Francisco Chronicle*, 12/10/22; *Palo Alto Times*, 12/1122.

108. *Holly Leaves*, 11/17/22.

109. *San Francisco Call*, 12/1/22.

110. Incomplete; no citation or date; approximately 12/14/22.

111. Undated clipping, pencil date 1922.

112. *Des Moines News*, 11/20/22.

113. Hicks, *Bohemian*, 109.

114. Charles Farwell Edson to Fritz Kreisler 11/25/22. Recommending HC to him; but since HC still had the letter, he may never have met Kreisler. On Schoenberg and Busoni, see "Composer-Pianist to Be Feted in New York," San Francisco *Journal*, 12/24/22.

115. SRC, Memoir IX, 32–33. However, SRC could have confused this with her contributions to New Music Society.

116. Doctor, *The BBC*, 337.

117. She played "Exultation" again in Los Angeles on April 5. *Los Angeles Times*, 4/6/23.

118. *Oakland Tribune*, 4/28/23 (date in pen).

119. *The North American*, 3/19/23.

120. HC to JOV, 5/23/23. Stanford, Green Library, Special Collections.

Chapter 10

1. An ancestor, General Wadsworth, was aide-de-camp to George Washington.

2. Olive, "My life with Cowells," undated. Olive Cowell papers. NYPLFPA, JPB 99-3.

3. Michael Hicks's *Henry Cowell, Bohemian* is fully focused on this idea.

4. Jones, "Henry Cowell and Halcyon."

Chapter 11

1. *Morning Post*, 5/15/23.

2. *Saturday Night*, 6/16/23.

3. JOV to HC, 5/23/23. Original: Stanford, Green Library, Special Collections.

4. Kuhnle to his mother, 05/18/23. From notes taken by Rita Mead at Wesley Kuhnle collection, California State University, Long Beach.

5. Kuhnle Brochure.

6. HC to BW, 9/3/27.

7. Wesley Kuhnle to his family, 5/28/23. Kuhnle collection, California State University, Long Beach.

8. SRC comments, ca. 1973, on Olive's biographical sketch, ca. 6/36.

9. SRC note on program of Tandler concert, 3/12/27.

10. Kuhnle to his family, 06/05/23, Kuhnle collection, California State University Long Beach.

11. Ibid.

12. HC to Harry, undated.

13. Kuhnle to his family, 06/11/23, Kuhnle collection, California State University, Long Beach.

14. HC to Harry, undated.

15. Kuhnle to his family, 6/11/23, Kunhle Collection, California State University, Long Beach.

16. HC interviewed by Beate Gordon, 12/17/62. CUOHROC, 96–97; HC to Harry, undated.

17. Kuhnle to his family, 06/20/23, Kuhnle collection, California State University, Long Beach.

18. Ibid. Program of the 11th Bachfest.

19. HC to Harry, early June 1923.

20. HC to Harry, 7/17/23; HC to Harry, typed transcript, undated, probably late July.

21. Buhlig to HC, 10/21/40.

22. Kuhnle to his mother, 7/28/23, Kuhnle collection, California State University, Long Beach.

23. Kuhnle to his mother, 7/24/23, 8/13/23, ibid.

24. Information from HC's passport; HC to JOV, undated. Original, Stanford, Green Library, special collections.

25. Kuhnle to his parents, 9/2/23, Kuhnle Collection, California State University, Long Beach.

26. HC To Harry, 9/12/23.

27. HC passport.

28. On the attendance, HC to Harry, undated from Vienna; Max Neuhaus, *Bayrischer Kurier*, 10/24/23, trans. JS.

29. *Munich Post*, 10/15/23, trans. JS.

30. *Volkszeitung*, 11/7/23, trans. JS.

31. *Leipziger Neuste Nachrichten*, 11/5/23; *Abendpost*, 11/5/23; trans JS.

32. NY *Evening Mail*, 2/8/24.

33. HC interviewed by Beate Gordon, 16/10/62. CUOHROC, 18–19.

34. SRC, 2/15/76, on HC's story of the riot.

35. HC to Wesley Kuhnle, undated, ca. 10/1/23. Kuhnle Collection, California State University, Long Beach. On the attendance, HC to Harry, undated.

36. Korngold wrote for Vienna's *Neue Freie Presse*.

37. HC interview by Beate Gordon HC, 16/10/62. CUOHROC, 22.

38. HC to Harry, undated, early fall, 1923.

39. Unidentified newspaper, 12/?/23.

40. W. Bauer, *Allgemeine Zeitung,* Vienna, 11/2/23.

41. *Wiener Morgenzeitung,* 11/7/23.

42. Undated postcards ca. 1923.

43. HC interviewed by Beate Gordon, 12/17/62. CUOHROC, 82.

44. Announcement, Paris, source illegible.

45. Olive, note on program for HC's concert.

46. HC noted "by Louis Schneider."

47. 11/23/23; HC note on copy of the review.

48. Raymond Petit, *Revue musicale,* 12/15/23.

49. HC to Harry, ca 11/23 or 12/23; erroneously dated 1924 in ink.

50. 11/24/23; author identified as M. Marchalk.

51. Trans. JS.

52. Trans. JS. Undated, probably 11/23.

53. 11/28/23, faulty English translation; original missing.

54. HC interviewed by Beate Gordon, 16/10/62. CUOHROC, 19.

55. HC to Harry, undated, from Nürnberger Str. 65, but he was writing from elsewhere.

56. George Cowell to Harry, 12/10/23.

57. HC to SRC, recollections, ca. 1945.

58. HC to Harry, 12/2/23.

59. *The Times,* London, 10/12/23, list of coming concerts.

60. George Cowell to Harry, 12/10/23.

61. HC to Harry, 12/2/23.

62. HC to Harry, from shipboard, 1/5/24.

63. HC interviewed by Beate Gordon, 12/17/62. CUOHROC, 79; "Bela Bartok and the Music of the Hungarian People," ca. 1950s.

64. SRC to Donald P. Croker, 6/15/74; on the theft, SRC conversation with JS.

65. Peter Bartok email to JS, 1/15/05: his father left his correspondence behind when he emigrated. It later disappeared.

66. SRC to Stanley Sadie, Editor, *Musical Times.* 4/9/75.

67. SRC, Locations of tours in Europe.

68. Henri Matisse to Igor Stravinsky, 12/12/23; CUOHROC, 98–99.

69. The presence of Prunières's card in Henry's papers implies that they met. A note on the back says Prunières invited HC to his home in 1924 [*sic*], to talk about modern music.

70. HC interviewed by Beate Gordon, 12/17/62. CUOHROC, 79–80; HC, "Bela Bartok and the Music of the Hungarian People," ca. 1950s.

71. SRC to Donald P. Croker, 6/15/74.

72. *New York Herald,* Paris, 12/19/23.

73. *New York Herald,* Paris, 12/18/23.

74. If it had, Henry's clipping service would have sent something.

75. "Miousique," *Ouest Eclair,* Rennes, 1/30/24.

76. *Republicain Orléanais,* 1/28/24.

77. HC to Harry, 1/5/24.

78. Ibid.

79. SRC conversation with JS.

80. HC to Harry, 1/5/24.

81. HC interviewed by Beate Gordon, 12/16/62. CUOHROC, 20.

Chapter 12

1. HC to SRC, recollections, about 1945.

2. Although HC's records no longer exist, Carnegie Hall's archivist approximated the cost from other sources.

3. Advertisement from a New York paper just before 2/4/23.

4. HC to Harry, on the back of a flier for his 2/4 Carnegie concert.

5. *Brooklyn Daily Eagle,* 2/9/24.

6. Brooklyn *Standard Union* and New York *Herald,* both 2/18/24. Lichtenwanger places the earliest known performance in Chicago, 2/18/24, probably because

there is no program for the Town Hall concert.

7. *Musical Courier*, 2/21/24.

8. New York *Herald*, 2/18/24.

9. *Montreal Star* 2/23/24. On HC's New York, "The New Way," United News, 2/21/24.

10. "World of Music" (unsigned), Brooklyn *Standard Union*, 2/24/24.

11. BW to HC, 4/7/24.

12. HC interviewed by Beate Gordon, 10/16/62. CUOHROC, 10.

13. *Daily Palo Alto Times*, 4/4/28.

14. On the Herzes, see Oja, *Making Music Modern*, and Tick, *Ruth Crawford Seeger*.

15. Tick, *Ruth Crawford Seeger*.

16. San Francisco *Journal*, 4/10/24.

17. John D. Barry, column "Ways of the World"—"A California Innovator," *San Francisco Call*, 4/21/24.

18. Olive, apparently to Gassner, ca. 1924 or 1925.

19. HC to Harry, 8/5/24.

20. The performers were Yoshi, shamisen; Yoshica, shakuhachi; Arjun Govind, sitar; Sarat Lahiri, esraj; Wang Kang Hou, wu con.

21. Dr. Adelaide Reyes, conversation with JS, 7/8/08.

22. HC to Harry, undated, ca. 1/?/25; HC to Mrs. Varian, 1/29/25. Stanford, Green Library Special Collections. Misdated by SRC on the Cowell papers copy.

23. According to Olive Cowell, Biographical Notes, chronology compiled ca. 1932.

24. HC to Varèse, undated. Basel, Sacher Stiftung. HC could not have been at the premiere, 3/24/23, but probably heard it in January 1924. Thanks to Dr. Felix Meyer.

25. New York *Telegraph* 2/8/25 identifies Cotapos as Chilean vice-consul in New York.

26. *New Yorker*, 2/21/25; *New York World*, 2/9/25.

27. SRC to Slonimsky, 4/24/79.

28. Tick, *Ruth Crawford Seeger*, 50–51; HC to Harry, 3/16/25.

29. Ruggles to HC, 3/16/25. The date must have been on an envelope which is gone; in pencil on letter.

30. HC to Ruggles, 6/1/25; Varèse to HC, 6/7/25; HC to BW, 6/20/25.

31. HC to JOV, 5/16/25.

32. HC to H&O, 2/1/25, but clearly 1926. HC frequently put the wrong year on letters early in a new year.

33. HC to Harry 1/27/[25].

34. Oja, *Making Music Modern*, chapter 11.

35. Gresham, "The International Society for Contemporary Music," passim.

36. Dane Rudhyar interviewed by Rita Mead, 11/18/75.

37. HC to Harry 1/27[25].

38. Olive, "Chronology."

39. Cheryl Lee Johnson, article on www.park2parkla.com, Web site of Los Angeles parks system [10/15/2003].

40. Anna de Mille to HC, 10/17/25.

41. HC to Kunhle, 9/1/25, Kunhle collection, California State University, Long Beach.

42. Rita Mead, *Henry Cowell's New Music*.

43. HC to H&O, 12/29/25.

44. Dane Rudhyar, interviewed by Rita Mead, 11/18/75.

45. Isabel Morse Jones, "New Music Society. Moderns to Have Their Hearing Thursday." *Los Angeles Times* 10/18/25.

46. Undated copy in Cowell papers.

47. "Novelty Pianist to Spend Day in Salt Lake," *Deseret News*, 11/7/25.

48. Salinas *News*, 11/25/25.

49. HC to H&O, 11/24/25. Nathan Leopold and Richard Loeb had been convicted of murder the previous year in a sensational case.

50. HC to H&O, 11/24/25.

51. Ibid.

52. Klara Lilien to Emma, her mother in Lvov, in Polish, introducing Henry, 11/30/25.

53. Claire Bloomfield to HC, 11/28/25.

54. Olive, Biographical Notes.

55. HC to Harry, 12/2/25; Montreal *Gazette*, 12/1/25.

56. Henry Brant interviewed by Andrea Olmstead, 8/8/77.

57. *McGill Daily*, Montreal, 11/28/25; "Record of Montreal Engagements."

58. D. McG., "Westward Trend of Music Indicated by Gradova's Program." *Musical Courier*, 12/17/25.

59. HC to Agnes Varian, 12/8/25 Original: Stanford, Green Library Special Collections. HC to Olive, 12/10/25.

60. *Musical America*, 11/28/25; HC to Harry, undated, ca. 12/25; HC to Olive, 12/10/25; HC to H&O, 12/17/25.

61. HC to Olive, 12/12/25.

62. Various letters, HC to Olive or to H&O, December 1925 and January 1926; Salzedo to HC, 1/29/26.

63. Management contract between Cowell and William Gassner for 1/1/26–1/1/29.

64. Bruno David Ussher, "Music," *Saturday Night*, 1/16/26.

65. HC to Ruggles, 6/1/25.

66. *Musical America*, 1/30/26.

67. HC to Harry, 2/3/26.

68. HC to Harry 2/3/26, 2/16/26; HC to H&O, 2/23/26; HC to JOV, 2/23/26. Stanford, Green Library, Special Collections.

69. HC to Olive, undated.

70. HC, "Music," 1927 supplement to *Encyclopedia Americana*.

71. HC to JOV, 2/23/26; HC to H&O, 2/16/26.

Chapter 13

1. HC to JOV, 2/23/26. Stanford, Green Library, Special Collections.

2. HC to Harry, 2/26/26.

3. HC to Harry, 3/09/26.

4. HC to Harry, 3/2/26, 3/9/26.

5. HC to Harry and Olive, 3/?/26.

6. Rudolph Kastner, "Henry Cowell. Der Musiker mit der Donnerkeule." Berlin *Morgen Post*, 3/25/26.

7. *Express Czerwony*, 4/2/26; translation by Andrew Dobrowolski.

8. Isabel Morse Jones, "Introducing the New, . . ." *Los Angeles Times*, 11/28/26.

9. In HC, "Moravian Music," *Pro-Musica Quarterly* 5/2, June 1927. HC identifies Uhlehla as a botanist.

10. Vladimir Ulehla to HC, 3/29/26; HC to Olive, undated.

11. Although Eva Drlíková, "Cowell . . .," 296, found no evidence of contact between HC and Pospíšil, it exists in the Cowell papers.

12. Vladimir Uhlela to HC, 3/29/26.

13. HC to Harry, 4/?/26.

14. Dr. Ludvík Kundera, *Hudební rizhledy* (1926): 127, quoted in and translated by Drlíková, "Cowell, . . ." 296.

15. HC to H&O, 4/15/26, to H&O; Isabel Morse Jones. "Introducing the New . . ." *Los Angeles Times*, 11/28/26.

16. HC: "Moravian Music," *Pro-Musica Quarterly* 5/2, June, 1927; HC to H&O, 4/15/26.

17. "flb," *Wiener Morgenzeitung*, 5/26/26.

18. Othmar Wetchy, "Wiener Konzertsaal," *Musikbote*, Vienna, 5/26/26.

19. "ah,"*Slovak Daily*, 4/25/26.

20. Bartók to HC, 3/28.

21. Thanks to Eugene Brogyanyi for translations.

22. Isabel Morse Jones. "Introducing the New . . ." *Los Angeles Times*, 11/28/26.

23. Frances B. Ackermann to HC, undated. A friend of Blanche Walton, she called Linder his own worst enemy and unworthy of Henry's friendship. Ackermann had donated to the trip.

24. Una Fairweather to HC, undated, 1926.

25. "Concerto Cowell," *Gazetto di Venezia*, 5/9/26.

26. Ibid.

27. HC to BW, 6/16/[26].

28. Linder to HC, 5/10/26.

29. HC to BW, 6/16/26.

30. HC to JOV, 5/20/26. Stanford, Green Library, Special Collections.

31. Schmolke to HC, 6/6/26.

32. EV to HC, 4/17/26.

33. JS heard the story in Lang's seminar, 1964. HC was on the faculty.

34. Information from a note on the back of a program from his Paris concert, 5/21/26.

35. Una Fairweather to HC, undated.

36. HC to H&O, 6/10/26.

37. Paul Bechert, "Cowellism," *Musical Times*, 6/1/26.

38. R. G., London *Daily Mail*, undated.

39. *Musical Herald*, 6/26/26.

40. *The Sackbut*, July, 1926.

Chapter 14

1. *Modern Music*, 3/3 (March–April, 1926), reprinted in Copland, *Copland on Music*, 146–47.

2. Mother Carrington to HC, 6/24/26; HC to JOV, 5/20/26. Original: Stanford, Green library, Special Collections.

3. Unnamed newspaper, possibly Carmel or San Jose, dated in pencil August 1926.

4. Evelyn Wells, Statement re: Henry. Seattle, 1970 or 1971; Evelyn Wells to SRC, 8/5/75; SRC to Evelyn Wells, 8/13/75.

5. Evelyn Wells to HC and SRC, 3/15/62.

6. Evelyn Wells, Re: Henry, ca. 1970–71.

7. Olive Cowell's commentary, dated "before 1927."

8. HC to SRC, recollections, ca. 1945.

9. *New York Times*, 11/14/26.

10. HC to Olive, 11/?/26.

11. *San Jose Mercury*, 12/16/26.

12. For a complete list, see Saylor, *Writings*.

13. *American Journal of Psychology*, 37, April 1926, 233–36.

14. HC to Slonimsky, undated, approximately later March 1929.

15. Memorial Resolution—Paul Randolph Farnsworth (1899–1978). http://histsoc.stanford.edu/pdfmen/farnsworthP.pdf.[6/16/09].

16. Dorotha Jensen to Terman, 12/10/26; Paul Farnsworth report, 12/10/26.

17. Paul R. Farnsworth, report on HC's talk, 12/15/26.

18. Gassner to HC, 9/13/28, 9/25/28.

19. SRC conversation with JS.

20. Confirmed by Henry Leigh, "American News and Notes," *Musical Standard*, London, 6/19/26.

21. Charles Seeger interviewed by Rita Mead, 11/17/74. SRC's comment about the 1915 project is a marginal note on the interview transcript.

22. Olive Cowell, "My Relations with Henry," est. 1932.

23. HC: History of New Music, typescript on the Shady letterhead, ca. 1961?

24. Charles Seeger interviewed by Rita Mead, 11/17/74.

25. HC to BW, 5/2/27.

26. Ruggles to HC, 5/13/27, 5/25/27.

27. Further on Walton and other patronesses, see Oja, *Making Music Modern*, chapter 12.

28. HC to BW, 7/3/27.

29. Charles Seeger interviewed by Rita Mead, 11/17/74.

30. Leo Ornstein to HC, 7/23/27.

31. Arthur Nikoloric to HC, 1/9/37.

32. Yale Oral History, Ives #46, interview with Mme. Nikoloric.

33. Cowell's speech on Ives to a dinner meeting of the National Institute of Arts and Letters, April 11, 1962. On Seeger and Ruggles negativism, see SRC to Gilbert Chase, 5/12/65.

34. SRC to Gilbert Chase, 5/12/65.

35. HC to CEI, 7/27/27.

36. CEI to HC, 8/16/27.

37. HC to CEI, 8/20/27.

38. HC interviewed by Beate Gordon, 12/17/62. CUOHROC, 100–101.

39. HC, "History of New Music." A typescript on the Shady letterhead, ca. 1961?

40. Olive to HC, 12/20/27; HC to BW, 8/27/27; BW to HC 9/3/27.

41. Olive Cowell: "My life with [the] Cowells," undated. Olive Cowell papers, NYPLFPA JPB 99-3. Also two handwritten sheets accompanying that statement.

42. Felix Deyo, "World of Music: A New and Notable Publication," *Brooklyn Standard-Union*, 10/2/27; *Ohio State University Journal*, 10/23/27.

43. HC to BW, 9/12/27; Rudhyar to HC, 9/27/27; HC: "History of New Music," typescript on the Shady letterhead, ca. 1961?

44. HC to J. J. Becker, marked October 1927?

45. HC to BW, 9/3/27.

46. Alfred Human to HC, 11/1/27; HC to BW, undated (1927).

47. HC to Becker, undated, ca. beginning of 1928.

48. Olive to HC, 1/19/28.

49. Virgil Thomson, "Cowell's Magazine," *New York Herald Tribune*, 11/2/47.

50. Charles Seeger interviewed by Rita Mead, 11/17/74.

51. SRC to Rita Mead, 12/21/74.

52. Alfred Frankenstein interviewed by Rita Mead, 11/7/75.

53. SRC to Vivian Perlis, 6/30/81.

54. Root, "The Pan American Association of Composers," 49.

55. Varèse to an unnamed journalist, quoted in L. Varèse, *Looking Glass Diary*, 279.

56. Press Release or announcement of PAAC.

57. HC to H&O, ca. 1/31/28.

58. HC to CEI, 2/28/28.

59. Carlos Chavez, New York, to Rudhyar, 3/15/28. Stanford, Green Library Special Collections, Rudhyar papers.

60. HC to H&O, 3/27/28.

61. HC to CEI, 3/27/28.

62. HC to CEI, 4/10/28.

63. Varèse to HC, 9/18/28.

64. HC to CEI, 3/27/28, 7/10/28.

65. HC to CEI, 11/24/28.

66. CEI to HC, 12/3/28.

67. Louise Varèse, *Looking Glass Diary*, 279.

68. HC to Ives 4/14/29.

69. Notes taken by Olive from HC's lectures at Schaeffer's, 1926.

70. Dora C. Hagemeyer," Modern Music Discussed by a Composer." *Carmel Cymbal*, 11/17/26.

71. Peter Goodman, *Morton Gould*, 39.

72. Tick, *Ruth Crawford Seeger*, 92–93.

73. HC to David Ewen, 12/7/54.

74. Payne, Gershwin, 83–87.

75. Ibid., 83.

76. HC to David Ewen, 12/7/54. Carbon copy. See also Carol Oja, "Gershwin and American Modernists of the 1920s."

77. HC to BW, undated, 1929.

78. Oja, *Making Music Modern*, chapter 12. She apparently was unaware of the annoyance to Henry caused by Cos Cob.

Chapter 15

1. HC to BW, undated, 1929.

2. HC to JOV, 3/3/29. Original: Stanford, Green Library Special Collections. Also HC to SRC, Recollections, ca. 1945.

3. Olive, "My life with Cowells." Olive Cowell papers. Undated. NYPLFPA JPB 99-3.

4. HC to BW, 4/7/29.

5. *Corriere della Sera*, 4/10/29. The other composers were Richard Hammond, Deems Taylor, and Saminsky himself, all of whom were comparatively conservative; the Russians—Vladimir Deshevov, Vladimir Shcherbachev, Prokofiev, and Joseph Schillinger, a recent emigré to the United States—had reputations as progressives.

6. Olive, "My Life with the Cowells." Undated. Olive Cowell papers. NYPLFPA JPB 99-3.

7. HC to CEI 4/14/29.

8. Mentioned by Olive, "My Life with the Cowells." Undated. Olive Cowell papers, NYPLFPA JPB 99-3. There is no program.

9. "Conservative Music in Radical Russia," *The New Republic*, 8/14/29; "A Musician's Experiences in Russia—Some First-hand and Unbiased Impressions," *The Churchman*, 4/26/30; "Adventures in Soviet Russia," *San Franciscan*, 12/30/ and 1/31; *Musical Courier*, 5/23/31; *Musyka I Revoliutsiia*, late 1929, reprinted in the New York Russian-language newspaper, *Russky Golos*, 2/30.

10. Amy Nelson, *Music for the Revolution*.

11. See Glinsky, *Theremin*, for superb detail.

12. Illegible signature, to HC, 2/10/27. Letterhead of USSR Trade Delegation in Canada (Montreal).

13. "Society for Cultural Relations," provided by the Soviet Union Information

Bureau, ca. 1929. From "The Soviet Union: Facts, Descriptions, Statistics," Chapter 24. http://www.marxists.org/history/ussr/government/1928/sufds/ch24.htm. [2/13/10].

14. Dr. Felix Meyer, Sacher Stiftung, to JS, 2/1/2005.

15. HC to Olive, ca. 2/23/28.

16. Rudhyar to HC, 7/10/28.

17. The correspondence between NS and HC began 2/15/28.

18. HC to BW, 2/10/[29?].

19. Varèse to HC, 9/10/28.

20. San Luis Obispo *Daily Tribune*, 12/20/28.

21. HC to JOV, undated, ca. late February–early March, 1929.

22. HC to BW, 4/7/29.

23. 4/22/29 calling card of Docteur R. Allendy, a Paris physician, recommending HC to Monsieur [illegible], USSR Embassy.

24. SRC, "About Olive & Harry." Statement for Rita Mead, 1975.

25. SRC, narrative of HC's trip to Russia. 1940s, acc. SRC conversation with JS, 1992.

26. Olive, "My life with [the] Cowells." Undated. Olive Cowell papers, NPYLFPA JPB 99-3.

27. See Amy Nelson, *Music for the Revolution*, 207.

28. SRC, Narrative of HC's trip to Russia, 1940s.

29. SRC, "About Olive & Harry," statement for Rita Mead, 1975.

30. HC to Yuri Shaporin, undated. Central Archive of Literature and Music, Moscow.

31. Olive, "My life with [the] Cowells." Undated. Olive Cowell papers, NYPLFPA JPB 99-3.

32. SRC to Joan Peyser, September 24, 1981, and conversations with JS. SRC claimed to have heard him tell it many times in lectures, but her colorful writing style may have inadvertently dressed up the story.

33. SRC narrative of HC's trip to Russia, 1940s. The comment about thirty days

is in HC interviewed by Beate Gordon, 1962, 21.

34. Amy Nelson, *Music for the Revolution*.

35. HC to BW, 6/1/29.

36. SRC, narrative of HC's trip to Russia, 1940s. Thanks to Eric Marinitsch for providing a copy of the Universal publication.

37. HC to BW, 6/1/29; also in his accounts of the trip and *New Musical Resources*.

38. Ada Hanifin, "Henry Cowell Will Give Piano Recital As Farewell Here."

39. Olive, "My life with [the] Cowells." Undated. Olive Cowell papers, NYPLFPA JPB 99-3.

40. HC to Yuri Shaporin, undated. Central Archive of Literature and Music, Moscow.

41. Typescript translation dated 6/3/29, probably by Nicolas Slonimsky. Another review may have appeared in *Vchernaya Moskva*, 6/4/29.

42. HC interviewed by Louis Vaczek for the New School, 1/62.

43. Szigeti, *With Strings Attached*, 219, 236.

44. HC to Olive, 9/28/29.

45. Olive, "My life with [the] Cowells." Undated. Olive Cowell papers, NYPLFPA JPB 99-3.

46. HC to BW, 6/1/29.

47. HC to H&O, 6/7/20.

48. HC to Chain, 6/29/29. Sacher Stiftung. Thanks to Dr. Felix Meyer.

49. The stamp in the passport is 6/18, but he originally told Blanche Walton June 19. (HC to BW, 6/12/29).

50. Olive, "My life with [the] Cowells." Undated. Olive Cowell papers, NYPLFPA JPB 99-3.

51. *The New Republic*, 59/767, 8/24/29: 339–41.

52. Amy Nelson, *Music for the Revolution*, 212–13.

Chapter 16

1. Vladimir Ulehla to HC, 3/29/26.

2. Olive, "Making a Living," 8/32.

3. HC to BW, 3/3/27.

4. HC to Olive, 2/50/28.

5. HC, "New Terms for New Music," *Modern Music*, 5/4 (May 1928): 21–27.

6. HC to Chávez, 3/13/30. The reader is identified as Harry Block, Dashiell Hammett's editor.

7. Alfred A. Knopf to HC, 3/13/29.

8. HC to Olive, 7/21/29.

9. David Nicholls, editor, Henry Cowell, *New Musical Resources*, 165.

10. HC to Olive, 1/?/30; HC to H&O, 4/26/30.

11. HC to Chavez, 2/5/1930.

12. *Musical Opinion*, 5/1930.

13. HC to H&O, 11/30/31.

14. *Musical Opinion*, 5/30.

15. *Modern Music*, 3/2 (April–May 1930): 43–45.

16. *American Mercury*, 9/1930.

17. SRC conversation with JS, 1992.

18. Dane Rudhyar, "The Relativity of Our Musical Conceptions," in *Musical Quarterly*, 8/1 (January 1922): 108–18.

19. Discussed by both Godwin and Nicholls.

20. Seeger to SRC, 8/23/70.

21. JS conversation, 7/24/08, with Seward's daughter Jean Seward Uppman and her daughter Margo Uppman Vincent. Both thought the idea highly plausible.

22. Nicholls, preface to Cowell, *New Musical Resources*.

Chapter 17

1. HC to BW, 10/11/29.

2. Folder "Temporary Biog Bits." A group of postcards all with return address "Cui Studios 489 Lighthouse Ave. Pacific Grove, CA" to HC, Community Hospital, Belmont, San Mateo, California.

3. HC to JOV, 10/14/29. Original: Stanford, Green Library, special collections.

4. SRC, statement, 3/12/73, on HC's entire health history.

5. Bill from Community Hospital of San Mateo County, Belmont, California, 10/25/29.

6. HC to H&O.1/5/30.

7. HC and Lewis Terman correspondence, 11/1929.

8. Bulletin of the New School for spring term, 1929.

9. Copland/Perlis, 138.

10. Johnson told the story to SRC, who related it to JS in a conversation 12/30/91.

11. Bulletin of the New School, February, 1929.

12. Alvin Johnson to HC, 3/9/29.

13. Olive, "A tabulation of some of the things which I have tried to do for Henry (roughly chronological)," 6/11/32.

14. SRC Conversation with JS, 12/30/91.

15. New School Bulletin XII, February 17–21. No year.

16. The full story of HC's career at the New School can be found in Edward Carwithen's *Henry Cowell: Composer and Educator*.

17. Johnson to HC, 4/123/30.

18. Caturla to HC, 9/18/28.

19. HC to Slonimsky, 1/25/29.

20. Maria de Quevedo to HC, 2/4/29.

21. HC to Ives, 10/24/30.

22. Maria de Quevedo to HC, 4/25/30.

23. Maria de Quevedo to HC, 6/10/30.

24. HC to H&O, 12/30/30; HC to Slonimsky, 2/11/31.

25. HC to H&O, 12/30/30.

26. HC to Chavez, undated, ca. 7/29.

27. HC to Slonimsky, 3/11/[30].

28. Weiss to HC, 4/4/30.

29. HC to H&O, 1/19/30; HC to NS, 2/11/31.

30. HC to NS, 2/14/31.

31. Ruth Crawford to HC, 3/29/31.

32. HC to NS, 4/29/31.

33. No program or review survives to identify all of the pieces on the second concert.

34. NS to HC, 6/23/31.

35. HC to CEI, 8/31/31. Henry is reiterating Ives's thought.

Chapter 18

1. HC to BW, undated; late spring, 1929.

2. HC to Olive, 11/26/31; program of Walton tribute, New School, 9/12/59.

3. Leta E. Miller, "Henry Cowell and John Cage."

4. Gustave Reese, "The American Musicological Society." *Music Journal*, 4/6 (November–December 1946): 71.

5. 11/11/20. "Snows of Fujiyama" was not composed until 1924.

6. See bibliography for items by Nancy Yunhwa Rao.

7. Christopher Yohmei Blasdel, "The Single Tone: A Personal Journey into Shakuhachi Music." Printed Matter Press [no location or date]: 139. Thanks to Ralph Samuelson. For Tamada's first name, Tamada to HC, 3/14/34.

8. HC interviewed by Beate Gordon, 10/16/62. CUOHROC, 45. The Cowell papers contain nothing from the lectures.

9. The meeting is unsubstantiated; referred to in a statement by SRC about HC's non-Western interests, Shady, 12/23/74.

10. Dr. Adelaide Reyes, email to JS, 7/7/08. On the 1924 event, see Chapter 12.

11. Program: 2/20/27. When Sidney interviewed Henry in 1961 about his early involvement with comparative musicology, he said that he first presented concerts of authentic performers from Asia, Africa, and the Balkans at The New School in 1926, "as he had done earlier from time to time in San Francisco." There is no evidence of that New School performance, and plentiful evidence that his first contact with The New School was in 1928, He may have been thinking of the performances at St. Mark's.

12. Allan Edwards, *Flawed Words*, 41–42.

13. See Part I, chapter 7.

14. HC: "Moravian Music." *Pro-Musica Quarterly*, 5/2 (June 1927): 25–29.

15. HC, "How Young Hungary Expresses Individuality," *Musical America* [June 4, 1927]: 11.

16. SRC on HC's involvement in non-Western music, 1969.

17. See Oja, *McPhee*, 63 and fn 35.

18. Ibid., passim.

19. HC interviewed by Beate Gordon, 16/12/62.

20. Archivist G. Thomas Tanselle's telephone conversation with JS, 6/14/04.

21. Application and plan of study, Guggenheim Foundation Archive.

22. Others included Herbert S. Langfeld (Princeton), R. W. Husband (University of Wisconsin), Walter Miles (Yale), and Homer Weaver (Oberlin).

23. Letter of recommendation from Terman's file. Marked "Written in Dec 1930."

24. Seeger to Guggenheim Foundation, 1/7/31.

25. Announcement of Guggenheim Fellowships for 1931, 3/30/31.

26. HC to Henry Allen Moe, 8/14/31; HC to H&O, 10/20/31.

27. HC to Walter Miles, 11/21/31. He told Miles that he hoped to maintain contact with Yale, but was hampered by the stodginess of the music department, which "as far as I can make out, has contributed nothing of any educational value in music. As is usual everywhere, one must look to the psychology dep't. for all interesting musical activities."

28. HC to CEI, 11/28/31; HC to H&O, 11/30/31.

29. http://gamelan.free.fr/Jodjanem.htm, [9/12/05]. Jodhjana (1893–1972), from Jojakarta, was renowned as a dancer. In Europe from 1914, he was one of the few Javanese performers there.

30. HC to H&O, 12/11/31.

31. On Sambamoorthy (1901–1973), http://www.chennaionline.com/musicnew/CarnaticMusic/190th.asp. [9/12/05].

32. HC to Olive, 11/21/31.

33. HC to CEI, and to H&O, 12/11/31.

34. HC to CEI, 8/31/31.

35. HC to CEI, 7/19/31.

36. HC to H&O, undated. Mailed, apparently, before sailing.

37. HC to NS, 10/23/31.

38. HC to NS, 10/16/31.

39. Pedro Sanjuan to HC, 10/20/31.

40. HC to NS, 10/24/[31].

41. HC to CEI, 10/31/31.

42. Ibid.

43. HC interviewed by Beate Gordon, 12/17/62. CUOHROC, 82–83.

44. HC to BW, 12/2/31.

45. HC interviewed by Beate Gordon, 12/17/62. CUOHROC, 97–98.
46. HC to NS, 11/2/31.
47. HC to NS, 11/14/31.
48. HC to NS, 11/11/31.
49. Pedro Sanjuan to HC, 11/24/31.
50. *La Voz*, Madrid, 11/24/31.
51. HC to Olive, 11/30/31.
52. HC to CEI, 11/28/31.
53. HC to BW, 12/2/31.
54. Undated proof sheet, "Konzert Hoch-flut in Wien."
55. Corrections by SRC to Oliver Daniel's article "Henry Cowell," *Stereo Review* 36/6 (December 1974): 72–82; SRC corrections on documents concerning a lawsuit against Oliver Daniel.
56. HC to NS, 12/14/31.
57. HC to NS, 5/23/32.

Chapter 19

1. www.bls.gov, Bureau of Labor Statistics.
2. Cornelius Canon, *Federal Music Project*, 1–9.
3. Stokowski to HC, 3/6/32.
4. Unsigned, undated.
5. HC to H&O, 3/20/32.
6. Doris Humphrey to HC, undated.
7. Clara W. Mayer to HC, 11/20/31. On her opposition, Olive, "Henry Cowell at The New School," 7/4/32.
8. "New Courses Planned by Social School," New York *Herald Tribune*, 12/31/31.
9. Olive, "Henry Cowell at The New School," 7/4/32.
10. Bulletin of The New School, Spring 1932.
11. Olive, "Henry Cowell at The New School," 7/4/32. Paul Farnsworth, the Stanford psychologist, had surveyed American institutions concerning teaching of rhythm.
12. Carwithen, *Henry Cowell*, passim.

Chapter 20

1. BW to Olive, 7/25/32, with note by SRC.
2. Schmolke to Olive, 1/1/32; HC to Olive, 2/3/32.
3. Obituary, the *New York Times*, 8/30/32.

4. HC to Olive, 8/5/32, 8/12/32.
5. For more detail see Pekka Gronow, "The Record Industry Comes to the Orient," *Ethnomusicology*, 25/2 (May 1981): 251–84.
6. HC: "Music around the World" in *Listen: The Guide to Good Music*, 9/4 (February 1947): 4–7; HC wrote that subsequently the importance of the records "was so little understood that they were later used to mark points on the floor in a folk dancing class and even danced on, and of course broken up, as a stunt." By 1947, only about sixty remained out of several hundred. He said that the Hornbostel Collection *Musik des Orients*, issued by Odeon in Europe and later reprinted in America by Decca, used the same source.
7. HC to Henry Allen Moe, 12/5/32; HC to CEI, 11/19/32.
8. Henry Allen Moe to HC, 3/11/33.
9. HC to Henry Allen Moe, early January 1932; Guggenheim Foundation archive. Moe to HC, 3/11/32; SRC to Luening, 8/31/70; SRC to Greta Sultan, 8/11/75.
10. HC to Henry Allen Moe, 1/10/33. Guggenheim Foundation Archive.
11. References in the book suggest that he took those notes in 1932. Prince Raden Mas is identified in the *Palo Alto Times*, 4/21/33.
12. "Henry Cowell Studies Music by Tribesmen. Cannibal Soup-Song among Records." *Palo Alto Times*, 4/21/33.
13. HC, "Hybrid Music," typescript. Possibly mid-1940s.
14. HC to H&O, 12/11/31.
15. HC to CEI, 8/30/32; HC to H&O, 9/3/32; HC to NS 9/23/32, 11/25/32, 12/30/32.
16. HC to Adolph Weiss, 10/28/32. Original in Moldenhauer Archive, Library of Congress.
17. Varèse to HC, 9/12/32; HC to Max Eschig Company, 12/6/32; HC to CEI, 9/10/32.
18. HC to CEI, 9/26/32.
19. Carbon copy of a letter informing various people about the International Exchange concerts.

20. Ibid.

21. Undated announcement or press release.

22. "Regulations of the Foundation for International Exchange Concerts."

23. HC to Chavez, 9/11/32.

24. HC to NS, 10/22/32.

25. HC to Olive, 8/26/32.

26. NS to Olive, 9/12/32. The article was probably written for *American Composers on American Music*, about which, see Chapter 24.

27. Aaron Copland, "The Composer in America (1923–22)," *Modern Music*, 10/1 (January–February 1933): 87–92.

28. HC to Weiss, 10/20/32.

29. HC to Olive, 8/7/32; HC to Harry, 9/14/32; HC to Becker, 9/25/32. Information about Schoenberg and tennis from Christian Meyer, Schoenberg Center, Vienna, 3/13/12. Concerning the 1926 dinner with Schnabel: Schoenberg's extant appointment book, at the Schoenberg Center, is blank for almost all of that year.

30. CUOHROC: 85–86. Henry told the story in the 1962 interview with Beate Gordon. Mrs. Gordon told JS in 2005 that effects of Henry's strokes did not seem at all evident in the interview. His memory seemed to be excellent. Nuria Schoenberg Nono, conversation JS, Los Angeles, 10/22/89.

31. HC to Olive 8/26 and 8/27/32.

32. Stuckenschmidt, *Schoenberg*, 339, said that he attended Schoenberg's course on musical analysis—given in Schoenberg's home—rather than the composition class, and that Henry was there.

33. HC to H&O, 9/3/32; HC to Becker, 9/25/32.

34. Ibid.

35. HC to Olive, 9/10/32.

36. HC to Weiss, 10/20/32. Original in Moldenhauer Archives, Library of Congress.

37. HC to Olive, 11/27/32.

38. HC to H&O, 12/11/32.

39. Henry Cowell, "Who is the Greatest Living Composer?" *Northwest Musical Herald* (January 1933): 7.

40. HC to Olive, 9/17/32.

41. HC to CEI, 8/30/32; HC to H&O, 9/3/32; HC to NS 9/23/32, 11/25/32, 2/30/32.

42. HC to Olive, October 9, 1932.

43. A calling card of Lars Eke bears a note to Henry enclosing the clippings and the compliments of the society. "Don't forget us now you created quite an impression."

44. HC to Olive, 10/9/32.

45. HC to Chávez, 10/10/32.

46. HC to Olive, 10/9/32.

47. HC to Weiss, 10/20/32.

48. HC to Olive, 10/9/32.

49. Invitation.

50. *Berliner Morgenpost*, 12/4/32.

51. *8 Uhr Abendblatt*, 11/27/28.

52. HC to Olive, 12/20/32 HC.

53. Sidney's notes on conversations with HC, 8/9/58 and sometime around 1963.

54. HC to Piston 5/5/32, 11/30/32, 12/13/32. Piston papers, Library of Congress.

55. HC to CEI 12/11/32.

56. *Hamburger Fremdenblatt*, 12/12/32.

57. HC to H&O, 12/27/32 from shipboard.

58. Invitation.

59. HC to Olive, 11/28/32.

60. HC to CEI, 12/5/32.

61. Grete Sultan to SRC, 4/14/77.

62. Szigeti, *With Strings Attached*, 305.

63. "Henry Cowell Studies Music by Tribesmen. Cannibal Soup-Song among Records," *Daily Palo Alto Times*, 4/21/33.

Chapter 21

1. HC to Olive, November 28; to H&O, 12/27/32 from shipboard.

2. According to SRC, in conversations with JS.

3. *25th Anniversary Survey of the Composers' Forum* (1961): 8. The anonymous author reminds that the founding of the Forum in 1935 was preceded by Henry Cowell's similar activity at The New School, 1931–34.

4. HC interviewed by Louis Vaczek, ca. June 1962.

5. Arthur Berger interviewed by Andrea Olmstead, 11/9/77.

6. HC to CEI, 5/16/33.

7. Daniel Gregory Mason to HC, 11/13/33.

8. Douglas Moore to HC, 10/27/[33].

9. Ernst Toch to HC, 4/1/33; Bulletin of the University of Exile; Clara Mayer, 5/4/33 to HC.

10. Seeger telegram to HC, 4/30/35.

11. Alvin Johnson to HC, 1/21/35, 4/27/35.

12. HC to H&O, 10/17/35.

13. HC interviewed by Louis Vaczek, ca. June 1962.

14. New School 20th Anniversary Booklet (1939): 13.

15. Information courtesy of Janice Braun, Special Collections, Olin Library, Mills College.

16. Irene Williamson to HC, 11/23/35.

17. Terman to Professor Eliot G. Mears, Stanford, 11/24/33.

18. Terman to HC, 12/4/33 and course descriptions; Terman to HC, 6/9/34.

19. "General Outline of Course on Music 120, Stanford University Summer session, 1934."

20. Eliot G. Mears, to HC, 9/12/34.

21. Olive's notes on her visit with HC on his birthday in 1934.

22. R. L. Wilbur, president, Stanford University, to HC, 11/9/34.

23. R. L. Wilbur to Douglas Moore, 10/31/3, thanking him for offering his opinion of HC as a lecturer in music.

24. Acting President R. E. Swain, Stanford to HC, 3/21/35.

25. Ruth Radir to HC, 11/1/35.

26. Purchase order, 12/6/34.

27. Ruth Radir to HC, 11/12/35.

28. HC to CEI, 1/22/35.

29. Ruth Radir to HC, 11/1/35.

30. Terman to HC, 11/21/33; HC to Terman, 10/18/33.

31. HC to CEI, 1/22/35.

32. HC to H&O, 10/17/35.

33. Newsletter "Dynamics," 1/10/35. Thanks to Juilliard archivist Jeni Dahmer.

34. For example, it is hardly mentioned by Hicks, *Bohemian*.

35. Leta E. Miller, "Henry Cowell and Modern Dance: The Genesis of Elastic Form."

36. Ada Hanifin, "Henry Cowell, Composer, Talks on Primitive Music and Modern Composers," *San Francisco Examiner*, 6/11/33.

37. The *Carmelite*, 5/6/32, reported about his lecture on the evolution of primitive music, which he illustrated with recordings of Hopi dances.

38. HC to NS, 11/16/34.

39. See Chapter 9.

40. About Horst and Sabin, see Soares, *Louis Horst*, 16.

41. Rudhyar to Ruth St. Denis, 11/24/[?]. The envelope is marked 1926 or 1927.

42. New York *Herald Tribune*, 2/1/28, calendar listing for 2/4/28.

43. "M.W.," New York *Herald Tribune*, 4/1/6/?

44. Doris Humphrey to HC, undated.

45. Program. According to a quote from *Dance Magazine* on the flier, HC had written special music for this dance. His participation could explain the incompleteness of the manuscript. Mary F. Watkins, "Current Events in the Dance World," New York *Herald Tribune*, 3/6/32.

46. HC to Harry and Olive, 3/20/30. For a small amount of information about Graham and HC: Lewis Stewart, "*Music Composed for Martha Graham*," 17–21. He did not mention *Synchrony*, however, probably because Graham never danced it.

47. Martha Graham to HC, 6/6/30.

48. HC to BW, 8/19/[30].

49. HC to H&O, 1/19/31.

50. HC to H&O, 1/21/31.

51. Lichtenwanger #464.

52. HC: "How Relate Music and Dance?" *Dance Observer* 1/5 (June–July 1934): 52–53.

53. HC to H&O, 10/20/31.

54. New School announcement, 10/10/31.

55. List of Gassner's artists from *Musical America*, 1/25/32. His small stable included Humphrey and Weidman, and HC.

56. Humphrey to HC, undated, "Monday."

57. Various newspaper listings in Cowell papers, 1/5/32.

58. HC probably to H&O, 3/21/31.

59. Riegger to HC, 1/4/34; Salzedo to HC, 1/8/34. John Martin, "The Dance" column, *New York Times*, 4/1/23; 11/13/34; HC, New School, to Olive 11/13/34; program, Martha Graham and Dance Group, 2/15/36.

60. Lehman Engel, NYC, to HC, 1/14/36; Tina Flade program of dance concert, Mills College, 11/20/36.

61. HC to Olive, 6/20/37.

62. Flier, 12/10/33, at the Civic Repertory Theatre; unnamed paper, 12/9/33.

63. Hanya Holm to HC, 8/17/36.

Chapter 22

1. *Modern Music* 8/3, March–April 1931.

2. Boris de Schloezer, "Man, Music, and the Machine," *Modern Music*, 8/3 (March–April 1933): 3–9.

3. Wilfried Bendell to HC, 9/30/35.

4. Gann, *Nancarrow*, 1–2.

5. HC to Joseph Schillinger, 1/30/38.

6. HC to Chávez, 5/5/32, and numerous subsequent communications.

7. HC to NS, 10/22/32.

8. HC to NS, telegram and postcard, 10/28/32.

9. Riegger to HC, 10/31/32; HC, presumably to CEI, 11/19/32.

10. HC to CEI, 12/11/32.

11. HC to H&O, 12/11/32; HC, to H&O? 1/8/33; HC to H&O, 1/12/33.

12. HC to CEI, 1/10/33, 2/16/33.

13. HC to Becker, 3/18/33. The details of the letter are not always clear; an earlier letter may be lost, or the two may have spoken on the telephone.

14. HC to PG, 3/27/33.

15. HC to CEI, 11/8/33.

16. HC to CEI, 11/14/33.

17. CEI to HC, undated, but doubtless November 1933. Reproduced by permission of the American Academy of Arts and Letters, copyright owner.

18. HC to Olive, 12/08/33.

19. HC to J. J. Becker, 12/28/33.

20. HC to NS, 11/22/33.

21. Riegger to HC, 12/29/33.

22. In Riegger to HC, 12/27/[34], Riegger talks to HC as a top manager would to the chief executive.

23. HC to CEI, 1/4/[34].

24. HC to CEI, 2/17/34.

25. CEI to HC, undated #6, on Ives & Myrick letterhead in pencil. Ives crossed out the address and he substituted 164 E. 74.

26. BW to HC, 2/14/34.

27. CEI to HC, undated #5. probably early 1934; Riegger to HC, undated, spring 1934.

28. Riegger to HC, 2/22/34.

29. Salzedo to HC, 6/20/35. On 8/27/35 he postponed recording it again because of touring.

30. Rudhyar to HC, 3/10/34.

31. HC to Weiss 3/23/34. Original in Moldenhauer Archives, Library of Congress.

32. Weiss to HC, 4/26/34.

33. HC to Weiss, 4/30/34. Original in Moldenhauer Archives, Library of Congress.

34. Piston to HC, 1/15/[34].

35. NS to HC, 12/13/34.

36. HC to CEI, 4/14/34.

37. Riegger to HC, undated; date in red crayon 2/21/34.

38. Laprade, *Broadcasting Music*, 1–10.

39. Mrs. A. D. Varian to HC, 1/29/25. Original: Stanford, Green Library, Special Collections. The copy in the Cowell papers was erroneously marked 2/19/25 by SRC.

40. Boris Hambourg to HC, 3/8/26.

41. HC to John Varian, 2/20/27. Original: Stanford, Green Library, Special Collections.

42. Boris de Schloezer, "Man, Music and the Machine . . ."

43. Thomas Glynn to HC, 2/14/30.

44. Laprade, *Broadcasting Music*, 9.

45. HC to H&O, 1/12/31.

46. HC to H&O, 6/7/29.

47. Adolph Weiss to HC, 7/12/31.

48. HC to Olive, 11/7/31.

49. HC, "Music," *Encyclopedia Americana*, annual supplement for 1929.

50. Doctor, *BBC*, passim.

51. HC to CEI, 1/5/33; HC to H&O, 1/8/33; HC to NS, 1/14/33.

52. Form letter in Van Loon's name, 1/17/33, calling an organizational meeting; poster for the WEVD University of the Air.

53. HC to NS, 10/22/32.

54. Poster for the WEVD University of the Air.

55. [Illegible], secretary of Hungarian New Society for Music, 3/2/33 to HC; Alexander Jemnitz to HC, 3/19/33.

56. HC to Chávez, 3/33/33, 4/7/33; HC to Adolph Weiss, 4/13/33.

57. Arthur Berger interviewed by Andrea Olmstead, 11/9/77.

58. The Austrian program: Berg: "Nacht" (from *Seven Early Songs*); Webern, two songs from Op. 4; Schoenberg, Suite Op. 25; Hans Pless's "Regenwetterlied." Concerning Sherman and Clay, see unnamed San Francisco newspaper, 2/18/33.

59. HC to CEI, 4/29/33.

60. HC to CEI, 5/30/33, 7/7/33.

61. Fliers.

62. Ruyneman to HC, 10/3/33.

63. F. Labunski to HC, 7/31/33; Jerzy Fitelberg to HC, 11/11/33.

64. Dan Ecker, New York University YMCA, to HC, 11/6/33.

65. HC, "Music," *Encyclopedia Americana*, annual supplement for 1933.

66. Laprade, *Broadcasting Music*, 45.

67. Weiss to HC, 1/28/34; Riegger to HC, 4/7/34.

68. See Chapter 12.

69. John Hawkins to SRC, 7/16/63. The first sound newsreel was shown in October 1927, just three weeks after *The Jazz Singer*.

70. HC to Mrs. A. D. Varian, 1/29/25.

71. HC to H&O, from shipboard returning from Europe 12/27/32.

72. HC to CEI, 1/5/33. This was not the current Film Forum, which opened in 1970.

73. HC to Schmolke, 2/8/34.

74. HC to H&O, 10/19/34.

75. HC to NS, 10/20/34.

76. HC to NS, 11/6/34; HC to Olive, 11/6/34.

77. HC to H&O, 10/27/34.

78. Theodore Alfred Benedek to HC, 11/7/34.

79. HC to Olive, 11/13/34.

80. CEI, undated draft, not in his hand, of a letter to Mr. Frederick E. Williamson, Executive Offices, New York Central Railway.

81. HC to NS, 12/10/34.

82. HC, "Music," *Encyclopedia Americana*, annual supplement for 1929.

83. For fascinating details see Glinsky, *Theremin*.

84. NS to HC, 10/12/28; HC to NS, 10/18/28.

85. HC to NS, 3/27/30, 4/27/30.

86. HC to NS, dated only September; New School Flier of Concerts, January–April 1931.

87. Receipt signed by Leon Theremin, 3/7/31, for $200 from HC "in full for a 'rhythm-instrument to be constructed by me." Also, the *Carmelite*, 3/24/32.

88. The *Carmelite*, ibid.

89. Excerpts from May Seagoe, *Terman and the Gifted*, Los Altos, CA: William Kaufmann, 1975. SRC has written on the copy that only the information about Farnsworth was accurate.

90. Szigeti, *With Strings Attached*, 227; SRC's marginal note on a copy of the excerpt.

91. HC to Olive, 11/7/31; HC to NS, 12/21/31, 1/14/32, 1/10/32, and undated.

92. Typed transcript of article from the *Carmelite*, March 24, 1932. The technology is described in the *Daily Mirror*, by Gustav Davidson, 3/11/32. See also Szigeti, *With Strings*, 227.

93. Bulletin of The New School, fall, 1931.

94. HC to NS, 1/21/32.

95. *Musical America*, 1/25/32; *Musical Leader*, 1/28/32.

96. *New York Times*, note, 3/10/32.

97. Arthur Berger in New York *Mirror*, 4/2/32.

98. Ibid.

99. *New York Times*, 4/2/32.

100. *Modern Music*, 10/3 (March–April, 1932).

101. HC to Olive, undated, early 1932?

102. Hans Mersmann to HC, 3/17/32.

103. Flier. The program also included quarter-tone music for two pianos, though the only quarter-tone piece announced was *Zanadu* by Mildred Cowper. Henry mentioned Ives's pieces in his lecture. HC to CEI, 5/26/32.

104. Olive's commentary, 5/15/32.

105. HC to CEI, 5/16/32.

106. *Argonaut*, 5/20/32.

107. HC to NS, 7/7/32.

108. NS to HC, 10/14/34.

109. NS to SRC, 12/9/58.

110. That last Rhythmicon has been housed in a Budapest museum. I am grateful to Guy Livingston for this information.

Chapter 23

1. Undated PAAC brochure, ca. 1933.

2. Director of Kulturabteilung, Lindstrom AG, to HC, 2/23/33.

3. HC to Luening, 6/19/33.

4. Ruggles to HC, 6/12/33.

5. Copland to Chávez, 12/16/33. Aaron Copland papers, Library of Congress.

6. HC to Weiss, 10/28/32. Moldenhauer Archives, Library of Congress.

7. HC to Weiss, 4/13/33. Moldenhauer Archives, Library of Congress.

8. Salzedo to HC, 12/30/33.

9. Varèse to HC, January 2, 1934.

10. Mattfeld, 1893–1968, was a writer on music and librarian at the New York Public Library.

11. Riegger's letters show his dislike of Salzedo. Salzedo to HC 1/8/33.

12. Varèse to HC, 1/2/34.

13. HC to NS, 1/23/34.

14. BW to HC, 2/14/34.

15. Riegger to HC 1/4/34.

16. Seeger to HC, 3/14/34.

17. HC to Weiss, 3/7/34. Moldenhauer Archives, Library of Congress.

18. Salzedo to HC, 3/14/34.

19. HC to CEI, 3/14/34.

20. HC to Becker, 3/21/34.

21. HC to Weiss, 3/23/34.

22. Riegger to HC, 3/14/34, undated, 1934.

23. Ruggles to HC, 4/19/34.

24. CEI to HC, undated No. 5. From the context, April 1934.

25. Weiss to HC, undated, 1934.

26. Riegger to HC, undated, 1934.

27. BW to HC, 4/23/34.

28. PAAC brochure for 1934; program and flier for April 22 concert. SRC to Chavez, 10/22/64, said that the Cowell papers have only those PAAC programs that had pieces by HC, which is understandable and explains the lack of a program for 4/15/34.

29. *New York Times*, 4/23/34.

30. Weiss to HC, 4/26/34.

31. HC to Becker, ca. March 1934.

32. HC to CEI, 6/19/34.

33. Salzedo to HC, 6/22/34.

34. Riegger to HC, 11/20/34.

35. Varèse to HC, 4/23/36.

36. Postcard announcement.

37. See, e.g., HC to Varèse, letters in 1934, Sacherstiftung, Basel. Thanks to Felix Meyer.

38. SRC conversation with JS.

39. Helen Mills to HC, 10/25/33.

40. Helen Mills to HC, 4/25/34, 5/25/34.

41. Helen Mills to HC, 9/4/34.

42. Helen Mills to HC, 5/25/34, 7/19/34.

43. Helen Mills to HC, 9/4/34.

44. Katz is discussed in Shannon L. Green, "Art for Life's Sake: Music Schools and Activities in the U.S. Social Settlements, 1892–1942" (Ph.D. diss., University of Wisconsin, 1998).

45. Hedi Katz to HC, 1/22/35, 2/28/35.

46. Hedi Katz to HC, 2/28/35.

47. Hedi Katz to HC, 3/12/35.

48. Minutes of IEC committee meeting, 5/22/35.

49. See, e.g., HC to Becker, ca. March, 1934.

50. Gerald Strang to HC, 11/4/35.

Chapter 24

1. The following summary is drawn from Barbara Zuck, *A History of Musical Americanism*.

2. Marc Blitzstein, "Popular Music—An Invasion: 1923–1933."

3. "Modern Amerikai Zeneszerzök [Modern American Composers]," *Uj Föld*, April 1927, 62–63.

4. Barbara Zuck (*A History of Musical Americanism*: 273, 277) also noted that HC's promotion of American music was distinct from Americanist music.

5. "Bericht aus Amerika," *Melos*, 9 (August, October, December 1930).

6. HC to CEI, 11/16/30.

7. HC to Olive, 11/13/32.

8. HC to Chavez, 6/5/31; HC to Olive, 11/7/31; HC to CEI, 2/16/33, 4/29/33.

9. HC to CEI, 11/16/30.

10. HC to NS, 5/23/33.

11. Alban Berg to HC, 7/28/33.

12. I. Amdur to Stanford University Press, 6/19/33.

13. Hicks, *Bohemian*, 121.

14. Stanford University Press to HC, 11/3/33, 1//15/35.

Chapter 25

1. HC, "Who Is the Greatest Living Composer?" in *Northwest Musical Herald*, 1/1933.

2. HC elaborated on them in "Vocal Innovators of Central Europe," in *Modern Music*, 7/2 (February–March 1930): 34–38, where he talks about innovators in vocal technique in Europe.

3. The *Carmelite*, 7/28/31.

4. HC, "Why Modern Music," *Women's City Club Magazine*, 5/11 (December 1931): 16–17.

5. HC, "Creation and Imitation: A Dissertation on New Music," *Fortnightly*, 1/6 (November 20, 1931): 5–6.

6. HC, "Music," *Encyclopedia Americana*, annual supplement for 1929.

7. SRC conversation with JS.

8. HC, "Irish Traditional Music," *Irish Review* (May 1934): 21, 30; "The Music of Iceland," *Musical Mercury*, 3/3 (September 1936): 48–50; "An American Composer on Yugoslav Folk-Music," *Balkan Herald*, 1/5 (August 1935): 5; "The 'Sones' of Cuba," *Modern Music*, 8/2 (January–February 1931): 45–47. In HC to Olive, 11/26/31, he says he did a version for an unnamed Austrian newspaper but it is not known if the paper accepted it.

9. HC; "Towards Neo-Primitivism," *Modern Music* 10/3 (March–April, 1933):149–53.

10. HC; "The Scientific Approach to Non-European Music," *Music Vanguard: A Critical Review*, 1/1 (Summer 1935): 62–67.

Chapter 26

1. SRC to Oakley C. Johnson, 7/7/67.

2. Olive Cowell interviewed by Rita Mead, 5/22/75, 11/8/75.

3. Russell Varian to his family, 1/24/21; Russell Varian to his mother, 9/15/31. Stanford, Green Library, Special Collections.

4. See Pescatello and Tick, passim.

5. For details, see Amy Nelson, *Music for the Revolution*, and Boris Schwarz, *Music and Musical Life*.

6. Nelson, *Music for the Revolution*, 93.

7. HC: "Kto Kompositori v'Amerikye" [Who Are the Composers in America], *Muzika i Revolutsiya* 6 (late fall 1929): 34–38.

8. Republished in New York's Russian newspaper *Russkiy Golos* [Russian Voice], 2/23/30, with a similar introduction but without the reference to class orientation. Henry sent a copy to

Ives; a translation is in the Ives papers, Irving S. Gilmore Music Library of Yale University. HC to CEI, 3/18/30.

9. HC to H&O, 1/5/30. The initial press run of 2,000 was immediately reduced to 1,500.

10. Dorothy Lawton to HC, 4/4/30.

11. Georges Rimsky-Korsakov to HC, 5/?/30.

12. HC to Olive, 11/21/31.

13. HC to NS, 11/2/31.

14. Szabó (1902–1969) had emigrated from Hungary to the USSR in 1931; Weisshaus had recently declared for communism and intended to move to the USSR.

15. *Encyclopedia Americana* annual supplement for 1931.

16. Pescatello, *Seeger*, 109.

17. Canon, "The Federal Music Project," 223.

18. Ibid., 240; see also Elliott Carter, *Essays*, 203, on the split of the new-music world in the United States.

19. Tick, *Seeger*, 189.

20. See, for example, Seeger's "On Proletarian Music," *Modern Music* 11/2 (March–April, 1934): 121–27.

21. Pescatello, *Seeger*, 109.

22. Comments by SRC attached to a clip from the *New York Times* 6/5/77.

23. Reuss and Reuss, *American Folk Music*, 24.

24. Elizabeth Clark to HC, 3/17/32.

25. Signed by Jack Scott, Corresponding Secretary, Workers Music League, 3/18/32.

26. Olive's notes on a lecture at the San Francisco YWCA, May 1932.

27. Dunaway, "The Composers' Collective," 1–3. Also Henry Leland Clarke, "Composers' Collective of New York," *New Grove 2*; HC to H&O, 1/17/33. See also Pescatello, *Charles Seeger*; Tick, *Ruth Seeger*; Gac, "Comrades"; Blitzstein in *Unison: The Organ of the American Music League*, 1/2 (June 1936), quoted in Copland and Perlis, *Copland, 1900 through 1942*, 223.

28. Blitzstein, *Unison*.

29. Reuss and Reuss, *American Folk Music*, 45.

30. 11/21/33, cited ibid., 48.

31. Dunaway, "The Composers' Collective," 14–15.

32. I. Amdur, VOKS, to HC, 6/19/33.

33. L. Cherniavsky, VOKS, to HC, 7/26/33.

34. I. Amdur to HC, 10/19/33.

35. See Montefiore, *Stalin*, p. 241n and passim.

36. HC to SRC, 6/15/55.

37. NS to HC, 11/18/33.

38. HC to NS, 11/24/33, 11/26/33.

39. NS to HC, 11/25/33.

40. L. Cherniavsky to HC, 1/17/34.

41. Mead, *Henry Cowell's New Music*, 298–301.

42. Lazare Saminsky, "Europe and America in Music Today," *Modern Music*, 10/1 (January–February 1933): 93–95.

43. NS to HC, 11/28/33.

44. Kuznetsov to HC, 3/3/34 and 3/24/34.

45. Kuznetsov to HC, 2/4/34.

46. L. Cherniavsky to HC, 3/25/34.

47. Kuznetsov to HC, 3/28/34.

48. Reuss and Reuss, *American Folk Music*, 64.

49. *Baker's Biographical Dictionary* (6th ed., 1971): 1536. Thanks to Laurel Fay for his death date.

50. Schneerson to HC, 2/23/34.

51. Schneerson to HC, April 29, 1934.

52. Clipping from *Moscow Daily News*, 6/2/34, marked with date in the usual purple pen of Kuznetsov, who probably sent it to HC.

53. Schneerson to HC, 4/29/34.

54. See Bruce Minton and John Stuart, *Men Who Lead Labor* (New York: Modern Age, ca. 1937): 135.

55. Lan Adomian to HC, 7/12/34.

56. Seeger to HC, 3/20/34.

57. Valdimir Lakond to HC, 3/7/34.

58. George Charles to HC, 12/24/34.

59. Olive's notes on a visit with HC, 3/15/34.

60. "Tribuna zarubezhnikh compozitorov," *Sovyetskaya Muzika* (October, 1934): 78–81. Translation by JS.

61. Schneerson to HC, 12/4/34.

62. HC to Schneerson, 1/6/35; Schneerson to HC, 2/17/35. Schneerson's copy: Glinka Museum, Moscow. The date on his copy of the letter to Henry, 2/17/35, suggests that Schneerson may have delayed sending it.

63. HC, "Kept Music," in *Panorama: A Monthly Survey of People and Ideas*, 2/15 (December 1934): 6.

64. Schneerson to HC, 5/14/35.

65. Sitsky, *Music*, 111.

66. Soviet music specialist Laurel Fay was unable to determine who Feldman might have been. Grigory Petrovich Feldman, a later Miaskovsky student, was only thirteen in 1933.

67. Frankenstein was not impressed. See Mead, *Henry Cowell's New Music*, 324.

68. Howard Taubman, "Problems of Soviet Style," *New York Times*, 8/5/35.

69. Schneerson to HC, 10/27/35.

70. It appeared as "'Useful Music'" in *New Masses*, 10/29/35. Strang wrote Henry, 11/4/35, that he grinned over this incident. "We also had some contacts with the longshore strike."

71. Schneerson to HC, 5/31/36.

72. *Pierre Degeyter Music Club News*, March 1936. (Pierre Degeyter Music Club of Philadelphia.) Seeger expressed similar thoughts in "On Proletarian Music," *Modern Music*, 11/2 (March–April 1934): 121–27.

73. Gabriel Braverman to HC, 6/24/36.

74. Reuss and Reuss, *American Folk Music*, 68.

75. See Canon, "The Federal Music Project," 39–59.

76. Grigory Schneerson, "The Changing Course of Soviet Music," *Modern Music*, 13/2 (January–February 1936): 19–24.

77. "O novoi musike—pis'mo Genri Cowella" [About New Music—letter from Henry Cowell] *Sovyetskaya Muzika*, 9 (September 1936), 92–94. Translation by JS.

78. Adomian to HC, 2/13/36 and 3/6/36.

79. Montefiore, *Stalin*, 183, 395.

Chapter 27

1. HC to Olive, 8/27/32.

2. HC to CEI, 1/10/31.

3. CEI to HC, undated. Pencil on yellow legal paper, mid-1930s.

4. HC to Moss Ives, 5/2/32, and SRC's note on that letter.

5. CEI to HC, 2/26/[35?]. Edith says she is now acting as her father's stenographer "in place of a wobbly pen!"

6. CEI to HC, undated #14, 13/50/[35?]. Reproduced by permission of the American Academy of Arts and Letters, copyright owner.

7. Evelyn Becker to SRC, undated.

8. HC, prefatory note, 12/45, to Lou Harrison, *About Carl Ruggles: Section Four of a Book on Ruggles* (Yonkers, NY: Bardinaky), 1946.

9. Frank Wigglesworth interviewed by Rita Mead, 4/15/75.

10. *New Music* printed *Density 21.5* in 1946.

11. Copland, "America's Young Men—Ten Years Later," *Modern Music*, 13 (May–June, 1936): 3–11.

12. Goossens to HC, 2/9/35.

13. Sabine Feisst, Henry Cowell und Arnold Schönberg—eine unbekannte Freundschaft, *Archiv für Musikwissenschaft* 55/1 (1998), 57–71; Feisst, *Schoenberg's New World*, passim.

14. SRC to Mrs. Hawkins, undated but shortly after 10/10/41.

15. HC to Harry, undated, clearly 1916. Comments by Henry around 1919 imply that they also were in contact then.

16. PG to HC, 1/31/33.

17. Bird, *Grainger*, 1–46; 229; also Photo 1.

18. HC to PG, 2/20/33. Original: Grainger Museum, Melbourne.

19. HC to Olive, 2/21/33; HC to PG, 2/22/[33].

20. PG to HC, 8/29/33.

21. Cage in conversation with JS, 1991.

22. Probably 12/16/29, for the Honorary Music Club at Claremont College.

23. Cage to HC, 10/26/33.

24. HC, in "Current Chronicle," *Musical Quarterly* 38/1 (January 1952): 123–34.

25. Mead, *Henry Cowell's New Music*, 227, 229.

26. Ibid., 60.

27. Cage to HC, 10/26/33.

28. Interviews, John Cage folder. Vignettes by SRC sent to WDR for its Cage 75th birthday program "Nachtcagetag," 2/14/87.

29. Kostelanetz, *John Cage: An Anthology*, 36.

30. HC in "Current Chronicle," *Musical Quarterly* 38/1 (January 1952): 123–34.

31. This confirms Leta Miller's suggestion that whether or not one ascribes Cage's development to Henry's influence, their interests converged. Miller, "*Henry Cowell and John Cage.*"

32. Lou Harrison interviewed by Rita Mead, 10/1/77: Lou's remarks at a bicentennial concert at Menlo Park, 10/10/76.

33. HC to Lou Harrison, 9/11/35. Sidney was probably wrong in thinking that the letter referred to Harrison's work on Ives's Robert Browning Overture. He would have been only eighteen at that time, and said he wrote Ives on Henry's suggestion in 1936.

34. See Chapter 5.

35. Charles Amirkhanian to JS, conversation, October 2009. Amirkhanian said Harrison told him the story several times.

36. Peter Garland, ed., *A Lou Harrison Reader* (Santa Fe: Soundings Press, 1987), 29.

Chapter 28

1. Schmolke to HC, 7/22/24.

2. Schmolke to HC, 6/6/26.

3. Schmolke to HC, 6/11/27.

4. Schmolke to HC, 2/2/28.

5. HC to Olive, 11/21/31.

6. Schmolke to Olive, 1/1/32, trans. JS.

7. HC to Olive, 8/5/32.

8. HC and Schmolke to CEI, 8/15/32.

9. Schmolke to HC, 2/6/33.

10. Schmolke to HC, 2/18/33.

11. Schmolke to HC, 2/8/34.

12. BW to HC, 2/14/[34].

13. Clarence Davidson to HC, 5/24/34.

14. Schmolke to HC, 6/10/34.

15. Schmolke to HC, 9/18/34, but from context certainly 7/18.

16. HC to Olive, 10/1/34.

17. Schmolke to HC, 10/16/34.

18. Schmolke to HC, 2/17/35.

19. Schmolke to HC, 5/18/35.

20. Schmolke to HC, 6/8/36.

21. Schmolke to HC, 10/16/34; her cousin Olga Roggenkamp to HC and SRC, 6/3/63.

22. Cowell papers, photographs.

23. SRC to Vivian Perlis, 10/12/73.

24. SRC to Hugo Weisgall, 2/3/71.

25. Olive to SRC, 11/23/76.

26. Olive to SRC, dated 1977. Notes by SRC.

Chapter 29

1. See David Nicholls, "*Transethnicism.*"

2. "Lou Harrison at the University of Illinois, with Tom Siwe." *Percussive Notes*, 18/2 (Winter 1980): 30–33, 57–61. In a private conversation, however, SRC told JS that she felt Harrison was unreliable as a witness.

3. Charles Seeger, "Henry Cowell," *Magazine of Art*, 33/5 (May 1940): 288 ff.

Chapter 30

1. H. Wiley Hitchcock, "Editing Ives' 129 Songs," in *Ives Studies*, ed. Philip Lambert (Cambridge: Cambridge University Press, 1997).

2. Paul Rosenfeld, "The Winged Mercury," in *New Republic*, 76/979 (September 6, 1933): 109.

3. Gerald Strang interviewed by Rita Mead, 10/29/75.

4. Dorothy Blaney to SRC, 9/4/[73?].

5. Dorothy Blaney to SRC, 10/18[73?].

6. Lehman Engel interviewed by Cole Gagne, 3/4/77.

Chapter 31

1. Michael Hicks, "The Imprisonment."

2. Ibid.

3. Leta E. Miller and Rob Collins, "The Cowell-Ives Relationship."

4. Undated petition, ca. 1935, requesting removal of one boy from the "Las Lomitas Boys' Club."

5. Elmo Robinson to HC, 5/4/36. He apparently is not the juvenile officer mentioned later.

6. *Statutes of California.*

7. Olive's mother to Olive, 7/9/36.

8. Alfred Frankenstein interviewed by Rita Meade, 11/7/75.

9. Alfred Frankenstein to SRC, 10/3/[41].

10. Gerald Strang to Wallingford Riegger, 10/4/36; Olive to Lilly Popper, 9/27/36.

11. SRC undated note, probably 1973, on a letter from Duncan Oneal to Olive.

12. *The Newsletter and Wasp,* 6/6/, 6/13, 6/20, 6/27, 7/11/36. The authors' names are John L. LeBerthon and Jean Nohtrebel, presumably pseudonyms for the same person.

13. Typescript list of reasons for asking for a pardon, and various tasks. Probably by SRC, 1942.

14. Charles Seeger interviewed by Andrea Olmstead, 7/7/77.

15. Olive, statement on HC's imprisonment, 7/62; Olive interviewed by Rita Mead, 5/22/75 and 11/8/75. Olive: "My life with [the] Cowells," 23–26.

16. Olive to SRC, 11/23/76.

17. Olive to Wolff, 6/25/36.

18. Ray Green interviewed by Rita Mead, 9/8/76.

19. Elizabeth Moss to HC, 5/27/36.

20. John Cage to HC, 6/18/36.

21. Jean Seward Uppman, "Memories of Henry Cowell." In possession of JS.

22. NS to HC, 6/27/36.

23. Bonnie Fox Schwartz, "Social Workers and New Deal Politicians in Conflict: California's Branion-Williams Case, 1933–34," *Pacific Historical Reviews,* 42/1 (February 1973): 53–73.

24. Pierce Williams to HC, 6/7/36.

25. "Mary" to Olive, undated.

26. John Kirkpatrick interviewed by Cole Gagne, 2/25/77; Feder, *Charles Ives, My Father's Song,* 345; HC to Olive, 5/29/36.

27. NS to HC, 6/27/36.

28. Harmony Ives to Mrs. Ruggles, 7/3/36. Typescript transcript. Original: MSS 26, The Carl Ruggles Papers in the Irving S. Gilmore Music Library of Yale University. Reproduced by permission of the American Academy of Arts and Letters, copyright owner.

29. SRC's account of her relationship with HC.

30. Sidney to HC, 6/4/36.

31. HC to H&O, 5/25/46.

32. Strang to HC, 6/23/36.

33. HC to H&O, undated; handwritten notes in HC's hand concerning his case. One small sheet and two sheets of *New Music Quarterly* letterhead. Undated, but the contents suggest late May/early June.

34. HC to Olive, 5/29/36.

35. Alvin Johnson to HC, 6/17/36.

36. HC to H&O, undated, late May 1936.

37. HC to H&O, "Some ideas concerning my case," on *New Music Quarterly* letterhead, directed to his parents, written soon after his arrest, perhaps even the same day.

38. SRC note, probably from 1973, on a letter from Duncan Oneal to Olive.

39. "Cowell Enters a Plea of Guilty." *San Francisco Examiner,* 6/23/36.

40. HC to Chávez, 5/30/36.

41. HC to H&O, "Some ideas concerning my case" (see note 37).

42. Elsa Schmolke to unnamed friend of Olive, 6/17/36.

43. Olive interviewed by Rita Mead, 5/22/75 and 11/8/75.

44. HC, "Synopsis of My Sex Life," June 1936.

45. On the Sullivan connection, see Chapter 43. One Sullivan child signed the petition cited in chapter 31, note 4.

46. William Justema to SRC, 5/22/79.

47. Seeger to HC, 6/13/36.

48. Olive: "My life with [the] Cowells," 23–26; Olive interviewed by Rita Mead, 5/22/75, 11/8/75.

49. HC, "Insurance against Return," 5/28/36.

50. SRC, 1/20/88, note written on Strang to Chávez, 8/30/36.

51. Olive to Lilly Popper, 9/27/36.

Chapter 32

1. HC to NS, 7/6/36.

2. David Rothman, *Conscience and Convenience*, chapter 3.

3. All quotations not otherwise attributed are taken from the record of the hearing, Superior Court, San Mateo County.

4. Dr. Joseph Wortis interviewed by JS, 7/12/94.

5. Olive to Wolff, 10/17/26.

6. Statement after conviction, in record of hearing, Superior Court, San Mateo County.

7. SRC note, about 1973, on a letter from Duncan Oneal to Olive. She says Henry told her this story, but considering the late date of the note, and Sidney's dislike of Harry, it must be taken under advisement.

8. Virgil Thomson interviewed by Cole Gagne, 2/28/77.

9. Carey McWilliams, a high state official in the late 1930s, felt the *Examiner* now had a vested interest in the conviction. McWilliams, *The Education of Carey McWilliams*, 81.

Chapter 33

1. HC to NS, 7/6/36; Olive to NS, 7/13/36.

2. HC to Becker, 7/7/36.

3. HC to NS, 7/8/36.

4. Schmolke to HC, 7/8/36.

5. Stanley, 241.

6. Ibid., 15.

7. Duffy, *The San Quentin Story*, 135.

8. Ibid., 20.

9. Ibid., 21.

10. Ibid., 27–28.

11. Ibid., 26–27.

12. Ibid., 58.

13. Ibid., 35–36.

14. Ibid., 24, 34, 35, 49, 131.

15. HC to H&O, 7/9/36.

16. SRC, account of her relationship with HC.

17. San Quentin visitor's permit, 1939.

18. HC to H&O, 7/11/36.

19. HC to H&O, 7/10/36.

20. HC to Olive, 11/21/36.

21. Duffy, *The San Quentin Story*, 48; Lamott, *Chronicles*, 206.

22. Duffy, 46.

23. Stanley, 147, 230.

24. HC to Olive, 9/7/36.

25. SRC's account of her relationship with HC.

26. Duffy, *The San Quentin Story* 107–8; Stanley, 201.

27. Duffy, 35–36, 160.

28. HC to H&O, 7/11/36; Olive to Ernst Wolff, 7/31/36.

29. HC to H&O, 7/25/36.

30. Duffy, *The San Quentin Story* 140.

31. HC to H&O, 7/11/36.

32. Duffy, 45.

33. HC to NS, 7/16/36.

34. Duffy, *The San Quentin Story* 139.

35. HC to NS, 7/16/36.

36. HC to NS, 8/13/36; HC to Becker, 8/5/36.

37. Harmony Ives to Charlotte Ruggles, 7/12/36. Yale University Library. Typed transcript. Original: MSS 26, The Carl Ruggles Papers in the Irving S. Gilmore Music Library of Yale University. Reproduced by permission of the American Academy of Arts and Letters, copyright owner.

38. HC to BW, 7/17/36.

39. BW to Olive, 7/24/36.

40. Judy Brown to Olive, 8/4/36.

41. Alvin Johnson to Olive, 7/30/36.

42. Postmark date 8/3/36.

43. HC to Adolph Weiss, 7/29/36. Partly printed in William George, *Adolph Weiss*, 293–94.

44. Alvin Johnson to Olive, 9/19/36.

45. HC to H&O, 7/25/36.

46. HC to NS, 8/13/36.

47. Olive to Ernst Wolff, 7/31/36.

48. HC to Olive, 8/15/36.

49. The only other Evelyn in HC's life was Becker's wife, but since she was not in California, this Evelyn is unlikely to have been Mrs. Becker.

50. Wolff to unstated recipient, 8/28/36.

51. Adler to Wolff, 9/21/36.

52. HC to Becker, 8/5/36.

53. HC to Olive, 8/15/36.

54. Ibid.

55. Otto Westfell to Olive, 8/14/36.

56. Strang to Chavez, 8/30/36.

57. HC to "Jean," 9/1/36.

58. SRC's account of her relationship with HC.

59. Strang to Chávez, 8/30/36.

60. HC to Lilly Popper, 10/3/36, in Olive Cowell papers, NYPLFPA.

61. SRC to Vivian Perlis, 6/6/81, 6/30/81.

62. Duffy, *The San Quentin Story* 35.

63. Stanley, 142.

64. HC to Olive, 12/11/36 and 3/26/36.

65. HC to Popper, 10/3/36; HC to Olive, 10/8/36, in Olive Cowell papers, NYPLFPA; HC to NS, 12/15/36.

66. HC to Olive, 9/26/36, HC to H&O, 10/1/36, and Hans Nathan to HC, 12/12/36.

67. HC to Popper, 10/3/36, in Olive Cowell papers, NYPLFPA; HC to Olive, 12/11/26.

68. NS to Olive, 11/9/36.

69. HC to Olive, 7/12/37.

70. Strang to Chávez, 8/30/36.

71. HC to Popper, 9/12/36.

72. HC to "Jean," 9/1/36, HC to Olive, 9/7/36, HC to Popper, 9/12/36 and 10/3/36. In Olive Cowell papers, NYPLFPA; HC to Harry, 10/16/36.

73. Rothman, *Conscience and Convenience*, 136.

74. HC to "Jean," 9/1/36; HC to Olive, 9/7/36.

75. HC to Popper, 9/12/36; HC to Olive, 9/26/36.

76. HC to Olive, 10/18/36, 11/6/36.

77. H.A. Shuder to Olive, 9/22/36.

78. Duffy, *The San Quentin Story* 142.

79. HC to Olive, 11/29/36.

80. HC to Olive, 12/11/36.

81. HC to Olive, 10/22/36, 10/28/26.

82. HC to NS, 8/28/36.

83. HC to Olive, 10/21/36, 11/6/36.

84. Lichtenwanger, p. 149. Unnamed newspaper, apparently California, 11/1/36 (based on story on the verso); undated full-page article, *Philadelphia Inquirer*, 1936.

85. HC to Popper, 9/12/36, 10/3/36; HC to Olive, 9/26/36.

86. HC to Olive, 10/8/36.

87. Duffy, *The San Quentin Story* 225–26 and passim.

88. HC to Olive, 11/29/36, 1/25/37, 3/10/37, 3/26/37.

89. PG to HC, undated.

90. HC to NS, 11/14/36.

91. HC to Dorothy Slonimsky, 1/20/37.

92. HC to Olive, 12/8/36.

93. HC to Olive, 1/29/36.

94. Rules as to What Prisoners Can and Cannot Receive, 12/36.

95. HC to BW, 1/5/37; HC to Becker, 5/28/37.

96. HC to Olive, 12/24/36.

97. HC to Olive, 1/25/37.

98. HC to Harry, 2/4/37.

99. HC to Olive, 2/22/37, 3/10/37; 5/4/37; HC to Popper, 7/31/37; HC to NS, 8/5/37.

100. Judy Brown to Olive, 9/18/36; conversations between JS and SRC.

101. Ralph Samuelson suggested that although playing the instrument in the visitors' area might have been forbidden, Tamada could have taught Henry a lot about breathing (conversation with JS).

102. SRC, account of her relationship with Henry, 2/11/71.

103. HC to Olive, 9/5/36.

104. HC to Olive, 9/26/36.

105. HC to H&O, 10/1/36.

106. HC to Harry, 6/27/37.

107. Edwin Hughes to HC, 4/5/37.

108. HC to Olive, 5/4/37.

109. HC to NS, 6/17/37.

110. HC to NS, 12/15/36.

111. HC to Olive, 12/11/36.

112. HC to Olive, 1/10/37.

113. Olive to Ives, 3/6/37.

114. Harmony Ives to Olive, 3/12/37.

115. HC to Olive, 4/10/37.

116. HC to Olive, 4/10/37, 5/4/37.

117. HC to Becker, 5/28/37.

118. HC to Olive, 5/29/37.

119. Clifton Furness to Olive, 8/23/37.

120. HC to NS, 8/5/37.

121. Judy Brown to Olive, 9/18/36.

122. HC to Luening, 10/12/36.

123. Luening to HC, 11/30/36.

124. HC to Copland, 10/23/36.

125. HC to Olive, 11/29/36.

126. HC to Luening, 8/4/37.

127. HC to NS, 8/5/37.

128. HC to Becker, 9/29/36.

129. HC to Luening, 10/12/36.

130. Luening to HC, 11/30/36.

131. HC to Weiss, 12/1/36. Also printed in part in William George, "Adolph Weiss," 323–24.

132. HC to Luening, 12/5/36.

133. HC to BW, 1/5/37.

134. Riegger to Becker, 2/7/37.

Chapter 34

1. For elaboration of these ideas see Rothman, *Conscience and Convenience*, chapter 2.

2. Lamott, *Chronicles of San Quenton*, 22.

3. Rothman, *Conscience and Convenience*, chapter 5, and passim; Strang to Riegger, 10/4/36.

4. Alvin Johnson to Harry Cowell, 9/8/36.

5. Undated carbon clipped to letter from Seeger to HC, 6/13/36.

6. Materials almost certainly from the files of John Douglas Short, concerning sentences for sexual offenses.

7. Duffy, *The San Quentin Story* 107.

8. Lilly Popper to HC, 9/27/36, sent via Olive.

9. NS to Olive, 10/13/36, 11/7/36.

10. HC to Chávez, 11/26/36.

11. HC to Popper, 5/16/37.

12. Popper to Olive, 5/2/37.

13. HC to Popper, 5/16/37.

14. Rothman, chapters 2 and 5.

15. HC to Grete Williams, 11/1/36.

16. Carbon of statement dated 3/3/37, with a note to Wolff re: Short.

17. BW to Olive and to the Board, 3/11/37.

18. Olive to Douglas Short, 1/10/37.

19. HC to Olive, 1/25/37.

20. Elizabeth Moss to Olive, 12/18/36.

21. Olive to Wolff, 1/17/36.

22. HC to Olive, 1/20/37.

23. HC to Olive, 1/10/37.

24. F. A. Cochran to Douglas Short, 2/20/37.

25. "Expert Opinion Without Remuneration given by Dr. Lewis Terman . . . in a statement to Ernest Wolff," 3/3/37.

26. Short to the Board, 4/19/37.

27. HC to Olive, 4/20/37.

28. HC to Short, 5/19/37.

29. The members of the Board were J. H. Stephens, Sacramento; David T. Bush, Oakdale; and Fred Esola, San Francisco. Short to Oneal, 5/25/37.

30. Pierce Williams to Olive, 5/27/37.

31. Short to the Board, 6/7/37.

32. David Bush, telegram to Douglas Short, 6/8/37.

33. Short to David P. Bush, Fred L. Esola, and Joseph F. Stephens, 7/28/37.

34. Helen Hope Page to HC, 7/19/37, doubtless via Olive.

35. Helen Hope Page to HC, 6/14/38. It is unlikely that she is the "Helen" mentioned in chapter 33, p. 303.

36. HC to Olive, 8/11/37.

37. Rothman, 162–65.

38. HC to Olive and Harry, 8/13/37.

39. HC to H&O, 8/14/37.

Chapter 35

1. HC to Luening, 9/15/37; HC to Copland, 9/17/37.
2. HC to Lilly Popper, 8/22/37.
3. SF *Chronicle*, 9/2/3.
4. SF *News*. 8/27/37.
5. Lou Harrison to Olive, 8/21/37.
6. NS conversations with JS, 1988.
7. NS to HC, 8/24/37.
8. Georgia Kober to Olive, 9/8/37.
9. Alvin Johnson to Olive, 9/14/37.
10. Judy Brown to Olive, 8/24/37.
11. PG to Olive, 8/15/37.
12. Olive to Beyer, 8/24/37.
13. HC to Popper, 8/22/37.
14. HC to Popper, 8/22/37.
15. HC to BW, 8/23/37.
16. HC to Copland, 9/17/37.
17. HC to Becker, 9/5/37.
18. HC to BW, 8/23/37.
19. Hicks, "Imprisonment," 100; Ziffrin, *Ruggles*, 146.
20. John Kirkpatrick interviewed by Cole Gagne, 2/25/77.
21. BW to Olive, 8/22/[37].
22. HC to Olive, 9/9/37.
23. William Lawson to Cyril Quill, copied to Douglas Short, 8/27/37.
24. HC to Olive, 9/9/37.
25. HC to Olive, 10/8/37.
26. HC to Olive, 9/9/37; HC to NS, 11/15/37; HC to BW, 8/23/37.
27. HC to Otto Luening, 9/5/37.
28. He wrote about this to several people, including Ernst Bacon, 9/29/38.
29. HC to Copland, 9/17/37.
30. HC to BW, 8/23/37.
31. HC to Olive, 10/7/37.
32. HC to Olive, 10/10/37.
33. HC to H&O, 1/27/38.
34. PG to Olive 8/15/37; HC to PG, 8/24/37; PG to Olive, 8/25/37; HC to Harry, 9/11/37; HC to Olive, 11/1/37; HC to PG, 11/2/37.
35. HC to PG, dated 1/2/37, but it must be 1938; Henry occasionally misdated letters early in a new year.
36. HC to PG, 1/7/38, 2/8/38.
37. HC to PG, 3/10/38.
38. SRC, account of her relationship with HC, 6–8.
39. HC to H&O, 3/3/38, 3/9/38.
40. The following is derived from numerous letters from the fall of 1937 to the late spring, 1938.
41. HC to H&O, 3/9/38.
42. HC to Olive, 12/29/37; Beyer to Luening, 1/3/38; HC to Harry, 2/2/38.
43. HC to H&O, 11/21/37; HC to NS, 2/26/28; HC to PG, 7/31/38.
44. HC to Harry 2/2/38.
45. SRC, account of her relationship with Henry.
46. HC to PG, 5/24/38.
47. HC to Copland, 2/10/38.
48. HC to BW, 6/8/38.
49. HC to PG, 7/4/38.
50. HC to NS, 7/12/38; HC to Grete and Pierce Williams, 7/17/38.
51. HC to H&O, 7/22/38.
52. HC to PG, 7/31/38.
53. Ernst Wolff to Helen Hope Page, 4/29/38.
54. Short to Mark Noon, secretary of the Board of Prison Terms and Paroles, 8/8/38.
55. Helen Hope Page to PG, 6/14/38.
56. See Rothman, passim.
57. Wortis to Adolph Meyer, 6/17/38; Wolff to Olive, 6/20/38.
58. HC to PG, 6/19/38, Alan Mason Chesney Medical Archive, Johns Hopkins University; HC to Wolff, 6/23/38; Wolff to Wortis, 6/23/38; HC to Short 6/24/38; HC to H&O, 7/7/38.
59. Mark Noon to Short, 6/22/38.

Chapter 36

1. HC to Olive, 11/25/38; HC to NS, 2/26/39.
2. Sidney to HC, carbon, 9/30/38.
3. HC to Sidney, 8/8/38; undated ca. 1938.
4. HC to Sidney, 3/17/39.
5. Milton Babbitt, conversation with JS.

6. HC to H&O, 4/6/39, 8/29/39; HC to Olive, 7/30/39. Henry could not take his list of visitors when he left San Quentin.

7. HC to BW, 7/11/38.

8. HC to H&O, 12/26/38; Milton Babbitt, conversation with JS.

9. HC to BW, 9/26/38; HC to Ann and James Mundstock, 7/8/38; HC to H&O, 7/7/38.

10. HC to H&O, 4/26/39; HC to BW, 5/3/39.

11. HC to PG, 9/2/39; HC to Olive, 9/6/39.

12. HC to H&O, 9/12/38; HC to Becker, 10/3/38; Olive to Otto Luening, 10/8/38.

13. HC to Olive, 11/9/38.

14. HC to Olive, 11/25/38.

15. HC to BW, 12/20/38.

16. HC to Ernst Bacon, 3/31/39.

17. HC to NS, 10/1/39; HC to Olive, 12/8/39.

18. HC to H&O, 6/15/39.

19. HC to Ruggles, 7/8/39.

20. HC to H&O, 7/7/38.

21. Certificates, 3/21/39 and 4/20/40.

22. HC to PG, 4/9/39.

23. HC to H&O, 4/26/39.

24. HC to PG, 5/16/39.

25. HC to Ruggles, 7/8/39.

26. HC to BW, 9/11/39.

27. HC to Olive, 7/30/39.

28. HC to PG, 8/13/39.

29. HC to Olive, 9/24/39.

30. HC to PG, 9/19/39.

31. HC to PG, 9/19/39, 10/22/39, 12/11/39.

32. HC to PG, 10/22/39.

33. HC to Olive, 10/6/38; Olive to Luening, 10/8/38; HC to Olive, 11/9/38.

Chapter 37

1. Nancy Yunhwa Rao, "American Compositional Theory . . ."; "Henry Cowell and His Chinese Music Heritage . . ."

2. HC to PG, 6/13/37.

3. Beyer to Luening, 11/27/37.

4. Lou Harrison, *Primer*.

5. Henry wrote his article on Icelandic music before being arrested.

6. *Dance Observer*, 4/1 (January 1937): 1, 7–9.

7. SRC note with a photo of Graham from the *New York Times*, 11/20/80.

8. HC to Olive, 4/10/37.

9. HC to Harry, 6/27/37, and to Olive, 8/11/37.

10. Stewart, *Dances*, 19.

11. Lynn Garafola, *José Limón*, 83.

12. I am very grateful to Aaron Sherber of the Martha Graham Company for providing a copy of Canto Hondo. It was discovered behind a desk by Terese Capucilli, who had restored the dance with Martha Graham but using other music, since Henry's score was still missing.

Chapter 38

1. Stanley, *Men at Their Worst*, passim.

2. Short to Meyer, 8/12/38; Alan Mason Chesney Medical Archives, Johns Hopkins University.

3. HC to Wolff, 8/13/38.

4. Helen Hope Page to Wolff, 9/11/38.

5. Wolff to Helen Hope Page, 9/13/38; Short to Page, 9/19/38.

6. Dr. Joseph Wortis interviewed by JS, 7/12/94.

7. Wortis, Expert Opinion, 11/15/38.

8. HC to Short, 11/24/38.

9. Adolph Meyer to L. L. Stanley, 11/20/38; Meyer's Expert Opinion without Remuneration, 11/30/38, Alan Mason Chesney Medical Archives, Johns Hopkins University.

10. HC to PG, 9/7/38, 9/20/38.

11. PG to HC, 10/6/38.

12. HC to PG, 11/19/38; Wolff to PG, 11/23/38; PG to Wolff, 1/17/38.

13. Carey McWilliams, *The Education of Carey McWilliams*, 80–81.

14. On Clark, see Lamott, *Chronicles of San Quentin*, and Duffy, *The San Quentin Story*.

15. Duffy, 37–38.

16. Mark Noon to PG, 2/7/39.

17. Clip from unidentified paper. A mark on the back implies the SF *Chronicle* during Governor Merriam's term.

18. Duffy, *The San Quentin Story*, 109.

19. Twitchell to Stanley, 1/30/39.

20. Stanley to Twitchell, 1/31/39.

21. HC to Olive, 3/4/39.

22. H.A. Shuder to HC, 3/11/39.

23. HC to PG, 5/16/39.

24. McWilliams, 81.

25. SRC, comments on a folder labeled "Cowell Case—Significant Papers from Files of Dr. Ernst Wolff, culled by SRC in 1973."

26. Wolff to Short, 6/2/39, 7/5/39.

27. HC to H&O, 8/29/39.

28. HC to PG, 9/2/39; HC to H&O, 9/6/39.

29. PG to State Parole Office, 9/26/39.

30. Meyer to Wolff, 10/23/29, Alan Mason Chesney Medical Archives, Johns Hopkins University; Wolff to Wortis, 11/1/39.

31. Wortis to Wolff, 11/9/36.

32. HC to Olive, 9/2/39.

33. Short to PG, 11/14/39.

34. HC to Olive, 11/16/39.

35. Olive to PG, 12/24/39.

36. Rothman, *Conscience and Convenience*, 136.

37. Olive to PG, 2/26/40; Henry to Harry, 3/15/40.

38. HC to Sidney, 4/11/40.

39. HC to Olive, 4/12/40.

40. Olive to Short, 4/13/40.

41. Olive to Wolff, 4/30/40.

42. Wolff to Meyer, 4/18/40, Alan Mason Chesney Medical Archives, Johns Hopkins University; also in Cowell papers.

43. Terman, "A Partial Psychological Survey of the Prison Population at San Quentin. . .," in *Surveys in Mental Deviation in Prisons, Public Schools and Orphanages in California*, 1918.

44. Lewis Terman to the Board, 4/22/40.

45. Summary of responses to questions about HC, answered by Meyer, Terman, Wortis, 1937–40; Dr. Edward Twitchell, 1/30/39; and Dr. Leo L. Stanley, 9/22/38.

46. Olive to Wolff, 4/20/40.

47. Carbon of a digest of the contents of forty letters on behalf of HC, prepared for the Board. Dated April–May 1940.

48. Florence MacFarlane to Wolff, 4/25/40, 4/26/40.

49. PG to HC, 5/23/40.

50. SRC, "Cowell Case: Significant Papers . . .": comments written on orange folder, 1973.

51. Robert Kenny to the Board, carbon, 5/8/40.

52. "Parole or Ticket of Leave . . . Parole Granted by the Board of Prison Terms and Paroles of the State of California." Parole granted 5/6/40.

53. John Gee Clark to Johanna Magdalena Beyer, 5/29/40.

54. McWilliams to Olive, 5/9/40.

55. HC to PG, 5/11/40.

56. HC to PG, 5/12/40.

57. Note by SRC on Wolff to Meyer, 5/13/40.

58. HC to PG, 5/14/40; Olive to PG, 5/14/40, 5/23/40.

59. HC to PG, 5/16/40.

60. HC to PG, 5/29/40, 6/5/4.

61. Program 6/2/40.

62. HC to Sidney, 6/9/40; HC to Olive, 6/10/40.

63. HC to Sidney, 6/9/40.

64. Carey McWilliams, *The Education of Carey McWilliams*, 81.

Chapter 39

1. HC to Becker, 6/29/40; HC to H&O, 7/10/40.

2. Arthur Berger interviewed by Andrea Olmstead, 11/9/77.

3. Olive to PG, 5/14/40, 5/23/40; HC to Sidney, 6/29/40.

4. HC to H&O, 7/26/40. The article: "Grainger Home Becomes 'Laboratory' for Exciting New Piano Technique," White Plains *Evening Dispatch*, 7/24/40.

5. Wolff to Wortis, 7/30/40.

6. Wortis to Wolff, 8/10/40.

7. Dr. Joseph Wortis interviewed by JS, 7/12/94.

8. H. A. Shuder to HC, 7/23/40; Shuder to Mary Macfarlane, 9/4/40.

9. HC to BW, 7/6/40; HC to SRC, 7/8/40; HC to H&O, 7/10/40, 7/19/40; HC to Becker, 7/11/40. The Graingers were reached through a neighbor who managed him.

10. Dr. Joseph Wortis interviewed by JS, 7/12/94, in JS collection.

11. HC to SRC, 7/10/40, 7/29/40; HC to Olive, 9/23/40.

12. HC to Olive, 8/5/40.

13. HC to H&O, 7/19/40.

14. HC to Becker, 8/6/40, 10/15/40; HC to H&O, 10/29/40; HC to Fabien Sevitzky, 10/18/40; HC to NS, 10/29/40.

15. HC to Becker, 7/11/40, 7/22/40, 8/30/40, 9/3/40, 10/15/40; Becker to HC, 7/16/40; 7/[?]/40, 8/9/40, 9/4/40; Mattfield to HC, 8/5/40; Salzedo to HC, 8/28/40.

16. Harmony Ives to HC, 8/14/40.

17. SRC conversation with JS.

18. See, for example, HC to Olive, 8/30/40, 10/13/40.

19. Lilly Popper to HC, 10/8/40.

20. Olive to HC, 8/8/40.

21. HC to Olive, 8/30/40, 9/4/40, 9/17/40, 11/25/40; HC to H&O, 9/10/4, 9/16/40.

22. Olive to HC, 8/8/40.

23. HC to H&O, 8/30/40.

24. HC to Olive, 9/27/40; Olive to HC, undated, apparently in response to that letter.

25. The concert took place 8/17/40.

26. HC to H&O, 8/23/40, 8/30/40.

27. HC to Olive, 9/17/40.

28. Note by SRC on the program.

29. PG to HC, 9/29/40.

30. PG to HC, 10/24/40.

31. PG to HC, 10/30/40.

32. SRC conversation with JS.

33. HC to PG, 11/1/40; PG to HC, 11/8/40; Ella Grainger to HC, 11/22/40.

34. SR to HC, undated, from late 1940 to early 1941.

35. HC to PG, 12/31/40. Regarding a possible job: M.W. Royse, US Dept. of Justice—Immigration and Naturalization Service, to HC, 12/[?]/40 (carbon, clipped to HC to SRC, 12/19/40).

36. NS to HC, 6/30/40.

37. HC to Richard Franko Goldman, 7/12/40.

38. HC to Olive, 7/31/40; HC to H&O, 12/20/40; HC to F. Sevitzky, 12/11/40 and 1/11/41 (accidentally dated 1940): Library of Congress, Sevitzky papers.

39. HC to H&O, 7/19/40.

40. HC to H&O, 7/24/40.

41. William Gassner to HC, 7/30/40, 8/11/40.

42. William Gassner to HC, 9/23/40.

43. HC to H&O, 8/30/40, 9/17/40; HC to Olive, 9/23/40.

44. HC to H&O, 8/23/40; HC to Grainger, 9/27/40.

45. Lan Adomian to HC, 7/15/40; Willard Van Dyke to HC, 9/9/40.

46. "Music in Films, a Symposium of Composers," *Films /A Quarterly of Discussion and Analysis* I/4 (Winter, 1940): 5–20. The other participants were Blitzstein, Bowles, Britten, Copland, Cowell, Eisler, Rathaus, Lev Schwartz, Shostakovich, William Grant Still, and Thomson. A bibliography lists no film music by HC.

47. HC to H&O, 8/30/40; HC to Olive, 9/4/40.

48. Tax records and royalty statements, Cowell papers.

Chapter 40

1. HC to PG, 1/6/41, 1/27/41.

2. PG to HC, 1/22/41.

3. HC to PG, 1/25/41.

4. William Gassner to HC, 2/21/41.

5. HC to H&O, 12/20/40; HC to PG, 1/5/41, 1/15/41; Howard Hanson to HC, 1/28/41.

6. H. A. Shuder to HC, 1/5/41.

7. Ted Stanich to HC, 1/2/41.

8. HC to Sidney, 4/3/41.

9. HC to PG, 2/5/41, with attached brochure for The New School.

10. HC to PG, 2/21/41.

11. HC to PG, 2/14/41.

12. HC to Olive, 2/7/41.

13. HC to Olive, 3/18/41.

14. HC to Olive, 3/6/41.

15. HC to Olive, 3/24/41.

16. HC to Harry, 3/31/41, with attached "Report of activities of Henry Cowell during the first six months of his parole."

17. HC to Olive, 3/31/41.

18. HC to SR, 4/5/41.

19. HC to SR, 4/7/41.

20. HC to SR, 4/10/41.

21. Mary J. Shelly to HC, 4/7/41.

22. Alfred H. Meyer to HC, 4/12/41.

23. HC to Olive, 4/15/41, 4/17/41.

24. HC to Olive, 4/24/41, 5/4/41; Daniel, *Stokowski*, 428–29.

25. HC to Olive, 5/4/41.

26. HC to Olive, 5/4/41; PG to John Gee Clark, 5/5/41.

27. Michael Myerberg to HC; on the orchestra: Opperby, *Stokowski*, 74–76.

28. John Gee Clark to Dr. Joseph Wortis, 5/18/41; John Gee Clark to Grainger, 5/20/41.

29. HC to Olive, 5/29/41; Wortis to HC, 6/21/41.

30. HC to PG, 5/29/41.

31. PG to HC, 6/7/41.

32. HC to PG, 6/22/41.

33. HC, "Drums Along the Pacific," *Modern Music* 18/1 (November–December 1940): 46–49.

34. Lichtenwanger, #609.

35. "New Sounds in Music for the Dance," *Dance Observer* 8/5 (May 1941): 64.

36. HC, "Creating a Dance: Form and Composition," *Educational Dance* 3/7 (January 1941): 2–3.

37. HC to H&O, 7/16/21; HC to PG, 7/21/41.

38. HC to SR, 8/19/41.

39. Joseph Brennan to HC, 11/6/41.

Chapter 41

1. Sources for this sketch include Nicholas Slonimsky's draft biography of SRC based on material she sent him, and presented by Slominsky to JS.

2. The Cowell papers have a program for the Castilleja concert dated only November 20. SRC supplied the year 1930; it could also have been in 1929.

3. Duveneck, *Life on Two Levels*, 151. Thanks to Kerry King and John Goodman.

4. HC to H&O, 9/10/41, says she divorced in 1930.

5. SRC, recollections, 7/11/70.

6. *American Folk Song and Folk Lore: A Regional Bibliography.* New York, 1942.

7. SR to HC, 8/23/40.

8. From an autobiography included with a letter, HC to John Marshall, Rockefeller Foundation, 4/13/56. Also SRC, curriculum vitae, about 1946. The reference to Koechlin and Fauré is in Charles Seeger interviews folder. In SRC to Rita Mead, undated, possibly 1970s (carbon); SRC says she started the Berkeley job in 1939, but it must have been a year earlier, since she started visiting Henry regularly in the late winter of 1938. She also says she moved to DC early in 1941, but letters show her there already well before Christmas 1940.

9. HC to SR, 12/3/40.

10. SR to HC, undated; SRC thought early 12/40.

11. HC to SR, 12/13/40.

12. HC to SR, 12/13/40.

13. SR to HC, 12/16/40.

14. HC to SR, 12/17/40.

15. HC to SR, 12/19/40.

16. HC to SR, 3/14/41.

17. SR to HC, 3/28/41.

18. HC to SR, 6/17/41.

19. HC to SR, 4/3/41.

20. HC to SR, 6/16/41.

21. HC to SR, 3/14/41.

22. HC to SR, 8/19/41.

23. HC to H&O, 9/8/41.

24. HC to H&O, 9/10/41.

25. HC to PG, 9/15/41.

26. HC to Olive, 3/31/41.

27. HC to PG, 5/29/41.

28. HC to Harmony Ives, 9/15/41.

29. CEI and Harmony Ives to HC, 9/18/41.

30. HC to CEI and Harmony Ives, 9/20/41.

31. SRC to Mrs. Hawkins, undated, but a few days after 10/10/41.

32. HC to H&O, 10/2/41.

33. HC to H&O, 10/2/41.

34. SRC to Mrs. Hawkins, undated, but a few days after 10/10/41.

35. HC to Olive, 9/19/41; HC to SRC, 9/27/41; SRC to Olive, 9/27/41; HC to H&O, 9/27/41.

36. SRC to Olive, 9/30/41.

37. SRC to HC, undated.

38. HC to Lewis Terman, 6/24/41; Wortis to Seeger, 8/15/41; HC to H&O, 8/27/41.

39. HC, "Improving Pan-American Music Relations," *Modern Music* 19/4 (May–June 1942): 263–65.

40. HC to Olive, 4/25/42; HC to H&O, 5/28/42.

41. SRC conversations with JS.

42. SRC to Olive, 7/2/42.

43. SRC to PG, 7/6/42.

44. HC to Olive, 8/15/42.

45. "Report of the Inter-American Activities of the Committee Members of the Music Educators National Conference" submitted by HC, chairman. Mid-1940s. Regarding the manuscript music, HC to H&O, 1/31/43.

46. Charles Seeger interviewed by Rita Mead, 11/17/74.

47. Ibid. In the 1977 interview with Andrea Olmstead, Seeger described the projects and Ralph Peer's activities more colorfully, and possibly fancifully.

Chapter 42

1. SRC to Frances Binkley, 4/11/43. Thanks to Paul and Peter Binkley for providing a copy.

2. Joseph B. Brennan to HC, 6/30/42.

3. SRC to Frances Binkley, 4/11/43.

4. SRC to HC, 11/4/42; dated from postmark.

5. Printed list of rules governing applications for executive clemency. Undated, but with the name of Governor Olson, thus after 1/39.

6. Sidney erroneously calls him Farrell.

7. Hicks, "Imprisonment," 109.

8. SRC to Frances Binkley, 4/11/43.

9. "Application for Executive Clemency," probably the model for the form submitted.

10. HC to SRC, 11/12/42.

11. SRC to HC, undated, mid-November 1942.

12. SRC to Frances Binkley, 4/11/43.

13. SRC, account dated 3/11/73.

14. Wolf, "Pardoning Power," 49.

15. SRC to HC, 11/16/42.

16. HC to SRC, 11/20/42; SRC to HC, 11/22/42. These events are not included in her 1973 account of the pardon.

17. Wolf, "Pardoning Powers," 60.

18. SRC to HC, from California, dated "Wednesday."

19. SRC to HC, dated Thanksgiving [11/26/42].

20. SRC to HC, 11/28/42.

21. John Gee Clark to SRC, 11/30/42.

22. SRC to HC, 12/3/42.

23. SRC to HC, dated "Tuesday"; from the context, 12/8/42.

24. SRC to HC, undated; the context implies 12/8/42, from Hotel Senator, Sacramento. Lupino probably was HC's secretary or assistant for the Latin American distribution project.

25. HC to SRC, 12/11/42.

26. Paul Yarwood to HC, 12/14/42.

27. SRC to HC, 12/11/42.

28. SRC to HC, 12/11/42.

29. SRC to HC, 12/11/42.

30. SRC to HC, 12/17/42.

31. SRC to HC, "Monday," from Hotel Senator, Sacramento. That would be 12/21/42. Michael Hicks, "Imprisonment," was

skeptical about SRC's account of Sullivan helping, but Sullivan sent her a note on the letterhead of Hotel Senator indicating that he had arrived, was going to bed, and would see her in the morning.

32. SRC to HC, probably about 12/23/42.

33. SRC to Frances Binkley, 4/11/43.

34. SR to "Adrian," 12/21/38, mentions seeing the Packards. Therefore she had known them for at least four years.

35. Carbon copy of the pardon paper, with the governor's signature and seal.

36. Stanley Mosk to HC, 12/29/42.

37. HC to Erminie Kahn, 6/16/45.

38. Statutes of California, 1943, chapter 400, enacted May 13, 1943. Discussed in Helen R. Mac Gregor, "Adult Probation, Parole, and Pardon in California," Texas Law Review, 38 (1959–1960): 887–914. Thanks for the assistance of G. Patrick Flanagan, reference librarian and lecturer in law, Columbia Law School.

39. Jack Beeson conversation with JC.

40. I have been unable to find that modification, which might have been a legislative recommendation.

41. John Gee Clark to HC and SRC, 2/2/43.

42. SRC, statement about Mrs. Kingsley Porter.

Chapter 43

1. HC to H&O, 1/31/43; SRC, statement about HC's government service, 4/8/75.

2. SRC; Bess Lomax Hawes interviewed by Andrea Olmstead, 11/18/77.

3. HC to Olive, 9/18/43.

4. HC to H&O, 9/9/43.

5. Amy Hostler to HC, 6/6/42; Mills School Bulletin for 1942.

6. Winkler, Politics of Propaganda, passim; Holly Shulman, The Voice of America, passim.

7. Bess Lomax interviewed by Andrea Olmstead, 11/18/77.

8. HC, "The Use of Music by the OWI," MTNA Proceedings, 1946 [no month]: 56–65.

9. HC interviewed by Beate Gordon, 10/16/62.

10. Bess Lomax Hawes interviewed by Andrea Olmstead, 11/18/77.

11. HC, draft of a description of his own position, possibly drawn up when promotion looked possible. SRC on HC's service at OWI.

12. Bess Lomax Hawes interviewed by Andrea Olmstead, 11/18/77.

13. Ibid., marginal comment by SRC.

14. Ibid.

15. HC interviewed by Beate Gordon, 10/16/62, in CUOHROC, 30.

16. "Hoosegow Harmony," Time Magazine, 2/7/44.

17. HC to H&O, 4/10/44.

18. HC interviewed by Beate Gordon, 10/16/62, in CUOHROC, 29.

19. Two communications, HC to Olive, 5/26/44.

20. HC to SRC, 6/6/44, 6/8/44, 6/9/44.

21. HC to H&O, 12/2/44.

22. HC to Olive, 2/28/45.

23. Winkler, Politics, 138.

24. HC, "The Use of Music by the OWI," MTNA Proceedings 1946 [no month]: 56–65.

25. HC to Olive, 5/12/44.

26. John K. Fairbank to HC, 4/3/45.

27. SRC statement about HC and the government, 4/8/75; also SRC, "Bio bits," typescript.

28. Bess Brown Lomax Hawes to HC, 8/14/45.

29. Bess Brown Lomax to HC, undated, fall, 1945.

30. SRC, "Bio bits," typescript. New York World Telegram, 4/23/45, "OWI Spends Millions on Radio Music for Foe. Programs Sent to Nazis and Japs Defended against Boondoggle Charge."

31. Shulman, The Voice of America, 184.

32. Bess Lomax Hawes interviewed by Andrea Olmstead, 11/18/77.

33. OWI, "Library of American Music Scores," 33-page catalogue of works by American composers, ca. later 1945.

34. New Yorker, 12/23/44; Christian Science Monitor, 11/21/44; New York Herald

Tribune, 12/12/44. They played "The Celestial Violin," an arrangement of his song "How Old Is Song," which in turn is based on "Aeolian Harp."

35. *Schenectady* (New York) *Gazette,* 1/23/45.

36. HC to H&O, 3/17/45; HC to Ives, 3/18/45, with SRC notes about the event. SRC, typescript, "Henry and Sidney Cowell at the White House."

Chapter 44

1. Further, see Sabine Feisst, "Henry Cowell und Arnold Schoenberg" and *Schoenberg's New World.*

2. HC to CEI, 4/6/34, 4/10/43, 6/4/43; Harmony Ives to HC, 9/12/43.

3. HC to CEI, 12/4/43.

4. Harmony Ives to HC, 12/8/43.

5. Harmony Ives to HC, 1/20/44.

6. HC to CEI, 6/4/43 and 6/9/43; for New York Philharmonic information, thanks to Rich Wandel, archivist.

7. HC to CEI, 7/27/43.

8. HC to CEI, 1/29/43. Jamie Jordan, New York Philharmonic archive, told JS that the librarians had been extremely diligent about noting encores.

9. HC to CEI, 9/21/44; Harmony Ives to HC, 9/29/44.

10. Harmony Ives to HC, 9/29/44.

11. HC to Harmony Ives, 10/8/44; Harmony to HC, 3/14/45.

12. Ruggles to HC, 12/3/44: "I should think you would be greatly cheered when you hear what the smart, slick Jews are doing. The two new works of Schoenberg are not worthy of him either."

13. MS with edits by SRC; Henry Cowell, prefatory note to "About Carl Ruggles: Section Four of a Book on Ruggles by Lou Harrison" (Yonkers, NY: Oscar Baradinsky, 1946).

14. Ruggles to HC, 5/30/45.

15. Harrison to HC, undated, but certainly 1940–1941, when HC was at the Graingers'.

16. Lou Harrison to HC and SRC, undated, late 1945?

17. Cage to HC, probably, mid-1940s, during one of HC's stays in California.

18. Further, Leta Miller and Frederic Lieberman, *Lou Harrison: Composing a World.*

19. John Cage conversation with JS.

20. Transcribed by S.C. F. Spackman. The books, in NYPLFPA, Reigger papers, run from 2/6/41 through 3/16/61. Also SRC to HC, 4/2/61.

21. Paul Farnsworth to SRC, 1/17/66.

Chapter 45

1. HC to Grainger, 4/10/45.

2. C. A. Hawkins to HC, 1/7/42.

3. C. A. Hawkins to HC, 10/13/44.

4. Unknown (probably Odeline Hawkins, Sidney's stepmother) to SRC, 3/10/45.

5. C. A. Hawkins to SRC, 6/9/45.

6. Lou Harrison to HC, undated, almost certainly 1946.

7. Arthur C. Berdahl to HC, 10/1/45.

8. HC to Richard Franko Goldman, 11/10/45.

9. SRC, statement, 3/12/73, on HC's entire health history.

10. Otto Bergen, MD, evidently a cardiologist, to an unnamed doctor, 3/5/46.

11. Otto Bergen to HC, undated.

12. HC to H&O, 1/18/46.

13. HC to Olive, 4/16/46.

14. Yellow sheet written by SRC.

15. SRC to Harmony Ives, 7/26/47.

16. SRC to Harmony Ives, 7/26/47.

17. SRC to Lou Harrison, 10/14/47.

18. HC to SRC, 10/27/47.

19. Kyle Gann, *Nancarrow,* 42–44.

Chapter 46

1. New School Bulletins. Additional information from Rita Mead's notes on Henry at The New School, which she took from other New School Bulletins.

2. From registration slips.

3. From grade sheets.

4. Vignettes sent by SRC to Westbeutscher Rundfunk for its celebration of Cage's seventy-fifth birthday.

5. New School Bulletins.

6. Jack Beeson conversation with JS.

7. Willard Rhodes to HC, 5/20/48.

8. Contract for 1952–53, accompanying Reginald Steward to HC, 5/13/52.

9. "Bio Bits," comment by SRC.

10. Dr. Stuart Feder in conversation with SRC, 11/20/74.

11. Lawrence Rasmussen to HC, 8/23/49.

12. Jauana de Laban to HC, 9/18/52, regretting HC's resignation from Adelphi and feeling they shall work together again.

13. Paul Dawson Eddy to HC, 7/27/50.

14. Program, 1/16/54.

15. SRC on HC's managers.

16. HC to SRC, 12/16/52.

17. HC to SRC, 6/21/56.

18. Moses Asch, "Henry Cowell (1897–1965)," *Sing Out* 16/1 (February–March): 96. Moses Asch interviewed by Cole Gagne, 3/15/77. The interview is filled with contradictions. By that time, Asch was—according to SRC—unwell.

19. HC to Harry, 1/91/52; Deems Taylor to HC, 4/18/53.

20. HC to Olive, 10/19/52, 6/4/53.

21. SRC to Mrs. Carleton Sprague Smith, 7/10/53.

22. From an unnamed newspaper clipping assigned the date 6/4/54. Cowell can be heard delivering the speech at http://thisibelieve.org/essays/fifties/page/11.

23. Marjorie Fisher, "Discs from Cowell to Coward," *San Francisco News*, 1/7/52.

24. W. F., "Henry Cowell Concert. New School for Social Research, Nov. 16." *Musical America*, 12/1/53.

25. Daniel Ruyneman to HC, 3/18/48.

26. HC, proposal to ISCM, undated.

27. HC to SRC, 9/18/51, 9/30/52; Odeline Hawkins to HC, 12/1/52; SRC to HC 12/12/52.

28. HC to Olive, 2/18/54 and 13/10/54.

29. SRC, sheet of paper, dated 12/6/[?].

30. SRC to JS, 12/12/89. In JS's possession.

31. SRC, "HC and SRC."

32. John Douglas Short to SRC, 1/16/47.

33. Copley, *Blacklisting*.

34. SRC to Vivian Perlis, 5/3/77. SRC contradicted Gerald Strang's and Hermann Langinger's idea that HC was the victim of an anti-communist frame-up.

35. SRC to Vivian Perlis, 5/3/77.

36. Parsons Smith, *Still*, 195–96.

37. Reprinted in Piero Weiss and Richard Taruskin, *Music in the Western World*, 2nd ed. (New York, 2008), 410.

38. Many documents on the new onslaught against unconventional music are translated and published in Nicolas Slonimsky, *Music since 1900*, 3rd ed., 1949, 684–710.

39. Boris Schwarz, 250.

40. Rita Mitsel, "The Anti-Jewish Campaigns Against the Musicians in Kiev in 1948–1953." DMA document, Juilliard School, 2010, 85.

41. Articles of Trust; John William Ham to Olive, 9/23/49.

42. HC to Harry, 10/17/50.

43. SRC to Olive, 2/10/54.

44. Drafts, 9/18/47, 11/9/46.

45. John William Ham to HC, 11/14/47, 12/19/47; Olive to HC, 11/24/47.

46. HC to George Tyler, 6/30/54.

47. HC to Olive, 1/6, no year, 1954 or 1955.

48. John William Ham to SRC, 3/26/54.

Chapter 47

1. Lichtenwanger, 198.

2. Thanks to George Boziwick, who in turn says he was guided to the Edson book by Jean Bowen at the time of Boziwick's 1997 Cowell centenary exhibition at NYPLFPA. See also Lichtenwanger, 199.

3. Virgil Thomson, *New York Herald Tribune*, 1/13/49, quoted in Lichtenwanger, 201.

4. Wayne D. Shirley, "The Hymns and Fuguing Tunes."

5. Edwin Gershefski, "American Composers, XXVI—Henry Cowell," *Modern*

Music 23/4 (fall 1946): 255–60. The Cowells originally asked Ruth Crawford Seeger to write it.

6. Jeremy S. Brown has written extensively about HC's band music.

7. Lichtenwanger, 235.

8. HC and SRC, "Our Country Music," *Modern Music* 20/4 (May/June 1943): 243–47.

9. HC, "Music in Soviet Russia," *The Russian Review* 1/2 (April 1942): 74–79.

Chapter 48

1. Edith Tyler to HC, 7/18/47.

2. Olive, "My Life with [the] Cowells," Olive Cowell papers, NYPLFPA: 39; Harmony Ives to HC, 10/25/48.

3. Munson to HC, 6/6/48; Henry James, Jr., to HC, 1/14/48, 5/3/48, 5/14/48.

4. Agnes Moynihan to HC and SRCs, 7/23/51.

5. Maynard Solomon, "Charles Ives: Some Questions of Veracity."

6. Harmony Ives to HC, 6/6/[?].

7. Harmony Ives to SRC, 12/20/53.

8. Louise Fletcher Herrmann to HC, 7/16/47.

9. SRC to Harmony Ives, 11/20/54.

10. Edie Ives Tyler to SRC, 2/3/55. R. S. Ives, "Cowells Write Study of Ives," *Musical America*, 2/1/56.

11. Saylor, *Writings*, lacks a few items.

12. In Crawford, Lott, Oja, *A Celebration*, 79–91.

Chapter 49

1. SRC on HC's government services, 4/8/75.

2. Weiss to HC, 3/3/55.

3. William Glock to HC, 4/13/55. Glock was also interested in Sidney's knowledge of old American hymns and fuguing tunes.

4. HC to Olive, 5/6 /55, 5/6/55.

5. Itinerary; HC's passport.

6. HC to Olive, 6/11/55.

7. HC to SRC, 6/11/and 6/12/55.

8. HC To Riegger, 6/12/55.

9. HC to Olive, 6/12/55.

10. HC to SRC, 6/15/55.

11. HC to Olive, 6/18/55.

12. HC to SRC. Undated except "Until June 23."

13. Douglas Mackinnon to SRC, 12/17/76.

14. HC, Zähringer Hof, Baden Baden, to SRC. Undated except "until June 23."

15. HC to Olive 6/18/55.

16. HC to SRC, 7/4/55.

Chapter 50

1. SRC statement, 3/12/73, on HC's entire health history.

2. Internal memo, RF, 4/12/56.

3. HC to John Marshall, 4/13/56; Marshall to HC, 4/16/56.

4. John Marshall to HC, 4/27/56; HC to Marshall, 4/28/56.

5. Charles Burton Fahs to John Marshall, 4/17/56 and 4/18/56.

6. HC to Olive, 3/14/56; Harmony Ives to SRC, 5/25/56.

7. Flora M. Rhind, RF, to HC, 5/9/56.

8. HC to Olive, 5/4/34, 7/26/56.

9. Grayson Kirk, "To Whom It May Concern," 1/14/56.

10. Library of Congress certifying SRC's qualifications in folk song, 3/6/56.

11. The Reverend Arthur L. Swift, statement 4/17/56.

12. Because USIS's cultural and educational programs were part of the State Department's Bureau of Educational and Cultural Affairs at that time, it is not always clear which agency employed some of the various participants.

13. HC to Olive, 4/24/56.

14. John Marshall to Chadbourne Gilpatric, 5/14/56.

15. HC to SRC in Ireland, 6/23/56.

16. Martha Geesa, to HC, 7/6/56; David Cooper to HC, 7/6/56.

17. HC to SRC, 6/27/56.

18. John Marshall to HC, 6/29/56.

19. Joint State Department—USIS notice to posts, 7/19/56.

20. N. Paul Neilson to State Department, 9/6/56.

21. David Garth to State Department, 9/20/56.

22. William Copeland to State Department, 7/31/56.

23. SRC, "Some remarks as remembered in '77 by SRC."

24. HC to SRC, 7/12/56; to Olive, 6/18/56.

25. HC to SRC, 7/16–8/14/56; SRC statement on HC's entire health history, 3/12/73.

26. SRC to HC, 7/16–8/14/56.

27. HC to John Marshall, 8/15/56.

28. SRC to "dears" (her California family), 11/1/56.

29. HC to SRC, 8/14/56.

30. SRC, typed card filed with Irish reviews.

31. E. Lee Fairley, to HC, 8/12/56; *Washington Post*, obituary, 5/25/07.

32. SRC, statement 3/12/73, on HC's entire health history.

33. HC to SRC, 9/20/56.

34. HC to Riegger from Hamburg, undated. Riegger papers, NYPLFPA.

35. HC to Olive, 9/22/56; HC to Luening 9/20/56.

36. Dr. Werner Karthaus to John Jones, America-House Cologne, 9/26/56.

37. HC to SRC, 9/24/56.

38. C. W., "Ein Musik-Pionier aus Amerika /Begegnung mit dem Komponisten Henry Cowell." *Stuttgarter Zeitung*, 9/29/56.

39. *Badische Zeitung*, 10/5/56.

40. HC to SRC, 10/1/56; HC to Olive, 10/1/56, assorted items from trip to Germany.

41. HC to John Marshall, 10/19/56; SRC reports to the RF, 1/19/60; John Marshall to HC, 11/30/56; SRC to John Marshall, 10/27/56.

42. SRC to John Marshall, 0/27/65; HC to John Marshall, 10/28/56.

43. SRC, undated.

44. HC to SRC, undated but certainly 11/1/56.

45. Donald Heath to State Department, 10/6/56 and 1/4/57.

46. John Marshall to HC, 11/13/56 and 1/15/57.

47. SRC to "dears" (her California family), 11/1/56.

Chapter 51

1. Re: Pahlbod, http://www.iichs.org/ index_en.asp?img_cat=1108&img_ type=0. [5/18/09].

2. Mehrdad Pahlbod interviewed by JS, 7/5/93.

3. C. Robert Payne to SRC, 2/17/75. This is not the same Payne mentioned on p. 158.

4. Mehrdad Pahlbod interviewed by JS, 7/5/93.

5. C. Robert Payne to SRC, 2/17/75.

6. SRC diaries of Iran trip.

7. John Foster Dulles to US Embassy, Tehran, 7/10/56.

8. Ibid.; HC to SRC, 9/17/56.

9. HC to Olive, 11/18/56; SRC to Milton Rosenfield (her grandfather), 11/23/56.

10. HC to John Marshall, 1/8/57; SRC's later report; Mehrdad Pahlbod interviewed by JS, 7/5/93.

11. C. Robert Payne, to His Excellency Naser Qoli Zolfoghari, 12/1/56.

12. Ibid.

13. HC to John Marshall, 1/8/57.

14. SRC report to RF, 1/19/60.

15. SRC diary, 11/18/56.

16. Ibid., 11/22/56.

17. Ibid., 11/23/56.

18. SRC report to RF, 1/19/60; SRC to Miss Lee, 1/26/57.

19. HC to Barret Parker and C. Robert Payne, reporting on activities 11/19 to 12/18.

Chapter 52

1. SRC to Paul Sherbet, undated, ca. 1962.

2. HC to Mary Stewart French, 11/23/56.

3. SRC diary, 12/24/56.

4. SRC diary (yellow sheet).

5. Narayana Menon to HC, 12/3/56.

6. See Chapters 12 and 19.

7. Brian Silver, "Henry Cowell and Alan Hovhaness: Responses to the Music of

India," footnote attributing the comment to a personal communication from SRC.

8. SRC to Paul Sherbet, Asia Society, undated, 1962; SRC report to RF on music in India, 1/6/60.

9. Silver, "Henry Cowell and Alan Hovhaness: Responses to the Music of India."

10. HC to Chadbourne Gilpatric, 1/8/57.

11. SRC to Paul Sherbet, Asia Society, undated, re: the Anniversary 1962 event.

12. "Oriental and Western Music," *The Indian Express*, 12/27/56.

13. SRC report to RF on music in India, 1/6/60.

14. "American Music /Oriental Influence Explained," *The Hindu*, 12/28/56.

15. Silver, "Henry Cowell and Alan Hovhaness: Responses to the Music of India."

16. SRC report to RF on music in India, 1/6/60.

17. Harold Tufty interviewed by JS, 10/30/95.

18. HC to Chadbourne Gilpatric, 1/8/57.

19. Harold Tufty interviewed by Andrea Olmstead, 11/18/77.

20. Claude B. Cross to HC, 12/6/56.

21. SRC report to RF, 1/19/60.

22. HC interviewed by Beate Gordon, 10/16/62. CUOHROC: 27.

23. Harold Tufty interviewed by Andrea Olmstead, 11/18/77. Tufty incorrectly thought Mysore was already governor at the time. Obituary of Maharajah of Mysore, *New York Times*, 9/24/74.

24. Silver, "Henry Cowell and Alan Hovhaness: Responses to the Music of India."

25. Harold Tufty interviewed by Andrea Olmstead, 11/18/77.

Chapter 53

1. SRC report to RF, 1/19/60.

2. SRC to her grandfather, draft, 1/31/57.

3. "Abadan Today," published for the employees of the oil companies NIOC (National Iranian Oil Company) and IORC (a defunct company that probably was called the Iranian Oil Refining Company.

4. Ibid.

5. SRC to Milton Rosenfield, 1/31/57.

6. Translation from "Ettela'at," Tehran, 2/9/57.

7. SRC report to RF, 1/19/60: "Persian Tales and Travelogue."

8. SRC note on letter from Dan Oleksiw to SRC, 10/28/77.

9. C. Robert Payne to SRC, 2/17/75.

10. Mehrdad Pahlbod interviewed by JS, 7/5/93.

11. www/rhythmweb.com/tonbak [7/13/10]. Quoted from Tehrani's memoir, *Amouzesh-e-tombak*.

Chapter 54

1. HC to John Marshall, 1/8/57.

2. From *Dawn*, Karachi, 2/14/57.

3. SRC to Miss Lee, 1/26/57; SRC to Milton Rosenfield, 1/31; SRC to Donald King, 2/6/57.

4. SRC statement, 3/12/73, on HC's health history.

5. Records from Seventh Day Adventist Hospital, Karachi, 3/6/57.

6. Ibid.; record from Kingston, New York, hospital, 5/4/58.

7. SRC, incomplete description of Karachi; SRC statement, 3/6/57, on HC's entire health history; records from Seventh Day Adventist Hospital, Karachi.

8. SRC report to RF, 1/19/60; SRC to Gilpatric, ca. 3/4/57.

9. SRC report to RF, 1/19/60.

10. The ship was the *Lloyd Triestino Victoria*; www.lastoceanliners.com. [9/9/09].

11. SRC to Gilpatric, ca. 3/4/57.

12. Gilpatric to HC, 3/8/57.

13. SRC to Charles Fahs, 1/6/60.

14. David S. Cooper to SRC.

15. SRC statement, 3/12/73, on HC's entire health history; HC's health history on the round-the-world tour; report to RF, undated.

16. SRC report to RF on music in India, 1/6/60.

17. SRC to Gilpatric, 3/1/657; Margaret Gonneratne to HC and SRC, 7/23/57;

SRC to Harold Schonberg, 3/12/62, marked "not sent."

18. HC to Olive, 3/8/57; HC to Olive, 3/18/57; SRC report to RF on music in Singapore; SRC to Gilpatric, 3/16/57.

19. SRC, statement, 3/12/73, on HC's entire health history.

20. Ibid.

21. SRC to Gilpatric, RF, 3/16/57; pp. 3–10 of what may have been a draft of a letter or report from Bangkok, possibly to the RF.

22. HC to Olive, 4/12/57.

23. SRC, report on music in Thailand; *Bangkok World*, 4/6/57.

24. Folder marked "Instruments."

25. "American Composer Studies Thai Music," *Bangkok World*, marked 4/5/57 in HC's hand. According to SRC, conversation with JS, 3/29/92, the instruments were purchased on behalf of Carroll Music Instruments Co. in New York.

26. HC to Gilpatric, 3/27/57.

27. Thomas P. Dillon, to State Department, 5/6/57; HC to Olive, 4/12/57.

28. HC, Hong Kong, to Olive, 4/12/57.

29. "The Enemy: Red Boom in Macao," *Time*, 8/20/51.

30. SRC report, 1/6/60, on music in Macao "with much irrelevant travelogue"; SRC, 3/12/73, on HC's entire health history.

31. Thomas P. Dillon, US Consul, Hong Kong, to State Department, Washington, 5/6/57.

32. SRC diary, typescript, originally written to her sister Anne.

33. SRC report to RF on music in Japan; SRC statement, 3/12/72, on HC's entire health history.

34. HC believed he was one of only two composers to have been invited twice; actually there were two others, Milhaud and Surinach. He must have been amused that Copland still had not been commissioned.

35. HC to Olive, 5/29/57; material for notes about *Ongaku*.

36. Ibid.

37. SRC report to FR on music in Japan; SRC's statement of 3/12/73 on HC's entire health history.

38. Typescript, unnamed source, "Deep Interest in Folk Music: Impression of Japan by Mr. Cowell, American Composer," 6/23/57; SRC to Antal Dorati, 6/3/57.

39. SRC typescript of letters to her sister Anne.

40. Itinerary, 6/12/57.

41. HC to Olive, 6/6/57.

42. SRC, typescript on their trip to Japan. (Begins: "Joke Dept"), with note that it was written to her sister Anne, ca. 1977.

43. SRC to Olive, 5/11/57; HC to Olive, 5/29/57.

44. Elaine Fry interviewed by Andrea Olmstead, 11/18/77.

45. Undated note to Milton Rosenfield.

Chapter 55

1. SRC statement, 3/12/73, on HC's entire health history.

2. Records from the Kingston Hospital.

3. Dr. Myron White, to whom it may concern, 6/12/58.

4. Private communication, SRC to JS.

5. SRC, "Material for Notes," on Japan trip.

6. Unidentified diplomat, communicated to JS by Raphael Mostel, email 2/3/2010.

7. SRC, telephone conversation with JS.

8. SRC, report to RF on music in Singapore; Wikipedia, 6/38/09, "Negaraku"; Thomas K. Wright to HC, 9/20/57.

9. Thomas K. Wright, ibid., Daniel Moore to HC, 12/10/57.

10. Felix Meyer to JS, email 4/27/09.

11. SRC report to RF on music in Singapore; "Bad Boy at 60," *Time Magazine*, 9/23/57.

12. Lichtenwanger, 283.

13. "Bad Boy at 60," *Time Magazine*, 9/23/57.

14. Yehudi Wyner interviewed by Andrea Olmstead, 5/8/78.

15. *Musical Quarterly*, 45/4 (October 1959): 484–98.

16. *Time Magazine*, 2/18/57.

17. "J. L.," *American Record Guide,* January–February, 1957.

18. Review of Records, *Musical Quarterly,* October 1969. French was vice-president and director of publications for Associated Music Publishers when it took on *Music for Orchestra 1957.*

19. Note by SRC; SRC, "The Cowells and the Written Word."

20. Letter from HC's class to HC, 5/14/58.

21. Jack Beeson conversation with JS.

22. *Contemporary Music Newsletter,* 1960; minutes of board meetings.

23. John Ensor Harr and Peter J. Johnson, *The Rockefeller Conscience,* 101.

24. Fritz Kuttner to HC, 10/5/60.

25. SRC to Elaine Fry, 11/12/59.

26. Mehrdad Pahlbod interviewed by JS, 7/5/93.

27. David Cooper to HC, 7/28/58, 8/12/58, 9/22/58, 10/17/58.

28. Elaine Fry to HC, 9/13/60; USIA shipment notice, 10/18/60.

29. HC to David Cooper, 6/10/59.

30. HC to Aileen (Harrison), 10/31/59. Original, Stanford University Library, Green Library, Special Collections. Russell died 7/28/59.

31. Terman to HC, 8/9/56.

32. Gifted Children program follow-up questionnaire, 4/28/60.

33. Olive, "My life with [the] Cowells," 35. Undated. Olive Cowell papers, NYPLFPA JPB 99-3.

34. SRC, "The Cowell Foundation," 7/5/88.

Chapter 56

1. Nicholas Nabokov to HC, 11/21/60.

2. HC to Robert Thayer, undated draft.

3. Theodore Wertime to SRC 3/15/61.

4. HC to SRC 4/1/61, 4/2/61; SRC to USIA, 4/19/61.

5. HC to SRC 4/4/61; HC to Olive, 4/4/61.

6. HC to SRC 4/6/61; SRC to USIA, 4/19/61.

7. HC to SRC, 4/7/61, 4/8/61.

8. HC's speech first was issued in a typed transcript of the conference talks edited by William Archer and distributed by UNESCO. The conference report was later published in *Music in Ghana* II, 5/1961, 36–49.

9. HC to SRC, 4/11/61.

10. SRC to USIA music unit, 4/19/61.

11. HC to SRC 4/12/61. (The love notes have not survived.) SRC to USIA music unit, 4/19/61.

12. SRC to USIA music unit, 4/19/61.

13. *Hongkong Standard* Sunday Magazine, 5/28/51.

14. HC to SRC, 4/19/61.

15. Frances Stonor Saunders, *Cultural Cold War.* She does not discuss the East-West Music Encounter.

16. The following account is primarily drawn from Stonor Saunders.

17. Harr and Johnson, *The Rockefeller Conscience,* 96–100.

18. Stonor Saunders, 252–78.

19. New York FBI office to the director, memo, 9/28/56.

20. The script, "Oriental Influence on the [*sic*] Western Music," is dated New York and Reykjavik, 3/63.

21. HC to SRC, 4/20/61, 4/22/61, 4/26/61.

22. Maple Quon to HC, 5/3/61.

23. E. J. Findlay to HC, 4/18/61; invitation to the concert.

24. Toshiro Mayuzumi to HC, 8/32/61.

25. HC to SRC, 4/22/61.

26. HC to SRC, 5/2/61, 5/3/61.

27. HC to SRC, 4/28–29/61.

28. HC to SRC, 4/19/61.

29. Akira Ohsawa to HC, 12/18/61; HC to SRC, 5/1/61, 5/3/61, 5/4/61, 5/8/61, 5/13/61.

30. E. J. Findlay to HC, 6/5/61.

Chapter 57

1. HC to Olive, 11/15/61.

2. Maureen Kershaw to HC, 10/21/62; HC to Blanche Walton, 8/2/62.

3. HC to Olive, 1/29/62.

4. Peter Yates to HC 4/15/62, 7/18/62.

5. *High Fidelity*, 7/62, review of Louisville recording of Symphony No. 15.

6. SRC's note on the *New York Times* article and accompanying folder.

7. Alvin Johnson to HC, 12/15/59.

8. Miscellaneous correspondence, 4/61.

9. SRC to HC, 4/26/61; Allen McHose to SRC and other documents from 2/61; Eastman announcement, 7/31/62.

10. HC to SRC, 5/28/61, 6/9/61, 7/10/61, 7/27/61, 7/28/61, 7/31/61; HC to Olive, 7/19/61.

11. HC: "Freedom for Young Composers," *Music Journal*, 3/1962, 29 ff.

12. HC to Mme. Raden Mas Jodjana, 12/6/62.

13. John Kirkpatrick to HC and SRC, 4/30/62, 3/9/63.

14. SRC, note on the invitations.

15. Typescript by SRC accompanying a *New Yorker* cartoon from early in the Jimmy Carter administration, when he abolished chauffeur-driven limos. It shows a sign to call for taxis on the upper floor of the White House.

16. SRC to Olive, 11/15/61.

17. HC to Olive, 11/15/61.

18. HC to editors of *Life* magazine, 11/30/61; Ellen Reeves to HC, 12/28/61.

19. C. Robert Payne to HC and SRC, 12/6/61.

20. *New York Times*, 3/3/62: "Concerts to Honor Henry Cowell at 65."

21. Carbon, SRC to unknown either Olive or SRC's family, 2/22/62.

22. SRC conversation with JS, 1994.

23. Harold C. Schoenberg. "The Cluster Man. Henry Cowell, 65, Remains One of Our Most Adventurous, Vital Composers," *New York Times*, 3/11/62. Press release for NYPLFPA exhibition, "Henry Cowell—Fifty Years of Creative Life and Influence."

24. New School Bulletin, 3/14/62.

25. Carbon, SRC to unknown, either Olive or SRC's family, 2/22/62.

26. JFK to HC, telegram, 3/7/62.

27. Nelson Rockefeller to HC, telegram, 3/9/62.

28. Savilla Millis Simons to HC, 3/11/62.

29. *Musical America*, 4/62 and 5/62; SRC to Everett Helm, 1/6/62.

Chapter 58

1. Stonor Saunders, 351–52.

2. George T. Moody to HC, 7/30/62.

3. SRC to Edward Alexander, 2/27/63.

4. HC to George T. Moody, 8/8/62.

5. Strickland to HC, 6/12/62, 10/10/62.

6. Strickland to HC 11/24/62; Lawrence Carlson, CAO, US Embassy Iceland, to State Department, 10/26/62; Lawrence Carlson to State Department, 10/26/62 and 11/20/62.

7. State Department to US Embassy, Iceland 12/7/62.

8. Ashley Pettis to HC, 3/4/36, reports having warned Blitzstein to stop doing it, as it posed a danger to the person whose signature he falsified.

9. US Civil Service Commission, Bureau of Personnel Investigation: Report about HC, 12/18/62.

10. Specialist's Grant, Department of State, Bureau of Educational and Cultural Affairs, 3/7/63.

11. Communications between US Embassy, Reykjavik, and State Department, 3/1, 3/4/63; G. K. Rosinus, Bonn, to State Department, 3/5/63.

12. Strickland to HC, 3/11/63.

13. Bohlen to HC, 3/5/63; HC to Olive, 3/2/63; US Embassy, Luxembourg, to State Department, 3/8/63 and 3/16/63.

14. SRC to William Deary, 4/6/63.

15. David Hall to HC, 3/10/63.

16. SRC statement on HC's government service, 4/8/75.

17. Amerika Haus, Hannover, flier, 3/63.

18. Holograph notes for HC's talks in Europe, 1963.

19. *Stars and Stripes*, 4/2/63. Copland, Thomson, Carter, and Gunther Schuller were expected later; SRC statement on HC's government service, 4/8/75; Edward Alexander to SRC, 3/5/63.

20. SRC statement, 3/12/73, on HC's entire health history.

21. HC, health records, Berlin Army Hospital.

22. SRC to Olive, 4/4/63.

23. SRC statement, 3/12/73, on HC's entire health history.

24. Note by SRC, 1/78.

25. HC to Mildred Wikins, 8/?/63.

26. Catherine Djurklou to HC, 3/27/63.

Chapter 59

1. HC to Olive, 6/24/63, 7/4/63; HC to SRC 6/27/63, 6/29/63.

2. SRC to Carl Haverlin, draft of telegram, 7/15/63.

3. SRC statement, 3/12/73, on HC's entire health history; Allen McHose ["Larry"] to HC, 7/28/63; Nob Jones to HC, 8/23/63.

4. HC to Olive, 9/4/63; HC to Avery Claflin, 9/7/63; Willard Rhodes to HC, 9/12/63; HC to Olive, 9/20/63.

5. SRC statement, 3/12/73, on HC's entire health history.

6. HC to SRC, 11/10/63; HC to Olive 11/16/63, 12/13/63.

7. Lichtenwanger No. 922.

8. Paul Arma to HC, 12/15/63.

9. HC to Margaret Cowell, 12/25/63.

10. HC to SRC, 1/10/64.

11. HC to Olive, 1/20/64.

12. HC to Avery Clafin, 3/1/64; William Mitchell to HC, 7/28/63; HC to Olive, 5/14/64. BMI no longer has the contract but told JS that it could not have revealed the amount HC was offered even if it had the contract.

13. HC to Olive, Athens, 5/14/64.

14. Charles Garland to HC, 4/14/64.

15. HC to Olive, Stockholm, 6/3/64.

16. SRC statement, 3/12/73, on HC's entire health history.

Chapter 60

1. HC to Olive, 7/27/64.

2. Mario Di Bonaventura to HC, 7/24/64; program, 8/12/64.

3. Edward McMenamin to HC, 10/6/64.

4. Dr. Morton Rosenfeld to SRC, 10/5/64.

5. SRC to Olive, 10/24/64.

6. Felicia Geffen to SRC, 10/28/64.

7. Program, Waltann School of Creative Arts; Grace Stanistreet to HC, 6/25; no year, clearly 1964 from context.

8. HC to Lan Adomian, 3/20/65. Courtesy of Jerusalem Library.

9. Olive interviewed by Rita Mead, 5/22/75, 11/8/75.

10. HC to Paul Farnsworth, 12/2/65.

11. Francis Thorne to HC, 12/7/65.

12. SRC to Francis Thorne, 1/26/66.

Chapter 61

1. Bess Lomax Hawes interviewed by Andrea Olmstead, 11/18/77.

2. Gerald Strang interviewed by Rita Mead, 10/29/75.

3. John Cage, *Silence* (Middletown, CT: Wesleyan University Press, 1961), 71.

4. Dr. Joseph Wortis interviewed by JS, 7/10/94.

5. Ibid.; Gerald Strang interviewed by Rita Mead, 10/29/75.

6. "Peter" [Mrs. James] Turnbull, statement dated 2/86.

7. William Justema to SRC, 5/22/79.

8. Charles Seeger interviewed by Andrea Olmstead, 7/7/77.

9. SRC to Evelyn Wells, 7/18/75.

10. "Peter" Turnbull, statement dated 2/86.

11. SRC statement on HC's personality, 4/70.

12. Ibid.

13. SRC, a chapter about HC and Evelyn Wells drafted subsequent to their conversations.

14. SRC to Dorothy Blaney, dated October, probably ca. 1973.

15. SRC statement about why HC did so many things.

16. Note by SRC, 1/78.

17. SRC, draft chapter about Evelyn Wells.

18. SRC, "HC and Olive Cowell," about 1969.

Epilogue

1. SRC to Angelo Eaton, 1/4/66. Cremation is stipulated in the 1958 will.

2. SRC identified "Curley" in a conversation with JS, 12/2/89.

3. SRC to "Curley," 8/5/67.

4. Peter Goodwin, *Morton Gould*, 39.

5. George Crumb, telephone conversation with JS, 7/18/10.

6. Gann, *Nancarrow*, 43. Nancarrow's Rhythmic Study No. 37, for example, proves Henry's point that with a player-piano one could coordinate rhythm even with the complex pitch ratios of the chromatic scale.

7. Henry Brant to SRC, 1/6/65, Sacher Stiftung, Basel.

8. John Edmunds to unknown addressee, 11/29/60, 12/24/59.

9. David Nicholls, "Transethnicism."

10. Quoted in Lichtenwanger, 317.

SELECTIVE BIBLIOGRAPHY

Note Concerning the Sources Listed

The sheer massiveness of the sources for this book makes it impossible to list all of the material consulted. Bruce Saylor's *The Writings of Henry Cowell: A Descriptive Bibliography* lists 237 items; a few more escaped his notice. Martha L. Manion's *Writings about Henry Cowell: An Annotated Bibliography* lists 1,359 items through 1974, and many more have appeared since then. Although all of Cowell's books and articles, and the vast majority of the writings about him, were consulted for this book, this bibliography can show only the ones that were most important. Writings devoted solely to his compositions are, in general, not included. Some references that were of momentary importance are listed in relevant endnotes only.

The interested reader should consult Saylor's and Manion's bibliographies for full coverage through 1974, and standard bibliographies and encyclopedias for newer literature.

Archives

Cowell family manuscript material, interviews, letters, and other writings reside in the Henry Cowell papers at the New York Public Library for the Performing Arts.

NEW YORK PUBLIC LIBRARY FOR THE PERFORMING ARTS AT LINCOLN CENTER

Henry Cowell papers
John Becker papers
Olive Thomson Cowell papers
New Music Society papers
Wallingford Riegger papers

YALE UNIVERSITY LIBRARY, MANUSCRIPTS AND ARCHIVE

Charles Ives papers
Anna Strunsky Walling papers
Carl Ruggles papers

LIBRARY OF CONGRESS

Aaron Copland papers
Sidney Robertson Cowell papers
Oliver Daniel papers
Richard Franko Goldman papers

Percy Grainger papers
Charles Seeger papers
Fabien Sevitzky papers

THE ALLEN MASON CHESNEY MEDICAL ARCHIVES, THE JOHNS HOPKINS
MEDICAL INSTITUTIONS
Adolph Meyer papers

STANFORD UNIVERSITY LIBRARY
Ernest Bacon papers
Varian family papers

JEWISH NATIONAL UNIVERSITY LIBRARY, JERUSALEM
Lan Adomian Collection

PAUL SACHER STIFTUNG, BASEL

ARNOLD SCHÖNBERG CENTER, VIENNA

Writings by Henry and Sidney Cowell

BOOKS

New Musical Resources. New York: Alfred A. Knopf, 1930; 2nd ed., with introduction by Joscelyn
    Godwin, New York: Something Else Press, 1969; 3rd ed., with introduction by David Nich-
    olls, Cambridge: Cambridge University Press, 1969.
American Composers on American Music. Stanford: Stanford University Press, 1933; reissue, New
    York: Frederick Ungar, 1961.
Charles Ives and His Music. New York: Oxford University Press, 1955.
The Nature of Melody (1937, unpublished).
Rhythm (late 1930s, incomplete).

Henry Cowell

ARTICLES BY HENRY COWELL OF SPECIAL RELEVANCE TO THIS BOOK
(LISTED CHRONOLOGICALLY)

"The Process of Musical Creation." *American Journal of Psychology* 37 (June 1926): 233–36.
"Modern Amerikai Zeneszerzők [Modern American Composers]." *Uj Föld* (April 1927):62–63.
"Moravian Music." *Pro-Musica Quarterly* 5/2 (June 1927): 25–29.
"New Terms for New Music." *Modern Music* 5/4 (May 1928): 21–27.
"Conservative Music in Radical Russia." *The New Republic* (August 14, 1929).
"Music." *Encyclopedia Americana*, annual supplements for 1929–36.
"Kto Kompositori v'Amerikye" [Who Are the Composers in America]. *Muzika i Revolutsiya* 6
    (Fall 1929): 34–38.
"Vocal Innovators of Central Europe." *Modern Music* 7/2 (February–March 1930): 34–38.
"A Musician's Experiences in Russia—Some First-hand and Unbiased Impressions." *The Church-
    man* (April 26, 1930): 10–11.
"Adventures in Soviet Russia." *San Franciscan* (December 1930): 16–17; (January 1931): 12.
"The 'Sones' of Cuba." *Modern Music* 8/2 (January–February 1931): 45–47.
"Creation and Imitation: A Dissertation on New Music." *Fortnightly* 1/6 (November 20,
    1931): 5–6.
"Why Modern Music." *Women's City Club Magazine* 5/11 (December 1931): 16–17.
"Who Is the Greatest Living Composer?" *Northwest Musical Herald* (January 1933): 7.

"Towards Neo-Primitivism." *Modern Music* 10/3 (March–April 1933):149–53.

"Irish Traditional Music." *Irish Review* (May 1934): 21, 30.

"How Relate Music and Dance?" *Dance Observer* 1/5 (June–July 1934): 52–53.

"An American Composer on Yugoslav Folk-Music." *Balkan Herald* 1/5 (August 1935): 5.

"The Scientific Approach to Non-European Music." *Music Vanguard: A Critical Review* 1/1 (Summer 1935): 62–67.

"O novoi musike—pis'mo Genri Cowella" [On New Music—letter from Henry Cowell]. *Sovyetskaya Muzika* 9 (September 1936): 92–94.

"The Music of Iceland." *Musical Mercury* 3/3 (September 1936): 48–50

"Drums Along the Pacific." *Modern Music* 18/1 (November–December 1940): 46–49.

"Creating a Dance: Form and Composition." *Educational Dance* 3/7 (January 1941): 2–3.

"New Sounds in Music for the Dance." *Dance Observer* 8/5 (May 1941): 64.

"Music in Soviet Russia." *The Russian Review* 1/2 (April 1942): 74–79.

"Improving Pan-American Music Relations." *Modern Music* 19/4 (May–June 1942): 263–65.

"A Conservative Interprets the Modern." *Saturday Review* 26/5 (January 30, 1943): 25.

"Report of the Inter-American Activities of the Committee Members of the Music Educators National Conference" submitted by Henry Cowell, chairman (Music Educators National Conference, mid-1940s).

"The Use of Music by the OWI." MTNA *Proceedings*, 1946 [no month]: 56–65.

"What Should Composers Study." *Peabody Notes* 6/3 (Fall 1952).

"How and Why I Compose," an address to the annual Conference of the National Committee on Art Education, 5/6/60, at the Museum of Modern Art. (Reprint of a 1953 interview).

"Freedom for Young Composers." *Music Journal* (March 1962): 29–30, 70.

"The Composer's World." In *The Preservation of Traditional Forms of the Learned and Popular Music of the Orient and Occident*, ed. William Kay Archer, 99–113. Champaign-Urbana: University of Illinois, Center for Comparative Psycholinguistics, Institute of Communications Research, 1964.

COLLABORATIVE ARTICLES

Henry Cowell and Robert Duffus. "The Process of Musical Creation." *The Freeman* 3/55 (March 30, 1921): 63–65; 3/56 (April 6, 1921): 85–87; 3/57 (April 13, 1921): 111–13.

Henry Cowell and Sidney Robertson Cowell. "Our Country Music." *Modern Music* 20/4 (May/June 1943): 243–47.

BIBLIOGRAPHIES OF COWELL'S WRITINGS AND WRITINGS ABOUT HIM

Manion, Martha. *Writings about Henry Cowell, an Annotated Bibliography*. I.S.A.M. Monographs No. 16. Brooklyn, NY: Brooklyn College, Institute for Studies in American Music, 1982.

Saylor, Bruce. *The Writings of Henry Cowell, a Descriptive Bibliography*. I.S.A.M. Monographs No. 7. Brooklyn, NY: Brooklyn College, Institute for Studies in American Music, 1977.

ANTHOLOGY

Higgins, Dick. *Essential Cowell: Selected Writings on Music by Henry Cowell, 1921–1964*. Kingston, NY: McPherson, 2001.

CATALOG OF MUSIC

Lichtenwanger, William. *The Music of Henry Cowell: A Descriptive Catalog*. Brooklyn, NY: Institute for Studies in American Music, Brooklyn College of the City University of New York, 1986.

INTERVIEWS CONDUCTED BY JOEL SACHS

Mildred Baker, Jack Beeson, Henry Brant, John Cage, Sidney Cowell, Lou Harrison, John Kirkpatrick, Mehrdad Pahlbod, C. Robert Payne, Karl Ulrich Schnabel, Nicolas Slonimsky, Harold and Barbara Tufty, Jean Seward Uppman, Frank Wigglesworth, Dr. Joseph Wortis.

Books

Anderson, Jack. *Ballet and Modern Dance: A History*. Princeton, NJ: Princeton Book Co., 1986.

Anderson, William. *The Mystery of Leopold Stokowski*. Teaneck, NJ: Fairleigh Dickinson University Press, 1990.

Angulo, Gui de. *The Old Coyote of Big Sur: The Life of Jaime de Angulo*. Berkeley, CA: Stonegarden Press, 1995.

Archer, William Kay, ed. *The Preservation of Traditional Forms of the Learned and Popular Music of the Orient and Occident*. Champaign-Urbana: University of Illinois, Center for Comparative Psycholinguistics, Institute of Communications Research, 1964.

Arndt, Richard T. *The First Resort of Kings: American Cultural Diplomacy in the Twentieth Century*. Washington, DC: Potomac, 2005.

Beach, Frank L. "The Transformation of California, 1900–1920: The Effects of Westward Movement on California Growth and Development in the Progressive Period." Ph. D. diss., University of California Graduate Division, 1963.

Beal, Amy C. *New Music, New Allies*. Berkeley: University of California Press, 2006.

Berger, Arthur. *Reflections of an American Composer*. Berkeley: University of California Press, 2002.

Bernard, Jonathan W. *Collected Essays and Lectures, 1937–1995*, ed. Elliott Carter. Rochester, NY: University of Rochester Press, 1997.

Bird, John. *Percy Grainger*. New York: Oxford University Press, 1999.

Blasdel, Christopher Yohmei. *The Single Tone: A Personal Journey into Shakuhachi Music*. Tokyo: Printed Matter Press, n.d.

Bostick, Daisy F., and Dorothea Castelhun. *Carmel at Work and Play*. Carmel: The Seven Arts, 1925; reprint, Monterey, CA: Angel Press, 1977.

Broadcast Music, Inc. *BMI: The Explosion of American Music, 1940–90: BMI 50th Anniversary Booklet*. 1990. New York: BMI.

Brown, Jeremy S. "A Selected Annotated List of Band Works by Henry Cowell and a Performance Edition of His *Hymn and Fuguing Tune No. 1* for Symphonic Band." DMA diss., Ohio State University, 1993.

Burke, Robert E. *Olson's New Deal for California*. Berkeley: University of California Press, 1953.

Burkholder, J. Peter Ives, ed. *Charles Ives and His World*. Princeton: Princeton University Press, 1996.

Cage, John. *Silence*. Middletown, CT: Wesleyan University Press, 1961; paperback, Cambridge, MA: MIT Press, 1966.

Canon, Cornelius Bond. "The Federal Music Project of the Works Progress Administration: Music in a Democracy." Ph.D. diss., University of Minnesota, 1983.

Carroll, Mark. *Music and Ideology in Cold War Europe*. Cambridge: Cambridge University Press, 2003.

Carwithen, Edward R. "Henry Cowell: Composer and Educator." Ph.D. diss., University of Florida, 1991.

Chasins, Abram. *Leopold Stokowski: A Profile*. New York: Hawthorn, 1979.

Copland, Aaron. *Copland on Music*. Garden City, NY: Doubleday, 1960.

Copland, Aaron, and Vivian Perlis. *Copland 1900 through 1942*. New York: St. Martin's Press/Marek, 1984.

Copley, John. *Report on Blacklisting*. New York: Fund for the Republic, 1956.

Cottle, Thomas J. *When the Music Stopped: Discovering My Mother*. Albany: State University of New York Press, 2004.

Cowell, Henry. *New Musical Resources. With Notes and an Accompanying Essay by David Nicholls*. Cambridge: Cambridge University Press, 1996.

Daniel, Oliver. *Stokowski: A Counterpoint of View*. New York: Dodd, Mead, 1982.

Denisoff, R. Serge. *Great Day Coming: Folk Music and the American Left*. Urbana: University of Illinois Press, 1971.

Dickinson, Peter, ed. *Cage Talk: Dialogues with and about John Cage*. Rochester, NY: Rochester University Press, 2006.

Doctor, Jennifer. *The BBC and Ultra-Modern Music, 1922–1936: Shaping a Nation's Taste*. Cambridge: Cambridge University Press, 1999.

Duffus, Robert. *Innocents at Cedro: A Memoir of Thorstein Veblen and Some Others.* New York: Macmillan, 1944.

Duffy, Warden Clinton T. *The San Quentin Story.* New York: Curtis, 1950; Pocketbook reissue.

Duveneck, Josephine Whitney. *Life on Two Levels: An Autobiography.* Los Altos, CA: William Kaufman, 1978.

Edwards, Allan. *Flawed Words and Stubborn Sounds: A Conversation with Elliott Carter.* New York: Norton, 1971.

Ewen, David. *A Journey to Greatness: The Life and Music of George Gershwin.* New York: Henry Holt, 1956.

Feder, Stuart. *Charles Ives, My Father's Song, a Psychoanalytic Biography.* New Haven, CT: Yale University Press, 1992.

Feisst, Sabine. *Schoenberg's New World.* New York: Oxford University Press, 2011.

Frémont, Marguerite. *La Vie du Dr. René Allendy, 1889–1942.* Castelnau-le-Lez: Éditions Climats, 1994.

Gann, Kyle. *The Music of Conlon Nancarrow.* Cambridge: Cambridge University Press, 1995.

Garafola, Lynn, ed. *Jose Limon: An Unfinished Memoir.* Hanover, NH: University Press of New England, 1998.

Garland, Peter, ed. *A Lou Harrison Reader.* Santa Fe: Soundings Press, 1987.

George, William Bernard. "Adolph Weiss." Ph.D. diss., University of Iowa, 1971.

Gilmore, Bob. *Harry Partch: A Biography.* New Haven, CT: Yale University Press, 1998.

Glinsky, Albert. *Theremin: Ether Music and Espionage.* Urbana: University of Illinois Press, 2000.

Godwin, Joscelyn. "The Music of Henry Cowell." Ph.D. diss., Cornell University, 1969.

Richard Franko Goldman: Selected Essays and Reviews, 1948–1968. Brooklyn, NY: Institute for Studies in American Music, Brooklyn College of the City University of New York, 1980.

Goldsmith, Peter D. *Making People's Music: Moe Asch and Folkways Records.* Washington: Smithsonian Institution Press, 1998.

Goodwin, Peter. *Morton Gould: American Salute.* Portland, OR: Amadeus Press, 2000.

Green, Shannon L. "Art for Life's Sake: Music Schools and Activities in the U.S. Social Settlements, 1892–1942." Ph.D. diss., University of Wisconsin, 1998.

Gresham, David. "The International Society for Contemporary Music, United States Section: 1922–1961." DMA document, The Juilliard School, 1999.

Harr, John Ensor, and Peter L. Johnson. *The Rockefeller Conscience.* New York: Charles Scribner's Sons, 1991.

Harrison, Lou. *Lou Harrison's Music Primer.* New York: C. F. Peters, 1971.

Hicks, Michael. *Henry Cowell, Bohemian.* Urbana: University of Illinois Press, 2002.

Hitchcock, H. Wiley, and Vivan Perlis, eds. *An Ives Celebration.* Urbana: University of Illinois Press, 1977.

Hyland, William G. *George Gershwin: A New Biography.* Westport, CT: Praeger, 2003.

Jorgensen, Elizabeth Watkins, and Henry Irvin Jorgensen. *Thorstein Veblen: Victorian Firebrand.* Armonk, NY: M. E. Sharpe, 1999.

Kinzer, Stephen. *Overthrow: America's Century of Regime Change from Hawaii to Iraq.* New York: Henry Holt/Times Books, 2006.

Koch, Frederick. *Reflections on Composing: Four American Composers.* Pittsburgh: Carnegie-Mellon University Press, 1983.

Kopp, Alexander. "Elastic Form. Henry Cowell's 'ganze Welt der Music.'" Diss., Technical University, Berlin, 1998.

Kostelanetz, Richard, ed. *Aaron Copland: A Reader. Selected Writings 1923–72.* New York: Routledge, 2004.

Kostelanetz, Richard. *Conversing with John Cage.* 2nd ed. New York: Routledge, 2003.

Kostelanetz, Richard. *John Cage: An Anthology.* New York: Da Capo Press, 1991. (Reprint of 1970 publication with new chronology and catalogs.)

Lambert, Philip, ed. *Ives Studies.* Cambridge: Cambridge University Press, 1997.

Lamott, Kenneth. *Chronicles of San Quentin: The Biography of a Prison.* New York: McKay, 1961.

LaPrade, Ernest. *Broadcasting Music.* New York: Rinehart, 1947.

Lederman, Minna. *The Life and Death of a Small Magazine (Modern Music, 1924–1946)*. I.S.A.M. Monographs, no. 18. Brooklyn, NY: Brooklyn College, Institute for Studies in American Music, 1983.

Leeds-Hurwitz, Wendy. *Rolling in Ditches with Shamans: Jamie de Angulo and the Professionalization of American Anthropology*. Lincoln: University of Nebraska Press, 2004.

Luening, Otto. *The Odyssey of an American Composer*. New York: Charles Scribner's Sons, 1980.

Magee, Gayle Sherwood. *Charles Ives Reconsidered*. Urbana: University of Illinois Press, 2008.

Martin, George. *The Damrosch Dynasty—America's First Family of Music*. Boston: Houghton Mifflin, 1983.

Mason, Daniel Gregory. *Tune in America*. New York: Knopf, 1931.

McWilliams, Carey. *The Education of Carey McWilliams*. New York: Simon and Schuster, 1978.

Mead, Rita. *Henry Cowell's New Music 1925–1936: The Society, the Music Editions, and the Recordings*. Ann Arbor: UMI Research Press, 1981.

Meyer, Felix, and Anne C. Shreffler, eds. *Elliott Carter A Centennial Portrait in Letters and Documents*. A publication of the Paul Sacher Foundation. Woodbridge, Suffolk: Boydell Press, 2008.

Miller, Leta E., and Frederic Lieberman. *Lou Harrison—Composing a World*. New York: Oxford University Press, 1998.

Mitsel, Rita. "The Anti-Jewish Campaigns Against the Musicians in Kiev in 1948–1953." DMA document, The Juilliard School, 2010, 85.

Montefiore, Simon Sebag. *Stalin: The Court of the Red Tsar*. New York: Knopf, 2004.

Nelson, Amy. *Music for the Revolution*. University Park: Pennsylvania State University Press, 2004.

Nicholls, David. *American Experimental Music, 1890–1940*. Cambridge: Cambridge University Press, 1990.

Nicholls, David. *John Cage*. Urbana: University of Illinois Press, 2007.

Nicholls, David, ed. *The Cambridge Companion to John Cage*. Cambridge: Cambridge University Press, 2002.

Nicholls, David, ed. *The Whole World of Music: A Henry Cowell Symposium*. Amsterdam: Harwood Academic Publishers, 1997.

Oja, Carol J. *Colin McPhee: Composer in Two Worlds*. Washington: Smithsonian Institution Press, 1990.

Oja, Carol J. *Making Music Modern: New York in the 1920s*. Oxford: Oxford University Press, 2000.

Oja, Carol J., and H. Wiley Hitchcock. *Henry Cowell's Musical Worlds: A Program Book for the Henry Cowell Centennial Festival*. Brooklyn, NY: Institute for Studies in American Music, 1997

Opperby, Preben. *Leopold Stokowski*. New York: Hippocrene Books, 1982.

Parker, Robert L. *Carlos Chávez—Mexico's Modern-Day Orpheus*. Boston: Twayne, 1983.

Partch, Harry. *Genesis of a Music*. New York: Da Capo Press, 1974.

Patterson, David W., ed. *John Cage: Music, Philosophy, and Intention, 1933–1950*. New York: Routledge, 2002.

Payne, Robert. *Gershwin*. New York: Pyramid, 1960.

Pescatello, Ann. *Charles Seeger: A Life in American Music*. Pittsburgh, PA: University of Pittsburgh Press, 1992.

Polisi, Joseph. *American Muse: The Life and Times of William Schumann*. Milwaukee, WI: Amadeus Press, 2008.

Pollack, Howard. *Aaron Copland: The Life and Work of an Uncommon Man*. New York: Henry Holt, 1999.

Reuss, Richard A., with JoAnne C. Reuss. *American Folk Music and Left-Wing Politics, 1927–57*. American Folk Music and Musicians Series, no. 4. Lanham, MD: Scarecrow Press, 2000.

Revill, David. *The Roaring Silence: John Cage, A Life*. New York: Arcade, 1992.

Rich, Allan. *American Pioneers: Ives to Cage and Beyond*. London: Phaidon, 1995.

Rosenfeld, Paul. *Discoveries of a Music Critic*. New York: Harcourt, Brace, 1936.

Rossiter, Frank. *Charles Ives and His America* New York: Liveright, 1975.

Rothman, David. *Conscience and Convenience: The Asylum and Its Alternatives in Progressive America*. Rev. ed. New York: Aldine de Gruyter, 2002.

Saunders, Frances Stonor. *The Cultural Cold War—The CIA and the World of Arts and Letters*. New York: New Press, 2000. Originally published as *Who Paid the Piper*. London: Granta, 1999.

Schiff, David. *The Music of Elliott Carter*. London: Da Capo Press, 1983.

Schimpf, Peter John. "A Transcultural Student, Teacher, and Composer: Henry Cowell and the Music of the World's Peoples." Ph.D. diss., Indiana University, 2006.

Schlesinger, Arthur M., Jr. *The Age of Roosevelt, Vol. I: The Crisis of the Old Order, 1919–1933*. Boston: Houghton Mifflin, 1957, 1985, 2002.

Schoenberg, Arnold. *Letters*. Selected and edited by Erwin Stein; translated from the original German by Eithne Wilkins and Ernst Kaiser. New York: St. Martin's Press, 1965; reprint, Berkeley: University of California Press, 1987.

Schwarz, Boris. *Music and Musical Life in Soviet Russia 1917–70*. New York: Norton, 1972.

Seeger, Charles. *Studies in Musicology II, 1929–1979*, ed. Anne M. Pescatello. Berkeley: University of California Press, 1999.

Shulman, Holly Cowan. *The Voice of America: Propaganda and Democracy, 1941–1945*. Madison: University of Wisconsin Press, 1990.

Sitsky, Larry. *Music of the Repressed Russian Avant-Garde, 1900–1929*. Westport, CT: Greenwood Press, 1994.

Slonimsky, Nicolas. *Music since 1900*. 3rd ed. New York: Coleman-Ross, 1949.

Slonimsky, Nicolas. *Perfect Pitch*. Oxford: Oxford University Press, 1988.

Smith, Catherine Parsons. *William Grant Still: A Study in Contradictions*. Berkeley: University of California Press, 2000.

Smith, William Ander. *The Mystery of Leopold Stokowski*. Teaneck, NJ: Fairleigh Dickinson University Press, 1990.

Soares, Janet Mansfield. *Louis Horst: Musician in a Dancer's World*. Durham, NC: Duke University Press, 1992.

Stanley, Leo L., with Evelyn Wells. *Men at Their Worst*. New York: D. Appleton-Century, 1940.

Starr, Kevin. *Americans and the California Dream, 1850–1915*. New York: Oxford University Press, 1973.

Stevens, Halsey. *The Life and Music of Béla Bartók*. New York: Oxford University Press, 1953.

Stewart, Louis C. "Music Composed for Martha Graham: A Discussion of Musical and Choreographic Collaborations." Ph.D. diss., Peabody Conservatory of Music, Peabody Institute of The Johns Hopkins University, 1991.

Still, Judith Anne, and Lisa M. Headlee, eds. *Just Tell the Story*. Flagstaff, AZ: Master-Player Library, 2006.

Stodelle, Ernestine. *Deep Song: The Dance Story of Martha Graham*. New York: Schirmer Books, 1987.

Stuckenschmidt, Hans Heinz. *Schoenberg: His Life, World, and Work.*, trans. Humphrey Searle. New York: Schirmer, 1977.

Swafford, Jan. *Charles Ives. A Life with Music*. New York: Norton, 1996.

Szigeti, Joseph. *With Strings Attached: Reminiscences and Reflections*. New York: Knopf, 1947.

Terman, Lewis M. *The Intelligence of School Children*. Boston: Houghton Mifflin, 1919.

Thomson, Virgil. *A Virgil Thomson Reader*. Boston: Houghton Mifflin, 1981.

Tick, Judith. *Ruth Crawford Seeger: A Composer's Search for American Music*. New York: Oxford University Press, 1997.

Varèse, Louise. *Varèse: A Looking-Glass Diary, Vol. I: 1883–1928*. New York: Norton, 1972.

Varian, Dorothy. *The Inventor and the Pilot (Russell and Sigurd Varian)*. Palo Alto, CA: Pacific Books, 1983.

Von Gunden, Heidi. *The Music of Lou Harrison*. Metuchen, NJ: Scarecrow Press, 1995.

Wells, Evelyn. *Champagne Days of San Francisco*. New York: D. Appleton-Century, 1939.

West's Annotated California Codes: Penal Code. Eagan, MI: Westgroup, 1999.

White, Charles W. *Alejandro García Caturla—A Cuban Composer in the Twentieth Century*. Lanham, MD: Scarecrow Press, 2003.

Winkler, Allan M. *The Politics of Propaganda: The Office of War Information, 1942–1945*. New Haven, CT: Yale University Press, 1978.

Wolf, Marcie Hancock. "The Pardoning Powers of the Governor of California." MA thesis, Political Science, Graduate Division, University of California, 1943.

Woodcock, George. *Anarchism*. London: Pelican 1962.

Yung, Bell, and Helen Rees, eds. *Understanding Charles Seeger, Pioneer in American Musicology*. Urbana: University of Illinois Press, 1999.

Ziffrin, Marilyn J. *Carl Ruggles: Composer, Painter, and Storyteller*. Urbana: University of Illinois Press, 1994.

Zuck, Barbara. *A History of Musical Americanism*. Studies in Musicology No. 9. Ann Arbor: UMI Research Press, 1980.

ARTICLES

Blitzstein, Marc. "Popular Music—An Invasion: 1923–33." *Modern Music* 10/1 (January–February 1933): 96–102.

Boziwick, George. "Henry Cowell at the New York Public Library—A Whole World of Music." *Notes* 57/1 (2000): 46–58.

Boziwick, George. Introduction to Clarissa Dixon Cowell, "Material for Biography." *American Music* 27/1 (Spring 2009): 1–3.

Brant, Henry. "Henry Cowell—Musician and Citizen." *Etude* (February 1957): 15; (March 1957): 20; (April 1957): 22.

Braudo, Eugen. "The Russian Panorama." *Modern Music* 10/1 (January–February 1933): 79–86.

Brown, Jeremy S. "An American Original: The Published San Quentin Wind Band Works of Henry Dixon Cowell." *Journal of the World Association of Symphonic Bands and Ensembles* (1997): 59–84.

Brown, Jeremy S. "The Grainger-Cowell Prison Dialogues and the Origins of Henry Cowell's *Celtic Set* (1938)." *Conference Papers of the International Society for the Investigation of Wind Music* (April 2006): 75–86.

Brown, Jeremy S. "Henry Dixon Cowell and Hymn and Fuguing Tune No. 1 for Symphonic Band (1944)." *Journal of Band Research* 32/1 (Fall 1996): 1–32.

Butting, Max. "Music of and for the Radio." *Modern Music* 8/3 (March–April 1931): 15–19.

Cage, John. "Counterpoint." *Dune Forum* 1/2 (February 14, 1934): 42–44.

Central Intelligence Agency. "Origins of the Congress for Cultural Freedom." http://web.archive.org/web/20060616213245/http://cia.gov/csi/studies/95unclass/Warner.html. [10/5/09].

Chang, Josephine. "Henry Cowell as Piano Pedagogue." Unpublished, sent by author to Joel Sachs. 2007.

Citkowitz, Israel. "Home Thoughts." *Modern Music* 10/1 (January–February 1933): 107–14.

Clarke, Henry Leland. "Composers' Collective of New York." *New Grove Dictionary of Music and Musicians*. 2nd ed. New York: Macmillan, 2001.

Copland, Aaron. "America's Young Men of Promise—Our Younger Generation: Ten Years Later." *Modern Music* 13/3 (May–June 1936): 3–11.

Copland, Aaron. "The Composer in America, 1923–1933." *Modern Music* 10/1 (January–February 1933): 87–92.

Cowell, Clarissa Dixon. "Material for Biography." *American Music* 27/1 (Spring 2009): 4–59.

Cowell, Sidney Robertson. "The Cowells and the Written Word." In *A Celebration of American Music*, ed. Richard Crawford, R. Allen Lott, and Carol J. Oja, 79–91. Ann Arbor: University of Michigan Press, 1990.

Daniel, Oliver. "Henry Cowell." *Stereo Review* 36/6 (December 1974): 72–82.

Drlíková, Eva. "Henry Cowell, Leoš Janáček and Who Were the Others?" *Studies in Czech Music: Janacek and Czech Music. Proceedings of the International Conference*, ed. Michael Beckerman and Glen Bauer, 295–99. Hillsdale, NY: Pendragon Press, 1995.

Dunaway, David. "Charles Seeger and Carl Sands, the Composers' Collective Years." *Ethnomusicology* 24/2 (May 1980): 159–68.

Dunaway, David King. "Unsung Songs of Protest: The Composers Collective of New York." *New York Folklore* 5/1–2 (Summer 1979): 1–19.

Eby, Clare Virginia. "The Two Mrs. Veblens, among Others." *International Journal of Politics, Culture and Society* 13/2 (1999): 353–61.

Feisst, Sabine. "Henry Cowell und Arnold Schoenberg—eine unbekannte Freundschaft." *Archiv für Musikwissenschaft* 55/1 (1998): 57–71.

Frischkopf, Michael. "Nationalism, Nationalization, and the Egyptian Music Industry: Muhammad Fawzy, Misrphon, and Sawt al-Qahira (SonoCairo)." *Asian Music* 39/2 (Summer–Fall 2008): 28–58.

Fürst-Heidtmann, Monika. "Henry Cowell und die experimentelle Klaviermusik." *Neuland* 2 (1982): 255–63.

Gac, Scott. "Comrades, the Bugles Are Sounding!" *Music Research Forum* (University of Cincinnati College-Conservatory of Music) 11/2 (1996): 20–43.

Gann, Kyle. "Regarding Henry." *The Village Voice* (April 1, 1997): 60.

Garland, Peter. "The Legacy of Henry Cowell in the Life and Work of Conlon Nancarrow." Unpublished talk delivered at Nancarrow Festival, Mexico City, 1998. (Copy provided by the author).

Gershefski, Edwin. "American Composers, XXVI: Henry Cowell." *Modern Music* 28/4 (Fall 1946): 255–60.

Gerschefski, Edwin. "Henry Cowell." *American Composers Alliance Bulletin* 3/4 (1953): 3–4, 18–19.

Gillespie, Don. "William Russell, American Percussion Composer." *Southern Quarterly* 36/2 (Winter 1998): 35–55.

Goldman, Richard F. "A New Day for Band Music." *Modern Music* 28/4 (Fall 1946): 261–65.

Good, Emily. "'The Composers Organize': Fifty Years of the American Composers Alliance." *Newsletter of the Institute for Studies in American Music* (Brooklyn College) 17/1 (November 1987): 1–2, 15.

Gronow, Pekka. "The Record Industry Comes to the Orient." *Ethnomusicology* 25/2 (May 1981): 251–84.

Gronow, Pekka. "The Record Industry: The Growth of a Mass Medium." *Popular Music* 3 (1983): 53–75.

Hammond, Richard. "Pioneers of Movie Music." *Modern Music* 8/3 (March–April 1931): 35–38.

Heinsheimer, Hans. "Film Opera—Screen vs. Stage." *Modern Music* 8/3 (March–April 1931): 10–14.

Helm, Everett. "Henry Cowell: American Pioneer." *Musical America* 72/4 (April 1962): 32.

Hicks, Michael. "Cowell's Clusters." *Musical Quarterly* 77/3 (Autumn 1993): 428–58.

Hicks, Michael. "The Imprisonment of Henry Cowell." *Journal of the American Musicological Society* 44/1 (Spring 1991): 92–119.

Higgins, Dick. "Cowell's Lost 'Fanati.'" *Musical Quarterly* 82/2 (Summer 1998): 232–50.

Higgins, Dick. "Henry Cowell—Some Personal Recollections. *Soundings* 14–15 (1986).

Hitchcock, H. Wiley. "Henry Cowell's 'Ostinato Pianissimo.'" *Musical Quarterly* 70/1 (January 1984): 23–44.

Johnson, Steven. "Henry Cowell, John Varian, and Halcyon." *American Music* 11/1 (Spring 1993): 1–27.

Kolodin, Irving. "Ten Years of Modern Music Recording." *Modern Music* 10/1 (January–February 1933): 103–6.

Kerti, Anton. "Henry Cowell, Enfant Terrible of American Music." Unpublished.

Lott, R. Allen. "'New Music for New Ears': The International Composers' Guild." *Journal of the American Musicological Society* 36/2 (Summer 1983): 266–86.

MacDougall, Laurie. "Henry Cowell and His Family (1819–1955), a Brief History." http://www.santacruzpl.org/history/people/cowell3.shtml. [7/15/07].

Mead, Rita. "The Amazing Mr. Cowell." *American Music* 1/4 (Winter 1983): 63–89.

Miller, Leta. "The Art of Noise: John Cage, Lou Harrison, and the West Coast Percussion Ensemble. In *Perspectives on American Music, 1900–1950*, ed. M. Saffle, 215–63. New York, 2000.

Miller, Leta E. "Henry Cowell and John Cage: Intersections and Influences, 1933–1941." *Journal of the American Musicological Society* 59/1: 47–112.

Miller, Leta E. "Henry Cowell and Modern Dance: The Genesis of Elastic Form."

Miller, Leta E., and Rob Collins. "The Cowell-Ives Relationship: A New Look at Cowell's Prison Years." *American Music* 23/4 (Winter 2005): 473–92.

Nicholls, David. "Defining American Music." *Newsletter for the Institute for Studies in American Music* (Brooklyn, NY) (Spring 1999): 1–2, 14.

Nicholls, David. "Henry Cowell." *New Grove Dictionary of Music and Musicians.* New York: Grove, 2001.

Nicholls, David. "Henry Cowell: A Call for Restitution." *Newsletter for the Institute for Studies in American Music* (Brooklyn, NY) 24/1 (Fall 1994): 1–2, 15.

Nicholls, David. "Henry Cowell's 'United Quartet.'" *American Music* 13/2 (Summer 1995): 195–217.

Nicholls, David. "Transethnicism and the American Experimental Tradition." *Musical Quarterly* 80/4 (Winter 1996): 569–94.

Oja, Carol J. "The Copland-Sessions Concerts and Their Reception in the Contemporary Press." *Musical Quarterly* 65/2 (April 1979): 212–29.

Oja, Carol J. "Cos Cob Press and the American Composer." *Notes*, 2nd series, 45/2 (December 1988): 227–52.

Oja, Carol J. "Gershwin and American Modernists of the 1920s." *Musical Quarterly* 78/4 (Winter 1994): 646–67.

Paul, David C. "From American Ethnographer to Cold War Icon: Charles Ives through the Eyes of Henry and Sidney Cowell." *Journal of the American Musicological Society* 59/2 (Summer 2006): 399–458.

Pettis, Ashley. "Marching with a Song." *New Masses* (May 1, 1934).

Rao, Nancy Yunhwa. "American Compositional Theory in the 1930s: Scale and Exoticism in 'The Nature of Melody' by Henry Cowell." *Musical Quarterly* 85/5 (Winter 2001): 595–640.

Rao, Nancy Yunhwa. "Henry Cowell and His Chinese Musical Heritage: Theory of Sliding Tone and His Orchestral Work of 1953–1965." In *Locating East Asia in Western Art Music*, ed. Yayoi Uno Everett and Frederick Lau, 119–45. Middletown, CT: Wesleyan University Press, 2004.

Reese, Gustave. "The American Musicological Society." *Music Journal* 4/6 (November–December 1946): 7.

"Renaissance of Religious Art and Architecture in the San Francisco Bay Area, 1946–1968." Interviews conducted by Michaela DuCasse and Suzanne B. Riess. With an introduction by Jane Dillenberger. Regional Oral History Office, Bancroft Library, University of California, Berkeley.

Root, Deane L. "The Pan American Association of Composers (1928–1934)." *Yearbook for Inter-American Musical Research* 7 (1972): 49–70.

Rosenfeld, P. "Cowell." *By Way of Art: Criticisms of Music, Literature, Painting, Sculpture and the Dance.* New York, 1928, 77–80.

Ross, Alex. "Appalachian Autumn." *New Yorker Magazine* (August 27, 2007): 34–40.

Rudhyar, Dane. "The Relativity of Our Musical Conceptions." *Musical Quarterly* 8/1 (January 1922): 108–18.

Sachs, Joel. "Henry Cowell." *Die Musik in Geschichte und Gegenwart.* Kassel: Bärenreiter, 1994.

Saminsky, Lazare. "Europe and America in Music Today." *Modern Music* 10/1 (January–February 1933): 93–92.

Saylor, Bruce. "The Tempering of Henry Cowell's 'Dissonant Counterpoint.'" *Essays on Modern Music* 2/2–4 (Boston, League of Composers-International Society for Contemporary Music, 1985): 5–11.

Schillinger, Joseph. "Electricity, a Musical Liberator." *Modern Music* 8/3 (March–April 1931): 26–31.

Schloezer, Boris de. "Man, Music and the Machine." *Modern Music* 8/3 (March–April 1931): 3–9.

Schneerson, Grigori. "The Changing Course of Russian Music." *Modern Music* 30/2 (January–February 1936): 19–24.

Schwartz, Bonnie Fox. "Social Workers and New Deal Politicians in Conflict: California's Branion-Williams Case." *Pacific Historical Review* 42/1 (February 1973): 53–73.

Seeger, Charles. "Henry Cowell." *Magazine of Art* 33/5 (May 1940): 288–89, 322–27.

Seeger, Charles. "On Proletarian Music." *Modern Music* 11/2 (March–April 1934): 121–27.

Sessions, Roger. "Music in Crisis. Some Notes on Recent Musical History." *Modern Music* 10/2 (January–February 1932): 63–78.

Shackelford, Rudy. "The Yaddo Festivals of American Music." *Perspectives of New Music* 17/1 (Autumn–Winter, 1978): 92–125.

Sheppard, W. Anthony. "Continuity in Composing the American Cross-Cultural: Eichheim, Cowell, and Japan." *Journal of the American Musicological Society* 61/3 (Fall 2008): 465–540.

Silver, Brian. "Henry Cowell and Alan Hovhaness—Responses to the Music of India." *Contributions to Asian Studies* 12 (1978): 54–78.

Slonimsky, Nicolas. "Henry Cowell." In *American Composers on American Music*, ed. H. Cowell, 57–63. Stanford, CA: Stanford University Press, 1933.

Solomon, Maynard. "Charles Ives: Some Questions of Veracity." *Journal of the American Musicological Society* 40/3 (Autumn, 1987): 443–70.

Thomson, Virgil. "Home Thoughts." *Modern Music* 10/1 (January–February 1933): 107–9.

Weisgall, Hugo. "The Music of Henry Cowell." *Musical Quarterly* 45/4 (October 1959): 484–98.

Weyl, Charles. "The Orchestra on the Air." *Modern Music* 8/3 (March–April 1931): 20–24.

"Who Was Henry Cowell." www.parks.ca.gov/default.asp?page_id=918. [7/25/07].

Yates, Peter. "Parsley for Henry." *Arts and Architecture* 47/10 (October 1950): 45–49.

INDEX